CHANCES FOR PEACE

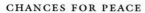

CHANCES FOR PEACE

Missed Opportunities in the Arab-Israeli Conflict

ELIE PODEH

UNIVERSITY OF TEXAS PRESS　*Austin*

First edition, 2015
First paperback edition, 2016

Requests for permission to reproduce material from this work should be sent to:
  Permissions
  University of Texas Press
  P.O. Box 7819
  Austin, TX 78713-7819
  http://utpress.utexas.edu/index.php/rp-form

♾ The paper used in this book meets the minimum requirements of ANSI/NISO
Z39.48-1992 (R1997) (Permanence of Paper).

LIBRARY OF CONGRESS CATALOGING-IN-PUBLICATION DATA

Podeh, Elie, author.
   Chances for peace : missed opportunities in the Arab-Israeli conflict / Elie Podeh. —
First edition.
      pages   cm
   Includes bibliographical references and index.
   ISBN 978-1-4773-0560-7 (cloth : alk. paper) — ISBN 978-1-4773-0561-4
(library e-book) — ISBN 978-1-4773-0562-1 (nonlibrary e-book)
1. Arab-Israeli conflict.   2. Conflict management—Middle East.   3. Middle East—
Politics and government.   I. Title.
   DS119.6.P63   2015
   956.04—dc23

                                                        2015023756

doi:10.7560/305607
ISBN 978-1-4773-1222-3 (paperback)

A pessimist sees the difficulty in every opportunity; an optimist sees the opportunity in every difficulty.
ATTRIBUTED TO WINSTON CHURCHILL

There is no privileged past . . . There is an infinity of Pasts, all equally valid . . . At each and every instant of time, however brief you suppose it, the line of events forks like the stem of a tree putting forth twin branches. ANDRÉ MAUROIS

Peace is only possible when one of the warring parties takes the first step, the hazardous initiative, the risk of opening up dialogue, and decides to make the gesture that will lead not only to armistice but to peace. . . . I am thinking here of the ongoing wars in the Middle East, I am thinking of Israel and Palestine. . . . The difference between an opening up and a closure depends on the risk taken, on the responsibility taken in the midst of risk, by someone who knows that, if he is not the first to address the other, if he is not the first to offer his hand, the war will not end.
JACQUES DERRIDA

CONTENTS

MAPS

TABLES

While writing this manuscript, I came across a short story by the French novelist André Maurois called "If Louis XVI Had Had an Atom of Firmness," published in 1931 in *If, or History Rewritten*, a collection of articles edited by J. C. Squire. I was intrigued by this imaginative piece, which begins with a tribute to the passing of a great historian who wrote on contemporary France, though his real expertise was the French Revolution. As the soul of the historian arrives at the Archives of Eternity in heaven, he finds himself in front of the "Archives of Unrealized Possibilities." Surprised, the positivist historian asks the young archangel accompanying him: "How can there possibly be Archives of 'unrealized' possibilities? Things that haven't happened can't leave traces, can they?" Amused, the archangel responds:

> O human presumption . . . Every thought that traverses the mind of God partakes *ipso facto* of a manner of existence no less real than that which you, mankind, ascertain through your five poor senses . . . There is no privileged past . . . There is an infinitude of Pasts, all equally valid . . . At each and every instant of Time, however brief you suppose it, the line of events forks like the stem of a tree putting forth twin branches . . . One of these branches represents the sequence of facts as you, poor mortal, knew it; and the other represents what History would have become if one single detail had been other than it was . . . These infinite branchings [*sic*] make up the Unrealized Possibilities, and I am here as their Curator . . . Do you understand? (Squire 1931, 112)

But the historian still does not fully understand: "If all Possibilities have the same validity," he asks, "why bestow the title of 'real' on the one which I have lived, and that of 'unrealized' on these others which, you say, are equally valid?" "Because," the archangel responds, "this is *your* Heaven . . . Paradise is individual" (ibid., 113). Perplexed, the historian is invited to step inside the Archives of Unrealized Possibilities; upon entering the "if France" library, he hurries to find "his" period, the French Revolution, to which he had devoted his earthly life. Among the many books in this library, the historian's eyes caught a volume which tells the possible and unrealized story of the reign of Louis XVI, 1774–1820. Captivated by this possibility, he is absorbed in this story, told in the following pages (ibid., 114–142).

This wonderful story can be added to another book I read many years ago, *The Wall of the Plague*. This novel was written by the South African author

André Brink during the apartheid years. Upon rereading the many quotations I have collected over the years, I was astonished to rediscover the following passage from Brink's book:

> At every crossroads on the way: those other options lurking in the shadows around one. In retrospect everything seems so simple and predictable: I drove that way, and then there, and there; here I turned left, there I kept straight on—Yet every single choice excluded innumerable others, changing the entire untravelled course ahead. What would have happened if I'd done this—or that—had gone here—or there? Even this is a simplification. The true question, it seems to me . . . is not what would have happened if I'd made different choices here or there. What matters is: which of those other options was I *conscious* [emphasis in the original] of from one instant to the next? Because . . . I carry within me not only those decisions taken but all the unchosen possibilities of myself. They are as much part of me as any choice made by chance at any given moment. (1984, 381)

These two passages made me realize that the notion of missed opportunities or opportunities that have not been realized—in life and politics—has always been a fascinating puzzle to me. Added to the famous and oft-quoted poem by Robert Frost, "The Road Not Taken" (a title borrowed by Itamar Rabinovich for his book on Arab-Israeli relations in the post-1948 period), the conclusion is that human beings are just as intrigued by the possibilities/alternatives/roads that were not taken as by those that were; that there is an innate curiosity and desire to get a glimpse of what would have been the results of traveling the untaken road. Regrettably, however, in contrast to what Brink thinks, I sense that most human beings—decision makers included—are not conscious of the different choices available while making their decisions and look only at immediate rather than long-term gains. This book is a small step toward arousing the reader's consciousness about the existence of other possible alternatives. It is also a small step toward offering a more systematic (or academic) approach to exploring the possibilities inherent in the road(s) not taken. A mission such as this is not regarded as part of the historian's domain, as his task is usually confined to the investigation of what happened and not what might or could have happened. This premise, however, has been challenged in recent years by social scientists, as will be seen in the Introduction, and it is challenged in this book as well.

The term "missed opportunity" is often used by historians, social scientists, and laymen. The problem is, however, that the use of this term is rather impressionistic; it is offered as a possibility without an attempt to define or measure it. This book seeks to rectify this omission by offering a theoretical framework enabling us to use the term in a more scientific way. On the basis of this framework, twenty-three episodes in the Arab-Israeli conflict are analyzed. The book is based only on secondary sources, as the length and width of the analysis precluded reliance on primary sources.

Now that this journey has come to an end, I would like to thank the following institutions and individuals who helped make it possible. The Harry S. Truman Research Institute for the Advancement of Peace, as always, was kind enough to support this research, which, in fact, is part of its academic mission. The Faculty of Humanities at the Hebrew University provided important financial support. I want to pay special tribute to Prof. Yaacov Bar-Siman-Tov of the Hebrew University, a good friend and colleague, who tragically passed away as I was completing the writing of this manuscript. Yaacov was involved in this project from the very beginning and contributed many insightful comments. Prof. Louis Kriesberg of Syracuse University and Dr. Yael Krispin-Peleg provided valuable help for the theoretical chapter of this book. I have also benefited from insights and talks on the subject by Prof. Avi Shlaim of Oxford University, Prof. Kenneth Stein of Emory University, Prof. Galia Golan of the Hebrew University and Herzliya Interdisciplinary Center, Dr. Neil Caplan of Vanier College in Montreal, Dr. Philip Matter, an independent scholar, and Mr. Walid Salem of al-Quds University. Last but not least, I want to thank all my students in my master's seminar, "Missed Opportunities in the Arab-Israeli Conflict," who stimulated my thinking with their original comments and questions while preparing the manuscript. Finally, I thank my two language editors, Lisa Perlman and Renee Hochman, who skillfully continue to polish my English. At the end of this journey, I would also like to express my appreciation to my book editor, Jim Burr, and my manuscript editor, Lynne F. Chapman, both of University of Texas Press, for their meticulous professional guidance throughout the process of publishing this book.

In October 2014, as I worked on the final draft of this book, my father, Schraga (Feivel) Podé, passed away at the age of ninety. As a Holocaust survivor, he did not have the luxury of following his heart in choosing a career for himself. Had he had the opportunity, he probably would have opted for studying history, which has always been his favorite hobby. Only recently did I realize that I have unconsciously followed the very path that he might have chosen for himself. Sadly, he did not live to see the publication of this book, which I dedicate to his memory.

Elie Podeh
Herzliya
February 2015

A STORY OF AN OPPORTUNITY NOT MISSED

A STUDY OF MISSED OPPORTUNITIES in the century-old Arab-Israeli conflict cannot ignore the oft-repeated aphorism, "The Arabs [or the Palestinians] never miss an opportunity to miss an opportunity." Abba Eban, the seasoned Israeli diplomat and foreign minister (1966–1974), gets credit for the quip. But when in fact did Eban coin it? And does it accurately sum up the broad tableau that is the world's most talked-about conflict?

This is the story of the search for the original source of the now-famous dictum and its implications. Heading first to the Internet, we find that it appears there an incredible 44,600,000 times (as of July 2014). Any serious website presenting famous quotes features numerous Eban gems, including this one. Myriad academic publications and journalistic pieces have used this saying in different ways, usually attributing it to the Arab or Palestinian side, as Eban did (e.g., Shlaim 2000, 489), but some have turned the maxim on its head and related it to Israel (Maoz 2004, 386–495), while yet others have adapted it to other conflicts and other circumstances. Like any good historian, I thought it necessary to trace the origins of this saying, not least because it plays an underlying and pivotal role in this study. None of the historical and contemporary sources had given any sure indication of the source or when it first appeared. According to Wikiquote, Eban proffered it following the Geneva Peace Conference, held on December 21–22, 1973.[1] Upon the statesman's death, Alexander Zvielli and Calev Ben-David published a eulogy (2002), which obliquely agreed with that time frame.

A check of this reference shows that in his speech at the Geneva conference, Eban mentioned the term "opportunity" twice early on, when he declared, "Today at last a new opportunity is born," and "We have no way of knowing whether this opportunity will be fulfilled or wasted . . . Israel for its part is resolved to seize the chance." Yet there is no reference to any *missed* opportunity. With the benefit of hindsight, I sense that the chances that Eban uttered these words at an international conference, in front of Egyptian and Jordanian representatives, are slim, as they could be construed as potentially insulting to the Arabs. A further check of the Israeli press following the conference did not yield any results.

Before examining Eban's own historical records, I decided that a meeting with someone close to him might help. I turned to two of his closest colleagues in the foreign office. The first was Eytan Bentsur, who was Eban's personal secretary at the Geneva conference and later rose up the ministry's ranks to become its director-general. He wrote a heartening tribute to Eban in a book dedicated to his memory and published by the ministry (Bentsur 2003, 161–166). Though of course familiar with the quote, Bentsur could not pinpoint its precise original uttering; nor could Moshe Raviv, Eban's political secretary between 1966 and 1968 and later Israel's ambassador in London. The problem was that since Eban, a sought-after speaker, gave so many speeches and interviews, it was truly like searching for a needle in a haystack.

My failure to find an answer in the diplomatic field led me to enquire among certain journalists who had used the adage in their newspaper articles. I approached Aluf Benn, today the editor of *Haaretz* and who for many years covered foreign policy and other topics for that newspaper. He in turn brought in his most senior journalist, the respected Yoel Marcus, who immediately pointed to an interview Eban gave to the German journal *Der Spiegel* in 1969; I was now confident that the missing statement was found. Since my German is weak, I asked my eighty-eight-year-old father, of Polish origin but fluent in German, to read the *Spiegel* piece. (My father has since passed away, in October 2014.) As an avid follower of history in general and Middle Eastern history in particular, he too enthusiastically joined the endeavor. After reading the text, his conclusion was that the famous maxim was not included in the interview. It is possible that Marcus remembered this particular interview because it includes another of Eban's famous quotations to the effect that the 1967 borders are tantamount to Auschwitz borders (the exact quotation is: "This map [of 1967 borders] reminds us of memories of Auschwitz"). My journey into the origins of this aphorism had reached another dead end.

It is not a coincidence that I left Eban's historical records to the last phase of my journey in the research of this book. Eban was a prolific writer; he left behind him two autobiographies (1977; 1993), several books on the history of diplomacy and international relations (1983; 1998), TV series, as well as many newspaper articles and interviews over the course of his long career. The saying was not found in either of his two autobiographies. Yet a similar quote appeared, for the first time, in his book on "new diplomacy," which came out in 1983. In a chapter on "the unending conflict in the Middle East," in a section dealing with opposition of the PLO to the Camp David Accords and the suggested autonomy plan for the Palestinians, Eban stated:

In the final resort the Arab cause in the West Bank and Gaza will stand or fall
by the decision of the Palestinian Arabs. Their diplomatic history refutes the
idea that nations usually act in their own best interest. *They have never missed
a chance of losing an opportunity* [my emphasis]. They have persistently rejected
proposals conceived largely in their own interest, only to look back to them
nostalgically when they have receded from view. (1983, 229)

Another possible source of information for Eban is his archival collection,
which was presented by his family to the Harry S. Truman Research Institute for the Advancement of Peace at the Hebrew University of Jerusalem. It
was a natural choice for the family following the establishment of the Abba
Eban Center for Diplomacy at the Institute in 1997. Luckily, there was no
need to pore over all the material. The librarian who catalogued the archive
cleverly indicated the term "opportunity" as a keyword in the digital lexicon
(certainly one of the perks of our age). One of the references related to a ne-
glected article, published by Eban in *The Jewish Frontier* (the journal subsequently folded) in 1987, under the title "An Opportunity Squandered?"[2] In
this article, Eban dealt again with the famous Israeli government decision,
made on June 19, 1967, to offer peace to Egypt and Syria in return for full
withdrawal from the occupied territories (see chapter 8). The article, the content of which had appeared in his autobiography (1977, 436), argued that the
offer was delivered to Egypt and Syria by the United States but was rejected
by the Arab states, as manifested in the resolutions of the Khartoum Arab
Summit in September 1967. Here, for the first time, Eban added the sentence
that "*[T]he Arab leadership has never lost a chance of missing an opportunity* [my
emphasis]. It was the first time in the history of war that the victor had sued
for peace while the vanquished demanded unconditional surrender" (Truman
Institute Library 1988, 10). Interestingly, in his updated version of his autobiography, Eban referred again to this episode and even quoted the same sentence above (about the victor and the vanquished), which appeared in the
article but not in the first biography (1977, 436), yet he omitted the reference
to the Arabs' constant missing of opportunities (1993, 450).

Thus, Eban used this quotation at least twice and in two different contexts:
one relating to the Palestinians and the autonomy plan; and the second to the
Arabs in the post-1967 period. Assuming that these are the sources of the famous dictum, it seems that it went through slight changes even under Eban's
hand, from "They [the Palestinians] have never missed a chance of losing an
opportunity" to "the Arab leadership has never lost a chance of missing an
opportunity." And so Eban's famous aphorism—it seems—has been refined
along the years and the new version—"never miss an opportunity to miss an
opportunity"—was accepted as the true quotation because, quite simply, it

sounds better. Eban himself did not repeat this saying in his latest autobiography, as noted above. My estimate is that in 1993, after the PLO recognition of UN Resolution 242 (which implied recognition of Israel) in 1988 and the announcement of the Oslo Agreements (though it is unclear whether Eban was aware of Oslo while writing his book in 1993), he thought that the maxim was no longer relevant. This assessment is validated by the journalist Akiva Eldar, who spent many hours with Eban as a *Haaretz* correspondent. According to his testimony, Eban thought late in his career that the maxim was more relevant to Israel than to the Palestinians or the Arab states.[3] Yet the quip had long left Eban's "possession"; many Israelis and others, believing that Israel has always presented peace initiatives while the Arabs and the Palestinians have rejected them, continued using this saying. Its use, therefore, is not so much related to factual information as to political proclivities. And thus we begin the story of missed opportunities in the Arab-Israeli conflict.

NOTES

1. http://en.wikiquote.org/wiki/Abba_Eban.

2. The article might have disappeared if the International Center for Peace in the Middle East had not collected three of Eban's articles, published in 1987 (Truman Institute Library 1988).

3. Interview with Akiva Eldar, March 1, 2013.

ON SEPTEMBER 1, 1982, US president Ronald Reagan outlined his plan for resolution of the Arab-Israeli conflict in a speech that would later be known as the Reagan Plan. Reagan ended his speech with the following passage:

> It has often been said—and regrettably too often been true—that the story of the search for peace and justice in the Middle East is *a tragedy of opportunities missed* [my emphasis]. In the aftermath of the settlement in Lebanon [following the Israeli invasion] we now face an opportunity for a broader peace. This time we must not let it slip from our grasp. We must look beyond the difficulties and obstacles of the present and move with fairness and resolve toward a brighter future. We owe it to ourselves, and to posterity, to do no less. For if we miss this chance to make a fresh start, we may look back on this moment from some later vantage point and realize how much that failure cost us. (cited in Quandt 1993, 482)

In this passage, Reagan used a term, "missed opportunity," that has since come into frequent use by academics and laymen both. Zeev Maoz, for example, asserts in his analysis of Israeli-Arab diplomatic exchanges that Israeli decision makers missed many opportunities to resolve the conflict. In his examination of the negotiations with Jordan's King ʿAbdallah, he states that the monarch "was clearly eager to make peace with Israel. Yet Israel turned a cold shoulder and perhaps missed an opportune moment, as had been the case with the [Syrian leader's] Zaʿim initiative" (2004, 398). Likewise, the so-called New Historians employ the term "missed opportunity" to denote the availability of an alternative policy choice that was not pursued by decision makers in Jerusalem. These studies usually place the blame for missing the opportunity for peace squarely and exclusively on Israeli shoulders (see, in particular, Shlaim 2000; Maoz 2004; Pappe 2006).

In contrast, the conventional Israeli position is that despite their own relentless and assiduous attempts to reach accord with the Arabs, long-sought peace has eluded Israel because of Arab intransigence. In this connection, the mythical dictum of Abba Eban, Israel's legendary foreign minister, that "the Palestinians [or Arabs] have never missed an opportunity to miss an opportunity" is often quoted as proof of Arab obstinacy and folly. Interestingly, David Ben-Gurion, Israel's first prime minister, discussed the cardinal significance of seizing historical opportunities. In a speech to the Knesset (Israeli parliament) delivered in August 1952, he said the following:

> All my life down to today—as a Zionist and as a Jew—I regarded peace and understanding with the Arabs as a basic and primary value . . . I would regard it as a grievous sin not only against our generation but also against future generations were we not to do everything possible to reach mutual understanding with our Arab neighbors and were the coming generations able to blame the Israeli government with missing any opportunity whatsoever for peace . . . I would not want to be the person that our grandchildren or great-grandchildren would charge with having missed, at some point, a possible chance for Israeli-Arab peace. (quoted in Morris 2001, 268–269)

On the Arab side, conventional wisdom has it that Israel's intransigent position has been responsible for missed opportunities for peace. Thus, for example, Hassan, then Jordan's crown prince and an avowed supporter of peace negotiations, asserted in mid-1980:

> Often, opportunities for peace have been there for the taking, but Israeli leaders have shown extreme reluctance to abandon the siege mentality and the irredentist claims that have characterized their politics. It is as though they do not want to live in the region as partners, but only as overlords. The state of Israel may be *in* the Middle East but its leaders do not wish to be *of* it. (1984, 121)

It is hard to concede that in any given conflict there is only one party to blame; logic dictates that missed opportunities occur on both sides, depending on the historical circumstances and the actors involved. The underlying assumption of this study is that both sides have missed opportunities for peace. By studying all the relevant episodes of Arab-Israeli negotiations on the basis of a theoretical definition developed for this purpose, it is hoped that the present volume will lead to a better understanding of the extent of the opportunity missed in each case and the party to be blamed for missing it.

The fact that the term "missed opportunity" is often associated with the new Zionist historiography is not surprising. Apart from the important analysis of a handful of case studies, the repeated use of this term probably reflects a certain political disappointment at the road not taken by Israeli and Arab leaders. More generally, the question of missed opportunities is raised "when observers are dissatisfied with a given historical outcome and argue that policymakers could have achieved a better one if they had acted differently" (George 2006, 87). It is surprising, however, that the term itself has not been adequately clarified or defined—either in relation to the Arab-Israeli conflict or in relation to any other conflict. One possible reason for this omission is that there are serious obstacles to proving that an opportunity has indeed been missed. As Alexander George and Jane Holl asserted, "It is often difficult to judge the degree of confidence that can be ascribed to what appears to have been a missed opportunity." The efforts to establish that a certain episode constitutes a missed opportunity, they continue, may be regarded as no more than an "academic exercise" (George and Holl 2000, 35).

Despite the academic hazards entailed, the analysis of historical episodes as possible missed opportunities can be related to the study of counterfactuals in the social sciences.[1] This kind of study involves "what if" or "if-then" statements, usually about the past. In Richard Ned Lebow's opinion, the researcher must construct a "plausible counterfactual," that is, a logical path between the counterfactual change and the hypothesized outcome (Lebow 2000, 565). To be sure, there have been some attempts at constructing alternative histories in recent years. Their aim was to imagine what might have happened at crucial historical moments had the known outcome not transpired (e.g., Waugh and Greenberg 1986; Roberts 2004; Cowley 2006; Rosenfeld 2005; Tetlock, Lebow, and Parker 2009). In Robert Cowley's opinion, this kind of writing "can be a tool to enhance the understanding of history, to make it come alive." In addition, "what ifs" can define true turning points and eliminate so-called hindsight bias (Cowley 2006, xiii–xiv; Taleb 2005, 56). This bias—"outcome knowledge"—leads people to see the future as more contingent than the past; that is, once we know what happened, it is difficult to recall that other possibilities were relevant at the time and that the outcome was not necessarily inevitable (Tetlock, Lebow, and Parker 2009, 17, 25). In the words of the editors of one of the "what if" collections, "The more people try to transport themselves by acts of imagination into counterfactual worlds . . . the more likely they are to realize that history could indeed have taken a different course" (ibid., 4). Such thinking refutes the notion of historical inevitability, as it involves also the realization of logically possible alternatives other than those which were in fact realized.

Attempts at constructing alternative imaginative historical accounts are more than problematic since "the sinuous paths of conditional events lead to accounts whose potential is nearly infinite. Every event can be retold, relived, and remembered as an 'opportunity' that was seized too early, too late, or not at all" (Serfaty 1988, 14). The difficulties inherent in writing alternative or virtual histories are clear: Lebow admitted that the outcomes in counterfactual experimentation in history and political science are always uncertain as "we can neither predict the future nor rerun the tape of history" (2000, 551). I. William Zartman called counterfactual analysis "a minefield" (2005, 3). Maoz added, "We can tell what happened, but we cannot tell what would have transpired" (2004, 387). In this, Maoz—perhaps unwittingly—followed the assertion of the well-known historian Michael Oakeshott: "The question . . . is never what must, or what might have taken place, but solely what the evidence obliges us to conclude did take place" (1933, 139). In his opinion, the historian differs from the eyewitness or the participant in that "he is never called upon to consider what might have happened had circumstances been different" (1933, 140). No wonder that many historians have rejected all kinds of counterfactual inquiry. E. H. Carr, for example, who disagreed with Oakeshott on many historiographical issues, shared his view on this matter, dismissing the "might-have-been school of thought" as no more than "a parlour game" (1990, 95–96).

Yet not all historians reject counterfactual reasoning. In response to Carr's dismissive view, Hugh Trevor-Roper wrote:

> I suppose that no phrase was more of an affront to my own historical beliefs than the phrase about the might-have-beens of history. Of course I agree that some historical speculations are useless, and some may reflect personal nostalgia. But at any given moment of history there are real alternatives, and to dismiss them as unreal because they were not realized—because (in Mr. Carr's phrase) they have been closed by the fait accompli—is to take the reality out of the situation. How can we "explain what happened and why" if we only look at what happened and never consider the alternatives, the total pattern of forces whose pressure created the event? (1981, 363)

Therefore, Trevor-Roper concluded, "History is not merely what happened; it is what happened in the context of what might have happened . . . it must incorporate, as a necessary element, the alternatives, the might-have-beens" (1981, 364). This alternative, in his words, is "a lost moment of history," which "was not a historical necessity, a consequence hanging in the stars, but the result, at first, of particular human accidents or decisions or events that in themselves were not necessary; it could have been otherwise" (Trevor-Roper

1988). This view dovetails with Isaiah Berlin's refusal to see history as inevitable, recommending the historian to mark the frontiers between reliable and unreliable history, that is, "the placing of what occurred (or might occur) in the context of what could have happened (or could happen)" (1955, 31). The reason for the refusal to contemplate the might-have-been, according to Jonathan Clark, is psychological: once a major decision has been taken, it has to be rationalized in retrospect as inevitable and rational in light of the prevailing circumstances (2004, 258). In contrast, however, the analysis of contingency shows the infinity of roads into the future that were open in the past.

In light of the apparent difficulties inherent in the construction of counterfactuals, the present work does not go so far as to develop an alternative historical narrative. My aim is more modest: to offer an educated assessment of whether certain episodes in the Arab-Israeli conflict can be defined as plausible missed opportunities. The book explores, on the basis of certain variables, whether other alternatives existed; these are choices that fall within "the horizon of the possibility" (quoted in Bunzl 2004, 857). This book is thus based on Max Weber's premise that history does recognize possibilities. In his view, "In every line of every historical work, indeed in every selection of archival and source materials for publication, there are, or more correctly, must be, 'judgments of possibility,' if the publication is to have value for knowledge" (1949, 173). We are primarily concerned with possibilities that seemed probable in the past.

In order to miss an opportunity, an opportunity must first present itself. Opportunities are occasions to "do something" or favorable moments for achieving a certain purpose. The opportune moment, according to Zartman, "is not just 'whenever' but is contextually determined, in relation to the conflict" (2005, 10). The opportunity may come from a lull in the fighting, a temporary cease-fire, or from a meeting of the parties. Such an opportunity, he writes, "offers an opening for specific measures, for it is not self-perpetuating and will fall apart at the next incident if not seized and solidified" (2005, 12). In a similar way, Ilan Peleg and Paul Scham emphasize that most breakthroughs in the Middle East peace process occur following some momentous political or military event that significantly affects the status quo. They call this variable "the trauma effect" (2010, 220). The invitation to seize the moment usually comes from a third party but it can also be presented by one of the rival parties. In any case, the moment must be seized and developed, as the situation would not produce its own solution. Zartman emphasizes that opportunities "are not revolving doors, where entry appears at regular intervals"; they constitute a period of time in the life of the conflict when diplomacy is possible (2005, 17). Thus, when a chain of circumstances produces an opportunity, a liminal period is created; this makes possible a certain breakthrough in the deadlocked conflict. If this moment—or opportunity—is not seized, it is likely to disappear. A different view, however, holds that opportunities do not "knock," but that political leaders and diplomats must create or develop them (Kurtzer et al. 2013, 269).

What turns a historical opportunity into a missed opportunity? The academic literature available on this issue is rather limited. The existing studies focus on two kinds of missed opportunities: for signing a peace treaty or advancing toward such an end (mainly with regard to the Arab-Israeli conflict); and for avoiding global and regional wars or crises before they started or for terminating them before they had run their course (see, e.g., McNamara et al. 1999; George and Holl 2000; Zartman 2005). This study is concerned with the first type. Deborah Larson offers the following definition for a missed opportunity:

> A missed opportunity for agreement is a situation where there was at least one alternative that the parties to a conflict preferred or would have preferred to nonagreement . . . Missed opportunities refer to what might have been, to possibilities that for one reason or another were never realized. Not all failures by states to reach agreements, therefore, qualify as missed opportunities. In the first place, both sides must have wanted an agreement. Second, one must show how changes in a set of historical conditions might have led to a different outcome. If structural constraints such as the balance of power, incompatible objectives, the deep-seated influence of the military-industrial complex, or strategic considerations prevented agreement, for example, then perhaps there were no lost possibilities. Finally, one should not have to rewrite *too much* history to achieve a different outcome: there must have been a plausible sequence of events that could have led to an accord. (Larson 1997, 702–703)

Larson suggested this definition within her analysis of the role of trust between the United States and the Soviet Union; specifically, she looked at the scope of missed opportunities to regulate the arms race and global competition during the Cold War years. Though useful and innovative, I find this definition too vague to apply to empirical cases. In addition, Larson's definition and other similar scholarly statements create a binary dichotomy between missed and unmissed opportunities: they either exist or they do not. A binary dichotomy between missed and unmissed opportunities, however, is likely to exclude historical episodes that can be seen as plausible not only in retrospect but also at the time of their occurrence. Yet since we cannot determine with certainty that a particular opportunity has been missed or not, perhaps we should assess the degree of its plausibility. This can be determined by the existence of certain variables, as suggested below. Avoiding a binary dichotomy, this model—called by Weber in a different context the "calculus of probability" (1949, 182)—offers a scale or continuum of plausibility of missed opportunities (ranging from nonexistent to highly plausible).[2] We therefore define the term *plausible missed opportunity* as a situation in which one party to the conflict or a third party offers a meaningful and attractive political alternative to the status quo, which embodies an option for resolving the conflict or moving toward that end, but this alternative is not pursued for various reasons. In order to identify more rigorously the set of plausible missed opportunities in the Arab-Israeli conflict, then, it is necessary to address three questions.

The first question we pose regarding each case is: To what extent does the analyzed case study constitute a historical opportunity? Evidently, not every historical moment or diplomatic initiative to solve the conflict constitutes a historical opportunity. To be determined as such, we should identify the existence of two elements:

1. *A formal and/or informal initiative presented by one of the parties to the conflict, or a trustworthy mediator, that has an element of attractiveness for the offered party (or parties)*. Since "attractiveness" cannot be objectively measured—what is considered attractive and generous by the offering party may be considered otherwise by the offered party—it is thus necessary to assess the extent to which the offer is an innovative or radical departure from the status quo existing between the conflicting parties. If the offer includes a significant incentive, or "mega-incentive"—that is, an offer that cannot be refused in terms of security and peace (Goren 2009)—then it may be defined as highly attractive to the offered party (or parties). Also, the attractiveness of an offer is enhanced if the offer, in one way or another, is presented repeatedly, implying that the offering party is consistent and serious in its effort.

2. *A significant historical process or event that creates a basis for the emergence of alternative conduct or reasoning about the conflict*. In other words, the convergence of certain historical processes and events—what Rosenfeld termed "points of divergence" (2005, 4, 11)—may help induce a convenient moment or circumstances for pursuing peace. Such developments, in American parlance, create a "window of opportunity" for a change in the conflict. These may include wars, revolutions, disintegration of states or regimes, as well as changes of governments and leaders. Such meaningful events may create a "trauma effect" that increases the receptiveness of leaders and society to the option of peaceful negotiations.

The convergence of these two elements may produce an "ideal" opportunity. Yet in the absence of the coalescence of certain historical processes or the "trauma effect," the mere existence of an attractive offer by the third party or one of the rivals may be sufficient for an opportunity to exist. Such an offer might be the result of a deliberate, proactive policy on the part of the third party to create an opportunity (Kurtzer and Lasensky 2008, 34) or a grand gesture of conciliation offered by one of the warring parties, such as Sadat's visit to Jerusalem in 1977 (Mitchell 2000).

According to this analysis, the existence of a historical opportunity is a product of an objective assessment of the processes, facts, and circumstances prevailing at any given moment. Yet the opportunity also includes a subjective element, which relates to the ability of the leader(ship) to identify the elements that create the opportunity and act to exploit it (Biran 2008, 39). Clearly, the inability of the leader(ship) to recognize the existence of a historical opportunity would result in its loss. It is possible that a seemingly attractive offer will not be pursued because its timing is not considered propitious by one party, but this will not detract from its being an opportune moment.

The second question is: If a historical opportunity has been identified, how plausible or feasible was it to seize the opportunity and realize the potential it embodied? Opportunity, wrote the American diplomat Richard Haass, "represents possibility; not inevitability" (2005, 4). Therefore, the seizing of the opportunity depends on the historical circumstances and the leaders involved. A historical opportunity is more likely to bear fruit if the time is ripe to solve the related conflict. A ripe moment, according to Zartman, is when the conflicting parties share two perceptual elements: a "mutually hurting stalemate" and a sense of a subjective "way out" (2000, 228–231; 2005, 10–11). Yet since it is difficult to weigh ripeness, particularly while the events are still taking place, it is suggested that the potentiality of the opportunity be examined. We therefore propose to assess the plausibility of a missed opportunity as a function of the following four variables:

1. *The degree of legitimacy that the political leadership enjoys, allowing it to promote new (and occasionally unpopular) initiatives.* Clearly, a leader enjoying legitimacy, respect, and seniority is in a better position to seize a historical opportunity than a counterpart who does not. Following this line of thought, when such a leader fails to seize the opportunity, the loss is that much greater. In contrast to the Israeli case studies where measurement of leadership's legitimacy is relatively feasible, the legitimacy of Arab leaders is more difficult to determine due to the lack of democratic institutions and reliable polls. In case such information is missing, this variable will be measured by the public image of the leader as a strong and legitimate leader. This variable posits that there must be strong, authoritative, and legitimate leadership on both sides that can negotiate an agreement, "sell" it to the people, and implement it (Peleg and Scham 2010, 218–219). When legitimate leadership fails to seize a historical opportunity, it enhances the plausibility of a missed opportunity.

2. The degree of the willingness, motivation, and determination of the leaders on both sides to take a bold step to change the course of events. Such willingness, which reflects a change in the leadership's state of mind, may be the result of a conviction that a peaceful solution is necessary because the continuation of the status quo (what Zartman termed "hurting stalemate") is detrimental to their state's interests. This position may be due to a change in the leader's belief system and/or pressure exerted by civil society elements. In such a case, the leader might even be willing to contemplate going the "extra mile" to achieve what he or she believes is essential for the state. One reliable indication of this willingness is the leader's persistence in proposing a peaceful solution. Another is the leader's perseverance in the negotiations despite gaps in the parties' positions. Plausibility is thus also a function of leadership's response to the offer.

3. The level of trust (or mistrust) existing between them, which may also be based on the history of past interactions. Ignorance or superficial acquaintance of the other party may lead to negative stereotypes and impede the potential for a positive development. In contrast, past interactions may reduce barriers and produce building blocks toward a certain trust between the conflicting parties. Mutual trust, built along a significant period of time, helps leaders ensure that they will not miss opportunities. Examples of constructive trust-building were Egyptian-Israeli relations following the Yom Kippur War and the concluding of two disengagement agreements between those two countries in the 1970s that culminated in the signing of the 1979 peace treaty, and Jordanian-Israeli relations that culminated in the 1994 peace treaty. However, past interactions may result in mistrust, as reflected in the case of Palestinian-Israeli relations since the signing of the Oslo Accords in the 1990s. The existence of trust when an opportunity is not seized enhances the plausibility of a missed opportunity.

4. The level of constructive involvement of a third party that exploits a historical opportunity to promote a dialogue. This is particularly relevant when the conflicting parties are unaware of the historical opportunity or feel insecure to move forward because of mistrust or uncertainty. When the third party is the initiator of the peace offer, it is expected to lead a balanced mediation process. If the offer has been presented by one of the conflicting parties, the third party is expected to fill the role of facilitator. Third-party involvement is not, in itself, a condition of a missed opportunity, but if a third party is involved, it is critical that such involvement is constructive. Thus, high-level involvement may contribute to a missed opportunity as a result of unbalanced mediation, mistakes, and insufficient preparedness on the part of the mediating party.

Finally, an analysis of the plausibility of a relevant case study is not complete without an assessment of the legacy effect of the event, which can only be evaluated in retrospect. It is therefore proposed to assess the degree to which some change or progress has been made in the conflict as a result of the offer. An offer may not necessarily result in the signing of a peace agreement but may trigger a paradigmatic change or the breaking of a certain taboo in the internal political debate that, in the long run, can bring peace. Thus, for example, if the failed negotiations between Egypt and Israel in 1971 ultimately contributed to the signing of the peace agreement in 1979, we may conclude that the opportunity in 1971 was not completely lost. Similarly, if the failed Camp David II negotiations in July 2000 did shatter the taboo in Israeli society regarding the negotiability of Jerusalem, then the opportunity was not completely missed. Observing such a long-term change—which may be a result of a deeper historical perspective that allows a better appreciation of a possible change—may reduce the perceived loss caused by the missed opportunity.

In sum, what is suggested is a three-tiered analysis for evaluating the plausibility of a given missed opportunity:

1. Identification of a historical opportunity
2. Assessing the plausibility of the missed opportunity
3. Evaluating the legacy effect of the missed opportunity

The continuum of plausibility of missed opportunities is divided into four levels for the sake of convenience: high, medium, low, and nonexistent, as shown in table 1.

Most of the case studies analyzed in this book unfortunately represent plausible missed opportunities. This finding highlights the importance of analyzing the few plausible opportunities that were not missed, such as the signing of peace treaties between Israel, Egypt, and Jordan. A greater understanding of such cases may contribute to a better understanding of the opportunities that were indeed missed.

To be qualified as a missed opportunity, should the alternative path be seen as possible at the time or only in retrospect? Niall Ferguson, in his collected volume on virtual history, included only plausible or probable alternatives "which we can show on the basis of contemporary evidence that contemporaries actually considered" (1997, 86; Weinryb 2003, 393). Likewise, Simon Serfaty argued that "hindsight, which shapes our memories of the past, permits the belated discovery of the missed opportunities that haunt our perception of the present" (1988, 13). A somewhat less compelling premise was offered by George and Holl, who argued that "missed opportunities that rest too heavily on hindsight carry less plausibility." Yet in their opinion, "An after-the-fact identification of an action or strategy not known or considered at the time can still be useful in drawing lessons" (2000, 35).[3] There can be no

Table 1. Level of Plausibility of Missed Opportunity Conditions

High	Existence of historical opportunity; high potential (3–4 variables); apathy on the part of the offered party; no or low impact on the ground.
Medium	Existence of historical opportunity; some potential (2 variables); some interest on the part of the offered party; no or low impact on the ground.
Low	Existence of historical opportunity; limited potential (1 variable); interest of the offered party; no or low impact on the ground.
Nonexistent	1. No historical opportunity. 2. Existence of historical opportunity; existence of potential; significant impact on the ground and/or the signing of an agreement.

denying that a historical perspective allows us to reassess events with the benefits it affords; thus, for example, the signing of the Egyptian-Israeli peace treaty in 1979 cast new light on President Sadat's sincerity in offering his peace initiative in February 1971 and the degree of Israel's missing an opportunity then. However, if there were other alternatives examined on the Israeli side at the time of the 1971 episode, their existence enhances our assessment that the event was indeed a missed opportunity.

Michael Greig's research on "moments of opportunity" offers several perspectives on the question of whether there are moments that can be identified as more likely to develop into missed opportunities and refers specifically to the mediator's role. First, mediation can be successful early in a conflict, before the disputants have built up high levels of hostility that make compromise difficult. Second, and in some contradiction to the first conclusion, mediation can become successful late in the conflict, after disputants have expended significant resources in conflict with one another and eventually become more willing to improve their relationship (Greig 2001, 715). Such an option is not surprising, taking into account the possibility that the rivals may have reached the point of a mutually hurting stalemate, according to ripeness theory. Third, when mediation was initiated by one of the rivals, the likelihood of achieving a mediated agreement significantly increased (Greig 2001, 716). As the Arab-Israeli conflict has been studded with many third-party interventions, it will be interesting to see whether local initiatives constitute missed opportunities more often than external ones.

When a certain episode in the conflict is defined as a plausible missed opportunity, it is important to explain why this alternative was not pursued. Tuchman usually attributes folly to mistakes made by decision makers (1984, 3–4). Zartman, on the other hand, gives leaders more credit, asserting that "Neglect, obliviousness, and stupidity always take their toll, but generally it can be assumed that policy-makers thought they knew what they were doing and why" (2005, 5). Indeed, the reasons for choosing a certain policy should be given due respect but evaluated critically all the same. This study does not claim that the proposed but unchosen course of action, on certain occasions, would have definitively ended in a peaceful agreement, but rather that an opportunity "to do something" to promote peace was missed. While it is possible that the other option could have negatively affected the course of events, it is generally believed that it offered a preferable policy choice. In this respect, the study of missed opportunities entails a value judgment on the part of the writer.

It is agreed that analyzing certain episodes in the Arab-Israeli conflict through the prism of missed opportunities may be merely "an academic exercise," to use George and Holl's term, or, as Michael Heim posited, the engagement in virtual history may be "real in effect but not in fact" (quoted in Weinryb 2003, 408). Nonetheless, it is my belief that the kind of intellectual experiment suggested in these pages has its benefits, as policymakers and the public in general may find in these missed opportunities educated lessons for future negotiations. This line of thought is succinctly argued by Niall Ferguson:

> Because decisions about the future are—usually—based on weighing up the potential consequences of alternative courses of action, it makes sense to compare the actual outcomes of what we did in the past with the conceivable outcomes of what we might have done. (Ferguson 1997, 2)

Seen in another context, veteran US diplomat Dennis Ross, who was involved in many American mediation attempts to solve the Arab-Israeli conflict, might have added that one requirement of statecraft is recognizing a strategic opening. In his opinion, "Being able to marshal the wherewithal to act on an opening and exploit it, in the final analysis, is one of the better measures of effective statecraft. By the same token, missing opportunities or squandering them may be one of the better measures of statecraft poorly executed" (2007, 22).

This kind of thinking is based on the assumption that history may offer us not only interesting stories but also lessons for the future. The eminent historian Eric Hobsbawm asserted, "Unfortunately, one thing historical experience has also taught historians is that nobody ever seems to learn from it." Perhaps so, but nevertheless he concluded, "We must go on trying" (1997, 35). Moreover, the lessons of history remind us of the choices that decision makers confronted, as well as the role of chance and accident in human affairs. The lessons of imaginary history, wrote Roberts, "make us eschew hubris, by reminding us what so easily might have been—and what still might be—around only the next corner" (2004, 6).

Many good historians have attempted to understand why we do not learn from history or, conversely, why we do not draw lessons from their studies (e.g., Liddell-Hart 1971; May 1973; McNamara et al. 1999; Shamir and Maddy-Weitzman 2005, 13; Cordesman 2007). This book is indeed an attempt to draw some lessons from the opportunities existing in the history of Israeli-Arab peaceful negotiations. Zeev Maoz once sarcastically noted that the Israeli way of learning is to study history and learn the lessons of its mistakes, only to repeat them the next time (2004, 208). On a more positive note, it is my hope that decision makers on both sides of the conflict will draw on the lessons of missed opportunities for peace, and, armed with this knowledge, will be in a better position *not* to miss opportunities once they appear; or, better still, that decision makers will propose attractive initiatives of their own that, in turn, will develop into new opportunities.

NOTES

1. Missed opportunities can also be analyzed in the exact sciences: thus, for example, Alexander Kohn (1989) investigated some historical episodes in which scientists missed the opportunity for a discovery that was later made by another scientist. On page 179 he presents a list of thirteen missed discoveries during the years 1242–1939.

2. A similar idea was suggested by George and Holl (2000, 35) when they made a distinction between outcomes that would *surely* have been achieved and outcomes that *might* have been achieved.

3. In contrast, one may refer to Barbara Tuchman's assertion that in order to define a certain policy as folly, it is imperative that its negative consequences are seen at the time (1984, 4).

CHAPTER 1

THE FAYSAL-WEIZMANN AGREEMENT

1919

IT IS COMMONLY BELIEVED that the modern Arab-Israeli conflict in the land of Palestine (Eretz Israel) began with the arrival of the first waves of Jewish immigration at the end of the nineteenth century. True, local Arab-Palestinian leaders occasionally submitted petitions to the Ottoman authorities, complaining about what they considered to be Jewish-Zionist provocations in the fields of immigration, land purchase, and labor (Ben-Bassat 2009, 43–62). These, however, did not deteriorate into open and wide clashes but were limited to local—albeit occasionally armed—disputes. At the same time, the pre-1914 period saw some peaceful Zionist-Arab contacts during which an agreement regarding the nature of their relations in Palestine was considered—without the knowledge of the Ottoman overlords (Mandel 1976, 165–207; Caplan 1983a, 10–27; Tessler 1994, 127–145). These contacts were interrupted by the outbreak of the Great War in August 1914, though in any case it seems that the gaps between the two sides' positions and aspirations were unbridgeable. The first formal attempt in the modern era to reach an understanding between Jews and Arabs was the Faysal-Weizmann Agreement, signed in January 1919; however, it was never implemented and was in fact repudiated by Faysal before the ink even dried. This chapter will analyze to what extent that agreement signified a missed opportunity.

THE EPISODE

The territory of Palestine had become an important bone of contention between the superpowers, the Arabs, and the Jews even before World War I. With numerous actors involved, a string of agreements made during the war only complicated Palestine's political fate. For example, there was the correspondence, exchanged in 1915–1916 between the British high commissioner in Cairo, Sir Henry McMahon, and the Hashemite leader in the Hijaz, Husayn bin 'Ali, which promised the land, according to the Arab interpretation, to the Hashemite Arabs upon the war's end (Antonius 1965, 164–183).[1] The Sykes-Picot Agreement, signed between Britain and France in April 1916, with Russia joining in immediately after, secretly pledged that Palestine would remain under international control. Then the British published the Balfour Declaration in November 1917, which promised to view with favor the establishment of a Jewish national home in Palestine (Tessler 1994, 145–150). When the war did end in August 1918, Palestine was under the control of British military forces. And by the time the Paris Peace Conference convened five months later it was clear that the British would remain the masters in Palestine, following the French willingness to withdraw any claims to the land, as reflected in the Lloyd George–Clemenceau Agreement of December 1918. Still, the fate of Palestine in terms of boundaries and the roles ascribed to the Arab majority and Jewish minority was nebulous.

In light of this background, almost any Arab-Jewish understanding was set to dovetail with certain Zionist and Arab interests: it could project legitimacy to the Zionist claim over Eretz Israel at a time when only eighty thousand Jews inhabited the land (in contrast to six hundred thousand Arabs) while simultaneously helping to secure the Arab claim over Syria, which was ruled by Amir Faysal, the third son of King Husayn of the Hijaz, since its capture in the summer of 1918 at the end of the Great Arab Revolt. Because that territory was accorded to the French in the Sykes-Picot Agreement, Faysal needed British support to achieve his goal of independence. Any Arab-Jewish agreement could also facilitate the task of the British in Palestine in implementing the promised Balfour Declaration. Zionist and Arab interests certainly converged when it came to the Sykes-Picot Agreement—both sides rejected it out of hand (Caplan 1983a, 37–38; Sanders 1983, 637). Indeed, early contacts between the Hashemites and the Zionists envisaged some form of cooperation regarding Palestine (Perlmann 1944, 130). This cooperation, however, rested on a mistaken Arab belief that Jewish settlement and colonization would be limited to "humanitarian grounds, subject to the limitations imposed by a proper regard for the warfare and the political and economic rights of the existing population" (Antonius 1965, 285).

In the second half of 1918, Dr. Chaim Weizmann, president of the World Zionist Organization (WZO) and the recognized leader of the Zionist movement, met Faysal twice. The first time was in early June, in the desert, near Aqaba, while commanding the Arab Revolt. Weizmann thought that this meeting "laid the foundations of a life-long friendship" (1949, 294). A second meeting was held in London in December. Both meetings were masterminded by the British—and particularly by T. E. Lawrence (Lawrence of Arabia), in his capacity as a liaison officer with the Arab Revolt. The British interest in promoting a Jewish-Arab dialogue was to forestall France's role in Syria, in contrast to the understandings penned in the Sykes-Picot Agreement. At the London meeting the main lines of the soon-to-be-signed agreement were drawn. Faysal's aspirations focused on Syria and Mesopotamia, not Palestine. Weizmann was charmed by Faysal's personality, thinking he had found an ideal Arab leader with whom a kind of Zionist-Arab entente could be worked out. He had good reason to believe that Faysal would offer him better terms than the Palestinian Arabs he had met shortly before who were averse to Zionist aims in Palestine. Likewise, there is ample evidence of Faysal's appreciation for the Jewish leader and his ability to elicit Jewish financial support for the anticipated Arab kingdom (Friedman 2000, 217–220, 225; Caplan 1983a, 36–37; Reinharz 1993, 253–256).

On January 3, 1919, days before the opening of the Paris Peace Conference, Faysal and Weizmann made history by signing the first Jewish-Arab agreement in the modern period. It was a formal confirmation of what had been concluded at their London meeting; between the lines one could detect the British desire to oust the French from Syria, or at least to weaken their position there. The agreement envisaged a high level of cooperation between two separate political entities, the Arab state and Palestine, the latter presumably under Jewish control; it expressed Arab willingness to implement the Balfour Declaration and encourage the immigration of Jews to Palestine on a large scale. The boundaries of the two entities were to be delineated by a special committee following the Paris conference, and provision was to be made for the protection of Arab peasants in Palestine and for Muslim custody of the holy places. As a quid pro quo, the Zionists promised to "use [their] best efforts to assist the Arab State in providing the means for developing the national resources and economic possibilities thereof." Finally, the parties agreed "to act in complete accord and harmony on all matters . . . before the Peace Congress." The last clause explained, in fact, the motivation of both sides to act in unison (Friedman 2000, 223–234; Sanders 1983, 639; Caplan 1983a, 36–38; Antonius 1965, 437–439; Flapan 1979, 43–44; Sykes 1967, 39–43; Cohen 1970, 141–142; Tibawi 1978, 332–333; Reinharz 1993, 273–274). Faysal, however, conditioned his agreement on the proviso that the Arabs would receive independence, according to the memorandum he submitted to the peace conference. A note to that effect was added to the agreement in his handwriting in Arabic. Were this demand not met, he wrote, "I shall not then be bound by a single word of the present agreement which shall be deemed void and of no account of validity" (quoted in Antonius 1965, 439). There is no doubt that Faysal "regarded the Zionists as the appropriate contractual party in any agreement on the future of Palestine" (Perlmann 1944, 137), but it is less clear what kind of entity for the Jews he had in mind when signing the agreement. Aware of the explosive nature of the agreement, Faysal and Weizmann both pledged to keep it secret; it became public only in June 1936, after Faysal's death in September 1933.

On February 6 Faysal testified before the peace conference, presenting the case for Arab independence based on the right of self-determination. He demanded an Arab kingdom stretching from Damascus to Arabia "reserving Palestine for the consideration of all parties concerned" and asked for an inter-allied commission to investigate the genuine desires of the populations (Flapan 1979, 46). At the same time, an independent Syrian delegation to the conference under the leadership of Shukri Ghanim stated its agreement to the settlement of Jews in "autonomous Palestine, connected with Syria by the sole bond of federation" (Sasson 2004, 22, 295). Jewish contacts facilitated a meeting between Faysal and US president Woodrow Wilson (Friedman 2000, 225–226). Faysal hoped to enlist US support for furthering Syrian independence. Wilson, though a believer in self-determination and a critic of colonialism, was nevertheless unwilling to interfere in the struggle between Britain and France in Syria. Later, in May, he agreed to send the King-Crane Commission to Syria to explore the views of the local inhabitants, but by then the Faysal-Weizmann pact was defunct.

The first signs that Faysal would recant the agreement came in March. In an interview with a French newspaper he was quoted to the effect that "If the Jews desire to establish a state and claim sovereign rights in the country [Palestine], I foresee and fear very serious dangers and conflicts between them and other races." This sparked a spate of Jewish inquiries; in response, Faysal wrote a letter to Felix Frankfurter, president of the Zionist Organization of America and a member of the American-Zionist delegation to Paris, reassuring him that "We Arabs, especially the educated among us, look with the deepest sympathy on the Zionist movement." He admitted that he was familiar with the Zionist demands from the Paris conference, regarding them as "moderate and proper," and promised that "we will do our best, insofar as we are concerned, to help." Frankfurter took care to give this letter the utmost publicity. He emphasized that it was "the first Arab voice which had expressed sympathy with national Jewish aims" (Friedman 2000, 228–229; Weizmann 1949, 245–246; Perlmann 1944, 139–140; Cohen 1970, 143–144).

Upon his return to Lebanon and Syria in late April 1919, Faysal felt the growing weight of Arab opposition to the separation of Palestine from the Arab lands. Though word of his agreement with Weizmann was not leaked, Faysal's public statements in favor of Zionist-Arab cooperation and the publication of his correspondence with Frankfurter aroused vehement criticism in Damascus and Palestine (Friedman 2000, 253–257). Yet Faysal was still not showing signs of abandoning his vision of Arab-Jewish cooperation. In mid-April 1919 he met a prominent Jewish delegation from Palestine, which decided to found a joint Arab-Jewish committee, tasked inter alia with creating a "rapprochement and an entente between the two communities in Palestine." This was meant to serve as the first step toward implementing the Faysal-Weizmann Agreement (Friedman 2000, 230–231).

This positive development in Arab-Jewish relations was not enough to stop Faysal from drifting away from the agreement. The appointment of the King-Crane Commission in May strengthened nationalist feelings among the Arabs, who considered Palestine as part of southern Syria. In early July the Syrian Congress declared its opposition to "the claims of the Zionists for the establishment of a Jewish commonwealth in that part of southern Syria, known as Palestine," demanding that "the unity of the country be maintained under any circumstances" (Antonius 1965, 441). Immediately after, in his testimony before the King-Crane Commission, Faysal declared that the separation between Syria and Palestine was unacceptable and that these areas, as well as Mesopotamia, should be placed under the auspices of the same power. He admitted that not long before he had been prepared to accept Zionism "in its limited sense," but that the wider Zionist aspirations "frightened the people." Faysal's testimony was received with great disappointment by the Zionists (Friedman 2000, 269). When he returned to Europe in the fall of 1919, it was already clear that the French were expected to take over Syria, and the British appeared ready to abandon Faysal and Syria to French interests. In the final analysis, the British-French political alliance proved more important than the Faysal-Weizmann Agreement.

In October Faysal told the *Jewish Chronicle* that he regarded Palestine not as an autonomous Jewish entity, but rather as a province of his future Arab kingdom. This statement would later become Faysal's official position (Caplan 1983a, 41). In response to Jewish demands for clarification, he noted that he needed to pay more heed to "the feeling among Arabs in Palestine" (quoted in ibid., 41; 1983b, 566; Khalidi 1997, 258). Upon returning to Damascus, Faysal faced an increasingly anti-European and anti-Zionist wave of nationalist feeling. In March 1920 the Syrian Congress proclaimed Faysal as the king of independent Syria, which included Palestine. Within weeks, however, the San Remo Conference allocated a mandate in Syria to France and in Palestine to Britain. In June a respected Palestinian representative in the Syrian Congress, 'Izzat Darwaza, declared that his countrymen would "not agree to Palestine being sacrificed on the altar of [Syrian] independence . . . the Government must deny the reports which have spread . . . and deliver specific instructions . . . to reject all the rumors connected with the Zionist question" (quoted in Porath 1974, 89; Caplan 1983b, 567). Faysal was then ousted by the French, which sealed the chapter of the Syrian Kingdom under him. A year later, he would be crowned as the king of Iraq. By then, his position was that

Palestine had not been excluded from the pledge given to the Arabs in the Husayn-MacMahon Correspondence (Sanders 1983, 645). Though another agreement was signed between the Zionist movement and certain Lebanese and Syrian nationalists in March 1920 (Sasson 2004, 23, 296–299), the Faysal-Weizmann Agreement was for all practical purposes null and void.

An interesting sequel to this episode is its place in Arab historiography. In fact, three approaches to the Faysal-Weizmann Agreement emerged in the Arab literature: the first treated the agreement as a piece of British-Zionist forgery out of the conviction that Faysal "could not possibly have put his signature on anything that would have harmed the Arab cause, because of his zealous nationalistic spirit, which was above suspicion." A second view was offered by the historian George Antonius, who accepted the authenticity of the document, crediting Faysal with "a positive belief in the possibility of Arab-Jewish cooperation in Palestine." The third approach blames Faysal for his own selfish ends at the expense of the Palestinian cause (Caplan 1983b, 562–563; Antonius 1965, 286; Tibawi 1978, 332–333; Cohen 1970, 142–143; Furlonge 1969, 71). Regarding the first, there is enough historical evidence to refute the allegation that the Faysal-Weizmann Agreement was a forgery (Friedman 2000, 232–237). It seems, therefore, that the changing historical circumstances, coupled by mounting Arab criticism of the relinquishing of Palestine, led Faysal to reverse his position. In order to keep his nationalist image intact he did not even reveal its existence — a decision that was honored by Weizmann. When the agreement was published, in 1936, at the peak of the Arab Revolt, it caused considerable embarrassment for the Palestinian Arabs and led to desperate calls denying its authenticity. Years later, however, in what became the accepted narrative of the Arab national movement, Antonius argued that Faysal had received from Weizmann "assurances that the Zionists had no intention of working for the establishment of a Jewish government in Palestine" (1965, 285). The Palestinian narrative either ignored the agreement or, at the very least, played down its importance (Kayyali 1978, 53, 65; 1990, 110).

ASSESSMENT

In his judgment of this episode, Caplan argues that "it is difficult to believe that anyone could have seriously contemplated a successful Arab-Zionist agreement at this time" (1983a, 43). This assessment was based, inter alia, on an oft-quoted British intelligence officer who opined that the agreement was "not worth the paper it [was] written on." In the officer's opinion, "No greater mistake could be made than to regard Faisal as a representative of Palestinian Arabs" (Caplan 1983a, 39–40). Yet if we assume, as Zartman advises us, that policymakers usually "knew what they were doing and why" (2005, 5), then both Weizmann and Faysal honestly and sincerely attempted to reach some kind of understanding serving respective Zionist and Arab interests. Both, however, made grave mistakes: Weizmann believed Faysal was "the then-acknowledged leader of the Arabs, the bearer of their hopes" (1949, 246). As such, he presumed he was also the spokesman of the Arabs residing in Palestine. Familiar as he was with the views of certain Palestinians, perhaps it was convenient for him to take Faysal as their spokesman. In addition, he may have not anticipated the level of opposition from the local Arab population. As argued by Perlmann, "During this early period, only a few Zionist leaders were alive to the difficulties which Arab resistance would place in their path" (1944, 128). Faysal, too, misjudged the extent of the opposition—inside and outside Palestine—to its exclusion from the Arab homeland. Undoubtedly, he overrated his own position (Sykes 1967, 43). More generally, the failure of the agreement can be attributed to the fact that the British too changed their position along the way. With the expulsion of Faysal from Syria and the establishment of the British Mandate over Palestine, the interests that lay behind the motives for signing the agreement simply evaporated.

Later, in the 1940s, during discussions within the Jewish Agency, a member of one of the leftist parties, Aharon Cohen, accused the organization of missing important opportunities with regard to the early contacts between Jews and Arabs (1970, 167). Walter Laqueur added that "Later critics of the Zionist executive have asserted that Weizmann and his friends did not try hard enough at the time to win the confidence and friendship of the Arabs" (1972, 238). Surprisingly, the agreement aroused little interest or enthusiasm among Zionists at the time. Christopher Sykes argued that "It was not what the Jews wanted. They wanted a State and they feared entering into any agreement which did not acknowledge their right to build one" (1967, 42). This is a strange explanation: the text of the agreement was explicit enough regarding the aims of the Zionists, as can also be deduced from the Arabs' complete rejection of it.

In retrospect, then, can the Faysal-Weizmann Agreement qualify as a plausible missed opportunity? It can certainly be defined as a historic opportunity as it occurred following a major turning point in the history of the Middle East, on the eve of the disintegration of the Ottoman Empire and the formation of a new political order. In many ways, it was a liminal period in which hitherto unthinkable changes might have been possible. An agreement between Jews and Arabs could theoretically fit in the new regional order. In addition, the offer presented to the Zionists seemed highly attractive at first, as it was thought to include the Arab party's formal approval of establishing a Jewish home in Palestine. As time went by, however, the offer's appeal was substantially reduced when it became obvious that it was not supported by the local Palestinians. At the same time, the Zionist offer—though important—was less attractive to the Arab side from the outset. It promised some tangible dividends to Faysal and the greater Arab nationalist movement, but it offered very little to the Arab population of Palestine. Although this population became aware of the agreement only in 1936, it had vehemently objected to Faysal's early positive statements regarding the Jewish aspirations in Palestine. From the time the Balfour Declaration was announced in 1917, the Palestinians feared the implementation of Jewish plans, which led to a wave of riots in 1920–1921—even absent any knowledge of a secret agreement.

So what was the potentiality level of the episode? The first element in our definition relates to the legitimacy level of the leaders. While Weizmann was the recognized—and, as such, the legitimate—leader of the Zionist movement, the extent to which Faysal represented the Arab Palestinians is less clear. He attempted, to a large extent successfully, to create the impression in the West that he truly represented the Arabs in Syria, Mesopotamia, Palestine, and perhaps elsewhere, though officially he only represented the Kingdom of Hijaz. It is true that in 1919 many Arabs (including Palestinians) were willing to become part of the Syrian Kingdom under his rule, but they were unwilling to accept any concessions made on their behalf, particularly if they involved separating Palestine from the Arab homeland. Henry Cattan, a Palestinian jurist, asserted that Faysal represented only the Hijaz and therefore "possessed no representative capacity that entitled him to speak on behalf of the Arabs of Palestine or of the Arabs generally" (1969, 259).[2] In a similar vein, renowned British diplomat Christopher Sykes (the son of Mark Sykes of the Sykes-Picot Agreement) wrote, "If Feisal had been a Palestinian Arab of Jerusalem his treaty with Zionism might have had some feeble hope of acceptance, but since he was who he was, it had none at all" (Sykes 1967, 43).

The second element relates to the willingness of a leader to take bold new moves on the basis of changes in his thinking. It seems that neither Weizmann nor Faysal were bold or determined enough to actually implement the agreement, even when it served certain aims. It was no coincidence, for example, that it was signed on the eve of the Paris conference—but even this broader context was not enough to give it the launching power it required. Faysal's handwritten condition in the margin of the agreement, giving him an early escape route, adds to this point. It is also noteworthy that Faysal quickly withdrew from the agreement in the face of vehement Arab and Palestinian opposition.

The third element relates to the impact prior contacts between the parties had on the negotiations and the existence of trust. The two leaders had no prior negotiating experience, though Jewish-Arab contacts often occurred in the pre-1914 period. Yet the historical evidence points to the existence of mutual respect and a certain trust between them. Faysal in particular was not averse to the Jewish aspirations, as manifested in his attitude toward the Jews while king of Iraq (1921–1933) and in the amicable relations that developed between his brother, Amir, later king of Jordan (1923–1951), and the Zionist movement (see chapter 4).

The fourth element pertains to the role of the third-party mediator. Initially, the British played a major role in facilitating the agreement, hoping that it would strengthen their claims in the Middle East at the forthcoming Paris conference. From the spring of 1919, however, the agreement threatened to undermine Britain's relations with France. Faysal's demand to establish an Arab kingdom based in Damascus contradicted the Sykes-Picot Agreement and therefore was opposed by Britain. Taking into account its decisive role in the Middle East in the aftermath of World War I, the fact that Britain did not embrace the agreement in Paris or act to implement it further eroded its significance and potentiality. In fact, when all is said and done, none of the parties involved directly or indirectly in the agreement were enthusiastic about seeing its fulfillment.

In sum, this agreement represented but a "window of opportunity," rather than an opportunity to be missed. The fact that Faysal suffered from legitimacy deficiency and that neither he nor his Jewish counterpart was determined enough to push their unprecedented pact, coupled with the declining British interest in implementing it, meant that the potential for opening that window was low. What was the legacy of the agreement? Antonius claimed that the main merit of the agreement lies "in the evidence it affords of the lengths to which Faysal was prepared to go in the sense of Arab-Jewish cooperation so long as that did not conflict with Arab independence" (1965, 286). Caplan argued that the unconsummated agreement "was to become a model for future Zionist suggestions for solving the Palestine problem" and a valuable lesson for future negotiations (1983a, 45–46). In reality, however, the agreement sank into oblivion, at least until 1936. For the Arabs and Palestinians it was a shameful reminder of an illegitimate offer made by an illegitimate Arab leader; for the Zionists—now backed by the British Mandate—it was superfluous. In hindsight, it seems a naïve and premature attempt, dictated by the exegesis of the hour, at solving the conflict.

NOTES

1. For an antithetical Israeli interpretation, see Friedman 1992, 65–96.
2. The same position was adopted by al-Hout 1981, 102–109; Cohen 1970, 143; Ben-Gurion 1975, 9.

CHAPTER 2

THE PEEL PLAN FOR PARTITION

1937

THE IMPOSITION OF THE British Mandate over Palestine spurred the local Arab-Palestinian population to riot against the British and the Jews in 1920–1921. The rest of the 1920s passed relatively calmly until the eruption of the Wailing Wall disturbances in August 1929, which began in Jerusalem but quickly spread, taking the most severe turn in Hebron with the massacre of sixty-seven Jews. Such tension erupting into violence underscored the essence of the conflict between the Zionist and Arab-Palestinian national movements. The conflict flared in 1933 and 1935 as a result of Palestinian frustration at the growing number of Jewish immigrants to Palestine and the expansion of Jewish land purchases. In April 1936 an Arab attack on a Jewish bus triggered yet another wave of aggression—later known as the Arab (or Palestinian) Revolt—which lasted until 1939. Aiming to organize themselves politically, the Palestinians set up a new institution, the Arab Higher Committee (AHC), composed of several parties and families loosely organized around Hajj Amin al-Husayni, head of the Supreme Muslim Council (SMC) and mufti of Jerusalem. The AHC declared a national civilian strike and proclaimed that it would not end until the British fulfilled three basic demands: cessation of Jewish immigration, an end to all further land sales to the Jews, and the establishment of a national (that is, an Arab majority) government. The strike was suspended in October, however, following a coordinated effort of several Arab leaders to resolve it. Husayni felt frustrated that his policy was not fully supported by the Arab leaders, who were in fact unwilling to confront the British on the Palestine issue. Shortly thereafter, the British nominated a commission of inquiry headed by Lord William Peel that for the first time raised the idea of partitioning the land between the disputants. This chapter will analyze if and to what extent the Peel Partition Plan was a missed opportunity.

THE EPISODE

The Peel Commission, after spending weeks in Palestine and many more months of deliberations back in London, published its report in July 1937. Key to the report was the call for the partition of Palestine into separate Jewish and Arab states. This was a logical derivation of the report's conclusion that the conflict was between two national communities with "no common ground between them" within "the narrow bounds of one small country." The contrasting aspiration of the two national movements, Peel and his associates emphasized, did not allow their fulfillment in a single state. Although the idea of the cantonization of Palestine was bandied in the report, it favored the division of the land into three separate zones: a Jewish state including mainly the coastal region from south of Tel Aviv to north of Acre, the Jezreel Valley, and the whole of the Galilee; an Arab state that would take in the rest of the country, joined to Transjordan; and a British enclave consisting of Jerusalem, Bethlehem, and a narrow corridor to the Mediterranean (see map 2.1). Because the Jewish entity, as delineated by the report, was to include some 225,000 Arabs, it recommended an exchange of population along the model of the Greek-Turkish transfer scheme of 1922. The linking of Arab Palestine to Transjordan was adopted as a result of the mufti's adamant opposition to any form of partition (Mahler and Mahler 2010, 69–79; Tessler 1994, 242; Flapan 1979, 254; Katz 1998, 1–14).

The British government and parliament approved the principle of partition, though not its precise details. This stemmed from interdepartmental disagreements, particularly between the Foreign and Colonial Offices, regarding the applicability of partition to the Palestine problem. The fact that the British did not adopt a clear-cut position opened the way for Zionist and Arab parties to press for changes in the policy. This domestic political bickering continued until the Foreign Office finally succeeded in sabotaging the plan (Cohen 1978, 38–49; Sykes 1967, 181–182).

The Zionist response to the Peel Commission Report was neither positive nor negative. The Zionist Congress, held in Zurich in August 1937, witnessed a heated debate between the supporters and opponents of the report. Chaim Weizmann, David Ben-Gurion, and Moshe Sharett led the moderate camp, which advocated making the "greatest possible use of historical opportunities" (Laqueur 1972, 519–520). This group viewed the boundaries outlined in the report as "a stepping stone to further expansion and the eventual takeover of the whole of Palestine" (Morris 2001, 138), suggesting the debate that ensued at the congress was essentially tactical. The Zionist hesitation was reflected in the concluding resolution of the congress—with 299 in favor and 160 against—which declared, "The scheme of partition put forward by the

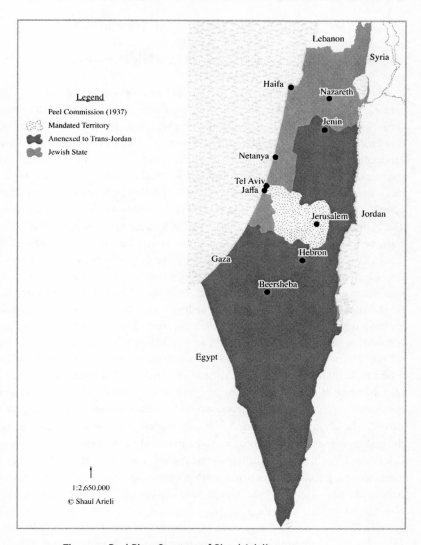

MAP 2.1. The 1937 Peel Plan. Courtesy of Shaul Arieli, 2013.

Royal Commission is unacceptable." Yet the principle of partition was not rejected, and the Zionist executive was empowered "to conduct negotiations for
the purpose of clarifying the specific content of the government's proposals of
a Jewish state in the Land of Israel (Galnoor 1995, 207). In another meeting
of the Jewish Agency Council the final statement reiterated many elements of
the Zionist Congress's declaration, but significantly added, as a result of the
strong opposition to partition, a demand that the British "convene a confer-

ence of the Jews and the Arabs of Palestine with a view to exploring the possibilities of making a peaceful settlement between Jews and Arabs in and for
an undivided Palestine on the basis of the Balfour Declaration" (Hurewitz
1976, 78).

The Palestinian-Arab response to the Peel Commission Report was, on the
surface, clear-cut, as all the local parties and institutions, as well as the Arab
states, publicly rejected the partition plan (Morris 2009, 98–107). In reality,
however, there was hardly unanimity. There was a major division between the
Husaynis and Nashashibis, the two most politically prominent families on
the scene, the first in control of both the SMC and AHC and the second organized around the National Defense Party. The differences emerged with Husayni's unilateral decision to boycott the Peel Commission from its inception.
The Nashashibis and perhaps other Arab leaders, as well as some British officials, believed that such a decision was harmful to Palestinian interests. As a
result, Husayni was persuaded to testify before the committee (Morris 1999,
138; Elpeleg 1989, 49–51; Nashashibi 1990, 52–54). Prior to the report's publication, there were indications that the Nashashibis, backed by Transjordan's
Amir ʿAbdallah, were in favor of the partition plan. That was the reason given
for the party's decision to withdraw from the AHC (Darwaza 1993, 2:418–420;
Nashashibi 1990, 55–56; Porath 1977, 229–230; Kayyali 1990, 283). However,
on July 21, two days before the official response of the AHC, the party published its formal position, which denounced and rejected the partition plan,
offering instead the establishment of a sovereign, democratic state in which
minority rights (that is, of the Jews) would be fully and constitutionally guaranteed. The about-face stemmed from the widespread public opposition to
the plan as expressed by various organizations and individuals wherever their
voices could be heard, including in the media. Thus, for example, 150 religious leaders published a petition stating that supporters of the plan would
be considered infidels. Also, several party leaders living in the northern Galilee
objected to the fact that their region was excluded from the Arab state and
given to the Jews (Swedenburg 2003, 160; Darwaza 1993, 2:424; Kayyali 1990,
284–285). Assassination attempts against opposition leaders may well have
frightened the Nashashibis too.

In contrast to the initial wavering position of the National Defense Party
and its supporters, the AHC was unequivocally opposed to partition from
the start. Husayni may have made the pragmatic decision to testify, but he
showed no signs of such pragmatism in his presentation before the commission (Sykes 1967, 174–175). Yet it took the AHC two weeks—which were exploited to coordinate policies with the Arab leaders and check any possible
Palestinian deviation from the official line—to issue a formal response to the
Peel recommendations. The statement expressed objection to the very idea of

a Jewish state, demanded the termination of the British Mandate and recognition of the Palestinians' right to complete independence, and insisted on the cessation of all Jewish immigration and land purchase. It also warned that any attempt to divide the country was bound to intensify Palestinian armed resistance. No doubt Husayni's fear of the recommended merger with Transjordan under the rule of his nemesis Amir 'Abdallah constituted a major reason for opposing the partition (Caplan 1986, 69; Hurewitz 1976, 79–80; Kayyali 1978, 207–208; 1990, 284–285) Yet the fact that the commission decided to opt for the merger was because of Hajj Amin's position: "Had the Mufti favored partition, the British would have preferred an Arab state under his rule than under Abdullah's" (Flapan 1979, 254). Husayni's position, however, was determined, according to his biographer, by the fact that he "was authoritarian and could not tolerate competition" (Mattar 1988, 66).

Hajj Amin was not wrong about 'Abdallah's pretensions; he hoped to use partition to advance his aggrandizement schemes in Palestine and Syria, indeed, to become king of the unified state. Already in the period preceding the Peel Report he tried to convince his Jewish interlocutors that only a merger between Palestine and Transjordan under his tutelage would enable him to deal effectively with the extreme Arab opposition to the partition idea. Undoubtedly, 'Abdallah stood to gain the most by the partition's implementation. He could have reached an accord with the moderate Nashashibis; then the merger of Transjordan with Arab Palestine, with 'Abdallah as monarch, would leave al-Husayni essentially powerless (Gelber 1997, 105–121; Avizohar and Friedman 1984, 212–217; Klieman 1980, 157).

Eventually, public opinion in Palestine and the Arab world was overwhelmingly against the partition scheme and in favor of Husayni's leadership (Darwaza 1993, 2:425–460; Kabha 2004, 195–202). The AHC invested major efforts in mobilizing the support of the Arab states. This campaign commenced as soon as the first rumors about the Peel Plan became public. Surprisingly, the first delegation visiting Damascus, under the leadership of Husayni, suffered a setback as Syrian national leaders advised the Palestinians to accept the plan (Porath 1977, 230). In Lebanon the Maronites initially also welcomed the prospects of a Jewish state, which would break the hostile ring of Muslim Arabs (Cohen 1978, 33; Caplan 1986, 61). However, with the official publication of the report, Syria, Lebanon, Iraq, and Saudi Arabia issued strongly worded declarations opposing partition ('Abd al-Hadi 1975, 6–47; Darwaza 1993, 2:425–460; Sheffer 1974, 72–77). 'Abdallah, who had the most to gain from the plan, was now forced to restrain his public enthusiasm. Moreover, the strong objection of the Arab states to any Hashemite aggrandizement plans in Palestine (or elsewhere) compelled 'Abdallah to reconsider his position, at least publicly. In private, he continued his secret contacts with the Zionists and the British while mulling a possible implementation of partition (Shlaim 1988, 57–65; Flapan 1979, 253; Gelber 1997, 105–121). He even tried to persuade the Palestinians to acknowledge the fact that the Jews were a power to be reckoned with, but to no avail (Gelber 1997, 106). The result, then, was the emergence of a collective Arab negative response, which was not necessarily shared by all, and certainly not by 'Abdallah.

The apex of the joint Arab coordination was the Bloudan Conference in Syria in September 1937. Some four hundred official and unofficial representatives from Syria, Iraq, Lebanon, Transjordan, Egypt, and Palestine took part in this conference. As expected, the concluding communiqué rejected the partition plan and declared instead that Palestine was an integral part of the Arab homeland, and that its preservation as an Arab country was the sacred duty of every Arab. Syrian and Palestinian delegates met on the sidelines of the gathering, deciding to prevent partition by armed resistance. In addition, it was proclaimed that "The friendship or the alliance which exists between them and Britain is on the verge of declension." This was a thinly veiled allusion to the ultimate weapon that the Palestinian leader and the Arab states could apply against Britain in the partition struggle (Porath 1977, 230–232; Kayyali 1978, 208–209). With the assassination of the acting district commissioner in the Galilee in September, the match was lit on the second, more deadly phase of the Arab Revolt, while London appointed a commission, headed by Sir Charles Woodhead, which allowed it to retreat from the partition plan.

ASSESSMENT

From the moment the Woodhead Commission was formed, wrote Yuval Arnon-Ohanna, "the opportunity was missed" (1984, 84). He did not lay the blame on any one party, nor did he explain exactly what was missed. Avi Shlaim was more explicit when he argued that the period 1936–1938 "can be seen as one of exemplary opportunity and unmitigated failure for the Zionist movement." In his opinion, "Had the Zionist movement accepted the proposal [i.e., the partition plan] spontaneously and without delay, and had it mobilized its support behind a clear-cut, straightforward policy in favor of partition, it is quite conceivable that it might have been implemented" (1988, 64). In this, Shlaim repeated almost verbatim the words of Nahum Goldmann, later to become president of the World Jewish Congress (WJC) (1969, 180). Aharon Klieman thought that the Peel Partition Plan "stands out as the earliest and the greatest single missed opportunity for avoiding the terrible Palestine tragedy" (2000, 56).[1] Rashid Khalidi entertained himself with various "what if" questions, such as what if the Palestinians had "compromised and accepted some form of Jewish national home within the context of an Arab state in Palestine before 1939?" His answer was not unequivocal: "Perhaps it might have been to their advantage, difficult though it is to imagine such an initiative in the circumstances of the time" (2006, 118–119).

Ben-Gurion thought that had the partition plan been carried out, "the history of our people would have been different and six million Jews in Europe would not have been killed—most of them would be in Israel" (quoted in Segev 2000, 414; Flapan 1979, 250). It is highly doubtful that the tiny part of Palestine offered to the Zionists in the Peel Report would have been enough to absorb millions of Jews in the pre-1939 period. In any case, Segev opined, there was no question of a missed opportunity: "By the time the principle of partition had been put on the table, there was no chance of resolving the conflict peacefully" (ibid.). A similar view was expressed by Christopher Sykes, the veteran British diplomat, who claimed it was difficult to believe that the Peel recommendations "could have succeeded, or have led to anything but violently intensified strife and bloodshed." The Peel Report, he continued, "has often been mourned as a last missed chance to bring a peaceful settlement to the Holy Land." However, the plan "belongs perhaps to that interesting category of unaccomplished things which often exert a great hold on the affection and imagination" (Sykes 1967, 189).

Was the Peel Plan a missed opportunity? It certainly constituted a historical opportunity. It was offered by Britain, the superpower in charge of the mandate; it was presented at a liminal period, following the cessation of hostilities after a turbulent period in Palestine; it was devised by a formal investigation committee that earnestly studied the problem; and the proposed solution constituted a significant departure from the status quo, which both sides were keen to change. In hindsight, the offer seems to have been attractive to both parties: for the Zionists, it was the first time they were offered a sovereign, independent Jewish state; for the Palestinians, it offered most of the territory constituting Palestine (80 percent) and the establishment of a new Arab state. Yet at the time the Zionists were disappointed by the promise of only 20 percent of the land, while the Palestinians complained about not getting the whole of Palestine, since the Jewish claim—in their opinion—was unjust and illegitimate. In some respects, the reaction of both sides was highly emotional. The criticism of Edward Keith-Roach, then British district commissioner of Jerusalem, seems highly relevant in this context: "Jews, Christians and Muslims are like three bewildered, disconsolate children at a party. 'We don't want jam; we don't want honey; we don't want cake. We want jelly.' Alas, there is no jelly" (1994, 190). Moreover, the partition envisaged a leading role for 'Abdallah at the expense of al-Husayni, which surely lessened its gleam for the Palestinians. It can be assumed that had the plan not envisaged a merger with Transjordan, it would have been perceived as more attractive in al-Husayni's eyes.

What was the potentiality level of the opportunity? The first element relates to the legitimacy level of the leaders. Both movements were headed by legitimate and/or powerful institutions and leaders. In the case of the Zionist movement, they were even elected to their posts. Except for the opposition Revisionist Party under the command of Ze'ev Jabotinsky, the Zionist Congress—with Weizmann and Ben-Gurion at the helm—represented the majority of the Jewish community in Palestine (and to some extent also the anti-Zionist Jews in the diaspora). It is more difficult to measure the legitimacy of Hajj Amin and the AHC in light of the internal divisions in Palestinian politics and society. Evidently, however, the latter possessed enough leverage to enforce its will on recalcitrant political elements in Palestine and outside the Arab world. According to Arnon-Ohanna, Hajj Amin "could have made any decision he chose and most of the Arabs in the land would have listened" (1984, 76). The public volte-face in the Nashashibis' position may attest to the influence and popularity of their rivals, the Husaynis. It seems, therefore, safe to assume that had Hajj Amin accepted the partition plan, he could have mobilized Palestinian support behind it.

The second element relates to the willingness of the leaders to take bold new moves on the basis of changes in their thinking. Though reluctant, the Zionist leaders—particularly Ben-Gurion and Weizmann—understood the magnitude of the hour; they thought it was unwise to reject the plan outright and therefore attempted to adjust it to their interests. In this respect, it seems that the Zionist Party was on the verge of willingness to adopt bold decisions. Yet the position of the Arab-Palestinian side did not leave much room for maneuver: though there were elements in Palestinian society and Arab leaders willing to work for partition, the opposing voices, first and foremost the AHC and the Husaynis, prevailed. In light of this adamant and unflinching Arab-Palestinian resistance, the chances of implementing the plan were dim.

The third element relates to the impact of prior contacts between the parties on the negotiations and the existence of trust. The history of past acquaintances did not augur well for reaching a Zionist-Arab accommodation. The period 1934–1936 witnessed numerous meetings between Zionists, Palestinians, and Arabs (Teveth 1985; Sela 1972–1973). Though high-ranking Palestinian leaders refused to take part in these meetings, the talks with junior leaders only deepened the gulf between the parties, exposed the real intentions of each party, and therefore unwittingly entrenched the opposition voices, particularly among the Palestinian-Arabs.

Finally, the fourth element pertains to the role of the third-party mediator.

In this case, interdepartmental divisions in Britain hampered the government's full backing of the Peel recommendations and actually played a destructive role. Had the British government fully endorsed and promoted the plan, it might have been able to implement it with the support of the local Zionists and those Arab forces that favored it, but indecisiveness and institutional disagreements ruled out this possibility (Klieman 1983, 120–127). Nor did the League of Nations play a helpful role by demanding a period of tutelage for the proposed state before granting independence (Flapan 1979, 240).

In sum, though the Peel Report constituted a historical opportunity, it seems that its potentiality level was low. Therefore, the apathy and indifference with which the Palestinian side treated the offer did not affect the degree of the missed opportunity. Among the four variables of the potentiality level, only one—the question of legitimacy and in a limited way—allowed for the possible exploitation of this opportunity; the others, particularly the role of the third party, refute that it constituted a missed opportunity. Thus, while Shlaim may have reached a contrary conclusion, a different Zionist policy would not have resulted in any meaningfully different course of events as the Arab-Palestinian position was not at all open to nuances or variations. With the wisdom of hindsight, it is clear that the Arab-Palestinian side made a formidable mistake by adopting the all-or-nothing approach (Khouri 1968, 40), yet under the prevailing circumstances it is difficult to imagine that a different type of behavior was possible.

NOTE

1. The same position was presented in his early book on the partition plan, which was published only in Hebrew (1983, 1). In contrast to the translated English title, the Hebrew title added the phrase "An Opportunity Missed?"

CHAPTER 3

THE UN PARTITION PLAN

1947

ON FEBRUARY 14, 1947, the British government announced its decision
to transfer the Palestine problem to the United Nations (UN). It was the beginning of the end of the British Mandate over Palestine. The UN appointed
a Special Committee on Palestine (UNSCOP), tasked to investigate the conditions prevailing in the land and recommend a comprehensive solution.
At the end of August the committee submitted its report, which then went
through a long period of debate before being approved by the General Assembly on November 29, 1947. UNSCOP recommended a partition plan that
would see the establishment of a Jewish state and an Arab state, but with differently delineated boundaries from the Peel Commission's plan presented a
decade earlier. Like its predecessor, the UN plan was not implemented. This
chapter will analyze if and to what extent this episode constituted a missed
opportunity.

THE EPISODE

The British decision to transfer the Palestine problem to the UN stemmed
from two basic reasons. First, it was part of the larger process of decoloniza-
tion, in which Britain—following the devastating results of World War II—
decided to evacuate many of its overseas colonies, foremost India and Burma.
By 1947, according to Michael Cohen, Palestine was "the major trouble spot
in the British empire, requiring some 100,000 troops and a huge budget to
maintain" (1987, 122). Second, the post-1945 era saw several international attempts to solve the Palestine problem, such as the Anglo-American Committee of Inquiry, the Morrison-Grady Plan, and the London Conference. All
these attempts, however, failed as a result of the disagreements between the
superpowers and the opposition of both the Zionists and the Arabs (Hurewitz 1976, 224–283; Cohen 1987, 106–112; Cohen 1982, 96–134; Morris 2001,
177–180).

Just as World War II had profound repercussions for the mandatory power, so also did it affect the two local warring parties, the Zionists and the Palestinians. The Holocaust, the full tragedy of which was still coming into focus, added a moral dimension to the Zionists' demand to immediately establish a Jewish state that would also solve the problem of more than 250,000 displaced persons in Europe, survivors of the brutal Nazi concentration camps. In addition, by May 1942 the Zionist movement was ideologically committed to the Biltmore program, which publicly demanded the establishment of a Jewish state over the whole of Palestine as part of the new world order after the war. The new policy was tantamount to rejecting the concept of partition (Hurewitz 1976, 195–211; Cohen 1978, 130–134; Laqueur 1972, 545–549).

Important changes also occurred on the Arab-Palestinian side. On the eve of the war, the Palestinians—fortified by the achievements of the Arab Revolt (1936–1939)—decided to reject the British 1939 white paper, which provided for the establishment of a Palestinian state within ten years and imposed heavy restrictions on Jewish immigration and purchase of lands (Cohen 1987, 93–94; Kayyali 1990, 300–303). In spite of his declining influence, Hajj Amin al-Husayni, head of the Supreme Muslim Council (SMC) and the Arab Higher Committee (AHC), succeeded in imposing his views on other members of the AHC, who had hitherto been willing to accept the terms of the white paper as a basis for further discussions with the mandatory power (Nevo 1984, 128–142; Kayyali 1990, 302; al-Hout 1986, 397; Khalidi 2006, 116).

Prior to the war, in 1937, Al-Husayni was expelled from Palestine; he eventually moved to Germany and collaborated with the Nazis during the war. The war years thus found the Palestinians disorganized and leaderless, and the Palestinian national movement fragmented. In addition, the consequences of the Arab Revolt had exhausted the Palestinian society and damaged their ability to prepare for the final showdown with the Zionists (Tessler 2009, 252–254; Khalidi 2006, 105–139). So the Arab states took over the responsibility for the Palestine problem. This was reflected in the decision of the newly established Arab League (March 1945) to appoint the Palestinian representative at the League (Musa 'Alami) and reorganize the membership of the AHC in such a way that assured the supremacy of the Husaynis in this institution. The net result was that major decisions regarding the Arab position toward Palestine were now taken at the League's headquarters in Cairo. No wonder that Khalidi spoke of Arab "tutelage" over the Palestine issue (2006, 125). Yet in a way, the Palestinian Arab cause was strengthened, "for the Arab governments could bring to bear the full weight of their diplomatic machinery, their resources in manpower and wealth, and their bargaining influence with the Big Powers" (Hurewitz 1976, 194). Reality, however, was to prove otherwise.

The Palestine problem was dealt with by the UN assembly during a session that lasted from April 28 to May 15, 1947. After weeks of deliberations it was decided to set up the special commission, UNSCOP, composed of representatives of eleven "neutral" countries. When the committee arrived in Palestine in June, it was notified of the AHC's refusal to testify before it. This was accompanied by a short civilian protest strike. The reason for boycotting UNSCOP was its alleged predisposition to accept a "Zionist solution" to the Palestine problem. The Arab League and certain Arab governments attempted to change the negative position of the AHC, considering it harmful to the Arab cause, but to no avail (Hadawi 1991, 65–66; Khouri 1968, 45–46). The Palestinian refusal to cooperate with UNSCOP stood in sharp contrast to the full cooperation the committee received from the Zionist leadership and community in Palestine. The disparity between the reactions of the two communities, according to Aharon Cohen, "could not fail to give the impression that the Jews were imbued with the sense of right and were prepared to plead their case before any unbiased tribunal, while the Arabs felt unsure of the justice of their case, and were afraid to bow to the judgment of the nations" (1970, 206). Yet it seems that the sense of existing bias was the very reason for boycotting the committee; some historians supported this decision on the grounds that "There was no point in meeting UNSCOP's members when it was clear that the creation of an independent Arab Palestine was not the committee's objective" (Pappe 1994, 23). Though there were indications that certain leaders and institutions were willing to cooperate with the committee, the AHC policy of intimidation and coercion was effective as it succeeded in silencing any opponents (Hurewitz 1976, 294).

The AHC may have successfully boycotted UNSCOP, but the Arab counterposition did not go completely unrepresented. Acting "independently," 'Alami and Cecil Hourani, secretary of the Arab Bureau in Washington, submitted a memorandum setting out the Arab viewpoint from their perspective (Morris 2001, 182). The committee learned more about the Arab-Palestinian position during its July 1947 meetings in Beirut with representatives of League members (except Transjordan). Bound by their official positions, the Arab delegates rejected the partition of Palestine, opposed further Jewish immigration or purchase of land, and demanded the establishment of an independent Arab state guaranteeing Jewish minority rights (Khouri 1968, 46; Hurewitz 1976, 295; Cohen 1982, 265). This indicates that in many ways the Arab states endorsed the AHC's position. The UNSCOP team then proceeded to Amman, where it met with 'Abdallah, who had just been crowned king of Jordan. At that point, 'Abdallah felt he could not deviate from the unified Arab stance. This infuriated the Zionists, who thought they had a prior agreement with him by which he would support the partition of Palestine and the merging of its Arab part with Transjordan (Shlaim 1988, 95). Instead, 'Abdallah sent a message to the British expressing his regrets that he was obliged to support the Arab position of an independent Palestine due to political and tactical considerations. He took the time to add his personal belief that partition was the only possible solution and that when the time was right he "would be perfectly willing to give his full cooperation and to take over all the Arab areas of Palestine, or as much of them as were offered to him." But, he lamented, since Jordan was the only Arab state to gain from partition, he could not publicly support this idea, as it stood in contrast to the official view of the Arab world (Shlaim 1988, 93–94). Interestingly, Musa ʿAlami, a former associate of Husayni, told the British, "The Mufti would accept partition if his position as head of the Arab state was to be recognized" (Cohen 1982, 267). Issa Khalaf responded to this point by claiming that though the mufti most certainly had the ambition to become the supreme leader of the Arabs in Palestine, "there is neither evidence nor indications to substantiate ʿAlami's claim that [he] would have, under certain circumstances, accepted partition" (1991, 157).[1] In his opinion, the mufti's uncompromising stand "represented the mainstream in Palestine and the Arab world. In such a case, even those who were willing to compromise with the Jews were [too] intimidated to do so" (ibid.). It is clear that beyond the resolute objection to a Jewish state on any part of Palestine stood Arab animosities and a specific fear of ʿAbdallah's rule extending to the Arab part of Palestine, as envisaged in the Peel Partition Plan. This fear was shared by the Palestinian leadership as well as most Arab states, so opposed were they all to Hashemite aggrandizement designs. The lack of unity among the Arab leaders and their inflexible positions, according to Shlaim, "created a very poor impression on members of the committee who had come with an open mind" (1988, 92; see also Pappe 1994, 27).

On August 30, 1947, the UNSCOP report was submitted to the UN. It called for the end of the mandate system and the creation of procedures that would lead to the independence of Palestine. The committee, however, split—8 to 3—regarding what type of state should emerge. The majority called for the establishment of Jewish and Arab states—politically independent but united economically—with Jerusalem and its environs internationalized. The Arab part, which would constitute some 45 percent of the Palestine territory, would include the Western Galilee, the hill country of central Palestine with the exception of the Jerusalem enclave, and a coastal plain between Isdud and the Egyptian border. The Jewish state, covering the other 55 percent of the territory, would encompass the Eastern Galilee, the coastal plain from the south of Acre until Isdud, and the whole Negev. The minority position favored the establishment of an independent federal state after a three-year preparatory stage under UN trusteeship. The state would include two separate entities with local administrative powers, but a united central authority would be divided between Jews and Arabs. The boundaries of the suggested federated state were somewhat different from the majority proposal, giving most of the Negev and Jerusalem (except for the Jewish parts) to the Arabs (Mahler and Mahler 2010, 99–105; Hurewitz 1976, 295–298; Smith 1996, 138; Pappe 1994, 31–32; Cohen 1970, 214–216) (see map 3.1).

In late September the UN General Assembly established an ad hoc committee to consider the UNSCOP report. This time a representative of the AHC, Jamal Husseini, did appear before the committee, justifying the Palestinian abstention on the grounds that all previous inquiry commissions ignored the rights of the Arabs of Palestine. In his opinion, both UNSCOP recommendations—that of partition or federation—could not become a basis for discussion as both were inconsistent with the UN Charter and Covenant of the League of Nations. Instead, he called for the establishment of an Arab state in the whole of Palestine, which would safeguard the rights of the minorities. He ended his presentation with a veiled threat that the Arabs of Palestine were determined to oppose, with all the means at their disposal, any scheme that provided for the dissection, segregation, or partition of Palestine (John and Hadawi 1970b, 197; Hadawi 1991, 68–69; Khouri 1968, 47–48; Yakobson and Rubinstein 2009, 28).[2] During the debate over the report held at the General Assembly in late November, the Arab delegates presented a unified position that fully supported the Palestinian claims (Hadawi 1991, 71–74; 'Abd al-Hadi 1975, 104–109; Yakobson and Rubinstein 2009, 44–45).

In a meeting between two Zionist leaders and 'Azzam Pasha, the secretary-general of the Arab League, in September 1947, in which the former suggested reaching an agreement between the Jewish state and the Arab League on the basis of the UNSCOP report, 'Azzam replied that "the Arab world is not in a compromising mood. . . . Nations never concede; they fight. . . . We shall try to defeat you. I'm not sure we'll succeed, but we'll try. We were able to drive [out] the Crusaders, but on the other hand we lost Spain and Persia. It may be that we shall lose Palestine. But it's too late to talk of peaceful solutions" (Horowitz 1953, 233; Cohen 1970, 217; Caplan 1986, 151). Yet the Arab-Palestinian side was thwarted in its attempt to undermine the UNSCOP report because of a lack of coordination and the existing mistrust between the Husayni and other leading Palestinian families, as well as several Arab leaders, particularly the Hashemites in Iraq and Transjordan (Khalaf 1991, 156). Moreover, as noted above, since 1945 the Arab League had gradually taken over the responsibility of Palestinian affairs; in a series of Arab meetings dealing with the Palestine problem, held over 1946–1948, the voice of the AHC was not treated seriously (Pappe 1994, 69–76; Maddy-Weitzman 1993, 48–70). When al-Husayni asked in October 1947 for the League's commitment to establish an independent administration in all Palestine on May 15, 1948, following the

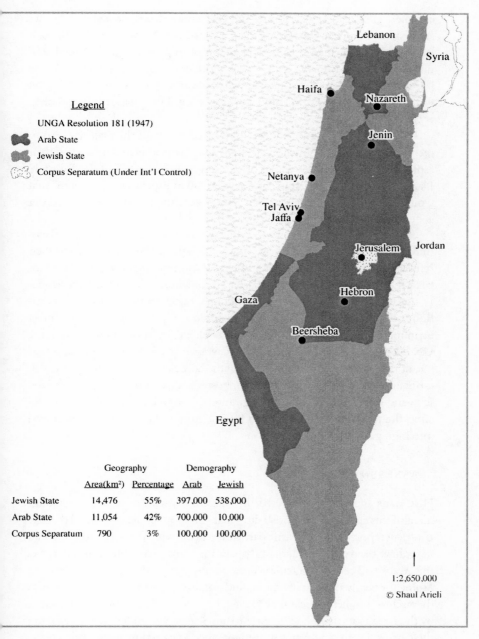

Legend

UNGA Resolution 181 (1947)

Arab State

Jewish State

Corpus Separatum (Under Int'l Control)

Lebanon

Syria

Haifa

Nazareth

Jenîn

Netanya

Tel Aviv
Jaffa

Jerusalem

Jordan

Hebron

Gaza

Beersheba

Egypt

	Geography		Demography	
	Area(km²)	Percentage	Arab	Jewish
Jewish State	14,476	55%	397,000	538,000
Arab State	11,054	42%	700,000	10,000
Corpus Separatum	790	3%	100,000	100,000

1:2,650,000

© Shaul Arieli

MAP 3.1. The 1947 UN Partition Plan. Courtesy of Shaul Arieli, 2013.

completion of British withdrawal, the Hashemite states persuaded the other Arab states to ignore the request (Pappe 1994, 74). No wonder that the collective Arab performance against the report during the lengthy UN deliberations was not coordinated and was therefore politically insignificant. At the last moment, the Arab delegates expressed willingness to consider the plan for a solution based on the minority suggestion, but it was too late (Cohen 1970, 233).

In contrast, the Zionist leadership resolved to accept the majority recommendations of the commission. Though the partition plan fell short of their aspirations regarding the whole of Palestine—as expressed in the Biltmore Plan[3]—the Zionist leadership considered it "an indispensable minimum" that would allow the establishment of a Jewish state in part of Palestine (Tessler 2009, 259–260).

On November 29, 1947, the General Assembly secured the necessary two-thirds majority needed to approve UNSCOP's report. The Arabs declared their refusal to recognize the validity of the resolution on the grounds that it violated the provisions of the UN Charter (Hadawi 1991, 76–77). On December 17 the Arab states published a communiqué rejecting the principle of partition and vowing to obstruct its implementation (Elpeleg 1995, 55). The almost unanimous Arab position also reflected a belief in the moral unjustness of the UN decision. "No one," Husayni later wrote, "ever accepted partition that meant the dismembering of the body of the homeland, so why should the Palestinian people?" (ibid., 54). By then, hostilities had already begun between Jews and Palestinians. It was the beginning of the civil war in Palestine. Hereafter, the preparations in the Arab League for a military showdown moved into high gear.

ASSESSMENT

Historians and diplomats are hardly unanimous with regard to their judgment of this episode. The British diplomat Christopher Sykes claimed that the UNSCOP report was "a fantastic partition scheme which, it is safe to say, could never have been put into successful operation" (1967, 335). He argued that "As the Arabs had refused to compromise in any way with the Jewish National Home for nearly thirty years they could not, except with great humiliation to themselves, publicly retreat now" (1967, 337). A similar argument was posited by the Israeli journalist and historian Tom Segev, who added that in rejecting the partition plan "the Arabs missed a chance to gain time to prepare to war. They had made a tactical error" (2000, 496).

The Palestinian side tended to support the policy adopted by its leadership. Segev quoted Anwar Nusseibeh as saying that "The Palestinians refused at any time to sign their own death warrant" (ibid.). The historian Walid Khalidi, in an article written on the occasion of the resolution's fiftieth anniversary, complained of the "historical amnesia" regarding the partition plan (2007, 98). In his opinion, the plan "was not the legal, moral, fair, balanced, pragmatic, practicable 'compromise' formula that it is made out to be." How fair could it be, he asked, if 55 percent of the total area was given to the Jews who constituted less than a third of the population and who owned less than 7 percent of the land? The Palestinians, on the other hand, who constituted more than two-thirds of the population and owned the vast bulk of the land, were awarded 45 percent (2007, 102–103; 2009, 26). In his opinion, the resolution was not a fair compromise: "A compromise does not come about if its putative provisions are congruent with the wishes of one side but anathema to the other" (2007, 109). It is clear, therefore, that Khalidi thinks that the Palestinian rejection of the partition plan was justifiable and the fact that later the Palestinians accepted it was not a "belated affirmation of its feasibility in 1947" (2007, 111). The same position was shared by Edward Said, who claimed that he would have objected to the partition plan because "it was an unfair plan based on the minority getting equal rights to those of the majority" (quoted in Yakobson and Rubinstein 2009, 46). Yet criticism of the Palestinian rigidity regarding the plan comes from Pappe, who claimed that its leadership "lacked the pragmatism and ability to seize the historical opportunity and failed to realize that instead of rejecting it out of hand, it was better to be a party to a settlement, even a minimal one" (1994, 23).

Was the 1947 UN Partition Plan a missed opportunity? No doubt, the episode constituted a historic opportunity; the fact that Britain finally decided to withdraw from Palestine and terminate the Mandate promised that the vacuum left by the British would have to be filled by the local players. The fact that the UN nominated an inquiry commission and was about to make a decision regarding the final status of the territory meant that the parties to the conflict confronted a real opportunity for a change. It was a window of opportunity on the scale of the disintegration of the Ottoman Empire following the end of World War I. In addition, the proposal was highly attractive to the Jewish side, which for the first time ever was offered the larger chunk of the land, in spite of the fact that the number of Palestinians was twice that of the Jews. Needless to say, the plan was less attractive to the Palestinian side, as it offered them substantially less than what was offered by Peel. On the other hand, the fact that the plan was disappointing from a Palestinian point of view should not obscure the fact that it did offer, and this was a precedent, the establishment of an independent Palestinian state on part of the land. In contrast to the Peel recommendations, the envisaged state was not meant to be associated with Jordan, but was economically linked with the Jewish state only. This positive side of the plan was lost on the Palestinians, as reflected in Khalidi's sharp criticism. Also, the fact that the proposal was adopted by the UN—an organization endowed with international recognition and legitimacy—should have lent added value to its attractiveness. The unequivocal negative response of the offered party—in this case the Arab-Palestinians—as well as the first sparks of a civil war in Palestine shut the door on any negotiations that might have addressed the implementation of the partition proposal.

What was the potentiality level of the episode? The first element relates to the legitimacy level of the leaders. David Ben-Gurion and Moshe Sharett represented the Jewish community and enjoyed wide legitimacy. Dissenting views, which were reflected in the Etzel and Lehi organizations, could not seriously challenge this legitimacy. In contrast, Hajj Amin al-Husayni suffered from legitimacy problems. Internal disputes within the Palestinian leadership and society, in addition to existing mistrust between Husayni and certain Arab leaders (particularly King 'Abdallah), damaged his credibility and limited his maneuverability in Arab affairs. In 1939, wrote Rashid Khalidi, "The Palestinians began a disorienting period of transition during which they lost control over their own fate" (2006, 124). However, his dwindling influence notwithstanding, Hajj Amin's radical postures were accepted by the AHC and most Arab leaders. This was the case with the rejection of the 1939 white paper and it was the case regarding his decision, against the better judgment of other Arab voices, to boycott UNSCOP. It must be admitted, therefore, that Hajj Amin still enjoyed enough leverage to impose his will on recalcitrant Arab players. Thus the net result was that the two conflicting parties possessed enough legitimacy and/or leverage to advance a solution.

The second element relates to the willingness of the leader to take bold new moves on the basis of changes in his thinking. The Zionist leaders were determined to seize the opportunity. In contrast to the hesitations that led to a lukewarm response to the Peel Plan, the UN Partition Plan was supported by most of the political forces in the Yishuv except for the right-wing organizations. They opposed the concession of so much land—80 percent of the territory known as Palestine (comprising Palestine and Jordan)—because, in their eyes, it was all part of Greater Eretz Israel. In contrast, the Palestinian leadership was bold and determined to reject the plan and continue the struggle by military means. If dissenting voices existed, they were silenced or chose to be silent.[4] The Palestinian rejection of partition was later reflected in the 1964 PLO National Charter, of which Article 17 stated, "The partitioning of Palestine in 1947 and the establishment of Israel are illegal and false" (Harkabi 1972, 28).

The third element relates to the impact of prior contacts between the parties on the negotiations and the existence of trust. The history of past interactions between Jews and Arabs did not contribute to a better understanding between the warring parties; on the contrary, being acquainted with the positions on the other side made each party more suspicious of the other's motives and sincerity (Sela 1972–1973). Moreover, the violent Arab-Jewish clashes during the Arab Revolt further alienated the two parties to the conflict.

The fourth element relates to the role of the mediator. The fact that Britain was adamant about withdrawing from Palestine, while the UN was responsible for the successful completion of its commission's work, strengthened the possibility that the partition solution would be implemented. In other words, the UN offered the power and legitimacy of its status as the world's leading international organization to the partition plan. In this respect the plan differed from the Peel Plan, which had been offered by a British commission, and its implementation was obstructed by certain British political interests. However, the problem was that the UN or any other superpower did not ensure the formation of a certain mechanism that would guarantee the successful implementation of the recommendations. Thus the British unilateral evacuation from Palestine in May 1948 left a vacuum that would soon be filled by the invading Arab armies.

This analysis suggests that the potentiality level of the missed opportunity in the 1947 UN Partition Plan episode was medium. Two of the variables presented in our definition support the conclusion that it was a plausible missed opportunity. That the Palestinians treated the offer with apathy, indifference, and disdain further increased the level of the opportunity missed. This, however, was somewhat offset by the fact that the principle of partition remained on the table, offered many years later in the Oslo Accords in 1993. But by then the territory offered to the Palestinians was significantly less than what was offered in 1947. With the wisdom of hindsight it is clear that the Palestinians, backed by most Arab states, made an undeniable mistake in rejecting the UN partition offer, which could have ensured the establishment of a nascent Palestinian state. Husayni, who possessed enough leverage to carry with him the Arab and Palestinian constituencies, should have grasped the magnitude of the hour. It should be remembered that the notion of partition was put on the table for the first time by the Peel Commission in 1937; it was a paradigm shift from previous diplomatic solutions. Therefore, the doubts of the conflicting parties were well understood at the time; ten years later, however, with the second partition plan, the adoption of the same policy in different historical circumstances might be considered a folly. "By adamantly insisting on all or nothing," concluded Fred Khouri, the Palestinians "ended up with practically nothing" (1968, 66). The assessment that it had been a mistake to reject the

UN Partition Plan does not ipso facto turn it into a missed opportunity; still, our analysis demonstrates that a certain potential for seizing the opportunity did exist and that it was missed by the Palestinian leadership.

NOTES

1. In 'Alami's biography (Furlonge 1969) there is no indication of this story.

2. For the official text of the presentation, see http://unispal.un.org/unispal.nsf/9a798ad bf322aff38525617b006d88d7/a8c17fca1b8cf5338525691b0063f769?OpenDocument.

3. The Biltmore Conference was convened by the American Zionists at the Biltmore Hotel in New York in May 1942. The conference adopted a program which demanded for the first time the establishment of a Jewish state in Palestine (Tessler 2009, 251; Oren 2007, 442–445).

4. For the possible existence of such voices, see Salem 2005, 183–185.

CHAPTER 4

ISRAELI-JORDANIAN NEGOTIATIONS
1946–1951

AFTER THE 1948 Palestine War ended, Israel and Jordan signed an armistice agreement on April 3, 1949; in the ensuing months the two countries went a step further and began secretly negotiating the terms of a peace treaty. These negotiations resulted in the drafting of a nonaggression pact, but it did not develop into an agreement. The assassination of King 'Abdallah in July 1951 sealed the fate of that episode. This chapter will analyze whether Israel and Jordan missed an opportunity to sign a peace treaty.

THE EPISODE

Relations between the Zionist movement and the Hashemite king in the pre-1948 period were characterized by cautious cooperation based on mutual interests. Both viewed the Husayni-led Palestinian national movement's aim to establish an independent Arab state as a threat. 'Abdallah aspired to annex the Arab part of Palestine, if not the whole of Palestine, to his kingdom, possibly to create a more comprehensive Arab union. As his attempts to take over Damascus had been persistently frustrated by the French and the Syrians, Palestine—and Jerusalem in particular—became his other coveted prize. 'Abdallah was not averse to the idea of Jewish autonomy in Palestine under his rule, but eventually he was compelled to accept the logic of Jewish independence. The Jews, for their part, wanted to establish an entity with as much territory in Palestine as possible. They saw 'Abdallah as a possible ally. They also hinged their hopes on the positive attitude of the Hashemite family toward the Jews and their aims, as reflected in the Faysal-Weizmann Agreement. Just as important, the two sides shared some economic interests such as the water supply, electricity, and the potash industry. Moreover, cooperating with the Jews could have benefited Jordan, which was in dire need of foreign capital and skills (Sela 1985, 11–13; Shlaim 1988, 43–46). Yet Jordan's policy toward the Jews was determined also by the interplay of three constraints:

its political and financial dependence on Britain, which made ʿAbdallah vulnerable to Western pressures; its involvement in the emerging Arab system (having joined the Arab League as a founding member in 1945 meant that Jordan was similarly vulnerable to Arab pressures); and finally, though the political system was based on patrimonial leadership, the Jordanian elite occasionally resisted ʿAbdallah, forcing him to adjust his policy preferences. ʿAbdallah, therefore, had to navigate delicately between his state interests and political constraints.

The separation of Transjordan from the Palestine Mandate in the 1922 white paper was grudgingly accepted by the Zionist labor movement, which hoped to establish a Jewish entity across the two banks of the Jordan River. The right wing continued to harbor hopes regarding the establishment of a Jewish state over the whole of Palestine (including Transjordan), as delineated in 1920. It was hardly a surprise, therefore, that the first contacts with ʿAbdallah in the 1930s related to possible plans for leasing lands in Transjordan and Jewish settlement there. A major episode in this connection was the obtainment of a Jewish lease in Ghaur al-Kibd, located in the central Jordan Valley between the Allenby Bridge and Salt (Shlaim 1988, 50–54; Ran 1991, 23–27; Gelber 1997, 7–22). With the institutionalization of the Jordanian polity and the diminishing chances of Jewish settlement, contacts focused their attempts to coordinate policies with regard to burning political issues in Palestine, such as the role of the Legislative Council, the Arab Revolt, and the Peel Commission. These contacts also included the exchange of information and the payment of certain fees to ʿAbdallah (Gelber 1997, 23–58, 83–144; Ran 1991, 23–104).

A new chapter in Zionist-ʿAbdallah relations commenced in late 1936. Coincident with the British government's appointment of the Peel Commission to seek a solution to the deadlocked Zionist-Palestinian relations and due to the reluctance of the Husayni-led Palestinian national movement to cooperate with it, ʿAbdallah and the Zionists found common interests. Indeed, when the Peel Commission recommended partitioning Palestine into a small Jewish state and a larger Arab Palestinian state integrated with ʿAbdallah's emirate, the king was the only Arab leader in favor of it; he even held secret negotiations with the Jewish Agency. Though ʿAbdallah considered Palestine only as a springboard to his ultimate aim—the Syrian throne—he was, from a Zionist point of view, the favorite partner for partition. British hesitancy, Arab obstinacy, and undecided Zionist policy, however, all helped to thwart this plan (Gelber 1997, 116–121; Ran 1991, 60–86: Shlaim 1988, 57–65; see also chapter 2).

Following World War II, with Britain's declared intention to withdraw from Palestine, the notion of partition reemerged. Once more, the Zionists' preferred candidate for partition was ʿAbdallah. Already in August 1946 a sort of understanding had developed: 'Abdallah consented to the partition of Palestine into a Jewish and Arab state in return for British, American, and Zionist agreement to annex its Arab section to Jordan (Caplan 1986, 145–147, 268–270). Despite expectations and their tentative agreement, however, 'Abdallah joined the Arab consensus against partition when UNSCOP published its recommendations in September 1947 (Gelber 1997, 217–230; Ran 1991, 201–214; see also chapter 3).

This did not stop 'Abdallah from continuing to support partition in his secret messages to the Jewish Agency. As a result, Golda Meyerson (later Meir), the acting head of the Political Department of the Jewish Agency, was sent to test the ground. At their meeting on November 17, 1947, the king declared his readiness "to partition which would not put me to shame in the eyes of the Arab world when I should have to defend it." The option he now proposed was "an independent Hebrew Republic in part of Palestine within a Transjordanian state that would include both banks of the Jordan, with me at its head, and in which economy, army and the legislature will be joint" (quoted in Shlaim 1998, 113). More crucially, the meeting apparently concluded with an understanding (Shlaim termed it a "firm deal") between the two parties to divide Palestine, as Mrs. Meyerson expressed her consent to the possibility that 'Abdallah would capture the Arab part of Palestine provided that it did not prevent the establishment of the Jewish state and did not involve a military clash between their mutual forces (Shlaim 1988, 113–116; Caplan 1986, 159–160; Bar-Joseph 1987, 8–11).[1]

Contacts between 'Abdallah and the Jewish Agency continued during the period of the Zionist-Palestinian unofficial civil war (December 1947–May 1948). A second meeting was held between Meyerson and 'Abdallah on May 10, 1948, on the eve of the Arab invasion of Palestine. For the Zionists, the aim of the meeting was to secure the king's confirmation of their earlier understanding. He did not deny its existence but emphasized that the political circumstances had changed since the November meeting; he was now only one among five Arab leaders. Updating his position, he suggested an undivided Palestine, with autonomy for the areas in which the Jews predominated. This was utterly unacceptable for Meyerson and thus the meeting failed to produce any agreement (Shlaim 1988, 205–210; Gelber 1997, 280–281; Sela 1985, 20–25; Meir 1976, 177–179). In fact, it left the Zionists somewhat confused with regard to the exact role 'Abdallah was about to play in Palestine in the anticipated Arab invasion. According to the Arab Section's assessment of the Jewish Agency's Political Department written on May 13, 'Abdallah "has not entirely betrayed the agreement, nor is he entirely loyal to it, but something in the middle. He will not remain faithful to the borders of 29 November [the partition boundaries], but nor will he try to conquer all our state" (quoted in Shlaim 1988, 211). With the wisdom of hindsight, Shlaim might have been correct in writing that "'Abdallah remained remarkably loyal to his original understanding with Golda Meir" (2000, 39), yet the Zionist leaders could not count on that at the time, as the assessment of the Jewish Agency's Arab Section reveals. In any case, the meeting had an aura of Greek tragedy as the two parties were opposed to war but were unable to swim against the popular tide on each side.

It is testimony to their shared desire for a solution that after the war 'Abdallah and the Israeli leaders resumed their secret contacts. The participants in these meetings from the Israeli side included Reuven Shiloah, Eliyahu Sasson, his son Moshe—all from the foreign office—and Moshe Dayan from the Israel Defense Forces; the Jordanians included Samir al-Rifa'i, the minister of court affairs; Fawzi al-Mulki, minister of defense; 'Abd al-Ghani al-Karmi, the king's personal secretary; and the king himself. The talks were held on two levels. The first led to the signing of an armistice agreement on April 3, 1949 (Shlaim 1988, 386–433). The second was meant to result in a peace treaty. In his discussions with Israelis between November 1948 and May 1949, 'Abdallah reiterated his desire to sign a peace agreement based on Israel's recognition of the West Bank's annexation and other concessions. Satisfied with the terms of the armistice agreement, Israeli leaders were unwilling to pay the price of a formal peace with Jordan (Rabinovich 1991, 114). Yet the failure of the Lausanne Conference regarding the Palestinian refugee problem, the political pressure from the United States, and the refusal of Egypt to enter into serious negotiations beyond the armistice agreement changed the Israeli position with regard to peace with Jordan.

When the negotiations began in late November 1949, 'Abdallah made it clear that he was not interested in partial arrangements but in a "general settlement in which he regained Arab territory large enough to enable him to ward off the criticism that a separate peace with Israel would receive" (quoted in Rabinovich 1991, 120). The initial Jordanian demand for withdrawal from Jaffa, Ramleh, and Lydda was quickly dropped as a result of Israeli objections. The talks focused on four issues: borders, Jerusalem, joint economic enterprises (such as the electricity project in Naharayim and the potash plant at the Dead Sea), and the refugees. A major problem throughout the negotiations was that "Israeli policy makers did not have a clear concept of the essence of peace or its price. Hence, they frequently shifted the focus of the negotiations from one issue to another" (Gelber 2004, 130). The Jordanian side was mainly interested in securing a corridor granting free and secure passage to a port on the Mediterranean and control of the Negev, enabling Jordan to be linked with the Gaza Strip and Egypt. As the second demand was immediately and

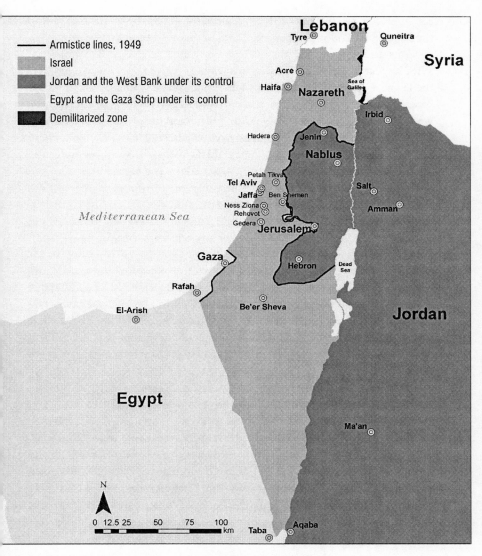

Map 4.1. The 1949 Armistice Lines. Courtesy of Shaul Arieli, 2013.

resolutely rejected by Israel, the first stage of the negotiations concentrated on the issue of a corridor (Gelber 2004, 131; Rabinovich 1991, 127–128).

Considerable progress was made at the meeting held on December 13. With respect to Jerusalem, Jordan was willing to give Israel sovereignty over the Jewish Quarter in the Old City but excluding the Wailing Wall, as well as secure access to Mount Scopus. It also agreed to hand over to Israel the entire western shore of the Dead Sea up to and including the potash plant. The two sides accepted the principle of mutual frontier adjustments subject to military and agricultural needs. Israel, in return for Jordanian concessions, agreed to grant a corridor from Hebron to the Gaza coast. The agreements were laid down in a paper entitled "Political Questions and Territorial Changes." Both Avi Shlaim and Dan Schueftan described the talks as a "major breakthrough" (Shlaim 1988, 528; Schueftan 1986, 197). Itamar Rabinovich, however, did not discern elation on the Israeli side or any sense of a turning point (1991, 129). The progress achieved in the negotiations was probably a result of the adoption of the UN General Assembly resolution regarding the internation-alization of Jerusalem just a few days earlier, on December 9, 1949. It stated that the city—with defined boundaries specified in a map—"shall be estab-lished as a *corpus separatum* under a special international régime and shall be administered by the United Nations" (Laqueur and Rubin 1984, 135). Thus, both Israel and Jordan shared a desire to frustrate the internationalization of Jerusalem.

In contrast to the expectations, however, the next round of negotiations in late December saw regress in the Jordanian position with regard to Jerusalem, the exact width of the corridor and its location, and the potash plant (Schueftan 1986, 203–204). Studies of Israeli-Jordanian relations are not unanimous in as-signing responsibility for this temporary deadlock in the negotiations. Shlaim throws the blame squarely on Ben-Gurion, arguing that the guidelines given to the Israeli delegation before the meeting "laid all the emphasis on Israel's demands and failed to take adequate account of Jordan's needs." In his view, Ben-Gurion "had clearly not learnt that negotiations consist of more than one-sided insistence on advantages that had not been achieved by war" (1988, 529–530). In contrast, however, both Rabinovich (1991, 128–130) and Gelber (2004, 135–136) posit that the two parties share equal responsibility for the failure to implement the promised concessions as a result of mutual domestic constraints and the unwillingness of both Britain and the United States to play an active part in the negotiations.

The next round of negotiations resumed a month later and focused solely on the issue of Jerusalem. During these talks several ideas were raised, but the Jordanian demand for a complete return of Arab quarters in the New City was rejected by Israel, while the counter-demand for Jewish territory in the Old

City was nixed by Jordan, which was only willing to consider free access to Mount Scopus, the Wailing Wall, and the Jewish Quarter (Shlaim 1988, 538–540; Gelber 2004, 141–143). During this round it became clear that the prime minister, the Palestinian Tawfiq Abu al-Huda, was opposed to any territorial concessions to Israel in Jerusalem. He even passed a resolution to that effect in his government, out of fear that any concession in Jerusalem might bring harsh Arab criticism and possibly lead to Jordan's expulsion from the Arab League (Gelber 2004, 141). Here, too, Britain and the United States refrained from involvement in the details of the negotiations.

Though the Jerusalem talks failed, 'Abdallah's determination to prevent the collapse of the negotiations did not: on February 17 he brought a detailed agenda to the table. Among his suggestions were that a five-year nonaggression pact be drawn up on the basis of the existing border lines and the possibility of signing a comprehensive agreement be studied; that negotiations continue for the renewal of trade relations and the creation of a free port for Jordan in Haifa; and that certain other terms pertaining to the property of the refugees be addressed (Rabinovich 1991, 134). This initiative gave the negotiations a "fresh impetus precisely when the dialogue appeared to be at a standstill" (Gelber 2004, 144). Israel was impressed, and surprised, by 'Abdallah's agenda; its importance was mainly symbolic since the principle of nonaggression existed already in the Israeli-Jordanian Armistice Agreement. On February 24 two ministers were forced by 'Abdallah to initial the principles of the draft agreement (for the text, see Schueftan 1986, 206–207). Soon after, the Jordanian government reluctantly approved the draft, though not before amending several clauses to ensure that the agreement would not constitute a separate peace treaty. In other words, Jordan "removed all the meat from the agreed statement" (Shlaim 1988, 543). When the new draft was presented to the Israeli side, they were unwilling to sign "a new edition of the armistice agreement" (Rabinovich 1991, 138; Sasson 2004, 45–46). The king himself was apparently caught unawares by the Jordanian draft and reprimanded his ministers in front of the Israeli representatives. A few days later, when 'Abdallah attempted to force the agreement on the government, Prime Minister Abu al-Huda resigned. Both Sa'id al-Mufti and Samir al-Rifa'i failed to set up a new government as a result of domestic opposition and organized campaigns in several Arab countries that spread rumors about Jordan's alleged signing of a peace agreement with Israel. Succumbing to the pressure, 'Abdallah backtracked on his intention to make peace with Israel. On March 7, Israeli representatives were notified that the negotiations were adjourned. It was expected that they would resume after the upcoming parliamentary elections and the next session of the Arab League, both scheduled for April. The suspension of the talks, in Shlaim's assessment, represented a draw in the tug-of-war between the government and royal court (1988, 548). What the episode made clear was that 'Abdallah was no longer the master in his own domain (Gelber 2004, 148; Rabinovich 1991, 140; Sasson 2004, 45–47; Schueftan 1986, 208–210).

The suspension of the negotiations did help 'Abdallah weather a small storm at the Arab League session. To further dodge Arab accusations of collaboration with Israel, he joined the resolution forbidding negotiations or the signing of any agreement with Israel; a violation of this resolution would lead to the expulsion of the dissenting state from the League (Rabinovich 1991, 143; Shlaim 1988, 553–555). On April 11 elections were held on both banks of the Jordan River, and the composition of the new parliament (divided equally between East and West Bank delegates) allowed 'Abdallah to declare the annexation of the West Bank on April 24. As a result of his acquiescence to the Arab League resolution regarding negotiations with Israel, the League members decided to recognize this step informally. Israel, for different reasons, adopted the same position. 'Abdallah's contacts with Israel resumed in late April, but they remained intermittent and inconclusive throughout 1950; this strengthened the Israeli conviction that "resumption of the dialogue did not hinge on a compromise between Israel and Jordan but on a compromise between the king and his government" (Gelber 2004, 169). Indeed, the composition of the new government—evenly divided between Jordanians and Palestinians—did not allow the continuation of the negotiations with Israel. With the assassination of 'Abdallah by a Palestinian on July 21, 1951, the dream of an Israeli-Jordanian peace treaty finally evaporated.

ASSESSMENT

Can the negotiations between Israel and Jordan during the years 1946–1951 be considered a missed opportunity? Many years ago, the philosopher Martin Buber was of the opinion that "by [taking] certain [Israeli] concessions it was possible to reach an agreement" (quoted in Mendes-Flohr 1988, 219). Likewise, Zeev Maoz was of the opinion that "'Abdallah was eager to make peace with Israel. Yet, in the early stages of the negotiations Israel turned a cold shoulder and perhaps missed an opportune moment" (2004, 398). Shlaim took a middle road, concluding that the quest for an agreement was doomed "because Israel was too strong and inflexible while 'Abdallah was too weak and isolated" (2000, 67). Rabinovich was more explicit, arguing that the question of a missed opportunity is not central to this episode, as an assessment of the forces operating at the time shows that "It was impossible to reach an acceptable agreement to Israel, which, at the same time, would be viable from the perspective of the Jordanian entity" (1991, 142).[2] Shimon Shamir concluded that the conditions were not ripe for a solution (2012, 26). Finally,

Moshe Sasson, whose father participated in the talks while he himself served as a young diplomat cadet, was convinced that an agreement would not have been signed even if ʿAbdallah had survived the assassination attempt (2004, 259).

According to our analysis, the episode did constitute a historical opportunity. The war and particularly its results created a new reality in which Israel and Jordan gained substantial territory: both were now in a position to strike a deal at the expense of the defeated Palestinians. The idea of such a deal was raised several times in the pre-1948 period but the international, regional, and domestic circumstances were not favorable enough to implement it. Both parties could have gained from such an agreement: Jordan, by acquiring additional territory and access to the Mediterranean, which is of political and economic importance; Israel, by securing peace along its longest border and winning recognition from an Arab state, thus breaking the wall of Arab rejection and boycott. In other words, the attraction here was not of a specific offer presented to the parties, but rather the very idea of reaching a peaceful settlement, the components of which would be decided following an intensive round of negotiations. The post-1948 talks were, in many ways, the consummation of a long process of negotiations between ʿAbdallah and the Zionists, which in fact extended for over two decades.

What was the potentiality level of the opportunity? In terms of legitimacy as leaders, our first variable, both sides enjoyed a significant measure of legitimacy: on the Israeli side, Ben-Gurion as the first Israeli prime minister and Moshe Sharett as the first foreign minister were fully in charge of the decision-making process, despite opposition forces operating on the left (Mapam Party and Communists) and right (Begin and the Revisionists), which objected to an agreement with Jordan (Gelber 2004, 148–149). Yet this opposition could not have prevented the signing of an agreement had the Israeli leaders chosen this road. On the other side, ʿAbdallah was considered a legitimate monarch in the pre-1948 period, yet the arrival of many Palestinians into the kingdom following the annexation of the West Bank changed the demographic balance and shook public opinion. "The country was still called 'Jordan,'" wrote Mordechai Gazit, "but in reality it had become Palestine" (1998, 410). Gazit exaggerated the extent of the change, but there is no doubt that the continued negative stance of several ministers in the government (some of whom were of Palestinian origin) was affected by the pressure coming from society. Jordan, in contrast to the Western thinking, was not a "one-man show" (Rabinovich 1991, 115–116). Even if ʿAbdallah had enjoyed absolute legitimacy, he still would have faced great difficulties in pursuing his policy with regard to Israel. "What ʿAbdallah seriously misjudged," wrote Shlaim, "was the strength of the internal opposition to his peace policy and the effect which the storm in the

Arab League had on the readiness of his ministers to carry out this policy" (1988, 560).

The second element relates to the willingness of the leader to take bold new moves on the basis of changes in his thinking. The Israeli side was interested in an agreement, yet it seems that it was not willing to pay a meaningful price to attain one. Shlaim thinks that a major factor in the failure was "Ben-Gurion's lack of commitment to a political settlement with Jordan" (2000, 67). Interestingly, he had never made an attempt to meet 'Abdallah. On the other hand, Sharett believed that Israel had nothing to give Jordan (Gelber 2004, 140). Moreover, the final draft of the nonaggression pact was perceived in Israel as not attractive enough. This suggests that the Israeli leadership lacked resolve and determination to take bold moves, even at the price of some generous concessions; peace with Jordan, in other words, was not considered urgent. It was 'Abdallah throughout the negotiations who appeared more resolute and determined to arrive at some accommodation. Whenever negotiations stalled, he came up with another initiative that aimed at preventing a possible deadlock in the talks. The problem, however, was that 'Abdallah's resolve was not matched by his ministers or the public in general. A big gap existed between the king's willingness and his ability; while he was sincere in his willingness to pursue the peace track, his ability to do so was limited due to the domestic and regional environments (Sasson 2004, 46–47). As time went by, the king's determination to conclude an agreement declined due to the growing domestic opposition and his deteriorating health.

The third element, the impact of prior contacts between the parties on the negotiations and the existence of trust, is particularly noteworthy in this case. Undoubtedly, previous negotiations between 'Abdallah and the Jewish Agency helped to build a certain trust that even the war was unable to break. Moreover, as the talks before and after the war were conducted by a limited group of diplomats and politicians, a certain personal intimacy likely developed between them, which helped smooth over some differences and disputes. This mutual trust would remain an important legacy for King Husayn (Sasson 2004, 260).

The fourth element pertains to the role of the mediator. Perhaps the most problematic aspect of the negotiations was the superpowers' low level of involvement in the talks. There is much evidence to support the argument that both the British Foreign Office and US State Department deliberately refused to intervene or advise the parties on how to proceed. This behavior had several possible explanations, such as an unwillingness to interfere in something seen as futile and bound to fail, or fear that such interference would weaken 'Abdallah and/or his government and adversely affect the superpowers' interests. The Israeli foreign office even went as far as assessing that "The British were not particularly interested in an Israeli-Jordanian settlement" (Gelber 2004, 158). In contrast, Shlaim absolves Britain of any responsibility, claiming, "The Israeli contention that Britain failed to encourage Jordan to negotiate . . . is without substance" (1988, 567). Britain and the United States were not responsible for the failure, but neither did their "hands-off" position contribute. It seems that both powers—and particularly Britain, which was the dominant power in Jordan—were hesitant to involve themselves more deeply in the negotiations out of fear for the king's very survival, and the assumption that any pressure would in any case be of no avail (Gazit 1998, 420).

The analysis above suggests that the talks between Israel and Jordan in the aftermath of the 1948 War constituted a historical opportunity. Yet the potentiality level of this episode was low, as only one variable—the level of trust—supported the missed opportunity thesis. As for the king's legitimacy and determination to conclude an agreement, there were serious doubts about his ability to deliver that end product. In this respect, his assassination only jolted the tip of the iceberg of resistance to Israel. On the Israeli side there were no doubts regarding the legitimacy of its leaders, yet it seems that Ben-Gurion was far from determined to pay the price of peace. In addition, the role of the mediator—Britain in particular—was unhelpful for a variety of reasons. And though a more generous Israeli offer to Jordanian demands would have improved the chances of a possible breakthrough, it seems inconceivable that a lasting agreement could have been signed and sustained in light of the widespread opposition to it.

NOTES

1. Most historians refute the thesis that collusion or anything resembling a deal concerning the Arab part of Palestine was made between the Jewish Agency and ʿAbdallah; see Shamir 2012, 22; Karsh 1999, 569–585.

2. The quote is taken from the Hebrew version. It is interesting to note that this conclusion was omitted from the English version, which usually is identical with the Hebrew version.

CHAPTER 5

ISRAEL AND SYRIA:
THE HUSNI ZAʿIM INITIATIVE
1949

HUSNI ZAʿIM, the Syrian chief of staff, executed a military coup on March 30, 1949, toppling the civilian regime headed by President Shukri al-Quwwatli and Prime Minister Khalid al-ʿAzm. At the time, the Israel-Syria armistice negotiations were about to begin. Zaʿim certainly surprised Israel and the United States when he swept in and promptly offered to sign a peace agreement with Israel and resettle some three hundred thousand Palestinian refugees in Syria in return for a substantial Israeli territorial concession along Lake Kinneret (Sea of Galilee) and some additional demands. The Zaʿim offer aroused much academic interest as a possible first Arab-Israeli peace agreement that might have been missed. This chapter will assess if and to what extent the Zaʿim episode was a missed opportunity.

THE EPISODE

The primary motives for Zaʿim's coup were a combination of personal ambition and the dissatisfaction of many officers with the civil government's performance. In particular, they were annoyed by what they viewed as Syria's mishandling of the 1948 Palestine War and the fact that the army was poorly equipped and supplied (Rathmell 1995, 25–26; Seale 1987, 41–45). Zaʿim was a professional French-trained soldier portrayed as an adventurer with dubious connections with Britain, France, the United States, and Israel at different times. In fact, there is strong evidence that the coup was instigated with the help of the CIA, as secret contacts between Zaʿim and the US agency commenced as early as November 1948. The US interest in promoting a pro-Western regime stemmed from the fear of a Communist takeover and a Syrian-Soviet "marriage of convenience." Another factor was the US interest in securing Syrian consent for the rights-of-way for the Trans-Arabian pipeline (TAPLINE) from the Dhahran oil fields in Saudi Arabia to the Mediterranean, particularly after obtaining the consent of Lebanon, Jordan, and Saudi Arabia

(Copeland 1969, 50–54; Little 1990, 53–56). Discussion of the matter had been deferred for several years in Syria's parliament. Being a Kurd by origin, Za'im did not harbor any commitment to pan-Arab ideology prevalent at the time. Yet the fact that he ended the 1948 War as a national hero established his reputation and initial legitimacy when he seized power (Rathmell 1995, 36–44; Seale 1987, 44–45).

Za'im's coup occurred after Egypt, Jordan, and Lebanon had already concluded armistice agreements with Israel. Za'im immediately started negotiations with Israel, which, in fact, had already been started by the previous regime on March 17; Za'im's policy toward Israel thus signaled continuity rather than change (Shalev 1989, 36–37). Khalid al-'Azm, Syria's prime minister before the coup, wrote in his memoirs that his government had decided to follow the lead of Egypt, Jordan, and Lebanon out of fear that Syria would be left on its own to confront Israel militarily (1973, 381). The main interest of Syria in the talks was to maintain its hold over the territories it gained during the war beyond the fixed 1947 international boundary and to improve its access rights to the region's scarce water resources—the Jordan River and Lake Kinneret. Israel, for its part, had opposite interests, particularly as the agreements with Egypt and Lebanon necessitated its complete withdrawal to the international boundary. Its policy now was based on the premise that "There was no point in making concessions on important issues when Israel enjoyed an overwhelming advantage over a weak Syria practically devoid of Arab support" (Rabinovich 1991, 68).

In contrast to the Israeli-Jordanian arena, where armistice and peace talks progressed in parallel, Za'im used the armistice talks to deliver his peace offer to Israel right off the bat. On April 15 the Syrian representatives to the armistice talks delivered the initiative, which included an offer to sign a full peace treaty with open borders and an exchange of ambassadors as well as economic and military cooperation. In return, Syria demanded border modifications along the Jordan River and control of half of Lake Kinneret. This demand, incidentally, had already been suggested by the previous government ('Azm 1973, 381). In order to conclude the deal without delay, Za'im suggested a personal meeting with Ben-Gurion. The latter's response was hardly encouraging; he dismissed the possibility of any meeting before a complete Syrian withdrawal to the international border within an armistice agreement. In private, he went further, entertaining the idea of expelling the Syrians by military force to the international border. Meanwhile, in early May, Za'im met the American chargé in Damascus and offered, within the framework of a comprehensive solution to the Arab-Israeli conflict, to settle as many as three hundred thousand Palestinian refugees—about half the estimated total—in the northeast Jazira area, on condition that Syria be given adequate financial aid to resettle them. This information, however, was not formally transmitted to the Israelis at the time. Za'im also reiterated his desire to meet Ben-Gurion or Sharett (Shalev 1989, 56; Rabinovich 1991, 68–71, 20; Shlaim 1986, 73–75). In order to enlist US support for his plan, Za'im arrested many alleged Communists and approved the long-delayed TAPLINE concession (Little 1990, 57).

Several considerations drove Za'im to seek peace with Israel. First was the fear of a renewed attack by Israel, which at that time enjoyed overwhelming military superiority. After all, Syria was left as the only neighboring Arab state confronting the Israeli threat after the others had signed armistice agreements. Second, Za'im wanted to withdraw his army from the front in order to consolidate his power in Damascus, allowing him to deal more effectively with potential rivals in the army and the political arena. Third, he contemplated taking some serious economic and social reforms, and peace with Israel might facilitate that process. Fourth, he feared deterioration in his relations with the Hashemites in Jordan and Iraq. Finally, the most important consideration for Za'im was the hope that an Israeli-Syrian peace treaty and a major contribution to the solution of the refugee problem would help win American financial support and general goodwill. Indeed, in late July he delivered a request for a $100 million military and economic aid package from the United States (Shlaim 1986, 72; Rabinovich 1991, 80–91; Little 1990, 57).

The UN mediator and the American diplomats attempted to persuade Ben-Gurion to meet Za'im, but to no avail; he insisted that he saw no purpose in such a meeting as long as Syria did not declare its forces' withdrawal to their pre-war territory (Rabinovich 1991, 72). At that time, even the moderate Sharett agreed that the time was not propitious for such a high-level meeting. Henri Vigier, the French diplomat who served as the adviser of the UN observers' headquarters, thought, however, that Sharett should have represented Israel in the armistice talks instead of the lower-ranked officials who did so, and that by insisting on the international border rather than the water line, the Israelis "missed a unique opportunity to come to a long-term agreement with the Syrians" (quoted in Rabinovich 1991, 73). Za'im expressed disappointment with Israel's intransigence; still in favor of peace with his neighbor, he told the American chargé on May 11 that "When candid men with the authority to settle things met, an agreement became feasible if they presented to one another reasonable requests that cannot be rejected" (ibid.). The UN and US diplomats were convinced that a high-level meeting (i.e., either Ben-Gurion or Sharett) should be arranged with Za'im and that the water line constituted a more reasonable border than the existing international border.

On May 17, General Riley, the UN chairman of the Syrian-Israeli armistice talks, told the legal adviser of the Israeli Foreign Office on behalf of Za'im that he was willing within the Lausanne talks—the ongoing conference held since April by the UN Palestine Conciliation Commission for the settlement of the Palestinian refugee problem—to resettle three hundred thousand refugees in Syria in return for a solution to the border issues. Ben-Gurion seemed unimpressed by Za'im's latest offer. At the other end of the spectrum, both Abba Eban, the Israeli representative at the United Nations, and Sharett were definitely impressed by the initiative. On May 25 the latter was quoted to the effect that Za'im's offer shows vision and courage and should be explored. Sharett then expressed his willingness to meet Za'im or his foreign minister 'Adil Arslan to discover Syria's true intentions (Shlaim 1986, 74–75; Rabinovich 1991, 74–75, 97–98). Za'im refused to meet Sharett because of his low seniority, while Arslan refused to meet Sharett because of his pan-Arab views and his unwillingness to recognize or negotiate with Israel altogether. In his memoirs, Arslan proudly stated that his refusal to meet Sharett succeeded in subverting the idea (1983, 2:841–842, 847). Not surprisingly, when Za'im was elected president by a referendum and Muhsin al-Barazi was appointed prime minister on June 25, 1949, Arslan was dismissed from his post (ibid., 848). When Syria's negative reply to the Israeli offer was delivered to Sharett, he felt deceived and humiliated. As a result of UN and US pressure, Ben-Gurion himself was persuaded to meet Za'im in early June. A few days later, however, the Syrian response was that issues pertaining to the armistice talks would be kept within the framework of the "mixed" committee while those pertaining to peace relations would have to be dealt with by other Arab states as well. It became clear now that neither Za'im nor any other senior Syrian politician would meet senior Israeli officials outside the established framework of the armistice talks. The Syrian behavior indicated either that Za'im had realized the constraints of the domestic and regional arenas compelled him to withdraw from his initiative, or that the sincerity of his initial offer was called into question. In any event, the possibility of a high-ranking meeting between Israeli and Syrian officials vanished, and with it the possibility of signing a separate Israeli-Syrian peace agreement.

After a month of suspension, the talks were resumed in mid-June. By now, however, Za'im's enthusiasm for a peace treaty had declined and he was willing to be satisfied with an armistice agreement, which was eventually signed on July 20. It would seem that the internal opposition to Za'im's moderate position vis-à-vis Israel and his domestic reforms compelled him to withdraw from his initial ambitious plans. The United States and the United Nations were also pleased enough with the signing of the armistice agreement, preferring to focus on the negotiations at the Lausanne Conference (Rabinovich 1991, 79–80).

Then, on August 14, after just four months in power, Za'im was assassinated by a group of officers under the leadership of Sami Hinawi. The main reason for Za'im's fall was the fact that he antagonized all the major groups that had supported him (Shlaim 1986, 79; Arslan 1983, 2:871; Seale 1987, 58–63). His assassination brought to an end the so-called Za'im Initiative.

Assuming that Za'im presented a unique—and sincere—offer to Israel, it is to be questioned why the response of its decision makers reflected skepticism, indifference, and doubt. There are several possible answers. First, the gap between the two parties was too wide to bridge; Za'im's demand for border modifications and particularly control of half of Lake Kinneret was anathema to Israeli leaders, as this water basin was the key to future national irrigation schemes all the way to the Negev desert. Za'im, for his part, needed to show territorial gains to justify his policy vis-à-vis Israel in Arab nationalist eyes. In this respect, Za'im was no different from King 'Abdallah, who demanded significant territorial concessions from Israel that would lift his stature in Jordan and the Arab world (see chapter 4). Although there was much logic in this demand, Israel never considered it as a serious or worthwhile proposition and therefore rejected it. Second, the fact that Za'im came to power through a coup and the stability of his regime was very much at stake raised doubts as to the wisdom of concluding an agreement with him. Moshe Ma'oz argued, "Ben-Gurion was not prepared to make important strategic concessions to Syria in return for a formal peace treaty signed by an unpredictable and corrupt Syrian dictator, who might not be willing or able to fulfill Syria's peace commitments to Israel in the future" (1995, 24). Third, there are indications that the Israeli leaders generally did not take Za'im seriously because they saw him as an ambitious adventurer motivated by personal greed. During the war, Za'im reportedly asked Israel for a million dollars to help him topple the Syrian government, put an end to the war, and reverse Syria's position toward Israel. If this information is correct, then it can explain the hesitation of the Israeli leaders to treat him seriously (M. Ma'oz 1995, 22; Rabinovich 1991, 99; Shlaim 1986, 68–69). In this regard one must also take into account Za'im's unpredictable decision making; upon seizing power he made an attempt to woo Iraq and Jordan, though he quickly made a complete volte-face when he was persuaded by Egypt and Saudi Arabia to adopt an anti-Hashemite position—a step that earned him their formal recognition of his rule (Seale 1987, 46–57). Finally, it is argued that Israeli decision makers, and particularly Ben-Gurion, believed that the armistice agreement satisfied Israel's immediate needs. "Although I'm prepared to get up in the middle of the night and sign an agreement," Ben-Gurion was quoted as saying, "I am not in a hurry and I am prepared to wait ten years. We are under no pressure to do anything" (quoted in Shlaim 1986, 77). Ultimately, Za'im's swift demise lends credibility to all the suspicions and concerns that surrounded him.

ASSESSMENT

Scholars are at odds over their assessment of the Zaʿim Initiative. In Shlaim's opinion, Zaʿim displayed a "flexible and conciliatory attitude" as opposed to the "unremitting Israeli intransigence" (1986, 78). He further argues that Zaʿim "gave Israel every opportunity to bury the hatchet and lay the foundations for peaceful coexistence." Moreover, "If his overtures were spurned, if his constructive proposals were not put to the test, and if an opportunity for a breakthrough had been missed, the responsibility must be attributed not to Zaʿim but to Israel." In this connection Shlaim particularly blames Ben-Gurion, who was the main proponent of the notion that time was on Israel's side and that it could manage without peace with the Arabs (2000, 53; 1986, 79). Simha Flapan too is critical of the Israeli response, which, in his opinion, "ranged from indifference to distrust to contempt, although a few scattered voices tried to stress the uniqueness of the opportunity" (1987, 210–211). Similarly, Zeev Maoz claimed that Ben-Gurion's eventual willingness to meet Zaʿim in June 1949 was "too little and too late" (2004, 394). The Zaʿim Initiative, in his assessment, was clearly a missed opportunity on the part of Israel (ibid., 398). Moreover, "had Israel been willing to adopt a more forthcoming position early on, the Zaʿim Initiative could have paved the way for a model of refugee resettlement that Israel could use as a precedent for other agreements with Arab states with large numbers of Palestinian refugees" (ibid., 395). Finally, Moshe Sasson cautiously remarked, "I had a most profound sense that a chance for peace had slipped away already in 1949" (2004, 258).

A different assessment, however, was offered by Itamar Rabinovich. In his view, "Ben-Gurion's refusal to meet Husni Zaʿim in April–May 1949 did not destroy the prospect of reaching an agreement that would have transformed Arab-Israeli relations" (1991, 109). It is difficult to believe, he argues, that Zaʿim would have survived in power even if he had reached an agreement with Israel and enjoyed massive US aid. While in his first days Zaʿim appeared to be a popular reformer, his image soon turned into one of a corrupt dictator who was consumed with grabbing prestige and status, and who thus lost the support of his allies. In other words, his offer was completely divorced from the prevailing public opinion in Syria and the rest of the Arab world. In this respect, Arslan was more representative of the public's voice than was Zaʿim. In Rabinovich's view, an Israeli-Syrian treaty would have more closely resembled the May 1983 Israeli-Lebanese Agreement than the Camp David Agreement (1991, 109–110).[1] Likewise, Shalev believes that a peace treaty might have precipitated Zaʿim's downfall (which was quick anyway). And yet both Shalev and Maʿoz think that though the prospects for an agreement were slim, Ben-

Gurion should have responded to Zaʿim's initial offer to meet so as to explore its validity and his seriousness (M. Maʾoz 1995, 24; Shalev 1989, 62).

To what extent is it plausible that the Zaʿim Initiative was a missed opportunity? There is no doubt that this episode constituted a historical opportunity. The war and its consequences created a new reality in which both Israel and Syria gained additional territory beyond their delineated international border. This created a bargaining chip for both countries in future negotiations. Moreover, a new military regime came to power in Syria, toppling an illegitimate civilian government that was considered responsible for the army's poor performance in the Palestine War in spite of the limited territorial gains. Shortly after his rise to power, Zaʿim gave the green light to the armistice talks and offered Israel what seemed to be an attractive and unprecedented initiative: the signing of a peace treaty with a possible solution for almost half of the Palestinian refugees. In return, Israel would have to pay no small price in terms of territory and water resources. Yet signing a peace agreement with the first Arab state was meant to offset the disadvantages of the territorial demand. In addition, the breaking of the taboo of signing a peace treaty with Israel might have given ʿAbdallah, who was then ensconced in negotiations with the Israelis, enough courage to take the bold decision of signing a second agreement.

What was the potentiality level of the episode? The first element relates to the legitimacy level of the leaders. As discussed in the previous chapter, the Israeli government was secure in its position. Under Ben-Gurion and Sharett, it enjoyed a comfortable majority in the Knesset. But it now had to negotiate with a regime that had come to power through a military coup. And though the just-deposed Syrian government had suffered from serious legitimacy problems, it was difficult to assess, at the time, to what extent the new regime enjoyed the legitimacy and support of its people. Initially, Zaʿim was surrounded by fellow army officers who supported him and his policy. In June he was elected president in a plebiscite—a measure that may attest to his popularity (Seale 1987, 59). At the same time, however, he belonged to the Kurdish minority and as such he was opposed by leading Sunni families, who were ardent Arab nationalists. They saw Zaʿim as a collaborator with foreign forces who had climbed the social ladder with French help (Rabinovich 1991, 81; Shlaim 1986, 79). Understandably, Israel did not know how to treat the new leader and his bold initiative, particularly in light of his prevailing negative image. No wonder that after the coup Ben-Gurion was quoted to the effect that "Israel must always ask itself whether the representatives of an Arab state really represent their country. [King] Farouk is apparently Egypt, but who is Zaim?" (Rabinovich 1991, 99). It was a false assumption with regard to Faruq, but it may have been right with regard to Za'im. As a result, Israel's response to Za'im's overtures displayed a mixture of caution and suspicion. As time went by, Za'im's unpredictable policy with regard to Israel, Arab neighboring countries, and domestic reforms antagonized even the forces that had supported his rise to power. Rumors regarding his alleged meeting with Ben-Gurion ('Azm 1973, 381; Seale 1987, 62) further weakened his position. The result was that he could not advance his initiative and Israel could not consider him as a legitimate partner.

The second element relates to the willingness of the leader to take bold new moves on the basis of changes in his thinking. Initially, Za'im displayed himself as a leader capable of making bold decisions in the realm of domestic and external affairs. He seemed intent on reaching an agreement with Israel and showed the eagerness and flexibility needed to do so. As time went by, however, his enthusiasm for implementing these assertive moves withered away. This stemmed from the growing opposition to his policy, particularly with regard to peace with Israel, and the internal struggle for power. An opposite trend occurred on the Israeli side; Ben-Gurion had the ability to make bold moves, but he thought that the Za'im offer was "too high a price to pay for a dubious agreement" (Ma'oz 1995, 22). Seeing the armistice agreements with Egypt, Jordan, and Lebanon as a preferred model, Ben-Gurion scoffed at Za'im's offer. After an initially lukewarm—almost indifferent—response to Za'im's innovative ideas, Ben-Gurion and Sharett became convinced that his ideas—particularly the resettlement of many Palestinian refugees in Syria—were worthy of exploration. By the time this shift had taken place, Za'im's room to maneuver was significantly circumscribed, leading to his demise shortly after.

The third element relates to the impact of prior contacts between the parties to the negotiations and the existence of trust. Prior contacts between Syrian and Zionist/Israeli leaders did not play a significant role here. Curiously, Weizmann, Ben-Gurion, Sharett, and other Israeli politicians and diplomats had met leading Syrian politicians during the French mandate period. From the Syrian perspective, these contacts were intended to help it win independence and acquire a possible foothold in the Palestine problem (Ben-Gurion 1975, 174–176; Khoury 1985, 334–337). Since these leaders did not play any role in the Za'im regime (they were either deposed or out of office by then), these early Zionist-Syrian contacts could not affect matters during the Za'im period. Yet in addition to rumors that Za'im collaborated with the CIA, during the 1948 War he secretly asked Israel for a million dollars to help him topple the Syrian government, put an end to the war, and bring about a change in Syria's policy toward Israel. The Israeli intelligence community was aware of Za'im's reputation as an opportunist. It is not known whether Ben-Gurion was privy to this information, but if he was it may explain his reluctance to meet the Syrian leader.

The fourth element relates to the role of the mediator. The United States, the United Nations, and France, all possible third partners, did not play a meaningful role in the negotiations, though all three did mediate between the parties at one time or another. They also exerted some pressure on Israel to present a more moderate position toward the Syrians and insisted on a favorable response to Za'im's request to meet Ben-Gurion. Yet the main problem was that the diplomatic efforts were not coordinated; each party was concerned with securing its own interests. Moreover, the involvement of the United States, the United Nations, and France was not consistent, nor did it include top decision makers. Thus, for example, Dean Acheson, the US secretary of state, was hardly involved in the negotiations. At a certain point, when the Israeli-Syrian Armistice Agreement was signed in July, the State Department was no longer eager for the parties to move on to a peace agreement, preferring instead to use the Lausanne Conference mechanism to solve the refugee problem. Za'im's offer to settle some refugees in Syria was now to be dealt with at Lausanne (Rabinovich 1991, 79–88). George McGhee, the special assistant to the US secretary of state responsible for aid to the Palestinian refugees, thought that Za'im's proposal had been one of the best opportunities thus far to resolve the refugee problem (1983, 36). Yet even that, not to mention Za'im's attempts to win over the United States by approving the TAPLINE concessions, his rounding-up of Communists, and his eagerness to come to a comprehensive agreement with Israel, was not enough to cause the United States to navigate the parties toward an agreement. It was satisfied that the fighting had ended. It seems that the United States was not involved in peacemaking for peace itself, but was rather hoping to create a firmer foothold in the Middle East through Za'im.

In sum, the Za'im Initiative was a historical opportunity, but its potentiality level was low. The legitimacy of the Syrian leader was questionable (and this deficiency increased as time went by), and there was no willingness or preparation on the Israeli side to take bold moves in favor of peace. Even Za'im's initial boldness dwindled as he succumbed to domestic and regional pressures. The lack of trust that already existed between the parties deepened, and previous contacts tended to confirm Za'im's untrustworthiness. The main factor that supports the missed opportunity thesis was the lack of or limited third-party role; evidently, the United Nations, the United States, and France did not play an effective role in attempting to further the negotiations. Yet a more assertive role by a mediator, including the personal involvement of senior US officials—which was not likely at the time—would not likely have changed the outcome.

Still, it can be argued that the Israeli decision makers made a mistake by not treating the Syrian proposal with the seriousness it deserved. In particular, they failed to respond quickly to Za'im's offer to meet. A meeting might have illuminated the gaps or led to further negotiations. Perhaps it was thought that a meeting with Za'im was still premature. Maybe the Israeli behavior stemmed from the logic of the parallel negotiations with 'Abdallah, where senior diplomats, not decision makers, met the king. It is also possible that Za'im's dubious image damaged his credibility in Israeli eyes. It should be remembered, however, that King 'Abdallah had received a "subsidy" on a regular basis from the Jewish Agency, but this did not tarnish his image in Israeli eyes. In other words, the Zionist policy toward the king was not motivated by moral considerations. But the fact that a mistake was probably made does not turn this case into a missed opportunity. On the contrary: our analysis does not support the thesis that the Za'im episode constituted a missed opportunity.

NOTE

1. Rabinovich refers to the notion that the Israeli-Lebanese Agreement cannot be considered a peace treaty in the full sense of the term. Moreover, it was nullified shortly after its conclusion in March 1984. See chapter 15.

CHAPTER 6

ISRAELI-EGYPTIAN RELATIONS: THE ALPHA PLAN AND THE ANDERSON MISSION 1949–1956

IN EARLY 1955 Britain and the United States devised a peace plan, code-named Alpha. It was an attempt to offer a partial solution to the Arab-Israeli conflict, though the eventual goal was a comprehensive settlement. The main incentive of the Western powers in launching this joint endeavor was to stabilize the region and thus maintain their own security and economic interests in the Middle East while damaging the developing Soviet-Arab relations. In addition, a settlement was seen as a prerequisite to the participation of the Arab states—particularly Egypt—in the organization of Middle East defense. It was the first Western attempt to reach an agreement between the new Egyptian regime, headed by Gamal 'Abd al-Nasser, and Israel. The failure of the Alpha Plan led the United States to send a personal presidential emissary, Robert Anderson, to mediate between the two parties. This chapter will analyze if the Alpha Plan and the Anderson Mission constituted historical opportunities for peace.

THE EPISODE

Until the outbreak of the Arab Revolt (1936–1939), Egyptian interest in the Palestine conflict was limited. Three major developments changed that. First, the rise and spread of the pan-Arab ideology in society encouraged leading Egyptian intellectuals to emphasize their association with the Arab world in terms of language, history, culture, and territory (Gershoni and Jankowski 1995, 117–142). Second, being part of the Arab world meant that Egypt, as a result of its self-perception of leadership based on its geographical location, human resources, Islamic centrality (al-Azhar), and other soft power capabilities, believed it was destined to lead the Arab world (Podeh 1995). Third, political rivalries existed between the royal court and the government.

The growing political commitment to the Palestine issue led Egypt to take part in the 1948 War. A major consideration in King Faruq's decision to enter the fray was his fear of a change in the Arab balance of power as a result of possible territorial gains in Palestine by Jordan's King ʿAbdallah. Though the army's performance in the war was poor, Egypt found itself in control of the Gaza Strip, which was populated by some three hundred thousand Palestinians, mostly refugees. Contacts between Israel and Egypt following the war were limited and held in secrecy. The main Egyptian demand was for Israel's withdrawal from the Negev in order to establish a territorial link with the Eastern Arab world and possibly gain land for resettling Palestinian refugees. Israel, for its part, considered Egypt to be the most important Arab state and the key to peace with the Arab world in general. Clearly, a sincere dialogue with Egypt was much preferred over Jordan's ʿAbdallah or Syria's Zaʿim (Rabinovich 1991, 115; Oren 1992, 98). Unwilling, however, to pay a realistic price for peace, both sides signed the armistice agreement on February 24, 1949. The agreement was roughly based on the cease-fire lines with the exception of establishing a demilitarized zone in al-ʿAuja (Rabinovich 1991, 172–177; Caplan 1997, 34–56). From the signing of the agreement until the collapse of the monarchy in 1952 there were further contacts, but they did not produce a breakthrough, as there was no incentive for both parties to deviate from their entrenched positions (Rabinovich 1991, 177–202; Oren 1990, 351–353). Under the shadow of the disastrous Palestine War, King Faruq faced growing domestic problems, which further hindered the promotion of any dialogue with Israel. Moreover, relations between the two countries soured as a result of Egypt's decision to block the Suez Canal to Israeli shipping. Though the UN Security Council considered this act a violation of the armistice agreement, according to Resolution 95 of September 1951, Egypt maintained that the agreement did not end the existing state of belligerency (Caplan 1997, 54).

The military coup, led by General Muhammad Naguib and Colonel Gamal ʿAbd al-Nasser on July 23, 1923, seemed to open a new chapter not only in Egypt's history but also in Israeli-Egyptian relations. Ben-Gurion welcomed the coming to power of the young officers, hoping that the perceived legitimacy of the new rulers would encourage moderation toward Israel. Meetings between representatives of the new regime and Israeli diplomats were held in Paris, London, and New York. These talks indicated that the Palestine question did not top the Free Officers' agenda and that they did not harbor any plans for war against Israel. Relations with Britain and socioeconomic reforms were of much more immediate concern to them. But the contradiction between Egypt's public denunciations of Israel and its more moderate posturing behind the scenes caused confusion in Israel; some thought that Egypt was playing a double game aimed at misleading Israel in order to prepare for the "second round" (Oren 1992, 100–101).

This pattern characterized Israeli-Egyptian relations in 1953. Contacts and venue options expanded while the new military regime simultaneously upgraded its support of armed infiltration through the border—particularly from Gaza—tightened blockade restrictions in the Suez Canal, and broadcast anti-Israeli propaganda in its radio transmissions (Oren 1992, 102–104; Tal 1998, 106–107). The diplomatic exchanges between Nasser and Prime Minister Sharett throughout 1953 were important in themselves, but in essence they achieved very little; by the end of the year, wrote Shlaim, "The high hopes that had been pinned on the Egyptian revolution [by Israel] had largely faded away" (2000, 81).

The signing of the Egyptian-British treaty in July 1954 raised apprehension in Israel as to the ramifications that the expected British withdrawal from the Suez Canal bases would have on future Israeli-Egyptian relations. The military presence in the Suez Canal zone constituted, in Israeli eyes, a buffer against a possible Egyptian offensive against the Negev. Two Israeli operations were aimed at subverting this development. The first was the reactivation of a Jewish intelligence underground cell, which was instructed to firebomb US and British institutions in Egypt, thereby shaking the West's faith in Egypt's ability to safeguard the canal against domestic upheaval. In mid-July a series of bombs exploded in British and US facilities in Cairo and Alexandria; they caused little damage and no fatalities. Egyptian authorities uncovered the plot and placed ten Egyptian Jews on trial for espionage (Morris 1993, 316–320; Sheffer 1996, 750–769). The second operation was the sending of an Israeli merchant ship, the *Bat-Galim*, through the Straits of Tiran and the Suez Canal, both of which Egypt had closed to Israeli vessels. The move was intended to test the Egyptian blockage. As expected, the ship was stopped on September 28, its cargo confiscated, and the crew arrested. Israel hoped that the whole matter would be brought to the United Nations and the International Court of Justice, leading to the condemnation of Egypt and the implementation of UN Security Council Resolution 95 (see above; Morris 1993, 320–321).

The *Bat-Galim* and the Mishap spurred the most intensive series of Egyptian-Israeli contacts since the beginning of the armistice agreement. An important role was played by British MP Dr. Maurice Orbach, who between November 1954 and January 1955 made several trips to Cairo to persuade Nasser to show clemency to the arrested Jews. The talks covered a wide range of subjects and included the submission of specific Israeli proposals. Nasser "expressed his wish for peace with Israel, but conceded that Arab pressure hindered it at the present" (Shamir 1989, 77). Nasser pledged to release the ship, reduce the blockage, and show leniency toward the Egyptian Jews. He also agreed to high-level talks, preferably in Paris (where most of the earlier meetings had been held), on condition that strict secrecy be observed. Sharett appointed Yigael Yadin, the former chief of staff, who was studying archaeology in London at the time, to represent Israel in the talks; the CIA was involved in coordinating the meeting. However, when the Egyptian military tribunal found eight of the accused Jews guilty and sentenced two of them to death on January 27, 1955, Sharett decided to suspend further contacts with Nasser. The episode certainly instilled mistrust between Nasser and Israeli decision makers (Oren 1992, 356; Rafael 1981, 36–39; Sheffer 1996, 760–761).

Relations were further aggravated when Israel launched the Gaza raid on February 28, 1955, which led to the deaths of thirty-eight Egyptians and eight Israelis. It was the most serious retaliatory attack by Israel since the 1948 War. The raid was primarily a response to several Egyptian provocations on the border, but it can also be seen as an attempt to raise Israel's domestic morale following the *Bat-Galim* episode and the execution of two Jews caught in the Mishap (Shlaim 2000, 123–128; Morris 1993, 324–350; Tal 1998, 181–208). In Nasser's mind, the Gaza raid and the signing of the Turco-Iraqi Agreement (later known as the Baghdad Pact)[1] that preceded it by four days were part of a "concerted Western plot to destroy the Egyptian revolution and to reassert the domination of imperialism over the entire Arab world" (quoted in Podeh 1995, 127).

The Gaza raid caught Nasser by surprise at a time when his domestic legitimacy was still at stake; as an officer, he felt humiliated by its consequences. It was hardly a surprise that it forced him to seek arms from whatever source possible to combat the Israeli menace; the result of this was the Czech arms deal in September 1955, which solidified Nasser's connections with the Soviet bloc. In addition, the raid also prompted Egypt to organize Palestinian *fedayeen* units in the Gaza Strip and other Arab countries as a retaliation instrument against Israel. Morris concluded that at that point Egypt and Israel "stopped toying with the possibility of a settlement and plunged headlong down the road to war" (Morris 1993, 334, 355).

Nasser now ruled out any direct contacts, even clandestine ones, with Israel. But he continued to sanction backdoor communication with Israel—through third-party mediators and emissaries—right up to 1956. A major episode in this regard was the Israeli-Egyptian indirect contacts surrounding a peace plan, code-named Alpha. It was a secret British-US plan devised in early 1955 by Evelyn Shuckburgh, the British Foreign Office assistant undersecretary of state, and Francis Russell, from the US Bureau of the Near East at the State Department. By offering a solution to the conflict, Britain under the premiership of Anthony Eden and the United States under President Dwight Eisenhower and Secretary of State John F. Dulles hoped to prevent the Soviet Union from exploiting the conflict to fortify its position in the Middle East. In addition, a settlement was seen as a prerequisite to the participation of the

Arab states—particularly Egypt—in the organization of Middle East defense, which was directed against what was perceived as the Soviet menace to the Free World (Caplan 1997, 68–69; Hahn 1991, 186–187).

The essence of Alpha can be summed up as follows: linking Egypt to Jordan by ceding to them two "kissing triangles" in the Negev near Eilat, with an east-west Arab corridor that would not cut Israel's north-south link to its important port city; ceding to Jordan some areas, such as Mt. Scopus and the Semakh triangle; ceding to Jordan an equivalent area south and west of Hebron should the Gaza Strip be given to Israel; free port facilities for Jordan in Haifa; dividing the demilitarized zones between Israel and its neighbors; repatriating some seventy-five thousand refugees to Israel over five years; resettlement and financial compensation for some 450,000 refugees in Jordan, Syria, Lebanon, Sinai, and Iraq; and compensation for those preferring resettlement with financial international help. The plan made mention of further negotiations on the Jerusalem and Jordan water issues but did not specify a solution. An end to the Arab economic boycott of Israel and shipping blockage in the Suez Canal was also referred to. The inducement offered to Egypt in return for agreeing to the plan was military and economic assistance, including $120 million in aid for the construction of the hoped-for Aswan Dam project. The main incentive offered to Israel was a security guarantee of its new borders (Caplan 1997, 73–95, 296–303; Shamir 1989, 82; Oren 1992, 109–117; Bar-On 1994, 83–98).

The plan did not envisage the signing of a peace treaty but aimed at achieving a "reasonable settlement." The two superpowers decided that Nasser would be approached first, in the hope that his agreement would induce other Arab states to follow. The ambassadors in Cairo were instructed not to present the plan as a whole, but to reveal it gradually "so that the solution should appear to emerge from the discussions with the parties rather than to have been worked out fully by the US and UK Governments in advance" (Caplan 1997, 297). The Israeli raid on Gaza delayed the introduction of Alpha. Eventually, it was revealed to Nasser in general terms in early April, upon his return from the nonaligned conference in Bandung, where he was exposed to the neutralist ideology. Nasser did not reject the notion of settlement outright, but emphasized that he could not commit himself to a negotiation process because of inter-Arab constraints. More particularly, he objected to the idea of a corridor through the Negev, insisting on full Israeli withdrawal. The British offered wider and wider triangles in terms of territory, with additional economic and military assistance, but Nasser refused anything less than the whole Negev. It seems that Nasser, particularly in the wake of the Bandung Conference, did not trust the Western powers and suspected that they were plotting behind the scenes to overthrow him. The US ambassador in Cairo,

Henry Byroade, assessed that the promotion of Alpha in this context was "unwise and useless" (Hahn 2004, 184). The Israelis were not officially notified of Alpha, but when certain elements were leaked out, Prime Minister Sharett made it clear that Israel would neither relinquish territory nor repatriate refugees. Moreover, he made it clear that no peace plan could serve as a precondition for the suggested security guarantee (Caplan 1997, 106–120; Oren 1992, 114–115; Shamir 1989, 82–83; Hahn 1991, 190–191; 2004, 184).

The plan went through two additional junctures: when Dulles made the first public proclamation of the essence of Alpha in a speech at the Council on Foreign Relations in late August 1955, and when Eden outlined a more explicit version in his Guildhall speech in November. Both statesmen expressed willingness to provide guarantees for the agreed-upon borders, as well as financial assistance for the reparation and rehabilitation of the refugees, but these ideas did not alter the basic reluctance of the two parties to accept the terms of the plan (Caplan 1997, 123–151, 175–186; Oren 1992, 115–120; Bar-On 1994, 90–95). Moreover, Nasser's drift toward neutralism and the Soviet Union—a process that accelerated following the Czech arms deal—reinforced doubts in Israel and the West regarding his sincerity and interest in cooperating with the West and working for a solution to the conflict.

Not deterred by the failure of the Alpha project, the United States initiated another diplomatic effort when it dispatched Robert Anderson, a personal friend of Eisenhower and former deputy secretary of defense, to the region. He shuttled between Cairo and Jerusalem in utmost secrecy from January to March of 1956. The protocols of the talks demonstrate that the parties had no intention of budging from their positions: Nasser insisted on Arab territorial continuity by ceding the Negev and allowing the refugees free choice between repatriation and resettlement; Ben-Gurion was willing to discuss only minor border changes and would negotiate the refugee problem only within the framework of direct peace talks. Likewise, Nasser was willing to discuss the lifting of the Suez shipping blockade and the Arab boycott only as part of the final settlement. He also rejected the idea of a top-secret encounter with Ben-Gurion on board a US Navy vessel on grounds of personal safety, recalling several times in this context the fate of Jordan's King 'Abdallah. Eisenhower thought that both Israel and Egypt contributed to the failure of the mission: Ben-Gurion by his adamant refusal to consider any territorial concession, and Nasser by his driving ambition to become the political leader of the Arab world (Caplan 1997, 220–242; Bar-On 1994, 99–113; Heikal 1996b, 92–102; Hahn 2004, 190–192; Sheffer 1996, 850–854).

ASSESSMENT

Historians of the Arab-Israeli conflict differ in their assessment of this episode. The first critical voice was that of Rony Gabbay, who wrote in his study of the refugee problem: "[H]ad Israel been able to conclude a peace settlement with Egypt . . . the situation would have been entirely different. . . . That was the golden opportunity of Israel, but it was lost due to serious miscalculations" (1959, 340). Many years later, both Avi Shlaim and Zeev Maoz criticized Israel's behavior toward Egypt in the years 1949–1954 (for some reason they do not analyze the Alpha project or the Anderson Mission). The high-level meeting that did not take place in late 1954 due to Sharett's suspension of the talks led Shlaim to question Israel's standard official version that it consistently strove for direct contact and was consistently met with Arab refusal:

> There is, of course, no way of telling what might have happened had the planned meeting [between Nasser and Yadin] taken place. Could it have led to a higher-level meeting with Nasser himself? Could it have prevented the subsequent escalation of the conflict? Could it have produced at least some of the ingredients for a breakthrough in the relations? . . . There are no answers to these questions. History does not disclose its alternatives. All one can say is that Nasser offered Israel a chance to talk and that this offer was spurned. One can add that Sharett's wavering played a part in missing this opportunity. Sharett did not rise to the occasion, displaying delaying tactics and timidity when boldness was called for. In the words of one of his own officials, Sharett failed to seize the bull by the horns when the bull offered his horns. (2000, 121–122; Kamil 2003, 99)

In Maoz's opinion, the contacts with Nasser "did represent a major opportunity. Yet the Israeli positions and its escalatory behavior may well have caused this opportunity to dissipate" (2004, 402). Most damaging, in his view, was the Gaza raid, which "closed the window of opportunity." Therefore, "The botched dialogue with the young regime in Egypt can be seen in retrospect as a missed opportunity" (2004, 403–404).

As for the Alpha Plan, Mordechai Bar-On thinks it was doomed to failure because it was based on three mistaken premises: that Israel was the major obstacle to Britain's restoration of its previous prominent status in the region; that Nasser could be persuaded to reconcile himself to Israel's existence; and that Israel could be persuaded to make substantive concessions. In his view, "No permanent settlement between Israel and the Arabs was feasible in 1955, because Israel would simply not make any far-reaching territorial, economic, or demographic concessions, certainly not in exchange for arrangements that fell far short of full peace and a final resolution of the conflict" (1994, 88–89). With regard to the possibility that the Egyptian-Israeli contacts in the 1950s constituted a missed opportunity, he asserted that the Anderson Mission proved that "From the 1948 Israeli War of Independence and until the 1967 Six-Day war, not even the barest condition necessary for a peace settlement . . . existed, not even a de facto state of non-belligerency" (1994, 112). Likewise, Michael Oren concluded that peace "was never a real possibility at any time in the period 1949–1956." In spite of Israel's intransigence on the territorial and demographic issues, he argued, "the responsibility for the failure of peace rests largely with Egypt." In his opinion, Egypt's demand for the Negev was unjustified and unrealistic; it was Egypt's consent and not Israel's that held the key to peace: "Given the green light from Nasser, the Powers would have placed tremendous pressure on Israel, forcing it to yield on all of Alpha's principal points" (1990, 365). A somewhat similar view was offered by Shimon Shamir, asserting that Nasser was interested in the benefits he could derive from the process of negotiations rather than in any concrete outcome from them (1989, 87–88). "In the year before the Suez crisis," he explained, "scoring points was 'the name of the game' and each player's purpose was to expose the other's intransigence" (1989, 100).

Did the Israeli-Egyptian contacts in 1949–1956, and particularly the Alpha project, constitute a missed opportunity? The immediate postwar period provided a chance to talk peace as the war and its significant consequences created new possibilities for change, similar to those existing with 'Abdallah and Za'im. However, this window of opportunity was quickly closed as Israel and Egypt found no incentives to go beyond the armistice agreement, in which each party achieved its immediate goals of a recognized cease-fire along the postwar borders. Though the state of belligerency did not end there, the agreement offered some form of tranquility and a mechanism—the Mixed Armistice Commission—to deal with violations of the cease-fire. The 1952 coup with the toppling of the monarchy offered another opportunity as the new rulers were not committed to the policies they had inherited and enjoyed a measure of legitimacy. In addition, the young officers were initially lauded by Israeli decision makers. Yet this window of opportunity was shut quickly as well, as it became evident that the new regime was concerned primarily with domestic political problems such as the power struggle between the main instigators of the coup, the need to introduce social and economic reforms, and the demand for a revision of the Anglo-Egyptian treaty. Moreover, the spiral of events between Israel and Egypt in 1954–1955 jeopardized the chances of the Alpha Plan from the very start: the Mishap, the *Bat-Galim* affair, the Gaza raid coinciding with the Turco-Iraqi Agreement, the Bandung Conference, and the Czech arms deal—all these meant that the timing of Alpha's launch was not propitious (Caplan 1997, 288).

In order to qualify as a real opportunity, however, it is necessary to identify the existence of an offer that the parties consider attractive enough to foster dialogue. An analysis of the contacts from 1952 to 1956 indicates that no attractive offer had been submitted either by Israel or by Egypt. The only possible exception is Nasser's offer in late 1954 to hold a high-level meeting, which might be considered as an attractive opening. Yet since the offer came on the heels of Egypt's fateful decision regarding the Jewish defendants in the Mishap trial, it is highly unlikely that any Israeli prime minister would have picked up the gauntlet. In contrast to Za'im's offer, which involved a possible meeting with Ben-Gurion and a generous offer in substance, the Egyptian offer was only for a lower-level meeting, which was not linked to an attractive new position. It is fair to speculate that had Nasser been serious in his offer, he would have reiterated it in the subsequent negotiations.

Similarly, the Alpha Plan could not really be considered attractive to any of the parties involved in the conflict. It demanded from Israel substantial territorial concessions and a major contribution to solving the refugee problem, but offered very little in terms of incentives and an attractive end result. True, a security guarantee was a desired aim, but it was not considered worth the price demanded by the plan. Since a peace treaty was not offered and many issues were left open (Jerusalem, refugees, water, final borders), the possibility of continued hostilities and violence remained open. In many ways, from an Israeli point of view the Alpha Plan was yet another version of "yesterday's peace plan," with little relevance to the post-1948 situation.

Nasser, for his part, needed a substantial Israeli concession—such as withdrawal from the Negev—that would allow him to deflect expected Arab opposition. In many ways, he resembled King 'Abdallah, who demanded from Israel a significant reward for peace, enabling him to proudly present it to the Arab world. Unlike 'Abdallah, however, Nasser did not want to end his career with a bullet to the chest. For him, then, Alpha's advantages were not worth the risks involved. Interestingly, such an assessment was written at the time by the State Department: "No Arab leader was likely in the foreseeable future to sponsor peace with Israel since in doing so he would risk almost certain assassination or would at least alienate all his domestic support and [be] regarded in other Arab countries as a traitor to the Arab world" (quoted in Caplan 1997, 83).

The role of the United States and Britain was paramount in this episode. They deftly combined techniques of mediation and conciliation (Caplan 1997, 269–289). However, the preceding analysis shows that no amount of realistic sticks and carrots could have compensated for the lack of trust between the leaders and the existing gaps between the parties' positions. The classification of this episode as a nonhistoric opportunity precludes the necessity of examining its potentiality level: since an opportunity did not exist, it could not have been missed.

NOTE

1. The Baghdad Pact was the organization formed to defend the Middle East against the Soviet menace. It was formally established in November 1955 and consisted of Britain, Iraq, Pakistan, Iran, and Turkey. See Podeh 1995.

CHAPTER 7

EGYPTIAN-ISRAELI CONTACTS

1965–1966

THE EPISODE

"NASSER WAS WAITING FOR ESHKOL." This was the headline of a feature in the daily *Ma'ariv* on June 5, 1987, the twentieth anniversary of the 1967 Six-Day War. The article revealed for the first time the story of a possible meeting that could have taken place in 1966 between high-level Israeli and Egyptian official envoys. "Had the late Prime Minister Levi Eshkol accepted the Egyptian invitation to send in 1965, two years prior to the war, a high-level delegation to Cairo," asked the reporter, "could the Six-Day War have been averted? And if so, could the bloody road to peace have been shortened and the 1973 Yom Kippur War prevented?" (Goldstein 1987). Only in the late 1990s did many of the elements of this cryptic report receive confirmation by Meir Amit, head of the Mossad, Israel's intelligence organization, from 1963 to 1968.

Given the relations between Israel and Egypt in the mid-1960s, the very existence of contacts was a surprise. In 1965, Nasser was considered Israel's most dreaded enemy; his image in Israel—among decision makers and the public alike—was that of a leader aggressively bent on the destruction of the Jewish state. Often enough, analogies were drawn to Hitler and Mussolini to depict his aims and behavior (Podeh 2004, 72–99). The fact that in the early 1960s he hired German experts—some of whom had served the Nazis during wartime—to build his long-range missile program was seen as a proof of this analogy. In addition, his intensive involvement in Arab affairs—the war in Yemen, the establishment of the PLO, the initiative to hold Arab summits, and the establishment of an Arab command to divert the tributaries of the Jordan River—all these were seen as evidence of his scheming to attain Arab hegemony. In short, Nasserism was perceived in Israel and the West as a dire threat that should be contained, if not eliminated. From their perspective, Nasser and the Egyptians had a similar negative image of Israel. The 1956 War served to them as proof that Israel was an imperialist stooge while the incidents along the Israeli-Syrian border in the demilitarized zones were seen as an indication of Israel's aggressive intentions (Heikal 1990).

In his memoirs, Amit recounts at length the story of the contacts, which began between a Mossad agent and one Mahmud Khalil, a general in the Egyptian air force with direct access to Nasser and ʿAmer, his minister of war. The first meeting took place in September 1965, when Khalil accompanied ʿAmer on a state visit to Paris. The crux of the meeting was an Egyptian request for Israeli support for a financial loan to the tune of $30 million to be credited by international institutions (Amit 1999, 209–212; Amit 1998, 284–294; Shalom 2001, 324). The financial support was to ameliorate Egypt's economic predicament caused by the huge costs of the military intervention in Yemen since 1962 and other unsuccessful expenditures.

Following a demand for a more explicit expression of support for the Egyptian request, a top-secret letter was prepared, which Prime Minister Eshkol personally authorized. It approved the continuation of the secret dialogue, which would focus on the following points: the opening of a covert direct channel between the two leaders, Israeli willingness to help Egypt obtain an international financial loan, an Egyptian undertaking to accept the 1955 Johnston Plan for the division of the water resources between Israel and its neighbors, the examination of means to prevent the unintentional outbreak of hostilities and their escalation, and any other subject of interest to the parties (Amit 1999, 213; 1998, 294–295).

In the following months two more meetings were held between Khalil, the Mossad agent, and others involved in the operation. Once it became clear that both Nasser and ʿAmer had given their consent—though not without doubting the seriousness of the Israeli response—Amit himself, as head of the Mossad, met Khalil in Europe in early February 1966. The meeting focused on the terms of the loan to be given by a European bank. Amit enumerated the Israeli demands that were expected in return: some tangible evidence of Egyptian willingness to accept the Johnston Plan, allowing the passage of foreign ships carrying goods to Israel through the Suez Canal, allowing Israeli flights over the Tiran Straits, the establishment of a hot telephone line between the leaders, the release of the 1954 "mishap" prisoners, and downgrading the tone of anti-Israeli propaganda. Khalil did not reject the Israeli demands, though he did stress the need for patience. The encounter revealed just how fearful the Egyptian side was about the possibility of being exposed by an Israeli leak (Amit 1998, 299–301).

Amit reported the gist of the meeting to Eshkol, and added a personal note to the effect that in his opinion Nasser was indeed interested in establishing contact with Israel and that this might present an opportunity to "make unprecedented history." "I know and recognize the difficulty and risk," Amit wrote to the prime minister, "but I believe that we have to show goodwill and make a gesture, even if only for the sake of history" (1998, 302). The Egyptian response to the Israeli demands was not discouraging: 'Amer expressed willingness to release the "mishap" prisoners on condition that they be transferred to a third country and that the matter remain secret. With regard to the water diversion plan, 'Amer claimed that Egypt had already halted the project. He also agreed to authorize Israeli flights over the Tiran Straits, but asked Israel to stop its support of the monarchists in the Yemen War. Finally, he insisted that the next meeting, slated to take place on February 12, 1966, be held in Cairo instead of Athens, as initially planned. The reason for this was fear that either Khalil or the dialogue would be exposed (Amit 1998, 303–304).

The initial response of Eshkol and Golda Meir was that the whole issue was "too good to be true" (Amit 1998, 305). As soon as Amit returned to Israel, a meeting was convened in Eshkol's office with several ministers and top advisers. The atmosphere at the meeting was cloudy with mistrust, fear, and hesitation of both Nasser and the Egyptian regime. The most vocal opposition came from Isser Harel, the prime minister's adviser and Amit's predecessor at the helm of the Mossad. Harel doubted the sincerity of the Egyptian initiative; he downplayed the importance of their concessions to Israel and insisted that guarantees be provided for the next meeting, since asking that it be held in Cairo might spell a trap, the aim being to kidnap the Mossad head. Harel's negative attitude may have reflected his personal rivalry with Amit,[1] but his position was supported—in one way or another—by most of the participants in the discussion. Thus the main issue was not the loan or the conditions to be met, but the venue for the next meeting. Eshkol, personally, did not think that a meeting in Cairo entailed any serious risks, but in light of the almost unanimous objection he decided to ask for it to be relocated outside Egypt, perhaps in Europe (Amit 1998, 307–310; Shalom 2001, 326–327). This Israeli response disappointed and humiliated the Egyptians. Consequently, the Cairo visit— or any other high-level meeting for that matter—was canceled. In the months that followed, the dialogue simply died out (Amit 1998, 311–313).

Amit, at the time and forever since, thought that Israel missed an opportunity (and this was the title of the article he published on the subject). He did not delude himself into thinking that a peace treaty was missed, but in his opinion this episode could have been "an important pillar in building peace," since, as he asserts with confidence, the contact with Khalil was more serious and significant than any other previous interaction with the Egyptians (Amit 1998, 316).

ASSESSMENT

In retrospect, did this episode constitute a missed opportunity? It certainly constituted a historical opportunity, since a dialogue with top-level Egyptian envoys representing Nasser—Israel's most threatening enemy—could have been seen per se as an attractive offer to Israel. The fact that Egypt did not reject out of hand Israeli demands for that dialogue should have strengthened its attraction. In addition, though the dialogue was not a result of a significant turning point in the conflict, it can be seen as a culmination of a certain historical process: the decline of Nasserism, and the economic recession resulting from the Egyptian involvement in the Yemen War and the failure of Egypt's second five-year economic plan.

What was the potentiality level of this episode? The two parties to the conflict were led by legitimate regimes: Nasser in Egypt and the Eshkol coalition in Israel. Their ability to take decisions and implement them seems to have been great enough, despite the presence of some dissenting voices in both countries. It is doubtful, however, that these leaders were willing to take truly bold decisions or change their position toward the enemy in a profound way. Since the offer came from Egypt, Eshkol was not resolute enough to pursue the initiative against some dissenting voices that were motivated by political and personal ambitions. A high level of mutual mistrust still prevailed, leading the parties to suspect the motives of the other side. The history of past contacts may have magnified this attitude, as each side was convinced that the other one deliberately misled it or evinced dishonesty. Unfortunately, third parties—as far as we know—did not play a significant role in this episode. It seems that one European country (France?) was somehow involved in the dialogue, as well as in the discussions over the possible loan, but there was no American—or any other—diplomatic attempt to affect the contacts. This perhaps emanated from the fact that it was a Mossad operation, which by nature did everything covertly, combined with Egypt's own insistence on maintaining complete secrecy. Thus, the potential for seizing the opportunity was not high, as the leaders were not resolute in their position, the history of past interactions was not encouraging, and the involvement of a third party was nonexistent. But in the final analysis, the existing legitimacy on both sides, the fact that the third-party variable was not relevant, and the attractiveness of the offer—a high-level meeting in Cairo with Israel's perceived archenemy—leads to the conclusion that the plausibility level of a missed opportunity in this episode was medium.

But what was missed, as Amit contended, was not a peace agreement; under the prevailing historical circumstances it is unthinkable that such a meeting would have led to the signing of an agreement ending the conflict.

And yet Israeli leaders missed an opportunity to do something here. Considering that the whole process would have been kept cloaked in secrecy, it is possible that some progress and trust could have been established between the two parties. Even if the 1967 War would not have been prevented, the negotiations between Israel and Egypt after the war would have started from a different point, as happened later with President Anwar al-Sadat, when the post-1973 negotiations were, in many ways, the continuation of the pre-1973 contacts.

NOTE

1. Harel resigned from the Mossad in protest at Ben-Gurion's policy regarding the Israeli attitude toward the issue of the German experts in Egypt. From then on, he repeatedly expressed animosity toward his replacement. In addition, he and Amit had a bitter row over the issue of the assassination of Moroccan opposition leader Mahdi Ben-Berka, in which Israel was allegedly involved. In his memoirs, Harel did not make mention of the 1966 contacts with Nasser (Harel 1989).

CHAPTER 8

ISRAEL'S PEACE OVERTURES IN THE POST-1967 PERIOD

The Six-Day War ended on June 10, 1967, with a stunning and decisive military victory for Israel over Egypt, Syria, and Jordan. Israel gained control of the Sinai Peninsula (including the Gaza Strip), the Golan Heights, and the West Bank (including East Jerusalem), thus tripling the size of its territory (see map 8.1).[1] In other words, the war ended with significant territorial gains which could serve Israel as a bargaining chip in negotiating a peace treaty with the Arab states. Indeed, following lengthy deliberations, on June 19 the National Unity government headed by Levi Eshkol adopted a formal resolution that reflected Israel's willingness to fully withdraw to the 1967 boundaries on the Egyptian and Syrian fronts in return for peace with these countries. The government was unable to reach a similar decision regarding the Jordanian front as a result of ideological divisions over the West Bank and doubts about the security implications of withdrawing from the Jordan River. Yet secret talks were held with King Husayn in 1968 regarding the Israeli Allon Plan. This chapter will discuss if and to what extent the Israeli post-1967 initiatives constituted missed opportunities for peace.

THE EPISODE

The National Unity government was hastily formed on the eve of the war as a result of the panic and fear that had engulfed Israeli society in the preceding weeks. It was composed of twenty-one ministers representing seven parties with different—even antagonistic—political and ideological hues, including Rafi, David Ben-Gurion's former party (headed by Moshe Dayan, who replaced Eshkol as minister of defense), and Menachem Begin's Gahal opposition party. In spite of its diversity, the government managed to survive until August 1970, making some important decisions along the way that enjoyed broad consensus. Such was the idea of uniting Jerusalem; disregarding the

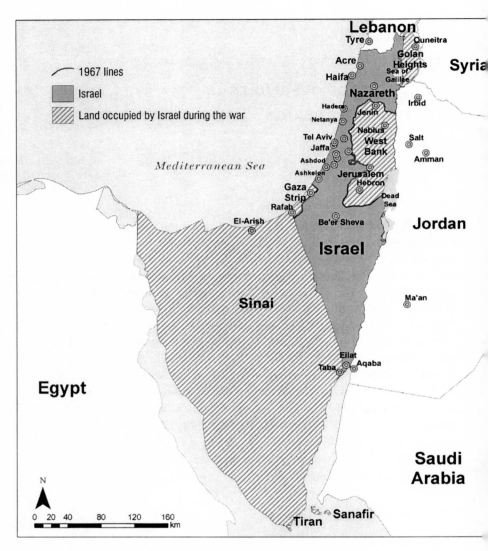

MAP 8.1. Israel's Post-1967 Boundaries. Courtesy of Shaul Arieli, 2013.

possible outcry from the international and Arab communities, on June 20 the government moved to annex the Jordanian eastern part of occupied Jerusalem with its Christian and Muslim holy sites. A few days later, Israeli law and administration were applied to this territory (Shlaim 2000, 250–251; Pedatzur 1996, 29). The consensus stopped there: differences of opinion, whether ideological or security-based, quickly arose regarding the future of other territories. The urgent need to adopt a clear position with regard to the newly occupied territories stemmed in part from the fact that on June 17 an emergency special session of the UN General Assembly opened at the behest of the Soviet Union. Four days earlier, Moscow had submitted to UN secretary-general U Thant a demand "to adopt a decision designed to bring about the liquidation of the consequences of aggression and the immediate withdrawal of Israel forces behind the [1949] armistice lines." The Soviet demarche at the United Nations also brought some pressure by the United States on Israel to offer a moderate position with regard to the territories, which would help to ameliorate the heated situation in the Middle East. As Israel needed US diplomatic support at the UN, it could not fail to deliver the expected result (Raz 2012, 39; 2013, 89–90; Korn 1992, 24–30).

The deliberations concerning the future of the occupied territories commenced on June 13 in an informal meeting at Eshkol's house with several top ministers, where the idea of peace with Egypt and Syria on the basis of the international border was parleyed for the first time. In this discussion, defense minister Moshe Dayan held that the time was not ripe for peace moves as the Arabs were in a state of shock following the defeat. In contrast, Foreign Minister Abba Eban advocated an activist peace policy, arguing that Israel should not miss the present opportunities, as "others would seize them with harmful consequences." Eban was likely referring to the 1956 War, when Israel was forced to withdraw from Sinai without any treaty. At that point, Eshkol sided with Eban without committing himself to any action (Rafael 1981, 170). Next, on June 14–15 the government's ministerial committee for security affairs discussed the matter. Since its members also could not reach a decision, their ideas and recommendations were submitted to the government, which debated the issue at length on June 18–19. The dispute centered on the territories that were considered by many in Israel as part of biblical Eretz Israel (the West Bank; that is, Judea and Samaria, and Gaza). Since some of the ministers—particularly from the right-wing Gahal Party but also from Labor— vociferously opposed concessions in these territories, it was decided to defer the decision, at least regarding the offer to be submitted to Jordan. As for Egypt and Syria, the disagreements were more focused on the wording of the respective offers than on the ideology. Two versions passed through the drafting stage, but neither was embraced by all present, so it was decided to set up a special subcommittee tasked to reach an agreed formula, which it did and which the government eventually accepted (Raz 2013, 90).[2]

The main part of Resolution 563 with regard to Egypt stated, "Israel proposes signing a peace treaty with Egypt based on the international frontier and Israel's security needs. According to the international frontier, the Gaza Strip is located within the area of Israel." In return, Israel demanded the following: freedom of navigation in the Straits of Tiran and the Bay of Solomon

[Aqaba]; freedom of navigation in the Suez Canal; freedom of flight over the Straits of Tiran and the Bay of Solomon; and demilitarization of the Sinai Peninsula. The same resolution applied to Syria, with the following demands on that front: demilitarization of the Golan Heights and an absolute guarantee of noninterference with the flow of water from the sources of the Jordan River to Israel. It was also emphasized that "until the signing of a peace treaty [with Egypt/Syria], Israel will continue to hold the territories it has held since 10 June 1967." The resolution made vague reference to the refugees, stating that the signing of peace agreements would open the way for international and regional arrangements for the solution of the refugee problem. The wording of the resolution purposefully allowed Israel some room to maneuver in terms of territory; the accepted formula, "based on Israel's security needs," could be used to legitimize certain territorial amendments (Pedatzur 1996, 55–56; Shlaim 2000, 253; Raz 2012, 43–45; Bavly 2002, 36).[3]

Curiously, there was no indication that either the resolution text or the minutes of the discussions were meant to be read in Cairo and Damascus. According to Avi Raz, who recently completed a study on what he termed "the generous offer that was never offered," "[t]here is nothing in the resolution to suggest an intention to convey the text as a peace proposal to the Arabs" (2013, 91). Instead, the text was delivered in utmost secrecy to Eban, who waited at the United Nations for further instructions from the Israeli government. The text was not even delivered to the Israeli army and intelligence chiefs. Chief of Staff Rabin learned about the resolution only when he was appointed ambassador to Washington a few months later (Raz 2013, 92; Bavly 2002, 37). On June 21, Eban delivered the Israeli proposal to Secretary of State Dean Rusk and other US diplomats. He would later write in his memoirs that "Rusk, Goldberg [US representative at the UN], and their colleagues could hardly believe what I was saying. Here was Israel, on the very morrow of the victory, offering to renounce most of her gains in return for the simple condition of a permanent peace." Eban added his assessment that the proposal was "the most dramatic initiative ever taken by an Israeli government before or since 1967, and it had a visibly strong impact on the United States" (1977, 436; Rafael 1981, 171). Interestingly, Rusk's memorandum of the conversation with Eban did not reflect any American admiration or astonishment at Israel's alleged magnanimity (Raz 2013, 93).

Yet the more important question remains whether Israel's bold offer was ever delivered to Egypt and Syria. Eban claimed that a few days after he presented the message, "replies came back from Washington stating that Egypt and Syria completely rejected the Israeli proposal" (1977, 436). In an updated edition of his memoirs published a few years later, Eban omitted the reference to the delivery of the peace proposal but asserted that the resolutions of the Arab summit at Khartoum in September, which negated the possibility of peace or direct negotiations with Israel, "seemed to leave no room for reconciliation" (1993, 450).[4] Eban's version was accepted at face value by some scholars (Pedatzur 1996, 57), but it was challenged by others (Shlaim 2000, 254; Bavly 2002, 37–38). According to Shlaim, there was no confirmation from Egyptian or Syrian sources that they had received a conditional Israeli offer of withdrawal through the State Department in June 1967. In his meticulous study of the Israeli resolution, Raz came to the conclusion that the "Abba Eban tale is nothing but a fiction"; the resolution, in his opinion, "was not a generous offer at all but a diplomatic maneuver to win over the one international player that really mattered to Israel—the United States" (2012, 47).

The official Israeli historical narrative follows Eban's account. On the fortyfifth anniversary of the war, in 2012, the Israeli State Archives uploaded the protocols of June 18–19 deliberations on their Internet site under the title "The Government Discusses Israel's Peace Plan, 18–19 June 1967." A short summary of the events and discussions is attached to the documents. According to this narrative, "The government decision was passed on to the US in secret. A positive answer was not received from either Egypt or Syria." The formal Arab response, the narrative continues, came with the resolutions of the Khartoum Arab summit, which adopted the "three no's: no peace with Israel, no recognition of Israel, no negotiation with it." In other words, Israel's official version is that the Arabs rejected its "generous" peace offer, yet there is no historical evidence to support the claim that this offer was indeed delivered to Egypt and/or Syria.

Within a short period of time, the consensus on complete withdrawal on the Egyptian and Syrian fronts was eroded. The ministers concluded that the offer to pull back to the international border (though with the caveat of "security needs") "had been too rash and too generous and that a higher price should be exacted from Egypt and Syria for their aggression" (Shlaim 2000, 254). The change of heart was also the result of a political shift to the right and the establishment of pressure groups that lobbied for retaining the territories either for ideological or security reasons (Tessler 2009, 411). Thus on October 17, 1967, the government adopted a new decision, which largely nullified the June 19 resolution: "Israel will demand continued control of Sharm al-Sheikh and a continuous strip of territory from Eilat as a condition for peace with Egypt." This formal decision was added to the general agreement in the government that Israel should not withdraw from the Golan Heights. The settlement activity that had begun in Sinai and the Golan was testimony to the change in Israeli policy, which now expected border modifications within any peace treaty. This tendency was reinforced by the perception that the Arab states were unwilling to negotiate with Israel, as expressed in the Khartoum resolutions (Bavly 2002, 42–46; Pedatzur 1996, 177–188, 244–255).

Though the Israeli government deliberately avoided reference to the West Bank in its June 19 resolution because of ideological differences, talks regarding its future were held behind the scenes. In general, there were three schools of thought among Israeli decision makers: keeping all the territory west of the Jordan River; settlement with the local Arab Palestinians, possibly by establishing autonomy; and pursuing the "Jordanian option," that is, a settlement—preferably a peace agreement—with King Husayn on the basis of new, agreed, and secure boundaries (Shlaim 2007, 280). In mid-July, Husayn told the United States and Britain that he was prepared to make a unilateral settlement with Israel. This message was relayed after receiving a green light from Nasser to proceed with his covert diplomacy on condition that there would be no direct negotiations with Israel and no peace treaty. Husayn's initial bargaining position was that in return for a bilateral settlement, Israel should withdraw to the June 4, 1967, lines, including East Jerusalem, though he was willing to make some minor reciprocal territorial adjustments (Ashton 2008, 122, 126; Raz 2012, 67–68; Golan 2015, 13–14). US secretary of state Rusk wrote to Eban that Husayn's initiative "offers the first important breakthrough toward peace," adding that in his judgment "it is an opportunity that must not be lost" (quoted in Ashton 2008, 127). Husayn's initiative caught Israel unprepared; it was too early for the government to make any concessions, particularly in light of the existing political and ideological differences, with regard to Jerusalem and the Jordan Valley. In spite of its initial enthusiasm, the Johnson administration was reluctant to put Israel under any significant pressure to compromise. Soon, however, Husayn backtracked, informing the United States that he was too weak to try to undertake bilateral negotiations with Israel at this moment (Ashton 2008, 128).

A more serious exchange of views between Israel and Jordan began on May 3, 1968, when Eban met Husayn secretly in London. Yet the lengthy proceedings of the talks revealed that the territorial gap between the parties was as wide as ever, with the question of sovereignty over East Jerusalem constituting the major stumbling block (Shlaim 2007, 278–282; Raz 2012, 220–222). The clandestine Israeli-Jordanian contacts continued during summer 1968, culminating in a meeting between Eban, Yigal Allon, the Israeli minister of labor, and Husayn on September 27 in which Israel presented, for the first time, the Allon Plan as a possible negotiation framework. This plan, submitted by Allon to the Israeli government on July 26, 1967, called for incorporating into Israel a ten- to fifteen-kilometer-wide strip of land along the Jordan River, most of the Judean Desert around the Dead Sea, and a substantial area in and around

Jerusalem, including the Latrun Salient. All in all, the plan envisaged Jordan ceding some one-third of the West Bank to Israel (see map 8.2). Initially, the plan called for a Palestinian autonomous regime in that enclave, but since the local Palestinian leaders refused to pursue this track, Allon switched his plan to the Jordanian option. The Allon Plan meant to safeguard Israel's security interests while retaining as few Arabs as possible in the areas claimed by Israel, envisaging the building of settlements and army bases in these areas (Shlaim 2007, 288; Raz 2012, 245; Allon 1989, 16–17; Cohen 1973; Golan 2015, 14–15; Pedatzur 1996, 126–145). The Allon Plan was discussed by the government but never formally approved, as Prime Minister Eshkol feared that a vote would lead to the breakup of the coalition. Therefore, it was agreed that the plan would be presented to possible interlocutors on an unofficial basis (Hadari 2011, 471). Thus when Allon met Husayn in late September 1968, he had an unofficial authorization to present his map. The king rejected the plan without any hesitation; in his written response to Israel, he asserted that "the plan itself is wholly unacceptable since it infringes Jordanian sovereignty. The only way is to exchange territory on the basis of reciprocity" (Shlaim 2007, 290; Pedatzur 1996, 141–145). The gap between the parties sealed the fate of the possibility of reaching a first Israeli-Arab peace agreement. And though secret Israeli-Jordanian contacts continued in the late 1960s and early 1970s, they thereafter focused on functional cooperation over matters of mutual concern, such as the tracking of Palestinian guerrilla activities (Ashton 2008, 135).

ASSESSMENT

The 1967 War caused dramatic changes in the Middle East. History shows that such formidable changes create opportunities. The conquest of the Arab territories gave Israel a bargaining chip that was not in its possession in the pre-1967 period. What was needed, therefore, was an attractive Israeli offer that would turn the episode into a historical opportunity for negotiations and possibly even lead to a peace agreement. Israeli leaders grasped the magnitude of the hour and endorsed a bold initiative—perhaps the boldest ever in Israeli history—by offering to fully withdraw on the Egyptian and Syrian fronts to the international border in return for the signing of peace treaties. Though a similar decision was not accepted with relation to Jordan, the offer was generous enough as a starting point. The problem was that this bold and courageous decision was delivered only to the United States and not to its intended recipients, Egypt and Syria. Not only that, but even the Israeli military and intelligence chiefs were not privy to the decision, and it was kept from the rest of the international community as well. Though Eban's speech at the United Nations promised that Israel "is now willing to demonstrate its instinct for

MAP 8.2. The 1967 Allon Plan. Courtesy of Shaul Arieli, 2013.

peace" (Mahler and Mahler 2010, 130), Israel was in fact—in the words of Eshkol—playing chess with itself (Rosenthal 2012, 579).

If the Israeli peace proposal was not delivered to Egypt and Syria, as the evidence shows, then an opportunity did not exist. Ironically, it was Israel that missed an opportunity here to exploit the dramatic changes in the region and submit a bold initiative, which, in fact, it had gone so far as to draft. The United States also missed the opportunity to take stock of the Israeli initiative: though it was asked not to deliver the proposal to Egypt and Syria, it could have secretly conveyed the ideas to them in a vague way and thus probed their reaction to it. Egypt and Syria might have rejected the proposal anyway, as the three "no's" in Khartoum indicate. Yet the Arab summit resolutions did give a "green light" to the confrontation states to initiate a diplomatic process in order to "eliminate the consequences of aggression." Moreover, both Egypt and Jordan accepted UN Security Council Resolution 242, which implicitly recognized the state of Israel (Sela 1998, 108–109). A bold Israeli peace initiative presented to both Egypt and Syria, with extensive US mediation, might have triggered a successful diplomatic process.

The June 19 resolution, then, constitutes a different kind of missed opportunity in the annals of the Arab-Israeli conflict. It could perhaps be termed an invisible missed opportunity, as the potential recipients of the initiative—and even some actors in the offering party—had no inkling of its existence. Israel can be blamed for missing this opportunity, though the level of its plausibility is difficult to measure, as it had never been formally submitted to the other side.

The opportunity that presented itself in the post-1967 period was also relevant to the Israeli-Jordanian track. In a recent study, Galia Golan concluded that Israel's startling victory in the war, the existence of a strong and legitimate government in Israel, and Husayn's peace offers created the potential for a breakthrough (Golan 2015, 24). Indeed, Husayn's initiative, presented through the United States after the war, could have been a serious offer at peacemaking, though Husayn himself immediately backtracked as he did not feel confident enough to pursue it due to the Arab position. Also, the unenthusiastic Israeli and to some extent American responses further eroded his self-confidence. In the next round of talks, held secretly and directly with Israeli representatives in 1968, Husayn received from Israel an offer that could not but be refused (Raz 2012, 245). The Allon Plan, which was unofficially proposed by Israel, betrayed Husayn's concept of a just and honorable solution. Moreover, being the first Arab leader asked to take the possible risk of signing a peace treaty with Israel, he did not consider the Allon Plan to be an attractive enough offer to warrant a continuation of the dialogue. Years later, he believed that the choice was there, but that the Israelis were "really impossible in terms of their attitude" (quoted in Ashton 2008, 135). In addition, it seems that Israel was not serious about negotiating a settlement with Jordan. The makeup of the coalition did not allow the government to submit a serious peace offer. The talks, according to Jack O'Connell, the chief of the CIA mission in Amman in the years 1963–1971, "turned out to be a subterfuge by Israel to eliminate pressure from the United States, by claiming that progress was being made secretly with the king, without conceding anything to the Jordanians." The Israelis, in his opinion, knew that the Allon Plan was a nonstarter (2011, 88). The time gained allowed Israel to establish facts on the ground in the West Bank, particularly in the Jordan Valley, Gush Etzion, and Hebron (Pedatzur 1996, 189–243). Indeed, years later, Allon himself confessed that "No Arab would ever accept the plan and nothing will come of it, but we must appear before the world with a positive plan" (quoted in Raz 2012, 247). O'Connell concluded that in this period "Israel missed its best opportunity for peace" (2011, 89). Yet our conclusion is that though the post-1967 period presented an opportunity to do something, the Allon Plan was not attractive enough to the other side and therefore could not be missed.

NOTES

1. Israel in the pre-1967 period encompassed 20,770 square kilometers. In the war it conquered Sinai (60,000 km²), Gaza (360 km²), the West Bank (5,860 km²), and the Golan Heights (1,250 km²).

2. The Israeli State Archives (ISA) recently published online the protocols of the discussions held on June 18–19. See http://www.archives.gov.il/NR/exeres/99B95-060B-40DE-B401-A2FD0DDDE07D,frameless.htm?NRMODE=Published.

3. The quotations were taken from the ISA website above.

4. The Israeli propaganda highlighted the negative aspects of the Khartoum summit (the three "no's"), while bypassing the fact that it authorized the beginning of a diplomatic process through a third party; see Riyad 1981, 52–57; Meital 2000, 54–82.

CHAPTER 9

THE ROGERS PLAN

1969

WILLIAM QUANDT, a member of the National Security Council staff during the Nixon and Carter administrations, noted in his book on US policy toward the Arab-Israeli conflict in the post-1967 period that "The eventual peace agreement between Egypt and Israel in March 1979 bore a remarkable resemblance to the principles of the Rogers Plan" (1993, 83).[1] Quandt's comment raises the notion that the Rogers Plan, presented in October 1969 by the US secretary of state, might have been a plausible missed opportunity. The plan was devised and submitted after the failure of UN special envoy Gunnar Jarring's mission and the resumption of the War of Attrition on the Egyptian-Israeli front. This chapter will discuss if and to what extent the Rogers Plan was a missed opportunity.

THE EPISODE

In January 1969, when Richard Nixon became US president, the Arab-Israeli conflict was at a deadlock: all post-1967 attempts to find a peaceful formula had failed, including the mission of UN mediator Jarring. The new president, with William Rogers as secretary of state and Henry Kissinger as national security adviser, was quickly occupied with the effects of the Cold War on the international arena, relations with the Soviet Union and China, and, of course, the United States' debilitating involvement in Vietnam. The Middle East was not at the top of Nixon's foreign policy agenda. Having said that, the US administration was certainly concerned by the global ramifications of the Arab-Israeli conflict and therefore sought a mechanism to reduce its explosive nature. The new thinking was that the United States should adopt an active diplomatic role in promoting a political settlement based on the principles of UN Security Council Resolution 242. The State Department in particular was keen to find an initiative that would reduce Soviet influence and improve Arab-US relations. It also favored the idea of an "evenhanded" approach to the conflict. This thinking, however, was not shared by Kissinger, who doubted the effectiveness of such an approach and was skeptical of the virtues of evenhandedness in this conflict, which tended to be interpreted by Israel as tantamount to being pro-Arab (Quandt 2005, 58–62; Spiegel 1985, 181–182; Korn 1990, 38–42; 1992, 31–57).

In Israel, Golda Meir replaced Prime Minister Eshkol following his death in February 1969. In contrast to Eshkol's moderate views in the Arab-Israeli conflict, Meir was known for her tough and rigid positions with regard to the Arabs; some saw her as the proponent of an extreme version of "Ben-Gurionism" (e.g., Brecher 1970, 308–311, 369); others depicted her as "the intransigent" (e.g., Shlaim 2000, 283–284). Though Meir's personal belief system played an important factor in the overall Israeli position regarding a possible settlement of the conflict, the Israeli elite and society in general was undergoing its own process of radicalization. Thus the June 19, 1967, resolution that proposed the conclusion of peace agreements with Egypt and Syria based on the international border and security needs of Israel was now replaced by the decision that peace agreements should give Israel "recognized secure borders" (see chapter 8).

Israeli policy toward a possible settlement was based on two premises: that there would be no return to the 1967 lines, which—according to the Israeli view—did not provide enough security; and that there would be no withdrawal without direct talks with the Arabs and the signing of peace agreements (Gazit 1984, 20). The newly established settlements in the occupied territories (in the Golan Heights and particularly in the West Bank) reflected this new Israeli thinking along the lines of the Allon Plan (Pedatzur 1996, 160–255). The formal position was supported by the public: polls showed that the majority of Israelis were against withdrawal from the occupied territories (Katz 2006, 30–31). These polls reflected two important trends. First, they showed the impact of the new right-wing organizations founded immediately after the war and the emergence of messianic voices within the National Religious Party (NRP) and its associated circles, which called for retaining the Jewish religious historical sites, particularly in Judea and Samaria. Second, they revealed disappointment with the Arab position as reflected in the Khartoum Arab summit, which nixed the possibility of direct talks and recognition of Israel (see chapter 8).

In Egypt and the Arab world, Nasser continued dictating the Arab discourse and action. Though his influence in the Arab world diminished following the defeat, he still remained the most important Arab leader. The resolutions of the Khartoum summit allowed him to maneuver between the radical camp, which supported the continuation of the armed struggle, and the more

moderate camp under his leadership, which sought a political solution entailing Israel's withdrawal from the occupied territories based on Resolution
242 (Sela 1998, 97–109). Though the resolution talked about "withdrawal of
Israeli armed forces from territories occupied in the recent conflict," the Arab
interpretation was that the text meant Israeli withdrawal from *all* the occupied territories. This, they claimed, was supported by the text in the preamble
emphasizing "the inadmissibility of the acquisition of territory in war" (Riyad
1981, 58–75). However, the first round of prenegotiations, mediated by special envoy Jarring, did not produce any results. The gap between the parties
regarding the possible elements of compromise was wide, and then Egypt also
insisted on the conclusion of a comprehensive rather than bilateral agreement
(Katz 2006, 61–86; Riyad 1981, 76–102). In the meantime, Nasser managed
to rebuild his army with Soviet support. Buoyed by that achievement and in
order to break the deadlock, he initiated a limited war in April 1969, called
the War of Attrition, intended to debilitate Israel and compel its withdrawal
from Sinai and perhaps from other occupied territories as well (Bar-Siman-
Tov 1980; Riyad 1981, 104–106). Yet the war did not prevent Egypt from continuing its use of the diplomatic card for achieving the same purpose.

The diplomatic stalemate, the escalation on the Israeli-Egyptian front,
and two pro-Egyptian military coups in Sudan (May) and Libya (September
1969) put the Nixon administration under pressure to turn its attention to the
Middle East and devise a new strategy for the conflict. In June 1969, Joseph
Sisco, the assistant secretary of state for Middle East affairs, presented Egypt
with a draft proposal for a solution to its problems with Israel that included
many of the points which would later be presented in the Rogers Plan. It was
an American attempt to test the waters before diving into the broader conflict. The Egyptian reaction at that point was decidedly negative (Meital 1997,
65–66). Nixon then sought the support of the Soviets in approaching the
parties—a step that might have a mitigating effect on the global Cold War as
well. In this way, the United States established a link between the Cold War
and the Arab-Israeli conflict. The extensive meetings that took place between
Rogers and Andrei Gromyko, the Soviet foreign minister, produced a joint
US-Soviet working paper, submitted to Nasser on November 10, 1969. The
ten-point plan called for the conclusion of a "final and reciprocally binding accord" between Israel and Egypt, to be negotiated under Jarring according to
the model of the 1949 armistice agreements. It envisaged the end of the state
of war and the establishment of a formal state of peace based on secure and
recognized boundaries to be agreed upon by the parties. It also specified the
establishment of demilitarized zones, special security arrangements in Sharm
al-Shaykh and the Gaza Strip, and freedom of navigation in the Tiran Straits

and Suez Canal for Israel. The Israeli-Egyptian agreement was devised as a package deal, to be followed by an Israeli-Jordanian accord including an agreement on a just solution to the refugee problem (Quandt 2005, 67–68; Riyad 1981, 110; Korn 1990, 47; 1992, 143–164; Daigle 2012, 58–65). Egypt's response was noncommittal: "Though we maintained reservations on a number of points," wrote Mahmoud Riyad, foreign minister at the time, "there were equally some positive points, most important of which was Israel's total withdrawal to Egyptian international boundaries and Rogers's admission of the necessity for a comprehensive solution." However, Egypt decided to hold off its final agreement until an "integrated formula" including the Jordanian and Syrian fronts was drafted (Riyad 1981, 110–11; Quandt 2005, 68).

When no reply came from Egypt or the Soviet Union, Rogers—with Nixon's approval—decided to outline the basic elements of the plan in a public speech on December 9, 1969 (Daigle 2012, 65–75). It was presented as an effort of the four powers—the United States, Soviet Union, France, and Britain—to assist Jarring's mission in working out a peaceful settlement based on Resolution 242. The eventual aim of the proposed ideas was "a binding commitment by Israel and the United Arab Republic [Egypt] to make peace with each other." To achieve this aim, Israel would be required to withdraw to the international border. With regard to the extent of Israeli withdrawal, Rogers stated that "any change in the pre-existing lines should not reflect the weight of conquest and should be confined to insubstantial alterations required for mutual security." The United States, Rogers continued, "does not support expansionism." The speech repeated in a somewhat confused way the main points appearing in the memorandum submitted to Egypt, including some ambiguous references to the issues of Jerusalem and the refugees (Korn 1990, 47; 1992, 160; Daigle 2012, 65–75).

To emphasize the "package deal" nature of the Rogers Plan, the United States presented on December 18 a parallel document outlining an Israeli-Jordanian settlement, with several points added or modified to suit the special circumstances on this front. The permanent border, for example, was to "approximate" the armistice demarcation line but would also allow alterations based on "administrative and economic convenience." On the matter of Jerusalem, it was proposed that the two countries recognize it as a unified city while sharing some civic and economic responsibilities, as already suggested in Rogers's speech. As to the refugee problem, an annual quota of refugees to be agreed upon by the parties would be allowed to repatriate while the rest would be compensated financially (Quandt 2005, 68; Korn 1992, 161–162).

Israel was informally updated by the United States regarding its diplomatic contacts with the Soviet Union and Egypt, including the proposal submitted to Nasser. When Rogers made the US plan public, Israel flatly rejected it, describing it as no less than "an attempt on the very existence of Israel" (Rafael 1981, 210). The Israeli ambassador in Washington, Yitzhak Rabin, was recalled for consultations. A cabinet meeting on December 22 issued a clear statement:

> [The plan] prejudices the chances of establishing peace; disregards the essential need to determine secure and agreed borders through the signing of peace treaties by direct negotiations; affects Israel's sovereign rights and security in its proposals for the solution of the refugee question and the status of Jerusalem. If these proposals were carried out, Israel's security and peace would be in a grave danger. Israel will not be sacrificed by any power policy, and will reject any attempt to impose a forced solution upon it. (Rafael 1981, 211)

The Rogers Plan created a sense of crisis within Israel, perceived as an "imposed settlement" threatening its very interests and values. In response, Ambassador Rabin was instructed to launch a public campaign on Capitol Hill and among agents of the Jewish lobby to undermine the plan (Rabin 1979, 1:272; Daigle 2012, 74–75).

Though the Israeli reaction was harsh, it was the Soviets and the Egyptians, noted Korn, "who dealt the Rogers' proposals their death blow" (1992, 163). The Soviets refused to associate themselves with the plan and notified the United States that Nasser too had turned it down, displeased with the language of peace it contained as well as the notions of demilitarization, free maritime passage, and security measures. Rogers and Sisco felt that the Soviets, in reversing their early expressions of cooperation, had let them down. They concluded that Nasser "was not ready to settle his differences with Israel peacefully, and the Soviets were not disposed to try to oblige him to do so" (Korn 1992, 164; Daigle 2012, 75–78). Egypt's foreign minister Riyad presented things a little differently. He argued that following Israel's rejection, "I saw no point in our accepting it [the Rogers Plan] for it would mean further concessions within the framework of a settlement which we were doubtful the US could get Israel to accept" (1981, 114). It was quite clear without this statement that Egypt opposed the plan, though for tactical reasons it preferred not to openly reject it. The Israeli rejection provided a convenient pretext (Heikal 1975, 91; 1996b, 148–149; Korn 1992, 163–164; 1990, 48). It is perhaps worth noting too that Egypt's ability to present a more moderate position was curtailed by its need to rely on Arab financial support, as discussed at the Arab Summit held at Rabat on December 21–23, 1969 (Sela 1998, 117–121). Ultimately, then, a rather complex web of interrelationships and a need for mutual support led Egypt to reject the plan and the Arab world to follow suit. Egypt's negative response was backed by a *fatwa* (religious ruling) issued by al-Azhar, which asserted that a peace treaty with Israel was forbidden by the holy *shariʿa* (Reiter 2008, 82–84).

Quandt concluded that the Israeli, Egyptian, and Soviet objections to the plan "put a sudden end to the first Middle East initiative of the Nixon administration" (2005, 68). With the failure of the Rogers Plan, hope died that "linkage diplomacy"—i.e., involving the Soviet Union in the negotiations—would help provide the key to peace. The United States turned its focus toward achieving a cease-fire in the War of Attrition, a limited goal that was eventually achieved by Rogers in August 1970 (Quandt 2005, 68–69).

ASSESSMENT

Maoz asserted that "Israeli decision makers failed to realize that the [Rogers] plan was one that Israel could live with in the long run." When we examine subsequent US proposals, he continued, the Rogers Plan can be seen as "a really good deal even from the perspective of today's hawks" (2004, 407). To what extent, then, did the Rogers Plan constitute a case of a missed opportunity?

The Rogers Plan can be considered a historical opportunity to solve the conflict for two reasons. First, it came after the initiation of the War of Attrition by Egypt, which was an attempt to break the diplomatic stalemate reached by the Jarring Mission, and following the election of a new US administration that was determined to promote a peaceful dialogue to ameliorate the effects of the Cold War. In addition, since no serious diplomatic process between Israelis and Arabs began after the 1967 War, this episode can be seen as a belated response to this major turning point in the conflict. Second, the Rogers Plan presented a positive—if not attractive—offer to the parties. Moreover, it constituted a revolution in American thinking, being the first attempt at presenting a blueprint for the resolution of the Arab-Israeli conflict. Israel, and to a lesser extent Egypt, did not see the plan in a positive light at the time, but hindsight suggests that it did contain some attractive elements—indeed, attractive enough to later be included in the Israeli-Egyptian peace treaty.

What was the potentiality level of this opportunity? The legitimacy of the two leaderships was high. In spite of the 1967 military disaster, Nasser was still considered a popular leader both in Egypt and the Arab world. By the end of 1969, it seemed that he was "riding a new wave of popularity" and that Egypt's role in the Arab world was on the rise (Sela 1998, 116). In Israel, Golda Meir led the Labor Alignment to a victory in the elections, held on October

THE ROGERS PLAN 99

28. She set up a National Unity coalition based on the same components of the previous government—Labor, Begin's Gahal, and the NRP. In fact, it was the largest-ever coalition with no fewer than 102 members—that is, 85 percent of the 120-strong Knesset. The fact that Moshe Dayan, the charismatic leader associated with the 1967 victory, continued serving as minister of defense strengthened Meir's position. Therefore, both the Egyptian and Israeli leaderships were powerful and legitimate enough to take bold decisions had they chosen to.

However, there were no signs that either leader was willing—or even thinking—in terms of taking bold decisions. There was no noticeable change in their worldviews toward the other. Under Meir's leadership, wrote Shlaim, "Israel's policy in the conflict consisted essentially of military activism and diplomatic immobility," adding that "intransigent" was not only her middle name, but the hallmark of Israel's policy (2000, 289). Meir presented herself as a peace-loving leader, but her perception of Israel's enemies was shaped by a mixture of hostility and contempt, while the conditions she outlined for peace were unacceptable to the Arabs (Meir 1976, 321–322). "Even if we have to stand for years," she said after Rogers's speech, "we would not accept something less than a real peace and a defensible border." In her opinion, Nasser and the other Arab leaders did not learn the lessons of the Six-Day War and did not forgo their vision to destroy Israel.[2] Meir's harsh position was also the product of her lessons from the 1956 War, which ended with no satisfactory agreement; had that result been different, it might have prevented the outbreak of another round of hostilities. The composition of Meir's National Unity government also made it difficult to move forward. She conveniently threw the blame for the diplomatic impasse not only on the intransigence of the Arabs but also on the "extreme" right-wing parties (1976, 322). It would be fair to conclude, however, that Meir was not alone in her harsh judgment of the Rogers Plan; for Abba Eban, the moderate foreign minister, it was simply "one of the major errors of international diplomacy in the postwar era" (1977, 464).

Nasser, for his part, had accepted Resolution 242, which in retrospect signaled Egypt's first move toward a peaceful solution (Meital 1997, 173–179). Yet his diplomatic moves did not then attest to a meaningful change in his position. Unwilling to relinquish his role as champion of radical Arab nationalism, Nasser was compelled to adopt a strident anti-American position (Kissinger 1979, 378). Moreover, the fact that he was committed to an all-Arab solution of the conflict limited his maneuverability in solving it (Heikal 1996b, 148). While the Jordanian track did not pose an obstacle, the Syrian refusal to recognize Resolution 242 blocked the possibility of a joint Arab diplomatic move. Thus, by insisting on an all-Arab solution, Nasser unwittingly tied himself to the Arab consensus and in such a way deprived Egypt of the advantages the resolution offered for an Israeli-Egyptian bilateral track.

Israeli-Egyptian relations—or rather relations between Nasser and Golda—suffered from the mistrust syndrome. The contacts between the two sides in the 1950s and 1960s left a legacy of apprehension and suspicion; they did not lay a solid basis for trustful negotiations.

In this connection the role of the mediator is highly important. As mediator, Rogers certainly attempted to offer an "evenhanded" posture, but this policy was not supported by Nixon or Kissinger. Kissinger was particularly opposed to Rogers's proposal, thinking it could not bridge the gap between the two sides. Instead, he advocated an interim settlement, which would lead the Arabs to realize in the long run that only the United States could deliver a deal entailing Israeli withdrawal (Kissinger 1979, 374–376; Daigle 2012, 79–80). In many ways, the Rogers Plan reflected a power play between the White House and the State Department. In addition, Nixon's rather ambivalent position weakened the plan. Nixon never publicly endorsed the plan, "nor did he send any signal to Moscow and Jerusalem that the plan was *his* and not just Rogers's" (Daigle 2012, 80). This bureaucratic and personal rivalry, coupled with Nixon's own ambivalence, meant that the plan was doomed from the start. In such a way, both Israel and Egypt received contradictory messages that each side used to its own advantage. This flawed conduct hampered the chances of the US initiative to solve the conflict (Quandt 2005, 69; Spiegel 1985, 187–188; Kissinger 1979, 373–379; Korn 1992, 277). No less important was the fact that though the Rogers Plan was meant to augment the Jarring Mission, no mechanism was set in order to establish clear spheres of activity and modes of cooperation between the two entities involved.

In sum, the potential for a missed opportunity was limited, confined to the existing legitimacy of the leaders to take bold decisions. In contrast, the rigid positions, the existing mistrust between the parties, and the undetermined nature of American policy meant that the plausibility level for seizing the historical opportunity was low. This assessment is strengthened by the fact that Israeli leaders at that time did not regard the Rogers Plan as an attractive offer and that the response of most relevant parties (except Jordan) ranged from objection to indifference. Thus, though the Israeli-Egyptian peace treaty resembled the Rogers Plan (Quandt 1993, 83), in 1969 it did not constitute a plausible missed opportunity. Yet the Rogers Plan should not be considered as a complete failure, as it provided the parties with the necessary framework for negotiations if and when the talks resumed (Daigle 2012, 81).

NOTES

1. Interestingly, this important sentence was omitted from the later, shorter version of his book used extensively in this research (Quandt 2005, 68).

2. Knesset speech on the occasion of the introduction of her government (*Divrei Haknesset* 56 [December 1969]: 192).

CHAPTER 10

THE JARRING MISSION AND
THE SADAT INITIATIVE
1971

On February 4, 1971, after barely six months at the helm of his country, Anwar al-Sadat astonished the Egyptian parliament with an initiative to negotiate an interim settlement with Israel. In an uncoordinated move four days later, UN mediator Gunnar Jarring presented Egypt and Israel with identical memoranda outlining his own proposals for resolving the conflict between them. Among the demands outlined therein, Israel was to declare its commitment to pull back to the 1967 border (including the Gaza Strip), in return for which Egypt would sign a peace treaty with its neighbor that extended free passage in the Tiran Straits and Suez Canal, termination of the state of belligerency, and recognition of Israel's right to exist. Thus by mid-February 1971, the Israeli-Egyptian scene was quite suddenly faced with two surprising initiatives. The aim of this chapter is to assess whether, and if so to what extent, these two interlinked episodes constituted missed opportunities.

THE EPISODE

In August 1970, just before Nasser's sudden death, Egypt and Israel had accepted the Rogers Initiative to terminate the War of Attrition. Exhausted by the war, both parties were willing to accept a cease-fire, confined initially to ninety days, and to resume Jarring's diplomatic mission (which had in fact begun after the 1967 War). The US mediation stemmed from its apprehension that the fighting along the Suez Canal and the growing role of the Palestinian resistance movement in Jordan (which eventually ended in Black September) would propel regional instability and, consequently, Soviet involvement (Quandt 2005, 75; Meital 1997, 70–76; Riyad 1981, 135–157; Gazit 1984, 53–68; Rafael 1981, 221–232). Upon the acceptance of the Rogers Initiative, the right-wing Gahal Party in Israel promptly quit the National Unity government formed before the 1967 War out of fear that the agreement implied future territorial concessions. That same day, Egypt violated the cease-fire by moving its missiles to the edge of the Suez Canal. This step intensified Israel's mistrust of Nasser and led to the suspension of its participation in Jarring's renewed mediation efforts. Only in late December, after receiving some assurances and weapons from the United States, did Israel agree to reverse this decision (Shlaim 2000, 296; Gazit 1984, 74).

The cease-fire allowed Nasser to briefly play a leading role in appeasing the Palestinian-Jordanian rift—until he suffered a fatal heart attack on September 28. Sadat, who had been appointed as vice president ten months earlier, was elected as Nasser's successor by popular referendum on October 15. And yet at home and abroad Sadat was considered a weak figure, a temporary compromise until the emergence of a new leader from the old Nasserist establishment. Kissinger related in his memoirs that when a journalist asked him about Sadat, "I said I thought he was an interim figure who would not last more than a few weeks" (1979, 1277).[1] The same assessment was shared by the Israeli intelligence and political elite (Maoz 2004, 418; Gazit 1984, 87). Not only was Sadat an enigma, but also his short flirtation with the Nazis during World War II aroused suspicion and mistrust (Sadat 1978, 13–28; Israeli 1985, 18–22; Beattie 2000, 17, 27, 35).

Sadat inherited a plethora of problems in the political, military, and economic spheres that needed to be dealt with immediately. In contrast to Nasser, he was not personally responsible for the humiliating 1967 defeat, nor was he committed to the Soviet Union. His succession did not change Egypt's overall strategic aims in the conflict, i.e., full Israeli withdrawal from the occupied territories; he believed, however, that since the prospects for achieving a comprehensive solution to the conflict were slim, the alternative was partial accommodation, setting in motion a process leading to the same end result. To attain this objective, Sadat was prepared to demonstrate a measure of flexibility, though not at the expense of what he considered to be vital Egyptian interests (Meital 1997, 79–81).

The first sign that Sadat was departing from Nasser's policy with regard to the conflict was seen in his interview with the *New York Times* on December 28, 1970. In return for the complete Israeli pullback from Sinai ("every inch"), Sadat was willing "to recognize the rights of Israel as an independent state as defined by the Security Council of the United Nations" and would welcome a guarantee by the four superpowers "of all Middle Eastern borders, including Israel," as a first step toward a peace settlement. At that point, Sadat rejected the notion of diplomatic relations with Israel, suggesting that this question be left to future generations (Israeli 1978, 14–15). A few days later, in an interview with Walter Cronkite on CBS, the president made it clear that he was "quite open-minded and open-hearted for a peaceful solution" (ibid., 17). These declarations were not accidental but part of a concerted, though still covert, move that differed in essence and in style from Nasser's policy.

When Sadat stunned the members of his parliament with an initiative to negotiate an interim settlement with Israel on February 4, 1971, he was nevertheless careful not to deviate from Nasser's legacy. He extended the cease-fire by thirty days and suggested a partial Israeli withdrawal from the east shore of the Suez Canal as the first step toward Israel's submission of a timetable for implementing the entire UN Resolution 242, leading to full Israeli withdrawal from Sinai. In return, Egypt would clear the canal and reopen it for international navigation. Again following Nasser, Sadat expressed a commitment to the return of all conquered Arab territories and the preservation of Palestinian rights. He did not specify the depth of the expected pullback, but two options emerged in later diplomatic exchanges and public declarations: the al-Arish-Ras Muhammad line and some forty kilometers to the strategic Gidi and Mitle passes. Sadat expected Egyptian military or police forces to cross to the canal's east bank once the Israeli withdrawal was completed so as to safeguard the clearing operations (Israeli 1978, 31–32; Maoz 2004, 412; Shlaim 2000, 302; Quandt 2005, 88–89; Gazit 1984, 97–98; 1997, 100; Rabin 1979, 2:330; Venetik and Shalom 2012, 150–151).[2]

Sadat hoped that his initiative would break the diplomatic deadlock. In hindsight, such "out-of-the-box" thinking characterized his decision making, as manifested too in the surprise attack on Israel in October 1973 and, by contrast, his visit to Jerusalem in November 1977. He did, though, have specific motives for launching the initiative. First, a positive outcome from the negotiations would enable him to take credit for starting the process of Israeli withdrawal. Second, Egypt would earn income from the traffic in the reopened Suez Canal. Third, it would gain Egypt points with the United States and lead to the resumption of diplomatic ties with the superpower, cut in 1967. Fourth, it would constitute a lever in Egypt's policy, which might elicit a more generous attitude to its arms requests from the Soviet Union. And, finally, in case the initiative failed, it would give Egypt more time to prepare for a military showdown while some of its forces constituted a vanguard on the east shore of the canal (Touval 1982, 179–180; Riyad 1981, 187–188; Meital 1997, 87). At the same time, though, as Sadat himself later admitted, he really had no option: it was the only alternative to the military one, which he was unable to undertake at that time (Sadat 1978, 221–222). Interestingly, Sadat had seized upon the same idea that Moshe Dayan, the Israeli minister of defense, had been quietly and privately exploring since September 1970. It offered a thirty- to forty-kilometer mutual withdrawal on both banks, the cleaning of the canal and its reopening for international shipping (including Israel's), the rehabilitation of the Egyptian cities along the canal, and a prolongation of the cease-fire. It was expected that such an initiative would stabilize the cease-fire through a disengagement of forces and alleviate the international pressure on Israel to fully withdraw from Sinai. But since the idea was not supported by most Israeli leaders, and since the United States believed that the idea of an interim agreement would be rejected by Egypt, it was summarily shelved (Touval 1982, 177–178; Kissinger 1979, 1280; Rafael 1981, 258; Venetik and Shalom 2012, 149).

Sadat knew that his initiative would be met with strong criticism: "My people will not like it," he said in one of his earliest interviews. "That is why Nasser was against it. But I will take that risk. And after that, if world opinion does not understand our attitude, we can then say we have done our best" (quoted in Israeli 1978, 33). But Sadat was not deterred by the expected opposition from the old Nasserist guard even though his own legitimacy was still mooted. He was adamant to offer the initiative—and in reality, no public protest was heard (ibid., 1978, 219, 280).

On February 8, four days after the announcement of the Sadat Initiative, Jarring—coincidentally, it should be noted—presented Egypt and Israel with an identical proposal of his own for resolving the conflict. It was a sudden, unexpected move since the Jarring Mission's first effort some weeks before had not brought any progress. For the first (and last) time, Jarring played a more active role in the peace process—a result of American pressure that his mission not be limited to carrying messages but that he act as a mediator, presenting the parties with papers that bore his own (or rather US-inspired) mark (Touval 1982, 157; Kissinger 1979, 1278). The document demanded that Israel declare its commitment to withdrawal to the 1967 border (including the Gaza Strip). In return, Egypt was directed to sign a peace treaty with Israel stipulating free passage in the Tiran Straits and Suez Canal, termination of the state of belligerency, and recognition of Israel's right to exist. Both countries would have to declare their recognition of the right of every country to live in peace within secure and recognized borders, the cessation of hostile activities, and the establishment of certain demilitarized zones (Gazit 1984, 77–78; Riyad 1981, 188; Rafael 1981, 254; Venetik and Shalom 2012, 145–146).

Thus by mid-February 1971 the Israeli-Egyptian scene was faced with two surprising initiatives: one, presented by Sadat, offered the opening of the Suez Canal in return for partial Israeli withdrawal that would constitute the first step on the road to a comprehensive agreement; the second, by Jarring, offered a peace treaty in return for full Israeli withdrawal from Sinai. The burden of response now fell on Israel as it did not present an initiative of its own.

The first official response to Jarring's proposal came from Egypt on February 15. Its document stated, inter alia, that "Egypt will be ready to enter into a peace agreement with Israel containing all the aforementioned obligations provided for in Security Council Resolution 242." In return, Egypt demanded full Israeli withdrawal from Sinai and the Gaza Strip, the establishment of de-militarized zones of equal size on both sides of the border, the formation of a UN peacekeeping force, and the settlement of the refugee problem according to UN resolutions. Its tone made it clear that Egypt "considers that the just and lasting peace cannot be realized without the full and scrupulous imple-mentation of Resolution 242 and the withdrawal of the Israeli armed forces from all the Arab territories occupied since 5 June 1967" (Meital 1997, 91; Gazit 1984, 82–83, 93–94; Riyad 1981, 188; Venetik and Shalom 2012, 146). The response deviated from the Jarring framework in several respects, par-ticularly regarding Gaza, the refugees, and the linkage to withdrawal on other fronts (Gazit 1984, 83). Yet, historically speaking, as the Israeli senior diplomat Gideon Rafael asserted, "It was a far-reaching development. For the first time, the government of an Arab state had publicly announced its readiness to sign a peace agreement with Israel in an official document" (1981, 255–256).

Israel was not caught unprepared; when news of the resumption of the Jarring Mission broke out, Prime Minister Meir nominated a high-level com-mittee to lay down possible concessions within a real peace process. The committee unanimously agreed on full withdrawal to the international line on the Egyptian and Syrian borders. Most members were also willing to cede the Gaza Strip, most of the West Bank, and East Jerusalem. When Meir met the committee in early January 1971, she expressed vehement criticism of the document and decided to shelve it.[3]

The first formal Israeli reaction to the idea of the Suez interim settlement came on February 9 during a Knesset debate on Sadat's initiative. There, Prime Minister Meir expressed willingness to discuss the initiative under cer-tain conditions, demanding the holding of direct talks and recognition of Israel's needs for secure and recognized boundaries, which meant for all in-tents and purposes a refusal to return to the prewar lines. Her main opposi-tion was to the idea that the interim settlement would not be part of a com-prehensive agreement leading to peace. On the other hand, she was afraid that a partial agreement would bring more pressure to bear on Israel to withdraw without receiving the desired peace. Her speech attempted to emphasize all the negative aspects of Sadat's initiative—the absence of a time frame, the depth of withdrawal, the crossing of the canal by Egyptian forces—without attempting to see its potential stabilizing effects on Egyptian-Israeli relations. She censured Sadat for his inability to use the term "Egyptian-Israeli peace treaty." Meir did not encounter any serious resistance in the Knesset; even the opposition party, Gahal, led by Menachem Begin, which, as noted earlier, left the unity government as a result of the Rogers Initiative, largely supported her position. It was only the parties on the extreme left that criticized the government for not responding positively to this historic initiative, which reflected, in their view, a significant change in the Arab position, and one that was begging for a counter-initiative (Gazit 1984, 97, 104–105; Venetik and Shalom 2012, 151–153).[4] The Israeli response did not reject the idea of a partial settlement mainly because it did not want to antagonize the United States, which supported the idea. But anyone reading between the lines would have sensed that the conditions raised and the reservations expressed were tantamount to a rejection of the initiative.

In tandem, on February 26 Israel delivered to Jarring its response to his document. Following extensive consultations within the Foreign Ministry and the government, and in contrast to veteran diplomat Gideon Rafael's recommendation that Israel should present a draft peace treaty, the paper reiterated the main principles of Israeli policy. To the somewhat ambiguous text, "Withdrawal of Israeli armed forces from the cease-fire line with Egypt to secure, recognized and agreed boundaries to be established in the peace process," a short but significant sentence was added: "Israel will not withdraw to the pre-June 5, 1967 lines" (Rafael 1981, 256–257; Meital 1997, 91; Venetik and Shalom 2012, 147).[5] Jarring did not hide his disappointment; in the report to the Security Council submitted in early March, he announced the mission's failure, laying the blame on Israel's refusal to fully withdraw from Sinai.

President Richard Nixon took Sadat's bid seriously and instructed the US State Department to begin work on the interim canal settlement. However, the cool Israeli response to the Egyptian overtures infuriated the United States. Ambassador Rabin was told by State Department negotiator Joseph Sisco that Jerusalem's response was inappropriate and that "Israel would be regarded responsible for rejecting the best opportunity to reach peace since the establishment of the state. Twenty years you did not know peace," he continued, "and if you continue in this way, Israel will never see peace. You [i.e., Israel] need to make some hard choices so as not to miss the big opportunity." Put another way, the United States saw the Egyptian position as positive in contrast to the negative Israeli stance (Rabin 1979, 2:333–334; Venetik and Shalom 2012, 153–154). With this, the Jarring Mission came to an abrupt end.

In spite of the disappointing Israeli response, the United States upheld the diplomatic dialogue. In the absence of any other alternative, the interim agreement was seen as the only avenue for a breakthrough. Rogers, his deputy Sisco, and the US representative in Cairo, Donald Bergus, saw Sadat's initiative as a major opportunity for peace and invested great efforts throughout 1971—termed by Sadat as "the Year of Decision"—to move forward. In various diplomatic exchanges, Israel was reproached both by the White House and the State Department for its negativism and inability to present unambiguous positions (Rabin 1979, 2:340–343). Attempting to break the ice, Sisco presented a proposal in March that included the following elements: Israel's withdrawal forty kilometers east of the canal; demilitarization of the evacuated area; the recruitment of Egyptian civilians to clear and operate the canal and to be allowed into a ten-kilometer-wide strip along the east bank; complete opening of the canal six months after the agreement; having the agreement constitute the first step toward the full implementation of Resolution 242; and providing both sides with the freedom to review the cease-fire after one year (Rafael 1981, 260–261; Gazit 1984, 105; Rabin 1979, 2:338–447). The document was drafted with Sadat's knowledge and encouragement. It seems that the US diplomats—in contrast to the common Israeli assessment—were convinced that Sadat was genuinely seeking peace.

At the same time, however, Sadat sent mixed messages in numerous directions, as he continued his contacts with the Soviets to purchase further arms. In addition, he did not renew the cease-fire, though he did not threaten to resume the fighting on the March 5 expiration date (that is, the final extension of the August cease-fire agreement). These steps were an attempt to signal to the United States and Israel that the military option had not faded (Rafael 1981, 262; Riyad 1981, 192).

The discussions in the Israeli government regarding Sisco's paper revealed the existence of two camps. The soft-liners, including Dayan, Eban, and Rabin, advocated it as a basis for negotiations, though with certain modifications. This group did not oppose the suggested withdrawal, which would turn the relevant territory into a demilitarized buffer zone, allowing the opening of the canal and thus reducing the risk of future war. Such an agreement would also serve as a test of the seriousness of the Egyptians (Eban 1977, 469–470; Ya'acobi 1989, 110–117; Rabin 1979, 2:344–345; Venetik and Shalom 2012, 156–157). The hardline group, primarily Golda Meir and several leading ministers, rejected any withdrawal without the signing of a full peace treaty. Even if a limited redeployment was agreed to, the distance of forty kilometers (encompassing the strategic Gidi and Mitle passes) was rejected. In addition, linking the Suez agreement to the full implementation of Resolution 242 — an Arab code word for the demand for complete evacuation of all the territories occupied in 1967—was vetoed. Finally, there was strong objection to the stationing of any Egyptian forces on the east bank. Rafael lamented that all these contentious issues were resolved to the full satisfaction of both Egypt and Israel—following the 1973 War (1981, 262).

On April 19 Israel submitted its reply to the American memorandum. It was a reflection of the position of the hardline group and included the following conditions: the clearing and opening of the canal within six months of the agreement; the unlimited duration of the cease-fire; the withdrawal of Israeli forces from the east bank to a distance to be specified; agreement to the entry of only Egyptian civilians to the evacuated area; the reduction of Egyptian forces west of the canal; and the exchange of prisoners of war. It was clarified that when agreement on a final boundary was reached in the framework of a peace treaty, the Israeli forces would withdraw to this line, but no link was made between the Suez deal and future agreements. In fact, to emphasize the disconnection, the suggested plan was termed a "special agreement" instead of an "interim agreement," which implicitly indicated continuity. Kissinger thought the Israeli paper was a nonstarter. Indeed, the US and Egyptian responses to it showed just how wide the gap between the parties was (Rafael 1981, 264–265; Ya'acobi 1989, 119–123; Quandt 2005, 90; Rabin 1979, 2:348–349; Venetik and Shalom 2012, 158–162).

But in contrast to Kissinger, Rogers thought the Israeli response did contain some positive seeds, and thus he was authorized by Nixon to visit the Middle East in early May. It was the first visit of a US secretary of state in the area since John Foster Dulles's visit in 1953. In Cairo, Rogers found a frustrated president preoccupied with domestic problems who merely reiterated the Egyptian position with regard to the Suez agreement (Riyad 1981, 197–201). As an incentive to the United States to pressure Israel for further concessions, Sadat told Rogers that once an interim agreement was signed, most of the Soviet experts stationed in Egypt would be asked to leave within a six-month period (Daigle 2004, 5–6). In Israel, Rogers encountered more difficulties; still haunted by memories of the detested Rogers Plan he had drafted (see chapter 9), decision makers there received him with suspicion. Though Meir remarked that he was "a very nice, very courteous and extremely patient" man (Meir 1976, 321), she assumed that his ultimate aim was to implement his plan. Rogers pressed his interlocutors not to miss the opportunity for peace and asked Israel to commit itself to pull back to the international border. In the absence of such commitment, he demanded a clear Israeli position with regard to the interim agreement. Meir again refused to link this agreement to a full withdrawal, objected to the crossing of any Egyptian forces to the east side of the canal, refused to clarify just how far Israel would be willing to pull back, and demanded an unlimited extension of the cease-fire without giving Sadat a guarantee that the withdrawal process would continue. The main problem, however, was that Meir mistrusted Sadat, believing that he, like Nasser, was bent on the destruction of the Jewish state by stages. It was a tough meeting that reflected not only the gap between the parties but also their ingrained negative perceptions of each other (Rafael 1981, 267; Ya'acobi 1989, 130; Meital 1997, 94–96; Venetik and Shalom 2012, 163–166). If that were not enough, Rogers and Sisco themselves played a double game: to the Egyptians, they tried to present Israeli proposals as more positive than they actually were; with the Israelis, the Egyptian position was cast in the best possible light. The result of these maneuverings was the loss of credibility all around. Add to this the fact that Kissinger and the White House remained skeptical regarding the chances of these diplomatic exchanges (Quandt 2005, 92).

Following Rogers's departure, two important developments occurred in Egypt. First, in mid-May, Sadat purged the Nasserist power centers (through what he called the Corrective Movement)—a step that uprooted the domestic challenge to his rule and strengthened, in the long run, his legitimacy (Sadat 1978, 204–231; Heikal 1975, 122–138). Second, on May 28, Egypt and the Soviet Union signed a Treaty of Friendship and Cooperation during the visit of Soviet president Nikolai Podgorny. Kissinger wrote that the treaty "was bound to alarm the Israelis and make the interim agreement even harder to achieve" (1979, 1284). But Sadat was quick to reassure the United States that the treaty did not signal a shift in Egypt's foreign policy and that its interest in concluding an interim agreement had not diminished (Sadat 1978, 222–224; Meital 1997, 96–97; Riyad 1981, 205; Daigle 2004, 8).

In the subsequent months, the indirect contacts between Israel and Egypt through US mediation continued, but the momentum had been lost. In late 1971, Kissinger rather than the State Department took over the execution of Middle East diplomacy. With the United States in an election year, Nixon did not believe he could risk recurrent crises in the Middle East, so he had Kissinger step in, "if only for the damage-limiting purpose of keeping things quiet until after the 1972 elections" (Kissinger 1979, 1287). Moreover, the war in Vietnam, the détente with the Soviet Union, and warming relations with China constituted more urgent problems on the US foreign policy agenda. The likelihood of a breakthrough on one of these fronts—with a possible positive effect on Nixon's election campaign—seemed greater than in the Middle East conflict. Kissinger believed that continuing the status quo in the Middle East served the United States well, as the Arab parties would eventually realize that only the United States—and not the Soviet Union—was capable of furthering the peace process. In any case, when Meir and Sisco met in early August 1971, they both agreed that "the interim settlement was virtually dead," though they did not want to announce that publicly (Venetik and Shalom 2012, 179–189).

In Israel, it soon became obvious that the chances for a diplomatic solution were fading. In late November 1971 the Labor Party held a convention that dealt with the political situation. Many participants expressed doubts regarding Sadat's sincerity and intentions, as well as Rogers's evenhandedness. The convention's final resolution attributed the failure of the Jarring Mission and the interim agreement to Egypt's insistence on prior Israeli commitment to full withdrawal to the 1967 lines. It was further stated that the party would identify with the government's position in its struggle for peace in secure and recognized boundaries, which necessitated a change in the armistice lines (Deutsch 2010, 91). In such a way, Labor (which in many ways represented the government) absolved itself of any responsibility for the diplomatic impasse.

Interestingly, when Golda Meir visited the United States in December that year, she presented a more moderate position in her meetings with Nixon and Kissinger, the elements of which included willingness to a limited cease-fire (of eighteen to twenty-four months); a certain linkage between the interim and final agreements in return for US abandonment of the Rogers Plan; withdrawal of some thirty kilometers (but not including the passes); and the crossing of limited Egyptian police forces to the east bank (Gazit 1984, 114; Rabin 1979, 2:367–370; Venetik and Shalom 2012, 194). Kissinger's testimony, however, did not give the impression of a breakthrough or a major change in Israel's position (1979, 1289). He did not even immediately report to Sadat on the new tone.

It seems that Kissinger decided to perpetuate the diplomatic impasse. Perhaps he did not want to antagonize the Soviets, who objected to the Suez interim settlement just before Nixon's planned visit in Moscow in May 1972. It is also possible that Meir became more flexible after her two demands were met: the final shelving of the Rogers Plan and the resumption of the sale of Phantom jets to Israel. But her change of heart, made after long procrastinations, did not satisfy the other side because Israel's policy still aimed at substantial territorial changes. Thus, Sadat's "Year of Decision" ended with no decision at all and no progress in the diplomatic field. Though contacts between Israel and Egypt continued through the following year, each party stuck to its own position, with the United States unable or perhaps unwilling to bridge the gap between them (Meital 1997, 98–102; Kissinger 1979, 285–300; Quandt 2005, 92–97; Riyad 1981, 209–242; Gazit 1984, 131–141).

In the absence of a meaningful diplomatic breakthrough in the Middle East, the United States was preoccupied throughout 1972 with other pressing problems. On the home front, Nixon's presidential campaign began in January, and in July the Watergate scandal began. On the foreign front, the escalation of the Vietnam War, the opening to China, and the arms reduction talks with the Soviet Union all contributed to the relative detachment from the Middle East. Even Sadat's daring decision to expel more than ten thousand Soviet advisers from Egypt in July was not met with an adequate American—or Israeli—response (Quandt 1977, 151–153; Parker 2001, 69). A few days later, Meir made a speech in the Knesset that reflected Israel's inflexibility with re-

gard to Sadat's peace overtures, which were considered inadequate and unsatisfactory. The session ended with the Knesset approving a resolution calling
on Sadat to start negotiations with Israel without prior conditions.[6]

A last-ditch effort to reach a settlement was made in February and again
in May 1973, when Sadat sent his national security adviser, Hafiz Isma'il, to
talks in Washington, which went beyond the Egyptian demands presented in
the February 1971 initiative. In return for full Israeli withdrawal to the international line, Egypt was willing to recognize Israel's existence, sovereignty,
and territorial integrity; end the state of war; allow Israel free passage in the
Tiran Straits and Suez Canal; and permit the stationing of international forces
in two locations in Sinai, including Sharm al-Shaykh. Hafiz did not dismiss
the possibility of normalization, including diplomatic and economic ties, but
only when the entire Arab-Israeli conflict and the refugee problem would be
resolved. Once again, Meir was suspicious of Sadat's motives and sincerity
and was unwilling to discuss full Israeli withdrawal even for the price of a
peace treaty. Also, the United States, and Kissinger in particular, did not treat
this round of discussions seriously. Kissinger saw them mainly as a tool to
keep the Soviet Union out of the conflict. In essence, he continued to believe
that maintaining the status quo was preferable to a possible treaty (Venetik
and Shalom 2012, 217–218; Kipnis 2012, 47–69; Gazit 1984, 135–140; Rabin
1979, 2:382–391). Though the Kissinger-Hafiz talks did not promise a peace
treaty to Israel, they included the seeds of a possible partial settlement that
could have delayed—if not prevented—the devastating 1973 War (Venetik
and Shalom 2012, 219; Kipnis 2012, 14–15). Uri Bar-Joseph asserted that
Sadat hoped this "far-reaching proposal for a comprehensive settlement of
the Egyptian-Israeli dispute would generate a diplomatic process that might
render war unnecessary" (2006, 549). Yet the failure to reach a settlement convinced Sadat that only a military showdown, however limited, would be able
to break the ice. In numerous interviews in 1973 he asserted that a resumption
of hostilities would be the only way to unfreeze the impasse (see, e.g., Venetik
and Shalom 2012, 232).

Both Israel and the United States were aware that the diplomatic stalemate
could lead to war. Thus, for example, in a high-echelon meeting at Meir's
house on April 18, 1973, Dayan, the head of the Mossad and the chief of staff,
concurred that war was the only way open for Sadat to ignite the diplomatic
process. One of the leading ministers argued that war could be avoided only
if Israel were prepared to negotiate with Egypt on the basis of full withdrawal
from Sinai (ibid., 229; Kipnis 2012, 97–100). However, Meir's government
was not prepared to do this. The road to the October 1973 War was thus paved.

ASSESSMENT

Diplomats, politicians, and academics have often commented on the February 1971 initiatives. David Korn, who served at the US embassy in Israel at the time (1967–1971), believes that the three years that preceded the 1973 War turned out to be "one of the great missed opportunities for peace in the Middle East" (1992, 274). In his view, "Ultimate responsibility for the missed opportunity lay with Golda Meir whose certainty in her beliefs instilled in her the conviction that by refusing any compromise she was saving Israel from great peril" (ibid., 277). Two Israeli diplomats also lay blame for failure on the Israeli side. Eytan Bentsur, Eban's political secretary and later the director-general of the Foreign Ministry, wrote, "History will judge if an opportunity had not been missed—one which would have prevented the Yom-Kippur War and foreshadowed the peace with Egypt. I truly believe that it was a historic mistake" (2003, 163–164). Likewise, Moshe Raviv, who later became Israel's ambassador in London, concluded that as a result of its shortsighted policy, Israel had missed an opportunity to advance toward peace in 1971 (2000, 176). On the other hand, Mordechai Gazit, who served as director-general of the prime minister's office under Meir, has remained adamant throughout the years that Sadat was not yet willing to make any compromise. In his opinion, "The question whether Egypt was ready to begin to move toward peace in 1971–2 is not a hypothetical one properly belonging to the category of the 'ifs' of history. It is, instead, a question of fact and one on which the available material is plentiful and unambiguous. Only those who choose to prefer mere impressions and flat assertions over all the existing evidence will grasp at the 'ifs' of history argument" (1997, 114). He acknowledges that something indeed was missed but that it was not a peace treaty—rather "an ambiguous and indefinite settlement" along the model reached in 1957 which proved unsatisfactory in 1967 (1984, 13). He further granted that the concessions made by the prime minister in December 1971 should have been made five or six months earlier (ibid., 119). Nevertheless, following his retirement, Gazit kept defending Meir's policy. This was clear in a series of letters he exchanged in the late 1990s with Michael Sterner, then head of the Egyptian desk at the State Department. Sterner did not agree. In his opinion,

> Israel began to see her improved strategic position as the result of the captured territories as more important than the dream of peace negotiations. By the time Nasser died this view was comfortably established in Israeli political and military circles, reinforced by the position that Egypt lacked the military capability to present any serious threat to Israel. Even the "opportunity" pre-

sented by the new leadership in Cairo was not enough to upset this compla-
cent outlook.[7]

Among the politicians, Gad Ya'acobi, who served as a young minister at
that time, thought the opportunity was missed because Israel and the United
States "did not possess enough imagination and determination to prevent
the tragic missed [opportunity]" (1989, 174). The lesson of this historical episode, he reflected, was that "Avoiding crucial decisions may bring deterioration with an unpredictable end" (ibid., 175). Shimon Peres, then minister
of transportation and communications, expressed a more cautious position,
though he, too, was critical:

> It is hard to judge today whether peace with Sadat might have been possible
> at that time on the terms that were eventually agreed to five years later. It
> would be irresponsible for me to pass judgment from the convenient perspec-
> tive of hindsight. I do feel, though, as I felt then, that the tentative proposals
> for an interim agreement were a beginning. I would have been happier if it
> had been explored more tenaciously, but I have to admit that the conditions
> that Sadat put forward at the time virtually forced the Government to reject
> his advances. (Peres 1995, 291)

On the other side of the conflict, Egyptian foreign minister Mahmoud
Riyad wrote in his memoirs, "Once again a golden opportunity for peace in
the area was dissipated by the Israeli compulsion for expansion" (1981, 189).
Likewise, Gamasy, who served as the chief of staff and minister of defense in
the aftermath of the 1973 War, blamed Israel for missing an opportunity in
rejecting the Sadat Initiative (1993, 171).

Academics offered contradictory assessments. "That this [the Sadat Initia-
tive] was a missed opportunity of major proportion is not a new idea," wrote
Zeev Maoz (2004, 416). "What could have been the first step in a peace process that would have averted the Yom Kippur War turned out to be a chief
motivating factor for the Egyptian decision to initiate the war" (ibid., 420).
Raymond Cohen thought that Sadat's Suez initiative "was the great missed
opportunity of the period between 1967 and 1973 wars." In his view, the cultural incompatibility between Israel and Egypt led the Meir government to
miss the tacit dimension of the Egyptian proposal (1990, 153–155). Other
studies lay the blame for the diplomatic impasse on Israel and thus contribute
to the assessment that the episode should be seen as a missed opportunity
on Israel's part (Shlaim 2000, 301–309; Bavly 2002, 88–89; Bar-Joseph 2006).
Venetik and Shalom argue that what was missed was an interim agreement
on the Suez Canal in 1971, which might have prevented the Yom Kippur War

(2012, 263). Similarly, Quandt (1977, 129) and Shafir (2006, 7) opined that Israel missed a nonbelligerency agreement that would have prevented the war. Moshe Gat thought that Sadat's peace was a "peace in name only," assessing, at the same time, that "both countries were equally culpable" in pursuing unrealistic and contradictory policies (Gat 2012, 230–231). Finally, Meir's biographer held that no opportunity was missed since Sadat never abandoned the military option. Meron Medzini suggests that Sadat's diplomatic initiative was "part of a deception campaign to blacken Israel and justify the resumption of war against it when the day comes" (2008, 502). Finally, Shimon Shamir claimed that though Sadat's initiative was a sincere offer, "there was really no chance for success," for Israel needed the October War in order to make peace with Egypt (1994, 38).[8]

The February 1971 initiatives of both Jarring and Sadat were classic examples of opportunity, as they entailed the two essential ingredients: a major historical turning point and an attractive offer. Nasser's sudden death and the rise of Sadat represented the turning point. To be sure, Nasserism—the movement embodied in Nasser's ideology and personality—had collapsed; it had been on the wane since 1967, but the death of the man was also the final blow to the movement. Though his successor was relatively unknown, the mere change created an opportunity. In many ways, the situation resembled the July 1952 Revolution, when an unknown group of officers seized power, a development Israeli leaders viewed as an auspicious start of a new era. In addition, what Sadat offered Israel, in his Suez initiative and in his reply to Jarring's memorandum, which included, for the first time, a willingness to sign a peace treaty, can be considered an attractive diplomatic offer. At the time, however, Israeli leaders did not identify a historical opportunity; they either underestimated or misinterpreted the offers. Rather than focusing on Sadat's new and revolutionary ideas, they emphasized what was missing and voiced their reservations in that context alone. Gazit, for example, wrote that a comparison between the Egyptian responses to Jarring's memorandums of 1969 and 1971 reveals that they were almost identical; the single change, he continued, "related to [Egypt's] willingness to conclude a peace treaty with Israel" (1984, 85). This odd description reflected the relative indifference with which the Israeli leadership received Sadat's initiative.

What was the potentiality level of the episode? The first element relates to the legitimacy level of the leaders. As shown in the episode surrounding the Rogers Plan (see chapter 9), the Meir government was highly stable and legitimate. Though the Gahal right-wing party quit the coalition following the cease-fire with Egypt in August 1970, the government still enjoyed a clear majority in the Knesset. In terms of ideology, it was more cohesive. Moreover, Meir had a strong personality. Her position, wrote Peres, then a young minister from the Rafi Party, was "beyond dispute. Members of the government look at her either with admiration, fear or else they have no choice. In spite of her old age (74), her talk is lucid and her memory is impeccable" (quoted in Medzini 2008, 472). Eban, her foreign minister, firmly believed that "her strength lay in the fact that she could always carry the domestic consensus, and there was no risk that we would be unable to take the Knesset and the Cabinet with us" (Shlaim 2003, 169). Both Eban and Dayan, who harbored more dovish approaches with regard to Arabs, were unwilling or incapable of confronting her. Since several innovative moderate ideas were suggested by Dayan in 1970–1971 (including Sadat's idea of the Suez interim agreement), it would seem that Meir's autocratic style impeded the expression of dissenting voices.[9] Moreover, her leadership perception, according to a veteran diplomat, was "to hold on doggedly to concepts, even if they had long been overtaken by events" (Rafael 1981, 381).

Sadat's legitimacy, by contrast, was unclear; in the shadow of the legendary Nasser, and having been elected as merely a temporary leader, there was much doubt about Sadat's ability to take bold decisions. The West and Israel shared this image. Kissinger said of him: "Who is Sadat? We all thought he was a fool, a clown. A buffoon who goes on every stage every other day to declare a war. We were convinced he was a passing episode. That his days were few" (quoted in Golan 1976, 145). This echoed the Egyptian view of the new leader; Saad al-Shazly, for example, wrote that in his first months in office "Sadat was a man without any real power." It was only after May 15—the Corrective Revolution—that he truly embraced power (1980, 92). The same opinion was voiced by Heikal (1993, 223). The Israeli view (which generally reflected the Western perception) was highly skeptical of his ability to survive in power more than half a year. Sadat was considered erratic and spineless. The May events did not change the assessment of the Israeli intelligence regarding the likelihood of his political survival (Maoz 2004, 418; Gazit 1984, 87; Kissinger 1979, 1277; Medzini 2008, 499). Yet it is important to note that Sadat's early pronouncements about change in Egypt's position toward a solution to the conflict were heard already in late 1970, when he had been in office only two months. The fact that in the first half of 1971 he continuously and consistently reiterated this position, adding or modifying certain nuances depending on the audience and fully aware of the existing opposition to his views, attests to his self-confidence and sense of strength. It seems, therefore, that following the purge of the Nasserist centers of power in May and the Soviet advisers in July 1972, Sadat became a stronger and more legitimate leader, allowing him to pursue peace negotiations with Israel (Parker 2001, 21).

The second element pertains to the willingness of the leader to take bold new moves on the basis of changes in his/her thinking. Sadat entered office with the conviction—or hope—that a political settlement was the way to regain the occupied territories. Perhaps this was an attempt to distance himself from Nasser's legacy. The fact that he conducted a "peace offensive" in the pre-war period and resumed it in the aftermath of the war, leading eventually to the signing of the Egyptian-Israeli peace treaty, attests to his sincerity from the very beginning (Bavly 2002, 87–89; Shamir 1994, 37). Some American diplomats (Rogers, Sisco, and others) believed that Sadat did contemplate peace seriously and they conveyed this impression to the Israeli leadership. Sadat himself saw his 1971 initiative as the beginning of his peace campaign; it was, in his words, a "test for peace" (1972–1973, 120). In his memoirs he wrote, "If the United States or Israel had shown enough interest in that initiative, the October War would not have taken place" (1978, 280). There is no knowing whether he was already prepared to sign a peace agreement at that time or to disengage the "Egyptian problem" from the other fronts, as he did eventually in 1979. His aim was to restore Egypt's desecrated honor, and this could have been accomplished by peaceful means. War was not his first priority. Meital claimed that "Sadat did not intend to make a move leading to a separate peace with Israel. Rather, the initiative was to serve as a starting point—a means to create a momentum for a process bound to lead to a comprehensive solution" (1997, 97). Such a scenario could have gathered momentum that would have averted the war.

On the other hand, rigidity and intransigence characterized Golda Meir. She saw the world in simplistic black-and-white terms. She had a negative perception of the Arabs in general, and this did not change during her tenure. The traumatic experiences of the Jews in the Russian pogroms, the Holocaust, and Israeli-Arab wars were the lens through which she viewed the Arabs, who in many ways replaced the role of the *goy* [gentile] in the Jewish Diaspora. She harbored a deep sense of mistrust toward Arab leaders, which turned every opportunity into a ploy and trap (Medzini 2008, 443, 449; Meir 1976, 336; Podeh 2004, 83–91). In Shlaim's opinion, Meir, more than any other Israeli leader, "exhibited the siege mentality, the notion that Israel had to barricade itself behind an iron wall" (2000, 283–284, 323). Even Foreign Minister Eban admitted that "For Mrs. Meir, there was something called 'the Arabs'—the adversary, the foe, the architect of our destruction." In addition, she was apocalyptic about the Arab world, not believing in the possibility of change (Shlaim 2003, 160, 169). This view was nixed by her biographer, who attempted to refute her rigid image, arguing that Meir went a long way in pursuing peace, particularly with regard to Egypt (Medzini 2008, 446). In reality, however, Meir did very little to advance peace. She stuck to the position of her predecessors, the Eshkol government, which opposed return to the 1967 borders on all fronts and insisted on direct talks with the aim of delineating "secure and recognized boundaries" only in exchange for a contractual peace. While this was legitimate as an opening gambit, the fact that Meir adhered to this position throughout the negotiations made it difficult, if not impossible, to advance with Sadat. She also forcefully objected to a partial settlement with Egypt, and when she finally agreed, it was attached to harsh conditions that the other side could not possibly have accepted (Raviv 2000, 173). No wonder that in her memoirs Meir dedicated only a few sentences to this important episode in Israeli diplomacy (1976, 334). In her presentation of its government in the Knesset in December 1969, Meir promised that it would "seek every way, every crevice through which it will be possible to talk about real peace."[10] Four years later she proudly announced that "During the whole term of this government we did not waste and did not reject any possibility of serious contact with our neighbors regarding peace."[11] The historical research does not support this assertion. It is a pity that major decision makers who disagreed with Meir's response to Sadat—such as Dayan, Eban, and Rabin—were not willing to confront her.[12]

The rigid Israeli position was a result of ideological and political changes that had taken place in society since the war. It was a self-satisfied complacency, which resulted from the astounding military victory of 1967 and the mistaken view that the War of Attrition had been won (Korn 1992, 276). Yet the formal position of the Israeli government immediately after the war indicated a willingness to withdraw to the pre-war borders in return for peace treaties with Egypt and Syria. This decision, however, was reversed in October 1967 (see chapter 8). It was not necessarily an irreversible decision. In May 1971, Ben-Gurion met with Rogers as a private citizen and told him that he was willing to return all the territories except Jerusalem and the Golan Heights in exchange for a peace treaty (Dayan 1976, 526). The United States believed, mistakenly, that in essence Israel was still willing to withdraw from the territories in return for peace (Rabin 1979, 2:331). In February 1971, Rogers lamented that "If, in 1967, we could have gotten from Egypt what they are now willing to give, Israel would have been delighted with it" (in Daigle 2004, 4). Therefore, a return to the postwar policy was not unthinkable.

The third element relates to the impact of prior contacts between the parties on the negotiations and the level of trust existing between the parties. This element is only indirectly relevant, as Israeli leaders had no experience in dealing with Sadat (and vice versa). While Nasser's negative image was entrenched in Israeli leadership and society (Podeh 2005, 151–208), Sadat's relative anonymity could have contributed to a "clean" start; yet his short flirtation with the Nazis during World War II cast a shadow on his image. Sadat was not a fascist, but any association—however brief—with Nazi Germany was seen in a highly negative view in Israel. Similarly, Sadat possessed negative images of the Jews and Israel (Sadat 1972–1973, 121; Israeli 1985, 10). Each side was a captive of its own negative perceptions of the other, and this damaged the chances for dialogue. As a result, each side tended to attribute evil intentions to any offer, however sincere or innocent, of the other. It appears that Sadat's initiative was an attempt to overcome his negative image, though during the negotiations it was his prior conception of Israel as an expansionist power that came to the fore. As for Israel, a large measure of skepticism and mistrust guided its thinking toward the Egyptian leader's intentions.

The fourth element concerns the role of the mediator. In this episode there were two: UN envoy Jarring and the United States. There is a general consensus among scholars and observers of the period that Jarring, in terms of his personality and mediation skills and style, was not a suitable choice for the mission. Another problem that handicapped his mission was that he represented the United Nations—a body with no resources or power of its own, and consequently little sway. In other words, both his and his backing organization's lack of muscle severely limited any possible influence on the final outcome (Touval 1982, 163; Mørk 2007, 116; Gazit 1984, 152; Parker 2001, 26). As for the United States, in the early 1970s it was preoccupied with ending the Vietnam War, the opening to China, the armament reductions negotiations with the Soviet Union, and Nixon's own personal political problems, which eventually led to his resignation. Still, the United States could have played a more significant role in the indirect Egyptian-Israeli negotiations. Its involvement in the diplomatic field, especially via the State Department, was, after all, extensive. However, as with the failure of the Rogers Plan, the bureaucratic and personal animosity between Rogers and Kissinger hampered the chances of the initiatives. Kissinger in particular played a disruptive role, with the blessing of Nixon. Kissinger's confidence that the diplomatic stalemate served US interests led him to play down the importance of noticeable changes in Israeli and Egyptian positions. Oscillating between Rogers and Kissinger, Nixon eventually decided to go against the State Department. The bottom line was that US policy during the years 1971–1973 was ineffective and inconsistent (Quandt 1977, 163). Peleg and Scham concluded that "Arab-Israeli agreements usually have involved energetic, focused, and personal US presidential leadership" (2010, 219). That was not the case with Nixon, who focused on the Cold War, relations with China, and the end of the Vietnam War before the Watergate scandal took hold of him. In addition, Nixon refused in an election year to apply pressure on Israel to modify its position. The idea of doing so was made moot by US officials, but Nixon and Kissinger were against such a step (Rabin 1979, 2:336). "The picture could have changed dramatically," wrote Maoz, "had the US decided to put pressure on Israel" (2004, 419). The outcome of these bureaucratic squabbles, foreign policy priorities, and Nixon's difficulties prevented the United States from playing a decisive role in promoting an Israeli-Egyptian dialogue.

In sum, three of the variables measuring the potentiality level of the opportunity were relevant: 1) the legitimacy of the Israeli leadership was high; that of Sadat partial, but from May 1971, when his initiative was still on the table, his domestic position improved; 2) there was a change in the Egyptian position toward Israel and a willingness to make bold moves, while in Israel peace rhetoric exceeded peace actions; and 3) the United States failed to play a meaningful role as mediator. Only the fourth element—image and previous contacts—might have been an impediment.

The response of the Israeli leaders to Sadat's initiatives was disappointing—a mixture of apathy, indifference, and opposition. At no point was there a feeling in Israel's highest echelons that what Sadat offered was a real opportunity that should be seriously discussed and reciprocated. The United States—which considered the episode a unique opportunity—complained that Israel had never submitted a detailed counter-proposal or clarified its position. "Keeping the status quo is not a policy," Rogers reproached Dayan in November 1972 (Rabin 1979, 2:379). Even the idea that Meir would send a secret message to Sadat was dropped (ibid., 368). The unenthusiastic Israeli response could not have triggered a serious negotiation process that might have evolved in the long run into a peace treaty. In late 1971, Meir for the first time displayed a more flexible position, but the United States—and Kissinger in particular—did not pursue the matter. It is a pity, as Gazit noted, that Meir did not present these views six months earlier (1984, 119). It should be recalled too that Hafiz Isma'il's offers in 1973 did not receive enthusiastic responses from the United States or Israel either.

The analysis of this case study, then, leads us to conclude that the plausibility level of a missed opportunity was high. The burden of responsibility for missing this opportunity falls squarely on Israel. The one thing that might mitigate this impression is that the initiative left an important legacy on the ground; it paved the way for future Israeli and Egyptian concessions (Touval 1982, 164; Shemesh 2008, 39). In other words, the initiative was an important milestone on the road to peace, culminating in the signing of the Israeli-Egyptian peace treaty in 1979. It is unclear what was missed—a peace treaty, a nonbelligerency agreement, or another limited arrangement—but whatever it was, it had the potential of preventing the 1973 War and paving the way to a more comprehensive and binding treaty in the long run.

NOTES

1. Kissinger added here: "That was among my wildest misjudgments" (1979, 1277). General Saad al-Shazly, who would be the Egyptian chief of staff during the October 1973 War, wrote that Sadat "came to power by mere chance" and the main reason for him becoming Nasser's deputy was because he was "nothing more than a yes man" (al-Shazly 1980, 91). Shazly was ousted by Sadat in 1978.

2. There are some differences between what was said in the speech and how Sadat described it in his memoirs. In his talk Sadat was more ambiguous, while in his memoirs he was more explicit, specifying that his initiative called for Israeli withdrawal to the passes and the crossing of Egyptian forces to the east bank (Sadat 1978, 219, 279).

3. This is called the "Yakinton Plan." The story became known only in 1999. See Bavly 2002, 82–83.

4. See the discussion in *Divrei Haknesset* 59 (February 9, 1971): 5302–5330; and the continuation of the debate in vol. 60, February 17, 1971, 1451–1459.

5. Foreign Minister Eban elaborated on the disagreements within the government regarding the exact wording, which did not change the final result, giving the reply "a more peremptory tone" (Eban 1977, 473). Shlaim asserted here that even Eban, the most moderate of Meir's ministers, "failed to appreciate the full significance of Sadat's statement" (Shlaim 2000, 301).

6. *Divrei Haknesset* 64 (July 26, 1972): 3601–3637.

7. Sterner to Gazit, March 16, 1999. See the whole correspondence, which is located in the Mordechai Gazit archive, the Truman Institute, Hebrew University of Jerusalem (quoted in Deutsch 2010, 108). Elsewhere, Sterner emphasized that he found the Israeli position "singularly inflexible, unresponsive, and unimaginative" (Parker 2001, 58).

8. For other views that repudiate the missed opportunity thesis, see Israeli 1985, 66, 73–100.

9. Eban relates the famous story in which Dayan raised within the government the issue of a thirty-kilometer withdrawal in Sinai, but since there was no consensus he did not want to antagonize Meir. "I have always regretted that he [Dayan] did not show his usual tenacity in support of this imaginative proposal, which could have averted the Yom Kippur War," he said later (1977, 476).

10. *Divrei Haknesset* 56 (December 15, 1969): 235.

11. *Divrei Haknesset* 68 (July 25, 1973): 4275.

12. Dayan is quoted to have said on one occasion: "If I am ready to admit one mistake, it is that we did not accept Sadat's initiative in 1971. This could have prevented the war" (quoted in Shamir 1994, 38).

CHAPTER 11

DISENGAGEMENT AGREEMENTS
WITH EGYPT AND SYRIA
1973–1975

THE 1973 WAR ERUPTED on October 6, when Israel came under surprise attack by a coalition of Arab states led by Egypt and Syria. Following the war (called the Yom Kippur War by Israel and the October War by Egypt), a frenetic diplomatic campaign, skillfully masterminded by US secretary of state Kissinger, led to the signing of four agreements and the convening of an international conference. It began with a six-point agreement between Israel and Egypt on November 11, 1973. Then the Geneva Conference on December 21, 1973, paved the way for the Israeli-Egyptian Disengagement Agreement, signed on January 18, 1974, and the Israeli-Syrian Disengagement Agreement on May 31. This round of diplomatic activity ended with the second Israeli-Egyptian Disengagement Agreement on September 1, 1975. The present chapter will analyze if and to what extent the signed agreements achieved all that was possible at the time, or whether an opportunity was missed to go beyond the partial agreements to a final peace treaty.

THE EPISODE

War had been raging for sixteen days when the UN Security Council adopted Resolution 338 on October 22, 1973, calling for all parties to immediately halt the fighting, commence negotiations to implement UN Resolution 242, and work toward a just and durable peace in the Middle East (Laqueur and Rubin 1984, 481). It would be another two days before the cease-fire went into effect, after the Israel Defense Forces crossed over to the west bank of the Suez Canal and encircled the Egyptian Third Army and Suez city. Each side claimed victory: while Egyptian forces had established a firm hold in the east bank, Israeli forces stood sixty miles from Cairo and twenty miles from Damascus. Thus, the results of the 1973 War, in contrast to 1967, were "much more balanced, not least at the psychological level." This even outcome promoted "a more realistic attitude on both sides and established a more promising basis for bargaining and compromise" (Shlaim 2000, 321).

The first diplomatic necessity was to separate the Israeli and Egyptian armies, which were still at a face-off. The superpowers were extremely concerned about a possible resumption of hostilities, knowing that this would cause regional instability and a further hike in oil prices, which, following the embargo called by the Arab oil-producing states, had already hurt Western economies. Egypt and Israel both preferred US mediation: the former because only the United States could deliver political concessions from Israel; the latter because of its dependence on US arms, economic aid, and diplomatic support. All three were not interested in seeing the Kremlin involved in the diplomacy to a serious degree. As a result, newly appointed secretary of state Kissinger became the chief negotiator. The fact that President Nixon was deeply mired in the Watergate scandal allowed Kissinger great latitude in shaping US policy. His strategy was to not link the initial diplomatic steps with the nature of the final peace agreement. "Step-by-step diplomacy," as it became known, was devised to avoid collapse of the talks in the event of insurmountable gaps between the positions of the parties. It was also meant to reassure Israel that a settlement would not be imposed against its will. The result was an unprecedented US role in mediating the Arab-Israeli conflict (Quandt 2005, 131–135; Kissinger 1979, 615–616).

The first achievement was the signing of the "six-point agreement" on November 11. This was an outcome of talks held between the Israeli representative, Major General (Res.) Aharon Yariv, and the Egyptian representative, Lieutenant General ʿAbd al-Ghani al-Gamasy, the head of military operations who would become chief of staff in December. They met at the 101st kilometer of the Cairo-Suez road. With the active mediation of Kissinger, who shuttled between Jerusalem and Cairo, an agreement was reached on the provision of supplies to the encircled Third Army, the exchange of prisoners of war, and the need to discuss the disengagement of both states' armed forces. The success of the talks owed much to the good rapport that developed between Yariv and Gamasy. Apparently, the talks were too successful; when the two began discussing the details of the planned disengagement on the eve of the Geneva Conference, Kissinger halted the negotiations (Stein 1999, 97–116; Kissinger 1979, 632–646; Golan 1976, 88–119; Touval 1982, 232–238; Fahmi 1983, 54–55; el-Gamasy 1993, 318–338).[1]

The idea behind the international conference was to create an opportunity to get Arab and Israeli delegations to meet under the auspices of the United Nations, the United States, and the Soviet Union to discuss a comprehensive peace settlement. Confident in the progress made through his step-by-step diplomacy, Kissinger saw the conference "as a symbol of our commitment to overall peace, as a means of keeping in touch with the Soviet Union during the delicate phase while the cease-fire hung in the balance, and as a fallback position if alternative routes failed" (1979, 749). The conference was meant to serve as an umbrella for bilateral talks on the Israeli-Egyptian track, the Israeli-Jordanian track, and, if possible, the Israeli-Syrian track. In this way, the United States believed it would reduce the role of the Soviet Union to mere spectatorship.

Sadat agreed to take part, seeing the conference as "a safety net, a forum to which he could appeal if all else failed" (Kissinger 1979, 748). Israel objected to it in principle out of fear of being subjected to international pressure to relinquish territory. But in light of the fact that elections were slated for December 31, ten days after the opening ceremony, Meir could not afford to reject the image of a peace-loving government. She insisted, however, that the Palestinians not attend, but agreed to leave open the possibility that they join in at a later stage—a compromise that was accepted by the Arabs. Jordan expressed willingness to take part in the conference, hoping to reverse the decision of the Algiers Arab summit that the PLO was the sole representative of the Palestinian people (Sela 1998, 165–70). Syria opted to abstain; in Kissinger's opinion, Hafiz al-Asad was "rejecting only the opening plenary session of the conference, not the concept of the negotiation" (1979, 783).

The conference lasted for two days (December 21–22); the eloquent speeches made by the participants could not conceal the fact that it was no more than a symbolic event. The conference was an opportunity to begin a meaningful diplomatic process, but the negotiations, as envisaged by Kissinger, were supposed to be held elsewhere, in the bilateral tracks (Stein 1999, 117–145; Touval 1982, 238–241; Quandt 2005, 138–141; Kissinger 1979, 755–798; Golan 1976, 120–141; Fahmi 1983, 60–65). The conference itself was adjourned without any meaningful result. "The endeavor had not all been in vain," wrote Quandt, "but one might wonder if the results were commensurate with the effort" (2005, 141).

The elections in Israel ended with another victory for Labor, but it lost power in the Knesset to the right-wing Likud Party. The change in the electorate reflected the protest and anger in Israeli society toward its leadership and its responsibility for the abysmal failure in the war. This trend would culminate in the May 1977 elections, from which the Likud emerged victorious. For the time being, the results were a clear signal that the Labor Party was no longer the only dominant force in the political system (Bar-Siman-Tov 1998, 8).

With the breakup of the Geneva Conference, the road was open for Kissinger to renew his step-by-step diplomacy; naturally, the Israeli-Egyptian track became the main zone of activity. His shuttle diplomacy led to the signing of the first Israeli-Egyptian Disengagement Agreement on January 18, 1974. His eagerness to conclude an early agreement reflected his intent to outmaneuver the Soviet Union while also providing a solution to the energy crisis, as OPEC had just doubled oil prices. Kissinger found that both Egypt and Israel displayed considerable flexibility, making concessions at a fairly rapid pace. Sadat's eagerness to sign an agreement was criticized by his foreign minister, Ismʿail Fahmi, who thought that Sadat "put aside his most important cards" while damaging Egyptian interests and weakening Syria's capacity to bargain at a later stage (1983, 71). Fahmi was not alone; other top officials opined that the terms of the agreement were "much less than what they thought they ought to get for having gone through the Bar-Lev line" (Stein 1999, 152). The agreement stipulated that the two parties would refrain from all military or paramilitary actions against each other. Israel was to withdraw to about twenty kilometers east of the Suez Canal; the area evacuated by Israel was to be divided into two roughly equal parts, one held by a limited contingent of Egyptian troops and the other a buffer zone overseen by UN forces. The agreement dealt primarily with military issues, but it contained a paragraph to the effect that although neither party considered the document as a final peace agreement, "it constitutes a first step toward a final, just and durable peace according to the provisions of the Security Council Resolution 338 and within the framework of the Geneva Conference." On the Israeli side there were expectations that the agreement would bring about the reopening of the Suez Canal to navigation, including the passage of Israeli cargo ships and the removal of a blockade threat at Bab al-Mandab Straits (Stein 1999, 146–155; Fahmi 1983, 70–80; Touval 1982, 241–248; Quandt 2005, 141–143; Kissinger 1979, 799–853; Dayan 1976, 565–570; el-Gamasy 1993, 331–338). This agreement was not enough to convince Meir that Sadat was willing to conclude a peace treaty. Indeed, until her death, wrote her biographer, fear and mistrust were so deeply ingrained in her that she remained suspicious of Sadat's motives (Medzini 2008, 600–601).

Thus, within a short period of time the two countries signed an agreement that had eluded both for over three years (1971–1973), for which both had paid a very high price. Interestingly, the concessions Israel made in 1974 were more significant than those it had refused to make in return for an interim agreement. Moreover, in contrast to Sadat's 1971 offer to reopen the Suez Canal, the disengagement agreement did not include any Egyptian quid pro quo and the two states remained in a state of war. For domestic reasons the government felt compelled to submit the agreement to the Knesset. On January 22, following a stormy debate, it was approved: 76 members were in favor while 35 members of the Likud Party opposed it. The decision to obtain Knesset ap-

proval became a precedent for future agreements involving territorial concessions (Bar-Siman-Tov 1998, 9).

With the conclusion of the Egyptian-Israeli Disengagement Agreement,
Kissinger aimed at brokering a similar Syrian-Israeli agreement. Such an
achievement, he surmised, would point to the continued dominant US role
in Middle East diplomacy and prevent the isolation of Sadat in the Arab world
(Kissinger 1979, 935; Stein 1999, 154–155). It could also help end the Arab oil
embargo and distance Syria from the Soviet Union. The opening conditions
were not auspicious: "Deeply distrustful of each other as only nations can be
that claim the same soil," wrote Kissinger, "they [Israel and Syria] had lived in
sullen enmity for a generation." And unlike Sadat, who had been negotiating
with Israel in one way or another since 1971, Asad was entering the process
for the first time (Kissinger 1979, 935–936). The first encounter (Seale termed
it a "duel") between Kissinger and Asad had taken place in mid-December
1973, but the latter refused to attend the Geneva Conference (Seale 1988, 230–
238; Kissinger 1979, 777–786). Another meeting was held immediately after
the signing of the Israeli-Egyptian agreement (Kissinger 1979, 848–852). Almost in parallel, the Israeli-Syrian front saw a limited war of attrition during
the spring of 1974, aimed at pressuring Israel to withdraw from the Golan
Heights. In preparation for a possible agreement, and in order to respond to
US demands, a small Arab summit was held in Algeria on February 13 with
Egypt, Syria, and Saudi Arabia participating. There it was agreed to lift the
oil embargo—a decision made public on March 18. In addition, Syria was persuaded to hand over to the United States the list of Israeli prisoners of war it
held as a confidence-building measure (Fahmi 1983, 83–92; Kissinger 1979,
945–953). These steps paved the way to face-to-face negotiations in late February 1974. Though Syria, unlike Egypt, did not succeed in capturing territory beyond the pre-October 6 lines—in fact, Israel managed to seize a salient
chunk of the Golan—it was essential for Asad to show to his public that the
war did produce gains, much like those Egypt had acquired in its agreement.
The problem was that the margin for compromise on withdrawal was narrow;
in contrast to the rather large Sinai Peninsula, much less territory was available
to bargain over, and in Israel's eyes, every single mile of territory had strategic
significance (Touval 1982, 253; Kissinger 1979, 937).

Meanwhile, the Israeli domestic scene underwent some important changes.
On April 1, 1974, only three weeks after Meir's new coalition government was
sworn in, the Agranat Commission published its interim report on the failures of the Yom Kippur War, which absolved the political leadership of any
responsibility and laid the blame squarely on the military and intelligence.
The report provoked mass demonstrations by a furious public that took to
the streets demanding the resignation of both Meir and Dayan. Nine days

later, greatly aged and wracked by guilt, Meir bowed to the pressure and tendered her resignation. She continued as head of a caretaker government until Yitzhak Rabin—the newly elected head of the Labor Party—presented his government on June 3. Rabin was the first prime minister to be born in Israel and the first to rise up from the ranks of the army rather than the Labor Party (Shlaim 2000, 323–325; Medzini 2008, 602–611). But until he took the reins, it remained the task of the weakened Meir government to continue the negotiations with Syria.

Kissinger's shuttle between Damascus and Jerusalem lasted for thirty-four weary days, from late April until the signing of the agreement on May 31, 1974. The protracted "duel" involved thirteen visits and 130 hours of face-to-face talks (Seale 1988, 244). The ultimate agreement stipulated that Israel withdraw to the October 6 lines (including the territory captured during the war), except for the city of Qunaytra and a narrow ribbon of territory looped around it, which were handed over to Syria as a gesture. Israeli and Syrian forces were to be separated by a narrow buffer zone several kilometers wide along the Golan Heights. In this area, a new UN force was established to monitor implementation of the agreement. In addition, limited-force zones of fifteen kilometers were set up along the two sides. Like the Israeli-Egyptian agreement, it was stipulated that the document was not a peace agreement but rather "a step toward a just and durable peace" on the basis of UN Resolution 338. In private, Asad gave Kissinger an assurance that Syria would not permit Palestinian raids to be launched from its territory into Israel. The agreement also included several secret commitments: Israel was promised that no other parties would be invited to the Geneva Conference without the consent of the initial participants; that any future initiative regarding Syria would be coordinated with Israel; and that its stance not to return to the 1967 borders in the Golan Heights would be recognized (Kurtzer et al. 2013, 65; Stein 1999, 155–162; Kissinger 1979, 1032–1110; Golan 1976, 177–212; Quandt 2005, 148–153; Seale 1988, 244–249; Touval 1982, 249–259; Fahmi 1983, 93–96, 277–280). In an interesting postscript, Asad asked Egypt to co-sign the accord under the pretext that Syria and Egypt had formed a unified military command under Egyptian leadership, and as long as this command was in existence it was logical that Egypt would be a signatory too. This Syrian attempt not to commit itself to an act which might embarrass it in the Arab world was flatly rejected by Egypt (Fahmi 1983, 95). Like the Israeli-Egyptian version before it, the Knesset approved this agreement by a majority of seventy-six against thirty-six (Bar-Siman-Tov 1998, 11).

In an attempt to reap the benefits of the two successful agreements, President Nixon—at the height of the Watergate scandal—visited the Middle East in June 1974. However, on August 8 he was compelled to resign under threat of impeachment. His vice president, the inexperienced Gerald Ford, replaced him. Kissinger, kept on by Ford as secretary of state, signaled continuation within the administration. Still riding the wave of success, Kissinger made an attempt in the autumn of 1974 to achieve another bilateral agreement, this time between Israel and Jordan. Inviting Jordan to participate in the Geneva Conference was meant to facilitate this task. Yet two obstacles impeded progress. First, for political and ideological reasons, the new Israeli government under the politically inexperienced Rabin was unable to contemplate concessions. Second, the Arab summits in Algiers (November 1973) and Rabat (October 1974) had decided that the PLO—and not Jordan—was the sole representative of the Palestinian people (Sela 1998, 165–170). As a result, King Husayn believed that in order to ward off the PLO's claims and win legitimacy, he would need to achieve a substantial Israeli withdrawal—something Israel was either unwilling or unable to give. In light of these serious structural problems, it was hardly a surprise that the US mediation on the Israeli-Jordanian track failed (Touval 1982, 259–261; Quandt 2005, 157–159). Shlaim was of the opinion that Rabin "did not display much statesmanship or foresight in relation to Jordan" (2000, 334), but the fact of the matter was that Rabin correctly judged that after Rabat, and in light of his domestic problems, Husayn was not the partner for a settlement over the West Bank and Gaza (1979, 448). Stein assessed that "creating a Jordanian-Israeli agreement was next to impossible" at that time, and that for Husayn signing such an agreement in the prevailing climate "would have been political suicide" (1999, 168, 172).

Kissinger correctly judged that it would be preferable to focus efforts on the Israeli-Egyptian track; estimating that a comprehensive agreement was still not feasible, he opted for a second disengagement agreement. In March 1975, Kissinger resumed his shuttling about, but he quickly realized that the gaps between the parties were too wide to be bridged. The main obstacle was the Israeli demand for a nonbelligerency treaty in return for another partial withdrawal. The Israeli insistence led Kissinger to suspend his mission, now blaming Israel for its failure. Moreover, Ford decided on reassessing US policy, which entailed a suspension of arms supplies to Israel (Shlaim 2000, 336; Quandt 2005, 163–164; Rabin 1979, 460–464).

Sadat once again proved his determination to pursue the diplomatic course when he opened the Suez Canal for shipping on June 5, 1975 (Sadat 1978, 295–296). Despite the recommendations of his foreign minister, Sadat did not extract any concession from Israel in return for this move (Fahmi 1983, 163). As will be recalled, the idea of opening the canal first arose in his February 1971 initiative (see chapter 10), but it was not implemented until after the war. And yet when Rabin met Ford in Washington in June, he argued that there was no Arab leader willing to sign a peace treaty and normalize relations with Israel. Like Golda Meir, he was suspicious of Sadat, whom he considered to be a "traitorous person" in light of his biography and diplomatic conduct (Rabin 1979, 470–471, 474).

This visit and subsequent diplomatic exchanges between Israel, Egypt, and the United States led to another round of shuttle diplomacy in August 1975. Realizing that the aim of attaining formal Egyptian agreement to end the state of belligerency was not feasible, Israel had to content itself with some functional equivalents. Only then could the second disengagement agreement — Sinai II — be signed, and this occurred on September 1. It stipulated Israeli withdrawal from the Gidi and Mitle passes as well as the Abu Rodeis oil fields. A UN buffer zone separating the two countries was set up, as well as limited armament zones on both sides (see map 11.1). It was also agreed that nonmilitary cargoes destined for or departing from Israel would be permitted through the Suez Canal. Article 1 stated that the conflict would not be resolved by military force, but by peaceful means. Two articles explicitly stated that the agreement was a significant step toward reaching a final and just peace settlement. To gain Israeli agreement, the United States offered certain inducements in the realm of military, economic, and energy (i.e., oil) needs. In this connection, Washington agreed to resume the weapons shipments to Israel, including the advanced F-15 jets. In addition, it agreed to station troops in the buffer zone and place civilian personnel at the Umm Khashiba early warning installation. Finally, the United States made certain secret promises to Israel, such as that the next agreement with Egypt would be a final peace agreement; that the current agreement stood alone and was not linked to any other agreement (in the Israeli-Egyptian or any other track); and that it would not recognize the PLO or negotiate with it as long as it rejected UN Resolution 242 and did not renounce terrorism. The US assurances to Egypt were more limited, including, inter alia, a promise to work toward a second Israeli-Syrian agreement (Stein 1999, 175–180; Touval 1982, 264–271; Quandt 2005, 166–170; Shlaim 2000, 337–340; Golan 1976, 213–251).

In terms of legitimacy, both sides suffered from profound problems. Fahmi thought that Egypt had paid an unnecessarily high price for the agreement and therefore was unwilling to sign it. As a result, Sadat was compelled to ask Prime Minister Salem to sign it (Fahmi 1983, 164–165). Sadat, however, saw the agreement as "the third stage of the peace process" that would eventually lead to a comprehensive agreement (1978, 296). In Israel, the agreement was approved by the Knesset, but it was less popular than its predecessors. All in all, 70 members voted in favor, 43 opposed, and 7 abstained (Bar-Siman-Tov 1998, 14).

In late 1975 it seemed that Kissinger's step-by-step diplomacy had exhausted itself. As 1976 was an election year in the United States, the chances

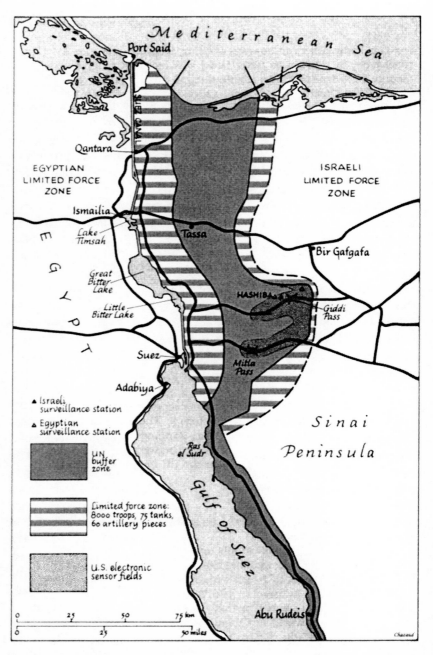

MAP 11.1. The 1975 Israeli-Egyptian Disengagement Agreement. From *The Iron Wall: Israel and the Arab World since 1948* by Avi Shlaim. Copyright © 2001, 2000 by Avi Shlaim. Used by permission of W. W. Norton & Company, Inc.

for another breakthrough in the peace process were slim. In addition, the harsh Arab responses to the last agreement, combined with the outbreak of the Lebanese Civil War in April 1975 and Rabin's domestic problems, all meant that the peace process was frozen. It would take another four years until the conclusion of an Israeli-Egyptian peace treaty.

ASSESSMENT

The signing of three disengagement agreements may suggest that opportunities were not missed in this case study. Having said that, what was arguably missed was a comprehensive peace agreement. "I felt deep regret," wrote diplomat George Ball, "as I watched the US turn its back on a serious effort to solve the overall problem in favor of a tactical maneuver that bought time at the expense of ultimate peace" (1976, 139; Touval 1982, 225). Edward Sheehan, who closely followed Kissinger's diplomacy, lamented that "The sort of settlement I have urged . . . might have been possible on the morrow of the October war had Henry Kissinger truly seized the opportunities of that period. But he feared then that to seek so much so soon was doomed to fail" (1976, 217). Kissinger, according to Sheehan, justified his policies with the philosophy of what is, not of what might have been. "What were the alternatives?" he asked. "The conflict in the Middle East has a history of decades. Only during the last two years we have produced progress. It's easy to say that what we've done is not enough, but the steps we've taken are the biggest steps so far. They were the attainable—given our prevailing domestic situation" (ibid., 201). A similar criticism of Kissinger was voiced by Stanley Hoffmann, who argued, "As much energy had to be spent on wresting a few miles of sand, or heights, or words, than would have been lavished on a far bigger settlement; and that the exercise ended up as a gigantic game of hide-and-seek, in which all the fundamental issues . . . were being postponed." The result was, in his opinion, "the neglect of opportunities that lay outside the current framework" (1978, 75). Finally, former Egyptian foreign minister Riyad commented that Kissinger was anxious to project himself as a great peacemaker, but in fact "he was sowing the seeds of discord and friction everywhere he went, deliberately aborting opportunities for a real peace" (1981, 285). An opposite assessment was offered by L. Steven Spiegel: in his opinion, Kissinger "exploited the opportunity provided by the October War," adding that "Perhaps Ford's reelection would have given Kissinger the opportunity to direct the parties onto a new track, but we will never know" (1985, 314).

As for the Israeli-Syrian track, Patrick Seale blamed Israel for missing the opportunity to sign a comprehensive agreement because of its refusal to fully withdraw to the 1967 borders and solve the Palestinian issue. In addition, he blamed the United States—and Kissinger in particular—for not playing the role of honest broker (1988, 265).

In the pre-1973 period, Israel was under no pressure and without incentives to move forward in the peace process. Undoubtedly, the war shattered the Israeli decision-making elite. Fahmi's description of the Israeli attitude is accurate:

> Egypt had not won the war in the sense of pushing the Israelis out of Sinai
> . . . but Egypt had scored a valuable political victory. The Egyptian assault
> had demonstrated to Israel and to the US that Egypt was now in a position
> to inflict heavy damage on Israel, making it pay very highly for the continued
> occupation of Sinai. It provided for the first time an incentive for Israel to
> negotiate and for the US to push Israel seriously towards negotiations. The
> task of finding a lasting solution to the ME conflict acquired a new urgency
> because of the war, and negotiations resumed in a totally different political
> climate. (1983, 34)

This quotation validates the assertion that the period after the war constituted an opportunity. As we have seen in this volume, wars in general offer windows of opportunity, but the 1973 War offered an even bigger than usual opportunity because Israel's sense of invincibility was shattered. In addition, the urgent need to disengage the armies served as a convenient trigger for resuming the diplomatic process, which had essentially begun prior to the war. Sadat, for one, considered the war as no more than a pretext to resume the negotiations. Though the new turning point was not accompanied by the submission of a formal US—or other—initiative, still the initiation of Kissinger's step-by-step diplomacy served both as an incentive and catalyst and thus constituted, according to our definition, an opportunity.

The first variable of the opportunity relates to the legitimacy of the decision-making elite. If Sadat suffered from lack of legitimacy in the pre-war period, his perceived victory enhanced his positive image and, as a result, his legitimacy in Egypt and the rest of the Arab world. This transformation was reflected in his determination to pursue his own policy and disengage himself from the Nasserist legacy. The October celebrations, which overshadowed Revolution Day (July 23) in the national calendar, were another symbolic indication of Sadat's newly acquired confidence (Podeh 2011, 87–91). Kissinger pointed out that Sadat never mentioned domestic obstacles to his policies. Even if they existed, he concluded, "He [Sadat] absorbed them in his own position; he acted in his own name, which is another way of saying that he assumed the responsibility for Egypt" (Kissinger 1979, 780–781). A similar scenario occurred in Syria, where Asad gained greater confidence—and probably legitimacy—following the war, which was depicted as his personal victory. In Israel, meanwhile, the Meir government suffered from a lack of legitimacy, or badly damaged legitimacy, as a result of the devastating political and psychological effects of the war. With Meir's resignation following the publication of the Agranat Commission's report, Rabin's position was not necessarily better, being a young and inexperienced politician compelled to navigate between the more experienced and sometime devious politicians in his own party. The fact that he was appointed and not elected further eroded his legitimacy (Rabin 1979, 433). Therefore, his level of maneuverability in the domestic political scene was circumscribed. Yet both Meir and Rabin managed to garner enough support in the Knesset to legitimize their policy. In many ways, their governments preferred to be perceived as being coerced by the United States to sign the agreements (Kissinger 1979, 608; Bar-Siman-Tov 1998, 8). As for the United States, Gerald Ford also suffered from a legitimacy deficit. The fact that he—like Rabin—was appointed rather than elected harmed his ability to initiate a major step and go beyond the disengagement policy.

The second variable relates to the ability and desire of the leader or leaders to take bold steps. We have seen already Sadat's determination to pursue peace, as reflected in his pre-1973 diplomacy. He was adamant to take advantage of his "victory" to achieve full Israeli withdrawal from Sinai. It is unclear, however, whether, at this stage, he was willing to pursue a separate peace with Israel. When Rabin raised that very question, Kissinger replied that "Sadat cannot make a separate peace" (Rabin 1979, 457). Indeed, Sadat's public declarations and secret diplomatic exchanges did not support the thinking that he would be willing to sign an agreement separate from the Syrian and Palestinian tracks. When Sadat, in his memoirs, related to Sinai II as "the third stage of the peace process," he was hinting that the whole process was predetermined (1978, 296). Yet he may have attempted to present his peace campaign as a more thoughtful plan than it was in reality. In contrast, Rabin was in favor of a second agreement with Egypt. Although he made it clear that a return to the 1967 borders was unthinkable, a meticulous reading of his memoirs reveals that he was willing to withdraw from most of Sinai (1979, 452, 458, 470–471, 496). As for Asad, his intentions remained an enigma to Western and Israeli officials. Seale wrote with certainty that Asad was in favor of a formal peace treaty (1988, 256). If that was the case, then he was highly successful in hiding this intention.

The third variable relates to the history of past interactions. The fact that Sadat had been negotiating with Israel since 1971 did not dissipate Israeli feelings of mistrust about his intentions. His brief flirtation with Hitler and the Nazis during World War II was brought up by every Israeli leader, including Rabin (1979, 474). Depicting Sadat's change of heart from supporting Husayn to 'Arafat on the question of Palestinian representation in 1974, Rabin wrote in his memoirs, "I felt a red light was lit: if Sadat is capable of violating an agreement with an Arab leader [Husayn] and turn his back to him with no hesitation, how would he treat an agreement with Israel, when and if he faced Arab pressure?" (ibid., 447). Rabin tended to accept the assessment of foreign observers that with Sadat it would be easy to sign a deal, but that he would not honor it; and that it would be more difficult to sign an agreement with Asad, but he would honor it (ibid., 474). Stein aptly summarized the picture Israeli decision makers drew of Sadat:

> Inconsistency, unpredictability, and uncertainty left mistrustful Israelis additionally skeptical about Sadat's intentions. Israel's extraordinarily cautious establishment judged Arab motivation through actions and verbal content analyses, not direct contacts, and found it difficult to read and believe Sadat. He confused the Israelis by keeping their decision makers off balance and inevitably in a quandary about determining the sincerity of his real intentions. (1999, 8)

Sadat, by contrast, often expressed his doubts regarding Israel's sincerity and true intentions. Fahmi was more outspoken than Sadat in his negative perception of the Israeli attitude. Thus, despite the positive progress in the negotiations during the years 1974–1975, negative images of the other continued playing a decisive role on both sides. In the long run, most Israeli fears and suspicions proved to be "totally unfounded" (Maoz 2004, 428).

The fourth variable relates to the role of the third party. The United States, Kissinger in particular, played a significant role, which surpassed by far any previous American diplomatic involvement in the Arab-Israeli conflict. For the first time, wrote Spiegel, "Management of the . . . dispute became America's top foreign policy priority" (1985, 312). Paradoxically, it was the weakness (Nixon) and inexperience (Ford) of US presidents that allowed Kissinger to play such an important role (Touval 1982, 282). He was without a doubt a gifted mediator. Quandt wrote that Kissinger's skills as a negotiator were unparalleled: "His originality, his sense of timing, his intelligence, and even his personality served him especially well" (2005, 172). He was criticized, however, as noted above, for his focus on achieving limited tactical goals instead of pursuing a grand strategy for solving the conflict. Touval argued, "The fact remains that partial settlements were easier and therefore more likely to be accomplished than a comprehensive agreement" (1982, 272–273). Yet it is possible that in his desire to be associated only with success, Kissinger deliberately avoided pursuing the option of a comprehensive agreement, fearing possible failure. Our assessment of Kissinger's contribution to the process should be qualified. "However impressive Kissinger's tactical skills, persuasive powers, and intellectual prowess," wrote Touval, "their impact upon the parties' positions should not be overemphasized. Much more important for bringing about concessions were the resources that Kissinger was able to wield. His arguments moved governments not because of their logic, but because he was the American secretary of state. It was the weight of American pressure and the lure of US incentives that produced the decisive impact" (1982, 281). Certain Arab circles criticized Kissinger for not being a neutral mediator but rather "Israel's envoy" (Fahmi 1983, 168; Seale 1988, 260).[2]

The initiative for the Disengagement Agreements came from the United States, with the active prodding of Sadat. Israel, in contrast to the past, did not respond with apathy and indifference, though it was far from enthusiastic. The Meir and Rabin governments attempted to walk on a tightrope between the need to respond to the changed reality after the war and a desire not to alienate the public, which was shuffling in the direction of the right-wing Likud Party. The Disengagement Agreements were an adequate measure as they conformed with Labor's ideology of not withdrawing to the 1967 borders. Also, Kissinger's step-by-step diplomacy dovetailed with the Israeli gradualist approach. In addition, Israel feared damaging its relations with the United States; the suspension of arms supplies in 1975 was a clear reminder of the tools that were in its possession to achieve its goals. In the long run, the agreements with Egypt were instrumental in advancing the prospects of an Israeli-Egyptian peace treaty. The same process, though, led neither to a second agreement nor to the signing of a peace treaty with Syria. It would seem that the enigmatic nature of Asad's personality, as well as the more strategically meaningful concessions demanded of Israel, constituted the main reasons for the failure in this track.

Ultimately, then, the post-1973 War period constituted a historical opportunity that the United States and Kissinger attempted to seize. The signing of the Disengagement Agreements suggests that the opportunity was not completely missed. But what about a more comprehensive agreement? The analysis of the potentiality level of this episode suggests that the possibility for more gains were slim, at best. Meir's and Rabin's governments were burdened by the weight of serious legitimacy problems, unable to deviate in any meaningful way from the almost unanimous position of refusal to withdraw to the 1967 borders. In spite of the disastrous results of the war, Israeli decision makers did not undergo a fundamental change with regard to the price needed to pay for a peace treaty. Suspicion and mistrust continued to govern their attitudes toward Sadat and Asad, who, in turn, suspected the motives and sincere desire of Israeli leaders to relinquish territories. It is possible that Sadat was still not prepared to sign a separate agreement with Israel; Asad, for his part, was unwilling to accept less than full Israeli withdrawal and progress on the Palestinian track (Seale 1988, 256). Finally, in spite of the fact that Ford was not considered a "strong" and legitimate president, the skills, talent, and intensive involvement of Kissinger in the negotiations facilitated the mediation of three disengagement agreements.

In assessing the plausibility level of the missed opportunity, it is important to note that neither party showed apathy or indifference toward the peace offers. And in fact, the Disengagement Agreements had a positive contribution in the long run as they largely paved the way for a peace treaty, which materialized when the historical circumstances allowed. The preceding analysis demonstrates that it would be a mistake to view this episode as a missed opportunity to sign a comprehensive peace treaty. Rather, Henry Kissinger accurately assessed the constraints and the limitations, particularly on the Israeli side, to extract the maximum gains possible in this episode.

NOTES

1. In his memoirs Kissinger wrote, "We were not, to be frank, too eager for a breakthrough at Kilometer 101 before the Geneva Conference" (Kissinger 1979, 752).

2. Seale went as far as writing, "In the service of the Jewish state, he [Kissinger] may one day be seen to rank only behind Theodor Herzl and David Ben-Gurion" (1988, 260).

CHAPTER 12

THE ISRAELI-EGYPTIAN PEACE TREATY: AN OPPORTUNITY NOT MISSED

1979

THE LEAD-UP TO THE Israeli-Egyptian peace treaty was almost as dramatic as the treaty itself. When Sadat landed in Tel Aviv in November 1977, he became the first Arab leader ever to officially visit Israel. The drama continued ten months later with the signing of the Camp David Accords on the White House lawn on September 17, 1978, culminating in the Israeli-Egyptian Treaty, sealed on March 26, 1979. The process through which the parties arrived at the treaty, with the intensive and extensive diplomatic involvement of the United States, was neither quick nor smooth. Yet the final outcome signified that for the first time in the modern history of the Arab-Israeli conflict, an opportunity for peace had not been missed. The aim of this chapter is to analyze the conditions that facilitated the attainment of this treaty. By focusing on the circumstances that helped the actors seize the opportunity, it will be possible to draw some important lessons with regard to why this opportunity had not been missed.

THE EPISODE

With the signing of the second Egyptian-Israeli Disengagement Agreement in September 1975, US president Ford and secretary of state Kissinger and Presidents Sadat and Rabin exhausted the step-by-step formula. Still, until the end of Ford's term the following year, Sadat and Rabin continued testing each other's readiness to move forward. But the meetings held between Israeli, Egyptian, and American officials through several intermediaries—the United States, Morocco, and Romania—did not yield any results. In addition, the Lebanese Civil War, which erupted in April 1975, had significant ramifications for the Arab world and prevented Egypt and the other Arab countries from serious further exploration of the road to peace. However, with the subsiding of the civil war at the end of 1976 and the growing stability in the oil market following the post-1973 energy crisis, Sadat and the Saudis again pursued, via the United States, a pragmatic position in the Arab-Israeli conflict (Quandt 2005, 179; Stein 1999, 184–185).

The election of Jimmy Carter as the new American president in January 1977 and the entrance of a democratic administration to office offered a possible change in the US position with regard to the Middle East. But Carter came to the presidency with scant experience in foreign affairs and even less knowledge of the Arab-Israeli conflict. The new secretary of state Cyrus Vance and national security adviser Zbigniew Brzezinski had similarly little exposure to the Middle East scene, though both had been involved in the Middle East study group at the Brookings Institution in Washington. The two, as well as William Quandt, played key roles in drafting the 1975 Brookings report "Toward Peace in the Middle East," which guided the new administration's thinking. The report adopted a comprehensive approach, calling for peace agreements between the parties based on an almost full Israeli withdrawal to the 1967 borders, the establishment of a Palestinian autonomy or entity federated with Jordan, resettlement of the Palestinian refugees, provision of UN guarantees, and Soviet involvement in the process (Stein 1999, 182, 188). In short, the new US administration was convinced that "the step-by-step approach had run out of steam" (quoted in ibid., 187). A return to the concept of an international conference seemed the most appropriate alternative.

Within a short time, the United States began to explore the possibilities with potential actors. Shuttle diplomacy was renewed with vigor. In February, Vance visited Amman, Cairo, Damascus, Jerusalem, and Riyadh; between March and May, Carter too met Israeli, Egyptian, Jordanian, Syrian, and Saudi leaders. Carter had a particularly disappointing meeting with Rabin, who gave him the impression that he was not prepared to enter serious negotiations. It is possible that Rabin's declared preference for Ford in the US elections had adverse effects on their relationship (Quandt 2005, 182; Stein 1999, 192; Margalit 1997, 12–13). Following the meeting, Carter declared that there would have to be a substantial Israeli withdrawal with only some minor adjustments to the 1967 borders. In addition, on March 16 he issued the Clinton Declaration, which supported the idea of a homeland for the Palestinians (Stein 1999, 193). Thus, the US position was in favor of reconvening the Geneva Conference; Israeli withdrawal, with only minor modifications, to the 1967 borders; and recognition of Palestinian rights. The new American policy undoubtedly alienated the Rabin government and damaged the Labor Party's prospects of winning the elections, slated for May that year. In contrast, Sadat expressed a more forthcoming position, including willingness to accept the idea that peace would entail recognition of Israel and normal relations with it (Quandt 2005, 183). It is possible that Sadat contemplated signing a separate agreement without completely resolving the Palestinian issue or worrying about Jordan's abstention from the peace process. In any case, it seems that Sadat and Carter developed excellent rapport from the outset (Stein 1999, 195–196).

The Israeli elections, held on May 17, 1977, resulted in the victory of the Likud Party, under the leadership of Menachem Begin. The results were not only a political "ballot box revolution" but also a major ideological shift, as Likud was more committed to the territorial preservation of Greater Eretz Israel, particularly the biblical areas of Judea and Samaria (the Jewish term for the West Bank) and the expansion of the settlements in this area. As heir to Ze'ev Jabotinsky's right-wing platform, and having sat in the opposition's stalls in Israeli politics for the better part of three decades (except when he was part of Golda Meir's National Unity government in 1967–1970), Begin was an enigma to all the actors involved in the peace process. Their initial reaction was a combination of astonishment, bewilderment, and disappointment at his election (Quandt 2005, 183; Stein 1999, 198; Shlaim 2000, 352–354). They soon discovered, however, that Begin was willing to display a certain flexibility regarding some issues that were outside his core ideological beliefs. Begin adhered to Jabotinsky's Iron Wall philosophy, which did not preclude the possibility of peace with the Arabs once they recognized the strength of the Jewish state. In his desire to be accepted as a legitimate prime minister, Begin offered the post of foreign minister to the Labor Party's Moshe Dayan—a revered hero of the 1967 War whose image was tarnished by the 1973 War, and who very much wanted to correct this. With the moderate minister of defense Ezer Weizman and the participation in the coalition of a new centrist party—the Democratic Movement for Change, under the leadership of renowned archaeologist and former chief of staff Yigael Yadin—Begin succeeded in softening the government's hawkish image.

Upon Begin's first visit to Washington (July 19–20), American officials were surprised to see "more flexibility in substance and procedure than they had anticipated" (Stein 1999, 199). He expressed a willingness to reconvene the Geneva Conference and presented a more moderate position than Rabin regarding withdrawal from Sinai. In general, he was opposed to partial agreements and favored comprehensive treaties. He was, however, opposed to recognizing Palestinian rights, either in the form of their having an independent delegation to the Geneva talks or the creation of a political entity in the West Bank and Gaza (Quandt 2005, 184–185; Stein 1999, 198–200; Tamir 1988, 32; Peleg 1987). Over the next few months the United States attempted to bridge the gaps between the possible parties to the conference, but Syrian insistence on a unified Arab delegation (to "supervise" a possible deviation of an independent Egyptian delegation) and Israeli refusal to include PLO members were considerable obstacles to any progress. Sadat was growing impatient with all the time-consuming discussions about the Palestinians, complaining that "peace is slipping through my fingers for procedural reasons" (Stein 1999, 208).

On August 25, Romanian president Nicolae Ceausescu met Begin and discussed the possibility of a meeting between Begin and Sadat in Bucharest.[1] According to Begin's biographer, he insinuated that he would be willing to accept full withdrawal for a peace treaty with Egypt (Shilon 2007, 283–284; Segev 2008, 175). Two months later, Sadat met the Romanian president, who told him emphatically that "Begin wants a solution" (Sadat 1978, 306). The meetings in Romania paved the way for several secret meetings between Israeli and Egyptian envoys in Morocco; this began in early July with a meeting between the head of the Israeli Mossad, Yitzhak Hofi, and Hasan al-Tuhami, Egypt's deputy prime minister, continued with King Hasan's meeting with Dayan in late August, and ended with the latter's meeting with Tuhami on September 16. In the last meeting, Tuhami made it clear that in return for full Israeli withdrawal from the occupied territories and a solution to the Palestinian problem (he mentioned here the establishment of an enclave connected with Jordan, Egypt, and Saudi Arabia), Egypt would be willing to sign a peace agreement that would surely be followed by Syria and Jordan. A controversial point was whether in return Dayan promised or signaled to Tuhami Israel's willingness to return all of Sinai (according to Egyptian sources), or merely pledged to convey Tuhami's ideas to Begin (according to Israeli sources) (Segev 2008, 173–181; Stein 1999, 206–207; Dayan 1981, 38–54; Shlaim 2000, 358; Shilon 2007, 285–286). These contradictory versions may be reconciled with the assessment that whatever Dayan told Tuhami, the latter's impression—conveyed to Sadat—was that Israel would fully withdraw from Sinai in return for peace.[2] All these positive signals affected Sadat's decision to go to Jerusalem (Fahmi 1983, 253; Boutros-Ghali 1997, 134; Dayan 1981, 87–88; Bar-Siman-Tov 1994, 244).

The lack of progress toward convening the international conference led the United States and the Soviet Union to issue a joint declaration on October 1 stating that "The only right and effective way for achieving a fundamental solution to all aspects of the Middle East problem in its entirety is negotiations within the framework of the Geneva Peace Conference," and that a comprehensive settlement should resolve key issues such as Israeli withdrawal from territories occupied in 1967 and resolution of the Palestinian problem, "including insuring the legitimate rights of the Palestinian people" (Stein 1999, 214–215). The United States might have hoped that Soviet involvement would bring in Syria and the PLO, but, regardless, the text infuriated Israel; Dayan was sent to Washington and managed, with the help of the Jewish lobby, to draft a six-point working paper, which served to water down the meaning of the joint declaration (Stein 1999, 218–219; Quandt 2005, 189–190).

At this point in late October 1977, when the road to the Geneva Conference was certainly bumpy if not blocked, Carter urged Sadat, in a personal and confidential letter, to take "dramatic action" to save the peace process (Carter 1982, 295; Stein 1999, 221; Sadat 1978, 301–302). This suggests the kind of intimacy the two had developed in the short period since Carter's election. And Sadat did not disappoint his new friend; he thought that to deal with the psychological barrier, "we ought to find a completely new approach that would bypass all formalities and procedural technicalities by pulling down the barrier of mutual mistrust" (Sadat 1982, 303–304). On November 3 he called for the convening of a multilateral peace conference in East Jerusalem,[3] to be attended by no less than ten members: the United States, the Soviet Union, China, France, Britain, Israel, Syria, Jordan, Egypt, and the PLO. The aim of such a meeting was to prepare the way for the Geneva Conference and persuade Israel that genuine peace would be possible only with full withdrawal to the 1967 borders and the acceptance of a Palestinian state (Carter 1982, 296; Stein 1999, 222; Sadat 1978, 306–308). After Carter convinced Sadat that this innovative idea was not practical, he thought of another groundbreaking idea: a personal visit to Jerusalem and a speech in the Knesset. Sadat was highly motivated in linking the visit to the Muslim holiday of 'Id al-Adkha, thus exploiting the opportunity to pray at al-Aqsa Mosque on this particular religious holiday (Sadat 1978, 308; Podeh 2011, 95).

Sadat announced his new initiative during his speech at the opening of the new session of the People's Assembly, on November 9. He offered "to go to the end of the world, not excluding Israel, in order to avoid the unnecessary wounding, not to mention killing, of a single soldier" (Sadat 1978, 308). Though taken by surprise, Begin was quick to respond and pick up the gauntlet: he invited Sadat to visit Jerusalem, and the same invitation was extended as well to King Husayn and the Syrian and Lebanese presidents. The United States had not been consulted in advance and feared that Sadat's initiative would sidetrack the concept of the Geneva Conference and might even endanger the possibility of peace (Stein 1999, 225). Many Egyptian officials did not treat Sadat's initiative seriously; they saw it as a "publicity stunt" (Fahmi 1983, 256). In more analytical terms, Sadat offered a "self-binding commitment." By making this offer in front of a worldwide audience, he chose public opinion as the outside third party with whom "insurance" was deposited. Reneging on such a commitment would have had a tremendous diplomatic price. With that, Sadat increased the costs of defection for himself and for Israel (Maoz and Felsenthal 1987, 191–192).

Begin's quick invitation and Sadat's immediate acceptance changed reality. As a result, Foreign Minister Fahmi submitted his resignation; Muhammad Riyad, the minister of state for foreign affairs, declined to accept the post and resigned as well (Fahmi 1983, 277–278). At the last moment before the visit, Boutros Boutros-Ghali was nominated as the minister of state for foreign affairs.[4]

On November 19, Sadat made history by being the first Arab leader ever to visit Israel; the following day he delivered a moving speech in the Knesset, in which the word "peace" was used no less than seventy-two times (Sadat 1978, 330–343). He made it clear that he did not come to sign a separate Egyptian-Israeli agreement or a third disengagement agreement. He offered a comprehensive peace agreement, based on the complete Israeli withdrawal from the territories occupied in 1967 and the attainment of rights for the Palestinians, including their right to establish their own state. The Palestinian issue was described as "the crux of the entire problem," which would prevent a durable and just peace if not solved. In return, Israel would be able to live in the region with its neighbors in security and peace. "Before us today," Sadat stated, "lies the appropriate chance for peace. If we are really serious in our endeavor for peace, it is a chance that may never come again" (Sadat 1978, 338). When it was Begin's turn to take to the podium, he acknowledged the differences between the Israeli and Egyptian positions but emphasized that "everything is negotiable."[5] Expecting a grand Israeli gesture equivalent in magnitude and significance to his visit, Sadat was disappointed by Begin's words. Avi Shlaim was of the opinion that Begin "was unable to rise to the historic occasion" (2000, 361). Perhaps the main problem was that Sadat and Begin, in contrast to Sadat and Carter, did not develop mutual trust and that the visit—in spite of its success and impact—"did not overturn deeply embedded fears about Arabs, in general, or remove anxieties that Israelis possessed for Egypt's leadership role in the Arab world" (Stein 1999, 229). Though Begin offered no gesture, it seems that some progress was made during the visit regarding the questions of Egyptian sovereignty over Sinai and its demilitarization (Stein 1999, 228–230; Shlaim 2000, 361; Dayan 1981, 81–86).

The ten months between the Jerusalem visit and the Camp David talks (November 1977–September 1978) saw a flurry of diplomatic activity. This began with a second meeting between Dayan and Tuhami in Morocco on December 2. Once again, Egypt, in view of Arab opposition, expressed its refusal to sign a separate bilateral agreement, insisted on complete Israeli evacuation of settlements in Sinai, and demanded a solution to the Palestinian problem (Shlaim 2000, 361–363; Dayan 1981, 91–97). The second round (December 13–15) was held at Mena House in Cairo; it was meant to be a preparatory meeting, with the participation of several Arab states and the superpowers, leading up to the Geneva Conference. Ultimately, only representatives from Israel, Egypt, the United States, and the United Nations attended; what is more, the talks were futile, though a direct communication line be-

tween Cairo and Jerusalem was established and some trust between the negotiators, particularly the military people, was built (Stein 1999, 236–238). The
third round was the Begin-Sadat summit, held in Isma'iliyya on December 25.
There Begin outlined the Israeli position regarding the bilateral peace treaty
and his limited self-rule plan for the Palestinians in the West Bank and Gaza.
He had already shown this autonomy plan to Carter in Washington a week
earlier. It was the first time that "Israel presented to the administration in
Washington a comprehensive peace plan" (Yaari, Haber, and Schiff 1980, 177).
In Bar-Siman-Tov's view, the autonomy plan was "Begin's most creative idea
throughout the peace process, and it enabled, with some changes worked out
at the Camp David summit, the achievement of peace" (1994, 246).

While some of the conceptual seeds for the Camp David Agreements were
planted here, the gap between the two parties was still wide, revolving around
four issues: the Israeli settlements in Sinai; the implementation of UN Resolution 242 on all fronts; the demilitarization of Sinai; and the need to find a
solution to the Palestinian problem. Begin thought the meeting was a success, while Sadat believed it was a complete failure. In any case, it was decided
that the political and military talks would be separated and held, respectively,
in Jerusalem and Cairo (Stein 1999, 241–243; Shlaim 2000, 365–366; Yaari,
Haber, and Schiff 1980, 182–201; Tamir 1988, 34–36; Kamel 1986, 21–27;
Dayan 1981, 102–105). While some progress was made on the military track,
the political talks ran into difficulties as Begin allegedly treated the Egyptian
foreign minister, Ibrahim Kamel, in a patronizing way—behavior that led
Sadat to recall his delegation. By taking this dramatic step, Sadat "sent a message to the Americans that the talks had reached a crisis and were in need of
rescue" (Stein 1999, 247; Kamel 1986, 53–71).[6]

Initially, the United States had difficulty adjusting to the new reality created after Sadat's visit; Carter's administration preferred pursuing the Geneva
Conference path instead of Sadat's bilateral diplomacy. By late 1977, according
to Carter's testimony, "It was becoming obvious that Sadat and Begin alone
could not go very far in resolving the basic problems that had not been
touched—the Palestinian issue, the withdrawal of Israeli forces from occupied
territory, Israeli security, or the definition of a real peace" (1982, 298). Meeting
Sadat in Aswan in early January 1978, Carter was impressed by the Egyptian
leader's conviction to move toward real and permanent peace (ibid., 302–303).
From that moment, wrote Stein, "Carter took it upon himself to keep the
negotiating process moving and to try to broaden the circle of negotiations
to include [other] Arab partners" (1999, 248). To that end, he met Sadat and
Begin in Washington in February and March 1978, respectively, offering renewed versions of ideas that had originated in the discussions at the White
House and the State Department. American pressure on Begin was particu-

larly unrelenting. It became obvious to Carter that Begin, in contrast to the moderate voices of Dayan and Weizman, "was becoming an insurmountable obstacle to further peace" (1982, 312). Meeting Begin on May 1 on the occasion of Israel's thirtieth anniversary, Carter told him that "peace in the Middle East was in his hands, that he had a unique opportunity to either bring it into being or kill it." Carter added, in his diary, that his guess was that Begin "will not take the necessary steps to bring peace to Israel—an opportunity that may never come again" (1982, 313). Another effort to bridge the gap was made in a tripartite meeting of Israeli, Egyptian, and American representatives on July 17–19 at Leeds Castle in England. These talks did not bring any breakthrough either, but, according to a top American official, they were "the best, freest, farthest-ranging and honest discussions of underlying issues" to date (quoted in Stein 1999, 250; Yaari, Haber, and Schiff 1980, 293–297; Kamel 1986, 208–219; Dayan 1981, 138–148).

In all the meetings held since Sadat's visit incremental progress was made in narrowing Egyptian and Israeli views, but it was not sufficient for an agreement. At this point Carter was in a quandary; many Democratic officials urged him to disengage himself from the peace process as a kind of damage control. Eventually, against the recommendations of Secretary of State Vance, Carter decided "it would be best, win or lose, to go all out." He then sent Vance to the Middle East to invite Begin and Sadat for an extensive negotiating session at Camp David. Both leaders were more than eager to receive the invitation. In his gamble, Carter demonstrated the profound US commitment to advancing the peace process (Carter 1982, 316; Quandt 2005, 197; Shlaim 2000, 371; Stein 1999, 251).

The Camp David talks extended from September 5 to 17, 1978, during which time no member of the negotiating delegations left the grounds of the presidential retreat to ensure that nothing would be leaked to the press. They concluded when an agreement was produced, which became the basis for the Egyptian-Israeli peace treaty, signed six months later. The analysis of the talks is beyond the scope of this research (Quandt 1986, Carter 1982, 319–403; Yaari, Haber, and Schiff 1980, 298–353), but it is important to highlight some of the points that ensured this opportunity did not slip away. Moshe Dayan gave a vivid account of the talks:

> It [i.e., the talks] proved the decisive, most difficult and least pleasant stage in the Egypt-Israel peace negotiations. The differences between the stands taken by Carter, Sadat and Begin were abundant, wide and basic, and all three parties had to resolve agonizing psychological and ideological crises in order to reach an agreed arrangement. It meant abandoning long-held traditional viewpoints and outlooks and taking up new positions. The deliberations were

marked by sharp and often bitter arguments between us and the Egyptians, and even more so with the Americans. (1981, 153–154)

In retrospect it is clear that each of the three leaders was earnestly coveting an agreement. This was manifested in the composition of their delegations and the seriousness with which all concerned took the discussions. On the Israeli side, Begin was considered tough, while his leading ministers Dayan and Weizman were more flexible (Shilon 2007, 302). The reverse was true for the Egyptian delegation: Sadat was the flexible one, and his team—mainly from the Foreign Office—quite steadfast. Sadat continued the talks even when his foreign minister, Ibrahim Kamel, and his advisers criticized his approach, particularly with regard to his concessions on the Palestinian issue (Boutros-Ghali 1997, 151). Interestingly, in terms of content, the first five days at Camp David were rather futile, but then the United States presented a draft paper on September 10 that became the basis for the final agreement, although its wording was fine-tuned some twenty-three times. Here, Carter's personal involvement and commitment in the mediation process was crucial: at times, he offered inducements or exerted pressure on the parties; but mainly he played on what he considered each side's main weaknesses (Shlaim 2000, 373; Carter 1982, 319–403; Touval 1982, 318–320; Boutros-Ghali 1997, 151).

The element of the talks relating to Egyptian-Israeli relations was less contentious than those concerning the Palestinian problem or its possible linkage to the bilateral treaty. They covered issues such as the demilitarization of Sinai, the dismantling of Israeli airfields and settlements there, and the supply of oil to Israel. The settlement issue was possibly the most difficult for Begin to stomach, as it could serve as a precedent to evacuating Jewish settlements in Judea, Samaria, and the Golan, so he made it conditional on ratification by the Knesset. Eventually, the section in the agreement that dealt with Egyptian-Israeli relations specified that a peace treaty would be signed within three months based on the following principles: complete Israeli withdrawal from Sinai and recognition of Egyptian sovereignty over it; demilitarization of most of Sinai; the stationing of UN forces to supervise demilitarization and to ensure freedom of navigation in the Suez Canal; and the establishment of normal relations, including full recognition, termination of economic boycott, and diplomatic relations. It was agreed that the same principles would apply to peace agreements on other fronts (Shlaim 2000, 375; Quandt 2005, 197–203; Kamel 1986, 294–382; Tamir 1988, 50–86; Dayan 1981, 153–180).

Most of the discussions at Camp David, however, revolved around the Palestinian issue, as it was crucial for Sadat to make a show of Arab solidarity and refute the recurring accusation that Egypt had abandoned the Palestinians. The section in the agreement on Palestinian autonomy was longer than that on Israeli-Egyptian relations and more ambiguous too. The responsibility for dealing with the issue was laid on Egypt, Israel, Jordan, and representatives of the Palestinian people from the West Bank and Gaza (but not members of the PLO). The agreement envisaged the establishment of "full autonomy" for the Palestinians (the Hebrew version of the term was the "Arabs of Eretz Israel" so as not to recognize a separate identity)[7] within a period of five years. The Israeli military government and its civil administration would withdraw as soon as a self-governing authority had been freely elected by the local inhabitants. This would be followed by a withdrawal of Israeli armed forces and redeployment of remaining forces in specified security locations. When the self-governing authority was established, the transitional period of five years would commence; as soon as possible, but not later than the third year, negotiations would be held to determine the final status of the area and its relationship with its neighbors and to conclude a peace treaty between Israel and Jordan. The question of Jerusalem was dealt with in two separate letters to Carter, in which each party stated its position on the subject. With regard to the settlements in the West Bank there was a vague promise by Begin to freeze additional construction, though later he claimed it was for only three months (Stein 1999, 253–255; Shlaim 2000, 375; Laqueur and Rubin 1984, 611–613). Though the Israeli-Egyptian and Palestinian autonomy sections were included in the one document, it did not make a direct link between the two or make the implementation of one part conditional upon the other; thus, the seeds of separation between the two issues were sown.

The signing of the Camp David Agreement on September 17, 1978, was an impressive victory for all, and certainly for American diplomacy. The Israeli Knesset ratified it by an overwhelming majority (eighty-four in favor, nineteen against, and seventeen abstentions), including many votes of the opposition Labor Party. This result more or less reflected the attitude of the Israeli public, as polls indicated that 82 percent approved of the agreement (Bar-Siman-Tov 1998, 18). Sadat was in a more delicate position: in contrast to the overwhelming joy of the American and Israeli delegations, "the Egyptian delegates were despondent" (Boutros-Ghali 1997, 151). Foreign Minister Kamel submitted his resignation in protest of the concessions made by Sadat; it was the third resignation of a foreign minister in a short time (Kamel 1986, 370–382). When Sadat returned to Cairo he was warmly received by the masses, but his welcome was probably staged. The People's Assembly received his speech with fanfare, but many Egyptians, according to Boutros-Ghali, "were negative about Camp David" (1997, 157).[8] Beyond its own borders, Egypt's diplomatic isolation in the Arab world was gaining momentum: much to Sadat's chagrin, Jordan, Morocco, and Saudi Arabia, the moderate Arab states that not long before had backed his policies, were now riled that the agreement

did not assert the Palestinians' right to self-determination through the creation of a Palestinian state, nor did it mention the PLO or the Arab right to
Jerusalem. By November this opposition crystallized in the resolutions of the
Arab summit in Baghdad, which disavowed the Camp David Agreement and
made public a list of sanctions on Egypt to be applied when a peace treaty with
Israel was signed (Boutros-Ghali 1997, 154–155, 162; Sela 1998, 202–203). In
order to strengthen his position domestically, Sadat named a new prime minister, Mustafa Khalil, and replaced Minister of War Gamasy with Kamal Hasan
'Ali, while Boutros-Ghali remained the acting foreign minister.

The final peace treaty was to be signed within three months, but the negotiations proved to be more difficult than expected, ending only on March
26, 1979. Talks resumed in Washington on October 12 at the foreign ministers' level; they were "protracted, arduous and punctuated by crises" (Shlaim
2000, 378; Quandt 2005, 205). Several key issues delayed the negotiations:
the timing of Israeli withdrawals in Sinai in relation to the establishment of
diplomatic ties with Egypt; the linkage between the Egyptian-Israeli peace
treaty and a comprehensive settlement in general and the Palestinian issue in
particular; and finally, the question of whether the treaty with Israel super-
seded Egypt's commitment, under the Arab League Security Pact, to help
other Arab states in case of war against Israel. In addition, there were the
questions of US financial and military commitments to both Egypt and Israel,
Israel's demand for guaranteed oil supplies, and compensation for Israel in
return for withdrawing from the strategic airfields in Sinai (Stein 1999, 257;
Shlaim 2000, 378–379; Quandt 2005, 209–228; Boutros-Ghali 1997, 166–167).
During this phase, Carter and his team played a crucial role in mediating between the parties; Carter in particular was committed to the process, and
in early March 1979 he visited both countries—"an act of desperation," he
wrote in his diary (1982, 416)—in a last-ditch effort to overcome the differences. His gamble now, according to Quandt, was less hazardous than his
decision to go to Camp David, since "he had every reason to believe his trip
would be crowned with success" after Sadat had given him carte blanche to
negotiate the final text of the treaty with Israel (2005, 228). Carter's talks with
Begin in Jerusalem proved to be nerve-wracking; while Sadat paid attention
mainly to the great picture, Begin was obsessed with the details. At one point,
Weizman was quoted to the effect that "I have had enough; because of all this
nonsense we are about to miss the opportunity for peace" (Yaari, Haber, and
Schiff 1980, 383). With his now established mediation skills, Carter managed
to finalize the agreement (Carter 1982, 228–235).

The peace treaty, in contrast to the Camp David Agreement, dealt exclusively with Egyptian-Israeli relations. The only reference to nonbilateral issues
was included in the preamble, where it stated that the treaty "is an important

step in the search for comprehensive peace in the area and for the attainment of settlement of the Arab-Israeli conflict in all its aspects."[9] In addition, a joint letter from Sadat and Begin to Carter promised to start negotiations on autonomy for the West Bank and Gaza within a month of the treaty's ratification. These references could not conceal the fact that essentially Sadat had consented to a separate deal with Israel, as his ministers and advisers had feared. The long document listed all the security arrangements, the timing and procedure of withdrawal, as well as various aspects of normalization and diplomatic relations. On March 22 the Knesset approved the peace treaty by an overwhelming majority: ninety-five in favor, eighteen against, and just two abstentions. It was a bigger majority than for the Camp David Agreement (Bar-Siman-Tov 1998, 18–19). In Egypt, the vote in the People's Assembly gave the impression of unanimous support: 329 approved, 15 opposed, and one abstention. But there the public debate revealed serious opposition to the separate nature of the treaty, which many worried would lead to Egypt's further isolation in and ostracism by the Arab world. And then it happened: on March 27, 1979, the Arab League meeting in Baghdad decided to expel Egypt and to transfer its headquarters from Cairo to Tunis. Most of the Arab states severed their diplomatic ties with Egypt and put in place certain political and economic sanctions that had been adopted in Baghdad (see above) (Sela 1998, 207–211).

But the treaty held. On February 26, 1980, long before the completion of Israeli withdrawal from Sinai, which would be checked off two years later (April 25, 1982), diplomatic relations between Israel and Egypt were established. In fact, the peace agreement proved strong and resilient enough to withstand two highly significant events: the assassination of Anwar Sadat on October 6, 1981, and the Lebanese War in June 1982. Yet these events contributed to the emergence of a cold peace between the two states. It was not long before the negotiations over autonomy stalled, mainly as a result of Israeli reluctance to advance any solution that might imply it was conceding sovereignty over Judea and Samaria.

Divergent views exist regarding the rewards of the treaty for both sides. Eliahu Ben-Elissar, the first Israeli ambassador in Cairo, expressed a common Israeli view: "Nobody won and nobody lost; everyone got what was dearest to him" (1995, 268). That was not the refrain heard on the other side of the border: "I was not the only one to feel," wrote Boutros-Ghali, "that Israel was the winner and Egypt the loser in this treaty" (1997, 203).[10] The academic assessment tends to support the Egyptian view; Shlaim, for example, concluded, "In the final analysis Begin got what he wanted: a peace agreement with Egypt that stood on its own" (2000, 380). Similarly, Shibley Telhami argued that there were two primary bargaining issues: the extent of linkage between normalization and progress on the West Bank and Gaza, and the question of Jewish settlements in the West Bank and Gaza. On both issues, he contended, the outcome decidedly favored Israeli preferences. In his opinion, "both issues . . . could have been settled in a manner favoring Egyptian preferences. . . . Sadat's personality and the Egyptian system of government were largely responsible for the Egyptian failure in this regard" (Telhami 1990, 201). Undoubtedly, this sense of failure contributed to the coldness of the peace treaty.

ASSESSMENT

During the talks of the Israeli-Egyptian Political Committee in Jerusalem in January 1978, Boutros Boutros-Ghali told Yigael Yadin that "Sadat has presented a unique opportunity for peace; it must be seized" (1997, 54). Indeed, the Israeli-Egyptian peace treaty was the first historical opportunity in the century-old Arab-Israeli conflict that had not been missed. It is imperative, therefore, to analyze the reasons and circumstances that allowed the actors to succeed with this opportunity. Maoz wrote in this connection that "Sadat's initiative was an opportunity that could not be missed" (2004, 434). This kind of historical inevitability, however, precludes the possibility that the opportunity could most definitely have been missed if any of a number of elements were different. So what were the forces at work in this specific case study that enabled this opportunity to be realized?

It is more than obvious that the Sadat visit to Jerusalem and its "spinoff" events signified a great historical opportunity for signing a peace agreement. His gesture was unprecedented in Arab-Israeli relations; it was the first time that an Arab leader—particularly the one heading the most important and strongest Arab state—was willing to grant Israel unconditional recognition. There is no question that an event of this magnitude has the potential to transform reality—and history (Touval 1982, 289; Bar-Siman-Tov 1994, 244–245). The event in itself was sufficient to constitute a historical opportunity, yet it was buttressed by two other important developments that preceded it and somewhat paved the way for Sadat's otherwise-sudden visit: the election of a new Democratic administration in the United States led by Carter, who proved to be committed to transform American policy vis-à-vis the Arab-Israeli conflict, and the surprising election of Begin as Israel's prime minister and the replacement of the stalwart Labor Party with the Likud-led government. After eight failures in the opposition, Begin felt a burning urge to leave his mark on history: the view from "the top" may well have changed how he saw the country's future unfolding, driving him to make some painful national decisions. In addition, Laura Zittrain Eisenberg and Neil Caplan believe that the aborted joint American-Soviet declaration in October 1977 "became the common catalyst that created one of the rare historic moments when two Middle Eastern leaders found the path of mutual recognition and direct negotiations preferable to all other available options" (1998, 31–32).

Thus 1977 saw several major turning points, which, taken together, served as the greatest historical opportunity in Arab-Israeli relations. In addition, Sadat's visit served as a highly attractive offer, though it did not entail, by itself, a well-thought-out peace plan. The visit can be seen as a kind of "mega-incentive" to the other party, as it could not be ignored or bypassed. Sadat was aware of the magnitude of his initiative and therefore was highly disappointed by the absence of a significant Israeli counter-gesture. The protracted negotiations over eighteen months that took place between the visit and the signing of the peace accord showed that "inevitability" was not a term that could define this process. The many personal accounts that describe the negotiations demonstrate that the possibility of failure could not be overruled (Dayan 1981; Kamel 1986; Boutros-Ghali 1997; Fahmy 1983; Riyad 1981).

Having established the existence of a historical opportunity, it is necessary to analyze the variables of a missed opportunity, which, in this case, operated in a way that enabled the actors to seize the opportunity. The first variable in our definition relates to the legitimacy level of the political leadership; both Begin and Sadat enjoyed a wide measure of legitimacy and were thought of as strong leaders capable of taking significant decisions. The fact that Begin enjoyed a clear majority in the Knesset following the elections suggested that his coalition too had the strength and confidence to endorse tough decisions. Moreover, being the leader of a right-wing government meant that Begin could count on the support of the leftist parties in questions relating to the peace process. While previous Israeli governments, particularly Rabin's, refrained from offering concessions for fear of criticism from the right-wing parties, the Likud government "embodied the right wing and possessed impeccable ultranationalist credentials" (Touval 1982, 287–288; Eisenberg and Caplan 1998, 33). Indeed, the Camp David Accords and the peace treaty received unprecedented support in the Knesset. At no point was there any real danger that the government would not be able to implement its peace policy because of domestic opposition (Bar-Siman-Tov 1994, 251). In addition, Begin enjoyed the position of an undisputed leader within his party: Ezer Weizman, upon retiring from the army and joining the Likud, wrote that he was surprised to find himself in a civil organization headed by a commander that everybody obeyed and with whom nobody dared to argue (1982, 100).

The Israeli public, according to polls, broadly supported the Camp David and peace treaties. The benefits of peace were perceived to exceed the costs, and the general feeling in society was that "Israel had to do its utmost not to squander a rare chance for peace" (Bar-Siman-Tov 1994, 248). Yet in spite of the wide support in government, the Knesset, and among the public of peace with Egypt, Begin needed and sought legitimacy during the phase in which his policy was being formulated. He invested efforts to acquire four types of legitimacy: governmental, factional (that is, of his Herut Party), parliamentary, and extra-parliamentary (ibid., 252–257). This strategy enhanced Begin's ability to successfully complete the process he had set in motion.

In contrast, Sadat, though not presiding over a democratic system, was generally thought of as a legitimate leader, particularly after the October War, the results of which boosted his leadership and legitimacy. His ministers and advisers were well aware of his tendency to exploit his position at the helm. Fahmi wrote that "politically, there was no internal pressure on Sadat. He was firmly in control and the opposition was negligible" (1983, 282). When Fahmi, who strongly opposed the Jerusalem visit, asked Sadat to consult with top members of the National Security Council about the move, he replied: "I will not discuss it with anybody, I don't care for anybody's opinion" (ibid., 275). Boutros-Ghali, who replaced Fahmi, admitted that he and his foreign affairs advisers "feared that Sadat would make concessions far beyond our worst fears." This stemmed from the fact that "Sadat was the boss. He could ignore his advisers, bypass the Assembly, override the wishes of the Egyptian people, and he enjoyed demonstrating his power" (1997, 165). Sadat was in a unique position to advance his policy, which was not necessarily supported by his ministers and certainly not by the public. In short, as Eisenberg and Caplan concluded, "This initiative was undertaken by heads of state whose leadership within their respective camps was virtually unchallenged" (1998, 32).

The second variable relates to the leaders' willingness to take bold steps. As demonstrated in previous chapters, Sadat saw his February 1971 initiative as the beginning of a journey to peace; the idea of visiting Jerusalem was imaginative and bold, but the road was actually paved during the six years preceding it. The harsh social and economic problems caused by the demographic explosion, which spurred the "bread riots" in Egypt in January 1977, served as a reminder of the necessity for stability and security. Sadat's inclination toward bold and dramatic decisions was also behind his decision to launch the October War. His ministers and advisers were very familiar with this tendency; criticizing Sadat, Fahmi wrote that the Israelis "must have known his weakness for the *grand geste*, for the unprecedented step and the dramatic move made regardless of risk" (1983, 283). The Jerusalem visit, in his view, stemmed from Sadat's desire to become an international hero and the lauded peacemaker (ibid., 283–284). It is highly possible that Sadat's character and behavior—particularly his flair for drama—drove his decision to visit Jerusalem. Fahmi was probably correct in assessing that Sadat had no good reason to make the visit since Egypt had already lost its main negotiating card: refusal to recognize Israel (ibid., 279). But at the same time, the peace treaty was the consummation of a long process, which attested to Sadat's sincere conviction to end the conflict. This commitment was echoed in Boutros-Ghali's assertion that the peace treaty for Sadat "was far more important than the details we kept raising with him. Sadat followed his vision" (1997, 196). Moreover, his vision was so broad that those involved throughout the negotiations could not help but notice that while Begin was obsessed with the smallest details (Sadat and Kamel described him as a "petty shopkeeper" [Kamel 1986, 31]), Sadat "had no patience with details" (Boutros-Ghali 1997, 46; Yaari, Haber, and Schiff 1980, 180, 186). It was in his character, then, according to Boutros-Ghali, that "Sadat wanted the Camp David meetings to end with an international document, no matter what the price" (1997, 137–138).

Begin could not have been a more diametrically different partner. In contrast to Sadat, Begin was a kind of enigma. He came onto this stage suffering from a negative image in the West and the Arab world because of his activist anti-British role as the leader of the militant Etzel organization during the Mandate period. In addition, Begin's right-wing ideology seemed a potential impediment to any future peace talks. Yet the makeup of the Likud government and Begin's early statements reflected a sense of unexpected moderation vis-à-vis possible negotiations with the Arab states. In this context, it helped that Begin transmitted an image of a sturdy and confident leader. Sadat told Dayan that the Romanian president, Nicolae Ceausescu, had told him that Begin was tough enough to take daring decisions (1981, 87; Grosbard 2006, 182). On another occasion, Sadat said that he could count on only two strong Israeli leaders: Begin and Golda Meir; Rabin, in his opinion, was "a weak man" (Ben-Elissar 1995, 152). Carter had the same opinion; in his diary he wrote, as early as July 1977, that "My own guess is that if we give Begin support, he will prove to be a strong leader, quite different from Rabin" (1982, 290). Moreover, there are indications that Begin entered office determined to leave his mark on history. Peace with Egypt did not contradict Jabotinsky's Iron Wall strategy of compromise with the Arabs on the basis of their recognition of Israel's strength (Shilon 2007, 277–278). This image of Begin would be validated; he was willing and capable of making bold decisions as long as they did not stand in contrast to his core ideology beliefs, particularly the preservation of the biblical territories of Judea and Samaria. The peace treaty with Egypt, dissociated as it was from the Palestinian part of Camp David, dovetailed with his interests and ideology.

The third variable is the history of past interactions between the parties to the conflict, which influenced the level of trust existing between them. By 1977, Egyptian-Israeli relations had gone through a decade of contacts and negotiations, culminating in the signing of two disengagement agreements and secret meetings held in Morocco and Romania. These talks were essential building blocks for developing confidence and mutual testing of intentions. They proved that the distance between the two states on bilateral issues was not wide (Stein 1999, 268; Quandt 2005, 236). During this period, then, a modicum of trust was built between them, particularly between the representatives of their military establishments (Ali 1993; Tamir 1988). Still, suspicion and mistrust prevailed; this was manifested, for example, in the public warning of the Israeli chief of staff, Mordechai Gur, that Sadat's visit was a shock ploy on the scale of the Yom Kippur War to deceive the Israeli army (Yaari, Haber, and Schiff 1980, 60). Sadat's claim was that the aim of the Jerusalem visit was to break the psychological barrier, which constituted, in his opinion, 70 percent of the conflict (1978, 336). In many ways, the gesture did much to cross the psychological threshold and even break down the emotional walls and barriers. Bar-Siman-Tov suggested that the visit "induced a peace ritual, a unique symbolic event that shattered many components of the Israeli belief system" (1994, 247). In addition, Sadat's "language, coupled with several emotional exchanges with leading Israeli personalities, touched a chord within the Israeli people, allowing Begin to be more forthcoming in negotiations than he might otherwise have dared to be" (Eisenberg and Caplan 1998, 39). Yet the protracted negotiations demonstrated that suspicion and mistrust did not completely evaporate after Sadat's visit. These emotions were apparent in the Sadat-Begin relations during the Camp David negotiations. In general, though, it is clear that the decade of contacts between Israel and Egypt, coupled by Sadat's grand gesture, helped mitigate the mutual suspicion and mistrust, and this, in turn, facilitated the realization of this historical opportunity.

The fourth variable is the level of the involvement of the third party that exploits the existence of a historical opportunity to promote a dialogue. The US involvement in the Arab-Israeli conflict was limited prior to the mid-1970s. It was Kissinger, under Nixon and Ford, who raised the US role to new heights and succeeded in concluding three disengagement agreements along the way. Yet Carter and his team played an even more significant role as mediators in the conflict. "Even after the [Sadat] visit," wrote Bar-Siman-Tov, "direct third-party intervention was needed in the peace process, a role that was fulfilled by President Jimmy Carter, without whose participation it would not have been possible to conclude a peace treaty" (1994, 245). Carter's extensive involvement stemmed from his inherently idealist nature; according to Quandt, he "deeply believed that men of goodwill could resolve problems by talking to one another." At Camp David, Quandt continued, "He initially thought he would need only to get Sadat and Begin together and help them overcome their mutual dislike. The agreement itself would then be worked out by the two leaders in a spirit of compromise and accommodation" (2005, 236). Beyond his idealistic character, Carter was committed to the mediation process out of conviction that the historical opportunity that presented itself should not be missed. He also appreciated the possible rewards he as president and the United States as superpower could reap by flying solo in leading the peace process. Upon the fall of the Iranian shah in 1979, hitherto the pillar of US policy in the Gulf, and the whiff of another approaching election year in the United States (1980), Carter was in dire need of a significant feat in the realm of foreign affairs. His mediation style included the use of both sticks and carrots (Touval 1982, 319). What also worked for Carter was the quick and satisfying rapport that he found with Sadat; in fact, the latter used to confide in Carter, revealing the lines that would not be crossed. Carter's relations with Begin were more formal and rigid. This fact did not always work to Sadat's advantage, as Carter also used this intimacy to elicit further concessions from Sadat. In contrast, Carter would intimidate Begin by pointing out how detrimental a failure would be to Carter himself and to Israeli-US relations. Since Begin and Sadat did not develop intimate and workable relations, Carter's role as mediator became even more important (Grosbard 2006, 211–212, 216–217; Dayan 1981, 145). At the signing ceremony of the Camp David Accords, both Sadat and Begin hailed Carter's role in their speeches; Begin even referred to Camp David as the "Jimmy Carter summit" (Grosbard 2006, 221). Years later, Shimon Peres acknowledged that "without the unique contribution of Jimmy Carter, there would have been no Camp David" (1995, 293). Carter, Sadat, and Begin were engaged in what Stein termed heroic diplomacy: "each took many risks; each was unconventional, creative, and committed to finding workable solutions. Vision, not fear of their shadows, guided them. They were leaders, not managers; statesmen, not timid politicians" (1999, 268).

The US mediation role was also important in minimizing the uncertainty problem, which caused anxiety on both sides. From an Israeli perspective, the acute problem was the exchange of territories, a tangible security asset, for peace, an abstract and intangible asset, as well as the fear that the peace might not outlive Sadat. From an Egyptian perspective, the main fear was that Israel would not fully honor its promise to withdraw from Sinai and evacuate the settlements. In a series of letters and oral promises, which also included political and financial support, the United States attempted to respond to these fears (Bar-Siman-Tov 1994, 248–250).

It should be emphasized, however, that although the mediator succeeded in inducing the parties to make concessions on issues that were associated with core values, those concessions did not involve basic policy changes. In most cases, the concessions represented only a willingness to accept ambiguous phrases as satisfactory or to agree to postpone the consideration of highly contentious problems. The really important ones—Israel's readiness to withdraw from Sinai and Egypt's readiness to recognize Israel—were made before the mediation began. "The mediator's contribution, however crucial and indispensable," Touval concluded, "did not bring about basic attitude changes or policy transformations, but only built on them" (1982, 319–320).

Some of the historical opportunities existing in previous episodes were missed as a result of the unsatisfactory response of the offered party. As we have seen, apathy, inaction, or indifference on the part of the offered party may seriously discourage the continuation of the dialogue regarding the offer. In many ways, Begin's reaction to Sadat's offer was swift, courageous, and bold. Yet the absence of a counter-gesture by the Israeli side left the Egyptian party disappointed and bitter. Moreover, Begin's lawyerly style of negotiations coupled with his tendency to be involved in every small detail often antagonized and even offended the Egyptian side; the eighteen months that lapsed between the Sadat visit and the signing of the treaty were fraught with setbacks and deadlocks. Yet the fact that the dialogue was never halted contributed to the feeling that all parties were interested in continuing the negotiations and probably in signing an agreement.

The Israeli-Egyptian negotiations, which culminated in the peace treaty, marked the first historical opportunity in the annals of the conflict that was not missed. An assessment of why this was the case shows that the very variables that led to wasting past opportunities now created a situation conducive to an agreement: the leaders on both sides were strong, enjoyed enough legitimacy, and were determined and committed to "heroic diplomacy." The past interactions between the parties were characterized by a minimum level of trust; added to Sadat's surprising gesture, the psychological barrier no longer constituted an impediment. In addition, a committed US president who was personally involved in the negotiations beginning at least with the Camp David summit helped facilitate the agreement. In short, all the ingredients that contributed in the past to missing opportunities worked now in the opposite direction.

It could be suggested that the Israeli-Egyptian negotiations also provided an opportunity to solve the Israeli-Palestinian issue. Yet in the absence of a recognized Palestinian representative and with Begin's ideological commitment to the Greater Eretz Israel platform, both the PLO and Begin had every reason to sabotage an agreement concerning the West Bank and Gaza. Begin's autonomy talks were only a ploy to show Sadat that the Palestinian element included in the Camp David Agreement had not been thoroughly abandoned. Once the bilateral peace treaty was concluded, Begin took various steps to impede the talks. He spelled his intention of claiming, at the end of the transitional period, Israeli sovereignty over the entire territory. This was the main issue that led to the resignation of both Dayan and Weizman from his government (Shlaim 2000, 381–383; Shamir 1988, 197–200). In other words, the autonomy talks were deadlocked long before the 1982 Lebanese War. Local Palestinian leaders in the West Bank and Gaza—under PLO pressure—also joined the chorus of Arab opposition. Thus, the Israeli-Egyptian talks, which had found common ground fertile enough to enable them to blossom into an agreement, were not the appropriate launching pad for an Israeli-Palestinian agreement. It would be another fourteen years before the world would learn of the Oslo Agreements.

NOTES

1. This idea was raised by Ceausescu for the first time when he met Golda Meir in 1971 (Segev 2008, 175).

2. Moshe Shachal, at that time member of the Knesset of the Labor Party and later minister in several governments, said that Dayan did mention full withdrawal in return for a full peace treaty (interview, December 31, 2012). It makes sense that if Begin had insinuated to the Romanian president his agreement to full withdrawal, as claimed by his biographer (Shilon 2007, 283), then Dayan may have reiterated this hint.

3. In his memoirs, Sadat speaks of a meeting in Jerusalem, at the Knesset and not East Jerusalem (1978, 306). Ism'ail Fahmi, the foreign minister, claims that it was his idea that Sadat accepted. He thought that the idea was "an effort to convince him [Sadat] to abandon his plan to go to Jerusalem" (1983, 255).

4. Boutros-Ghali was never nominated as minister of foreign affairs because he was a Copt, something which he openly resented throughout the period.

5. For the text, see http://www.jewishvirtuallibrary.org/jsource/History/begintoknes setsadat.html.

6. Kamel himself thought that the idea to recall the delegation was political and not connected to the incident, which only constituted the pretext (1986, 66–67). For a different version, see Tamir 1988, 44. Kamel's memoirs are a scathing criticism of Sadat and the agreement. In contrast to the rather neutral English title, the Arabic version is titled *The Lost Peace* (2003).

7. In a letter attached to the agreement in English, Carter acknowledged that the term "Palestinians" was construed by Begin as "Palestinian Arabs" and "West Bank" as Judea and Samaria. See Eisenberg and Caplan 1998, 178–179.

8. Personally, and in spite of his criticism of Sadat, Boutros-Ghali thought that "the Camp David agreement had many faults, but we had achieved an important step on the road to peace, perhaps not only to Jerusalem, but beyond Jerusalem" (1997, 152).

9. For the text, see http://www.mfa.gov.il/MFA/Peace%20Process/Guide%20to%20 the%20Peace%20Process/Israel-Egypt%20Peace%20Treaty.

10. In spite of his criticism, Boutros-Ghali wrote that "Egypt had sacrificed enough lives and money for the Arabs and the Palestinians. The time has come for Egypt to think of itself. Sadat's commitment to 'Egypt first' is justified, I thought" (1997, 207).

CHAPTER 13

THE ARAB PEACE PLAN AND THE REAGAN PLAN

SEPTEMBER 1982

WHEN SAUDI CROWN PRINCE Fahd gave an interview to the Saudi Press Agency on August 7, 1981, he unexpectedly announced an eight-point program for solving the Arab-Israeli conflict. The Fahd Plan, as it became known, was submitted for approval to the Arab summit in Fez, Morocco, but sharp Arab divisions over its terms led to the summit's collapse. A revised version—called the Arab Peace Plan—was submitted to the reconvened Fez summit on September 9, 1982, and unanimously approved by all the Arab states. Meanwhile, a week earlier, on September 1, US president Ronald Reagan published his plan for solving the conflict. The convergence of these plans was not coincidental, as the United States and the Arab states attempted—each according to its interests—to capitalize on the changes in the regional system in the aftermath of the Lebanese War (June–September 1982). This chapter will analyze if and to what extent these two plans constituted missed opportunities to solve the conflict.

THE EPISODE

The Saudi peace plan was born out of a combination of long- and short-term interests. Prior to its announcement, the Saudis had been playing different roles in three arenas: strategic partnership with the United States in the international system; a balancer in the Arab system; and leader in the Arabian Peninsula, perceived as its immediate sphere of influence (Gause 2002, 193). Saudi foreign policy reflected its security dilemma: the wide gap between its newly acquired economic and financial capabilities—a result of the oil boom—and its weak military capabilities highlighted the kingdom's vulnerability in the face of potential threats from the Soviet Union, Iran, and radical Arab neighbors (Safran 1988, 1–6; Quandt 1981, 1–12). Geographically remote from the Arab-Israeli stage, Saudi Arabia confined its support to subsidizing the Arab confrontation states according to the resolutions of the Arab summits. This was a kind of "insurance policy" aimed at securing the Palestinian flank of Saudi foreign policy. Yet, fearing that deterioration in the Arab-Israeli conflict would lead to a regional upheaval, Saudi Arabia's new wealth allowed it to deviate from its traditional balancing role and play a more prominent position in the Arab system in the post-1973 period. The change in the Saudi role stemmed from several developments. First, its economic capabilities were already being used as an instrument of influence in Arab politics. The power of the "purse strings" would remain acute as long as the oil boom continued. Second, following the 1967 and 1973 wars, Egypt became more dependent on the oil states, and its ability to pose a credible claim for Arab leadership was substantially reduced. Moreover, following the peace treaty with Israel, Egypt was marginalized in the Arab system as a result of the sanctions imposed by the Arab summits. Third, Iraq, another potential Arab power with military and economic capabilities, had been engaged in a war with Iran since September 1980. Thus Saudi Arabia emerged as a regional power by default, buoyed by the oil boom and the marginalization of both Egypt and Iraq (Kerr 1982, 1–14; Dessouki 1982, 319–344).

Thus, the Saudi elite increasingly developed a self-perception as leader of the Arabs, based on Saudi Arabia's tangible economic capabilities. This perception was magnified by the United States, which encouraged a "Pax Saudiana" in the Middle East (Binder 1982, 1–3). It was also a product of several relatively successful Saudi mediation attempts in the 1970s; in the realm of the Arab-Israeli conflict, Arab decisions were rarely taken without consulting Saudi Arabia or in the absence of its participation (Dawisha 1983, 678). Saudi Arabia also played a key role in the Lebanese crisis of spring and summer 1981, brokering a cease-fire between Israel and the PLO (Safran 1988, 249–256, 329–331). In the absence of any other credible Arab leader due to Iraq's war with Iran and Egypt's exclusion from the Arab system, these episodes led the Saudis to believe that indeed the "Saudi era" had finally dawned (Ajami 1999, 130).

The Fahd peace plan was a product of several Saudi interests. First, it aimed at securing the approval of the US Senate for selling AWACS aircraft and F-15 equipment to Saudi Arabia. After Reagan's authorization of these transactions was overridden by the Senate in June 1981, the Saudis invested considerable efforts to reverse the decision in the final vote. Second, by initiating a moderate plan that implicitly recognized Israel, the Saudis hoped to entice the United States to forge closer relations with it, the greater goal being to eventually bring about a US-PLO dialogue. Third, the plan meant to secure the support of Western European countries, which had attempted unsuccessfully to promote a joint peace initiative of their own during 1980–1981. In fact, the

Saudi plan incorporated certain elements of the European initiative and the Venice Declaration.[1] Finally, the plan offered an alternative framework to the Camp David Accords and the autonomy talks between Israel and Egypt, which reached a deadlock in 1980. The Saudis feared that the unresolved Palestinian issue might fester again once Israel completed its withdrawal from Sinai in April 1982. A peace plan based on recognized elements could perhaps bring a renewed Arab consensus under Saudi leadership (Safran 1988, 332–333; Dawisha 1983, 681; Podeh 2003, 3–7). Thus, the new Arab balance of power led the Saudi elite to believe that the time was propitious for a more ambitious role. Yet its traditional cautious behavior led to the publication of a vague and uncommitted plan that would enable the Saudis to "test the waters" and backtrack should circumstances demand.

The Fahd Plan called for Israeli withdrawal from all Arab territory occupied in 1967, including Arab Jerusalem; the dismantling of all Israeli settlements; affirmation of the right of Palestinian refugees to return to their homeland and of compensation for those unwilling to return; a transition period of regime transfer for the West Bank and Gaza, not exceeding several months, under the auspices of the UN; and the establishment of a Palestinian state with Jerusalem as its capital. Of the eight articles of the Fahd Plan, the most controversial was number seven, which said: "All states in the region should be able to live in peace"—an implicit recognition of Israel. With the exception of Egypt, no Arab state had hitherto been willing to recognize Israel's right to exist, even in such a vague formula (Podeh 2003, 40; Kostiner 2009, 419; al-Madfai 1993, 101–102, 127; Dajani and Daoudi 1986, 67). Essentially, the plan did not offer new elements. In an effort to forge a broad international and regional consensus, Fahd mixed Arab and UN resolutions; even the language of Article 7 was reminiscent of UN Resolution 242.

The Fahd Plan caught the Arab states and the PLO by surprise. Initially, Arab leaders received it with little enthusiasm and even disinterest. Logically, President Sadat should have supported the plan, since it legitimized the peaceful path that Egypt had taken. But Sadat feared it would divert the peace process from the Camp David track and therefore refrained from endorsing it publicly. The main opposition to the plan came from the Steadfastness and Rejection Front (SRF) states—Syria, Libya, Algeria, South Yemen, and certain Palestinian elements—who saw Article 7 as an unnecessary concession to Israel and the whole plan as an abandonment of the Palestinian cause. The PLO adopted a more cautious position for obvious reasons—it was dependent on Saudi financial support. For the same reason, Iraq also could not openly oppose the plan during its war with Iran. Jordan, Morocco, Tunisia, and the Gulf Cooperation Council (GCC) members generally supported the plan, but since their weight in the Arab system in terms of power, influence, and legitimacy was significantly less than the SRF countries, they were unable to tip the scales in favor of the Saudis (Podeh 2003, 7).

The unenthusiastic Arab response, coupled with a lukewarm US reaction and absolute Israeli rejection, led to the temporary shelving of the plan. In mid-October, however, the Arab and Western dialogue was revived. Of particular impact was Sadat's assassination on October 6, 1981, which signaled a death knell to the Camp David track and the autonomy talks. The timing of the renewed dialogue served the Saudis well in the late October vote over the AWACS deal in the US Senate and the scheduled Arab summit a month later. Of particular importance was the call for the plan's endorsement by the Arab summit. The Saudis hoped that the "Arabization" of the plan would result in a new resolution replacing Resolution 242. Successful implementation of this great plan could have consolidated Saudi Arabia's leading role in regional and international politics. When the Arab foreign ministers convened in Fez on November 22–23 to prepare the summit, wide divisions became visible. The GCC states, as well as Jordan, Tunisia, and Morocco, supported the plan; in contrast, the SRF countries opposed it. Realizing the potential of Syrian veto power, the Saudis sent Prince 'Abdallah to Damascus to work out a deal. All diplomatic efforts, however, failed to bridge the gap. Since the foreign ministers could not find a common formula, it was decided to leave the issue for the presidents and kings. On November 25, King Hasan opened what became the shortest summit ever; only four hours were needed to understand that the disagreements over the Fahd Plan were too wide to bridge. King Hasan could only hope that some face-saving formula would be found. However, the unwillingness of the SRF countries to approve the Fahd Plan left him no choice but to adjourn the event. Undoubtedly, the Saudis were greatly disappointed and embarrassed by the Fez fiasco (Podeh 2003, 9–11; al-Madfai 1993, 122; Dawisha 1983, 679–681).

Israel, for its part, received the Fahd Plan with surprise and disbelief. The first informal reaction was that the Saudi plan constituted "a ploy to destroy Israel's existence." It was compared with the 1965 Bourguiba Plan, which, according to the Israeli interpretation, meant a phased annihilation of Israel.[2] Over the following days, the negative Israeli reaction crystallized; Foreign Minister Yitzhak Shamir proclaimed that the Saudi plan was dangerous and contained no new elements. Even Shimon Peres, leader of the opposition Labor Party, stated that it should be rejected outright. Only the radical leftist parties expressed support for the plan (Podeh 2003, 11–12). The Israeli media generally reflected the formal position; only the daily *Haaretz* criticized the negative response. An editorial emphasized that the Israeli response "exposes the ineptitude and embarrassment of Israeli diplomacy in the face of changes in the basic Arab perceptions, whether real or imaginary" ("What Is Dangerous to Israel?" *Haaretz*, August 10, 1981). One of the paper's influential journalists explained the panicked response by the fact that Israel had always been prepared to retaliate against Arab missiles carrying warheads but not missiles carrying peace plans (Marcus 1981).

The Israelis' dismayed and dismissive response stemmed from two reasons. First, the government led by Begin, who had just been reelected in June, feared, like Sadat, that the Saudi plan would provide an alternative to the Camp David process. Any other peace channel—such as the Fahd Plan—would presumably force Israel to address itself to the notion of a Palestinian state. Second, Israeli belief that the Arabs desired to annihilate Israel had not diminished. This ingrained negative perception brought many Israelis to suspect every Arab move, even when couched in peaceful and nonbelligerent terminology (Podeh 2003, 12–13).

The US reaction to the Fahd Plan was similarly unenthusiastic, though for its own reasons. A State Department official stated that the plan "appears to be largely a restatement of previously known Saudi government decisions of principles outlined in Resolutions 242, 338 and other UN resolutions relating to the Arab-Israeli conflict" (Reich 1984, 104). This anemic reaction stemmed from the Reagan administration's reluctance to get embroiled in the Arab-Israeli conflict, which, at that point, was considered a low priority in Washington. And the United States too was reluctant to deviate from the Camp David track. Instead, its main goal was to construct a geopolitical grouping to contain what was perceived as an imminent Soviet threat to the Gulf stability following the Iranian Revolution and the Soviet invasion of Afghanistan, both in 1979. In this respect, Saudi Arabia was considered as playing a pivotal role "because of its geopolitical position, its oil and petrodollar reserves, its dependence on Western military equipment . . . and its fervent anti-Communism" (Reich 1984, 94; Ben-Zvi 1993, 123–126). The AWACS and F-15 equipment sale, which was finally approved by the Senate that October, was connected to Reagan's determination to strengthen US-Saudi ties.

The revival of the dialogue over the Fahd Plan in the wake of Sadat's assassination found a more responsive US administration. On October 29, both Alexander Haig, the US secretary of state, and President Reagan welcomed elements of the plan they viewed as a possible basis for negotiations. The deadlock in the Camp David track and the desire to enhance the Saudi role in the Arab system constituted important considerations for the United States (Reich 1984, 107).

In contrast, Israel received with grave concern the plan's revival and demanded that the United States reject it. The fact that the Reagan administration—in contrast to its previous stand—now saw "some positive elements" in the plan threatened to actualize those fears that the United States might abandon the Camp David track. Israel worried that with Sadat's disappearance, the plan would become a viable framework for the peace process. This concern seemed particularly acute as a result of the Senate decision to approve the AWACS sale to Saudi Arabia. Perhaps even more worrying, Israelis perceived this US-Saudi alliance as a possible substitute for the Israeli-American connection (Safran 1988, 335; Schoenbaum 1993, 274–275). On November 2–3 the Israeli Knesset held a lengthy political debate, which opened with a statement by Begin. After expressing his deep sorrow at Sadat's slaying and praising his leadership, he moved on to the Saudi plan. Begin rejected the interpretation that Article 7 meant recognition of Israel, describing it as a plan instead for its gradual annihilation. Begin's speech reflected a patronizing attitude toward the Saudis: "A desert petro-dollar state, where the darkness of the Middle Ages still exists, with the amputation of hands and heads, with unheard of corruption, speaking of arrogance, while she is attempting to dictate to us, to the old Jewish people, our borders, and to reap from us our capital. There is no more to be said."[3]

Begin concluded his speech by calling the Saudi plan "a sophisticated and rational method for the complete annihilation of the Israeli State."[4] Even opposition leader Peres agreed, adding that the plan was a "decorated version of extreme Arab positions, which pay some pale lip-service to world public opinion."[5] In the ensuing discussion, many Knesset members echoed their fears regarding the possibility that the United States would adopt this plan and toss away the Camp David track. Apart from the radical left parties, the Knesset was unanimous in rejecting the Saudi plan. A resolution was adopted stating that the Saudi document could not be regarded as a peace plan but should be seen as a threat to Israel's existence, and that the Camp David Accords were the only basis for regional peace and a solution to the Arab inhabitants of Judea and Samaria.[6]

As the Arab summit approached, Israel closely followed the Arab dialogue regarding the Fahd Plan. When the summit collapsed, a sigh of relief was heard from Jerusalem. In an attempt to capitalize on the Arab failure, Begin expressed willingness to meet King Khalid if the Fahd Plan were abrogated (Podeh 2003, 16).

The Saudi perception that the failure of the Fahd Plan stemmed from timing and tactics meant that the plan would be raised again at the next opportune moment. This moment presented itself when the Knesset passed a law annexing the Golan Heights in December 1981. Next, the completion of Israeli withdrawal from Sinai in April 1982 served as another opportunity for the Saudis to renew their call to convene an Arab summit and discuss the plan; but the Israeli invasion of Lebanon in June suspended further discussion—

though only for three weeks. From a Saudi point of view, the conditions were suddenly more propitious: the PLO was defeated in Lebanon; Syria had received a blow from the Israeli air force, its position in Lebanon was shaken, and its financial dependence on Saudi Arabia was greater than ever. This situation limited Palestinian and Syrian ability to torpedo the Saudi plan again. Indeed, Syria even expressed willingness to hold a summit and approve an agenda that included the Fahd Plan, though hinting at certain desired amendments (Podeh 2003, 16–17; Dawisha 1983, 684–685).

The Arab summit convened on September 9, 1982, but it was preceded by the launching of another peace plan by President Reagan on September 1. During his first year in office after his 1980 election, Reagan evinced little interest in Middle East policy. Along with his secretary of state Alexander Haig and his secretary of defense Caspar Weinberger, he viewed the Middle East primarily through the prism of the US-Soviet rivalry. Though Reagan was considered a staunch ally of Israel, bilateral relations went through several crises during 1981: the battle over the AWACS sale to the Saudis was the first. The acquisition of this sensitive technology was met by strong opposition from the Israeli lobby in the United States, and was made possible only after Reagan intervened in the Senate. The idea behind supporting the sale was to ensure the participation of moderate Arab countries in efforts to achieve peace in the Middle East. Begin's attempt to sabotage the deal on Capitol Hill was seen by Reagan as a betrayal (Reagan 1990, 415; Kostiner 2009, 419). In addition, Israeli bombing of the Iraqi nuclear reactor and the annexation of the Golan Heights, which led to the suspension of the US-Israel strategic agreement signed in November, further soured relations (Quandt 2005, 246–249; Reagan 1990, 411–419). Reagan was infuriated by Begin's reaction, which amounted to: "Mind your own business. It is up to Israel alone to decide what it must do to ensure its survival" (Reagan 1990, 419).

When Israel invaded Lebanon in early June 1982 in response to the assassination attempt on the Israeli ambassador in London by a radical Palestinian group, the United States seemed to back a limited Israeli military operation aimed at eliminating the threat posed by the PLO to northern Israel. Soon, however, as the IDF engaged with Syrian forces in Lebanon and the operation expanded, Reagan sent a harsh personal letter to Begin, demanding an immediate cease-fire; "a refusal by Israel to accept a ceasefire," he wrote, "will aggravate further the serious threat to world peace and will create extreme tension in our relations" (quoted in Quandt 2005, 252; Naor 1993, 302–303). Begin, led by Minister of Defense Ariel Sharon and Chief of Staff Rafael Eitan, continued and escalated the war with the tacit agreement of Secretary Alexander Haig. Due to personal and political differences, Reagan decided to replace Haig with George Shultz in late June. Unexpectedly, the newly appointed secretary of state immediately turned his attention to the long-neglected peace process. Fearing that the Lebanese War would shake the fragile Israeli-Egyptian peace treaty and destroy the chances for peace in the Middle East, he secretly gathered a group of senior officials from the State Department to discuss "a fresh start to the Middle East process" (Shultz 1993, 85; Quandt 2005, 253). Shultz's thinking was that the end of the war, with the evacuation of the PLO fighters from Beirut, would present an opportunity for the United States to launch a peace initiative. The deliberations of the group, which also included officials involved in the past (such as Carter and Kissinger) and experts from the private sector, highlighted the fact that in light of the PLO setback in Lebanon there must be a Jordanian role in any solution to the Palestinian problem. Such a role necessitated a reversal of the 1974 Rabat declaration, which recognized the PLO as the sole representative of the Palestinians. It was estimated that the PLO ousting from Lebanon and the loss of its territorial base invalidated its veto on any decision concerning the Palestinians (Shultz 1993, 87–89; al-Madfai 1993, 102).

To test the reactions to the plan, the United States diplomatically engaged with the relevant actors. It was imperative to find a credible Arab partner. The consent of Jordan's King Husayn was essential. It was believed that Jordan could be drawn into the process by appropriate American incentives and with backing from the moderate Arab states. It was hoped that revealing the plan to Husayn before it was introduced to Israel would demonstrate that it was an American initiative and not a joint American-Israeli endeavor (al-Madfai 1993, 101). A special envoy sent to the Jordanian king did not bring a conclusive answer; walking on a tightrope, Husayn urged the United States to negotiate with the PLO, abandon the Camp David Accords, and pressure Israel to withdraw from the West Bank and Gaza. The United States estimated that Husayn was laying the groundwork to back out if he did not get an Arab consensus behind him. A more resolute negative reaction came from Israel, apprehensive that a peace plan would help to revive the crushed PLO or, as discussed, deviate from the Camp David path. Sharon even secretly sent a warning that if the United States published a peace plan that Israel would find antagonistic to its interests, it would annex the West Bank (Shultz 1993, 91–94).

Before the plan was published, it was delivered to the main actors; Fahd was disappointed that it did not recognize the PLO. Saudi Arabia was in a delicate position, as it had been sponsoring an Arab plan that was to be discussed and approved within a few days at the Arab summit (see below). Prince Bandar, the Saudi ambassador in the United States, clarified that Fahd's statement in his plan on "the right of all people in the area to live in peace" was a deliberate effort to show that Saudi Arabia was willing to live in peace with Israel (Shultz 1993, 86). The attitude of the new Egyptian president, Husni

Mubarak, was "generally positive," while Husayn continued to display an undecided position due to his sensitive relations with the PLO. He saw the negotiations as a kind of trap and thought that in order to survive "he had to appear willing while simultaneously planning his escape" (ibid., 95). Begin was briefed on the plan a day before its publication by US ambassador Samuel Lewis, minutes before his meeting with the newly elected Lebanese president, Bashir Gemayel, in the northern Israeli city of Nahariya. Begin reacted, according to Shultz, with "shock and outrage," as he saw it as "a significant departure from the Camp David accords" (ibid., 94; Reagan 1990, 431–432). Begin was furious that he had not been consulted in advance and that instead of exploiting the weakening of the PLO to strengthen Israel's hold over the West Bank and Gaza, he would have to confront an American plan that implied the renewal of the battle over Greater Eretz Israel (Schiff and Ya'ari 1984, 288–289). The rather cold water spilled on the plan before its publication did not deter Reagan from proceeding with the expectation that "leadership from the United States might be able to break through the endless intransigence" (Shultz 1993, 95).

On September 1, the day marking the end of the evacuation of the PLO from Beirut, Reagan delivered his speech, presenting what later became known as the Reagan Plan (Laqueur and Rubin 1984, 656–663; Shultz 1993, 96–98; Reich 1984, 119–123; Tessler 2009, 600–604). In historical terms, it was the first peace plan for the Middle East ever publicly proposed by a US president (Laham 2004, 35). Reagan stated that during the recent war the United States was engaged in "a quiet, behind the scenes effort to lay the groundwork for a broader peace in the region." The Lebanese War, said Reagan, "tragic as it was, has left us with a new opportunity for Middle East peace. We must seize it now and bring peace to this troubled area so vital to world stability."

Reagan repeated the phrase "opportunity not to be missed" several times in his speech. The plan followed the outline agreed to at Camp David: the Palestinians would get autonomy after a five-year transition period beginning with the free elections of a self-governing authority—a process that would prove that the Palestinians could run their own affairs and that the new authority did not constitute a security threat to Israel. The United States made clear that it would not support the formation of an independent Palestinian state in the West Bank and Gaza or the annexation of the territory by Israel. Therefore, the plan assessed that "self-government by the Palestinians of the West Bank and Gaza in association with Jordan offers the best chance for a durable, just and lasting peace." In addition, the plan called for the "immediate adoption of a settlement freeze by Israel" to raise Arab confidence in the peace process, and it clarified that UN Resolution 242 applied to all fronts, including the West Bank and Gaza. Yet, "The extent to which Israel should be asked to give

up territory will be heavily affected by the extent of true peace and normalization and the security arrangements offered in return." Finally, it was determined that Jerusalem must remain undivided until its final status was decided
through negotiations. Reagan ended his speech with the following passage:

> It has often been said—and regrettably too often been true—that the story of
> the search for peace and justice in the Middle East is *a tragedy of opportunities
> missed* [my emphasis]. In the aftermath of the settlement in Lebanon we now
> face an opportunity for a broader peace. This time we must not let it slip from
> our grasp. We must look beyond the difficulties and obstacles of the present
> and move with fairness and resolve toward a brighter future. We owe it to
> ourselves, and to posterity, to do no less. For if we miss this chance to make a
> fresh start, we may look back on this moment from some later vantage point
> and realize how much that failure cost us. (Laqueur and Rubin 1984, 663)

In a way, the Reagan administration attempted in this plan to introduce
certain changes to the Camp David Accords, which seemed necessary in light
of changing reality. "The absence of Jordan and representatives of the Palestinian inhabitants of the occupied territories from the negotiations," said
Shultz on September 12, "has been the crucial missing link in the Camp David
process" (quoted in Reich and Hollis 1985, 144). Indeed, the Reagan Plan can
be seen as an extension of the Camp David Accords.

The reactions to the Reagan Plan in the United States and the West were
favorable. In the Arab world the most encouraging response came from Husayn, who described it as "The most courageous stand taken by an American
administration since 1956" (quoted in Sahliyeh 1988, 292; Hassan 1984, 125–
126). Egypt and Saudi Arabia also expressed some support, if lukewarm, for
the plan. Meanwhile, vociferous criticism came from two different directions: Syria and the radical organizations within the PLO (al-Madfai 1993, 106;
Laham 2004, 42–43), and Israel, which, according to Shultz, "was going all
out to strangle the infant initiative in the cradle" (1993, 98; Quandt 2005, 255).
On September 2 the Israeli government decided to reject the plan outright;
after enumerating all the differences between the texts of the Camp David Accords and the Reagan Plan, the communiqué stated that because of the contra-
dictions between the two documents, Israel had decided not to enter into any
negotiations, offering to renew the autonomy talks on the basis of the Camp
David Accords (Lukacs 1992, 200–203; Laham 2004, 53–56).

In a secret letter to Reagan, Begin did not mince words:

> Mr. President, you declare that you will not support the creation of a Pal-
> estinian state in Judea, Samaria, and the Gaza district. The Palestinian state

will rise of itself the day Judea and Samaria are given a Jordanian jurisdiction; then in no time, you will have a Soviet base in the heart of the Middle East. Under no circumstances shall we accept such a possibility ever arising which would endanger our very existence. We have chosen for the last two years to call our countries friends and allies; such being the case, a friend does not weaken his friend, an ally does not put an ally in jeopardy; this would be the inevitable consequence of the positions transmitted to me on Aug. 31 to become a reality. (Reagan 1990, 434; Shultz 1993, 98; Naor 1993, 328–329)

Shultz correctly assessed that Israel felt at the height of its power following the Lebanese War: the PLO was crushed, a pro-Israeli president and government were installed in Beirut and an Israeli-Lebanese peace treaty was in the offing, and the Israeli-Egyptian peace treaty remained intact despite Egyptian denunciation of the war. As they saw it, wrote Shultz, we "have suddenly pulled the rug out from under them" (1993, 99). Moreover, the Israelis felt betrayed, as a unilateral American approach violated in their eyes the spirit and letter of the pledges given in the second Israeli-Egyptian Disengagement Agreement in 1975 to consult with Israel in advance before launching any new policy regarding the conflict (Reich and Hollis 1985, 141).

Meanwhile, the Arab summit, which reconvened in Fez on September 6–9, adopted a modified version of the Fahd Plan and renamed it the Arab Peace Plan. Five differences existed between the two documents. First, the controversial Article 7 was amended so that its new wording did not entail recognition of the Israeli state, not even implicitly. Moreover, the reference to the Security Council accorded a certain role in the peace process to the Soviet Union and Western Europe—actors that traditionally were more sympathetic to the Arab cause. Yet in contrast to the original plan, the wording was changed from "*the* states" to "*all* the states in the region," which tacitly also referred to Israel. Second, in contrast to the disregard of the PLO in the Fahd Plan, the new Article 4 referred to the right of the Palestinians to self-determination, under "the leadership of the PLO, its sole legitimate representative." Third, the wording in Article 4—"the inalienable national rights" of the Palestinians and "compensation for those who do not wish to return"—may be interpreted as a reference to the Palestinian "right of return." Fourth, while the text of the plan called for Israeli withdrawal to the 1967 borders, the reference in the preamble to Bourguiba's Plan may have suggested an Arab call for Israeli withdrawal to the 1947 boundaries. Finally, Article 6 stated that Jerusalem (and not Arab Jerusalem, as stated in the Fahd Plan) would be the capital of the Palestinian state (Podeh 2003, 17–18, 41; Dawisha 1983, 685; al-Madfai 1993, 121–127).

In the American mind, by introducing the Arab Peace Plan, "the Arab world was doing its own job of making the peace process more difficult" (Shultz 1993, 100). The summit did not provide the desired mandate for Husayn; secretly, he expressed unhappiness with the outcome in Fez and suggested that he might make a move on his own, akin to Sadat's visit to Jerusalem. The Saudis, for their part, emphasized that the sentence in the Arab plan dealing with the rights of all the states in the region to live in peace amounted to recognition of Israel's right to exist (ibid.). According to al-Madfai's analysis, "The Fez Plan accepted the principles of resolution 242 and Israel's right to exist within secure and recognized boundaries, without making explicit reference to them" (1993, 127). This was not the way Israel saw the Fez resolutions; the government declared that "The belligerent anti-Israeli decisions adopted at the Fez Arab summit are anchored in previous Arab summits' decisions, which determined that their aim was actually the annihilation of Israel."[7] Prince Hassan, the Jordanian crown prince, thought that the Arabs and Israelis exchanged their traditional roles: the three no's of Khartoum 1967 were replaced by Israel's three no's to the Palestinians and the PLO following the Fez summit (1984, 109).

Thus in early September 1982, shortly after the end of the Lebanese War, there were two peace plans on the table. Yet Gemayel's assassination just three weeks after assuming power and the Sabra and Shatila massacre shifted the attention away from the peace plans to the Lebanese quagmire. Contacts regarding the possible promotion of the plans were nevertheless held with Husayn and the Arab League during the rest of 1982 (al-Madfai 1993, 107). The United States attempted to find some common ground between the two plans, hoping that a positive response by Husayn and/or the Arab League would help bring about a change in the Israeli position. The Jordanian king may have entertained the idea of devising a Jordanian-Palestinian formula that would meet the Reagan Plan without deviating from the Fez principles (al-Madfai 1993, 134). For that purpose he even met Reagan in December 1982. Husayn was tempted, but he could not move ahead without a mandate from Yasser 'Arafat as the PLO was recognized as the sole representative of the Palestinian people. The final straw came with the formal rejection of the Reagan Plan by the Palestinian National Council on February 22, 1983, and the declaration of the Jordanian government on April 10 "to leave it to the PLO and the Palestinian people to choose the ways and means for the salvation of themselves and their land, and for the realization of their declared aims in the manner they see fit" (Laqueur and Rubin 1984, 679–683, 686–691; Sahliyeh 1988, 293; al-Madfai 1993, 107–108). On October 27 that year, in his address to the nation, Reagan said he thought his plan "still offers the best hope for bringing peace to the region" (quoted in Reich and Hollis 1985, 149), but this was no more than wishful thinking.

ASSESSMENT

The Reagan and Arab Peace Plans were presented at the end of the Lebanese War. Content aside, their presentation highlighted the fact that Israel was the passive actor in the diplomatic field. The United States and the Arab world thought that the war provided a historical opportunity to solve the Arab-Israeli conflict, particularly the Israeli-Palestinian conflict. The repeated statements of Reagan and Shultz, as well as the discussions of the group that initiated the Reagan Plan, attest to their belief that the war's end, the evacuation of the PLO, and the reinstatement of a new Lebanese regime constituted a "window of opportunity" for a "reshuffling of the cards" in the realm of the Arab-Israeli peace process. Indeed, our analyses in previous chapters show that wars and revolutions often constituted turning points that were exploited to launch new diplomatic initiatives. Therefore, it seems that while American officials exaggerated the magnitude of the opportunity presented in the wake of the war, they were nevertheless correct in seeing the existence of a historical opportunity that should be seized. Neither plan was seen as highly attractive by the parties to which it was offered: the absence of the PLO and the rejection of the establishment of a Palestinian state in the Reagan Plan lowered its attraction in Arab eyes, while Israel's hawkish government considered the two plans far from attractive and was therefore unwilling even to consider them. Yet Jordan, Egypt, and Saudi Arabia—the major players in the Arab system— would have been willing to proceed with the Reagan Plan had Israel and the PLO softened their positions. The significant change in the region following the war was sufficient, however, to offer an opportunity to pursue a peaceful dialogue.

To what extent were these historical opportunities missed? The first variable relates to the level of the legitimacy of the leaders. One plan was launched by a popular US president, Reagan, who presented, in this case, a bipartisan position; the second was pitched by the highest Arab institution and as such was considered to express, to a large extent, an Arab consensus. So both plans enjoyed broad general support. Meanwhile in Israel, Begin, who was once more elected prime minister in August 1981 following a fierce election campaign in which Likud and Labor received a like number of seats (forty-eight and forty-seven, respectively), headed a narrow coalition government with the religious and other right-wing parties. With Sharon as minister of defense and Shamir as foreign minister, it was considered a radical right-wing government. Although it confronted strong leftist opposition, Labor leader Peres's view of the Reagan and Arab Peace Plans did not substantially differ from Begin's. Thus, except for the radical left parties, the Knesset was unanimous in rejecting the Reagan and Arab Peace Plans. It seems, therefore, that

Begin enjoyed the legitimacy of the majority in the Knesset as well as in the general Israeli public.

The second variable relates to the willingness of leaders to take a bold step. Among the relevant actors, only Reagan was willing to take such a step, though he himself did not invest much effort in pursuing his plan. Both he and Shultz lacked the conviction and the tenacity needed to advance it; discouraged by the opposition (Israel) and lack of enthusiasm (Arab states) of the parties involved, Reagan and Shultz simply gave up. The Arab Peace Plan was adopted by the Arab League, but there was no Arab partner willing to lead it; Saudi Arabia originally initiated the plan, but it demonstrated a kind of reluctant leadership when it was modified and accepted as an Arab plan. Another possible leader, Egypt, was still ostracized by most Arab states. And King Husayn, the most logical partner, continued to "sit on the fence," unwilling to go head to head with the PLO. In the absence of a reliable Arab partner willing to lead the peace plan, it soon sank into oblivion. But the player most reluctant to take bold steps was Begin and his government. The Reagan Plan was not a complete deviation from the Camp David Accords and the autonomy plan, as they had feared. Still, Begin was unwilling to pursue any plan that implied the loss of control and sovereignty over the West Bank and Gaza, as well as the complete halt of settlements. Even the tilt toward Jordan was rejected by Israeli leaders who reckoned that Jordan was in fact the Palestinian state. The Arab Peace Plan, which offered the establishment of a Palestinian state and attached an important role to the PLO, was seen in Israel—particularly after the results of the Lebanese War—as the incarnation of their worst fears. The fact that the plan implicitly recognized Israel was lost in the cacophony of statements that the plan was contrary to Israeli interests and beliefs.

The third variable relates to the level of trust between the parties as a result of their past interactions. Israel-US relations had improved considerably since the mid-1970s and the signing of the Israeli-Egyptian peace treaty. Fully committed to ensuring Israel's survival, Reagan had been sympathetic to its security concerns—as reflected in the text of the Reagan Plan. Yet he chose some measures that soured relations between them, such as the sale of AWACS radar planes to Saudi Arabia, the support of a UNSC resolution condemning Israel for bombing the Iraqi reactor (June 1981), and the suspension of Israeli-US strategic cooperation following the formal Israeli annexation of the Golan Heights (December 1981). Begin also felt betrayed when Reagan did not consult with him in advance regarding his plan. Its publication, therefore, rocked the foundations of trust between the two leaders. As for Israel and the Arab League, they had no history of negotiations; the League had a highly negative image in Israel, as is clear in most of its past decisions, which were anti-Israeli and anti-Zionist, reflecting an amalgamation of the lowest common denominator in the Arab world. Similarly, the Israeli image of Saudi Arabia, which initiated the Fahd Plan, was of a primitive and barbaric Islamic country.

The level of involvement of the third party is the fourth variable of missed opportunities. In the case of the Reagan Plan, the United States, acutely aware of the possibility of a historical opportunity, offered its plan and mediation expertise. Since it initiated the plan, the United States had to offer a balanced mediation process. Israel, however, expecting closer cooperation with the United States, was disappointed that the details of the plan had not been discussed with it and that Jordan and Saudi Arabia, due to their major role in the plan, were given more information in the preliminary stages; it did not matter that the plan was submitted simultaneously to Jordan, Egypt, Saudi Arabia, and Israel a day before its publication. As soon as the plan was made public, however, the United States did relatively little to promote it; Reagan, in fact, "never committed the resources to a serious follow-through" (Eisenberg and Caplan 1998, 51; Sahliyeh 1988, 294). One Arab writer claimed that the plan "represented a vague outline" rather than an outlined formula to achieve peace." He concluded, therefore, that the Reagan Plan "was [a] public relations ploy designed to create the illusion that the President was seeking to advance the peace process" (al-Madfai 1993, 37, 71). This is a harsh judgment; it was certainly not a ploy but a sincere—however flawed—attempt at offering a peace plan with carrots and sticks to both parties. Though the Reagan Plan was favorably received in the United States, it seems that outright Israeli rejection and the Jordanian and Saudi wavering threw cold water on the initiative. In his memoirs, Shultz described in detail the process of devising the plan, but offered very little on the marketing process (1993, 85–100). Despite the plan's failure, he was content that "For the first time in this administration, we have a Middle East policy" (ibid., 100). It should be emphasized, however, in all fairness, that given the gaps between the parties and the ideology of Begin's right-wing government, even a well-implemented marketing strategy would probably not have changed the outcome. As for the Arab Peace Plan, the United States was unwilling to promote it as the Reagan administration was persuaded by Israel that it was a nonstarter.

A summary of the variables analyzed above shows that the relevant leaders enjoyed sufficient legitimacy to advance the peace plans, yet they were unwilling to take bold decisions. In addition, a sense of mistrust developed between Begin and Reagan, while Israelis had a negative image of the Arab League and Saudi Arabia. Although the United States as a third party did initiate a peace plan, it did not exert much effort in Israel and the Arab world to promote it. There, in spite of the existence of a historical opportunity following the Lebanese War, the potential for seizing it was low, and this precluded the possibility of a diplomatic breakthrough. Israel, in contrast to the Arab side, did not initiate its own plan and showed clear opposition to the plans offered by the other parties, which stymied any serious dialogue regarding the offers. Instead, Israel turned its attention to the limited goal of attaining a peace treaty with Lebanon (see chapter 14).

In retrospect, the Arab Peace Plan left one important legacy: it was the first time that Saudi Arabia formally played a role in the Arab-Israeli conflict by offering a peace initiative. Twenty years later, in February 2002, Crown Prince ʿAbdallah would offer another peace plan, which became the second Arab Peace Plan (see chapter 21).

NOTES

1. The Venice Declaration was adopted by the nine EEC countries on June 13, 1980. See the text in Laqueur and Rubin 1984, 621–622.

2. The Tunisian president, Habib Bourguiba, made a series of declarations in March–April 1965 in support of a peaceful solution to the conflict on the basis of the UN 1947 partition plan. Israel rejected this proposal outright.

3. *Divrei Haknesset* 14–15 (November 2–4, 1981): 307.

4. Ibid., 336.

5. Ibid., 308.

6. Ibid., 341–343. The vote in the Knesset was 55 in favor, 18 against, and 27 abstentions.

7. *Maʿariv*, September 13, 1982.

CHAPTER 14

THE ISRAELI-LEBANESE PEACE AGREEMENT
MAY 1983

IN TANDEM WITH THE presentation of the Arab Peace Plan and the Reagan Plan in September 1982, attempts were made to produce a peaceful solution to the Lebanese imbroglio. Following the 1979 Israeli-Egyptian peace treaty, there were hopes in Israel that Lebanon—under the lead of the pro-Western Christian Maronites—would be the second Arab state to sign a peace agreement. Indeed, on May 17, 1983, the United States succeeded in brokering an Israeli-Lebanese agreement; in contrast, however, to the successful Israeli-Egyptian peace treaty, this agreement was annulled less than a year later. The agreement had become, in the apt terminology of two scholars, a "perfect failure" (Eisenberg and Caplan 1998, 43). This chapter will analyze how and why this opportunity was not missed—although its short duration may lead to the conclusion that perhaps it was an opportunity that should have been missed.

THE EPISODE

The agreement came in the wake of the Lebanese War, euphemistically termed by Israel "Operation Peace for Galilee." Its major aim was to secure Israel's northern border from attacks by Palestinian terrorist organizations. Other, more comprehensive goals, which Minister of Defense Ariel Sharon and others in the cabinet and army entertained, were the destruction of the PLO infrastructure in Beirut, the expulsion of Syrian forces from Lebanon, the establishment of a new political order based on the Phalange forces, and the signing of an Israeli-Lebanese Peace Agreement. Sharon's grand design may have also included turning Jordan into a Palestinian state and the absorption of the West Bank into Greater Eretz Israel (Shlaim 2000, 396; Eisenberg and Caplan 1998, 43; Inbar 1991, 73; Parker 1993, 176).

Initially, the war was planned and conducted in collaboration with Bashir Gemayel, the charismatic leader of the Phalange forces, an ultranationalist

Maronite militia. Contacts between Israel and the Phalange strengthened from the mid-1970s as a result of their mutual opposition to the growing role and impact of the PLO in Lebanon. Now frequent, these contacts led Israel to believe that "Once installed as president of a PLO- and Syria-free Lebanon, Gemayel would commit his country to an open peace with the Jewish state" (Eisenberg and Caplan 1998, 44; Shlaim 2000, 398). There are indications that Israeli prime minister Begin also felt a moral obligation to defend its Christian ally surrounded and threatened—like the Jewish minority—by Muslim neighbors. An analysis of the war and its ramifications for Israel, Lebanon, and the region is beyond the scope of this chapter; it is important, however, to analyze the process that led to the conclusion of the agreement.

On August 23, 1982, Gemayel was elected president; the road was now open, in Israeli eyes, to consolidate the ties with Lebanon by signing a peace treaty. In a sense, "it was what the war was all about" (Schoenbaum 1993, 293). On September 1, following the agreed-upon departure of PLO fighters from Beirut, Begin and Sharon secretly met Gemayel in the Israeli northern coastal city of Nahariya; Israeli leaders were angry to find that Bashir was anxious to demonstrate his independence, keen to broaden his domestic political base, particularly among the Muslim population, and to emphasize his link to the Arab world while downplaying the Israeli connection. More concretely, he was not willing to go beyond the signing of a nonaggression pact and insisted on putting on trial Major Saʿad Haddad, the Christian militia leader in southern Lebanon financed by Israel (Shlaim 2000, 414; Schiff and Yaʿari 1984, 288–290). Later, Gemayel's senior adviser said that Israel's insistence at the meeting on signing a peace treaty was unreasonable because a "peace treaty should emanate from your heart and it is not understandable how the other side is being pressured to sign it. With whom do you want to sign a treaty, with Bashir or with Lebanon?" In this regard, he noted in particular the difficulty the Muslim community had with the possible treaty (quoted in Tamir 1988, 182–183). In contrast to Israeli expectations based on mutual coordination prior to the war, the military cooperation of the Phalange with the IDF during the war was disappointing. Thus the meeting with Gemayel, which coincided with the publication of the Reagan Plan, caused great consternation in Israel regarding the political dividends of the war.

Israel's concern turned into panic when Bashir Gemayel was assassinated on September 14, probably by Syrian agents. In spite of his hesitations and procrastinations, Israeli policy largely depended on Gemayel's personality, and he was still trusted by Israeli leaders. His unexpected elimination threatened to exacerbate confessional divisions and domestic instability while allowing Syria to reemerge as the power broker. Syrian forces had entered Lebanon following the decision of the Arab summit in Cairo (November 1976) to form an

Arab Deterrence Force (ADF) to supervise the end of the civil war. Since then, Syria had succeeded in imposing its hegemony over Lebanon—a position that the Israeli invasion initially managed to erode. As revenge against Gemayel's killing, the Phalange forces entered the Palestinian Sabra and Shatila refugee camps and ran amok, causing mass carnage (September 16–17). Israel was implicated as a collaborator since the IDF—according to the accusation—was aware of the atrocity and in a position to prevent the killings. As a result, the Israeli government came under heavy international and domestic criticism and pressure to withdraw from Beirut and Lebanon. The sense of shock and revulsion forced the government to appoint an inquiry commission (Shlaim 2000, 416; Schiff and Ya'ari 1984, 313–357; Schulze 1998, 137–139). In light of its growing difficulties at home and negative perception worldwide, Israel hoped that the signing of a peace agreement with Lebanon would serve as a tangible political achievement.

On September 21 Amine Gemayel was elected president; in contrast to his younger brother Bashir, Amine was known for his pro-Syrian proclivity. At the outset, it was clear that Amine would be more cautious and less enthusiastic to forge relations with Israel. Like Bashir, he understood the limits imposed by the Lebanese and Arab political systems on the president's ability to maneuver vis-à-vis Israel. Therefore, his main goal was to achieve full withdrawal of all foreign troops from Lebanon. Any contacts with Israel would have to be developed cautiously and secretly. For that purpose, the United States—which had played a significant role in ending the war—was perceived as a credible mediator (Inbar 1991, 74).

Realizing that the rules of the game had changed, the Israeli government approved its guidelines for the envisaged political and security agreement with Lebanon on October 11, 1982. In terms of security, Israel demanded the establishment of a security zone forty-five to fifty kilometers wide, defended by the Israeli-backed militia of Major Haddad, three early warning stations, freedom of air surveillance, and the absence of any UN forces. The plan saw the early withdrawal of the PLO, preceding the simultaneous withdrawal of Israeli and Syrian forces. The agreement was seen as a prelude to negotiations—with the possible participation of the United States—leading to the signing of a peace treaty (Tamir 1988, 184–187; Inbar 1991, 75; Schiff and Ya'ari 1984, 360–361). The initial Israeli contacts with Amine Gemayel demonstrated certain flexibility on his part regarding the security zone. He rejected, however, the presence of any Israeli forces on Lebanese soil and the attaching of any role to Haddad, who was considered a renegade; instead, he was in favor of stationing UN forces in southern Lebanon. Because of domestic and regional considerations, it became clear that a peace treaty was not feasible; instead, Gemayel preferred indirect talks aimed at working out a withdrawal schedule and details of the proposed security zone (Inbar 1991, 75). In late October, following the meetings of both Foreign Minister Shamir and President Gemayel with US president Reagan and secretary of state George Shultz, the United States decided to start a low-key mediation process that mainly dealt with procedural questions. At the same time, Gemayel's representative and Minister of Defense Sharon held secret talks in late December, which led to the drafting of a "document of principles." Surprisingly, the Lebanese envoy accepted many of the Israeli demands, such as the placing of normalization on the agenda (in addition to security arrangements and withdrawal), the establishment of a liaison office in Beirut, the establishment of three warning stations, the integration of Haddad's militia into the Lebanese army, and a withdrawal schedule in line with the Israeli plan. However, Gemayel refused to sign the document, though he promised it would serve as a blueprint for his negotiating team (Inbar 1991, 77; Tamir 1988, 193–196).

The formal negotiations commenced on December 28, alternating between Khalde in Lebanon and the border town of Kiryat Shemona in Israel; heading the delegations were diplomats David Kimche, director-general of the Israeli Ministry of Foreign Affairs; Antoine Fattal, a veteran Lebanese diplomat; and US special envoy Morris Draper. The Lebanese delegation included a Sunni and Shi'i, reflecting the mosaic nature of that society; this composition circumscribed Gemayel's ability to respond to Israeli demands but added legitimacy to any step taken. The first round of formal negotiations revealed that the understandings included in the "document of principles" could not serve as a basis for the talks. The United States found itself heavily drawn into the negotiations, often allying itself with the weaker side so as to offset the imbalance between Israel and Lebanon (Inbar 1991, 78; Schiff and Ya'ari 1984, 366). In February 1983 the United States presented the parties with drafts that dealt with two contentious points: the scope of normalization, and the agreements in the security zone. The tripartite talks made it clear that a peace treaty along the Israeli-Egyptian model was not feasible and that Lebanon would not agree to Israeli military presence on its territory. Under pressure from Syria, Saudi Arabia, and the Muslim community in Lebanon, the Christians—particularly the Maronites and Phalange—were obliged to limit the scope of normalization; it was no coincidence that the model of the 1949 armistice agreement was seen as a desired end. Some progress was made in mid-March, when the Israeli and Lebanese foreign ministers were invited to Washington for intensive talks. It is possible that Sharon having to resign after the report of the Kahan Commission on Sabra and Shatila may have eased the negotiations (Inbar 1991, 78–79; Tamir 1988, 198–202; Schiff and Ya'ari 1984, 366–370; Parker 1993, 179–192). Sharon was replaced by Moshe Arens, former ambassador in Washington.

When an agreement seemed within reach, Shultz decided to personally intervene; on April 24 he arrived in the Middle East. The timing was complicated: a terrorist bombing of the US embassy in Beirut had killed sixty-three people, and King Husayn had announced his final rejection of the Reagan Plan. Shultz might have thought that in these circumstances a Lebanese-Israeli agreement was desirable and feasible, and that it would offset some of the damage to US interests. He might also have been driven "by a desire to have his own Camp David" (Parker 1993, 210; Seale 1988, 406). He may not have realized how slim the chances were for real peace. Yet he sensed that Syria was the greatest stumbling block to any agreement; playing the role of the spoiler, the Syrians, he wrote, "were pulling the rug out from under any effort" (Shultz 1993, 197). And, he continued, the Israelis were not far behind the Syrians in obstructing the process, as they did not realize that in contrast to Egypt, which was large enough, strong enough, and independent enough to withstand the temporary Arab estrangement, Lebanon did not have those attributes. Moreover, some thought that Israel "has squandered much of the goodwill their expulsion of the PLO leadership had generated among some of the Lebanese, and they had emerged in the eyes of much of the world as heedless, dangerous, and arrogant" (ibid., 198). For two weeks, Shultz shuttled between Jerusalem and Beirut, with occasional side detours to Cairo, Riyadh, and Damascus. The negotiations proved to be debilitating, as the Israeli position was unyielding, while the Lebanese were backing away from commitments already made. They wanted Israeli withdrawal for the minimum political price. Meanwhile, Syria made it clear that the withdrawal of its forces would not be linked to or discussed within the context of Israeli withdrawal. President Asad considered the Israeli-Lebanese draft worse than the Camp David Accords and threatened to harm Lebanon if an agreement was signed. As a result, the Lebanese chose to avoid putting anything in writing, while the Israelis wanted everything in writing (ibid., 206–213).

Such contradictory aims did somehow end in the signing of an agreement on May 17, though it more closely resembled a nonaggression pact than a peace treaty.[1] The agreement proclaimed the termination of the state of war and recognized the international border as inviolable. The parties undertook to prevent the use of their own territory for terrorist activity against the other. Israel was to withdraw all its forces from Lebanon within eight to twelve weeks from the signing of the agreement; a security zone was to be established in the area south of the Awali River, with certain security arrangements. Major Haddad's militia was defined as the "Lebanese Army territorial brigade," which, in addition to another regular army brigade, was to be responsible for the security in this zone. These forces, it was stipulated in an annex to the agreement, would be integrated into the Lebanese army. Article 8 stated that a Joint Liaison Committee would be established and among its tasks would be the initiation of "*bona fide* negotiations in order to conclude agreements on the movement of goods, products and persons." The agreement did not specify the establishment of diplomatic relations between the countries, nor did it commit Lebanon in any way to normalization. It included several secret understandings, which were quickly leaked to the Arab press, such as the permission of Israeli observation flights over Lebanon and the operation of joint Israeli-Lebanese surveillance patrols. Most important was a private pledge by Shultz that Israel would not be obliged to implement the accord so long as the Syrians and Palestinians had not withdrawn from Lebanon. This last assurance gave Asad a veto over the fulfillment of the agreement (Eisenberg and Caplan 1998, 53–54, 192–194; Schiff and Ya'ari 1984, 377–378; Tamir 1988, 210–213; Parker 1993, 195–196; Seale 1988, 407–410; Kimche 1991, 169; Schulze 1998, 140–142).[2]

The agreement was ratified by the Lebanese parliament on June 14 (Saba 2000, 42). As the ink was drying, Israeli leaders felt that it might just work out (Rubinstein 1992, 195). They soon discovered, however, that Syria and other opposition forces in Lebanon had other plans.

Having obtained Egyptian consent, the United States also attempted to solicit the blessing of Jordan, Syria, and Saudi Arabia. While kings Husayn and Fahd expressed cautious support, Asad was adamantly opposed; in his opinion, the agreement was a "submission" and an unacceptable reward for aggression; he was also upset that Israeli withdrawal was linked to a Syrian withdrawal, which meant an end to Syrian presence in Lebanon. "An agreement reached at gunpoint is not an agreement," he told Shultz (Shultz 1993, 217; Seale 1988, 408). It became clear that Syria would do its utmost to sabotage the Israeli-Lebanese agreement; seeing Lebanon as part of his *lebensraum*, Asad was furious that the negotiations largely ignored him, though he was continuously updated by US and Lebanese envoys. In addition, a second agreement with an Arab country meant the continuation of the momentum established with the Israeli-Egyptian peace treaty, which would further isolate Syria.

By January 1983 Syria was in a better position to play a major role in Lebanon after being supplied by the Soviets with an advanced anti-aircraft missile system (Parker 1993, 196–197). In addition, Moscow gave Syria a commitment to come to its aid if it were attacked by Israel—a vital element in Asad's search for strategic parity. Both Syria and the Soviet Union were one in seeking to deny Israel the achievement of its war aims, to reassert Syria's influence in Lebanon, and to prevent the conclusion of an American-brokered Israel-Lebanon peace treaty that would open the door for Israeli-US regional hegemony (Seale 1988, 399–400). To achieve these aims, Syria assembled a coalition of Sunni-Shi'i-Druze representatives, as well as some Christian forces under the National Salvation Front, which vowed to sabotage the accord (Seale 1988, 410–418; Tessler 2009, 627).

Eventually, on March 5, 1984, the Syrian pressure came to bear as the Lebanese parliament nullified the agreement. Its annulment served Gemayel well in his reconciliation talks with other Lebanese leaders that began in Lausanne a week later. Israel, for its part, decided to withdraw in stages without waiting for concurrent Syrian withdrawal. This decision was made as a result of domestic pressure on the National Unity government headed by Shimon Peres. It began in September 1983 and was completed in June 1985; with this, the story of the Israeli-Lebanese agreement came to an end (Tamir 1988, 214–215; Kimche 1991, 173–174).

ASSESSMENT

Though the Israeli-Lebanese-US negotiations ended in agreement, it is clear that this episode was an abysmal failure—a "perfect failure," some say (Eisenberg and Caplan 1998, 43), a case in which the operation succeeded but the patient died (Inbar 1991, 81), or simply a miscalculation on the part of the United States (Parker 1993, 204–211). The agreement did not survive a year and was largely ignored during its short existence. The fact that an agreement was signed excludes the possibility that an opportunity was missed; but some scholars and observers have suggested that had it been signed sooner, its chances might have been better. They note that as Syria was the main force sabotaging the agreement, an earlier conclusion of the agreement—when "the Syrians had been badly mauled and pushed back by the Israelis and were thought to be *hors de combat*"—might have yielded a different outcome (Parker 1993, 194–195; Inbar 1991, 81). Patrick Seale, for example, wrote in his authoritative biography on Asad, "Had Israel imposed its 'order' on Lebanon in early September 1982 when it was at the height of its power, Asad could have done little about it. But nine long months elapsed before a Lebanese-Israeli agreement was concluded, by which time he was strong enough to contest it" (1988, 400). Similarly, Avraham Tamir, who took an active part in the talks on the Israeli side, argued that eight months were wasted in futile negotiations and this had a tremendous impact on the ability to implement the agreement in light of the swift consolidation of Syria's power (1988, 197). The US ambassadors in Beirut and Tel Aviv agreed that "What was possible in the fall of 1982 was not possible in early 1983" (Parker 1993, 198). In other words, what was missed was an opportunity to sign an early agreement that would have had better chances of survival.

The Lebanese War, as we posited with regard to the Reagan and Fahd Plans, provided a historical opportunity to resolve the Arab-Israeli conflict, particularly the Israeli-Palestinian conflict: the evacuation of the PLO from Beirut, the blow to the Syrian forces, and the formation of a new Lebanese regime constituted a "window of opportunity" in the realm of Israeli-Lebanese relations. Our analyses in previous chapters showed that wars and revolutions constituted turning points that were exploited to launch new diplomatic initiatives. Therefore, the United States was correct to see this episode as a historical opportunity that should be seized. In reality, as noted, it was not missed, as an agreement was signed; yet its swift demise necessitates an analysis of the variables of the missed opportunity.

The first variable deals with the level of the legitimacy of the leaders. By all accounts, Amine Gemayel's hold was tenuous at best; many in Lebanon and the Arab world thought that his government represented only narrow Maronite and/or Christian interests. The fact that he had to draw representatives from all the major sects into the negotiating process was an indication of the government's fragility. Caught between the domestic anvil and the Syrian (and all Arab) hammer, Gemayel could move only on the basis of consensus (Eisenberg and Caplan 1998, 49; Shultz 1993, 206). In his memoirs, Gemayel largely evades this event, blaming Israel for acting against the spirit of the agreement by making its withdrawal conditional on the withdrawal of Syrian forces (1992, 25).[3]

Israel was ruled by a government whose legitimacy had significantly eroded since the war. The domestic protest—described for the first time as a war by choice (*milhemet breira*)—commenced immediately but grew in scope and intensity following the massive Israeli bombardment of Beirut, the assassination of Bashir Gemayel, the massacre at Sabra and Shatila, and the rising numbers of Israeli casualties. An indication of the public anti-war mood was a mass rally of four hundred thousand people in Tel Aviv on September 25, 1982. The findings of the Kahan Commission in February 1983, which led to Sharon's resignation, further eroded the government's legitimacy (Eisenberg and Caplan 1998, 55; Shlaim 2000, 417). Shortly after the signing of the Israeli-Lebanese agreement on August 28, 1983, Begin announced his intention to resign—though it had been clear to people around him that for some time he was physically and mentally unfit to rule.[4] In sum, on both sides stood governments that possessed little, if any, of the legitimacy required for making serious decisions.

The second variable relates to the willingness of leaders to take bold steps. Clearly, Gemayel wanted to pay the lowest possible price for the withdrawal of all foreign troops from Lebanon, avoiding any steps that could be interpreted as normalization, as this would complicate his position in the domestic and regional arenas. By using the tactic of the "blackmail of weakness," Gemayel managed to successfully oppose the demands of a stronger party or at least delay compliance (Inbar 1991, 81–82). In contrast, Begin and Sharon sought to dictate their version of peace on a recalcitrant party; not fully realizing— or unwilling to admit—the weaknesses of the other party, Israel thought it would be able, with American support, to impose its terms and, as such, to acquire at least some political dividends of a domestically contested war. Israel, as Seale noted, had gone to war for the bigger prize of a peace treaty with a client state. And the more casualties its Lebanese adventure took, "the more Israel felt it had to justify it by securing a fully-fledged treaty" (1988, 404). When signed, even Begin understood the futility of the agreement; upon submitting it to the president, he said, "Here is the agreement, which is not worth the paper it's written on" (quoted in Shilon 2007, 415). Eventually, both Begin and Sharon resigned under the cloud of this episode, and their successors were more concerned with safe withdrawal than with the prospects of an Israeli-Lebanese peace. Therefore, on both sides there were absent leaders willing to pursue bold decisions. In fact, both sides held negotiations for different reasons, "none of which was the quest for an honorable and mutually satisfying peace" (Eisenberg and Caplan 1998, 47).

The third variable relates to the level of trust between the parties as a result of their past interactions. Contacts between Israel and the Maronite community, particularly the Phalange movement, were not a unique phenomenon. In fact, Lebanese-Zionist relations predated the establishment of Israel. They were partially based on a romantic view of the "minorities' alliance," which united the Jews with non-Muslim minorities in the Middle East (Rubinstein 1992, 196; Erlich 2000, 25–29; Schulze 1998, 146–157). Since the 1930s, Zionist leaders were in contact with leaders in the Maronite community, which culminated in a treaty, signed in 1946, between the Maronite Church and the Jewish Agency, but it failed to produce a meaningful political alliance (Eisenberg 1994, 117–146; Erlich 2000, 33–47). In many ways, it resembled the May 1983 agreement, as both "were meticulously negotiated, signed, and accepted by the respective leaderships—and soon after disavowed by the Lebanese side" (Eisenberg and Caplan 1998, 44). Following the 1948 War, a Mixed Armistice Commission was set up in 1949 to monitor border violations; it functioned effectively until 1967. In addition, Israel developed contacts with the Phalange movement in the late 1940s and early 1950s. Morris claimed that this served as the foundation of the Israeli-Phalange relationship in subsequent years (1984, 142).[5] The contacts widened and intensified in the period following the 1976 civil war, as the Christian militia forces were looking for external allies. By 1982 the Maronite-Israeli relationship became an open secret (Eisenberg 2010a, 63–71; Schulze 1998, 26–44, 81–112). Therefore, it seems that "lack of familiarity was *not* a factor accounting for the ultimate failure of the 1983 negotiations to produce a lasting agreement" (Eisenberg and Caplan 1998, 45). Yet it should be emphasized that these contacts were held mainly with the Christian-Maronite forces and occasionally with the Druze, while Sunni and Shi'i leaders were left out of this equation. Thus the past inter-actions between Israel and the Maronites did not serve the parties as they were negotiating in a different reality, in which the Muslim community played a more dominant role. Moreover, the limited cooperation of the Phalange with Israel during the war and in the aftermath of Bashir Gemayel's assassination again aroused mutual mistrust.

The fourth variable is the level of involvement of the third party. The United States was involved in the mediation process from the outset. Its in-volvement became more intensive as time went by, ending with Secretary of State Shultz's personal mediation, which succeeded to induce the parties to sign the agreement. Yet US behavior was characterized by a certain ambiva-lence and irresoluteness. In addition, a major player in the Lebanese arena—Syria—did not consider the United States a trusted mediator. There are indi-cations, moreover, that for Israelis and Lebanese the success of the agreement "lay more in terms of enhancing (Lebanon) or repairing (Israel) relations with the US than in dealing with one another" (Eisenberg and Caplan 1998, 51–52). By opting for an Israeli-Lebanese agreement, the United States may have mis-calculated; in Parker's opinion, "If the Americans had had the courage to tell the Israelis unambiguously early in the game that they could not support an agreement they knew the Syrians would not accept, it would then have been up to the Israelis to work out a more realistic set of arrangements" (1993, 210). Yet when Shultz came to the Middle East in April 1983, he had no attractive alternatives in his pocket and his prestige hinged on the successful conclusion of an Israeli-Lebanese agreement (ibid., 204). With the devastating bombing of the US Embassy in Beirut in April and the US Marines' barracks in October 1983, American enthusiasm for a successful agreement apparently gave way to a desire for quick withdrawal from the Lebanese quagmire.

The preceding analysis suggests that the four variables pertaining to a missed opportunity were not relevant in this case study; therefore, while a historical opportunity did exist, there is no reason to suppose that if an agree-ment was not signed, it would have been considered a missed opportunity. And, still, an agreement was signed. It can be concluded, then, that if an agree-ment was being imposed, at least on one of the parties involved, the chances it would endure were slim. Thus Inbar's conclusion that "The delay in producing an agreement seemed to be a major reason for its failure afterwards" (1991, 81) does not hold water. The variables operating against a successful agreement were relevant all along and a mere few months earlier would not have changed the outcome. Therefore, the assertion of one American diplomat—that no matter how the agreement looked and whatever the timing, it would not have survived—was correct. In his opinion, "That type of juggernaut imposition of foreign interests . . . on a small, defenseless foreign state simply won't last in this period" (quoted in Parker 1993, 199).

Ironically, we can say that the Israeli-Lebanese agreement was an opportunity that should have been missed, but in fact it was simply a mistake. Instead, an Israeli-Lebanese security agreement preventing future attacks from Lebanese territory would probably have endured longer (Saba 2000, 68–69).

NOTES

1. Quandt wrote that "Lebanon and Israel signed an agreement that was just short of a peace treaty" (2005, 258); Eisenberg and Caplan, echoing Parker, said that "The May 17 document was a peace treaty in all but name" (1998, 54; Parker 1993, 195); in Schiff and Ya'ari's opinion, the agreement "was merely the wrapping around a series of secret understandings" (1984, 378).

2. Inbar claims that the Lebanese made last concessions such as an agreement to put in writing a commitment for future normalization with Israel (1991, 80), but I have found no proof for this assertion. For a full version of the agreement, including annexes and explanations of the different clauses, see Rubinstein 1992, 310–343; Saba 2000, 81–88. For a highly critical appraisal of the agreement from a Lebanese perspective, see Saba 2000, 39–80.

3. This was not part of the agreement but a secret caveat made during the negotiations. Eventually, Israeli withdrawal was disengaged from the Syrian withdrawal and finalized in 1985.

4. Begin resigned in October 1983 as a result of depression, which worsened following the Lebanese War and the death of his wife in November 1982. See Grosbard 2006, 273–314; Shilon 2007, 415–435.

5. For an opposite view, see Eisenberg 2010a, 54–78; Zisser 1996, 47–84; Erlich 2000, 571–575.

CHAPTER 15

THE LONDON AGREEMENT

APRIL 1987

ISRAEL AND JORDAN had been enemies for forty years, but secret contacts between King Husayn and various Israeli politicians had continued throughout the period. London was the port of choice for a covert meeting between Israeli foreign minister Shimon Peres and Husayn on April 11, 1987; the meeting produced a joint document, known as the London Agreement. This document has never been signed or ratified by the Israeli government; domestic political disagreements between Prime Minister Shamir and his Likud Party, on the one hand, and Peres and the Labor Party, on the other—the two wings of the National Unity government—hampered the conclusion and implementation of that agreement. With the wisdom of hindsight, it is clear that the London Document was the last attempt to revive the Jordanian option with regard to the solution of the Palestinian problem in the West Bank and Gaza. The eruption of the Intifada (Palestinian uprising) in December 1987 and Husayn's decision to disengage Jordan from the West Bank in July 1988 led some to conclude that in rejecting the London Agreement, Israel missed an opportunity to solve the Palestinian problem. This chapter will analyze if and to what extent the episode did indeed represent a missed opportunity.

THE EPISODE

The Israeli elections in July 1984 produced a draw between the two leading parties, Labor and Likud. The result was the formation of a National Unity government with a twist: it was agreed that the premiership would rotate between the two parties' leaders. Peres would serve as prime minister for the first two years, with Shamir—Begin's successor—serving as his deputy and foreign minister; and after two years they would rotate. Rabin was to serve as minister of defense for the whole term. Although the government had the support of no less than 97 Knesset members (out of 120) for this arrangement, the parliament was composed of parties with different ideologies, particularly in the realm of Arab-Israeli relations (Shlaim 2000, 424–425).

No sooner did the National Unity government take office than it was preoccupied with completing Israel's withdrawal to the security zone in Lebanon and the stabilization of its economy, particularly the problem of soaring inflation. Regarding the Arab-Israeli conflict, Peres hoped to renew the dialogue with Husayn on the fate of the West Bank. Jordan, as will be recalled, in September 1982 accepted the Reagan Plan, which accorded it an important role in the negotiations. The defeat of the PLO in the Lebanese War and the fact that that organization was unwilling to recognize UN Resolution 242 and renounce terrorism left Jordan—at least in Israeli and US eyes—as the only viable partner for dialogue. And indeed, King Husayn attempted to seize the opportunity and reenter the diplomatic process; when the Reagan Plan was launched, he initiated a series of talks with 'Arafat to discuss the federation of the two banks of the River Jordan and to form a joint team to negotiate with Israel; these talks, however, ended in failure (Sahliyeh 1988, 293–295).

In 1984, Husayn opted to resume the talks with the PLO as a result of several developments. First was the weakening and isolation of the organization, following the expulsion of 'Arafat's troops from northern Lebanon in December 1983; second were expectations that a Labor-led government would be more inclined to a solution based on the Jordanian option. Finally, it was understood that the reelection of Reagan placed him in a better position to advance his peace plan. Jordan's renewed interest in the Palestinian arena was reflected in several ways: in January 1984 Husayn issued a decree to reconvene parliament after a suspension of ten years; with 50 percent of its members drawn from the West Bank, Jordan thus reestablished its constitutional link to the occupied territories. In addition, in November Husayn allowed the PLO to hold the Palestinian National Council in Amman. He hoped that the weakened PLO would adopt a more moderate position that would enable its participation in the peace process (Sahliyeh 1988, 295–298). The revived contacts between Jordan and the PLO led to the signing of the Amman Agreement in February 1985, in which it was agreed, inter alia, that peace negotiations would take place under the auspices of an international conference with the participation of the five permanent members of the Security Council and the parties to the conflict, including the PLO, within a joint Jordanian-Palestinian delegation (ibid., 298, 473; al-Madfai 1993, 151–152). The aim was Palestinian self-determination exercised through a Jordanian-Palestinian confederation, and the method was a Jordanian-Palestinian delegation to negotiate with Israel at an international conference. The three demands that the PLO was expected to meet to qualify for participation at a later stage were to accept Resolution 242, recognize Israel's right to exist, and renounce terrorism. Husayn could not embark on separate negotiations with Israel, particularly after the 1974 Rabat Arab summit, where it was determined that the PLO was the sole legitimate representative of the Palestinian people, or the Fez summit, which accorded the PLO a significant say in the formation of a Palestinian state. An international conference, Husayn hoped, "would enable him to remain within the limits of the inter-Arab consensus while providing a cover for the direct talks that the Israelis wanted so badly" (Shlaim 2000, 431). After a year of debilitating negotiations, however, the king suspended the agreement, ostensibly because of the PLO's objection to the demands. In addition, in July 1986 he closed down the PLO's offices and ordered the expulsion of its leading officials (al-Madfai 1993, 158–178). Concomitantly, Jordan found another opportunity to further weaken the PLO's position in the West Bank by rebuilding its patronage system with the help of Israel (Garfinkle 1992, 127–131).

Meanwhile, the Jordanian option was revived in the Israeli political system and public discourse. In his memoirs, Peres admitted that he had always considered an Israeli-Jordanian-Palestinian triangle (1995, 297). A top-secret memorandum prepared by Avraham Tamir, director-general of the Prime Minister's Office (under Peres), in July 1985 assessed that the developments over the previous two years in the Middle East, particularly the blow the PLO had received in Lebanon and the resultant Amman Agreement, paved the way for the resumption of the peace process. The most preferable option for Israel, it was estimated, was to open direct peace negotiations with a Jordanian delegation including Palestinians, not members of the PLO. It was further recommended that the final settlement would be either a confederation between Israel and a Jordanian federation including the Palestinian autonomy, or an Israeli-Jordanian confederation, which would jointly administer the autonomy (Melman 1987, 154–156; Shlaim 2000, 432). The idea of an international conference was not popular in Israel; it was equated with imposed solutions and thus was rejected by all mainstream parties. The challenge facing Peres was to find a formula to enable the king to open talks with Israel under an international umbrella and to set up a Jordanian-Palestinian team for the talks, bypassing the PLO (Shlaim 2000, 431).

In order to advance the Jordanian option, Peres met with Husayn in July 1985—their first meeting in ten years. In principle, Peres was opposed to the idea of an international conference, but he was willing to accept a formal opening session—termed an "international forum"—similar to the Geneva Conference. After all, within the framework of that conference Israel had negotiated two disengagement agreements with Egypt and one with Syria. Such a conference would provide the Arabs with the legitimizing fig leaf they needed and allow Husayn, under the joint Jordanian-Palestinian delegation, to play a role in the West Bank without contradicting the Rabat resolutions (Peres 1995, 305). On the basis of this understanding, the assistant under-secretary of state, Richard Murphy, produced in January 1986 a ten-point document on the procedures for negotiations, which resembled the old concept of the Geneva Conference: convening a festive opening followed by the holding of negotiations in bilateral committees independent of one another, with UN Resolutions 242 and 338 and the renouncing of terrorism as the basic guidelines. These conditions, in fact, excluded the participation of the PLO, though they allowed pro-Jordanian Palestinians to take part in a joint Jordanian-Palestinian delegation. But the Murphy document was soon shelved as a result of three developments: the abrogation of the Amman Accord in February 1986, the replacement of Peres by Shamir—who was very much opposed to the idea of an international conference—as prime minister in October, and the discovery of US involvement in the Iran-contra scandal ("Irangate") in November.[1] All these led to a temporary halt in the Israeli-Jordanian-American contacts regarding the international conference, but the road was paved for a more serious attempt (Zak 1996, 264–265; Shlaim 2000, 436–437; Lukacs 1997, 170–171; al-Madfai 1993, 186–190).

The breakdown of the Amman Accord was received with pleasure in Israel. Defense Minister Rabin thought it provided "an historic opportunity for advancing peace in the Middle East" (quoted in al-Madfai 1993, 188). From an Israeli perspective, it was a chance to revive the Jordanian option while bypassing the PLO, which was considered a terrorist organization.

The moment to be exploited came when Peres and Husayn met in London that chilly April day. There are several colorful accounts of the meeting, which produced the London Agreement (Peres 1995, 305–312; Shlaim 2000, 443–445; 2007, 440–446; Zak 1996, 266–270; al-Madfai 1993, 235; Raviv 2000, 254–255). The basic principles of the agreement were as follows. First, there was to be an international conference, with the participation of the five permanent members of the Security Council and the parties involved in the Arab-Israeli conflict, aimed at attaining comprehensive peace and "granting the Palestinian people their legitimate rights." Second, the conference would invite the parties to set up regional bilateral committees to negotiate bilateral issues. Third, the conference participants would not be in a position to impose a solution and would not veto any agreement reached by the sides. Fourth, the Palestinian issue would be discussed in a meeting of the Jordanian, Palestinian, and Israeli delegations, and the Palestinians would be included in the Jordanian-Palestinian delegation. Finally, participation in the conference would be based on UN Resolutions 242 and 338 and the renunciation of violence and terror. The document was subject to the approval of the Israeli and

Jordanian governments. Peres promised Husayn that if Shamir and the Likud rejected the agreement he would risk dismantling the government over this issue.

Maoz called it a "path-breaking agreement" (2004, 445), but in essence the document (not "agreement," as it was not signed by Peres or Husayn) dealt only with procedural matters pertaining to the planned international conference and was not a substantive agreement relating to Israeli-Jordanian or Palestinian relations (Zak 1996, 270). Still, it was an important milestone on the road to the eventual signing of a peace treaty between Jordan and Israel in 1994.

Peres's and Husayn's problem was how to "sell" the London Document to Shamir and his Likud ministers on the one hand, and to the PLO and Arab world on the other. In order to legitimize their move, Peres immediately sent his aide, Yossi Beilin, to Helsinki to report to US secretary of state Shultz, en route to Moscow. Exaggerating its significance, Beilin described the document as "the most historically significant step for Israel since the Biltmore Conference in May 1942,"[2] suggesting that the international conference proposal "be taken over as the initiative of the United States." Shultz refused to take part in this kind of political maneuvering, which would entangle him in domestic Israeli politics. In his memoirs he wrote, astonishingly: "The foreign minister of Israel's government of national unity was asking me to sell to Israel's prime minister, the head of a rival party, the substance of an agreement made with a foreign head of state—an agreement revealed to *me* before it had been revealed to the Israeli government itself!" (1993, 938–939). Upon his return from London, Peres updated Shamir on the agreement but refused to leave him a copy of the text for fear of leaks. Peres preferred that the text would be delivered by the United States, a step that would help impress upon Shamir the need to take a favorable stand (Peres 1995, 309). On April 22, Shultz spoke with Shamir and offered to come to the Middle East to "seize upon this very positive moment to go forward in the peace process" (Shultz 1993, 940). But Shamir splashed cold water on Shultz's proposal. His objection stemmed from two reasons. First, he thought that the conference would impose on Israel an unwanted solution, lead to its isolation, bring the PLO into the international arena through the back door, and eventually lead to Israel's withdrawal from Judea and Samaria, which he regarded as part of Greater Eretz Israel (Shamir 1994, 167–168). The second reason was linked to his suspicion of Peres, described in his memoirs as "operating behind my back and always disregarding the resultant damage to the coalition" (ibid., 167). Undoubtedly, Shamir was appalled that Peres was unwilling to show him—the prime minister!—the text of the agreement; he also feared that he had made some secret concessions to Jordan (Shlaim 2000, 446). It can be speculated too that, in light of Shamir's subsequent contacts with Husayn (see below), he was jealous of Peres. For Shamir, the London business smacked of conspiracy. In his desire to frustrate the initiative, he sent Minister of Defense Arens to convey to Shultz the impropriety of Peres's behavior, as well as his substantive opposition to the international conference concept. Shultz, however, was not easily put off; he thought that the agreement "represents a possibility that never existed before," and that the time was propitious "to try to come to terms with each other before real trouble [in the West Bank] breaks out" (1993, 941). Yet the inner squabbles between Peres and Shamir convinced Shultz not to embrace the London Document, though he felt that Shamir was wrong (Quandt 2005, 272; Peres 1995, 310).

In his communications with Shultz, Peres recognized that he would have to risk dismantling the government over this issue, emphasizing that he would not be a party to "Israel's missing this opportunity" (Shultz 1993, 940). On May 6, Peres presented to the inner cabinet a detailed proposal based on the London Document; as expected, it met with unanimous opposition from the Likud ministers. Peres decided not to put it to a vote because the outcome was certain to be a draw (which meant, in fact, rejection). Despite promises made to both Husayn and Shultz, Peres decided not to resign over the issue because such a step would have entailed giving his reasons in public, which would be an even greater violation of the pledge of secrecy given to Husayn in London (Shlaim 2000, 447, 446; Peres 1995, 311–312).[3] Peres's decision to remain in the government sealed the fate of the London Document.

The London Agreement had an interesting sequel, which has evaded scholars dealing with this episode and may throw some light on its potential. On July 18, 1987, Shamir too met Husayn in London; the Jordanian and Israeli reports on the meeting diverge, but it seems that Shamir expressed a more moderate position with regard to the international conference idea. Shultz was under the impression that "It was obvious that Shamir wanted to focus on his own private contacts with the king." Husayn, however, thought that Shamir was hopeless as a potential partner and opined that he could not work with him (Shultz 1993, 943; Shlaim 2000, 448–449; Quandt 2005, 272–273).[4]

As this channel closed down, another was opened; on September 11, Shultz presented Reagan with the idea of inviting Husayn and Shamir and representatives of Egypt, Syria, and Lebanon to meet in Washington under the two superpowers' auspices and the participation of the UN secretary-general. The aim was to achieve a peace treaty between Israel and the Arab states through direct negotiations. In this way, Shultz believed, Shamir would see the gathering as a summit (and not as an international conference), while Husayn would accept the international cover he needed for direct negotiations with Israel. This approach gave the Soviets some status in the summit but restricted their substantive influence. Reagan authorized the initiative, but added that "the first guy who vetoes it kills it" (Shultz 1993, 945).[5] On October 18, when the idea was presented to Shamir, he was both "attracted and appalled by it," according to Shultz's testimony. After some brief hesitation, he gave the green light to proceed; Shultz felt that "a sense of trust was evident and essential" in Shamir's response (ibid., 947). The surprise, however, came the following day, when Husayn gave a negative reply; the main reason for his refusal was his belief that Shamir would not relinquish an inch of territory and would not be willing to work on a final status agreement for the territories. In addition, he was convinced that Syria—backed by the Soviet Union—would oppose and obstruct the move (ibid., 948; Quandt 2005, 273). So this time it was Husayn, and not Shamir, to blink first and kill the idea.

Two months later, the Intifada erupted; the occupied territories, wrote Shlaim, "were like a tinderbox waiting for a spark" (2000, 450). The uprising brought the PLO back to center stage, rendering the Jordanian option largely irrelevant. Still, two diplomatic initiatives—one by Shultz (March 1988) and one by Shamir (May 1989)—attempted to offer a solution to a pre-Intifada reality.[6] This new reality led Husayn to declare, on July 31, 1988, that Jordan was disengaging itself from the West Bank by severing all economic and administrative ties. This decision, wrote Maoz, "put the tombstone over the grave of the Jordanian option" (2004, 446).

ASSESSMENT

Peres, the Israeli architect of the London Document, lamented in the 1990s that "We could have saved ourselves and the Palestinians six years of Intifada, and the loss of so much human life, had the former head of the Likud-run government not undermined the agreement I had worked out with King Hussein of Jordan" (1993, 16). Peres, in other words, was saying that by not endorsing the London Document, Israel missed an opportunity to prevent the uprising and, perhaps, to sign an agreement with Jordan. Taking into account his personal involvement and disappointment with his failure, Peres's assessment should be treated with caution.[7] Still, Shlaim thought that "the London Agreement was another missed opportunity of great importance," pointing the finger mainly at Israel for missing it (2007, 447). Moshe Raviv, who was the Israeli minister in London at the time, wrote, "In the catalogue of missed opportunities, the failure of the London Agreement has a respected place" (2000, 255). On the other hand, Eisenberg and Caplan's analysis of this episode as "premature peacemaking" suggests that the London Agreement paved the way for the Israeli-Jordanian peace treaty signed seven years later, but that it was not, per se, an opportunity missed for signing an agreement (1998, 60–71).

The London Document constituted a historical opportunity on two grounds. First, both Israel and Jordan estimated that developments in the region offered an opportunity to do something. In particular, the weakening of the PLO following the Lebanese War obliged 'Arafat to seek Jordanian support. This revival of the Jordanian option, which had led to the introduction of the Reagan Plan in September 1982, still seemed relevant a few years on. The failure of the Palestinian-Jordanian talks raised doubts regarding Husayn's ability to speak on behalf of the Palestinians, but since the United States and Israel saw the king as a reliable partner for negotiations, they deluded themselves into believing that he could deliver. Second, the fact that the London Agreement was not a one-sided offer but a joint Israeli-Jordanian initiative made it, at least in theory, an attractive offer that the United States (and perhaps other powers) could promote. Seeing the agreement as an opportunity to be seized, Shultz urged Shamir to respond to it favorably (Shultz 1993, 940). In October 1987, when he visited Israel on the occasion of receiving an honorary degree from the Weizmann Institute, Shultz said that "Serious opportunities for peace must be explored with energy, unity and resolve. For failure to do so may turn out to be that one serious mistake" (quoted in Shamir 1994, 170). At that time, before the eruption of the Intifada, Shultz believed that the opportunity still existed.

The first variable pertaining to missed opportunities relates to the level of legitimacy of the leaders. On the Israeli side, there was a serious problem as the government was composed of two rival parties in terms of politics and ideology. Peres, as foreign minister, did not represent Prime Minister Shamir and other Likud members in the government. In other words, Peres had no mandate for agreeing to an international conference (al-Madfai 1993, 190). Moreover, the timing of the accord could not have been less propitious, as Shamir was about to replace Peres as prime minister. This created a "schizophrenic Israeli diplomacy," as the foreign minister was promoting a policy that the prime minister opposed. With each attempting to win the battle, Shamir and Peres appealed to the United States to impose his preferred solution upon the other, sending separate envoys to argue their positions (Eisenberg and Caplan 1998, 66–67). Yet it is safe to assume that even if Peres had remained prime minister, the fact that he was presiding over a National Unity government "might have been enough to nix the plan" (ibid., 68). On the other hand, Maoz asserted that "Peres made a strategic mistake by not resigning and bringing down the national unity government" (2004, 447). He certainly could have done so, but the results of a similar move—his resignation from Shamir's National Unity government in early 1990—paradoxically led to the setting up of a narrow Likud-led right-wing government.[8]

On the Jordanian side, Husayn's legitimacy was assured, but he did not enjoy an Arab mandate to represent the Palestinians. In fact, though certain moderate Arab leaders (such as Mubarak, Fahd, and Hasan) would have preferred Jordan in the role, the Rabat summit deposited the Palestinian problem solely in the hands of the PLO. By the time Peres and Husayn reached their agreement, "the Jordanian option had long been a dead letter" (Schiff and Ya'ari 1984, 322). The majority of the Palestinians in the West Bank, as far as we can judge in the absence of reliable polls, supported the PLO as their representative and supported too the establishment of an independent Palestinian state. It was only by default, as a result of the Lebanese War, that Jordan had emerged as a possible interlocutor with regard to the Palestinians. Husayn attempted to exploit this historical opportunity to return to the Palestinian arena from which he was expelled in 1974. The London meeting offered him the role of a major Arab peacemaker and a method of talking to Israel that was relatively risk-free because it would be under US and Soviet patronage. Such a method assured him that Syria and the PLO, from which Husayn had suffered so much, would be less likely to accuse him of betraying the Palestinian cause (Shamir 1994, 169). Indeed, Syria and other Arab states initially supported the idea of an international conference, but the failure of the Jordanian-Palestinian talks and the abolition of the Amman Accord placed the king in a corner, where he "could neither replace 'Arafat, nor win his blessing for Jordanian-Israeli talks" (Eisenberg and Caplan 1988, 68).

The second variable is the willingness of leaders to take a bold step and change the course of events. In this episode, none of the leaders involved were willing to take risks. Peres, for one, when blocked by Shamir and the Likud, was unwilling to disband the government, providing various excuses for his behavior (Peres 1995, 311–312), which probably contradicted the promises he had given Husayn and Shultz. Husayn was unwilling to confront the PLO and Syria, particularly when he realized that Peres could not deliver and that Shamir enjoyed veto power. In addition, it was clear that Husayn, in contrast to Egypt's Sadat, could not risk the political and economic isolation of Jordan in the Arab world as a result of an agreement with Israel. And, finally, Shultz, though committed to the peace process, was unwilling to become embroiled in domestic Israeli politics. The fact that he and Reagan were less than enthusiastic about the concept of the international conference from the start, because of their reluctance to bolster the role of the Soviet Union, did not enhance its prospects.

The third variable relates to the history of past interactions between the parties to the conflict, which influences the level of trust (or mistrust) existing between them. Relations between Jordan and Israel were characterized by such terms as "hostile partnership" (Melman 1987) and "the best of enemies" (Bar-Joseph 1987). Husayn had met with every Israeli prime minister over the years, "creating ongoing relationships that have weathered wars and regional crises." By the 1980s, fifty years of high-level Israeli-Jordanian contacts were an open secret (Eisenberg and Caplan 1998, 62). These contacts created a sense of trust between the two sides, despite their still being officially at war. This trust was manifested in the London meeting, though its results—and the fact that Peres did not bring down the government as promised—damaged his credibility in Husayn's eyes. In fact, Husayn did not meet Peres again until the signing of the Oslo Accords in 1993 (Zak 1996, 278; Shlaim 2007, 447). In many ways, the London Agreement was a result of the trust that had been built over the years between the leaders of the two states, but this was not sufficient to overcome many other hurdles.

The fourth variable relates to the level of involvement of the third party. The United States had never been enthusiastic about convening an international conference, because such an enterprise entailed inviting the Soviet Union back into the Middle East. When, however, Shultz realized that some kind of international forum was needed to serve as a cover for Husayn, he played the role of trusted facilitator, with Egypt and Saudi Arabia being involved as well. Yet in spite of the US support of the London Document, the White House was unwilling to stake its prestige on what it feared might become yet another failed Middle East peace plan and hesitated to interfere in the domestic tug-of-war between Peres and Shamir (Eisenberg and Caplan 1998, 66). Probably the failure of the Reagan Plan contributed to the US hesitancy to promote the document. The result was, therefore, a lack of commitment on the part of the mediator to promote a joint plan that was endorsed by the parties to the conflict. In this regard, Shultz's lack of enthusiasm was criticized, for example, by Peres, who later wrote that with Shultz's decision not to interfere in Israeli politics, the London Agreement "was asphyxiated at birth" (1995, 310). From a different angle, an American diplomat, Robert Neumann, asserted, "A negotiator waits until the moment is right. A statesman ripens the moments. Shultz was not a statesman" (quoted in al-Madfai 1993, 194). If the Reagan Plan and the London Document were extensions of the Camp David formula, then what was missing here was a determined president like Jimmy Carter. Reagan's assessment seemed to be correct, however, as the chances for seizing this opportunity—according to our analysis—were not high.

The analysis of the four variables above suggests that the potentiality level of the London Document was low. The parties suffered from serious legitimacy problems; they were not willing to take bold and courageous steps; and the third party—the United States—was not fully committed to the process. The only variable that worked in favor of the pact was the length and depth of past interactions, through which a certain level of trust had been built between the parties. The plausibility level of the missed opportunity was low, since neither party showed apathy, indifference, or inaction on his part. In fact, the London Document was a product of a joint endeavor. Yet the reality was more complicated because of the National Unity government, meaning that the willing party (Israel/Peres/Labor) included also an element (Israel/Shamir/Likud) that attempted to sabotage the agreement. In addition, the assessment that the London Agreement constituted an important milestone on the road to the signing of the Israeli-Jordanian peace treaty further reduces the plausibility level of it as a missed opportunity.

Moshe Zak, an Israeli journalist well acquainted with Israeli-Jordanian relations, poses the important question of whether Husayn was ripe to sign a peace treaty in 1987, but he does not give a clear answer (1996, 273). No less important, however, is the question whether Israel was ripe to sign a peace treaty. In contrast to the accepted wisdom (reflected, for example, in Shlaim's assertion above), the analysis of the London Document shows that the plausibility level of a missed opportunity in this case study was low: neither party was truly ready to sign an agreement, nor was the mediator fully committed to this process. And yet it served as another brick in the edifice of the peace treaty that was completed in 1994.

NOTES

1. "Irangate" was the term used to describe the conspiracy in which Israel, with the knowledge of officials in the CIA and elsewhere, secretly delivered US-made arms to Iran during its war with Iraq. The money received went to fund aid to the Nicaraguan contras, which the US Congress prohibited. See Shlaim 2000, 439–442.

2. The Biltmore Conference was convened by the American Zionists at the Biltmore Hotel in New York in May 1942. The conference adopted a program that for the first time demanded the establishment of a Jewish state in Palestine (Tessler 2009, 251; Oren 2007, 442–445).

3. For the text of the proposal submitted to the inner cabinet, see Melman 1987, 157. In his memoirs, Peres wrote that he seriously considered resigning, but he does not mention any earlier promises to Husayn or Shultz to take this step (Peres 1995, 311–312).

4. Interestingly, Shamir failed to mention the encounter with Husayn in his memoirs.

5. In his memoirs, Shultz presents the idea as his; however, Quandt writes that the idea was initially pitched by Peres (2005, 273). Peres confirmed this in his memoirs (1995, 310).

6. These two initiatives will be discussed in the next chapter.

7. Peres repeated this argument in an interview he made with Amira Lam; in response to the question "What do you consider your biggest failure?" he answered: "The London Agreement. I reached an agreement with the king, which everyone thought was the best

agreement, but it was torpedoed, and this was the nation's biggest loss" (*Yedioth Ahronoth*, Seven Days magazine, July 30, 2010).

8. In March 1990 the National Unity government was brought down by Peres. The pretext was Shamir's rejection of Secretary of State James Baker's proposal that Israel negotiate with a Palestinian delegation composed of delegates residing not only in the West Bank (Judea and Samaria) but also East Jerusalem. Peres was given the mandate to form a government, but he failed. In June 1990 Shamir succeeded in setting up a narrow right-wing coalition. See Shlaim 2000, 471–472; Tessler 2009, 735.

CHAPTER 16

THE SHULTZ INITIATIVE AND
THE SHAMIR PEACE PLAN
1988 AND 1989

ON DECEMBER 9, 1987, a car accident in Gaza sparked off demonstrations there, spilled over to the West Bank, and quickly spiraled into what would soon become known as the Intifada, or Palestinian uprising. The uprising was triggered by a combination of factors, such as the economic and political repercussions of the Israeli occupation as well as the absence of any semblance of a peace process, which in turn led to growing despair and frustration, particularly among young people. The Intifada brought the PLO back to center stage, while concomitantly diminishing Jordan's role on the Palestinian scene. This development was reflected in King Husayn's decision to formally disengage Jordan from the West Bank in July 1988 and the Palestinian Declaration of Independence that November. During the Intifada, which continued for over six years, two attempts were made to revive the peace process. In March 1988, US secretary of state George Shultz launched a peace initiative, described by Quandt as "the most important US involvement in Arab-Israeli peacemaking since Reagan's initiative" (2005, 275). In May 1989, Israeli prime minister Yitzhak Shamir made public his peace plan—the first-ever formal Israeli peace initiative![1] The two attempts were linked not only by their substance but also in their attempts to respond to the changing reality. This chapter will analyze if and to what extent these initiatives constituted missed opportunities.

THE EPISODE

The eruption of the Intifada in 1987 was a major turning point in the annals of the Israeli-Palestinian conflict. Although it began due to an accident, tension and frustration had been growing for some time. Now, for the first time since the occupation began in 1967, the local population in the West Bank and Gaza rather spontaneously initiated a series of demonstrations, strikes, and riots that compelled the Israeli authorities to respond harshly. The disturbing pictures of Israeli troops firing on stone-throwing demonstrators caused great damage to Israel's image in the West and the Arab world; "The biblical image of David and Goliath," wrote Shlaim, "now seemed to be reversed, with Israel looking like an overbearing Goliath and the Palestinians with the stone as a vulnerable David" (2007, 454). The Intifada came as a surprise to Israel, Jordan, the United States, and even the PLO—all unaware of the deep social and economic forces that had been bubbling up from below (Schiff and Ya'ari 1984, 17–50). Though these events did not have any clear leaders, Yasser 'Arafat and the PLO were quick to realize the political potential of the uprising; having lost ground to Husayn and Jordan following the Lebanese War, they were keen to reap its dividends.

The Intifada brought about a reevaluation of the US policy toward the Arab-Israeli conflict in general and the Israeli-Palestinian conflict in particular. Shultz, the dominant architect of the Reagan administration's approach to the peace process, thought that "The Intifada created a wholly new situation, one that in its own way altered the fundamental concept of the peace process" (1993, 1016). It posed a "fresh opportunity," he believed, that could drive changes in a far more rapid way than the usual pace of the peace process. Shultz's premise, however mistaken in the long run, was that since the PLO did not initiate the grassroots uprising, it bore the promise of a new generation of Palestinians, with new leaders trying to take hold of their own affairs. This development coincided with the Israeli desire to talk to indigenous leaders, but not members of the PLO. Shultz reckoned that the United States could help identify local leaders who would participate in the dialogue (ibid., 1017). He was affected not only by the Intifada, but also by the calls from Israeli and Jewish leaders as well as Egyptian president Mubarak to take the initiative "to ward off a radicalization of the entire region" (Quandt 2005, 274). The fact that Shultz had taken the unusual step of launching a peace initiative in an election year in both the United States and Israel was testimony to the urgency the administration felt with regard to the magnitude of the opportunity. He thought that by creating an active and visible peace process, he would be able to "lessen the dangers of escalating violence" (1993, 1020).

In late January 1988, Shultz gathered a group of officials together with the aim of repackaging and streamlining the missing Palestinian element in the Camp David framework, forcing its pace and speeding up its implementation. Launched in March, the Shultz Initiative included the following elements. First, the process was to begin with an international conference, held in mid-April; to allay Israeli fears and reminiscent of the London Agreement, the conference was planned only as a "ceremonial kickoff event" and had no power to impose solutions or to veto any agreements previously reached by the parties. Second, two weeks after the conference, negotiations would begin

between Israel and each of the willing parties. The plan envisioned talks between Israeli and joint Jordanian-Palestinian delegations, with US involvement, working on the parameters of a transitional self-rule for the Palestinians in the West Bank and Gaza. These talks were expected to end within
six months (November). The transitional period would begin three months
later (February 1989) and would extend for three years. The plan then proposed that the final talks would be held seven months after the negotiations
on the transitional period began (in September 1989), and would be completed within one year. This was a new element termed "interlock": a built-in
connection between the transition period of self-rule and talks on the final
status, aimed at allaying Arab fears that the transitional period would last forever. The abbreviated timetable had clearly been prepared to coincide with
the January 1989 deadline for the end of the Reagan administration's term
(Spiegel 1990, 17–18; Shultz 1993, 1018–1019; Quandt 2005, 275).

Shultz was astonished to learn that only Mubarak and Israeli foreign minister Peres supported his initiative. As before, Shamir was opposed to the very
idea of an international conference, however ceremonial; he also objected in
principle to the exchange of territory for peace and to the linkage between the
transition and final talks, and he feared that the Jordanian-Palestinian delegation would be used as a cover for PLO members to wend their way into the
talks. Shamir's position was dictated by not only his ideological stand but
also political expediency: with elections scheduled for November, he thought
that diplomatic concessions would jeopardize his chances to win. Though the
United States did not apply pressure on Shamir, both Reagan and Shultz attempted to convince him of the international conference's benefits by emphasizing its ceremonial and procedural character (Shamir 1994, 175–176; Spiegel
1990, 19–20; Shlaim 2007, 456). Shultz was highly critical of the Israelis, accusing them of "using this issue [the international conference] as an excuse
to deflect the real concept and opportunity. I was throwing them a life jacket,
but they were refusing to put it on" (1993, 1026). He was particularly annoyed
by Shamir's intransigence and the fact that he did not give him anything to
work with (ibid., 1030).

Husayn, for his part, adopted a position that neither endorsed nor rejected
the initiative. While skeptical that Israel would give up any territory in the
West Bank, he thought that the PLO should play a leading role in the negotiations (Spiegel 1990, 20; Shultz 1993, 1025–1027). In hindsight, it is clear that
the Jordanian king was the first to understand—long before the United States
and Israel—that he could no longer negotiate the Palestinian cause on behalf
of the PLO. Indeed, the game was changed once the Arab summit in Algeria,
held on June 7–9, 1988, affirmed Arab support for the right of the Palestinians
to independence under the leadership of the PLO. From that point on, for ex-

ample, all Arab aid to the Intifada was to be channeled through the PLO and not, as previously, through a joint Jordanian-Palestinian committee (Shlaim 2007, 460–461). The process of Jordan's disengagement was finalized with Husayn's decisions in July to terminate the five-year development plan for the West Bank, sever all legal and administrative ties, dissolve Jordan's parliament (half of whose members were Palestinians from the West Bank), and more. On August 7, Husayn declared that Jordan would never again speak on behalf of the Palestinians. All these steps and statements signaled the demise of the Jordanian option. The decision to disengage from the West Bank disappointed Shultz as his initiative largely depended on Jordan's cooperation and participation (ibid., 462, 465; Quandt 2005, 277; Schiff and Ya'ari 1984, 270–273). In his memoirs, he wrote candidly that the king's decision "appeared to mark the end of my initiative" (1993, 1033).

The failure of the Shultz Initiative was also due to opposition from the PLO, which was disappointed that even as the uprising raged it was given the role of junior partner to Jordan in the plan (Quandt 2005, 276). Riding the wave of the Intifada, the PLO had rehabilitated its place in the Arab and international arenas; it now succeeded in thwarting the US initiative and eliminating Jordan as a spokesman for the Palestinian cause. Thus, for example, when Shultz tried to meet local Palestinian leaders in East Jerusalem, the PLO instructed those leaders to boycott the meeting—and they did.[2] Jordan's departure from the diplomatic lexicon meant that the United States and Israel would have to engage directly with the PLO. While Israeli leaders were still far from thinking in such terms, the United States was almost racing to that end; the major impediment was Kissinger's pledge to Israel in 1975 that the US would not recognize or negotiate with the PLO unless it acknowledged Israel's right to exist, accepted UN Resolutions 242 and 338, and renounced terrorism (Quandt 2005, 278; Spiegel 1990, 26). Yet 'Arafat, in his desire to enjoy the political fruits of the Intifada, realized that in order to open a formal dialogue with the United States he would have to acquiesce to these demands. At the Palestinian National Council meeting in Algiers on November 15, 'Arafat proclaimed an independent state of Palestine with Jerusalem as its capital (Lukacs 1992, 411–415). The ambiguity of the statement, however, with regard to UN Resolution 242, the recognition of Israel, and the renouncing of terrorism, led the United States to insist on a clearer formulation. This came in 'Arafat's address to the UN General Assembly and his press statement, both made in Geneva on December 13 and 14 (ibid., 420–434; Gazit 1990, 90–94; Quandt 2005, 282–285). The United States immediately announced that it was now prepared to begin a substantive dialogue with the PLO, though it did not recognize the declaration of an independent Palestinian state (Shultz 1993, 1044; Sayigh 1997, 624). In such a way, Reagan, shortly before leaving office, bequeathed this new reality to his successor, George H. W. Bush, who was elected in November. Shultz thought that a similar change would have to occur in Israel as well; at some point, he predicted, "Israel would have to face up to this truth" (ibid., 1045).

In Israel the November 1988 elections forced the two rival political blocs, Likud and Labor, to form another National Unity government, though this time Shamir served as the prime minister for the whole term, Peres was minister of finance, Moshe Arens foreign minister, and Rabin remained the defense minister. In early 1989, Shamir became convinced that Israel should advance a peace proposal of its own. This unprecedented move had its roots in several developments. First was a desire to bypass the PLO, following the US decision to open a dialogue with the organization—causing Israel to fear that it might become a legitimate player in the peace process. Second, he assessed that the intensity of the Intifada could be reduced by military means, but that only a political settlement could terminate it completely. Shamir understood that the Intifada, like the change in the PLO's position, which he described as deceitful promises and declarations, was damaging Israel's image and necessitated a response that would present the "truth" to the world and push the Arabs to a defensive position. In this connection, Shamir particularly emphasized the recent changes in world affairs—the decline of the Soviet Union and its withdrawal from Afghanistan, as well as the end of the Iran-Iraq War—which were now virtually over, redirecting world attention to the Middle East. And, finally, he estimated that there was general support in Israeli society for some peaceful process (Lukacs 1992, 246–248; Shlaim 2000, 466–467; Rubinstein 1992, 129–131). The main points of the plan, which were formulated by Shamir and Rabin during the first months of the year, were presented to Bush in April 1989 and were received with general support.

On May 14, 1989, the initiative was formally introduced.[3] Presented as an elaboration of the Camp David path, it called for elections in the West Bank and Gaza to select non-PLO Palestinians with whom Israel would negotiate, along with Jordan and Egypt, a five-year transitional agreement on self-rule. The elections were to be held in an "atmosphere devoid of violence, threats and terror"—phrasing that spelled the cessation of the Intifada. The interim period was supposed to provide a vital test of coexistence and cooperation to be followed by negotiations for a permanent solution. An interlock—the main novelty of the initiative—between the two stages was to be assured by a timetable limiting the transitional period. During the second stage, "all the proposed options for an agreed settlement" would be examined. In addition, the initiative called for the strengthening and expansion of the peace treaty with Egypt; a change in the nature of relations between Israel and the Arab states by abolishing the Arab boycott and by adopting other confidence-building measures; and an international effort to solve the problem of the Palestinian refugees. The initiative was intended as an indivisible whole: no progress in one area meant no movement in other areas either (Gazit 1991, 70–71, 94–96; Shlaim 2000, 468; Lukacs 1992, 236–239, 246–247; Rubinstein 1992, 134–140; Shamir 1994, 194–195; Schiff and Ya'ari 1984, 318–319; Ross 2005, 55–64; Arens 1995, 53–111).

Shamir's main problem was the opposition to the peace plan within the government and his party, led by ministers Ariel Sharon, David Levy, and Yitzhak Moda'i. At the Likud Party convention in June, Shamir had to accept four points that effectively muted any possibility that the Palestinians might accept the proposed elections: Arab residents of East Jerusalem could neither vote in nor run for the elections; there would be no elections until the Intifada ended; Israel would not relinquish any territory and no Palestinian state would ever be established; and settlements would continue to be built (Spiegel and Pervin 1991, 22; Arens 1995, 64–68). In addition, Shamir had to face the fact that Peres—in spite of his endorsement of the plan—was attempting to promote his ideas in the United States behind Shamir's back (Arens 1995, 78). In the long run, this domestic opposition would lead to Shamir's downfall.

The United States generally endorsed the initiative, though it tried to make it more appealing to the Palestinians. The new US secretary of state, James Baker, called on Israel "to lay aside, once and for all, the unrealistic vision of a greater Israel" and to "forswear annexation, [and] stop settlement activity" (quoted in Gazit 1991, 72). Nevertheless, Bush and Baker expressed their willingness to play a mediating role. The problem was that Israel saw the election proposal as a means of finding authentic non-PLO Palestinian leaders, while the US was looking for ways to involve the PLO in the process.

In addition to the United States, Mubarak became another potential mediator. Following its full return to the Arab League in the Casablanca summit in May 1989, Egypt felt more confident in playing a leading role in the peace process. Having established good rapport with 'Arafat, Mubarak now attempted to bridge the gap between the Israeli and Palestinian positions. Even the US found Mubarak to be a more effective channel than the formal US-PLO dialogue. Following a meeting with Rabin in September, Mubarak published a ten-point plan that called for the participation in elections of all citizens of the West Bank and Gaza, including the residents of East Jerusalem; agreement to international supervision before and during the elections; an Israeli commitment to accept the results of the elections, which would be the starting point to the final negotiations; and the prevention of settlement activity during this period. It was believed that these points were accepted by 'Arafat (Gazit 1991, 80–81, 96; Ross 2005, 57–60). Shamir and his dissenting ministers in the Likud, however, rejected Mubarak's plan, mainly because it called for the exchange of territory for peace. As a result, the cabinet reaffirmed Shamir's May 14 initiative without additions or changes. When Egypt officially delivered its plan in early October, it almost caused the breakup of the National Unity government, as Rabin, Peres, and the Labor Party supported it while Shamir and the Likud opposed it. As expected, the cabinet vote ended in a tie, meaning that the Egyptian proposal had been defeated. As with the London Document in 1987, Labor's threat to quit the government was not fulfilled; instead, it asked the United States to become directly involved in the peace process.

Without much enthusiasm, Baker stepped in and on October 8 proposed a five-point plan that suggested a mechanism to advance the Israeli-Palestinian dialogue based on the Israeli peace initiative: a meeting of Israeli and Palestinian delegations in Cairo. To soften up the Palestinians, it was noted that they would be able to raise issues pertaining to their views on how to make the elections and subsequent negotiating process succeed. In order to facilitate the process, Baker invited the foreign ministers of Israel, Egypt, and the United States to meet in Washington (Gazit 1991, 75–76; Quandt 2005, 298; Ross 2005, 60–64). Egypt declared that 'Arafat had accepted the Baker formula; Shamir's government consented but added six demands which—if accepted—would bind the US to unconditional support for Israel's positions. Consequently, the PLO responded with a set of conditions of its own. Baker was particularly frustrated with the Israeli politicians, thinking they had impeded the wheels of the peace process: Shamir was hard-pressed between intransigent Likud ministers accusing him of adopting a soft line and the Labor Party supporting both Mubarak's and Baker's plans. In March 1990, Peres attempted to do what he had failed to do at least twice before: to dismantle the coalition and form a government that would kick-start the peace process; however, his secretive attempt ended in a shameful failure (Rabin called it "the dirty trick"), which led to the formation in May of a narrow, right-wing Shamir-headed coalition. Shlaim assessed that it was "the most right-wing government in Israel's history and certainly the most hard-line when it came to relations with the Arabs." This government, continued Shlaim, allowed Shamir "the freedom of inaction" (2000, 471–472). With this, the halfhearted peace process that commenced with the Shamir Initiative, continued with Mubarak's ten-point program, and ended with Baker's five-point plan once more reached an impasse. The suspension of the US-PLO dialogue in June 1990, following a terror attack by a splinter Palestinian organization, sealed this chapter (Quandt 2005, 300–301).

ASSESSMENT

Ze'ev Schiff, a leading Israeli journalist and military expert, assessed that the Palestinian Intifada "created an opportunity for the parties to resume the peace process and re-examine a number of basic premises." The situation in 1988–1989, in his opinion, was akin to the time after the 1973 October War, when certain existing conditions made possible a series of interim agreements that led to a peace treaty (1989, ix). Similarly, Philip Mattar, a Palestinian academic, wrote in 1989 that "The US is again in danger of missing an opportunity for peace in the Middle East." In his opinion, "Never in recent years have peace prospects in the Middle East been better" (Mattar 1989, 141).

To what extent did the Shultz Initiative and Shamir Peace Plan constitute historical opportunities? Undoubtedly, the Intifada can be identified as a significant watershed in the conflict, creating a basis for the emergence of an alternative. Moreover, the change in the PLO position in late 1988 regarding recognition of Israel, the acceptance of Resolutions 242 and 338, and the renouncing of terrorism further contributed to the assessment that a major turning point in the Israeli-Palestinian conflict had occurred. As we have seen, the two US administrations in office during this period were convinced that the Intifada created a window of opportunity, and therefore called for a new initiative. The problem was that the two plans analyzed in this chapter had a measure of attraction for Israel, Jordan, and Egypt—but not for the PLO, which was emerging as an important player. The United States, wrote Shlaim, "recognized that the situation in the territories had been fundamentally altered by the Intifada, but it failed to understand the implications. Consequently, the Shultz Initiative continued to promote the Jordanian role in negotiations and to exclude the PLO" (2007, 456). This assessment is even more valid for the Shamir Plan, which completely ignored the PLO while giving prominent roles to the Palestinian inhabitants of the territories, Egypt, and Jordan—the preferred partners of Israel and the United States. Thus, while the Intifada and the new PLO position shattered some well-established premises, the peace plans did not reflect this and even lagged behind reality. In other words, the new circumstances produced a historical opportunity, which was exploited to present two peace plans in "a formula that proved unworkable a decade ago" (Mattar 1989, 141).

To what extent was this opportunity squandered? The first variable relates to the legitimacy of the leadership. As far as we can judge, 'Arafat and the PLO enjoyed broad legitimacy; though not directly responsible for the outbreak of the Intifada, both succeeded in reaping the political dividends of the uprising, culminating in the disengagement of Jordan from the West Bank, the declaration of independence, and the opening of the dialogue with the

United States. This legitimacy was further strengthened by the Arab summits in Algiers (November 1988) and Casablanca (May 1989), which gave the
PLO full support as the sole legitimate representative of the Palestinian people
(Sela 1998, 312–313). The legitimacy issue on the Israeli side was more problematic. Seemingly, Shamir's coalition was suited to grappling with fateful decisions, both because it incorporated Israel's largest parties and because many
of its ministers were highly experienced in matters of national security. Yet
the cabinet was deeply divided on how to tackle the Palestinian issue, though
occasionally its members found common ground on which to cooperate (like
Shamir and Rabin over the Israeli peace initiative). Each party was further
divided into competing camps that could balance and cancel each other out
whenever it appeared that an impending decision would be to their rival's advantage. This was particularly true with regard to Likud, where leading ministers constantly challenged Shamir's authority and legitimacy to offer concessions. The greatest enemy, wrote Rubinstein, was the internal divisions (1992,
141). The National Unity government did eventually collapse, attesting to the
personal and ideological differences that existed between Likud and Labor.

The second variable relates to the willingness of the leaders to take bold
decisions and steps necessitated to change the course of events. There is no
denying that by meeting the American demands, 'Arafat made a significant
shift in his policy, and perhaps even in ideology. Mattar thought that the
Algiers statement represented "a fundamental, even radical, change in Palestinian thinking" (1989, 142). It was the success of the Intifada that gave 'Arafat
and his followers the confidence needed to moderate their political program
(Shlaim 2000, 466; Mattar 1989, 142, 151). Yet Shamir and many members of
the coalition saw the change as a rhetorical ploy aimed at upholding the PLO
in the international arena and not a sincere change of heart (Rubinstein 1992,
130). It is clear that 'Arafat made a bold move though there are contradictory
assessments regarding its sincerity.

On the other hand, the Shamir Peace Initiative could hardly be described
as a bold move, as it did not significantly deviate from the traditional Israeli
policy. Moreover, many Israelis and Palestinians saw the plan as merely a
political tactic or ploy. Shamir himself was quoted as saying that his plan
was "largely a public relations exercise designed to take the heat off Israel"
(Mattar 1989, 144). The initiative, indeed, can be seen as a media spin aimed at
easing the international pressure on Israel to do something concerning Israeli-
Palestinian relations in light of the changes in the region following the outbreak of the Intifada. In his initiative, Shamir made it clear to the Palestinians
that Israel would not negotiate the establishment of a Palestinian state; that
Israel would not sit down with the PLO or anyone appointed by it; that the
residents of East Jerusalem would not be permitted to run for office and vote

for the institutions of the yet-to-be-established autonomous administration; and that the negotiations would not begin until the Intifada had ended (Schiff and Ya'ari 1984, 320–321). With such a clear position, Shamir's ideas could not be considered attractive enough from a Palestinian point of view. Mattar noted in this regard: "Truly free and democratic elections should and would be welcomed by the Palestinians, but no Palestinian, however moderate, can be expected to accept Shamir's scheme" (1989, 144). His lack of assertiveness with regard to his own initiative was manifested when he did not put up a fight and allowed the opposition within his own party to constrain him. Shlaim described this situation in a picturesque way: "By a neat sleight of hand, the master magician Shamir managed in rapid succession to launch and shoot down his own peace plan, making it look suspiciously like a clay pigeon devised for nothing more than a bit of harmless sport" (2000, 470).

The third variable relates to the history of past interactions, which affects the level of trust existing between the parties. In contrast to Israeli-Egyptian, Israeli-Jordanian, and even Israeli-Syrian relations, there was little history of formal Israeli-Palestinian relations until the late 1980s. The opposite was true with regard to nonofficial meetings, as Israeli and Palestinian civilians met on different occasions and at various locations, though these contacts had no political effect. Some rare examples of official contact were the meeting of Israeli officials with leaders of Palestinian refugees at the 1949 Lausanne Conference and with local Palestinian leaders from the West Bank following the 1967 War. The reason was that the Palestinian official representatives— whether the Arab Higher Committee during the Mandate period or the PLO since the mid-1960s—were regarded by Israel as terrorist organizations. Between 1986 and 1992, any contact between Israelis and the PLO was prohibited by law, though certain nonofficial meetings between those parties did take place (Tessler 2009, 728). The change in the PLO's position in 1988 did not change the negative image most Israelis had of the organization and of 'Arafat. As a result, all the initiatives concentrated on the grooming of local Palestinian leaders from the occupied territories, but the potential leaders refused to play a part in the Israeli game. It is also possible that they remained aloof because they had been intimidated by the PLO. The lack of contact and the negative image each party had of its adversary did not enable the development of any confidence-building measures, which would create some trust between the two parties.

The fourth variable pertains to the role of the mediator. During the Reagan era, Shultz dominated the diplomatic field. Quandt found that Shultz seemed to hesitate when opportunities opened up and that policies emerged more often as reactions to events in the Middle East than as part of a grand design (2005, 288). Still, his initiative was an attempt to seize the historical opportunity that accrued as a result of the Intifada. Spiegel thought that the initiative was "breathtaking in its attempt to square the circle of differing Israeli and Arab conceptions of how the peace process should be conducted" (1990, 17). Yet with the wisdom of hindsight it is clear that the Shultz Initiative, much like the Shamir Plan, "was a formula that proved unworkable a decade ago" (Mattar 1989, 141). When Bush entered office, he was guided by the premise that the Arab-Israeli conflict was not ripe for a solution and therefore the parties should be encouraged to engage in a prenegotiation phase of confidence-building measures (Quandt 2005, 293; Mattar 1989, 147–148). This is the reason why Bush and Baker were reluctant to lead the peace talks, but expressed interest in offering mediation, though without much enthusiasm. Baker, unlike Shultz, was willing to visit the Middle East only if there was a real chance of progress. However, as there were "no heroes for dramatic breakthroughs such as Sadat," in the words of peace-broker Dennis Ross, the Middle East expert on the National Security Council staff, the US involvement was limited. In addition, neither Bush nor Baker trusted Shamir, thinking he "had been stringing us along" (Ross 2005, 53, 64). Having established direct dialogue with the PLO, the United States was in a position to mediate between Israel and the PLO, but the Israeli position ruled out this eventuality. To be fair, it should be stressed that even a more energetic administration would have failed to bridge the gap between the parties over the Shamir Initiative. Interestingly, this episode saw the appearance of Egypt as a new actor in the mediation field. Having returned to a leading Arab role and enjoying 'Arafat's confidence, Egypt was even in a better position than the United States to serve as a mediator. The problem was that both mediators were suspected of being impartial: the US was suspected of backing Israel in Arab/Palestinian eyes, while Egypt was suspected of backing the PLO in Israeli eyes.

In sum, though the repercussions of the Intifada and the changes in the PLO's attitude offered a historical opportunity for doing something about the peace process, the initiatives put on the table by the United States and Israel held little attraction for the Palestinians or the PLO. In addition, none of the four variables analyzed above suggested that there was any significant potential for seizing this opportunity. The conclusion is, therefore, that the Shultz and Shamir initiatives did not in any way constitute a plausible missed opportunity.

NOTES

1. Actually, the first Israeli peace plan was adopted in June 1967, but it was never submitted to the Arab side. See the discussion in chapter 8.

2. In a somewhat bizarre scene, Shultz delivered his message to the Palestinian local

leaders, despite their being absent, in the flowering courtyard of the American Colony Hotel (Spiegel 1990, 18).

3. Rubinstein, who was intimately involved in the discussions as Shamir's cabinet secretary, claims that the term "initiative" instead of "plan" was deliberately used to maintain the necessary flexibility in light of the complexity of the situation (1992, 133).

CHAPTER 17

THE MADRID CONFERENCE
AND THE OSLO AGREEMENTS

1991 AND 1993–2000

IN 1991 A CONVERGENCE of dramatically shifting circumstances, primarily the end of the Gulf War and the crumbling of the Soviet Union, made possible an international conference on the Israeli-Arab conflict. The three-day parley, hosted by the Spanish government in Madrid and cosponsored by the United States and the Soviet Union, was unprecedented in its broad participation. Opening on October 30, it marked a concerted attempt to revive the peace process with Israeli, Syrian, Lebanese, and Jordanian-Palestinian delegations. The conference and the ensuing ten rounds of bilateral and multilateral negotiations did not produce an agreement, but they did facilitate a breakthrough on the Palestinian and Jordanian tracks. This chapter will deal with the Palestinian track, which led to the dramatic signing of the Oslo Accords. The term "Oslo" refers to a series of agreements that commenced with the Declaration of Principles on Interim Self-Government Arrangements, signed between Israel and the PLO on September 13, 1993, and ended with the Sharm al-Shaykh Memorandum in May 1999. The six years of intermittent negotiations in fact produced several agreements: the Paris Economic Protocol (April 1994); the Gaza and Jericho Agreement (May 1994); Preparatory Transfer of Powers and Responsibilities (August 1994); the Interim Agreement on the West Bank and the Gaza Strip (September 1995, also called Oslo II); the Hebron Protocol (January 1997); and the Wye River Memorandum (October 1998). The Oslo period ended with the Camp David talks (July 2000); within weeks of their collapse, the second Intifada erupted. In contrast to previous case studies bound by time and geography, the Oslo Accords were more complex, as the negotiations lasted for some seven years and involved many actors. The aim of this chapter is to offer a concise historical analysis of the period (excluding the Camp David II episode, which will be analyzed separately; see chapter 20) and to consider if and to what extent an opportunity arose, and was missed, to reach a final peace treaty between Israel and the Palestinians.

THE MADRID CONFERENCE AND THE OSLO AGREEMENTS 209

THE EPISODE

A recurring feature of Arab-Israeli negotiations throughout the 1980s, as we have seen in this volume, is the sense among decision makers and diplomats that an international conference is needed to kick-start a peace process. All such efforts failed due to the intransigence of key regional actors, most notably Israel and Syria, each for its own reasons, as well as a lukewarm US response.

The international conference idea was revived during the war against Iraq (January 1991). Just like with the 1982 Lebanese War, the State Department assessed that the war in Iraq might create conditions for a solution to the Arab-Israeli conflict (Quandt 2005, 303; Ross 2005, 65). Secretary of State Baker was convinced that "there are some new realities that make progress possible and we owe it to ourselves and everyone to make the effort" (1995, 443). No wonder that Bush conveyed this sentiment to Congress, on March 6, 1991, in the aftermath of the victory in Iraq: "We must work to create new opportunities for peace and stability in the Middle East. On the night I announced Operation Desert Storm, I expressed my hope that out of the horrors of war might come new momentum for peace" (quoted in Kurtzer et al. 2013, 15).

The convening of the Madrid Conference was the result of several major developments in the international and regional arenas. The first was the demise of the Soviet Union and the end of the Cold War; this profoundly affected the region, eliminating the patrons of the Arab Rejection Front — Syria, Iraq, Libya, and the PLO — which could no longer rely on the Soviet Union to back their often antagonistic policy toward peace with Israel. In addition, the fact that the crumbling superpower had opened its gates to some million Jewish immigrants strengthened Israel economically and demographically. The second development was the victory of the United States and the supporting coalition in the Gulf War against Iraq and the liberation of Kuwait. On the one hand, the war weakened Jordan and the PLO because of their support of Saddam Hussein's annexation of Kuwait; it was estimated that they might respond positively to any serious diplomatic overture in order to break out from their siege. On the other, the war strengthened the US determination to resolve the Arab-Israeli conflict. Becoming a hegemon in the international system, the United States saw the moment as propitious to establish a new order in the Middle East, with peaceful relations between Israel and the Arabs enabling it to more effectively support the policy of "dual containment" of both Iran and Iraq. Finally, though the Intifada had largely exhausted itself, it had greatly affected the Israeli public, which was more willing now to resume the Israeli-Palestinian peace process and not necessarily through the

Jordanian channel, understanding that the role of the Palestinians and the PLO cannot be ignored (Eisenberg and Caplan 1998, 77–79; Quandt 2005, 303–310; Hirschfeld 2000, 69–75; Ross 2005, 67–87; Kimmerling and Migdal 2003, 317–330; Karsh 1994, 143–156; Arens 1995, 218–244; Kurtzer et al. 2013, 22–30; Khatib 2010, 51–58).

It took Baker eight months of shuttle diplomacy to persuade all the relevant players to seize the opportunity and take part in the suggested international conference (Baker 1995, 443–469, 487–513). The regional countries responded to the idea with varying degrees of interest: Egypt was enthusiastic as it confirmed the choice Anwar al-Sadat had made by linking Egypt to the United States and following the peace path. Jordan and the PLO, in their desire to rehabilitate their images and redress their mistake of supporting Saddam Hussein, were happy to participate even at the price of a joint Jordanian-Palestinian delegation, absent any PLO, diaspora, or East Jerusalem representatives. Syria and Israel hobbled to the conference reluctantly for different reasons: the first made a strategic choice before the war when it joined the US coalition against Iraq. Facing the reality that the possibility of military parity with Israel had faded away with the disappearance of his Soviet patron, President Asad decided to continue his struggle to liberate the Golan Heights by other means—i.e., diplomacy. Israel, on the other hand, led by Shamir and the Likud, had always opposed the idea of an international conference, fearing an imposed solution. However, when Bush decided to delay the approval of $10 billion in loan guarantees for the purpose of dealing with the Jewish immigration from Russia over the following five years, Shamir had to rethink his position. In addition, Bush and Baker made it clear that they considered Israel's ongoing settlement activity as a major obstacle to peace (Eisenberg and Caplan 1998, 79–81; Shlaim 2000, 485–487; Quandt 2005, 307–309; Kurtzer et al. 2013, 28–30; Khatib 2010, 64–67).[1] The unusual use of the financial stick by the United States convinced him to participate in a ceremonial conference that would be stripped of coercive authority. "We had to go on with the negotiations," Shamir lamented in his memoirs, "and there was no other broker in sight. So I comforted myself with the knowledge that we couldn't be made to accept the unacceptable or to agree to our own destruction" (1994, 235). The fact that Asad—the "permanent spoiler"—agreed to attend the conference really left Shamir no choice. Saudi Arabia and other Gulf states also decided to attend as observers as a token of their gratitude to the United States in defending their territories against the Iraqi threat. The result was an impressive and unprecedented gathering, which, according to Shlaim, "presented the most serious attempt ever on the part of the United States to promote a comprehensive settlement of the Arab-Israeli conflict" (2000, 485). It was the result of determined presidential leadership, a strong secretary of state enjoying full presidential backing, and positive regional and international environments (Kurtzer et al. 2013, 29).

The conference opened ceremonially on October 30, 1991. It immediately turned into a stage on which each party presented its own historical narrative, colored by the personality and posture of the presenter before the international press. Thus Shamir and Syrian foreign minister Faruq al-Shara' delivered defiant and truculent speeches, while Dr. Haidar 'Abd al-Shafi, head of the Palestinian delegation, gave an eloquent and moderate presentation. It was the first time that the Palestinians—not official members of the PLO—were represented at an international conference, though not on an equal footing with the other participants. Following the plenary session, a series of meetings between Israel and each of the Arab delegations took place (Shlaim 2000, 488–492; Shamir 1994, 237–242; Quandt 2005, 310–313).

The conference was followed by five rounds of bilateral talks in Washington, which did not bring any breakthrough. Against Israeli wishes, the joint Palestinian-Jordanian delegation was soon separated into a Jordanian and a Palestinian track, with the Palestinian delegates sanctioned by the PLO and their activity fully coordinated with it; these factors marked an important step on the road to holding direct PLO-Israel talks (Shlaim 2000, 492–497; Hirschfeld 2000, 76–83; Abbas 1995, 85–101; Ashrawi 1995; Arens 1995, 245–263; Khatib 2010, 67–76; Pundak 2013, 37). The Madrid Conference also offered a new multilateral channel that included some twenty states and dealt with regional issues such as water, environment, economic development, arms control, and refugees. The first round of the talks was held in Moscow in January 1992.

The futile bilateral negotiations in Washington were interrupted by elections in Israel on June 23, 1992, which brought to power for the first time since 1977 the Labor Party, led by Rabin (prime minister) and Peres (foreign minister). The ideology and aims of the new government were markedly different from its predecessor; upon presenting his coalition, including the leftist Meretz and the ultra-Orthodox Shas Party, in the Knesset on July 13, Rabin stated that the government's main goal would be "to promote the making of peace and take vigorous steps that will lead to the end of the Arab-Israeli conflict." He called upon the leaders of the Arab countries to follow Sadat's example and visit Jerusalem, while expressing his readiness to travel to Amman, Damascus, and Beirut for the purpose of peace, as "everyone is a victor in peace." Rabin promised to continue the Madrid track and put more substance into achieving peace. Undoubtedly, the composition of the new government and its platform reflected a change in the national priorities in the realm of Arab-Israeli relations.

The change in the Israeli policy was not noticed immediately. Though the atmosphere in the Washington talks—resumed for the sixth round in August 1992—considerably improved, and though the government abolished the law prohibiting any contacts between Israeli citizens and the PLO (adopted in 1986), the talks in December were virtually at a dead end, as each side steadfastly clung to its position. The Palestinians wanted an end to the occupation while negotiating an interim agreement that would lead to an independent Palestinian state; the Israelis wanted to retain as much control as possible for as long as possible, without dismantling settlements, while preventing the mushrooming of the interim agreement into the nucleus of a Palestinian state. In addition, the Palestinian delegation lacked a mandate to negotiate (Shlaim 2000, 509; Savir 1998, 5). The eighth round ended abruptly on December 16 when Rabin decided to deport 416 Hamas activists to Lebanon in reaction to a terrorist operation perpetrated by that organization. The unexpected move discredited the peace process and strengthened the extremists on both sides. The next round of negotiations was delayed for another four months and produced no results. After twenty months and ten rounds of negotiations, wrote Shlaim, it was clear that "the Madrid formula was not capable of ushering in a new era of peace in the Middle East" (2000, 511).

Though unproductive, these talks were continued by the new US administration under Bill Clinton, who entered office in January 1993. Clinton, who had served as the governor of Arkansas and had little experience in foreign affairs prior to becoming president, initially relied on Secretary of State Warren Christopher and four Middle East experts who had served during the Reagan and Bush administrations—Dennis Ross, Martin Indyk, Samuel Lewis, and Edward Djerejian. Given his limited experience with the region, it seemed that Clinton did not at first consider the Middle East an important US strategic interest (Quandt 2005, 321–324; Kurtzer et al. 2013, 35–36).

The deadlock in the talks convinced Rabin and Peres that their preferred partners—Jordan and the local Palestinian leaders—were unable to deliver an agreement. At the same time, the setbacks suffered by the PLO led the organization to consider a more conciliatory approach. Thus Israelis and Palestinians appeared of one mind in sensing the futility of the Washington talks. This served as a background to the opening of a secret channel in Oslo in January 1993. It was initiated by Yossi Beilin, the Israeli deputy foreign minister, and Terje Larsen, a Norwegian social scientist, who headed FAFO, a peace research institute in Oslo. The informal talks were held between two Israeli academics, Dr. Yair Hirschfeld and Dr. Ron Pundak, and three Palestinian officials, PLO treasurer Ahmed Qurei (Abu 'Ala), Hasan Asfour, and Maher al-Kurd, who regularly updated 'Arafat and Abu Mazen. By sending senior officials, the PLO was conveying the message that it was willing to negotiate and compromise. On the Israeli side, Beilin was fully informed of the proceedings and updated Peres; Peres, for his part, reported to Rabin, who showed little interest, though he did not object to the exploratory nature of the meetings. In May, realizing that the talks were indeed advancing, Peres decided to upgrade the level of representation, sending Uri Savir, director-general of his ministry, and Yoel Singer, a highly respected legal adviser, to join them. Thus the Israeli-Palestinian secret channel became formal in all but name. Norway, through Larsen and Foreign Minister Johan Jørgen Holst, hosted and facilitated the talks, though they were rarely present in the negotiating room. The United States was not involved in the negotiations, though it was intermittently briefed by the Norwegians. It seems that Washington took little interest in the Oslo talks because this was not considered a channel that could yield concrete results. In all, fourteen sessions were held in Oslo between January and August 1993. Several vivid accounts of the talks, written by the participants or close observers, indicate that in addition to the interests that drove the parties to sign the agreements, the personal ties which developed between the negotiators (termed "the Oslo spirit") were highly important in overcoming the hurdles along the way (Savir 1998, 3–89; Beilin 1997, 61–164; Hirschfeld 2000, 106–145, 280–281; Abbas 1995, 111–183; Qurei 2006, 34–283; Pundak 2013).

As the negotiations in Oslo progressed, Rabin and Peres saw that a serious opportunity to strike a deal with the PLO was in the offing. A major factor in their decision to pursue this track was the intelligence assessment that in light of the dire situation in the occupied territories a political solution to the Palestinian problem was urgent, and that the rising prestige of the Islamic Palestinian organizations—Hamas and Islamic Jihad—made ʿArafat the most convenient interlocutor for Israel at that juncture. Hamas had emerged during the years of the Intifada as an Islamic alternative to the PLO; its local popularity was based on the use of violence and its call for the liberation of the whole of Palestine. Hamas gradually mounted an unprecedented challenge to the PLO's exclusive claim to the leadership of the Palestinian people (Kristianasen 1999, 20–21). This caused ʿArafat and Rabin "to look upon each other through new eyes" (Eisenberg and Caplan 1998, 107). In addition, coincidence played a role: simultaneous with the Israeli-Palestinian breakthrough, the talks with Syria—Rabin's initial preferred channel—stalled due to Asad's insistence on full Israeli withdrawal from the Golan Heights and his disappointing response to Rabin's "deposit" offer (see chapter 19). As a result, Rabin decided to change his priorities and focus on the Palestinian track, which seemed to offer an immediate political reward. Agreement with the Palestinians would have meant that he almost kept his word to his voters to sign an interim agreement within six to nine months of the elections.

In late July 1993, Israelis and Palestinians involved in the negotiations sensed the existence of a genuine opportunity for signing an agreement (Savir

1998, 38; Pundak 2013, 180–183, 257). When at a certain juncture the talks were deadlocked, Savir invoked the legacy of the conflict as seen from an Israeli perspective: "Perhaps those who say that you never miss an opportunity to miss an opportunity are right!" (This was a reference to Abba Eban's famous dictum.) Continuing with the historical lesson, Savir added, "We, too, have made mistakes. In 1971 President Sadat offered a temporary settlement on the Suez Canal. We rejected it, and in 1973 a war broke out. Nineteen-ninety-three is your 1971" (Savir 1998, 48; Pundak 2013, 337).

On August 20, 1993, Savir and Abu 'Ala signed, in a confidential ceremony in Oslo, the Declaration of Principles on Interim Self-Government Arrangements (DOP). On September 9, Israel and the PLO exchanged letters of mutual recognition (Pundak 2013, 361–379; Ross 2005, 114–120). Though Norway was the main facilitator of the negotiations, it was suggested that the United States announce that it had brokered the agreement and hold a signing ceremony in Washington. Secretary of State Christopher refused to take credit for a role he did not play, but the ceremony did take place at the White House on September 13 (Christopher 2001, 200). The Palestinian letter, consisting of 256 words, stated that the PLO "recognizes the right of the state of Israel to exist in peace and security." In addition, the PLO renounced the use of terror and all forms of violence, accepted UN Resolution 242, and promised to remove all the articles in the Palestinian National Charter that denied Israel's right to exist. In another letter submitted to the Norwegian foreign minister, the PLO called on the Palestinians in the West Bank and Gaza to "take part in the steps leading to the normalization of life," which meant a call to end the Intifada. Though the letter did not define which Israel was being recognized, the reference to Resolution 242 meant that the PLO had limited its future aspirations to the 1967 boundaries. The Israeli letter, only fifty-six words long, recognized the PLO as the representative of the Palestinian people and vowed to commence negotiations with it within the framework of the peace process. Beyond that, Israel recognized no rights belonging to the Palestinian people. Clearly, the recognition letters were not even, reflecting the asymmetry between the parties and the weakened position of the PLO (Golan 2007, 14–15, 165–167; Shlaim 2000, 518).

The DOP was not a peace agreement, but rather a blueprint for temporary arrangements by which the territories were to be administered pending the determination of their final status. The main premise expressed within it was graduality, with a peace process moving in stages from occupation to self-rule and then permanent solution. The stated aim was to establish a Palestinian Interim Self-Government Authority (PA) and an elected council for the Palestinian people. The basic elements of the DOP were as follows: Israeli withdrawal from the Gaza Strip and Jericho within six months; redeployment of Israeli troops in other areas of the West Bank and the holding of elections to the Palestinian Council under international supervision and within nine months; and negotiations on the permanent status to begin as soon as possible but no later than two years after Israel's withdrawal. These talks would include the issues of Jerusalem, refugees, settlements, security arrangements, borders, and relations with other neighbors.[2] Civil authority and powers would be transferred gradually to the Palestinians in the spheres of education and culture, health, social welfare, direct taxation, and tourism; security powers would gradually be transferred to a Palestinian police force, while Israel would retain responsibility for the overall security of Israelis, for the settlements, and for defense against external threats. The border passages with Egypt and Jordan would remain under Israeli control (Golan 2007, 15–16, 169–183; Savir 1998, 59–60; Shlaim 2000, 516–523; Khatib 2010, 77–102).

The DOP laid down three guiding principles, which became significant in the long run: first, that nothing done or agreed upon during the interim period was to prejudice or preempt the outcome of the final status negotiations; second, that the area referred to as being under the jurisdiction of the elected council, with certain exceptions left for the final status, was to be the West Bank and Gaza, which were viewed as "a single territorial unit, whose integrity should be preserved during the interim period"; and third, that disputes regarding the interpretation or implementation of the DOP were to be resolved via an Israeli-Palestinian liaison committee or by arbitration. These principles, concluded Galia Golan, illustrated the lack of trust between the parties, as they were meant to ensure that neither side would take advantage of the transitional period to improve its own position (2007, 19).

The DOP was approved by the Knesset by a vote of 61 to 50, with nine abstentions. The margin of victory for Rabin's government was impressive. A similar margin existed in society: a poll indicated that 53 percent supported the agreement while 45 percent opposed it (Bar-Siman-Tov 1998, 23). 'Arafat, on the other hand, encountered vociferous opposition. It included, on the one hand, leading officials of the PLO establishment, as well as many Palestinian intellectuals such as Edward Said and Mahmud Darwish who did not necessarily object to the idea of a two-state solution, but scathingly criticized what they regarded as a humiliating agreement that gave Israel tactical and strategic aims at the expense of Palestinian demands such as sovereignty, territories, and Jerusalem (e.g., Said 1996).[3] On the other hand, this opposition included the Islamic and left-wing organizations, which opposed any recognition of the Zionist state (e.g., Kristianasen 1999). In addition, 'Arafat had to face the ire of the radical Arab states, led by Syria.

Following the agreement, negotiations commenced between the two sides pertaining to its implementation. These were interrupted by the massacre of twenty-one Muslim worshippers at the Tomb of the Patriarchs (Ibra-himi Mosque) in Hebron by Baruch Goldstein, an American-born settler and member of the racist Kach Party, on February 25, 1994. Though the party was swiftly outlawed, Rabin refused to remove the settlers from Hebron on the grounds that the Oslo Agreements did not oblige Israel to evacuate any settle-ments during the interim period. Israel did, however, agree to the stationing of international and Palestinian police forces in the contested city (Savir 1998, 121–133; Hirschfeld 2000, 156). Hamas and Islamic Jihad retaliated to the slay-ings by launching two suicide operations in April that killed thirteen Israelis. It was the beginning of a new cycle of violence, which continued throughout the Oslo period.[4] Israel retaliated by initiating border closures, which natu-rally led to a major decline in the inhabitants' standard of living—an unex-pected development that stood in contrast to their expectations following the agreement. 'Arafat was unwilling to or incapable of directly confronting the Islamic groups, preferring instead to co-opt or divide them (Ross 2005, 190).

Soon after the PLO's return to the negotiation table, two agreements were concluded. The Paris Protocol, signed in late April 1994, dealt with eco-nomic relations between Israel and the Palestinians, including limited cus-toms union, transfer of goods, taxes, and monetary relations. The second, the Gaza and Jericho Agreement, was signed in Cairo on May 4. This docu-ment, as Golan concluded, had not been called for in the DOP but was the result of repeated delays, disputes, and haggling over implementation pro-cedures. Since the scheduled withdrawal from the Gaza Strip and Jericho, which was to signal the commencement of the timetable, had not yet begun, the agreement called for an accelerated withdrawal within three weeks. It also had a clause regarding "prevention of hostile acts," which was meant to pro-tect both Israelis and Palestinians from terrorist attacks. It also included some confidence-building measures, such as the release of prisoners. As the perma-nent peace treaty according to the DOP was to be concluded within five years, the fixed target date was May 4, 1999. The countdown to full peace had begun (Golan 2007, 19–20; Savir 1998, 138–143; Shlaim 2000, 525–527; Hirschfeld 2000, 157–159; Ross 2005, 122–136; Khatib 2010, 108–121). Significantly, the Cairo Agreement was supported by only fifty-two members of the 120-strong Knesset. The opposition boycotted the vote to show that there was no ma-jority in the public for the agreement (Bar-Siman-Tov 1998, 22). In any case, a new era was ushered in when 'Arafat entered Gaza with a token police force on July 1, 1994. This new zeitgeist was also reflected in other spheres, as Jordan concluded a peace agreement with Israel in October (see chapter 18) and an international economic conference took place in Casablanca in November. The new Middle East, which Peres had envisaged, was under way, or so it seemed (Peres 1993; Savir 1998, 151–153).

The most important agreement was the Interim Agreement on the West Bank and the Gaza Strip ("Oslo II"), signed in Washington on September 28, 1995. Comprising an astounding 410 pages and eight maps, it specified a timetable for the withdrawal (euphemistically called redeployment) of the Israeli army. In stage one (October–December 1995), the Israel Defense Forces (IDF) was to withdraw from six cities in the West Bank (not including Hebron). These cities would be under full Palestinian military and civilian control (area A); the IDF was to withdraw from 465 villages that would remain under Israeli security responsibility (area B). All in all, Palestinians would control 27 percent of the territory in the West Bank and 90 percent in Gaza, leaving Israel holding 73 percent of the West Bank (area C) and 10 percent of the Gaza Strip. Israel would also retain all security responsibilities regarding the movement of people and goods to and from the West Bank and Gaza. In stage two (January–February 1996), free and democratic elections for an eighty-eight-member Palestinian Legislative Council (PLC), as well as the chairman of the PA, were planned. Two months after the council's inauguration, it was to pass a resolution nullifying the clauses in the national charter calling for Israel's annihilation. Six months later, Israel was to withdraw from Hebron, retaining only the security control of an enclave of Jewish settlers and the Cave of the Patriarchs. In stage three (May 4, 1996), negotiations on the permanent settlement were to begin, with the aim of concluding them by May 4, 1999. In the final stage, Israel was to withdraw from unpopulated territory in three phases of six months each. The Palestinians agreed that the question of Jerusalem would be dealt with separately from the rest of the West Bank in the final status negotiations. East Jerusalemites, however, were permitted to vote for the PLC. The agreement barred either side from "any step that will change the status of the West Bank and Gaza Strip." While the exact timing and scope of Israeli withdrawals was left ambiguous, provisions for security were detailed and exhaustive; Israel was to maintain all external security, which included not only border areas but also the borders or edges of area A. In addition, Israel was to provide security for all the settlements in area B, where Palestinian police were operating as well. Undoubtedly, this complicated set of security regulations spelled problems for the future (Savir 1998, 240–242; Golan 2007, 20–24; Shlaim 2000, 527–528; Hirschfeld 2000, 159–167; Ross 2005, 188–215; Khatib 2010, 121–136).

In Israel, the Knesset ratified the agreement on October 5 by the narrowest of majorities: 61 to 59. Right-wing elements called the agreement illegitimate because it relied on the vote of Arab Knesset members. Some radical right-wing MKs equated Rabin to Neville Chamberlain's appeasement policy of Hitler at Munich (Shlaim 2000, 528–530, 551). The next day, a major rally was held in Jerusalem with the participation of tens of thousands of right-wing demonstrators demanding Rabin's dismissal. The leader of the opposition, Benjamin Netanyahu, called the agreement "an act of surrender" and a "danger to the existence of the State of Israel." Some protesters depicted Rabin as a "traitor" and "Nazi" (Savir 1998, 248–249). The rally was a genuine reflection of the deep divisions engulfing Israeli society with regard to the peace process. According to polls, Oslo II was supported by only 51 percent of the public while 47 percent opposed it—figures not unlike the margin in the Knesset (Bar-Siman-Tov 1998, 23). On the Palestinian side, 'Arafat was able to "sell" Oslo II to the population by emphasizing its symbolic gains; a public poll showed 66 percent support for the agreement and the peace process in general (Khatib 2010, 135–136).

The deep gulf in Israeli society was fatefully expressed in the assassination of the country's prime minister. Yitzhak Rabin was felled by the bullet of a right-wing extremist on November 5 at the end of a peace rally. Ironically, on the stage just minutes earlier, Rabin expressed his belief that "There is a chance for peace now, a great chance, which must be seized" (Shlaim 2000, 546–551). Dennis Ross hoped that the tragedy might produce an opportunity for consolidating the peace (2005, 209–216). Indeed, in the immediate aftermath of the assassination, public support of the peace process peaked. In hindsight, however, the horrific act dramatically changed the course of events, and the Oslo process went astray.

Amidst the shock of the assassination, Peres took over as acting prime minister and minister of defense; Ehud Barak, the former IDF chief of staff, became foreign minister. Though 112 out of 120 members of the Knesset recommended that President Ezer Weizman assign to Peres the task of forming a new government, he received a vote of confidence of only sixty-one members—a sign of his precarious hold on power. Still, Peres vowed to continue the peace process and implement Rabin's legacy. He had the option of skipping the Interim Agreement and moving straight to the permanent status negotiations, based on the draft of the Beilin–Abu Mazen understandings, which had been concluded just days before Rabin's assassination and was not yet public knowledge (it was published by a journalist only in 1997). The agreement, presented to Peres for the first time on November 11, 1995, was a result of secret talks held between four Israeli and Palestinian academics in Stockholm since September 1994 (Beilin 1997, 167–218; Agha, Feldman, Khalidi, and Schiff 2003, 71–90; Eriksson 2013, 209–224). More cautious than ever as a result of the traumatic event, Peres preferred implementing the Interim Agreement while simultaneously advancing the Syrian track.

Thus in late 1995 Israel withdrew from the Palestinian cities (except Hebron), in line with Oslo II. This enabled the holding of elections for the chairmanship of the Palestinian Authority (PA) and the PLC on January 20, 1996.

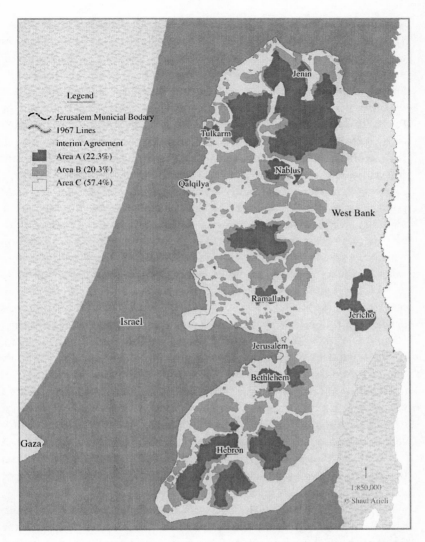

MAP 17.1. The Oslo 1995–1998 Interim Agreements. Courtesy of Shaul Arieli, 2013.

As expected, 'Arafat won a clear majority of 88 percent, and his Fatah organization gained the majority of seats in the council. This gave 'Arafat the necessary legitimacy to move ahead with the peace process (Steinberg 2008, 329–351). Yet the power of the Islamic organizations challenging him rapidly grew, in word and deed. Following the killing of Yihye 'Ayyash, a leading Hamas terrorist responsible for the murder of sixty Israeli civilians, a wave of retaliatory terrorist attacks in Israeli cities saw fifty-two people killed and hundreds wounded during February–March 1996 (Kristianasen 1999, 28–29). These attacks damaged Peres's credibility and shattered Israeli public support for the peace process. In a desperate attempt to shore up the Peres government and the peace process, an antiterrorist summit was held in Sharm al-Shaykh on March 13. Led by US president Clinton, the summit drew representatives from twenty-seven countries, including several Arab states and the Palestinians, though it produced no significant results beyond the expression of international solidarity with Israel in its fight against Islamic terror (Shlaim 2000, 557–558). In addition, on April 24 the PLC formally abrogated the offensive clauses against Israel and Zionism in the Palestinian National Charter.

Peres felt no choice but to call elections. Held on May 29, 1996, it saw the political scales tilt. This was the first time Israelis were choosing the prime minister directly, separately from their Knesset vote. Netanyahu beat Peres by a margin of less than 1 percent, though he was able to form a coalition with a comfortable majority of sixty-six in the Knesset. The victory of Netanyahu—a staunch advocator of Ze'ev Jabotinsky's revisionist ideology—was tantamount, in Shlaim's opinion, to a "declaration of war on the peace process" (2000, 568).[5] It should be emphasized, however, that the Oslo process did not end with Netanyahu's election, even if its progress would be halting. Naturally, with the Israeli "founding fathers" of Oslo out of office, or dead, Netanyahu did not feel committed to the process, which he had ideologically opposed from the very beginning. The Israeli withdrawals were stalled, and the standard of living in the West Bank and Gaza deteriorated. The situation was volatile; it exploded with Netanyahu's hasty decision, on September 25, to open the Hasmonean tunnel under the Temple Mount in an effort to provide better access to Jewish archaeological sites. The result was the most violent confrontation since the Intifada: some seventy Palestinians and fifteen Israelis soldiers were killed in its wake (Golan 2007, 27; Shlaim 2000, 576–577; Ross 2005, 263–266).

Hoping to arrest the escalation, Clinton immediately invited both Netanyahu and 'Arafat to a summit in Washington. This meeting resulted in the signing of the Hebron Protocol on January 17, 1997, according to which Israel had to withdraw from the Muslim area of Hebron (constituting 80 percent of the territory) while maintaining security in the "Jewish zone" (the remaining territory, which included some thirty thousand Palestinians). The agreement bound Israel to three further redeployments over the next eighteen months.[6] In addition, it was decided to release Palestinian prisoners, resume talks regarding the safe passage between the West Bank and Gaza; restart the construction of the Gaza airport and port; and resume permanent status negotiations within two months after implementation of the Hebron Protocol.[7] It was agreed to deploy a token Temporary International Presence (TIP), manned by Norwegians, to maintain order in the city. The Palestinian side reaffirmed its commitments to complete the process of revising the National Charter, fighting terror and preventing violence as well as curbing incitement and hostile propaganda (Shlaim 2000, 579–581; Golan 2007, 27–28; Quandt 2005, 345–348; Ross 2005, 269–322).

The importance of the agreement pertained not only to its contents but to the fact that it was the first time a right-wing government agreed to relinquish lands in the heart of Eretz Israel. In addition, the United States returned to play a leading role in the negotiations. With the Netanyahu government, Ross testified, he "was about to become a broker, negotiating with each side, finding out what they could do, drafting for them, and brokering the compromises" (2005, 268). The agreement was met with strong criticism in the Israeli government, but it was eventually approved by a majority of eleven to seven. The Knesset, by contrast, endorsed it by a clear majority (87 in favor, 17 opposed, and 15 abstentions). Again, this mirrored public opinion: according to a poll, 66.7 percent supported the agreement, while 26.8 percent opposed it. These numbers indicated a broad national consensus in favor of continuing the Oslo process. On the Palestinian side, too, the agreement was ratified by a large majority in the PLC (Bar-Siman-Tov 1998, 26).

Though the Israeli withdrawal from Hebron was completed, other commitments specified in the agreement were not implemented. Netanyahu's excuse was that the Palestinians had not dismantled terrorist infrastructure, though in fact the number of attacks and casualties had considerably declined (Ross 2005, 353–356). The Palestinians' main complaint was that Israel continued to expand settlement building in the West Bank, particularly in and around East Jerusalem. Following the first redeployment, Netanyahu announced the construction of housing in the neighborhood of Har Homa. This became a recurring pattern in Netanyahu's behavior: "Whenever he sought to reach out to the Palestinians, he would seek to offer his action with steps that would appease his right wing constituency. Yet it was precisely those steps that would inflame Palestinian opinion" (ibid., 263). More generally, the number of settlers grew rapidly during the Oslo years: in September 1993 there were approximately 110,000; in 1996 they numbered 143,000; and by 2000 there were some 200,000 settlers (excluding East Jerusalem; http://www.peacenow.org .il/node/297. See also in this connection Rabbani 2001, 75; Oren Barak 2005, 731). This trend, in parallel with the repeated delays in the redeployments, gave rise to Palestinian suspicions that the Netanyahu government's aim was, in fact, to undo Oslo.

The animosity and mistrust between Netanyahu and ʿArafat were further exacerbated when Israel carried out a botched attempt to assassinate a Hamas leader, Khaled Mashaʿl, in Jordan in late September 1997; the incident resulted in a severe crisis with Jordan and the release from prison of Hamas leader Shaykh Ahmad Yassin. And thus, wrote Ross, "An operation ill-conceived from the beginning ended with yet another blunder, strengthening Hamas in the process" (2005, 358). The United States tried again to breathe life into the peace process by offering a second redeployment ("in the low teens") in return for dropping the third and the beginning of the negotiations over the permanent status. In order to achieve that goal, Clinton was willing to offer Israel a formal defense treaty and the Palestinians a commitment to support the idea of Palestinian statehood in the final talks. These innovative ideas, however, failed to entice either Netanyahu or 'Arafat (Ross 2005, 369–384).

With the original deadline (May 4, 1999) for ending the permanent status talks rapidly approaching, Clinton, by now well into his second term, invited the parties to a Carter-style summit, this time at the president's Wye River retreat, on October 15, 1998. There, the Wye Memorandum was concluded by Netanyahu and 'Arafat on October 23. Based on the notion of reciprocity, its main points included a transfer of 12 percent of the land of area C to B, 1 percent from C to A, and 14.2 percent from B to A. Further redeployments were to be determined by a joint committee. This territory was to be delivered in three installments, each contingent on the PA's performance of certain tasks, such as prohibiting illegal weapons, outlawing and combating terrorist organizations, and preventing incitement—all subject to CIA verification. This was the first time that a third party—the United States—was nominated to be actively involved in monitoring the implementation of the agreement; the US, which had hitherto played the role of facilitator and mediator, now assumed the role of referee and arbitrator (Lasensky 2004, 224). The redeployments were also pegged to a reaffirmation by the PLC of the nullification of the anti-Israeli clauses in the National Charter. Ironically, the agreement reiterated the commitment "immediately to resume" final status negotiations, and to conclude them within the now-unrealistic original deadline: May 4, 1999. It was also agreed that the United States would facilitate these talks (Golan 2007, 29–31; Aruri 1999, 17–28; Shlaim 2000, 603–606; Quandt 2005, 354–355; Ross 2005, 415–459; Albright 2003, 306–318; Clinton 2004, 814–820).

"Wye was not off to a great start," wrote Quandt (2005, 355). It took Netanyahu more than two weeks to get a narrow majority in his government to approve the agreement. Moreover, most of its provisions were not implemented: Israel transferred only 2 percent of the West Bank from area C to area B, and 7 percent from area B to area A. In early December the government decided to suspend further implementation as a result of a terror incident in Ramallah—an unfortunate decision, according to Ross, "because the Palestinians were working diligently to carry out most of their commitments under Wye, particularly in the area of making arrests and fighting terror"

(2005, 478; Kristianasen 1999, 32–33). Still, on December 14, 'Arafat convened the Palestinian National Council (PNC),[8] with Clinton as guest of honor, to grant Israel a renewed cancellation of the offensive clauses in the National Charter, as promised at Wye.

A major problem facing Netanyahu was that despite the general public support for peace talks, his right-wing government wanted to spike the Oslo Accords. So Netanyahu adopted a defensive policy to appease his opponents; he "chose to see Wye as a problem, not an asset," wrote Ross. In this, Ross estimated, Netanyahu "made a strategic mistake because with Wye he was in a powerful position to sweep up public opinion by moving to the center and thus gaining a commanding position in Israeli politics. His policy, ultimately, cost him his job" (2005, 461). On December 23, Netanyahu tendered his resignation. The fall of his government, concluded Shlaim, "was probably inevitable because of the basic contradiction between its declared objective of striving for peace with the Arab world and its ideological makeup, which militated against trading land for peace" (2000, 606).

Ehud Barak, the new head of the Labor Party, was elected prime minister in May 1999, scoring 56 percent of the total vote due to the two-ticket vote (one for prime minister and one for the Knesset). The election produced a highly divided Knesset; though the government enjoyed a comfortable majority, it was in fact an amalgamation of seven parties with disparate aims and ideologies, which compelled Barak to constantly maneuver. Still, he entered office with great expectations; with his military background and political views, he enjoyed an image of a credible and legitimate leader capable of fulfilling Rabin's legacy. Indeed, upon his election, Ross wrote somewhat naïvely, "We [the US] were back in business" (2005, 494). Barak saw a window of opportunity lasting no more than two years to transform the region before Iran and/ or Iraq acquired nuclear weapons—a development that would make Israelis more fearful and less prone to making concessions. Barak's tight schedule coincided with that of Clinton, who was to end his second presidential term within seventeen months (ibid., 498–500). The new era was to begin at the Sharm al-Shaykh summit on September 4, 1999—exactly four months after the original date set for signing the permanent-status agreement—with the participation of US secretary of state Madeleine Albright, Egyptian president Mubarak, the newly crowned Jordanian king 'Abdallah, 'Arafat, and Barak. The resultant Sharm al-Shaykh Memorandum called for Israeli withdrawal from a further 11 percent of the West Bank; the release of 350 Palestinian prisoners; the opening of safe passage between the West Bank and Gaza; and a seaport to be built in Gaza. There was also a timetable for final status talks to deal with Jerusalem, borders, refugees, and settlements: a framework agreement on permanent status was to be achieved by February 2000 and permanent agreement by September that year. Barak, however, shelved the schedule because of his negotiations with Syria's Asad (see chapter 19). After the release of prisoners and the conclusion of the first stage of redeployment, disagreement arose regarding how much and which territory was to be handed over to the Palestinians in the second stage. Moreover, time was wasted in several unfruitful rounds of preliminary final status talks. A new wave of Palestinian terrorist attacks inside Israel caused further delays and bad blood. In December 1999 the Palestinians suspended the negotiations, blaming Israel's continued settlement expansion. Thus it was hardly a surprise that the two sides failed to reach a final draft as agreed in Sharm al-Shaykh (Golan 2007, 33; Ross 2005, 502–508).

The final attempt to save the Oslo Agreements was in July 2000, when Clinton invited Barak and 'Arafat to Camp David to negotiate the final status agreement. This important episode (addressed in chapter 20) failed miserably. The eruption of the second Palestinian Intifada in September 2000—exactly seven years after the signing of the DOP—meant, for all intents and purposes, the end of the Oslo process.

ASSESSMENT

The historiography of the Oslo process tends to focus on questions such as "what went wrong?" "why did it go wrong?" and "who should be blamed?" for what are seen as mistakes and failures (Kimmerling and Migdal 2003, 315–397; Maoz 2004, 470–477; Golan 2007, 33–35; Rynhold 2008, 1–26; Rabbani 2001, 68–81; Oren Barak 2005, 726–734; Seliktar 2009; Pundak 2001, 31–45; 2002, 88–113; Hassassian 2002, 114–132; Rothstein 2002, 161–169).[9] These important questions, however, are not the subject of this chapter, which attempts to assess to what extent Oslo constituted a missed opportunity.

The Oslo episode is one of the most complicated case studies because of its long duration (seven years), the many actors involved, the frequent changes in Israeli leadership, and the assassination of Rabin—perhaps the most important actor in this episode. Of course we cannot know what would have happened had Rabin not been slain, yet it is clear by the various accounts of the participants—as well as the post-Oslo assessment—that this tragic moment dramatically changed the course of events. Therefore, the question whether this opportunity had been missed should be separated into two—one dealing with the period up to November 4, 1995, and the second with the period since then.

The end of the Cold War and the defeat of Saddam Hussein in the Gulf War in 1991 created a new opportunity for Arab-Israeli peace diplomacy. With the disappearance of the Soviet Union—the patron of the radical Arab states—

and the need of Jordan and the PLO to reposition themselves in the wake of their mistaken decision to support Iraq, an opportunity presented itself to gather the warring parties. The dominance of the United States in the international system allowed it to play a major role in convening the Madrid Conference. It was US president Bush and secretary of state Baker who were credited with the idea of holding an international conference—an idea that had floated for most of the 1980s but was blocked by superpower rivalry or regional and domestic animosities. Yet the failure of the Madrid Conference to achieve a breakthrough, combined with the feeling that the Intifada had exhausted itself and the election of a more moderate Labor government in Israel, created a rare opportunity that brought the PLO and Israel to a new threshold. On the Israeli side, both Rabin and Peres came to the conclusion that the coalescence of changes in the international and regional arenas created a unique chance for peace that should not be missed (Dalal 2012, 155–156; Peres 1995, 325). Based on William Zartman's ripeness theory, Alan Dowty concluded that a "mutually hurting stalemate" produced a possible "way out" for both Israelis and Palestinians (2006, 26). Indeed, there is strong evidence that both sides, in real time, sensed the existence of "historical ripeness" to solve the Israeli-Palestinian conflict (Pundak 2013, 69–82, 180–183; Savir 1998, 38).

The success of the Oslo talks came as a surprise to all concerned, but with the wisdom of hindsight it is clear that a series of processes and events coalesced at this point, producing a unique opportunity to solve the Israeli-Palestinian conflict, and perhaps the entire Arab-Israeli conflict. As well as representing a turning point in the conflict, the Oslo track offered an attractive alternative to both sides. In contrast to past history, the agreement did not emanate from an initiative of one of the parties to the conflict or a third party, but was the product of secret bilateral negotiations, beginning as an academic exercise and ending in a political agreement. In other words, none of the parties was coerced into the agreement. Its terms also constituted a major deviation from the status quo, as they entailed mutual Israeli-Palestinian recognition and the backbone of a solution to the century-old conflict. The historical changes in the international and regional systems, as well as the great attraction of the agreement, meant that Oslo constituted a major historical opportunity.

To what extent was this opportunity missed? The first variable relates to the level of the legitimacy of the leadership. 'Arafat and the PLO enjoyed the legitimacy of most of the Palestinians, the setback suffered in the aftermath of the Gulf War notwithstanding. 'Arafat was the "symbolic leader" of the Palestinian people whose legitimacy rested on tradition and charisma. As such, he was the sole Palestinian leader capable of making concessions (Pundak 2013, 83; Steinberg 2008, 329–351; Grinberg 2007, 336; Hirschfeld 2000, 185). In the Madrid Conference, 'Arafat was compelled to accept a joint Jordanian-Palestinian delegation, which did not include official PLO members. Still, it was an open secret that the Palestinian members had received their instructions from PLO headquarters in Tunis. Thus through Oslo's backdoor channels the PLO succeeded in entering the diplomatic front door. Oslo, in general, also enjoyed extra-parliamentary support: according to Palestinian polls, the agreement unmasked a large, if dwindling, majority favoring a negotiated settlement (Rabbani 2001, 69). According to Khalil Shikaki's findings, support for the peace process went from a low of 37 percent in the aftermath of Goldstein's 1994 massacre to a peak of 82 percent in early 1997 (1998, 9). In his opinion, the Palestinian elections ipso facto legitimized the Oslo Agreements. On balance, therefore, Baruch Kimmerling and Joel Migdal rightly concluded, "The popular foundation for proceeding with negotiations was quite strong" (2003, 335–338). Many Palestinians believed that peace and economic well-being were imminent. Yet a hardcore minority voiced vitriolic opposition; it included the leftist organizations, the Islamists, some leading Fatah officials, as well as well-known intellectuals in the diaspora who seemed to hold a personal vendetta against 'Arafat (e.g., Said 1996, 165–185). Nevertheless, in January 1996, he was elected chairman of the PA by a majority of 88 percent. 'Arafat largely relied on his personal ability to convert individuals rather than depending on the support of groups or institutions. Seldom would he convene the PLC to legitimize his moves (Aburish 1998, 264). 'Arafat was constantly challenged by the Hamas movement, which offered an opposite ideology and means to liberate the occupied territories. Hamas's legitimacy and popularity grew in direct proportion to setbacks in the peace process. Thus 'Arafat faced an insurmountable problem: in order to confront the Islamist challenge, he had to take measures on a scale that "could not but translate into dangerous political instability" (Kristianasen 1999, 33). The result was the adoption of a policy of "revolving doors" with respect to the arrest and punishment of Islamic activists—a policy that led many Israelis to doubt 'Arafat's sincerity and integrity. What began as optimism and support for 'Arafat soon evaporated as revelations emerged that the Palestinian leadership was "compromised, corrupt, dependent on Israel, incapable of facing challenges, and most important, oppressive in its response to public criticism" (Khatib 2010, 172).

On the other hand, Rabin's government had a narrow majority in the Knesset, yet Rabin himself, who enjoyed the image of "Mr. Security" (having served as chief of staff during the 1967 War and minister of defense between 1984–1990), seemed to enjoy the respect and legitimacy of broader sectors of Israeli society (Grinberg 2007, 339; Inbar 1999). In fact, Rabin attempted to create a "peace camp"—a political identity that included not only leftist voters but also right-wing moderates who spoke his "security discourse." The charismatic leader in such a case, according to Grinberg, is the source of legitimacy in the new order. This is why Rabin's death largely denied further legitimacy to the peace process (2007, 154). In addition, Rabin and Peres at the helm made a perfect couple, each complementing the other: the one was "a guarded analyst of the present, obsessed by details," and the other "a cosmopolitan conceptualist who sees history in terms of processes and is obsessed by the future" (Savir 1998, 25; Hirschfeld 2000, 160; Pundak 2013, 300). Together they constituted a perfect team to market the compromise to the Israeli public.

The government seemed to possess extra-parliamentary legitimacy: polls conducted during the Oslo years show that support of the peace process did not drop below 50 percent even during the harsh period of terror bombings in 1995–1997. On certain occasions, such as immediately after Rabin's assassination and upon Barak's election, it even rose to 70 percent (Kimmerling and Migdal 2003, 338–340; Hirschfeld 2000, 322–324; Bar-Siman-Tov 1997, 177; Arian 1995, 57–59). Yet these numbers are somewhat misleading, as the opposition to the peace process was vehement, led by right-wing and religious elements that conducted an organized and systematic campaign against the Oslo Agreements. In addition, Rabin and Peres had great difficulty in legitimizing the peace policy in the Knesset: while Oslo I received an impressive margin, Oslo II had the narrowest possible majority (61 to 59). Yaacov Bar-Siman-Tov asserted that it marked "the first time since 1974 that the support for Arab-Israeli agreements was so minimal" (1998, 22). The lack of sufficient legitimacy was a result of the lack of clear-cut peace policy and the failure to manipulate symbols, language, and rituals in the pursuit of peace. Netanyahu's electoral victory signaled the declining legitimacy in Israeli society of the peace process. Yet even the right-wing Netanyahu suffered from legitimacy deficiency, as he managed only with great difficulty to get the approval of his government for the Wye Agreement. Barak's subsequent election seemed to reverse this trend, but this proved to be a short-lived phenomenon.

The second variable relates to the willingness of the leaders to take bold decisions. There are contradictory assessments in this regard. Uri Savir, who was close to the leaders, concluded that Rabin, Peres, and 'Arafat "had some things in common—they were strong and experienced leaders not easily shaken by the tremors of change." In his opinion, they were "all lonely and driven, convinced of the justice of their cause, and bent on achieving their goals" (1998, 79). The three became political bedfellows, perhaps by necessity, but Rabin's assassination changed the balance of power in this triangle. 'Arafat was an enigmatic figure; his biographers found it difficult to decipher his thinking and behavior (Rubinstein 2001, 11; Aburish 1998; Rubin and Rubin 2003). Often enough, he would make diametrically opposed declarations to appease disparate constituencies. This kind of "yes-and-no" attitude raised doubts in Israel regarding his true motives. Just how determined 'Arafat was to follow the path of peace is hard to estimate. In his memoirs, Pundak often quoted 'Arafat saying: "Where there is a will, there is a way to implement it" (2013, 76, 327, 333). He therefore concluded that "reality showed that 'Arafat was willing, capable and courageous enough to sign" (ibid., 354), yet "it was difficult for him to give up his position as a revolutionary and freedom fighter and to stand up to the level of a statesman building a new state and society" (ibid., 304–305). Indeed, 'Arafat was not determined enough to contain the peace spoilers intent on sabotaging the process. This could be the result of his leadership deficiencies or his frustration at the lack of progress on the ground, or both.

Similar doubts exist regarding Rabin's determination to pursue the peace path. Efraim Inbar argued that "The transition to the role of peacemaker was not easy for Rabin." In his opinion, Rabin failed to instill the Israeli public with sufficient faith in the correctness of the peace course because "he himself was not sure of the path chosen" (1999, 169). When he faced the question of evacuating the Jewish settlers from Hebron following Goldstein's massacre in February 1994, he refused to take the step out of fear of the opposition (Steinberg 2008, 391). It seems that the gradualist approach of the Oslo process suited Rabin well, as he could cautiously move from one phase to another, while delaying the settlement of the final questions to a later period. Still, in Beilin's opinion, Rabin was the real "hero of Oslo" because on his shoulders rested the responsibility of the decision and its subsequent events. Otherwise, continued Beilin, it would have been another missed opportunity (1997, 162–163).

The third variable relates to the history of past interactions, which affects the level of trust existing between the parties. The post-1948 period saw only a handful of contacts between Israelis and Palestinians. In addition, the fact that the PLO was perceived in Israel as a terrorist organization prevented the development of any serious Israeli-Palestinian talks. Between 1986 and 1992 any contact with the PLO was prohibited by law in Israel. In contrast to the Egyptian and Jordanian cases, there were no opportunities to build mutual trust. The century-old history of avoidance contributed to the easy demonization of the other, creating a psychological barrier to peace. The formal talks in Washington following the Madrid Conference were the first attempt to build some trust on a personal basis. But these contacts were limited due to fears of being accused of illicit contacts with their adversaries and of arousing suspicions of their own colleagues on the team. The result was that many opportunities were lost for unofficial exchanges of ideas that might have led the two sides to reach an understanding (Abbas 1995, 215). Therefore, the signing of the DOP and the Oslo Accords were tantamount to the shattering of a taboo in Israeli and Palestinian societies. The reluctance of Rabin to shake ʿArafat's hand at the signing ceremony in Washington on September 13, 1993, as seen by the world in his body language, illustrated in many ways the Israeli difficulty to overcome past animosities.[10]

Yet the lack of contacts did not hamper the success of the Oslo channel. In fact, the personal accounts of the participants reveal the existence of shared respect, and even trust, between the members of the delegations; they called it the "Oslo spirit." Yet relations between the leaders were more problematic; Clinton observed that Rabin and ʿArafat developed "a remarkable working relationship, a tribute to Arafat's regard for Rabin and the Israeli leader's uncanny ability to understand how Arafat's mind worked" (2004, 545). Rabin's wife, Leah, was also of the opinion that her husband developed a certain appreciation of ʿArafat (1997, 273). Yet this assessment was not shared by Israelis involved in the negotiations (Hirschfeld 2000, 153; Halevy 2006, 119). A study of the level of trust between Rabin and ʿArafat revealed that it was initially frail (Autumn 1993–Spring 1994), developing slowly to "limited" (Spring 1994–Autumn 1995). This in turn resulted in the adoption of limited political goals (Krispin-Peleg 2010, 204–207, 303). In addition, the fact that on the other side of the Jordan River stood a trustworthy leader—Husayn (see chapter 18)—radiated on ʿArafat in a negative way (ibid., 305). This sense of mistrust, however limited, filtered down to society through the media. The violations of the accords by the two sides—terrorist operations, ongoing settlement activity, delaying scheduled withdrawals—all contributed to the building of mistrust rather than the opposite (Enderlin 2003, 111–176). Kimmerling and Migdal concluded that the basic idea of Oslo was "to create trust and confidence between the two peoples. But the leaders of both peoples were hesitant to make hard and fateful decisions on real issues, which undermined the process" (2003, 361–363).

The fourth variable relates to the role of the mediator. In contrast to the hands-on mediation during Kissinger's and Carter's time, the United States did not play a meaningful role in the Oslo negotiations. In fact, Norway and Israel misled the Clinton administration regarding the seriousness of the talks (Agha, Feldman, Khalidi, and Schiff 2003, 52–54; Ross 2005, 101–107; Kurtzer et al. 2013, 42; Pundak 2013, 150–151), although a senior official in the administration was regularly apprised of developments. It all began when Norway, with little experience in mediation, initiated a secret back channel in parallel to the formal Israeli-Palestinian talks in Washington. Norway's past close ties with Israel and its reputation for a balanced position made it an attractive mediator for the PLO too, despite the fact that it was one of the last European countries to establish contact with it. Being a relatively powerless international actor, Norway had no leverage on the warring parties and no incentives to offer them. Yet it had its own interests in promoting peace in the Middle East by creating an image of having a mission in the world in the field of political morality and conflict resolution. It also bestowed fame and prestige upon Norway; not only was Oslo the home of the Nobel Peace Prize, but now it was also the venue of peace talks (Wagge 2004, 4; 2005, 7; Pundak 2013, 54–57, 88). The government's view was that "a different type of mediation was needed" to contrast that of the United States, which was perceived as biased. Officially, the government stayed out of the talks and delegated its management to a semi-academic foundation—FAFO. Norway saw itself playing only the role of a facilitator and therefore refrained from intervention; when circumstances dictated, it was prepared to step in as a mediator. Otherwise, it was providing content, as well as key logistical and security services (Agha, Feldman, Khalidi, and Schiff 2003, 49–52; Wagge 2004, 1–11; 2005, 6–24; Kriesberg 2001, 385). Stockholm replaced Oslo as the venue for final status negotiations, yet the Swedish role never exceeded that of a sponsor providing moral and material support. The successful conclusion of the Oslo Accords and the Stockholm talks was proof that once the involved parties are bent on finding a solution to their conflict they can do so, regardless of the mediator's skills or experience.

Still, the implementation of the Oslo Accords—particularly in an asymmetrical conflict such as this one—does necessitate the presence of a strong mediator who can force a solution on unwilling parties or offer incentives to weaker players. Clinton, to a large extent, enjoyed the fruits of the Oslo channel; the problem here was that the United States inherited an agreement that had been brokered by others, without any ability to change or adjust it according to its own interests, thinking, and experience. Daniel Kurtzer et al. admitted that "It is doubtful that the US could have addressed fully the deficiencies of the Oslo DOP, even if US resolve and determination had been greater than it proved to be" (2013, 50–51). Aaron David Miller complained that the United States was enchanted by the Oslo process without seeing its pitfalls; moreover, the US was left outside the implementation process, its role being confined to a "handmaiden, treasurer and crisis management." The main problem, in his view, was the lack of any supervisory system on the fulfillment of the provisions of the agreement (2008, 267). Following Rabin's assassination, the United States felt compelled to intervene more intensely. Ross, the chief American negotiator, admitted that after Netanyahu's election he became a full-time mediator:

> No longer would we be in the business of helping the parties, easing their efforts, reassuring them at critical moments, bringing them together at

times, and pressuring when necessary to get them to cross thresholds and make decisions. I was about to become a broker, negotiating with each side, finding out what they could do, drafting for them, and brokering the compromises. (2005, 268)

Similarly, Clinton became personally involved in the negotiations that led to the signing of the Hebron and Wye Agreements, though in the Sharm al-Shaykh memorandum the United States, along with Egypt, played a low-profile role of encouragement (Kriesberg 2001, 385). In spite of the growing involvement all around, US policy—according to Miller's testimony—suffered from a certain bias toward Israel, did not apply enough pressure on the parties, and in general did not invest enough effort to solve the problems (2008, 247, 249, 257, 268; Pundak 2013, 402).

Clearly, Oslo did not produce the expected result—an agreement between Israel and the Palestinians. Yet the opportunity that evidently existed in the Middle East in the post–Gulf War period was not fully missed, as a mutual recognition agreement was signed between Israel and the PLO, followed by several agreements that were at least partially fulfilled. In such a situation the question is whether and to what extent more could have been achieved. In this respect, the Oslo years should be divided into two periods, separated by the assassination of Rabin. The first period saw the leaders on both sides of the conflict enjoying a respectable measure of legitimacy. True, the agreement was repeatedly challenged by inter-group entrepreneurs (Oren Barak 2005, 728), but the leaders were committed to a gradual implementation of the Oslo process and were sufficiently bold to pursue the peaceful track. In spite of the political opposition existing on both sides, it seems that a majority existed in both societies supporting the peace process. Past acquaintances had not adversely affected the parties, which still benefited from the aura of the "Oslo spirit." In addition, it seems that a measure of trust developed between Rabin and ʿArafat from the spring of 1994. Though no one mediator played a significant role, the parties showed that they were resolved to move forward regardless of third-party intervention. With Rabin enjoying a strong sense of credibility among the Israeli public, it is highly plausible that he could have achieved more had he survived; had the Beilin–Abu Mazen understandings for the permanent status been presented to Rabin, he might have advanced it (Beilin 1997, 214). The assassination altered Israel's domestic political scene, preventing the hope embodied in the Stockholm document from materializing (Agha, Feldman, Khalidi, and Schiff 2003, 83).

The analysis above suggests that the potentiality level of this opportunity during the Rabin years was between medium and high. But in contrast to past and future episodes, the missing of this opportunity was not a result of leadership failures or mistakes but rather Rabin's unforeseen assassination. At this particular juncture the role of the leader was critical, and his elimination blocked the process, which was after all fraught with problems along the way. Even if Rabin and 'Arafat had not fully embraced the concessions included in the Beilin-Abu Mazen talks as a basis for final status negotiations, the chances for progress in the diplomatic process at a slower pace were still relatively high, particularly had Rabin been elected to a second term on the basis of a perceived popular successful first term. This conclusion dovetails with Pundak's assessment that Rabin and 'Arafat would have signed a peace agreement had the Israeli leader not been assassinated (2013, 387). The magnitude of the opportunity missed may be reduced due to the fact that a paradigmatic change in the Israeli-Palestinian conflict had indeed been achieved: mutual recognition, direct negotiations, partial Israeli withdrawal, and the modification of the Palestinian National Charter.

The post-Rabin period, however, saw a decline in the potentiality level of the missed opportunity. Peres enjoyed broad legitimacy in the immediate aftermath of the assassination. However, it quickly evaporated as a result of the repeated Hamas terror operations in early 1996. Peres also was not resolute enough in pursuing the peace process; when he was presented with the details of the Beilin–Abu Mazen understandings, he felt unable to adopt a controversial policy in such a traumatic period for Israeli society. In addition, the trust between the parties substantially declined as a result of the Palestinian suicide attacks that—in Israeli eyes—did not receive an adequate response from 'Arafat. Peres's attempt to proceed on the Israeli-Syrian track also aroused the suspicions of the Palestinians and further damaged their trust in him. Beilin, the architect of the Beilin–Abu Mazen Agreement, thought that Peres "missed a huge opportunity" to promote it (quoted in Eriksson 2013, 218). Yet Peres's declining legitimacy and resoluteness, the lack of trust, and the effects of the Rabin trauma contributed to a low potentiality to seize the opportunity. All in all, while Peres's premiership was too short to bring major changes, it seems that the potentiality level of this period was low.

The "window of opportunity" existing during the Rabin-Peres years all but closed during the Netanyahu period (1996–1999). Though he enjoyed a comfortable majority in the Knesset, Netanyahu was not driven to advance the Oslo Accords as a result of his ideological convictions. The concessions he made in the Hebron and Wye Agreements were largely forced upon him by the United States, which decided to play a more prominent role as a mediator. Moreover, the fact that these agreements had to be balanced by one-sided steps aimed at pacifying his right-wing constituency aroused suspicion and mistrust on the Palestinian side. Netanyahu's behavior toward 'Arafat was also characterized by a deep sense of mistrust. 'Arafat's approval of Oslo was seen as part of his phased strategy to take over the whole of Palestine. Add to this the unrelenting growth of the number of Jewish settlers in the West Bank on the one hand, and 'Arafat's inability or unwillingness to curb terror activity on the other, which only served to widen the gulf between the parties. The two sides were, in fact, engaged in the process of "building mistrust" (Enderlin 2003, 111–176). Though two variables—legitimacy and third-party involvement—were relevant during the Netanyahu period, it seems that his reluctance to advance Oslo and the high level of mistrust existing between the parties outweighed the positive variables, making the potentiality level of this missed opportunity low.

When Barak was elected, the political situation in the region may well have been ripe for a breakthrough. Yet the legitimacy that he appeared to enjoy was not accompanied by a resolute conviction to terminate the Israeli-Palestinian conflict. By adhering to the right-wing discourse code and wavering between the Syrian and the Palestinian tracks, he gradually lost the legitimacy and credibility of both the Israeli public and his Palestinian interlocutors. In many ways, therefore, the Barak period resembled Netanyahu's. In any case, the period between Barak's election and the Camp David summit was too short to offer a missed opportunity. In the final analysis, the mistakes made by both sides contributed to the undoing of the Oslo Accords. Former Israeli foreign minister Shlomo Ben-Ami, who was intimately involved in the diplomatic process, admitted that the "Israelis and Palestinians jointly killed Oslo" (2005b, 76).

NOTES

1. Both houses of Congress ultimately approved the $10 billion guarantees in October 1992.

2. As the Israeli withdrawal began on May 4, 1994, the permanent status negotiations would have to begin on May 4, 1996, and to be concluded by May 5, 1999.

3. A good description of the opposition and its arguments against the Oslo Agreements was provided by Hanan Ashrawi, a Palestinian member of the Palestinian-Jordanian delegation to the Washington talks (1995, 273–303). She wrote that it was clear that "the ones who initialed the agreement have not lived under occupation. You postponed the settlement issue and Jerusalem without even getting guarantees that Israel would not continue to create facts on the ground that would preempt and prejudge the final outcome" (ibid., 260). The DOP was ratified by a 63 percent majority in the PLO Central Committee (ibid., 278). A public poll indicated that 68.6 percent supported the agreement, though several PLO opposition factions objected; see Khatib 2010, 105–107.

4. For a list of terrorist attacks in Israel, see http://en.wikipedia.org/wiki/List_of_Palestinian_suicide_attacks; see also the numbers cited in Hirschfeld 2000, 307, note 35.

5. Ross wrote that with the election of Netanyahu, "The prospects of peace had been dealt a serious setback" (2005, 258).

6. This was included in a "Note for the Record," written by Ross, then the US special Middle East coordinator. Netanyahu was reluctant to put his name to a document committing Israel to further withdrawals, but he was prepared to let Ross pen a note stating that Israel would remain committed to Oslo II "on the basis of reciprocity" (Quandt 2005, 346).

7. The talks should have started on January 27, 1997, but they never did.

8. In contrast to the PLC, which is the institution that represents only the Palestinians in the West Bank and Gaza, the PNC also represents the Palestinians in the diaspora. Since the PNC drafted the charter in 1968, Israel demanded that this institution—and not the PLC—would annul the controversial clauses in the charter.

9. Kimmerling and Migdal also posed the less asked question "What went right?"

10. In his memoirs, Clinton relates how Rabin reluctantly agreed to shake 'Arafat's hand but refused any kissing, which is a traditional Arab greeting (2004, 543).

CHAPTER 18

THE ISRAELI-JORDANIAN PEACE TREATY

1994

ISRAEL AND JORDAN sealed their peace treaty at a dusty desert border point called Wadi Arava on October 26, 1994. The ostentatious ceremony, Avi Shlaim remarked, was "the culmination of thirty-one years of secret dialogue across the battle lines" (2007, 534). This dialogue turned public following the 1991 Madrid Conference, which led to bilateral Israeli-Jordanian talks. Though these negotiations made significant progress in 1992, it was only with the conclusion of the Israeli-Palestinian Declaration of Principles on September 13, 1993, that King Husayn expressed willingness to "go all the way." It was not a surprise, therefore, that on the morrow of the Oslo Agreements the Israeli-Jordanian Common Agenda was also signed. This paved the way for accelerated negotiations, which resulted in the signing of the Israeli-Jordanian peace treaty. Much like the Israeli-Egyptian one, it marked an opportunity that was not missed. This chapter will analyze the reasons that brought Rabin and Husayn to seize the historical opportunity.

THE EPISODE

In the spring of 1991, following the Gulf War, King Husayn "stood alone, more isolated internationally than he had ever been in his forty-year reign" (Ashton 2008, 284). The king had earlier attempted to serve as a mediator between Saddam Hussein and the West following the Iraqi conquest of Kuwait in August 1990. But when his position was mistakenly perceived as pro-Iraqi, he lost credibility in Western and some Arab eyes. Jordan's decision to adopt a middle ground stemmed from its economic dependence on Iraq (which provided 95 percent of its oil imports and accounted for 45 percent of its exports) and the fact that many Palestinians—Jordanian citizens—supported Saddam's policy. The result was Jordan's estrangement from the United States and Britain, as well as Egypt and Saudi Arabia—all of which strongly supported a military operation to liberate Kuwait (Shlaim 2007, 480–506). The cost of the crisis to Jordan, including UN sanctions, climbed to $5 billion; in addition, it was compelled to receive three hundred thousand Palestinian refugees from Kuwait (ibid., 507). Both the diplomatic isolation and the deteriorating economic situation led Husayn to enthusiastically embrace the idea of holding an international conference—the very idea he had promoted, in vain, during the 1980s. With that, the process of Jordan's rehabilitation in Western (and particularly American) eyes began.[1]

A joint delegation represented Jordanian and Palestinian interests at the Madrid Conference. When the parties were invited to hold bilateral talks, the delegation split into two tracks—one dealing with Israeli-Jordanian concerns and the other with Israeli-Palestinian affairs. From this point, wrote Shlaim, "Jordan was free to pursue its own peace diplomacy in conformity with the general Arab consensus rather than in defiance of it" (2007, 515). The talks were held infrequently from December 1991 to September 1993. The first six rounds of bilateral Israeli-Jordanian talks made little headway (Majali, Anani, and Haddadin 2006, 23–125). A breakthrough was achieved in the seventh round, on October 28, 1992, with the completion of a common agenda draft. It explicitly stated that the aim of the negotiations was "the achievement of just, lasting and comprehensive peace between the Arab states, the Palestinians and Israel." It specified the basic components of the expected Israeli-Jordanian peace negotiations in the realm of security, water, refugees and displaced persons, borders and territorial matters, as well as the spheres of future bilateral cooperation (Majali, Anani, and Haddadin 2006, 329–330; Zak 1996, 290–291; Rubinstein 2004, 151–153; Shlaim 2007, 518; Lukacs 1997, 189). In the absence of any news regarding other tracks, the two sides decided not to make their progress public. It was nevertheless leaked to the Jordanian press, arousing vehement criticism from the PLO and the political opposition in Jordan. Responding to the censure, the government refused to approve the common agenda. This setback and the Israeli deportation of Hamas activists to Lebanon in December 1992 led to a deadlock in the bilateral talks. The head of the Jordanian delegation, ʿAbd al-Salam al-Majali, was instructed "to spin the negotiations out" by focusing on technicalities rather than substance (Ashton 2008, 299). In spite of the impasse, wrote Shlaim, "It was essentially a matter of marking time, of waiting for a breakthrough on the Palestinian track" (2007, 518; Majali, Anani, and Haddadin 2006, 221–232).

Indeed, the Oslo Accords, signed on September 13, 1993, provided the necessary turning point. The king's first reaction was of surprise and anger at the PLO's secretive diplomacy—particularly as he had provided an umbrella to the Palestinian delegation in Madrid. Soon enough, however, Husayn realized that the accord helped clear the way for Jordan to pursue its own interests through a bilateral peace agreement as ʿArafat himself had broken the taboo on making peace with Israel. In the words of Queen Noor, "Because Arafat had made the first move, however flawed, Hussein felt free to proceed" (2003, 525). It was not a coincidence, therefore, that a day after the signing of the Oslo Accords on September 14, Elyakim Rubinstein and Faiz Tarawneh, the respective heads of the Israeli and Jordanian delegations, signed the common agenda in a modest ceremony at the State Department. Only now did Husayn feel confident enough to publicly commit himself to the document concluded a year earlier (Majali, Anani, and Haddadin 2006, 239–240; Shlaim 2007, 524; Ashton 2008, 300–301; Rubinstein 2004, 152–153; Shamir 2012, 59–60).

The signing of the Oslo Accords between Israel and the PLO raised Husayn's fears that Israel might abandon its policy of partnership with Jordan in favor of a new partnership with the PLO and 'Arafat. In particular, he feared that Jordan's special historical role in Jerusalem would be sacrificed. It was true that Israel did seem focused on the Palestinian track, but Rabin attempted to allay the king's fears regarding Israel's intentions; this was the aim of their secret meeting in Aqaba on September 26, 1993. Undoubtedly, the mutual trust and respect that developed between two leaders significantly contributed to the eventual success of the negotiations. "It was at this meeting," wrote Queen Noor, "that the two leaders would begin to know each other and to establish the personal trust and respect, differences notwithstanding" (Noor 2003, 529; Shlaim 2007, 25; Rubinstein 2004, 153; Ashton 2008, 303; Shamir 2012, 61). As a confidence-building measure, a tripartite US-Israel-Jordan economic working group was established, chaired by US envoy Dennis Ross. This was followed by another secret meeting between Peres and Husayn in Amman on November 2, which led to the initialing of a four-page document dealing with several key issues: land and borders, the establishment of diplomatic relations, and future cooperation in the fields of agriculture, transport, tourism, and energy. In addition, Peres suggested that Amman host an international economic conference with senior businessmen from Israel and the Arab countries (this was eventually held only in October 1995, coinciding with the first anniversary of the Israeli-Jordanian peace treaty). Unable to curb his enthusiasm, Peres leaked news of the meeting to the Israeli media. This only reinforced Husayn's mistrust of Peres, which began with his failure to deliver the London Document in April 1987 (see chapter 15). Rabin, peeved that Peres had received most of the credit for the breakthrough in the Palestinian track and highly suspicious of his motives, decided to take the lead in the Israeli-Jordanian talks. He was concerned, however, that in spite of his warm, developing ties with Husayn, the Jordanian leader might get cold feet and change his mind, as he had done on past occasions (Shlaim 2007, 527–530; Ashton 2008, 302; Halevy 2006, 77, 90–91; Shamir 2012, 62–65). Lending some perspective, Shimon Shamir, the first Israeli ambassador to Jordan, claimed that

238 CHANCES FOR PEACE

at this point King Husayn was still hesitating over whether or not to sign a full peace treaty (2012, 66).

Meanwhile, at home, Husayn prepared the way, taking various steps to strengthen the domestic legitimacy for his peace policy. In August 1993 he amended the electoral law to limit the strength of the Islamic opposition. The results of the elections held on November 8—the first multiparty election since 1956—produced an amenable parliament, allowing him to continue with the negotiations and conclude a peace treaty with Israel (Shlaim 2007, 530–531; Ashton 2008, 301).

Mutual contacts behind the scenes continued throughout the first half of 1994. However, with the signing of the Gaza-Jericho Agreement in May, Husayn realized that the progress on the Israeli-Palestinian track might severely affect Jordanian interests. As a result, a secret meeting was held between him and Rabin in London in late May, with key actors in the peace negotiations also attending, such as Crown Prince Hasan on the Jordanian side and Rubinstein and Efraim Halevy, the deputy head of the Mossad, on the Israeli side. At this meeting, Husayn heard for the first time that Israel would be willing to grant Jordan a privileged position in the Muslim holy places in Jerusalem in any future peace settlement. In return, Husayn agreed to begin working on a draft agreement in a place on the Israeli-Jordanian border. It was agreed that the talks would be bilateral but the Americans would be kept informed. The US involvement was crucial since Jordan was expecting its debt in the amount of $700 million to be waived and Rabin promised to further lobby for this request in the White House and Congress (Shlaim 2007, 533–534; Ashton 2008, 303–304; Halevy 2006, 75; Shamir 2012, 66–67). Interestingly, a few days later, and perhaps in order to conceal the progress made on the Jordanian track, Rabin publicly stated that he "had hoped that Jordan would be the first, or at least the second, state to sign a peace treaty, but there is no room for hopes now. Jordan had opportunities in the past and it missed them all" (quoted in Zak 1996, 294). He thus thrust the responsibility of past failures squarely on the Jordanian side. A meeting between Prince Hasan and the head of the opposition Likud Party, Netanyahu, reassured Husayn that the idea of an Israeli-Jordanian peace treaty enjoyed wide support (Shamir 2012, 68).

Husayn's June visit to Washington was meant to coordinate his moves with the Clinton administration and make his case regarding the erasure of Jordan's debt and the renewal of US economic and military aid that had been cut off during the Gulf crisis. Two Israeli emissaries—Halevy and Ambassador Rabinovich—also pleaded the Jordanian case to US officials. The United States, however, was adamant that only a dramatic shift in Jordan's policy (Ross's terminology was that Husayn "has to pull a Sadat") would convince Congress to write off the debt and authorize aid. Greatly impressed by Clinton, the king realized that the time was propitious for a grand gesture (Ross 2005, 170–176; Shlaim 2007, 534–535; Ashton 2008, 305; Halevy 2006, 76–77). He wrote a personal letter to the president, in which he promised to move forward in the peace process and recalled his grandfather's commitment to peace, which cost him his life (Shamir 2012, 73). Husayn also suggested that Christopher take part in a trilateral meeting at the Dead Sea with the Jordanian and Israeli prime ministers. Husayn pledged to work for peace in the spirit of his meeting with Clinton. The fact that the king consented "to go public" was a clear sign that he had "crossed the Rubicon" (Ross 2005, 176–178).

To prove his sincerity, Husayn made a speech in parliament on July 9 in which he stated that it was time for Jordan to pursue peace with Israel and that he was willing to meet Rabin publicly. The speech was meant to prepare the Jordanian public for the move. Though thrilled by this development, the United States was anxious that this kind of meeting should take place in Washington; yet the parties decided to hold it at their shared border. Ross asserted that such a sequence "would rob the Washington event of its drama — and drama with the Congress was a must." He further complained to the Israelis that they had better treat the US "as something more than 'the kosher caterer.'" Rabinovich was told that if Israel counted on debt forgiveness for Jordan, then Rabin should assent to a summit taking place in Washington with an air of drama and fanfare (Ross 2005, 178–180). The US pressure succeeded in changing the sequence of events; on July 18 the bilateral negotiations were launched in Wadi Arava, followed by a meeting between Majali, Peres, and Christopher two days later. These exchanges set in motion a process that culminated in the publication of the Washington Declaration on July 25, delivered in the presence of Clinton, Husayn, and Rabin. The details of the document were hammered out secretly between Husayn's and Rabin's personal emissaries without the knowledge of the State Department or even leading Jordanian and Israeli politicians. The declaration terminated the state of belligerency between the two countries, committing them to seek a just, lasting, and comprehensive peace based on UN Resolutions 242 and 338. It also stated that when the final negotiations on Jerusalem took place, "Israel will give high priority to the Jordanian historic role" in the Muslim holy shrines. The declaration signaled the beginning of the process of normalizing ties by setting up two border crossing points and the establishment of a coordination hotline between the police forces. As a postscript to the ceremony, Husayn and Rabin addressed a joint session of Congress, hoping to persuade it to agree to debt forgiveness and to a new economic and military aid package for Jordan (Ross 2005, 181–185; Ashton 2008, 306–308; Shlaim 2007, 536–539; Halevy 2006, 77–86; Rubinstein 2004, 155–157; Shamir 2012, 74–79).

Following the Washington Declaration, the United States still refused to confirm the assurances given regarding Jordan's debt and the military aid. A senior Jordanian sent to Washington was notified that nothing short of a peace treaty would satisfy the Americans. In addition, the involvement of Rabin and the pro-Israel lobby group AIPAC were crucial in winning congressional support (Noor 2003, 537). The Washington Declaration did not elicit strong domestic Jordanian criticism, except from the direction of the Islamic forces. In the Arab world, the Syrian press voiced some disapproval, though Asad himself refrained from any public criticism, perhaps because of his own expectations regarding the possibility of progress on the Israeli-Syrian track (see chapter 19). The strongest reaction came from the PLO, which resented the envisaged special Jordanian role in Jerusalem (Ashton 2008, 308; Shamir 2012, 79–82).

In the wake of the ceremonial festivities, the actual negotiations on the specifics of the peace treaty were conducted bilaterally in August–October 1994. Teams of experts worked out the details of water allocation, border demarcation, and mutual security. Often enough, Husayn and Rabin were called in to resolve outstanding problems. On October 16, for example, the two leaders worked through the night, going through the draft agreement paragraph by paragraph. When the border issue came up, wrote Shlaim, "They got down on their hands and knees to pore over a huge map laid out on the floor. Together, they worked out the whole line from Eilat and Aqaba in the south to the point of convergence with Syria in the north" (2007, 542). The treaty was initialed the following day. Regarding water allocation, Jordan received a generous offer from Israel, which promised to increase its water supply by more than 25 percent by tapping an extra 165 million cubic meters of water from the Yarmuk and Jordan Rivers annually. Israel also agreed to supply Jordan with fifty million cubic meters a year. In terms of the border demarcation, Jordan asserted its territorial sovereignty over some disputed lands, though the local Israeli farmers were permitted to stay and continue to work there. With regard to Jerusalem, the relevant clause in the Washington Declaration was inserted in the treaty. Finally, to allay Jordanian fears regarding the possible forced emigration of Palestinians from the West Bank to Jordan, the treaty stipulated that "Involuntary movements of persons in such a way as to adversely prejudice the security of either party should not be permitted." Interestingly, the security part of the treaty did not entail the involvement of the United Nations or any other third party, which attested to the amount of trust existing between the parties. The treaty was finally signed in Wadi Arava on October 26, 1994 (Ross 2005, 186–187; Shlaim 2007, 541–543; Ashton 2008, 308–311; Zak 1996, 296–298; Majali, Anani, and Haddadin 2006, 289–305, 329–340; Halevy 2006, 95–98; Noor 2003, 548–549; Habashana 1999, 77–122; Shamir 2012, 82–97).

The Knesset endorsed the peace treaty by an overwhelming majority. Even the Likud Party and Netanyahu were fully behind it. As for the public, 91.5 percent supported the agreement (Bar-Siman-Tov 1998, 24). Following the official signing ceremony, Clinton appeared before a joint session of parliament in Amman, declaring that the United States would meet Jordan's military needs. All the king's political maneuvers came to bear as the lower house of the Jordanian parliament approved the treaty 54 to 25, with one member absent. The upper house followed suit. Husayn could shake off any naysayers who called it "the king's peace." The treaty was ratified by the two countries at another official ceremony at Beit Gabriel, on Lake Kinneret, on November 11, 1994.

ASSESSMENT

Immediately after the conclusion of the peace treaty, Husayn claimed in an interview that there were "many opportunities [for peace] in the past that had been missed" by Israel and Jordan as a result of mistakes made by both sides.[2] Our analyses of two major episodes—with King 'Abdallah in 1950 and the London Document in 1987—indicated that the level of plausibility for a missed opportunity in these events was low (see chapters 4, 15). In contrast, however, the Israeli-Jordanian peace treaty embodied an opportunity that was not missed. There is no doubt that this episode constituted a historical opportunity; for years the Hashemite Kingdom had waited for a suitable opportunity to sign a peace treaty with Israel. Given the magnitude of the Palestinian population in Jordan and its long-standing public commitment to the Palestinian cause, it was clear that only a breakthrough on the Palestinian track would open the door for Jordan to advance its considerable interests vis-à-vis Israel. The Gulf War and the Madrid Conference were instrumental in creating the historical opportunity. Yet it was the Oslo Agreements that provided Husayn with the necessary legitimacy to promote a separate Israeli-Jordanian peace treaty. After his initial anger at the PLO's unilateral move, Husayn realized that Oslo offered the chance he longed for. In this specific case, there was no need for a significant peace offer by either side, since the agenda on the Israeli-Jordanian track was well known and had in fact been secretly approved already in October 1992.

In terms of legitimacy—the first variable of our definition—both Husayn and Rabin enjoyed considerable political and public support. The king's political maneuvers led to the election of a rather docile parliament; in addition, Husayn, approaching the age of sixty after forty-one years of rule (since 1953) and suffering from a terminal illness, was an experienced, trustworthy, and somewhat charismatic leader in the eyes of his people. For example, upon his return to Jordan from medical treatments abroad in September 1992, nearly a third of the kingdom's population poured into the streets to greet him in a spontaneous demonstration of affection and support (Shlaim 2007, 519). Following this exhilarating reception, Husayn admitted, "There are so many tragic cases of leaders losing their people as time goes on, but to have my relationship with the people grown even stronger after so many years is truly a blessing" (Noor 2003, 520). This image enabled him to proceed with implementing a policy that was not uncontroversial. In fact, Shamir contends that public opinion in Jordan received the treaty "with mixed feelings or even evident hostility" (2012, 93). Yet the support voiced by the East Jordanian elite, as well as the promises of expected economic rewards, helped overcome the suspicions and doubts. On the other side, Rabin enjoyed a comfortable majority in the Knesset, which also included—in contrast to the Oslo scenario—many Likud members. A dalliance with Husayn was considered acceptable policy across the divided political spectrum. It was not a coincidence, therefore, that the treaty was endorsed almost unanimously by the Knesset. In fact, it was one of the rare occasions in which, on both sides of the conflict, the incumbent leaders enjoyed wide popularity and legitimacy.

In terms of the willingness of leaders to take a bold step and change the course of events—the second variable in our definition—both Rabin and Husayn demonstrated that they were determined to exploit the opportunity and implement what in their eyes was an overdue historical mission. Having signed the Oslo Accords, Rabin felt confident enough to pursue the Jordanian track. Moreover, since Peres was perceived as the driving force behind the Palestinian breakthrough, Rabin took it upon himself to personally sew up the treaty directly with the king. Likewise, Husayn felt confident and courageous enough to pursue a policy that he considered part of the historical legacy of his grandfather, King 'Abdallah. Signing the treaty represented, in his eyes, the "crowning achievement" of his career (Shlaim 2007, 519–520, 532).[3]

The third variable relates to the history of past interactions; the Israeli-Jordanian connection was unique, having existed since the establishment of the two entities in the 1920s. Their mutual concern about the Palestinian problem and other bilateral interests kept these contacts alive even when they suffered temporary setbacks. These rather expansive relations included tacit alliances, clandestine cooperation, and informal agreements. This "wealth of experience" produced an evident measure of trust between the parties, though it did not extend to all leaders, e.g., Peres, Netanyahu, and Shamir, who were suspect in Jordanian eyes. But even the unhappy end of the London Document in April 1987 (see chapter 15) did not prevent the beginning of another round of negotiations when circumstances seemed propitious. The combination of these two elements—the long mutual history and trust—created a certain ripeness that paved the way for a quick negotiation process. The high level of trust between Husayn and Rabin played a crucial role on the road to peace: the two men had known each other for more than twenty years, shared a military background, and were discreet and committed. At the height of their careers, both realized that they would not have better partners. Husayn described their relationship as that "between two military men who dealt directly, and often bluntly, with each other" (Noor 2003, 547; Halevy 2006, 96). In his speech at the signing ceremony, Rabin stated, "Peace between states is peace between peoples. It is an expression of trust and esteem" (quoted in Ashton 2008, 314). Attending Rabin's funeral in Jerusalem, Husayn admitted: "We had a unique relationship" (Shlaim 2007, 527). The personal touch, added to the legacy of past interactions, greatly contributed to the potential of this historical opportunity.

The level of the involvement of the third party—the United States—was not extensive, but this proved to be less crucial since the parties themselves were keenly interested in concluding a deal and did not need external help. In fact, most of the Israeli-Jordanian negotiations were held on the bilateral level, with the US merely playing the back-burner role of facilitator. Indeed, the US did not attach much importance to the Jordanian track since Husayn's behavior seemed to be characterized by his habitual indecision. In early 1994, Ross estimated that the king "had no plans to move toward a formal agreement anytime soon" (2005, 167). This mistaken assessment was modified after the signing of the Gaza-Jericho Agreement in May and Husayn's highly successful visit to the United States in June. Yet the drafting of the Washington Declaration was a product of secret Israeli-Jordanian talks; the text was delivered to the US only a day before the ceremony! The US initially felt disappointed and somewhat humiliated to find itself playing little more than the caterer (Ross 2005, 181–185), though it took on a more meaningful role in the last stages of the negotiations. The services that it could provide were important, first by giving the stamp of approval to the bilateral agreement, and then by providing financial and military incentives. Husayn noted accurately that "The Americans played a very important role but we ourselves [Israel and Jordan] had done most of the job."[4]

In conclusion, the Israeli-Jordanian peace treaty was an opportunity that could not be missed. To begin with, the parties themselves were cognizant of the existence of a historical opportunity that should be seized. The fact that on both sides of the conflict stood legitimate leaders strong enough to take bold decisions and who trusted each other reduced the chances that this opportunity would be missed. Moreover, the long historical record of contacts between Israel and Jordan created a mutual and trustful basis for negotiations. Finally, the United States as a third party was committed to the process, even though its task was limited to the role of a facilitator rather than a mediator.

In any case, the US played a more meaningful role than in past negotiations with Jordan, and in such a way helped the parties to smooth differences along the way to concluding the treaty. In many ways, the Israeli-Jordanian peace treaty is an ideal case study in which all the variables needed in order not to miss an opportunity were fulfilled.

NOTES

1. For more on the reasons for Jordan's participation in the Madrid Conference and the peace process, see Habashana 1999, 51–74.

2. Husayn's interview with Smadar Peri, *Yedioth Ahronoth*, October 25, 1994.

3. The title of Ross's chapter on the Israeli-Jordanian peace treaty is "King Hussein Fulfills His Grandfather's Legacy" (2005, 164). See also Husayn's interview with Smadar Peri, *Yedioth Ahronoth*, October 25, 1994.

4. Ibid.

CHAPTER 19

ISRAELI-SYRIAN NEGOTIATIONS

1991–2000

SYRIA'S DECISION TO PARTICIPATE in the 1991 Madrid Conference set in
motion a process of peace negotiations with Israel that lasted almost a decade,
until the death of Syrian president Hafiz al-Asad in June 2000. The negotiations went through several phases. The first included the Madrid Conference
and ten subsequent rounds of bilateral meetings in Washington, which commenced during Shamir's and Bush's terms in January 1992 and ended during
Rabin's and Clinton's terms in June–July 1993. The second, between Rabin
and Asad, was particularly intensive, beginning in the summer of 1993, not
long before the signing of the Oslo Agreements, and ending with Rabin's assassination in 1995; this stage included two rounds of talks between the Israeli
and Syrian chiefs of staff. The third phase commenced with Peres as prime
minister (November 1995) and culminated in several high-level talks at Wye
River (December 1995–March 1996). The fourth stage was a brief Israeli flirtation with Asad during the Netanyahu premiership. The final stage was held
during the Barak period, climaxing in talks in Washington and Shepherdstown, West Virginia (December 1999–January 2000), followed by a summit
between Clinton and Asad in Geneva in March 2000. In contrast to the Palestinian and Jordanian tracks, the Israeli-Syrian track did not result in the
signing of any agreement, yet the two sides "did break considerable new
ground in the effort to build a lasting peace between them" (Cobban 1999, 4).
The aim of this chapter is to assess if and to what extent an opportunity in any
of these stages was missed by the parties to the conflict.

THE EPISODES

Peaceful interactions between Israel and Syria prior to 1991 were limited.
Some noncommittal contacts were held between Zionist and Syrian national
leaders in the pre-1948 period. Following the 1948 War, Israel negotiated armistice agreements with four Arab states, of which Syria was the last to sign,

in July 1949. The fact that during the war it captured certain Israeli territories beyond the international border complicated the negotiations and resulted in the establishment of three demilitarized zones. Earlier, in March 1949, the chief of staff, Husni Za'im, seized power and offered Israel a surprising initiative: a peace treaty and partial settlement of the Palestinian refugees in return for a meaningful Israeli territorial concession in Lake Kinneret (see chapter 5). Tension and animosity characterized Israeli-Syrian relations during the years 1949–1967. Vying for sovereignty over the demilitarized zones, both sides engaged in acts that violated the armistice agreement. These violations were supposed to be dealt with by the Mixed Armistice Commission (MAC), which was formed as part of the armistice agreement. Syrian attempts to divert the tributaries of the Jordan River and its support of the Fatah organization further contributed to the escalation on the border, eventually leading to the outbreak of the 1967 War, which ended with the Syrian loss of the Golan Heights. Syria's refusal to accept UN Resolution 242 led to its exclusion from the diplomatic process in the post-1967 period (Rabil 2003, 14–20; Kipnis 2009, 23–64).

Asad, who seized power in November 1970, adopted a more pragmatic attitude toward Israel, but only after the 1973 War, when he felt confident enough to accept Resolution 338 (which implied recognition of Resolution 242). This shift paved the way for Kissinger—the US mediator—to negotiate a Syrian-Israeli disengagement agreement in May 1974 (see chapter 11). Meeting President Nixon in June, Asad expressed readiness to sign a peace treaty with Israel, provided it withdrew to the pre-1967 borders and restored Palestinian rights. Syria's use of the good offices of the United States did not harm its friendship with the Soviet Union. In contrast to Sadat, Asad was unwilling to move to a second disengagement agreement; he was suspicious of Egypt, Israel, and the United States, which were trying, in his eyes, to divide the Arabs and isolate Syria. While the Syrian-Israeli border remained calm, Lebanon turned into their main battleground. During the Lebanese Civil War (1975–1976), following the intervention of the Syrian army, a "deterrence dialogue" had emerged, with the conclusion of an unwritten agreement concerning "red lines" Israel expected Syria to observe in return for tolerating its role in Lebanon. It indicated that the two sides shared a stake in Lebanon's stability and could bargain rationally while respecting the other's interests. In accepting Israel's red lines, Syria tacitly acknowledged Israel's legitimate security needs (Evron 1987, 54, 203; Rabil 2003, 50–53).

Following the failure to reach a second Israeli-Syrian Disengagement Agreement, Asad opposed the Israeli-Egyptian peace and joined the Arab Steadfastness and Resistance Front, which attempted—with Soviet blessing—to contain the growing influence of Israel, Egypt, and the United States in the Middle East. Once again, Lebanon became Israel and Syria's main battle-ground. During the 1982 Lebanese War, Israel inflicted a heavy military blow on Syria, which significantly diminished its influence in Lebanon. Syria never-theless managed to quickly regain its hegemonic position, which included also the abolishing of the Israeli-Lebanese peace treaty, signed in May 1983 (see chapter 14). Thus through a shrewd combination of proxies and Soviet backing, Asad succeeded "to snatch a victory from the jaws of defeat" (Drys-dale and Hinnebusch 1991, 128).

A decade later, however, Asad agreed to participate in the multinational Madrid Conference (October 1991). His changed posture was due to the fact that his aim of achieving strategic parity with Israel had evaporated with the collapse of the Soviet Union and the Gulf War, which left the United States as the hegemonic power in the international and regional systems. Syria's par-ticipation in the US-led coalition against Iraq paid off handsomely: a new relationship with the US was formed; Saudi Arabia provided support in the sum of $3 billion; and Syria tightened its control over Lebanon. Realizing that the option of retrieving the occupied Golan by force was no longer feasible, Asad opted for a peace process led by the US (Rabinovich 1998, 36–39; Rabil 2003, 94–100; Zisser 2001, 104–105). Madrid opened the way for ten rounds of Israeli-Syrian bilateral talks in Washington. The first five, held during Shamir's premiership, were led by Yossi Ben-Aharon on the Israeli side and Muwaffaq 'Allaf on the Syrian side. But Shamir was unwilling to accept the Syrian for-mula of "land for peace," and Israel considered Asad's definition of peace to be "evasive and unclear" (Ben-Aharon 2000). From a Syrian perspective, the Madrid Conference and the subsequent talks were an exercise in "futile diplo-macy" (Shaaban 2013, 46–49). Itamar Rabinovich adds, probably correctly, that neither delegation came to Washington "to look for the middle ground on which a deal was to be made." Rather, their leaders sent them "with a mes-sage defined by reluctance, skepticism, and suspicion" (Rabinovich 1998, 40).

The election of Rabin as prime minister in June 1992 brought some changes to the natural course of the negotiations. In his election campaign, Rabin attached more importance to the Palestinian, rather than the Syrian, track. Upon entering office, however, he was told by Secretary of State Baker that Asad was seriously interested in making peace with Israel and that the United States was ready to make a significant investment in securing a peace treaty. Rabin was impressed and ready to explore Syria's position. He probably saw the advantages of a "Syrian-first" policy: he would be dealing with an authori-tative head of state rather than with the diffuse Palestinian polity; a problem seemingly simpler to resolve than the complex Israeli-Palestinian dispute. In addition, Syria posed a greater threat to Israel, with its growing army and long-range missiles (Rabinovich 1998, 47, 54–55; Bregman 2014, 202). With the nomination of a new head of delegation—Rabinovich, a renowned expert on Syria—some progress was made during the next five rounds of bilateral talks, which started in August 1992. The first change was Israel's decision to view UN Resolution 242 as applicable to the Syrian track. This meant that Rabin's government, in contrast to Shamir's, "did not support the notion of 'peace for peace' and was ready to seek a settlement with Syria that would include an element of withdrawal" (Rabinovich 1998, 57–58; Pressman 2007, 357; Ross 2005, 100). In return, the Syrians submitted a document, "Draft Declaration of Principles," which was tantamount, in Israeli eyes, to "a glorified non-belligerency in return for full withdrawal," but at the same time indicated Syria's determination to seek a peaceful settlement (Rabinovich 1998, 62).

From the outset, the Syrians demanded full Israeli withdrawal from the Golan Heights to the June 4, 1967, boundary. The question of withdrawal to which boundary would prove contentious in the negotiations, as Israel referred to the international line drawn by the British and the French in 1923. The difference between the two lines is not significant—some eighteen square kilometers—but the 1967 line gives physical access for Syria to the northeast corner of Lake Kinneret and the upper Jordan Valley. In contrast to the demarcated 1923 boundary, the 1967 line was never officially set (Daoudy 2008, 222–223; Pressman 2007, 355–358; Kipnis 2009, 63–64).[1]

While the Syrians focused on the territorial dimension, Israel paid more attention to the nature of the peace (normalization), security matters, and linkage to other tracks. The negotiations began auspiciously but soon reached a deadlock. The election of Clinton as US president in November 1992 aroused some concern on both sides, but he quickly demonstrated his commitment to the continuation of the Arab-Israeli peace process. When the new secretary of state, Christopher, returned from his first Middle East tour, he declared that there was "a tremendous opportunity to make progress, an unusual moment to achieve Middle Eastern peace," and he recommended it as a good place for the president to invest his prestige and influence. Since the Palestinian track was considered less ripe and more complicated, Clinton adopted a "Syria-first" policy, as it was estimated that the collapse of the Soviet Union left Asad with only one recourse: to follow the Egyptian model and rely on the United States as a mediator. In contrast to the Palestinians, Asad was perceived as a strong leader, capable of delivering a deal, and trustworthy enough in light of the longevity of the 1974 Disengagement Agreement. According to this logic, a breakthrough in this track was seen as the key to attaining a comprehensive settlement and forming a new geopolitical realignment in the Middle East. In addition, it was estimated that a deal with Asad would bring also an

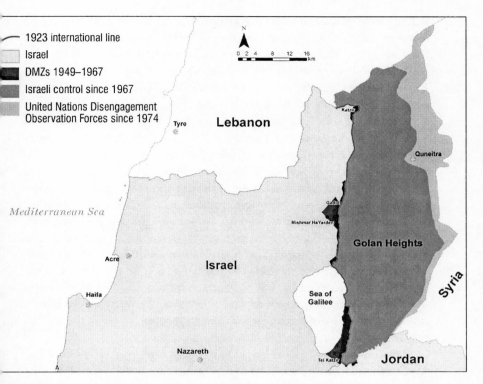

MAP 19.1. The Israeli-Syrian Border, 1923–2012. Courtesy of Shaul Arieli, 2013.

Israeli-Lebanese agreement. Not all the members of the US peace team shared the conviction and logic of the Syria-centric policy, but it gained prominence until the revelation of the Oslo channel (Indyk 2009, 18–19, 23–25; Rabinovich 1998, 85, 91–92; Miller 2008, 247, 252–253).

In the following months, both Rabin and Asad used language that offered some promise to diplomatic progress; in early November, Rabin suggested a formula that "the depth of withdrawal will reflect the depth of peace" (Rabinovich 1998, 83; Pressman 2007, 357). Perhaps not unrelated, in mid-November the head of the Syrian delegation used, for the first time, the "hypothetical question" technique, stating: "Supposing I satisfy you in the area that is of interest to you [namely, the nature of peace], would you be ready to satisfy me in the area that is of interest to me [namely, withdrawal]?" Moreover, ʿAllaf insisted that Israel provide an answer (Rabinovich 1998, 77). During 1992, Asad made a gesture of goodwill by allowing most of the Jewish community in Syria (estimated at four thousand) to leave the country (Zisser 2001, 106).

Before the year's end, however, Syria suspended the talks as a result of Israel's controversial decision to deport 415 Hamas activists to Lebanese territory on December 17 in retaliation against the organization's terrorist activities.

When the deportation crisis evaporated, the Israeli-Syrian talks resumed in January 1993 at the ambassadors' level but yielded no results. The first change occurred when Clinton and Rabin met for the first time in Washington in March, and the president attempted to convince the prime minister of the advantages of the Syria-first strategy. Rabin admitted that a peace treaty with Syria was impossible without full withdrawal from the Golan. In the first hypothetical questions that would accompany the process, Rabin told Clinton that he did not discount the possibility of full withdrawal in return for a genuine Syrian offer of peace, unconnected to other tracks, if backed by the necessary security arrangements. Rabin thought that a meeting with Asad—similar to the Sadat-Begin meeting—was necessary and that in any case a referendum would be required to approve a treaty with Syria because Rabin felt he did not have the mandate to make a decision on his own. "Clinton knew [then]," wrote Martin Indyk, "that if Asad was ready for peace, Rabin was ready to come down from the Golan Heights." The meeting was important as the two leaders developed trust and respect toward each other (Indyk 2009, 28–29).

The ninth round of Israeli-Syrian talks opened on April 27, preceded by Asad's renewed gesture to allow Syrian Jews to emigrate. In addition, he offered in public interviews a new formula: "full peace for full withdrawal," which was meant to respond to Rabin's earlier formula: "the depth of withdrawal will reflect the depth of peace." The Israeli assessment—confirmed by a Syrian interpretation—was that the term "full withdrawal" meant withdrawal from the Golan only and not from all the occupied territories, as previously demanded by the Syrians (al-'Azm 2000). In light of these exchanges, it is perhaps surprising that this round ended without any real progress. The tenth round, in June, did not produce any results either. In sum, wrote Miller, "In ten rounds of post-Madrid negotiations there were no relaxed coffee breaks, few handshakes, and no quiet bilateral meetings, let alone consequential secret or public diplomacy. Asad seemed to want us simply to deliver the Golan to Syria" (2008, 253).

The diplomatic impasse led Christopher to bring in Dennis Ross as special Middle East coordinator.[2] In late June the peace team attempted to revitalize the process, but developments in Lebanon once more intervened. In response to Hizballah's repeated Katyusha rocket attacks on the Galilee, in late July Israel launched a limited military action in southern Lebanon called Operation Accountability. Christopher managed to broker a cease-fire that included tacit understandings with Asad, Hizballah, and the Lebanese government regarding rules of conduct in southern Lebanon (Ross 2005, 109–110; Rabino-vich 1998, 102–104). This enabled Christopher and Ross to make a fresh start; the meeting with Rabin, on August 3, proved to be highly important. Rabin thought that the cease-fire might signal that Asad was ready for something larger and more strategic. In his opinion, opportunities are sometimes born out of crises and therefore the United States "should find out if there was an opportunity with Syria now." According to Christopher's testimony, Rabin posed a hypothetical question to Asad:

> What was Syria willing to do in exchange for Israel's full withdrawal from the territory in the Golan Heights seized by Israel in the 1967 war? More specifi-cally, was Assad willing to (a) sign a stand-alone treaty with Israel, i.e., one without linkage to the Jordanian and Palestinian negotiating tracks; (b) join in personal, public diplomacy to reassure the Israeli public of Syria's com-mitment to peace, including a meeting with Rabin; and (c) agree to a five-year timetable for Israel's full withdrawal from the Golan, with incremental normalization of relations between the two countries, such as the exchange of diplomats, as the withdrawal progressed? (2001, 221; Bregman 2013, 227–228)

Christopher was stunned: "Rabin was entrusting me with what should have been the ultimate winning hand on the Syrian track: Israel's departure from the Golan Heights" (ibid). It was the first time an Israeli prime minister had explicitly offered full withdrawal—albeit contingent on fulfilling certain Israeli needs. "We felt," Indyk wrote, [that] "we were on the threshold of a momentous breakthrough" (2009, 83). Rabinovich, however, asserts that Rabin did not give a commitment but rather deposited with Christopher a hypothetical, conditional willingness to withdraw from the Golan as part of a peace settlement (Rabinovich 2006, 277–279). Rabin's offer would hereafter become known as the "deposit."

The next day, when Christopher presented Asad with Rabin's hypothetical question, the latter's response "was a series of nitpicking questions and con-tentious pronouncements that I tried to answer without displaying my irrita-tion" (2001, 221). According to Christopher, Asad said that public diplomacy would come only after a peace agreement; that he would not meet Rabin until the Golan had been fully returned to Syria; that he would not resist a separate peace agreement, though he could not agree to early normalization measures; and that Israel must withdraw within six months instead of five years (ibid., 221–222). After four hours of discussions, Christopher concluded, "Rabin's risky, visionary step had not found reciprocity in Damascus" (ibid., 222). The Syrian narrative gives a somewhat different account: it emphasizes that Asad treated Rabin's offer with utmost seriousness, as he read his response from a paper—a rare occasion—after consulting Chief of Staff Shihabi, Defense Minister Tlass, and Foreign Minister Faruq al-Shara'. Asad expressed satisfaction with Rabin's proposal but wondered to which borders—1967 or 1923—Israel planned to withdraw; he then went on at length to describe the security arrangements with Israel he envisaged and clarified that all settlements would have to be evacuated within six months of signing a peace treaty (Shaaban 2013, 102; Bregman 2013, 228; Shara' 2015).[3] Regardless of the exact details of the meeting, the question is whether Asad's response was generous enough to continue the dialogue. In Ross's opinion, it "was not historic in nature" (2005, 112). Asad's rather indifferent approach is substantiated by the personal diary of his interpreter, Bouthaina Shaaban; Asad, she wrote, "seemed not to be impressed by the deposit. Although he appreciated its importance, he did not see it as groundbreaking or great as the Americans thought it was" (2013, 100). By all accounts, Rabin was disappointed by Asad's response; he was hoping for a counter-offer matching what he saw as a bold Israeli move (Christopher 2001, 222). It is possible too that he felt somewhat betrayed by Christopher, who delivered the "deposit" to Asad instead of keeping it in his "pocket" (Sagie 2011, 45). Later accounts also partially blame Christopher for mishandling the "deposit affair" (Kurtzer et al. 2013, 75–76; see below).

Asad's rejoinder was, in essence, not negative; in line with his character, he responded in a cautious, subdued manner, preferring to move in stages instead of taking a giant leap. He was not a leader bent on offering mega-incentives or showing high drama. The fact that Rabin's "deposit" did not make clear to which line Israel was about to withdraw—1923 or 1967—was probably a major reason for his unenthusiastic response (Shaaban 2013, 99; Pressman 2007, 359). The timing, however, proved crucial, and this Asad did not know. Israel and the Palestinians were on the brink of a historical breakthrough in Oslo. In light of the disappointing Syrian response, Rabin gave Peres the green light to conclude the Oslo negotiations. Patrick Seale argues that Rabin's indirect, oral, and secret offer to Asad was no more than "a political deception, a ruse of war," tailored "to engage Asad just enough to blunt his attack on Oslo, while, at the same time, frightening the Palestinians into concessions" (2000, 68). This thesis is supported by Indyk, who argues that since Rabin knew well the benefits of playing one off against the other, he used the Syrian offer to put pressure on the Palestinians—agreement with whom was his first priority (2009, 83–87). But Rabin was not the kind of leader who engaged in dubious and tricky diplomacy. It seems rather that in light of the imminent breakthrough on the Israeli-Palestinian track, he was probing the possibility that Asad would come with an attractive offer à la Sadat that would tip the scales in favor of a Syrian deal; but such a bold step could not have been expected by the wary and introverted Asad. Rabin was in a hurry to show his public results, and the Palestinian track looked set to deliver an immediate reward.

With the surprising signing of the Oslo Agreements in September 1993, the Israeli-Syrian negotiations were pushed to the back burner. Rabin explained to the United States that since the Israeli public would need time to absorb the agreement with the Palestinians, Israel would have to slow the pace on the Syrian track. Rabin even asked Clinton to convey to Asad his commitment to sign an agreement, but asked for a few months' delay (Rabinovich 1998, 118). Indeed, a traditional foreign policy maxim was that Israel could not proceed on two tracks simultaneously because of domestic opposition (Ross 2005, 137; Miller 2008, 255). The Oslo Agreements infuriated Asad for two reasons. First, he was angry because Rabin opted for the Palestinian track despite his on-the-surface inclination for a Syria-first policy. In light of their delegations' relative progress in August, the timing of Oslo just a month later was indeed unfortunate. Second, 'Arafat—his archenemy—had succeeded in bypassing Syria and signing a separate pact with Israel. According to a Syrian source, Asad regarded Oslo as not only a setback but a catastrophe for the Palestinians and the Arab world. In his opinion, Oslo "proved to us what we had been saying for years, that is, that the Israelis were playing one party off against the other, trying to gain world-wide media attention, and were firmly uninterested in real peace with the Arabs—and certainly not with the Palestinians" (Shaaban 2013, 76; Seale 2000, 68). The feeling that Rabin was deceiving him caused Asad to suspect his overall sincerity; but Uri Sagie, then head of IDF Military Intelligence (MI), argued in an honest and self-critical assessment of the talks that Rabin had no intention of deceiving Asad; he had been truly undecided on the question of which track to advance (2011, 45).

As expected, the Israeli-Syrian talks remained low in profile until the end of 1993. Hoping to revive this track, Clinton met Asad in Geneva on January 16, 1994. There, Clinton sought to convince Asad that Rabin's commitment to full withdrawal was in his pocket but that it would not be taken out until Asad filled the other pocket with Syrian commitments on security arrangements and normalization. Indeed, Clinton managed to extract two important concessions from Asad: willingness to accept "normal peace relations" with Israel; and willingness to make peace before a final settlement of the Palestinian issue (Clinton 2004, 883).[4] At a joint press conference they held, Asad spoke of "a just and comprehensive peace with Israel as a strategic choice." The US peace team was elated by what they saw as a major achievement. But to Rabin's mind the meeting did not produce enough "meat" to persuade the

Israeli public about the merits of an agreement (Ross 2005, 139–141; Rabinovich 1998, 128–130; Indyk 2009, 104–108; Pressman 2007, 360; Shaaban 2013, 79–88).

Following the signing of the Gaza-Jericho Agreement in May 1994 (see chapter 17), another breakthrough occurred on the Israeli-Syrian track. Meeting Christopher on July 18, 1994, Rabin clarified for the first time that his "deposit" referred to withdrawal to the June 4, 1967, lines, as Asad had insisted, but that "Israel will not spell this out before knowing that our needs will be fulfilled" (quoted in Bregman 2013, 229; 2014, 204; Kurtzer et al. 2013, 77–78). Still suspicious of whether the Israeli offer was a serious one, Asad agreed to resume the talks on the ambassadors' level. In addition, he offered minor concessions regarding the questions of normalization and the withdrawal timetable. The ambassadors' channel began in July and lasted almost a year. The talks dealt with what Rabin termed the "four legs of the table": withdrawal, normalization, security arrangements, and timetable for implementation (Rabinovich 1998, 147–158; al-Moualem 1997, 84). During this period, both Rabin and Asad were also engaged in public diplomacy, which was meant to prepare their public for the concessions entailed in signing a peace treaty.

The signing of the Israeli-Jordanian treaty in late October provided an opportunity to move forward also in the Israeli-Syrian track. Following his attendance at the ceremony, Clinton flew to Damascus and met with Asad—their second meeting in a year and the first visit of an American president in Syria since Nixon in 1974. Though Asad made some additional small concessions, their joint press conference was a media mishap that embarrassed Clinton.[5] It was this, perhaps, that led Asad to agree to the meeting of senior military officers as a kind of compensation. Both countries were represented by their chiefs of staff: Ehud Barak on the Israeli side and Hikmet Shihabi for Syria. This decision, wrote Ross, "was the most serious step Asad had taken in the negotiations" (2005, 152). Since Shihabi was a Baʿth Party member and a trusted confidant of Asad, his participation in the negotiations was a sign of earnestness on his part. Yet the talks, held on December 21–23, failed to achieve any breakthrough. With both men unaware of the "deposit," Barak focused on the security issues while Shihabi refused to discuss them as long as the border line was not specified. As a result, Asad refused to send Shihabi for a second round of talks (Ross 2005, 151–153; Rabinovich 1998, 173–175; Bregman 2013, 229–230). The Barak-Shihabi talks, wrote Shaaban, were "yet another missed opportunity" (2013, 121).

The next round was held in February 1995 at the ambassadors' level and focused on producing a document on security arrangements. The problem was how to devise a document that would diminish Syrian suspicions that

Israel wanted to neutralize Syria militarily and secure its own dominance, and at the same time would allay Israeli fears regarding Syria's future aims. In any case, Syria demanded that the security arrangements be equal, reciprocal, and mutual. Two major stumbling blocks were the size of the demilitarized zones on both sides of the border and the question of an early warning station in the Golan. In May a one-page non-paper, "Aims and Principles of Security Arrangements," was finalized (Rabinovich 1998, 176–180; Ross 2005, 153–161; Pressman 2007, 362; Seale 2000, 70–74; Kurtzer et al. 2013, 78–79).

These talks served as a basis for a second meeting between the Israeli and Syrian chiefs of staff—with Amnon Lipkin-Shahak replacing Barak—held in Washington on June 27–29. At the end of the talks, wrote Rabinovich, "We parted with a clear sense that a genuine negotiation between the Israeli and Syrian military establishments had begun" (1998, 185). Indeed, the account given by Ross indicated an agreement on some fifteen points, which the senior military experts could follow up on in their future meetings. Asad, however, decided to bring matters to a head; he demanded that Israel drop altogether the demand for a warning station and refused to send a senior military officer to continue the talks. Infuriated, Rabin suspended the talks. In light of the anticipated signing of the Cairo Agreement with the Palestinians (see chapter 17) and growing domestic opposition to any compromise regarding the Golan,[6] perhaps Rabin found this a convenient pretext to halt the talks. He "was ready for a domestic political crisis over a real issue [Oslo II]," according to Rabinovich, "but he was not willing to risk his government over a negotiation that, he suspected, Asad was not really determined to bring to conclusion" (1998, 191). In contrast, Seale thought that "Rabin was in no hurry to make peace with Syria and was certainly not willing to pay a fair price." In his opinion, Rabin's double-talk suggested that he "deliberately deceived both the Americans and Asad" (2000, 71).

Once more, a stalemate between Israel and Syria occurred as progress was being made on another track. As the Oslo II Agreement was ratified in the Knesset by only a slim majority, Rabin had to take into consideration the vocal domestic opposition to any future deal with Syria. Meanwhile, behind the scenes, Egyptian president Mubarak arranged a meeting between Syrian foreign minister Shara' and Moshe Shachal, a minister and confidant of Rabin. Mubarak's surprising involvement in the diplomatic process was due to his interest in ensuring that Asad would not receive from Israel more than Egypt had received in the peace treaty—as it was, Asad's prestige looked set to rise in the Arab world. A meeting was scheduled for December 5, 1995, in Geneva, but Rabin's assassination on November 4 put an end to this unknown episode.[7] The next meeting, between Shara' and a senior Israeli politician, would have to wait another four years. With this, the first chapter of the Israeli-Syrian peace talks was sealed. Unlike the Palestinian and Jordanian tracks, the Syrian track produced no significant result, though Rabin left a significant legacy that his successors would carry on. His assassination ended the first chapter of Israeli-Syrian negotiations; the plausibility level of a missed opportunity in this period will be analyzed below.

In Jerusalem, with many of the world's leaders to pay their last respects to Rabin by attending his funeral, Clinton and Ross informed Peres, now the designated prime minister, of Rabin's "deposit" delivered to Asad. Though surprised, Peres expressed willingness to honor Rabin's promise. He understood that the window of opportunity was small: in October 1996 there would be elections in Israel, and Clinton was facing an election year as well. In contrast to Rabin, Peres had a penchant for bold, ambitious moves. He was inclined to "think big," as reflected in his promotion of the Oslo track and his vision of the "New Middle East," which had opened new vistas for Israel in the economic sphere. In this case, he viewed an Israeli-Syrian peace treaty as a stepping stone toward a comprehensive settlement of the Arab-Israeli conflict. He also raised the possibility of Israeli-American and regional security pacts in this connection. This is the reason why Peres enthusiastically embraced Rabin's deposit, which added an aura of legitimacy to the negotiations on the Israeli-Syrian track. In his desire to stage a "high drama," Peres insisted on holding a summit with Asad as an essential component for a swift agreement. Perhaps he wanted to imitate the precedent of the Begin-Sadat meeting, which helped mitigate fears in Israeli society and paved the way for successful completion of that treaty (Ross 2005, 216–217; Rabinovich 1998, 196–206; Indyk 2009, 81; Cobban 1999, 105–114).

It quickly became clear that Asad would not agree to an early summit with Peres, which was tantamount, in his eyes, to a sign of normalization with Israel. He also objected to the idea of a tripartite meeting in Washington with Clinton. In short, Asad opposed the kind of "blitz" peace campaign Peres was suggesting (Shaaban 2013, 131–132). However, there were still indications that an Israeli-Syrian deal might open the way for a more comprehensive settlement. King Fahd of Saudi Arabia notified the United States that "If we miss the moment, it may not come again for a very long time." Fahd expressed readiness to "work" on Asad and offered to make peace with Israel once the Syrians did. The Saudi announcement was important since it signaled Arab support of Asad and provided an attractive incentive to Israel to advance along the Syrian track (Ross 2005, 217–218). Like Peres, Uri Savir, who had replaced Rabinovich as the chief negotiator with the Syrians, also endorsed this view. Indeed, conversations with Peres at the time reveal that he was determined to change the regional landscape with a dramatic move (ibid., 221–228; Savir 1998, 265–291). For his part, Asad also concurred with the assessments that there existed a moment that could be lost if not seized. He saw Peres as "a leader with vision, imagination and creativity" who could pursue peace. Ross thought that Asad wanted an agreement as a means to bolster his relationship with the United States, but an agreement "in content and process that sets him apart" (Ross 2005, 223). That Asad agreed to exert pressure on Hizballah to stop the violence in Southern Lebanon was seen, in American eyes, as a real turning point. Indeed, Asad considered this as a gesture of good-will toward Peres (Shaaban 2013, 133). With that, Peres was convinced that an Israeli-Syrian deal was in the realm of the possible, telling Clinton that he was ready "to fly high and fast, or low and slow, to an agreement," according to Asad's wish (Ross 2005, 234). Christopher also returned from Damascus with a new sense of optimism regarding the ability to reach an agreement within the suggested time frame. He felt that Peres "had a real partner" in Damascus (Rabinovich 1998, 217).

On the basis of these newly developed expectations, three rounds of Israeli-Syrian talks with US mediation began at Wye River on December 27, 1995, and lasted until mid-February 1996. The delegations coming to Wye, wrote Rabinovich, "were clearly seeking an agreement" (1998, 210). Savir too thought that "both sides meant business" (1998, 283). The talks focused, as before, on the Syrian desire to demarcate the border according to the 1967 line, while Israel insisted on defining the nature of the normalization, phases of withdrawal, and maintaining security and water interests. A new topic discussed in the talks was the possibility of building economic cooperation by devising trilateral projects in the Golan (Ross 2005, 238–240; Rabinovich 1998, 210–216; Savir 1998, 273–281; Kurtzer et al. 2013, 81–84). In the second round, opened on January 24, Asad dispatched two generals to take part in the military talks. All in all, the atmosphere at Wye was promising, leading Ross to tell Savir that "we might just make it" (2005, 242). Publicly, Ross was quoted to the effect that "More was accomplished during these six days [the first two rounds of Wye] than in the previous four years of negotiations" (quoted in Indyk 2009, 176).

Unbeknown to the Syrian delegation, the Wye talks were held under the shadow of a looming decision on Israeli elections. Peres was under pressure to decide whether to keep the original date of October 29, 1996, or to bring the elections forward to May 29 to take advantage of his substantial lead in the polls. Establishing whether or not a swift agreement with Syria was fea-sible was a crucial element in the decision. The fact that Asad was unwilling to hold a public summit and that Clinton was unwilling to launch a major plan bearing his name tended to support the argument for an earlier election date (Rabinovich 1998, 211). A few days after the beginning of the second round, Peres notified the United States that he had decided to move up the elections. He was willing to change his mind only if Asad was prepared to meet him and push for an agreement. Asad, however, thought that the talks had not reached a point where he could make a summit understandable to his own people (Ross 2005, 243). And thus once more domestic politics on both sides determined the outcome. Though the Wye talks continued, the new timetable, as well as Palestinian suicide bombings in Israel which the Syrians refused to denounce, undermined their success. The string of terrorist attacks in February–March 1996 perpetrated by Hamas led to the convening of an international conference in Sharm al-Shaykh on March 13, with the participation of Western and Arab leaders, to denounce terrorism and thereby to boost Peres's chances of reelection. The Syrians complained that the Arabs were asked to pay the price of Rabin's death "by being constantly asked to walk that extra mile and make the extra gesture to reach peace and 'uphold Rabin's legacy'" (Shaaban 2013, 139).

A last-ditch attempt to set up a Peres-Asad meeting was made by Daniel Abraham, a Jewish billionaire and self-appointed messenger, but it failed (Abraham 2006, 106–111). Several weeks later, the Israeli operation "Grapes of Wrath" against Hizballah (which unintentionally led to a massacre in the Lebanese village of Qana) caused a rupture in the Israeli-Syrian negotiations. Yet Asad's involvement in reaching the April understanding for the end of the violence enhanced his regional reputation and stature (Shaaban 2013, 137–155). The violence on the Palestinian and Lebanese fronts undermined Peres's electoral campaign and led eventually to his defeat. On May 29, 1996, Benjamin Netanyahu, the young leader of the Likud Party, won by the slimmest of margins. Peres's short premiership constituted the second opening for a Syrian-Israeli agreement, which might have been missed. The plausibility level of this possibility will be analyzed in the last section of this chapter.

Netanyahu's election constituted a setback to the peace process on the Palestinian and Syrian tracks. His public statements regarding refusal to withdraw from the Golan and his unwillingness to honor Rabin's deposit reflected the hardline position of his right-wing government. During his three-year premiership, there was one noteworthy attempt at reaching a deal with Asad: Ronald Lauder, a Jewish billionaire and a US ambassador in Vienna during the Reagan period, was sent, with a nod from Netanyahu, to Damascus on a secret mission in the summer of 1998, during which he had nine meetings with Asad. The details of these contacts were revealed only later, when Lauder admitted to Clinton that Netanyahu had negotiated a ten-point document, entitled "Treaty of Peace between Israel and Syria," which stipulated, inter alia, that "Israel will withdraw from the Syrian land taken in 1967 . . . to a commonly agreed border based on the line of June 4 1967" (Indyk 2009, 250; Ross 2005, 511–512, 528; Sagie 2011, 33, 43; Yatom 2009, 194–198, 210–212; Kurtzer et al. 2013, 84–85). Thus, in contrast to his rigid image and repeated denials, it seems that Netanyahu did accept Rabin's "deposit." However, when Netanyahu was asked by Asad to deliver a map showing the extent of withdrawal, he demurred (Shaaban 2013, 167–168). Netanyahu's hesitancy, as well as the opposition in his coalition, led by Minister of Agriculture Ariel Sharon and Minister of Defense Yitzhak Mordechai, stymied Lauder's mission. Understandably, Netanyahu later did not want to admit that he had accepted the deposit, particularly as the initiative was stillborn (Pressman 2007, 364; Ross 2005, 528).

In May 1999, Ehud Barak, the new leader of the Labor Party, defeated Netanyahu in the elections. This change, according to Ross, "gave me and everyone else a renewed sense of hope," as Barak was believed to be "everything Bibi was not" (2005, 495). He formed an uneasy coalition between the religious and secular parties. Upon assuming office in July, Barak publicly pledged to achieve comprehensive peace on all fronts within fifteen months and withdraw the IDF from Lebanon within a year. He recognized that a chance for peace existed as long as 'Arafat and Asad were alive and only until Iraq or Iran acquired weapons of mass destruction. In Barak's view, a deal with Syria was preferable, because Syria constituted a strategic threat to Israel and because Asad was everything 'Arafat was not: "one who kept his word and was respected and feared by others in the region" (Ross 2005, 500, 509). Realizing that the Israeli-Syrian track was riper, Barak and Asad were engaged in an exchange of mutual praise—orchestrated by the journalist Patrick Seale—with Asad describing Barak as a "strong and honest man," while the latter credited the former with creating a "strong, independent and self-confident" country. This kind of public flirtation—termed by Shaaban "newspaper diplomacy" (2013, 173)—added to the ambitious goals set by Barak, creating a new atmosphere in the peace process that led many to believe that a golden opportunity to solve the conflict was within reach (Rabil 2003, 216–217; Ross 2005, 496–497, 510; Pressman 2007, 365–366).

And yet it took six months of US-led secret contacts to resume the negotiations. Despite the auspicious start, Barak was unwilling to commit himself to Rabin's deposit, for several reasons: a desire to keep this important concession for a later stage in the negotiations, concern over domestic opposition, and certain disbelief that Rabin had indeed made such a concession. Eventually, ambiguity was used to bridge the gap, as Barak admitted, "We cannot erase the historical record." It was agreed, therefore, to "start talks where they had left off" (Ross 2005, 498–499; Indyk 2009, 259; Pressman 2007, 366; Swisher 2004, 67–69). When the American peace team met with Asad in December 1999, he expressed readiness to hold a political meeting "at a level below the highest level" and to act quickly (Indyk 2009, 244). He decided, for the first time, to send Foreign Minister Faruq al-Shara᷾ to negotiate directly with Israel. This decision was interpreted by US officials as readiness to conclude an agreement (Ross 2005, 536–538; Indyk 2009, 245; Pressman 2007, 367).

Asad's decision to move quickly stemmed from his deteriorating health. At sixty-nine and seriously ill, his two top imperatives had become making peace with Israel and the succession of his son, Bashar. He probably assumed that given his proven authority and perceived legitimacy in public, it would be easier for him to deliver a peace treaty than his newly appointed and inexperienced son (Indyk 2009, 242–243).[8] Well understanding the magnitude of the Syrian offer, Barak decided to lead the Israeli delegation to the talks at Blair House, the US president's official guesthouse, on December 15–16, 1999. In the run-up to the talks, he showed great enthusiasm. "From my military experience," he told Ross, "I know that when you have an initiative you must capitalize on it or lose the momentum and the opportunity." Barak proposed holding sustained talks until an agreement had been reached (Ross 2005, 538). At the same time, the Israeli professional delegation, headed by MI chief Sagie (himself an expert on the question of the Syrian border), began intensive preparations for the talks (Sagie 2011, 77–113). The ground, it seemed, was ready for a breakthrough.

Upon arrival in Washington, however, Barak got cold feet. He told Indyk that he would not be able to deal with the substantial issues and refused to meet Shara᷾ in private. His hesitancy stemmed from the growing criticism mustered by the Golan lobby in the Knesset, which attempted to pass a referendum law, and from polls indicating that the Israeli public preferred a tough negotiating process and objected to full Israeli withdrawal from the Golan in return for a peace treaty (Indyk 2009, 251–252; Ross 2005, 539; Drucker 2002, 71–73; Swisher 2004, 71–72). During the talks, four committees were set up—boundary, water, security, and normalization—though the first two issues were hardly discussed. For his part, Shara᷾ made it clear that no progress could be made without the Rabin deposit. Since the June 4, 1967, line did not exist on the map, he suggested that the two sides delineate it together. The one concession made by Barak was a vague willingness to deliver Rabin's deposit in the next round of talks. Despite the Syrians' disappointment, there was still a shared feeling that a breakthrough was imminent, so much so that Shara᷾ informed a group of Arab ambassadors in Washington following the Blair House talks that Syria was about to make peace with Israel (Indyk 2009, 253–257; Ross 2005, 538–543; Sagie 2011, 113–117; Rabil 2003, 218–219; Yatom 2009, 218–227; Clinton 2004, 884–885; Bregman 2013, 233–234; 2014, 207–208).

In spite of the failure of the first-ever high-level Israeli-Syrian talks, Barak pressed Clinton to resume talks with the Syrians "as quickly as possible in order not to lose the momentum" (quoted in Bregman 2014, 208). Clinton agreed, and it was decided that another round of talks would start on January 3, 2000. The fact that the talks were held during 'Id al-Fitr (the holy Islamic holiday ending Ramadan) attested to the urgency Asad attributed to them. The talks, which lasted for eight days, were held in Shepherdstown, a sleepy town on the Potomac River chosen because of Barak's insistence on avoiding leaks to the media. The differences between the adversaries, so it seemed, were not wide; Israel demanded a narrow strip off Lake Kinneret and the Jordan River, a presence in the Mount Hermon early warning station, the exchange of embassies in the first phase of implementation, and three years for implementing the withdrawal. The Syrians, meanwhile, expected Barak to deliver the Rabin deposit as promised; they were willing to accept an Israeli withdrawal to "a line based on the line of June 4 1967" and agreed that "sovereignty on the lake is Israel's; sovereignty on the land is ours." In addition, on the lake's northeast shoreline, Syria accepted that the 1923 international boundary would apply—that is, Syria would be at least ten meters away from the shoreline. As for the early warning station, Shara' accepted that it would be under the "total auspices and responsibility of the US and France for the first five years." Regarding withdrawal, they were willing to prolong the period to eighteen months. But Barak still refused to budge on any substantive issue. He wanted to show the Israeli public that he was securing Israel's needs before making any territorial concessions. After four days of talks with only limited progress, Clinton presented a seven-page draft treaty specifying points of agreements and disagreements between the parties. While progress was made on the security and normalization issues, the boundary remained the bone of contention. Barak insisted that Israel should gain sovereignty over a line stretching five hundred meters east of the water line. He said that he would be ready to reaffirm the Rabin deposit in the next round of talks if the Israeli demands in the realm of territory, normalization, and intelligence would be met and if Asad agreed to allow the Israeli-Lebanese negotiations to recommence at the same time. In any case, he clarified that his last concession would be made only at the end of the process, upon meeting Asad. In addition, Barak expected that the United States would compensate Israel militarily for the security risks inherent in withdrawing from the Golan and would persuade other Arab and Muslim states to join the peace process. The Syrians viewed Barak's attempt to control the northern strip of the lake as both a lack of seriousness and a form of Israeli avarice (Ross 2005, 549–565; Indyk 2009, 257–268; Pressman 2007, 367–370; Rabil 2003, 219–221; Sagie 2011, 121–127; Yatom 2009, 228–255; Clinton 2004, 885–887; Swisher 2004, 77–89; Kurtzer et al. 2013, 89–92; Shaaban 2013, 171–186; Bregman 2013, 234–236).

The final dinner at Shepherdstown was an embarrassing event; according to Indyk's description:

Barak repeated his now worn-out words about his admiration for Syria and its great leader . . . Sharaa responded eloquently, warning of the historic opportunity for peace they were all missing. He explained to Barak that the Israeli prime minister had made a liar out of him with his president because, after the meeting at the Blair House, Sharaa had convinced Asad that Barak was serious about making peace based on full withdrawal. Now, Sharaa argued, he had done his best to meet Israel's concerns but had heard nothing in response from Barak. He concluded by saying he didn't know whether it would be possible to continue the negotiations. (2009, 263)

Sharaʿ's disappointment in Barak was understandable, as he went home empty-handed. From a Syrian perspective, "Israel was unwilling to give up anything at Shepherdstown" (Shaaban 2013, 184). The US leaders, too, were highly critical of Barak; neither Clinton nor Madeleine Albright, the US sec- retary of state, minced words as they lay the blame for the failure squarely on his shoulders. Perhaps surprisingly, the top Israeli officials there also found Barak's hesitancy—driven by his concern of Israeli public opinion— unwarranted. Many participants and observers of the Shepherdstown talks were of the opinion that the Syrians showed flexibility while Israel displayed intransigence (Indyk 2009, 263–264; Albright 2003, 476; Ross 2005, 565; Drucker 2002, 87–88; Yatom 2009, 251; Clinton 2004, 886–887; Kurtzer et al. 2013, 92). The parties left Shepherdstown without any closing ceremony or press conference, planning to reconvene a week later. Meanwhile, however, the text of the draft treaty was leaked and appeared on January 9 in *al-Hayat*. This upset the Israelis, who claimed that the published text was inaccurate and biased; four days later, a fuller version was published in *Haaretz*. The publication was disastrous from a Syrian perspective because the text showed that Israel had wrung concessions from the Syrians without getting Israel to declare its commitment to a withdrawal from the Golan to the June 4 lines. Because of these revelations, wrote Rabil, "The Syrians apparently felt humili- ated" (2003, 221). Clinton thought that "the Israeli rebuff in Shepherdstown and the leak of the working document in the Israeli press had embarrassed Assad and destroyed his fragile trust" (2004, 903). Asad was furious and called off the next round; in Indyk's opinion, the publication of the draft treaty "had the effect of sabotaging the Israeli-Syrian negotiations at a critical moment" (2009, 268).

Barak's insistence on distancing the Syrians beyond the ten-meter line of the lake was to prevent Syrian access to the water. In reality, however, since 1967 the shoreline had receded as much as 470 meters at the northern tip. Even if Asad would have settled for nothing less than all the territory around the lake up to the ten-meter mark, "there would still be enough dry land around the lake for Barak" (Indyk 2009, 273). Ross added that a line drawn exactly where the shore existed on June 4, 1967, would be several hundred meters off the current waterline in the northern corner of the lake (2005, 574). Thus not only was the territorial gap between the parties small, but it was meaningless from the political, military, and economic points of view. Therefore, it would seem that Barak's intransigent position was a response to a psychological Israeli need rather than security or economic interests.

The denouement of this episode came when Clinton was persuaded by Barak to meet Asad. In the short period between Shepherdstown and Geneva, Barak changed his mind again, believing that it was in fact possible to reach an agreement quickly with the Syrians and take it to a referendum within forty-five days. In contrast to his thinking only two weeks earlier, wrote Indyk, Barak "now believed that such a deal would produce a landslide victory in the referendum and thereby act as an accelerator for the Palestinian negotiations" (2009, 271). The time pressure stemmed from reports received from top Egyptian and Saudi officials that Asad's health had deteriorated but that he was still determined to strike a deal (ibid.; Ross 2005, 568–569). At the same time, the Israeli and American peace teams drew the line of the suggested Israeli withdrawal five hundred meters from the shoreline. In return, Barak was willing to concede the al-Hama area in the southern part of the lake. In addition, details of the early warning and security arrangements were laid, as well as time frames and withdrawal phases (Indyk 2009, 274; Bregman 2013, 236–238). Deflecting opposition in the cabinet and from the public, Barak decided that he must exhaust every option to clinch a deal with Syria: "Maybe it won't be possible," he told Ross, "but at least I will know and our people will know there was no other way" (2005, 572). Barak's bottom line, as revealed to Clinton just before his meeting with Asad, was this: the border had to be at least four hundred meters from the shoreline, there must be a token Israeli presence in the Hermon early warning station, and Israel would have at least twenty months to withdraw from the Golan (ibid., 582–583; Bregman 2013, 238). If he was entertaining any other concessions then he was saving them for the endgame, upon meeting Asad. The problem was that the deal Barak now pitched to Clinton was not the one Asad expected.

Striving to persuade Asad that Barak was now sincere, Clinton turned to Bandar bin-Sultan, the Saudi ambassador in Washington who had previously been involved in related secret missions. Clinton now asked Bandar to notify Asad that the deposit was in his pocket (Swisher 2004, 95; Kurtzer et al. 2013, 96–97).[9] On January 18, 2000, Clinton spoke with his Syrian counterpart on the phone and assured him that Barak—recognizing the mistakes made at Shepherdstown—was ready to reconfirm the Rabin deposit. Clinton ended the conversation by expressing the hope that "this opportunity will not get wasted, Mr. President, because we are very close to reaching a deal. We have a government in Israel that is ready for an agreement and ready to mark the borders. We need to grab at this opportunity" (quoted in Shaaban 2013, 222; Shara' 2015).

Asad then agreed to meet Clinton in Geneva on March 26, 2000; in fact, he went to Geneva for Clinton's sake, according to the Syrian version (Shaaban 2013, 190). But the short meeting ended in a fiasco. When Clinton stated that the Israelis "are prepared to withdraw fully to a commonly agreed border," Asad retorted, "They [Israel] don't want peace" (Swisher 2004, 100–101; Ross 2005, 584; Shara' 2015). When told later about Asad's reaction, Barak, who was anxiously waiting to hear positive results that would enable him to join Clinton and Asad in Geneva for a summit, responded similarly: "Asad doesn't want peace" (Indyk 2009, 277). In Geneva, Clinton told Asad that given the narrow differences between the parties, "historians would have a hard time explaining why there was no peace deal with Syria" (ibid.). But to no avail. Sick, tired, but mainly humiliated, Asad felt deceived by both Clinton and Barak.[10]

Following the meeting, two narratives emerged: one argued that Asad, preoccupied with the questions of succession and his mortality, thought that now was not the time to do a deal (Ross 2005, 588; Indyk 2009, 278; Ben-Ami 2005b, 245; Rabinovich 2004, 139–140); the other held that Asad was ready to sign a deal, but he retracted when he realized that Clinton was not delivering the deal he expected from Barak (Daoudy 2008, 228; Ross 2004, 588; Pressman 2007, 375; Sagie 2011, 167–169; Drucker 2002, 109–110; Swisher 2004, 110–130; Shaaban 2013, 187–195). On balance, it seems that coming to Geneva despite his personal and state problems attests to the fact that Asad had hoped to close the deal based on the assurances he believed he had received from Clinton, Bandar, and others. Says Indyk: "When Asad was ready, Barak was not; and when Barak was ready, it was too late for Asad" (2009, 278). Other accounts, though, indicate that even when Barak was ready, the problem was that he felt unable to pay the price he knew he had to pay (Ross 2005, 583–587; Indyk 2009, 275–258; Yatom 2009, 256–273; Pressman 2007, 372–375; Rabil 2003, 224–225; Albright 2003, 480–481; Sagie 2011, 167–169).

Ten weeks after Geneva, on June 10, 2000, Asad died. Though the transfer of power to his son Bashar went smoothly, the fact that he was a young and inexperienced leader lacking the power, authority, and legitimacy his father had enjoyed made an Israeli-Syrian peace deal a more remote possibility, just as his father had predicted.

ASSESSMENT

The fact that the ostensible bridge separating Syria and Israel was apparently not wide led to a repeated use of the term "missed opportunity" with regard to this episode (Rabil 2003, 241–266). The Israeli-Syrian negotiations, wrote Jerome Slater, "came much closer to producing a comprehensive peace treaty than did the Israeli-Palestinian process. Their eventual failure is the latest in a long series of lost opportunities for peace" (2002, 79–80). Many participants and observers of this track have supported the argument that Israel missed an opportunity to sign an agreement with Asad, particularly during Barak's tenure (see, in particular, Bregman 2014, 215).

Uri Sagie, head of the Israeli delegation under Barak, was unequivocal in his assessment that Israel had missed a historical opportunity to reach an agreement. The Hebrew title of his book, *The Frozen Hand*, refers to the Israeli hand that was unwilling or incapable of signing the required document (2011, 12, 162–163, 169). Shlomo Ben-Ami, the foreign minister, felt that the opportunity was greatest at Shepherdstown, where Asad was willing to strike a deal but Barak's "unexplainable tactics" regarding the border issue alienated the Syrian leader and thwarted the goal (2004, 477–478). Danny Yatom, Barak's military secretary, displayed a more cautious approach, though he, too, thought that Barak should have demonstrated more flexibility regarding the territorial question since it might have led Asad to sign an agreement that would transform the entire Middle East (2009, 271). Raviv Drucker, in his biography of Barak, speculated, "It is possible that the cold feet that Barak got at Shepherdstown caused him to miss the chance to change the face of the Middle East for future generations" (2002, 109). Uri Savir, head of the Israeli delegation under Peres, took it back further, arguing that Peres's hesitations and eventual decision to move up the elections also contributed to the missed opportunity to sign a treaty with Syria (Caspit 1997).[11] Rabinovich, however, stressed that at no time between August 1992 and March 1996 were Israel and Syria on the verge of a breakthrough. The potential of reaching that point, in his view, existed only twice—in August 1993 (the "pocket" exchange) and during the first few weeks of Peres's tenure in November–December 1995 (1998, 235, 241–242).

The American position usually laid the blame for missing the opportunity squarely on Asad. Thus Christopher opined that Asad had missed a historic opportunity to achieve the return of the Golan during Rabin's term (2001, 224). Ross described Asad as "ever the one to miss opportunities" (2004, 501), but he also wrote that if not for Barak's cold feet, "there might have been a deal in January of 2000" (2004, 589; Clinton 2004, 904).[12] Indyk concurred: "Much of the blame [for missing the opportunity] has to be attributed to the lack of

266 CHANCES FOR PEACE

leadership on the part of Hafez al-Asad . . . he continually demonstrated a cautious, grudging approach to peacemaking" (2009, 278). In contrast, in Jeremy Pressman's opinion it was the United States that "missed some opportunities that are part of the role of any mediator" (2007, 352). A more scathing criticism of the US role is offered by Kurtzer et al.:

> Israeli-Syrian peace could have been achieved in the 1990s, not easily, not on the cheap, but with a sophisticated and sustained dose of US-led diplomacy . . . Historians of the future will look back and wonder why a difference of a few hundred meters along the shore of the Sea of Galilee was allowed to block the way to a peace agreement . . . Syrian-Israeli peace was within reach in 1999–2000. We had a chance to help them transcend their parochial concerns, but we failed. (2013, 103–104)

The Syrian narrative laid the blame on Israel. Marwa Daoudy asserted that the negotiations until 1995 were "a story of a missed opportunity" caused by Israeli refusal to withdraw fully from the Golan and relinquish control of the waters (2008, 216). Seale too suggested that it was Israel rather than Syria that missed the boat of peace: "Peace was within Israel's grasp, yet it wanted more than that: It wanted hegemony" (1996, 37). In 1999 Seale lay the blame squarely on Peres (quoted in Rabil 2003, 249). Walid al-Moualem, the head of the Syrian delegation to the talks, hinted that Peres was the one who missed this opportunity (1997, 87; Rabil 2003, 246). And, finally, Shaaban, who accompanied Asad during the whole decade of Israeli-Syrian negotiations, emphasizes the Syrian leader's sincere willingness to sign a peace agreement in contrast to continued Israeli intransigent behavior.

The Israeli-Syrian negotiations extended over a decade from the Madrid Conference in 1991 and until Asad's death in 2000. During this period, there were at least three significant occasions on which a peace treaty could have been clinched: the first was during Rabin's tenure, the second was during Peres's short premiership, and the third was under Barak. Though the Syrian side enjoyed stability in terms of leadership and its set of priorities remained largely unchanged, Israel experienced significant changes in terms of leadership and domestic political setting. As a result, the analysis of the Israeli-Syrian negotiations as a plausible missed opportunity must not relate to the period as a whole but to each episode, though certain features will surely remain constant in all three episodes.

The common denominator of all these episodes is that each constituted a historical opportunity. Following the disintegration of the Soviet Union and Saddam Hussein's 1991 defeat, it became a common truism, as succinctly summarized by Indyk, that the parties to the conflict "were witnessing a rare moment in Middle Eastern history when a window of opportunity opens wide." Indyk told Clinton that if he "put his mind to it, he could achieve four Arab-Israeli peace agreements in his first term as president" (2009, 16). The fact that the Labor Party, led by both Rabin and Peres, replaced the intransigent Shamir government strengthened the impression that a ripe moment was there, waiting to be seized. When Christopher unwittingly delivered the Rabin deposit to Asad, he tabled an attractive offer to Syria that could serve as an incentive for serious negotiations. The Rabin assassination created another turning point. With opposition rising against the right-wing extremism that led to his slaying, the post-traumatic Israeli society was perhaps more primed to discuss serious peace overtures. Indeed, the energetic Peres presented Asad with innovative ideas that could have been perceived as attractive enough to reach an agreement. And, finally, following the political stagnation characterizing the Netanyahu period, the election of Barak with his grandiose ideas about a comprehensive agreement on all fronts, beginning with Syria, created a new fork in Israeli-Syrian relations. The fact that Asad's clock was ticking served as an incentive on both sides to accelerate the pace of the negotiations. Barak and his advisers, as well as leading US officials, imparted a sense of urgency that a historical moment was there and must be quickly and cleverly seized (e.g., Ross 2004, 538; Yatom 2009, 218–220). The sense of an existing historical opportunity could be detected in Clinton's rhetoric in real time.[13] Even voices outside the official establishment, such as Henry Kissinger's, called for a leading US mediation role because Barak's election posed "an unprecedented opportunity for breakthrough toward Middle East peace" (Kissinger 1999).

In terms of legitimacy—the first variable of our definition—it is important to assess whether Rabin, Peres, and Barak on the Israeli side and Asad in Syria enjoyed sufficient legitimacy to allow them to pursue a peaceful course. Rabin had the benefit of a comfortable majority in the Knesset, and his military background and uncorrupted personality gained him a respectable image in Israeli society. Yet in terms of public support the Syrian track stood between the Jordanian track—which enjoyed wide support—and the Palestinian track—which was controversial. While ideology played a minor role, many Israelis developed an emotional attachment to the Golan after its occupation in 1967, and it soon became part of the Israeli ethos (Sagie 2011, 93–112, 137–142). What made the Golan issue domestically explosive and psychologically wrenching, wrote Rabil, was not the number of settlers (estimated at twenty thousand [Kipnis 2009, 263; http://www.golan.org.il]), but rather their ability "to strike a chord with the population at large on account of water and security issues" (2003, 164). Capitalizing on these emotions, the settlers succeeded in forming a lobby in the Knesset that traversed the political

268 CHANCES FOR PEACE

spectrum and consistently attempted to block any peace initiatives. Feeling this public sensitivity, Rabin promised to hold a referendum should an agreement be reached—a promise upheld by all his successors. Thus it became clear that peace with Syria would require any government to invest great efforts in persuading the public of the advantages of leaving the Golan. Upon Rabin's murder, Peres initially rode a wave of public support. Hoping to take advantage of his substantial lead in the polls, he opted to move up the elections, but a series of terrorist operations by Hamas and the decision to launch Operation Grapes of Wrath against Hizballah severely eroded his legitimacy, allowing Netanyahu to slide in, albeit by a slim majority.

The stalemate that characterized the Netanyahu period caused Barak to win an impressive majority, allowing him to form a wide coalition. It was an indication that the people were hungry for progress on the peace front after all. It was estimated that he enjoyed "real credibility in Israel and internationally" (Ross 2005, 502). However, his government was composed of too many antagonistic parties with ideological and political objections to any territorial concessions in the Golan and the West Bank. At Shepherdstown, it is argued, Barak hesitated because domestic politics and polls indicated a lack of support for a treaty involving full withdrawal from the Golan (Pressman 2007, 369–370; Ben-Ami 2005b, 244; Rabinovich 1998, 72–73). When he returned to Israel, he faced a demonstration of one hundred thousand right-wing Israelis vociferously opposing any compromise on the Golan (Swisher 2004, 88). Though domestic considerations played a vital role in Barak's thinking, one should take into account the fact that three months later, in Geneva, he asked Clinton to convey to Asad his readiness to immediately sign an agreement in spite of the domestic opposition at home. Moreover, Barak was convinced that the possible fruits of peace with Syria on the Lebanese and Palestinian tracks, as well as compensation promised by the United States, would persuade the Israeli public of the merits of a Syrian-Israeli treaty (Yatom 2009, 216). Indeed, while questioning the validity of polls with regard to foreign affairs, Clinton asserted, "If Barak made real peace with Syria, it would lift his standing in Israel and across the world, and increase the chances of success with the Palestinians." He also promised Barak to travel to Israel to help him sell the agreement (Clinton 2004, 886; Indyk 2009, 262; Cobban 1999, 3; Kurtzer et al. 2013, 93). Finally, Barak could have said that Rabin, Peres, and, most importantly, Netanyahu had committed to withdrawal to the 1967 border. Barak was in a position to say: "How could I offer less to Asad if even the Likud prime minister had committed to this?" (Ross 2005, 577). All this suggests that the domestic factor, in my estimate, should not have deterred Barak from crossing the Rubicon.

On the Syrian side, Asad had to deal with four Israeli prime ministers with varying degrees of legitimacy. He himself was considered to be the "one un-questioned leader of a personalized one-party regime" (Rabinovich 1998, 43; Ross 2004, 161). At the same time, Asad was "always looking over his shoulder," fearing domestic or external forces conspiring behind his back. This was the lesson he had drawn from the way he himself seized power in 1970 (Ross 2004, 141, 222; Savir 1998, 272). Indeed, domestic considerations be-came an obstacle to peacemaking in Syria as well. The opposition came from Hafiz's brother, Rif'at, who returned to Syria in 1992 after a period in exile;[14] the Islamist forces—particularly the Muslim Brotherhood—and other ele-ments that contested Asad's succession by his son, Bashar, after the death of the heir-apparent, Basil. As Asad grew sick and frail, the question of succes-sion took most of his attention, making his involvement in the peace process precarious. By committing Syria to peace, Asad ran the risk of alienating some of the regime's veterans. Being an 'Alawite, he and fellow officers feared that peace with Israel would alienate the Sunnis.[15] In short, peace with Israel might have threatened some of Asad's sources of legitimacy (Rabil 2003, 132–143; Indyk 2009, 280). All in all, the Syrian view was that only Asad, at the peak of his prestige, power, and control, could make peace with Israel (Azm 2000, 7). His biographer, Seale, concluded in 1996 that "Asad's position appears as strong as ever. Heading an authoritarian regime now well into its third de-cade, he may not be greatly loved, but he is respected and trusted, largely it would seem for his proven ability to steer his country through the dangerous shoals and rapids of the region's politics" (1996, 40). Likewise, Shaaban, who had been close to Asad, wrote that by the end of the 1990s, "The man could do just about anything he pleased—domestically—with no questions asked by the Syrian people. Nobody would doubt his wisdom and nationalist creden-tials . . . the majority of ordinary Syrians believed that Assad knew what was in their best interest and trusted him wholeheartedly when it came to foreign affairs" (2013, 188).

In terms of the willingness of the leaders to take a bold step and change the course of events—the second variable in our definition—such determi-nation was evidenced, for the most part, on both sides. The statements of Rabin, Peres, and Barak early in their terms indicated willingness and desire to make tough decisions. History attests that all of them made bold decisions and therefore were seen to be capable of concluding peace agreements. Yet Rabin procrastinated because he felt he could not move simultaneously on two tracks and because his "deposit" proposal had received, in his view, an unsatisfactory response from Asad. Peres appeared more eager than Rabin to conclude a treaty with Syria, though his condition of a summit with Asad was rebuffed. As for Barak, Sagie, his chief negotiator, asserted that he did want a settlement with Syria (2011, 18), but his adamant opposition to complete withdrawal infuriated Asad. Thus in spite of their ability and willingness, the three Israeli leaders, for one reason or another, did not ultimately take the truly tough but bold decision required to close a deal.

The question of whether Asad was as committed to a peaceful solution and willing to make a bold decision produced two answers. According to the first view, he was more interested in the peace process, which would bring diplomatic dividends with the United States and the West in general, than in actually signing a peace agreement, which would expose him to domestic criticism (Indyk 2009, 281; Rabinovich 1998, 108, 149, 240; Miller 2008, 256–257; Zisser 2001, 113).[16] The other view was that Asad had made a strategic choice for peace. This argument recurs through Shaaban's diary of the Israeli-Syrian negotiations (2013). It was also the view of several Israeli officials who dealt with Asad. Thus, for example, Uri Savir, the chief negotiator under Peres, argued that in deciding to move toward peace, Asad "had made what was a revolutionary decision from his standpoint, yet he remained conservative in his tactic" (1998, 272). His counterpart under Barak, Sagie, was also an ardent advocate of this school of thought (2011, 21–22). The problem, however, was that Asad's bold change of strategy was not matched by bold policy moves. Many of the diplomats involved agreed that Assad was "narrow, excessively tactical, and appears capable of only small, incremental moves. He is extremely cautious. He never initiates, he only responds." His introverted character too suggested that he would not repeat Sadat's virtuoso public diplomacy (Ross 2005, 141–142, 222; Indyk 2009, 97, 279–281; Savir 1998, 272; Rabinovich 1998, 74–75; Zisser 2001, 119). But from a Syrian perspective, Asad was the right man for the job:

> The image of Asad as a self-defeatingly cautious, reluctant, suspicious, procrastinating, formalistic leader, ruler, politician, and player can be quite misleading. In Damascus, there is no question that these qualities are all highly prized when brought to bear on Syria's dealings with Israel and the US. But people in Damascus also know that at critical moments, Asad has shown himself politically of bold decisions, daring initiatives, and decisive actions that have ultimately proved successful and far-sighted, even if unpopular at the time of their initiation. (Azm 2000, 17–18)

On balance, it seems to me that Asad was indeed determined to sign an agreement with Israel. His personality and characteristics dictated a kind of behavior occasionally seen not to support this thesis, but his actions—and particularly the talks at Shepherdstown and his venturing to Geneva a mere three months before his death—attest to his sincerity (Swisher 2004, 110–130).

The third variable relates to the history of past interactions between the parties to the conflict, which influences the level of trust existing between them. In contrast to the Jordanian case, Israeli and Syrian leaders had little negotiating experience, particularly during the indirect talks leading to the signing of the 1974 Disengagement Agreement (see chapter 11). The talks in the 1990s, then, marked the first time when a direct channel of communication was established that could facilitate a process of de-demonization between the leaders and their publics (Rabinovich 1998, 42, 63). Rabin, Peres, Barak, and Asad developed a mixed feeling of trust, suspicion, and respect. The fact that Asad had strictly upheld the 1974 agreement and stabilized the regime was translated in Israel as an indication of his trustworthiness and ability to enforce his policy (ibid., 43, 164, 238–239). From a Syrian perspective it seems that a certain trust existed between Rabin and Asad (Shaaban 2013, 96). The exchange of praise between Peres, Barak, and Asad was an indication of the positive perception each held of the other. At the same time, however, they all misinterpreted the intentions of the other side. Also, the centrality of the role of dignity and honor eluded the participants (Rabinovich 1998, 74–75, 237; Albright 2003, 481–482; Ross 2005, 142; Sagie 2001, 85).[17] On the public level, there were indications of some willingness to accept peace: on the Israeli side, polls indicated that half the population still opposed full withdrawal from the Golan (Drucker 2002, 75–86); on the Syrian side there were no polls, but Azm asserted that the answer to the question whether Syria—and not only the regime and government—was ready for peace is "a cautious and qualified yes." In his opinion, the mood in Syria concerning peace during the period from the Madrid Conference and Netanyahu's election was "of stoic resignation before a necessary evil." Azm admitted that voices of rejection and fears of Israeli hegemonial aspirations still exist in Syria, though in his opinion "they are in a minority now," as the entire debate was conducted on the assumption that a peace treaty with Israel had become inevitable (2000, 1–2, 6, 10). Moreover, the Syrian media made an attempt to transmit the message that peace with Israel was a strategic choice (Rabinovich 1998, 148; Azm 2000, 11; Seale 1996, 36–37; Moualem 1997, 87; Zisser 2001, 108). Thus in contrast to the view that the few meters of land separating Israel and Syria were only "a symptom of both countries' state of quasi-unreadiness for peace" (Rabil 2003, 266), this study estimates that Israeli and Syrian societies were ready for a peaceful solution. In any case, every Israeli prime minister was committed to holding a referendum before approving an agreement.

The fourth variable relates to the extent of the involvement of the third party in the negotiations. In contrast to the Palestinian and Jordanian track, where the United States initially played a minor role, it was active in the Israeli-Syrian talks from the outset. Asad and Clinton met three times in the 1990s. Clinton was perhaps the most trusted US president (Shaaban 2013,

96, 178). This was in spite of the fact that Syria was still included in the US list of states sponsoring terrorism and that the US did not always play the role of honest broker in the Israeli-Syrian conflict (Daoudy 2008, 229; Seale 2000, 75; Pressman 2007, 353–354; Aruri 2003).[18] Indyk admitted that Rabin "had shown how effectively the Israeli tail can wag the American dog," explaining that the United States had "an inherent tendency to defer to Israel because its smaller ally is the one that has to make the tangible concessions of territory" (2009, 89, 91). In any case, senior Israeli and American diplomats—Rabinovich, Sagie, Ross, Indyk, Miller, and Albright among them—were all critical of the way Clinton handled the negotiations, particularly at Shepherdstown (Rabinovich 1998, 237; Sagie 2011, 161). In hindsight, wrote Ross, "We shouldn't have allowed Shara to go home empty-handed. Clinton should have pressed Barak to be more forthcoming at that moment, not later" (2004, 501). Likewise, Indyk concluded, "Given the narrow gaps separating the substantive positions . . . one can look at that moment in mid-January 2000 and see that it was the right time for Clinton to have summoned Barak and Asad to a summit to conclude the agreement" (2009, 264). In his opinion, Clinton should have offered Israel some major incentives or simply walked away from the negotiations and left the parties to their own fate. Whether in Shepherdstown or Geneva, Indyk concluded, "It should not have been beyond the capabilities of American diplomacy to bridge the gap" (ibid., 287). Miller admitted that "the fact is that we didn't know how to close the deal" (2008, 257). Even Secretary Albright indirectly attacked Clinton, arguing that both Barak and Shara' believed that Clinton would intervene to force concessions on the other (2003, 479). A recent study by Kurtzer et al. emphatically argues that Clinton should have intervened more forcefully at least twice: first, with the breakthrough of the Rabin deposit; second, telling Barak that the US would not waste time on trying to clinch the deal unless he was prepared to accept the Syrian demand for withdrawal to the June 4, 1967, line (2013, 75–76, 95). On balance, the United States did play a significant role in the negotiations, yet it was not an even-handed one and it certainly did not use every tool at its disposal, including the flexing of its muscles in order to elicit concessions from the parties. In other words, the US failed as a formulator, mediator, and manipulator (Pressman 2007, 351–354; Rabinovich 1998, 253; Rabil 2003, 243–244, 257–258). Yet this position probably emanated from the conviction that the US would never be able to impose an agreement on the warring parties (Rabil 2003, 254).

An analysis of the four variables of a missed opportunity shows that though the leaders on both sides of the conflict were concerned with the domestic political scene, they enjoyed sufficient legitimacy to allow them room to maneuver. In addition, they seemed to be ready to take bold decisions even if their tactics differed. The measure of acquaintance and trust was not high, yet there was a modicum of respect toward the ability of the other to take decisions, and to implement and honor them. Finally, the United States was intensely involved in the process, though it made—according to the assessment of most participants—some mistakes along the way that caused their failure. All in all, the plausibility level of the missed opportunity in this episode is high.

This episode is divided into three sub-episodes, in which the actors played different roles. During the first, Rabin was in no hurry to conclude an agreement with Syria because the Oslo Agreements, peace with Jordan, and some normalization with the Arab world were not a bad record for one term (Rabinovich 1998, 239). Moreover, his enthusiasm for the agreement diminished because of Asad's disappointing response to his offer. This may suggest that the chances of this opportunity were the lowest among the three episodes analyzed in this chapter. In any case, the fault for missing this opportunity falls on Asad, as his unsatisfactory response led Rabin to prefer the Palestinian track over the Syrian. It is clear that Asad understood the magnitude of the Israeli offer, yet his response did not deviate from the traditional Syrian approach and he did not walk the "extra mile" needed to seize the Israeli initiative. Clinton and Christopher contributed to this miss by not building the necessary momentum to pursue the potential breakthrough (Kurtzer et al. 2013, 75–76). In addition, Rabin's assassination prevented the scheduled meeting between the Syrian foreign minister and Rabin's personal envoy, Moshe Shachal, which might have developed into a serious negotiation track.

A better chance occurred during Peres's premiership. After Rabin's assassination, Ross assessed, "There was a moment. Asad was not up to moving quickly, but the original talks at the Wye River plantation showed great promise. If not for the four Hamas bombings in Israel in nine days in 1996, there might well have been an agreement in that election year" (2004, 589; Clinton 2004, 904). Asad made a mistake by being unwilling to meet Peres, though his decision was consistent with his behavior throughout the years of negotiations. Peres missed the opportunity when he decided to move up the elections. "I am convinced," wrote Ross, "that had Peres been elected in 1996, we would have been able to conclude a Syrian deal within a year's time" (2005, 244). The net result was that in this case both Peres and Asad are to blame for missing this opportunity.

The greatest missed opportunity in the Israeli-Syrian talks occurred twice during Barak's term: in the Shepherdstown talks and when Asad met with Clinton in Geneva. In both cases Barak's insistence on holding to a position that had been consistently rejected by the Syrians was detrimental. For some reason he believed that he could successfully tread the threshold, and that it would be Asad who would cave in at the last moment. Barak's inflexibility is particularly inexplicable in light of the fact that a return to the June 4, 1967, lines was Asad's consistent position since the negotiations on the Disengagement Agreement in 1974. Indyk wrote that the lesson of this episode for the United States was that "When the moment arises that an Arab leader indicates a willingness to make peace, and reveals a sense of urgency, it is essential to capitalize on it immediately and pursue the opportunity relentlessly until the breakthrough is achieved and the deal is closed" (2009, 286). The question of timing was also underscored by Ross, who wrote, "The history of peacemaking, especially between Israel and Syria, suggests that opportunities are fleeting and fragile. They are easily lost" (2005, 589). Barak, it seems, was aware of the historical opportunity hovering before him but failed to understand Asad's motivation, thinking, and limitations (Siegman 2000, 2–9). Had he done so, he might have gone the extra mile—or rather the few hundred meters—required to conclude the agreement.

Miller, who had always been skeptical of the chances of an Israeli-Syrian deal, concluded, "Never has so much time and energy been expended on a process that produced so little in the end" (2008, 254). Yet the failure of the Israeli-Syrian negotiations is a result of mistakes made by leaders who failed to seize the opportunity even though they knew of its existence. It can be hoped that by learning the lessons of this episode, as Sagie wrote, "Perhaps we will know next time to take the road that will ensure a different outcome" (2011, 19). On this issue there is agreement on both sides of the conflict; Bouthaina Shaaban concludes her book with a personal hope "that the frustrating experience of those years will be a lesson for forthcoming generations to learn from, so they do not repeat our mistakes" (2013, 199).

NOTES

1. Bouthaina Shaaban indicates that the difference between the two lines is about sixty-six square kilometers or twenty-five square miles (2013, 127, 163). The 1923 line delineated the Syrian boundary ten meters from the lake, while the 1967 boundary reached the water's edge. But one has to take into account that the lake has shrunk since 1967 and the shoreline has shifted westward, away from Syria (Pressman 2007, 357).

2. The peace team included Martin Indyk, Aaron Miller, Gamal Helal, Mark Parris, Jonathan Schwartz, Bruce Riedel, David Satterfield, Robert Malley, and Toni Verstandig (Ross 2005, 105–107).

3. Based on a summary of Shara''s memoirs, *al-Riwaya al-Mafquda* [the Missing Narrative], *al-'Arabi*, January 30–February 1, 2015. According to Shara', Asad was confident that Rabin's deposit (*wadi'a*) meant Israel's full withdrawal from the Golan to the June 4, 1967, boundary.

4. From a Syrian point of view, there is a significant difference between the establish-

ment of "regular relations" (*'alaqat 'adiyya*) and "normalization" (*tatbiʿ*), which signifies a stronger bond, as stipulated in the Israeli-Egyptian peace treaty.

5. Christopher even went so far as to say, "Of all the missed opportunities, none was more frustrating than that presented in the Clinton visit to Damascus" (2001, 223). See, in contrast, the Syrian narrative, Cobban 1999, 65, and Shaaban 2013, 107–113, where only a positive description of the meeting is given.

6. Part of the opposition's campaign against the Syrian talks was the leak of official documents to the press and Netanyahu's reference to that in a speech in the Knesset (Rabinovich 1998, 182–183; Cobban 1999, 94).

7. Interview with Moshe Shachal, December 31, 2012. Shachal updated Peres regarding the scheduled meeting in Geneva, but Peres canceled it.

8. Both Shaaban and Sharaʿ did not think that Asad's health played a role in his decision making (2013, 188–189; Sharaʿ 2015).

9. Sharaʿ (2015) blames Bandar for misleading both the Americans and the Israelis as to the Syrian position.

10. According to Albright, Sharaʿ said: "The problem is not a matter of kilometers. It is one of dignity and honor" (2003, 481).

11. Interestingly, in his book (1998) Savir does not lay the blame on anyone for missing the opportunity.

12. Elsewhere Ross treated the Shepherdstown talks as a missed opportunity without appointing blame for the failure. See Swisher 2004, 112.

13. Shaaban presents several original documents by Clinton, written in different periods (1993, 1999, 2000), which attest to his realization that a historic opportunity to achieve peace between Israel and Syria did indeed exist (2013, 209, 218, 222).

14. The struggle between Hafiz and Rifʿat came to a head in 1998–1999, when the latter was stripped of his title as vice president and a major hub of his supporters was raided (Rabil 2003, 142).

15. It is told that when Asad entertained the thought of concluding peace with Israel through Clinton, a prominent Syrian officer came to him and said: "What are you doing? We will be lost if you make peace. We will be accused of treason" (Totten 2011, 289).

16. At the same time, Rabinovich wrote elsewhere that "Asad was apparently serious in his decision to make peace with Israel. But he was determined to obtain from Israel a commitment to full withdrawal from the Golan as a precondition for any discussion regarding the nature of peace" (1998, 56).

17. Shaaban wrote in this regard of Asad, who said before the Madrid Conference: "If I were an ordinary citizen, I would say that Syria without the Golan—but with dignity—is better than Syria with the Golan, deprived of its dignity" (2013, 30).

18. For a different Syrian view, see Moualem 1997, 91.

CHAPTER 20

THE CAMP DAVID SUMMIT, THE CLINTON PARAMETERS, AND THE TABA TALKS

JULY 2000–JANUARY 2001

With the failure of the Israeli-Syrian negotiations and the death of Asad, the focus of the peace process again shifted to the Israeli-Palestinian track. Though there was no sign of any breakthrough on the horizon, President Clinton invited Prime Minister Barak and Palestinian leader ʿArafat to a summit at Camp David, which extended from July 11–25, 2000. In contrast to the first Camp David summit where President Carter succeeded in brokering an agreement between Egypt and Israel, this summit failed to produce an agreement. An immediate result was the eruption of the second Palestinian uprising, al-Aqsa Intifada, in October. Still, attempts to reach an accord continued under fire until the very last days of Barak's and Clinton's terms, with the Clinton Parameters (December 2000) and the Taba Talks (January 2001). In the aftermath of Camp David, the parties were engaged in what Clayton E. Swisher termed "the politics of blame" (2004, 335–405) as each side published its own version of the events. As will be shown, the differences between the narratives do not necessarily lie in the exact historical details, but rather in their interpretation. The aim of this chapter is to assess whether the drama of Camp David and the two subsequent episodes constituted plausible missed opportunities.

THE EPISODES

When Barak was elected prime minister in July 1999 he demonstrated determination to move forward on the peace process, on both the Syrian-Lebanese and Palestinian tracks. Though he decided to give priority to the first track against the better judgment of some of his ministers and aides, he was also keen to explore possibilities on the other track. Opposed to the principle of gradual progress embedded in the Oslo Accords, Barak sought a negotiation process leading to a final settlement that would entail the end of all claims. His logic was that if Israel implemented all its commitments in a transitional period, it would have no further bargaining chips with which to obtain concessions from the Palestinians. Therefore, his talks with the US officials focused on the modalities of what became known as the Framework Agreement on Permanent Status (FAPS). In practice, Barak preferred to minimize the involvement of the United States (Ben-Ami 2004, 21–26; Beilin 2001, 75–78; Sher 2001, 17–29; Qurei 2008, 83–85).

The Palestinians received Barak's election with relief, perceiving it as "no less than a counter-revolution against the putsch" of Netanyahu in 1996 (Qurei 2008, 83). In principle they agreed with the logic of pursuing a final agreement, though 'Arafat expected Barak to fulfill the remaining elements of the Wye Agreement (which included Israeli withdrawal from 11 percent of area C) before moving to final negotiations. Yet friction existed within 'Arafat's inner circle regarding the talks; an undeclared struggle, according to Ahmed Qurei's testimony, emerged between the senior members of the leadership over who would take responsibility for the negotiations. This made it difficult for the Palestinians to pursue a unified position vis-à-vis Israel (2008, 85–86).

On July 29, 1999, the Israeli-Palestinian negotiations, led by Gilead Sher on the Israeli side and Sa'eb Erekat on the Palestinian, commenced in Jerusalem. These talks, which required American mediation, culminated in the Sharm al-Shaykh Memorandum on September 4—exactly four months after the original date set for signing the permanent-status agreement—with the participation of Secretary of State Albright, Egyptian president Mubarak, the newly crowned Jordanian king 'Abdallah, 'Arafat, and Barak. This agreement called for Israeli withdrawal from a further 11 percent of the West Bank, the transfer of another 8.1 percent from area B to A, the release of 350 Palestinian prisoners, the opening of safe passages between the West Bank and Gaza, and the construction of a seaport in Gaza. There was also a timetable for final status talks to deal with Jerusalem, borders, refugees, and settlements: the FAPS was to be achieved by February 13, 2000, and a comprehensive agreement on permanent status (CAPS) by September 13, 2000. The Knesset ratified the agreement by a majority of 54 to 23. On September 13, 1999, the FAPS negotiations officially commenced. However, with the signing of the Sharm al-Shaykh Memorandum, Barak shifted his energy to the Syrian track. His flirt with the "other woman"—as the Palestinians referred to Asad—aroused suspicions that Barak was looking to undermine their position by isolating them in the Arab world. Barak's attempts to assuage Palestinian fears were to no avail (Golan 2007, 33; Ross 2005, 502–508; Indyk 2009, 292; Sher 2001, 41–58; Qurei 2008, 87–90; Beilin 2001, 81–82, 89–91; Bregman 2014, 218–220).

An Israeli-Palestinian back channel was established in early November 1999 that operated in parallel to the official channel, dealing with the final status issues. The parties managed to agree on some principles and issues, but the differences regarding the details remained wide. As a result, the first FAPS deadline—February 2000—was not met. Consequently, 'Arafat threatened that he would declare the establishment of a Palestinian state on September 13—the original date fixed for signing the CAPS. This date would now constitute the main deadline for the parties. The Palestinians became frustrated by the Israeli inability, or unwillingness, to abide by the fixed deadlines and their wariness of Barak's motives grew. On the ground there were first indications that the despair on the Palestinian side might lead to the eruption of another violent uprising since, in their view, Netanyahu's three years in power and Barak's first year had proved to be a waste of time (Qurei 2008, 91–107; Beilin 2001, 93–105).

When the Syrian option evaporated in March 2000, the Palestinian track remained the "only game in town." A new round of negotiations began between Shlomo Ben-Ami and Abu 'Ala in Jerusalem on March 28 and lasted some six weeks.[1] In late April an abortive attempt was made to reach a FAPS in marathon discussions in Eilat. The Palestinians clarified that they opposed further interim agreements, preferring instead to move directly to a final settlement. As to substance, they insisted on only minor, and mutual, modifications of the 1967 borders, which, in their view, reflected their major concession at the Oslo Agreements—that is, the establishment of a Palestinian state on only 22 percent of the historical Palestine. In addition, they demanded formal Israeli recognition of the Palestinian Right of Return and the division of Jerusalem into Arab (East) and Jewish (West) parts. The gap between the parties was as wide as ever (Ben-Ami 2004, 32–36; Beilin 2001, 106–107; Ross 2005, 596–612).

On the basis of these talks, Israeli and Palestinian delegations headed by Ben-Ami and Abu 'Ala held two intensive rounds of negotiations in Stockholm between May 12 and 22. The choice of a remote site in Scandinavia for talks, reminiscent of the Oslo channel, was meant to allow the parties to consider secretly some daring solutions to the most sensitive permanent status issues in the conflict, namely, borders, security, refugees, and Jerusalem. In his opening remarks, Ben-Ami—a historian by profession—emphasized that the participants "should do their utmost not to regret for the rest of their lives having missed the opportunity" (2004, 45). Yet two unexpected developments put a spoke in the wheels of the talks: first, news of the secret channel was leaked; second, on May 15, the day the Palestinians commemorate the 1948 War (called Nakba Day), widespread demonstrations began in the West Bank and Gaza in solidarity with a hunger strike by Palestinian prisoners in Israeli jails. It was the most violent day in the territories since the opening of the Western Wall tunnel in 1996. These events affected the dynamics of the negotiations and led the parties to present more extreme views for fear of being accused of presenting a too-moderate position by groups opposing the peace process. To assuage Israeli public opinion, Barak temporarily suspended the talks and delayed the transfer of three Palestinian villages near Jerusalem (including Abu Dis, which was mentioned in the past as a possible substitute for the capital), though the decision was approved by the government. That was a secret commitment given by Barak to ʿArafat in February 2000. The villages were important to ʿArafat because his authority would then extend right up to the gates of Jerusalem. Barak never delivered on this commitment. Thus, wrote Martin Indyk, "A gesture that had been intended to build confidence . . . boomeranged, convincing Arafat that Barak's word was unreliable" (2009, 293). But perhaps the most significant gap hovered over the philosophy of the negotiations: while Israel focused on the mechanisms of implementation and procedural details, the Palestinians argued that any agreement on technicalities and mechanisms would be meaningless in the absence of an agreement on principles. Still, the talks were important as they clarified the gaps between the parties regarding the permanent status issues and signaled possible areas of agreement (such as the question of boundaries), which laid the basis for further negotiations (Ben-Ami 2004, 44–54; Qurei 2008, 108–123; Sher 2001, 86–96; Beilin 2001, 114–116; Ross 2005, 612–626).[2]

Meanwhile, Israel withdrew its forces from southern Lebanon. Having failed to clinch an agreement with Syria, Barak decided to go ahead with his election promise, though the timing and the swift implementation of the withdrawal came as a surprise. The Palestinians and ʿArafat received the move with mixed feelings: on the one hand, withdrawal to the international line was another precedent (following the Egyptian and Jordanian examples) that Israel was following UN resolutions (425) and, as such, was committed to implement Resolution 242, which meant the 1967 boundaries. This reinforced the Palestinian sense of entitlement to all the territories occupied in 1967. On the other, Hizballah presented a successful model of resistance, which the Palestinians were encouraged to follow instead of endless and futile diplomatic negotiations (Ross 2005, 626; Indyk 2009, 296). ʿArafat expressed a sense of betrayal and despair by the Israeli unilateral move, which, in his eyes, weakened his position on the Palestinian street (Qurei 2008, 121–124, 129; Beilin 2001, 117–118; Sher 2001, 97).

The last round of the "Swedish track" was held in early June, not in Stockholm but in Jerusalem, with the same participants. This round proved to be, according to Abu ʿAla, "difficult, tense and frustrating" while the atmosphere "was made worse by mutual suspicion and security problems" (Qurei 2008, 123). Abu ʿAla, who had just returned from Saudi Arabia, delivered Crown Prince ʿAbdallah's promise that if Israel would reach a settlement with the Palestinians, he would attempt to persuade the whole Muslim world to support it. But in terms of substance the gap was no closer to closing, and in

Ben-Ami's view even widened. In particular, it seemed that the Palestinian demand for the partitioning of Jerusalem and a reasonable implementation of the Right of Return could not be bridged (Ben-Ami 2004, 72–84; Qurei 2008, 122–137). And, according to Abu ʿAla, what the Israelis were proposing was "far from our perception of what was possible" (2008, 132).

As Israeli-Palestinian diplomatic interactions continued to lead nowhere, the idea of a tripartite summit seemed the only way to break the deadlock. Barak, who entertained the thought of a "Ben-Gurion style of decision" of ending the conflict once and for all, was the most enthusiastic. Clinton, too, was in favor of a grandiose move that would crown the end of his term, but he wanted to ensure the summit's success by another round of pre-negotiations. In contrast, ʿArafat opposed the idea, fearing a trap that would impose an un-satisfactory solution on him. He also worried that the Palestinians would be blamed for any failure at the summit. In any case, he wanted to first see Israel's fulfillment of the provisions made in Sharm al-Shaykh regarding withdrawal and the prisoners' release—provisions Barak tried to eschew (Qurei 2008, 136–137). At that time, the Palestinians considered a "negotiating summit," that is, a series of meetings that would eventually yield an agreement (Indyk 2009, 295). Therefore, the Israeli-American-Palestinian contacts concentrated on exploring the chances of a summit. Theoretically, a summit is designed, according to Maoz, to resolve substantial differences between the parties and initiate a mechanism to pull the process out of a stalemate. This was to be achieved by convening the principal decision makers who had the authority to make daring, far-reaching, binding decisions (2005, 205).

On June 5, Secretary Albright came to the region to prepare the ground for the summit and urge both sides to make concessions. But Barak was unwilling for tactical and domestic politics reasons to hand over the three Palestinian villages and decided to free only three prisoners—something the Palestinians considered to be an insult rather than a gesture of goodwill. Abu ʿAla and Ben-Ami held another round of talks at St. Andrews Air Force Base in Wash-ington, while Saʿeb Erekat and Oded Eran held parallel talks at nearby Bolling Air Force Base. The assessments of these meetings vary: one side argued that the gap was too wide to bridge in a single summit (Qurei 2008, 137–138; Ben-Ami 2004, 87–97; Sher 2001, 122–127); the other saw some chance in light of informal ideas that arose during the talks. At one point Erekat told Ross, "Dennis, it is possible. And we cannot miss the opportunity. We will never have an Israeli government like this one" (2005, 635). Indyk summarized the optimistic view: "So on all the key substantive issues—Jerusalem, terri-tory settlements, security, and refugees—we believed we could see a way to bridge the gaps through a variety of technical mechanisms" (2009, 304). The same view was expressed by Egyptian president Mubarak, who thought that "The Clinton-Barak combination is a fantastic opportunity which must not be missed" (quoted in Bregman 2014, 222).

On the road to the summit an important meeting took place on June 25 in Nablus, between 'Arafat and all the Palestinian leadership and an Israeli delegation led by Ben-Ami. There it became obvious that even if in the territorial field there was some room to maneuver, the gaps in the refugee and Jerusalem issues remained wide. 'Arafat made it clear that the crux of the problem was the question of Palestinian sovereignty over al-Haram al-Sharif (the Temple Mount) and the Old City, while Israel would retain sovereignty over the Western Wall and the Jewish Quarter (Ben-Ami 2004, 113–118). 'Arafat and Abu Mazen thought that the meeting showed some progress. In protest against this flawed assessment, Abu 'Ala tendered his resignation, but this step was rejected by 'Arafat (Qurei 2008, 148–160). A careful analysis of the detailed positions of both parties in the run-up to the summit reveals that, at this stage, the differences between the parties were gaping and the chances of narrowing them were slim, unless one party was hiding some major concessions in its pocket (Qurei 2008, 163–170; Ben-Ami 2004, 84–85; Sher 2001, 142–143). In addition, the mistrust and suspicion—even disdain—existing between Barak and 'Arafat threatened to undermine the summit from the very beginning. The Palestinian side was particularly critical of what was perceived as Barak's condescending behavior and tendency not to honor promises (Beilin 2001, 125; Indyk 2009, 289, 291, 294; Ben-Ami 2004, 118; Drucker 2002, 189–192).

In spite of the uncertainties, on July 4—American Independence Day—Clinton sent the parties an invitation to a summit at Camp David. In his memoirs, he confessed that "There was not a high probability of success," adding that he called the summit because he "believed that the collapse of the peace process would be a near certainty if I didn't" (2004, 912). It was a kind of "now or never" feeling that many of the American and Israeli negotiators shared that convinced them to hold the parley, its low prospects notwithstanding (Ross 2005, 645–647; Indyk 2009, 305). Though Barak was still enthusiastic, 'Arafat came to the summit "with a profound sense of gloom and suspicion." It was Clinton's task, Ross wrote, to convince 'Arafat that this was not a trap Barak was setting to corner him, but an opportunity to fulfill Palestinian aspirations (2005, 649). On the Palestinian side there was a feeling that conditions were not yet ripe for a summit (Hanieh 2001, 76). On the Israeli side this was interpreted as if 'Arafat did want a summit but for domestic reasons needed to be seen being dragged there "kicking and screaming" (Sher 2001, 122, 142). Thus the parties arrived at Camp David with a sense of anxiety and apprehension. They acknowledged that in theory at least they faced a historical opportunity; whether they would miss it depended on the dynamics of the negotiations and the ability of the leadership to take bold decisions.

Though Barak appeared to be the keenest player at Camp David, his position at home was tenuous. On the summit's eve his coalition cracked; several ministers of the religious parties (Shas and the National Religious Party) as well as the Russian Party (Yisrael Be'aliyah) resigned. So did David Levy, the foreign minister from Barak's party, who was not involved in the talks. In the Knesset a motion of no confidence received a slight majority (54–62).[3] While this vote did not affect Barak since he had won the premiership by the direct election method, it still meant that he did not enjoy the legitimacy of the Knesset. Thus within a year in office he managed to lose his parliamentary backing (Sher 2001, 146, 151; Drucker 2002, 178–188; Beilin 2001, 129; Meital 2006, 73). No wonder that Ben-Ami titled his book (in Hebrew) *A Front without a Rearguard* (2004, 129). It was plain for all to see that Barak's government "was on its last legs since he no longer commanded a majority in the Knesset" (Indyk 2009, 288). Though negotiating his country's future at Camp David, Barak had to constantly follow the mood in Israeli politics and public. Nevertheless, he did not show overt signs of concern when he issued a statement marking his departure to Camp David: "This is a moment of opportunity that will not reoccur. It is accompanied by major risks. And if, God forbid, we should fail, then the risks, and not the opportunities, will come true."[4]

Barak was not the only one facing legitimacy problems. 'Arafat well understood that he was sitting on a powder keg, as the recent riots demonstrated. If a proposed deal would be rejected by the Palestinian street now, violence could erupt and threaten the very survival of his increasingly unpopular regime. In addition, within the Palestinian leadership there were generational (old vs. young) and personal rivalries (e.g., Abu Mazen vs. Abu 'Ala). It was part of a struggle between those who considered themselves as the rightful heirs to 'Arafat. All this meant that his room for flexibility at Camp David was significantly constricted (Indyk 2009, 297; 2005b, 101–102).

The Camp David summit lasted fifteen days (July 11–25) before ending in naught.[5] A good deal of scholarship was subsequently dedicated to the questions of what went wrong and which party should be blamed for the summit's failure (Rabinovich 2004, 160–180). It seems that the controversy is not so much about the accuracy of the facts, but rather their interpretation. What will follow, then, is a short summary of the parties' positions on the four major issues of the permanent status: borders and settlements, security, refugees, and Jerusalem.

Regarding borders and settlements, in the preliminary talks in advance of

Camp David, Israel offered between 70 percent and 87 percent of the occupied territories, while the rest—including the major settlement blocs—was to be annexed to Israel. At the summit, Israel offered 91 percent of that territory (plus 1 percent in a land swap) for a Palestinian state, while the rest would be annexed to Israel. In all, 80 percent of the settlers were to be included in the annexed territory (including Ariel, the Latrun salient, and Etzion bloc). Over the course of the negotiations some sources claimed that Israel raised the offer to 94 percent. A corridor was to connect Gaza with the West Bank under Palestinian control but Israeli sovereignty. The Palestinians demanded full Israeli withdrawal to the 1967 borders, based on UN Resolution 242, but were willing to accept the concept of a one-to-one land swap, not to exceed 2.3 percent of the territory. It was unclear whether Jewish settlers not included in the annexed blocs would be able to remain in the Palestinian state. Yet according to Pressman's account, the 91 percent of the Israeli offer was tantamount, in fact, to only 86 percent from the Palestinian perspective. Also, Israel demanded to retain control over the Jordan Valley for six to twenty-one years to protect against a possible Arab invasion, meaning that during this period the Palestinians would have control of only 77 percent of the territory. In addition, the Israeli territorial offer was not contiguous, breaking the West Bank into two, if not three, separate blocs (2003, 17). The Palestinians agreed that Israel would retain only the areas allocated for settlement blocs, which would constitute no more than 4 percent of the area, with a further 1 percent for security purposes, in addition to the areas inhabited by Jews in Jerusalem (Qurei 2008, 251).[6]

On security, Israel insisted that the future Palestinian state would be demilitarized, while the Palestinians opted for "a state of limited arms." The Palestinians accepted the Israeli demand for three early warning stations in the West Bank. There are conflicting versions regarding the Palestinian position toward the Israeli demand for a network of security roads in the Palestinian state and the right of the IDF to enter Palestinian territory and airspace in case of emergency.[7] A contested issue was the question of Israeli control of the Jordan Valley. Israel demanded control (though not necessarily sovereignty) for a period lasting between six and twenty-one years. The Palestinian position was that an Israeli force, under the flag of an international peacekeeping force, would be stationed along the Jordan River. Israel was apparently willing to accept this idea, though it is unclear whether it was willing to renounce the notion of control.

The problem of the Palestinian refugees was not a major issue on the Camp David agenda and, in any case, little progress was made. In principle, the Palestinians insisted that Israel accept responsibility for creating the refugee problem—and for resolving it—as well as recognize the inalienable right of

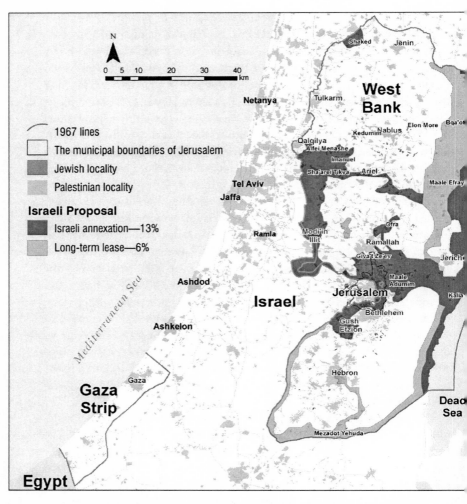

MAP 20.1. Camp David, July 2000: The Israeli Proposal. Courtesy of Shaul Arieli, 2013.

all refugees to return to Israel (Palestine in the pre-1948 period). This was far from the Israeli position, which was, at most, to express sorrow at the suffering of the refugees and to participate in an international effort to financially compensate them. In addition, Israel was willing to permit a small number of refugees to enter Israel under family reunification mechanisms. The Palestinians agreed that the right of return should be implemented in a way that protected Israeli security and demography. The impression of both Israelis and Americans was that the Palestinians attached more importance to the question of symbolic responsibility than to the actual mechanisms of return and, in any case, would not insist on actual return to Israel (Sher 2001, 156; Golan 2007, 42). This allegation, however, is not supported by Abu ʿAla's account of the Palestinian position, which insisted that 250,000 refugees from the Lebanese camps be permitted as a matter of priority to enter Israel and that the Palestinians who owned land in historic Palestine shall have the right to purchase lands and new homes (Qurei 2008, 252–254).

The Jerusalem issue was undoubtedly the most contentious at Camp David. Early on in the deliberations the gap between the parties was wide, as the Palestinians demanded the partition of Jerusalem into Arab (East) and Jewish (West), which meant full Israeli withdrawal from all the Jerusalem territory beyond the 1967 border, including the Old City. The Israelis offered Palestinian sovereignty only in the remote Arab suburbs surrounding Jerusalem and insisted on Israeli sovereignty in East Jerusalem. In the pre–Camp David talks Ben-Ami pitched the idea of establishing two capitals, while the Palestinian al-Quds would be based on Abu Dis and several other Palestinian neighborhoods inside and outside the current municipality boundaries (2004, 112; Klein 2001, 29–30). At Camp David the two sides did indeed agree that Jerusalem would function as two capitals for two states. The Israeli offer included the establishment of al-Quds with full sovereignty in the outlying areas of East Jerusalem (Abu Dis, al-Azariyya, Isawiyya, Shuʿafat, and more). In return, Israel would annex Maʿale Adumim, Givʿat Zeʾev, and Gush Etzion. The inner Arab neighborhoods in East Jerusalem (Shaykh Jarrah, al-Tur, Silwan, etc.) would enjoy self-rule (or functional autonomy) under Israeli sovereignty. Their situation would resemble the Palestinian territories in area B in the Oslo Agreements. With regard to the Old City and the Temple Mount/al-Haram al-Sharif area, Israel suggested several options that were not mutually exclusive: the first was formal Israeli sovereignty with functional Palestinian sovereignty over the Muslim and Christian Quarters, free access to the Haram from the Muslim Quarter, which would continue to be administered by the Waqf of the Palestinian state, and the establishment of a sovereign presidential compound in the Muslim Quarter. The second offer was the deferral of the question of sovereignty of the Haram for a limited or unlimited period of time. Finally, ʿArafat was offered "permanent custodianship" over the Haram, which would be conferred by a committee composed of five members of the UN Security Council, the Vatican, and Morocco as the chair of the Jerusalem Committee of the Organization of Islamic Countries. In return, Israel asked for a "prayer corner" on the site and residual sovereignty, which would include limitations on archaeological diggings in the area. Clinton added another creative idea— the vertical division of sovereignty; that is, while the Palestinians would enjoy sovereignty over the land, the Israelis would get sovereignty under the Temple

Mount and the adjacent Wailing Wall. 'Arafat, however, refused to share the sanctity of al-Haram, insisting on full Palestinian sovereignty there. The sides did agree that the Old City's Jewish Quarter, the Wailing Wall, and the Jewish neighborhoods in East Jerusalem would remain under Israeli sovereignty (Pressman 2003, 18–19; Klein 2001, 43–56; 2003, 71–81; Hanieh 2001, 83–84; Indyk 2009, 312–340; Qurei 2008, 254–256; Kurtzer et al. 2013, 136–142; Lehrs 2011, 22–34).[8] By proposing to divide sovereignty in Jerusalem, Barak ostensibly went further than any previous Israeli leader.[9] The Palestinians, for their part, also made some important concessions, though they were unable to offer a formula sharing sovereignty over the Temple Mount/al-Haram al-Sharif. In the final analysis, the summit collapsed due to the parties' inability to bridge the gap over this issue. In Clinton's words, "it was all about who got to claim sovereignty" (2004, 916).

In the days that followed, a battle over the memory of Camp David ensued between Israelis and Palestinians, in which the Americans also took part. Each side now presented its own version of the events with the aim of pinning the blame on the other. The Israeli narrative spoke of a generous Israeli offer that was unilaterally rejected by the other side—proving the nonexistence of a Palestinian partner (Morris 2002; Barak 2005, 117–150; Rabinovich 2004, 160–166; Drucker 2002, 286–288; Kurtzer et al. 2013, 142–147). Clinton too ascribed the blame to 'Arafat, in contrast to his earlier promise to the Palestinians. The Palestinian counter-narrative insisted that the Israeli position was neither generous nor an offer at all and that the failure was in fact Barak's (Hanieh 2001, 75–97; Qurei 2008, 267–272). At least one American diplomat participating in Camp David supported this perspective (Malley 2005, 108–114; Malley and Agha 2001; 2002). This "memory battle" remains yet another historiographical debate in the annals of the Arab-Israeli conflict (Pressman 2003; Shamir and Maddy-Weitzman 2005; Pundak 2001, 31–45; Kacowicz 2005, 343–360).

The attempts to reach a solution continued until Clinton's departure from the White House on January 20, 2001. The immediate Israeli and American goal was to persuade 'Arafat not to make good on his threat to declare a Palestinian state on September 13, the deadline set in Oslo II for a permanent status agreement. The tripartite diplomatic activity thus endured. By mid-August, Barak indicated for the first time his willingness to relinquish Israeli sovereignty over the Temple Mount. After consulting with the chief Sephardic rabbi, Eliyahu Bakshi-Doron, Barak was now prepared to explore the idea of ceding sovereignty to God, provided 'Arafat was prepared to do the same with his claim to Palestinian sovereignty on al-Haram al-Sharif. Unfortunately, 'Arafat rejected the innovative idea on the pretext that it would lead to an argument over whose God had the sovereignty. The suggestion of 'Amr

Musa, the Egyptian foreign minister, that no one would have sovereignty was rejected (Indyk 2009, 346–348).

On September 6–8, both Barak and ʿArafat spoke at the UN Millennium summit, but Clinton was unable to arrange a tripartite meeting. In contrast to the grim reality on the ground following the Camp David fiasco, Barak tried to assure the audience that "The opportunity for peace in the Middle East is now at hand and must not be missed" (quoted in Beilin 2001, 150; Ben-Ami 2004, 268–728). The next two weeks saw hectic diplomatic activity aimed at reviving the talks, culminating in the friendliest meeting ever between ʿArafat and Barak at the prime minister's home in the Israeli town of Kochav Yaʾir on September 25. Daniel Abraham, the Jewish billionaire who orchestrated the meeting, wrote that "this certainly [has] been the finest and the warmest" encounter (2006, 164). It was expected that the United States would soon submit to the parties a take-it-or-leave-it package deal, based on consultations made in Camp David's aftermath. There was a sense, at least on the Israeli side, that a major breakthrough was in the offing (Ben-Ami 2004, 279–285; Sher 2001, 260–287). Four days later, however, Ariel Sharon, the head of the opposition Likud Party, decided—for purely domestic political reasons—to visit the Temple Mount. But the act itself was considered highly provocative and it ignited demonstrations and riots in al-Haram al-Sharif, beginning at al-Aqsa mosque and quickly spreading across the West Bank. Naturally, the uprising was also an outcome of the frustration and despair felt in Palestinian society due to the deadlock in the peace process and the failure of Camp David. In fact, a popular uprising was long anticipated by the intelligence community in Israel and signs of it were detected in the pre-summit period. Many Israelis believed that the Intifada was premeditated, but the Palestinians saw it as "a spontaneous reaction to the long history of oppressive Israeli practices" fired by Sharon's visit (Qurei 2008, 264).

Curiously, while the violence in the West Bank continued (spreading also to Israel, where thirteen Arabs were killed in demonstrations in October), there was no let-up in the attempts to revive the Israeli-Palestinian talks by various international and regional channels. Yet the immediate focus of the contacts was to achieve a cease-fire; on October 16, Mubarak hosted Clinton, Barak, ʿArafat, and King ʿAbdallah at a summit in Sharm al-Shaykh, which adopted a fragile truce. Though the violence did not subside, Israeli-Palestinian talks continued. Even Barak's decision to resign, on December 9, as a result of continued criticism of his policy and his failure to enlarge his coalition did not stop that wheel from turning. Barak now gambled on a final deal with the Palestinians as the only way to arrest his plummeting popularity in the polls. He hoped that the elections, scheduled for February 6, would turn into a referendum for peace (Ben-Ami 2004, 403; Enderlin 2003, 339).

On December 19, high-ranking Israeli and Palestinian delegations met at the Bolling Air Force Base. On December 23, the last day of the talks, Clinton met the delegations and informed them of his bridging proposals (later to become known as the Clinton Parameters). According to Indyk, the document "had been meticulously prepared after extensive consultations with Israeli and Palestinian negotiators and leaders." In addition, all the important Arab leaders had been briefed on the details and had endorsed the plan (2009, 366). Clinton presented the parameters as his own ideas, noting that they remained on the table only so long as he was in office. He emphasized that they were non-negotiable. The gist of the parameters, as recorded in Clinton's memoirs, were as follows:

> On territory, I recommended 94 to 96 percent of the West Bank for the Palestinians with a land swap from Israel of 1 to 3 percent, and an understanding that the land kept by Israel would include 80 percent of the settlers in blocs. On security, I said Israeli forces would withdraw over a three-year period while an international force would be gradually introduced, with the understanding that a small Israeli presence in the Jordan Valley would remain for another three years under the authority of the international forces. The Israelis would also be able to maintain their early-warning station in the West Bank with a Palestinian liaison presence. In the event of an "imminent and demonstrable threat to Israel's security," there would be provision for emergency deployments in the West Bank. The new state of Palestine would be "non-militarized," but would have a strong security force; sovereignty over its airspace, with special arrangements to meet Israeli training and operational needs; and an international force for border security and deterrence.
>
> On Jerusalem, I recommended that the Arab neighborhoods be in Palestine and the Jewish neighborhoods in Israel, and the Palestinians would have sovereignty over the Temple Mount/Haram and the Israelis sovereignty over the Western Wall and the "holy space" of which it is part, with no excavation around the wall or under the Mount, at least without a mutual consent.
>
> On refugees, I said that the new state of Palestine should be the homeland for refugees displaced in the 1948 war and afterward, without ruling out the possibility that Israel would accept some of the refugees according to its own laws and sovereign decisions, giving priority to the refugee populations in Lebanon. I recommended an international effort to compensate refugees and assist them in finding houses in the new state of Palestine, in the land-swap areas to be transferred to Palestine, in their current host countries, in other willing nations, or in Israel. Both parties should agree that this solution would satisfy UN Security Council Resolution 194.
>
> Finally, the agreement had to clearly mark the end of the conflict and an

end to the violence. I suggested a new UN Security Council resolution saying that this agreement, along with the final release of Palestinian prisoners, would fulfill the requirements of resolutions 242 and 338. (2004, 936–937)[10]

Clinton asked the parties to give him a final answer (yes or no) within five days. For that purpose he was willing to meet the two leaders separately. On that day, the Israeli cabinet decided to accept the Clinton Parameters as the basis for negotiations, provided that the Palestinians accepted them too.[11] Still, there were certain reservations, including the very idea that the Palestinians would enjoy full sovereignty over the Haram/Temple Mount. It was decided that these reservations would be shared with Clinton, though they would not affect Israel's overall endorsement of the parameters in principle (Sher 2001, 366–374; Klein 2003, 110; Indyk 2009, 367). Ben-Ami claimed that the issue of sovereignty on the Temple Mount remained open but that the reservations were "pretty minor and dealt mainly with security arrangements and deployment areas and control over passages" (quoted in Swisher 2004, 399). Undoubtedly, it was a historic decision; the Israeli government, wrote Beilin, "which said 'no' to the Rogers Plan in 1969 and 'no' to the Reagan Plan in 1982, said 'yes' to the Clinton Plan in 2000" (2001, 193). Historic or not, the decision was made in the face of heavy right-wing opposition, buttressed by the voices of Chief of Staff Shaul Mofaz and head of the General Security Services Avi Dichter, expressing concern at the inherent military and political risks (Sher 2001, 367; Ben-Ami 2004, 397; Indyk 2009, 369).[12]

In contrast to the swift Israeli reply, 'Arafat dragged his feet and equivocated; on December 28 he faxed a long letter to Clinton outlining some fiftytwo reservations, including the Palestinians' demand for sovereignty over the entire Haram (Qurei 2008, 285–293; Ben-Ami 2004, 394–395; 2005b, 83–84). What followed was an international effort in which recognized Western and Arab leaders were approached by the United States and Israel and asked to bear down on 'Arafat to accept the parameters. "It is doubtful," wrote Ben-Ami, "whether history has seen a case of such global mobilization to persuade a local leader of a national movement to make a decision, to overcome his fears" (2004, 400; Ross 2005, 755). This pressure, however, yielded very little; ten days after the deadline, on January 2, 2001, 'Arafat arrived for a meeting with Clinton. The reservations the chairman raised there with regard to the parameters were tantamount to their rejection; Ross called them "dealkillers." In fact, on some points 'Arafat even retreated from previously accepted positions, such as the question of Israeli sovereignty over the Western Wall and the Old City division (Ross 2005, 756; Indyk 2009, 370; Clinton 2004, 943–944; Sher 2001, 382). "There was more divergence than convergence," according to another American report (Ben-Ami 2004, 404). At the end of the meeting, Clinton was thoroughly confused as to 'Arafat's position: "His body language said no, but the deal was so good I couldn't believe anyone would be foolish enough to let it go" (2004, 944). Indeed, a careful reading of Abu 'Ala's documented reservations demonstrates that the Palestinians flatly rejected the parameters under the façade of a favorable response (Qurei 2008, 285–293). Clinton summarized the Palestinian leader's response: "Arafat never said no; he just couldn't bring himself to say yes" (2004, 944). At this point, Prince Bandar and Nabil Fahmi, respectively the Saudi and Egyptian ambassadors in the United States, were called to intervene and persuade 'Arafat to accept the deal (Kurtzer et al. 2013, 150). Bandar recounts telling the Palestinian leader: "Since 1948, every time we've had something on the table we say no. Then we say yes. When we say yes, it's not on the table anymore. Then we have to deal with something less. Isn't it about time we say yes? We've always said to the Americans, 'Our red line is Jerusalem. You get us a deal that's O.K. on Jerusalem and we're going, too.'" Bandar and Fahmi advised 'Arafat to accept the deal, but still he wavered. According to his testimony, Bandar finally told 'Arafat: "If we lose this opportunity, it is not going to be a tragedy. This is going to be a crime; a crime not only against the Palestinians but against the entire region" (Walsh 2003; Simpson 2006, 264–265). Barak also attempted to persuade Mubarak to pressure 'Arafat, but to no avail (Bregman 2014, 264).

Klein offers a softer version of the Palestinian rejection, though conceding that Israel's "yes" to Clinton's ideas "was stronger and speedier than that of the Palestinians." He holds that while the Palestinian "yes" was indeed hesitant and reserved, it was the first official "yes" ever given to the permanent status agreement in general and Jerusalem in particular (2003, 111). Swisher went further, arguing for symmetry in the Israeli and Palestinian responses: "Eventually both would accept the parameters, but both would express reservations" (2004, 397; Pressman 2003, 20). A careful reading of all the available accounts, however, does not support the symmetrical approach. All in all, the only way to bring an agreement twelve days before the end of Clinton's presidency was to give an unequivocal "yes" to his parameters; any other response could not be interpreted as anything other than a rejection of his ideas. The Israeli impression that the Palestinians rejected Clinton's parameters was reinforced at a top-level Israeli-Palestinian team meeting on January 11 and a Peres-'Arafat meeting on January 13 in Gaza (Sher 2001, 387–390; Enderlin 2003, 346). The Clinton era thus ended with no Israeli-Palestinian final status agreement. With this added to his failure on the Israeli-Syrian track, Clinton left office utterly disappointed.

The final chapter in the Israeli-Palestinian negotiations saga was written in Taba from January 21–27, 2001, just as George W. Bush entered office and a few days before the elections in Israel. While the Intifada was still raging (a brutal Palestinian terror operation even led to a temporary suspension of the talks), top-level Israeli and Palestinian delegations attempted a last-ditch effort to arrive at an agreement. The new US administration preferred to abstain from participating in the talks and was only briefed of the proceedings. In the absence of official documents (except pertaining to the refugee problem), the account of the Taba Talks is largely based on a non-paper, prepared by European Union observer Miguel Moratinos. Though his draft was contested by some participants, it is generally considered as a fair reflection of the proceedings.[13] Moratinos's draft covered the following topics:

Borders and Settlements. For the first time, the parties agreed that in principle the 1967 lines would be the basis for the borders between Israel and Palestine. Also, for the first time maps delineating the boundaries were exchanged. The Israeli map presented a 6 percent annexation (the higher limit of Clinton's parameters) to include some 80 percent of the settlers, with the maximum of 3 percent land swap (that is, a ratio of 1 : 2), while the Palestinians agreed to 3.1 percent annexation on the basis of an equal swap.[14] They also insisted that the corridor ("safe passage") linking Gaza and the West Bank (under Israeli sovereignty) would be included in the calculation of the swap. Israel requested the leasing of 2 percent of the land—something the Palestinians were willing to discuss only after the establishment of a Palestinian state. In contrast to previous agreements, the Palestinians retracted their earlier readiness to include Ma'ale Adumim and Giv'at Ze'ev in the settlement blocs annexed to Israel after realizing that Israel insisted on annexing also the large tract that adjoins them (meaning that many Palestinians would find themselves in sovereign Israeli territory).

Security. Israel demanded that the Palestinian state be nonmilitarized, while the Palestinians were willing to accept limitations on the acquisition of arms and be defined as a state with limited arms. Israel agreed to recognize that Palestine would have sovereignty over its airspace. Israel requested access to Palestinian airspace for military operations and training, but this was rejected on the basis that it was inconsistent with the neutrality of Palestine. Israel agreed, as in the Clinton Parameters, to a withdrawal from the West Bank over a thirty-six-month period, with an additional thirty-six months for the Jordan Valley. The Palestinians agreed to an eighteen-month withdrawal under the supervision of international forces, while in the Jordan Valley it would accept an additional ten-month period. Israel requested to maintain and operate five emergency locations on Palestine territory (in the Jordan Valley), but the Palestinians agreed to only two, to be run by an international presence, and for a limited time only. The Palestinians refused to deploy Israeli armed forces on their territory during emergency situations but were willing to consider ways in which international forces might be used in that capacity. The question of monitoring and verification at Palestine's international crossings was not resolved. The Palestinians accepted the Israeli demand for three early warning stations in Palestinian territory, subject to certain conditions yet to be discussed.

Refugees. The greatest progress was made in the refugee group, chaired by Yossi Beilin and Nabil Sha'ath, where non-papers were also exchanged. A first attempt was made to formulate a joint historical narrative of the refugee problem, though no agreement was reached. Largely based on the Clinton Parameters, the talks offered five options: the return and repatriation to Israel of a limited number of refugees, return to Israel's swapped territory, return to Palestine, rehabilitation and relocation in host countries, and relocation to a third country. Preference in all these programs would be accorded to the refugees in Lebanon. Informally, Israel suggested a three-track fifteen-year absorption program. The first track referred to the absorption in Israel of twenty-five thousand refugees in the first three years (or forty thousand in the first five years). The second track referred to the absorption of refugees into the Israeli territory transferred to Palestinian sovereignty, while the third track referred to absorption in the context of family reunification schemes. Both sides agreed to the establishment of an international commission and an international fund as a mechanism for dealing with compensation issues. It was agreed that the United Nations Relief and Works Agency (UNRWA) should be phased out with an agreed timetable of five years. When the Israeli side raised the issue of compensation for former Jewish refugees from Arab countries, the Palestinians argued that this was not a subject for a bilateral Israeli-Palestinian agreement.

Jerusalem. Both parties accepted that the city of Jerusalem would be the capital of the two states: Yerushalayim the capital of Israel, al-Quds the capital of Palestine. Both sides supported the idea of an open city, though they diverged on its boundaries: Israel favored the Old City and an area defined as the Holy Basin; the Palestinians rejected the Israeli geographical boundaries and called for the full municipal borders of East and West Jerusalem. Both parties accepted Clinton's principle of Palestinian sovereignty over Arab neighborhoods and Israeli sovereignty over Jewish neighborhoods, except for Palestinian rejection of Israeli sovereignty in Jabal Abu Ghneim (Har Homa) and Ras al-Amud, as well as Ma'ale Adumim and Giv'at Ze'ev. The Palestinian side understood that Israel was ready to accept Palestinian sovereignty over the Arab neighborhoods of East Jerusalem, including part of the Old City; the Israeli side understood that the Palestinians were ready to accept Israeli sovereignty over the Jewish Quarter of the Old City and part of the Armenian Quarter. Both sides agreed that the question of Temple Mount/al-Haram al-Sharif had not been resolved. Both sides were close to accepting Clinton's ideas regarding Israeli sovereignty over the Western Wall and its surroundings, as well as Palestinian sovereignty over al-Haram. An informal suggestion was raised that for an agreed period of time the Temple Mount/al-Haram would be under the international sovereignty of the five permanent members of the Security Council plus Morocco (or another Islamic presence), with the Palestinians acting as the "guardians/custodians" during this period. All in all, many of the issues still remained unsettled.

At the press conference following the talks, the delegations announced that "The sides declare that they have never been closer to reaching an agreement and it is thus our shared beliefs that the remaining gaps could be bridged with the resumption of the negotiations following the Israeli elections" (Beilin 2001, 216). True, assessments of the degree of progress achieved in the talks varied: while Beilin (2001, 215–216) gave a positive account, Sher, Indyk, and others (who were not there) thought otherwise (Indyk 2009, 372; Ben-Ami 2004, 446–447; Sher 2001, 400–401; Rabinovich 2004, 159; Drucker 2002, 401). On the Palestinian side, Abu ʿAla listed some ten points of progress made at the talks (Qurei 2008, 323–324). On balance, it seems that the Israeli and Palestinian positions became closer, particularly with regard to the borders, security, and refugee problems, though much work remained, particularly with regard to the Jerusalem issue (Golan 2007, 61; Ben-Ami 2004, 446–447).

On February 6, 2001, however, Ariel Sharon, head of the Likud Party, was voted in as Israel's new prime minister. In many ways, Sharon's landslide victory (62.39 percent to 37.61 percent for Barak) was testimony to the Israeli disappointment with Barak and disbelief in the peace process as a result of the continuation of the Intifada and the incessant daily terrorism. Ironically, Barak's "no partner" propaganda campaign after Camp David helped Sharon to delegitimize the peace process and win the election. The combination of a hard right-wing prime minister in Israel and a new Republican administration in the United States that was unwilling to be burned in the conflict left little option but a suspension of the peace process.

ASSESSMENT

The Israeli-Palestinian negotiations during the Barak period (1999–2001) went through three stages: the Camp David summit, the Clinton Parameters, and the Taba Talks. This section will attempt to assess to what extent an opportunity to sign an agreement was missed during this period. Ben-Ami, head of the Israeli delegation to the talks for most of the period under review and himself a historian and diplomat, expressed in his memoirs a sense of frustration and despair. Lamenting the historical opportunity missed by the Palestinians, he invoked the mythological saying attributed to the legendary Israeli foreign minister Abba Eban that "The Palestinians had never missed an opportunity to miss an opportunity" (2004, 447). The quotation entered the Israeli discourse and mythology, and it is no wonder that Barak and others have often repeated it in relation to this episode and subsequently (Ehud Barak 2005, 120, 130; Pressman 2003, 10).[15] Ben-Ami thought that "Camp David was not really the deal the Palestinians could have accepted. The real lost opportunities came later on" (2005, 82). The opportunity lost, in his opinion, was connected to the Palestinian position regarding the Clinton Parameters. However, Ben-Ami did not absolve Barak of at least partial responsibility for the missed opportunity, which he believed had existed at Camp David, not at Taba (2004, 478; 2005, 82). From a different perspective, Prince Bandar, the Saudi ambassador to the United States, thought that 'Arafat's rejection of the parameters in January 2001 was "a tragic mistake—a crime really." He told a journalist, "I still have not recovered from the magnitude of the missed opportunity in January" (Walsh 2003). Another top Israeli negotiator, Gilead Sher, felt that had the Clinton Parameters been presented to the parties five months earlier, at Camp David, the opportunity would not have been missed (2001, 364). He added that upon meeting one of the Palestinian leaders, he was told that the Palestinians were now wondering whether missing this opportunity might outweigh their missed opportunity in 1947 (that is, the UN Partition Plan) (2001, 382).[16] Finally, a recent study of Ahron Bregman concluded that undoubtedly the verdict of history will show that with the Clinton Parameters, "Arafat missed an opportunity to have an independent Palestine with Arab East Jerusalem as its capital" (2014, 265).

The Camp David summit and its sequels (the Clinton Parameters and the Taba Talks) constituted a historical opportunity to arrive at an agreement. The opportunity presented itself as a result of the coalescence of three developments. The first was the return of the Labor Party to power in May 1999, with Barak as prime minister; he was committed to the pursuit of peace with Syria and the Palestinians, presenting himself as the true heir of Rabin. Second, there was an American president, in the last year of his second term, determined to leave his mark on history in the realm of the Arab-Israeli conflict, whether on the Syrian or the Palestinian track. It was part of his "personal journey of atonement" following the Monica Lewinsky sex scandal (Walsh 2003). Clinton realized that the convening of a summit was a risk, but it was, in own judgment, a calculated risk. And, finally, the failure of the Israeli-Syrian track in March 2000 and the death of President Asad in June left the Israeli-Palestinian talks as the only possible avenue for achieving a crowning success. And all the while, the September 13 deadline loomed on the horizon along with the fear that 'Arafat would fulfill his threat to declare the establishment of an independent Palestinian state.

Though no party presented an attractive offer to the other, the mere fact that an American president invited Barak and 'Arafat to a summit was seen as an opportunity to achieve a breakthrough in the negotiations, if not actually to sign an agreement. The parties developed expectations with regard to the concessions the other side would make. Undoubtedly, the legacy of the successful first summit at Camp David in 1978 strengthened these expectations. The sense of the existing historical opportunity at the outset of the summit was well illustrated in the speeches of the American and Israeli delegations, particularly of Clinton, Barak, and Ben-Ami (Indyk 2009, 325; Sher 2001, 80, 83, 123, 137, 158; Enderlin 2003, 174; Ross 2005, 757). This sense was even stronger with the publication of the Clinton Parameters, as by then it was clear that Clinton would be replaced by Bush (and not Al Gore), which meant the end of the Clinton era of negotiations since Bush was likely to demonstrate a less enthusiastic approach toward the Middle East, and in parallel there were growing estimates that Sharon would replace Barak as the next Israeli prime minister (Ben-Ami 2004, 379, 400–402). Interestingly, the sense of a historic opportunity did not exist on the Palestinian side. In their view, the time was not ripe for a summit; rather, it was seen as an "ectopic pregnancy." As a result, they did not feel that they were involved in history making (Ginnosar 2005, 55; Munther Dajani 2005, 71; Hanieh 2001, 76). Malley, who generally supported the Palestinian version of Camp David, was critical of 'Arafat for being fixated on potential traps and for not being able to see the potential opportunities: "He ['Arafat] never quite realized how far the prime minister [Barak] was prepared to go, how much the US was prepared to push, how strong a hand he had been dealt. Having spent a decade building a relationship with Washington, he proved incapable of using it when he needed it most" (Malley and Agha 2001).

In terms of legitimacy—the first variable of our definition—Barak began his term with a broad coalition, which indicated that he enjoyed wide legitimacy for his policy. As time went by, however, the coalition began to crack as Barak moved forward with his peace overtures to Syria and the Palestinians. On the eve of Camp David three parties defected from Barak's coalition. He gradually lost his Knesset majority and was eventually supported by only thirty members (one-fourth of the house). Leading ministers resigned from the cabinet, which shrank from twenty-three when his term began to fourteen. The legitimacy crisis deepened as Barak was accused of pursuing a policy that was supported neither by the public nor the Knesset. With so little support at home, Barak had limited maneuvering scope (Ben-Ami 2004, 465–468; 2005,

79; Shikaki 2002, 39). After declaring his resignation in late November 2000, Barak was accused of pursuing a policy that was morally unjustified in light of coming elections, though the Supreme Court of Justice ruled that the talks were constitutionally flawless. In a way, Barak's lack of legitimacy was part of what drove him to strike a deal in his last days in office; there are many indications that he thought—or rather hoped—that a deal with the Palestinians, which would entail the end of the conflict, would tip the scales in his favor in the elections (Clinton 2004, 943). This is why Barak continued the talks until his last day in office, in spite of the continued Palestinian terror attacks, which further eroded his legitimacy at home. Perhaps he was acquainted with the famous dictum of US president Andrew Jackson in the 1830s that "one man with courage makes a majority" (Ben-Ami 2004, 467).

'Arafat, on the other hand, seemed to enjoy wider legitimacy in Palestinian society, though he too was somewhat constrained by his constituency. The fact that he symbolized the Palestinian struggle for liberation and independence set him beyond and above any other would-be Palestinian leaders. Thus the younger generation participating in Camp David, which opted for a more moderate and flexible position, preferred to fall in line with its leader. But 'Arafat had to cautiously maneuver between his close aides Abu Mazen and Abu 'Ala—the two veteran Palestinian leaders who considered themselves as the rightful heirs to the throne. Though these old comrades displayed complete loyalty to 'Arafat, they were occasionally also critical of his policy.[17] Clinton wrote, for example, that he believed that Abu Mazen and Abu 'Ala would have agreed to a deal, but they did not want to be at odds with 'Arafat (2004, 944). Both leaders thought that only 'Arafat was capable of making the necessary compromises on the existential issues (Ross 2005, 768). Publicly, therefore, they did not dare challenge him. It is no wonder that Abu 'Ala, at the end of his book, praised 'Arafat: "His courage, and the admiration he inspired amongst his people, made him the leader most able to sign such a crucial document on behalf of the Palestinians" (Qurei 2008, 327). With the outbreak of the Intifada, 'Arafat had to be more responsive to the opposition voices coming from the younger generation in the field, the Fatah Tanzim and Hamas. They usually expressed more militant views, calling for the adoption of violent means to end the occupation. It is unclear if and to what extent 'Arafat was involved in the initiation and financing of terror operations, but it is obvious that in order to shore up his legitimacy he needed to demonstrate allegiance to the rebels' cause (Shikaki 2002, 39).

In terms of the boldness and determination of the leaders to pursue the peace trail—our second variable—it is beyond dispute that Barak was determined to reach a deal. Amnon Lipkin-Shahak, the tourism minister and a former chief of staff, one of the dovish Israeli members at Camp David, wrote that Barak "was truly and genuinely ready to reach a settlement, believing he had the solution to the conflict and the ability to implement it" (2005, 44). Maoz concluded that his impression was that Barak really wanted to conclude an agreement and well knew that this would require concessions (2005, 209). In his praise, Indyk wrote that he felt admiration for Barak's boldness and courage, as he had broken the Israeli taboo on dividing Jerusalem (2009, 323). Indyk's colleague Aaron David Miller wrote: "Bold, brave, and reckless, Barak wanted an end to conflict and all claims with the Palestinians" (2008, 297). Malley and Agha, who presented a critical view of the so-called "Israeli generous offer," admitted that Barak was "a man with a mission" who "genuinely wanted a historic deal" (2001). Even Sari Nusseibeh, the Palestinian president of al-Quds University, claimed that Barak had made an unexpected leap. It was abundantly clear, Nusseibeh acknowledged, that the Israeli and American interlocutors wanted to close a deal, but the Palestinians "were skeptical from the outset and therefore perhaps not tuned to the same mode" (2005, 20). By his own testimony, which in this case seems realistic, Barak claimed he was convinced that Israel could not afford the luxury of standing around passively without making a genuine attempt to achieve peace (Ehud Barak 2005, 146). He was aware of the risks involved and understood that he alone would pay the price of failure but was determined to continue (Sher 2001, 137). He felt that possible failures should not deter leaders from doing what they think is right (Ehud Barak 2005, 147). My impression is that his failure on the Israeli-Syrian track, which he might have considered at the bottom of his heart as a missed opportunity, drove Barak to explore yet another avenue with the same zeal with which he attacked the enemy during his celebrated military career.

Clinton, like Barak, came to Camp David determined to strike a deal. I believe that the Monica Lewinsky affair and the failure of the Israeli-Syrian track emboldened him to take the risk. There could have been no better trophy than an Israeli-Palestinian deal at the end of his second term. Miller may not agree with this thesis: "It was Bill Clinton now, and the inherent optimism deeply encoded in his political DNA, and his confidence that maybe, just maybe, he could pull this off" (2008, 295). Indyk thought that Clinton, like Barak, was confident that an agreement with 'Arafat was within reach (2009, 318).

In contrast, 'Arafat's arrival at Camp David did not derive from his determination to sign a deal but rather from a desire to avoid an Israeli-American trap (Hanieh 2001, 76; Indyk 2009, 338). He did not conceal his concern about the premature convening of the summit. He told Clinton on June 15, 2000, that he "would not wish to attend a summit that has not been prepared well enough to succeed." 'Arafat was particularly apprehensive that the United States would blame him if the summit failed (Qurei 2008, 161).[18] Miller concluded that the notion that 'Arafat was dragged kicking and screaming to the summit was exaggerated, yet at the same time he came neither to make sweeping concessions nor to negotiate in a meaningful way (2008, 297). Following the Camp David washout there were divergent analyses pertaining to 'Arafat's aims and intentions; he remained a kind of enigma to both participants and followers. However, on the eve of the Clinton Parameters and Taba Talks there were certain Israeli and American officials who believed that 'Arafat was at that moment intent on cutting the deal (Indyk 2009, 364; Ben-Ami 2004, 361; Enderlin 2003, 326–327, 332). It is possible, therefore, that 'Arafat arrived to this "second round" more prepared psychologically to sign, though the final decision was still dependent on the attractiveness of the offered proposal. Apparently, what seemed attractive to Israel and the United States was not attractive enough in Palestinian eyes, or at least in 'Arafat's.

The third variable relates to the history of past interactions between the parties to the conflict, which influences the level of trust existing between them. By the year 2000 the Israelis and Palestinians had a decade of negotiations behind them and several interim agreements within the Oslo framework. While some of the negotiators became intimately acquainted with each other, the continuation of the settlement activity and the frequent delays in the implementation of agreements on the Israeli side and the sporadic use of violence on the Palestinian side were responsible for the building of a wall of mistrust (Enderlin 2003, 111–176). Particularly significant were Barak's and 'Arafat's growing mistrust and animosity toward each other, which was noticed by all involved (Ginnosar 2005, 56–57; Miller 2005, 96; Enderlin 2003, 162, 165; Pundak 2001, 37; Malley 2001; Kurtzer et al. 2013, 119–121, 133). Erekat, 'Arafat's chief negotiator, argued that "The main problem is the lack of trust between our two leaders," stemming from the fact that Barak had not stood by his commitments made at the 1999 Sharm al-Shaykh meeting (Enderlin 2003, 283). And when Barak refused to meet 'Arafat face to face at the Camp David summit, this betrayed the very essence of the term "summit," though it accurately reflected their relations. Later, Barak would shrug that he never concealed his view that he found 'Arafat "an unsuitable partner" (Ehud Barak 2005, 144). In addition, Barak's habit of speaking in a right-wing code and not always honoring his commitments called into question his readiness to reach a permanent status agreement. Likewise, 'Arafat's double-talk and ambiguous positions raised doubts regarding his true intentions. His success in developing a reliable connection with Clinton could not compensate for the lack of trust between the Israelis and Palestinians.

The fourth variable relates to the extent of the involvement of the third party in the negotiations. In contrast to some previous historical episodes where the third party played a minor role, in this case the United States—Clinton in particular—played a highly significant role. At the end of his presidential term, the enthusiastic Clinton became intimately involved in the details of the Israeli-Palestinian conflict. As he met 'Arafat some thirteen times, more than any other US president, he was in a position to fill the role of a broker. The president was assisted by an impressive peace team that was acquainted with the Israeli and Palestinian negotiators. The problem was that the Palestinian party felt that the US did not play the role of an unbiased broker. The pre–Camp David summit negotiations, wrote Abu 'Ala, "strengthened the suspicion we had that the Americans and the Israelis were coordinating their positions in advance" (2008, 136). This impression intensified during the summit, as the Palestinians felt that the Americans "embraced the Israeli demands and considered them a basis, if not a ceiling, for negotiations" (Hanieh 2001, 80). Hanieh even went so far as to describe the Israeli-American coordination as "collusion" (ibid., 84). Abu 'Ala added that the United States "was always too keen to achieve success at any price, with the result that pressure was always exercised on the weaker of the two negotiating parties, namely the Palestinians" (Qurei 2008, 326). Malley, a member of the US peace team, acknowledged that the US "ended up (often unwittingly) presenting Israeli negotiating positions" (2001; 2005, 110). The Americans did not hide their bias; Indyk admitted that "Clinton would coordinate the American positions with Barak before they were presented to the Palestinians." This was justified on the grounds that "Israel was our ally and Clinton strongly committed to its security" (2009, 308–309; 2005b, 103). Clinton's performance at Camp David was criticized by certain Israeli negotiators, who blamed him for not applying enough pressure on 'Arafat or not imposing a solution on him (Yatom 2005, 40; Ginnosar 2005, 56). Sher acknowledged that the United States cannot be blamed for the failure, but added that their insufficient resolve as mediators hampered the chances of a deal (2001, 130). Some members of the American peace team were also critical of Clinton. Miller, for example, concluded: "Lacking Kissinger's deviousness, Carter's obsessive focus, and Baker's no-nonsense toughness, Bill Clinton was in no position to help close the deal unless Barak and Arafat were literally ready to do it themselves" (2008, 315). Daniel C. Kurtzer and his coauthors argue that the failure of Camp David was a function of Clinton's personality and style: he simply lacked the ability to twist arms (2013, 147). Yet in spite of all this criticism, it should be remembered that the presentation of the Clinton Parameters was a well-conceived American attempt to reconcile the differences on the basis of previous talks; it was an attempt to learn the lesson of a failed attempt (Ross 2005, 771). Moreover, the parameters constituted "the most detailed American vision for the outline of a two-state solution that any administration had developed before or since" (Kurtzer et al. 2013, 148).

Apparently, the United States was not the only mediator in the Israeli-

Palestinian conflict, though it was certainly the major one. At times, President Mubarak, King ʿAbdallah, and Crown Prince ʿAbdallah were called in to intervene, to apply some pressure on ʿArafat and soften his position. The Arab role during the Camp David summit was negligible due to American neglect to use the Arab card, but it grew following the publication of the Clinton Parameters. Though these leaders acknowledged that the parameters constituted an opportunity ʿArafat should not refuse (at least according to the American version), they were unwilling to pressure him or to embarrass him publicly. Therefore, their mediation was limited and ultimately unsuccessful.

Among the three episodes presented in this chapter—the Camp David summit, the Clinton Parameters, and the Taba Talks—it seems that a missed opportunity on the medium level occurred in the second case. The summit cannot be considered as a missed opportunity because the Israeli position was not attractive enough for the Palestinians and because neither side was actually ready to sign a deal. Though it did represent a major shift with regard to the Israeli position on territories and Jerusalem, it was still far from the minimum Palestinian demands (Bregman 2014, 244). In addition, the Palestinian side, and ʿArafat in particular, was not yet secure in pursuing the peace path, while the United States, especially Clinton, did not play the role of an honest mediator and did not make serious attempts to offer bridging proposals. In contrast, the Clinton Parameters should have been considered as attractive enough for the Palestinian leadership. If at Camp David Israel did not present a generous offer, according to the Palestinian narrative, then the Clinton Parameters went a reasonable distance in meeting Palestinian demands in the fields of security, territory, and Jerusalem. The suggested compromise with regard to the refugee problem did not satisfy Palestinian hopes and demands, yet a realistic assessment (as made at the Taba Talks) would have led to the realization that no Israeli government would ever cross the threshold offered by Clinton. The fact that the parameters were presented by Clinton as his own bridging ideas and the fact that he was at the end of his term boosted the chances of this opportunity.[19] Beyond that, the five months that elapsed from the Camp David summit to the Clinton Parameters allowed ʿArafat enough time to assess the maneuverability of the Israeli leadership. The major variable downgrading this missed opportunity from high to medium was Barak's ostensible narrow base of support and legitimacy. Still, one should take into account that a major deal would have turned the elections into a referendum, in which the Israeli public would have been presented with an offer that was hard to reject. Palestinian acceptance of these parameters would have gone a long way in allaying Israeli fears regarding Palestinian intentions, and an agreement would have constituted a bulwark against the developing mutual mistrust. The responsibility for missing this opportunity falls on ʿArafat. Nabil ʿAmr, a minister in ʿArafat's cabinet, was courageous enough to ask: "How many times did we agree to compromises, which we later rejected in order to miss them later on? And we were never willing to draw the lessons from our behavior" (quoted in Ben-Ami 2005, 79).[20] Reuven Merhav, a top-level Israeli Foreign Ministry official who closely followed the talks as an expert on Jerusalem, concluded:

> At historic junctures, leaders must sometimes take crucial, painful decisions, which we refer to as "Ben-Gurion style" decisions. Ben-Gurion, when offered the partition plan in 1947, had to forsake Jerusalem, but he said, "Let it be so; we need a Jewish commonwealth in Palestine. For that I am willing to pay a price and let us see what the future brings." Arafat may have been seen a successful leader until the [Camp David] summit, but unfortunately in the summit he showed himself to be a complete failure. He had great achievements while struggling uphill, yet turned out to be a terrible disappointment upon reaching the peak. He was no Ben-Gurion. He could have assumed what is called in Arabic the *burda*, the cloak of the leader, and brought his people to the Promised Land, but he missed the opportunity. (Merhav 2005, 175)

The historical analysis demonstrated that any attempt to draw symmetry between the Israeli and Palestinian responses to the Clinton Parameters is unfounded. At no point did the behavior of ʿArafat and his negotiating team reflect determination or urgency. Perhaps they were under the impression that the Bush administration would offer them a better deal, while Sharon's election was considered less ominous. In contrast, Barak and his "peace team" were highly aware of the time factor and therefore were racing to close a deal before the end of Clinton's term. Nabil Shaʿath commented that if what was proposed at Camp David "was too little, [then] Taba, was too late" (quoted in Meital 2006, 89). Indeed, at Taba Clinton was no longer in office and the new Bush administration was just learning the ropes. In contrast, the Clinton Parameters, standing between these two events, was a propitious moment for a deal—but it was missed. Nevertheless, the parameters did leave an important legacy for future negotiations.

Another factor that reduced the missed opportunity to medium level was that though an agreement was not signed, significant progress was achieved. Most of the negotiators agreed that any future settlement would have to rely on the understandings reached based on the Camp David summit, the Clinton Parameters, and the Taba Talks. A typical assessment was made by Malley: "Taboos were shattered, the unspoken got spoken, and, during that period, Israelis and Palestinians reached an unprecedented level of understanding of what it will take to end the conflict" (2001; see also Indyk 2009, 337–338; Klein 2003, 192). Matz was even more assertive: "Israeli concessions around and after CD II, and President Clinton's guidelines will be seen in the view of history as the largest step toward finding the acceptable ground for settlement. Taba will be seen as the occasion on which the negotiators demonstrated that an agreement between them was, probably, reachable" (2003b, 98).[21] Thus the debate surrounding the episode is not merely academic but has relevance to the ongoing conflict.

NOTES

1. Ben-Ami was the minister of internal security. Though David Levy was foreign affairs minister, it was Ben-Ami—considered close to Barak—who was involved in the negotiations with the Palestinians. In November 2000, upon Levy's resignation, he was given charge of that ministry as well.

2. It must be emphasized that the Israeli sources gave a more positive account of the Stockholm channel than did their Palestinian counterparts.

3. Sixty-one votes were needed to topple Barak.

4. http://www.mfa.gov.il/MFA/Government/Speeches%20by%20Israeli%20 leaders/2000/Statement%20by%20PM%20Barak%20prior%20to%20Departure%20 for%20the%20C.

5. There are numerous accounts of the proceedings, some providing a day-by-day account (Ross 2005, 650–711; Qurei 2008, 176–249; Ben-Ami 2004, 129–232; Sher 2001, 153–235; Indyk 2009, 306–340; Enderlin 2003, 177–260). For a thoughtful analysis of the US role, see Kurtzer et al. 2013, 105–153; Bregman 2014, 217–246.

6. In this account Abu 'Ala is more generous, as Indyk claims that the Palestinians' map presented to Clinton offered the Israelis less than 2 percent of the West Bank for settlement blocs (2009, 334).

7. Indyk claimed that the Palestinians agreed to unimpeded Israeli use of West Bank space and IDF access to designated areas in the Jordan Valley on specified roads in the event of an emergency arising from an eastern front threat (2009, 331). Qurei did not mention these clauses in his most detailed unofficial draft summary of the talks (2008, 251–260).

8. Formally, the Palestinians offered Israeli self-rule at the Wailing Wall and in the Jewish Quarter, but members of the Israeli delegation in Camp David understood that 'Arafat would be willing to accept Israeli sovereignty there (Klein 2001, 51–52).

9. There is a hint that Barak may have contemplated the idea of conceding sovereignty in the Temple Mount to the Palestinians should this lead to an agreement (Drucker 2002, 207).

10. The quote gives the gist of Clinton's remarks. Because there is no written document, there are some differences between the versions presented by the participants and observers. See Shamir and Maddy-Weitzman 2005, 251–255; Klein 2003, 100–111, 199–203; Sher 2001, 360–363; Indyk 2009, 366, 441–445; Ross 2005, 748–753; Qurei 2008, 279–285; Golan 2007, 49–54; Ben-Ami 2004, 380–381; Beilin 2001, 191–193, 289–293; Rabinovich 2004, 156–158; Enderlin 2003, 334–339; Kurtzer et al. 2013, 147–151; Bregman 2014, 262–267.

11. Ten voted in favor, two against, and two abstained (Sher 2001, 369).

12. Ben-Ami wrote that the chief of staff's going public to criticize the government's

endorsement of the parameters as an existential threat to Israel was "tantamount to a coup d'état" (2005, 79).

13. For the non-paper by Moratinos, see http://www.mideastweb.org/moratinos.htm, accessed April 20, 2012. See also in Qurei 2008, 352–364. For other accounts, see Golan 2007, 55–61; Ben-Ami 2004, 433–451; Indyk 2009, 371–372; Klein 2003, 111–126; Qurei 2008, 294–327; Sher 2001, 397–415; Beilin 2001, 198–222; Matz 2003a, 96–105; 2003b, 92–98; Enderlin 2003, 351–357. Barak claimed that Moratinos "fabricated the so-called Taba understandings" (2005, 141).

14. Matz claimed that the Palestinians agreed to the Israeli annexation of 3.1 percent, while Israel demanded 8 percent, with 2 percent of that being in the form of lease (Matz 2003a, 101–102).

15. This quote served as the motto of a very long academic article by Zeev Maoz: "Never Missing an Opportunity to Miss an Opportunity: The Israeli Nonpolicy of Peace in the Middle East" (2004, 386–495). Elsewhere (2005, 203–209), Maoz referred to Camp David as an Israeli missed opportunity. Interestingly, this quote entered also Malley and Agha 2001.

16. The comparison with 1947 has been made several times by Israelis and Palestinians. See Meridor in Shamir and Maddy-Weitzman 2005, 232; Merhav in ibid., 175; Maoz in ibid., 204; and Enderlin 2003, 344.

17. At one point, Ben-Ami quoted Abu 'Ala to the effect that "All this obsession with al-Haram al-Sharif is all 'Arafat's business; the rest of the Palestinian leadership does not share [his view] in this regard" (2004, 446).

18. Clinton did indeed promise 'Arafat he would not be blamed in case the summit failed, but he broke the promise (Qurei 2008, 161).

19. This view is not shared by Kurtzer et al.: "One can argue that the parameters were almost bound to fail because they were put forward just before Clinton left office" (2013, 149). They speculate, however, that the parameters would have stood a better chance had they been put on the table immediately after Camp David (ibid., 153).

20. Interestingly, this quote resembles one of Abba Eban's statements: "They [the Palestinians] have persistently rejected proposals conceived largely in their own interest, only to look back to them nostalgically when they have receded from view" (1983, 229).

21. Here Matz added a more controversial sentence: "I think there will never be a better opportunity than was present at Taba to reach an agreement" (2003b, 98).

CHAPTER 21

THE ARAB PEACE INITIATIVE

2002–2014

THE ARAB SUMMIT held in Beirut on March 27–28, 2002, adopted an initiative to solve the Arab-Israeli conflict, which would soon become known as the Arab Peace Initiative (API). This was a modified version of a Saudi proposal devised by Crown Prince ʿAbdallah and outlined in an interview with American journalist Thomas Friedman a month earlier. The API was presented to Israel at the height of al-Aqsa Intifada and therefore did not elicit a serious Israeli response. It has actually remained on the Arab agenda since, to be regularly reconfirmed by successive Arab summits, but successive Israeli governments have either ignored it or have not recognized it as a viable peace initiative. This chapter will attempt to analyze if and to what extent the API has been a plausible missed opportunity.

THE EPISODE

The election of Ariel Sharon as prime minister in February 2001, the relentless terror attacks of the Intifada, and Israeli military retaliation operations in the areas of the Palestinian Authority (PA) effectively ended any further peace negotiations. The United States, as mediator, was not engaged in pursuing peace talks but rather in seeking a formula for ending the violence. During 2001–2002 there were three attempts at reaching a cease-fire. The first was led by US senator George Mitchell, whose report was published in April 2001; the second was by the head of the CIA, George Tenet, who issued the Tenet Plan in June 2001; and the third was General Anthony Zinni's "Joint Goals" plan in March 2002. All these endeavors failed to achieve the declared target of an Israeli-Palestinian cease-fire (Golan 2007, 63–68). In light of the continuing violence, the timing of the peace overture offered by the Saudi crown prince ʿAbdallah—no less than the initiative itself—caught many by surprise.

On February 17, 2002, in the interview with Friedman, the crown prince revealed the premise of the plan that later became known as the Saudi Initiative: full Israeli withdrawal from all the occupied territories in accordance with UN resolutions, including in Jerusalem, in exchange for full Arab normalization of relations with Israel. ʿAbdallah told Friedman that his aim was "to find a way to make it clear to the Israeli people that the Arabs don't reject or despise them. But the Arab people do reject what their leadership is now doing to the Palestinians, which is inhumane and oppressive. And I thought of this as a possible signal to the Israeli people" (Friedman 2002a). The Saudi idea was not created in a vacuum; according to Friedman's testimony, Jordan, Morocco, and some key Arab League officials had been deliberating on it in private but had not dared to broach it publicly until one of the "big boys"— Egypt or Saudi Arabia—took the lead. Marwan Muasher, the Jordanian ambassador in the United States and later foreign minister, relates that King Husayn was in fact the originator of the multilateral Arab approach, as early as 1998, which stipulated that in return for full Israeli withdrawal from the occupied territories and the founding of a Palestinian state, the Arab states would establish diplomatic ties with Israel, initiate trade relations, and sign a security pact. Husayn thought that only Mubarak could sponsor this idea but, in any case, a lukewarm US response and Husayn's illness and death foiled the effort (Muasher 2008, 106–107).[1] In other words, Crown Prince ʿAbdallah refined an idea that had been floated though not pursued. In describing the plan as a "trial balloon," he employed a face-saving formula that would enable him to immediately withdraw it in case reactions were too harsh and critical. Significantly, the initiative was directed at the Israeli people and not the government.

Four goals may explain the Saudi move at this particular juncture. First, as indicated above, it was meant to solidify the Saudi image as a loyal American ally. The involvement of Saudi citizens in the 9/11 terrorist attacks had seriously damaged the Saudi image in the United States. The initiative was meant to demonstrate that the Saudis (and Arabs and Muslims in general) are a peace-loving people. In fact, ʿAbdallah's interview with Friedman was part of the Saudi campaign to better explain themselves to the world in light of the fact that Saudi citizens were involved in the devastating attacks several months earlier. Second, the continuation and escalation of al-Aqsa Intifada was causing rising instability throughout the Middle East, threatening to erode the legitimacy and credibility of moderate pro-Western Arab regimes. A successful Saudi Initiative might stabilize the region, it was thought. Third, in the absence of any serious Arab role in the peace process, the Saudis chose to fill what they perceived as a leadership vacuum in the Arab world. Finally, perhaps ʿAbdallah thought that such an initiative would strengthen the moderate faction within the Saudi elite against the radical fundamentalists challenging the legitimacy of the al-Saʿud dynasty (Podeh 2014, 586; 2007a, 6; Kostiner 2009, 422–423).

At that point, Jerusalem did not respond, as the Saudi Initiative—it was argued—was not officially presented to Israel. It soon became known, however, that Israel could not accept the initiative because the call for full Israeli withdrawal posed a threat to its security. Indeed, Sharon ideologically could not endorse an Arab initiative that would commit him to relinquish parts of Greater Eretz Israel. However, the positive and sometimes enthusiastic reactions to the initiative in the international arena did not allow for an immediate rejection, since this could have left the impression that Israel was a peace spoiler. There are indications that Sharon in private tried to learn more about the initiative though various intermediaries, including the Jewish billionaire Daniel Abraham, who visited Riyadh at his behest. According to one testimony, Sharon met Turki al-Faysal, the Saudi head of intelligence.[2] When President Moshe Katsav suggested meeting 'Abdallah in Saudi Arabia, his offer was rejected because it was interpreted as an Israeli attempt to achieve normalization before actually signing any agreement. As it became clear that the Saudis would not follow Sadat's model, the Israeli position hardened.

Regardless of the unencouraging Israeli position and in light of the upcoming Arab summit in Beirut, a vivid Arab dialogue erupted concerning the possibility of adopting a modified version of the initiative as an all-Arab peace plan. 'Abdallah had caught even the Arab states by surprise; mindful of the lessons of the fiasco of the first Fahd Plan in 1981 (see chapter 13), the Saudis hoped to form an Arab consensus prior to the convening of the summit. They foresaw two possible spoilers. The first was Egypt's Mubarak, who did not display enthusiasm because it was a Saudi-led initiative with the potential to undermine Egypt's perceived leading role among Arab nations and its status as the United States' best Arab ally. The second was Syria, which had already demonstrated its ability to frustrate Saudi moves with the Fahd Plan. The task of persuading Mubarak to support the initiative was easier, since he could not in principle oppose a move that dovetailed with the Camp David I policy, though he did express his uneasiness by not attending the summit. Like Egypt, Syria's discomfort stemmed from not having been consulted in advance. It particularly feared that the Saudi Initiative would not address the issue of Israeli withdrawal from the Golan Heights. It also objected to normalizing relations with Israel, preferring the term "normal relations" ('alaqat tabi'iyya). In addition, Lebanon, under Syria's sway, feared that the issue of the four hundred thousand refugees in its territory would not be addressed by the initiative either. As the summit's host, Lebanon felt in a position to press the issue. In the first half of March, top-level Syrian, Lebanese, and Saudi consultations were held, with the participation of Jordan as an avid supporter of the initiative. President Asad endorsed the initiative after receiving promises that his demands would be addressed. The Palestinian response was encouraging; a senior minister described the initiative as "the most important in the Arab world since the Madrid Conference." 'Arafat too saw it as a "strong platform for achieving a comprehensive peace." Yet the PLO was also disturbed by the absence of a reference to the refugee question. Surprisingly, Iraq and Libya voiced only mild criticism (Podeh 2014, 587; Muasher 2008, 118–124).

Israel, for its part, continued to focus on quelling the Intifada. Following a series of bombings, Sharon decided to ground 'Arafat in Ramallah in his presidential compound. On March 11, Israel launched the largest military offensive in the West Bank since 1967. The next day the UN passed Security Council Resolution 1397, calling for an end to the violence and implementation of the Mitchell and Tenet recommendations. No less important was the fact that the resolution, for the first time, supported the establishment of a Palestinian state, affirming the vision that "two states, Israel and Palestine, live side by side within secure and recognized boundaries" (Muasher 2008, 123; Meital 2006, 149). As the summit approached and it became clear that the initiative would be the main item on its agenda, Sharon adopted a more moderate position, at least publicly. On March 23 he expressed readiness to present his terms for peace before the Arab summit and asked the United States to arrange this visit. Arab leaders ridiculed the idea, interpreting it as a public relations ploy and another attempt to receive Arab recognition without reciprocating. In an interview on the occasion of the Jewish holiday of Passover, Sharon called the initiative a positive development; he added, however, that its terms were too vague and that the reference to Israeli withdrawal to the 1967 borders was unacceptable (Caspit 2002). An editorial in the Israeli daily *Haaretz* on the eve of the summit was not impressed by Sharon's "moderation" and stressed that Israel was missing an important opportunity for peace.[3]

On March 28 the Arab summit unanimously endorsed the Arab Peace Initiative, based on the Saudi Initiative with certain modifications. It called for full Israeli withdrawal from all the territories occupied since June 1967 and Israel's acceptance of an independent Palestinian state with East Jerusalem as its capital, in return for the establishment of normal relations between the Arab states and Israel in the context of a comprehensive peace. The plan explicitly stated that Israel should withdraw from the Golan Heights and the remaining occupied territories in Southern Lebanon. With regard to the Palestinian refugees, the achievement of a just solution to this problem would have "to be agreed upon in accordance with UN General Assembly Resolution 194." This short and somewhat ambiguous phrasing was the product of long Arab deliberations, which attempted to find a formula that would also allay Israeli fears of full implementation of the Palestinian Right of Return (Muasher 2008, 120–128). By declaring that the agreement would have to be agreed upon, the Arab states gave Israel a say (if not actual veto power) on the implementation of this right. Yet in order to assuage Lebanese apprehensions, it was added that the plan "assures the rejection of all forms of Palestinian patriation which conflict with the special circumstances of the Arab host countries." In return, the Arab states offered to "consider the Arab-Israeli conflict ended, and enter into a peace agreement with Israel, and provide security for all the states in the regions." The plan was directed not only at the Israeli government but also at the Israeli public, with a view to allow the Arab countries and Israel "to live in peace and good neighborliness and provide future generations with security, stability and prosperity" (Podeh 2014, 588–589; Kostiner 2009, 423–424; Muasher 2008, 127–128). No less important was the Saudi king 'Abdallah's speech at the opening session of the summit, which was also directed at the Israeli public:

> Allow me at this point to directly address the Israeli people, to say to them that the use of violence, for more than fifty years, has only resulted in more violence and destruction, and that the Israeli people are as far as they have ever been from security and peace, notwithstanding military superiority and despite efforts to subdue and oppress. Peace emanates from the heart and mind, and not from the barrel of a cannon, or the exploding warhead of a missile. The time has come for Israel to put its trust in peace after it has gambled on war for decades without success. (quoted in Meital 2006, 151)

"For the first time since the start of the Arab-Israeli conflict," wrote the Jordanian king 'Abdallah in his autobiography, "Arab states had formally and unanimously made an offer to Israel for normal relations as a basis for ending the conflict" (Abdullah 2011, 205).

The publication of the API regrettably coincided with a horrible terrorist attack, carried out on the eve of Passover, when families would be sitting down to celebrate the seder. A Hamas suicide bomber killed twenty-nine and wounded about 150 Israelis celebrating the holiday in a hotel in the beachside city of Netanya. The timing of the operation was carefully chosen by Hamas to hit the Israeli people during a major celebration and to stymie the launching of the API. On March 31 another terrorist operation by Hamas killed fifteen people in a restaurant in Haifa, raising the toll of Israelis killed in suicide operations during March to 130 (Meital 2006, 152). The Sharon government felt compelled to retaliate, announcing the decision to launch a massive military operation (called Defensive Shield) against the PA aimed at uprooting terrorism and isolating 'Arafat. In this atmosphere of violence and hatred, the Israeli response to the API was understandably not encouraging. One unofficial reaction was that "there was nothing new in the resolutions" and that Israel could not accept a resolution calling for the return of the Palestinians and withdrawal to the 1967 borders. Both the API and the military action were launched when the Israeli Knesset was in recess. Upon a special call from the opposition, Sharon delivered a statement in the Knesset, explaining the reasons for launching the military operation. With regard to the API, he acknowledged the existence of the "first seeds of change" in the age-old Arab conception that negated the Israeli State. Though the Arab position in Beirut included "extreme demands," he welcomed the first-ever Saudi recognition of Israel's right to exist in safe and recognized boundaries. He expressed willingness to unconditionally meet any moderate and responsible Arab leader and called on the United States to lead this initiative; personally, however, he opted for "an interim long-term solution." In the political debate that followed, only the leftist parties called for a clear Israeli acceptance of the API; they ridiculed Sharon's call for a meeting with Arab leaders as hollow rhetoric. The head of the opposition, Yossi Sarid, called for the convening of an international conference based on the API. The Likud-led statement adopted by the Knesset at the end of the debate ignored the API, referring only to Sharon's call to other moderate Arab states to act for peace (Podeh 2014, 590).

The US response to the API was not enthusiastic. The Bush administration's first fourteen months in office were characterized by a "hands-off approach" to the Middle East. In the immediate post-9/11 period, Bush was preoccupied with fighting against international terrorism and the Afghanistan War (Bush 2011, 126–151; Rice 2011, 71–121). Moreover, his determination to seek out and destroy Iraqi weapons of mass destruction meant that Middle Eastern problems, even the peace process, were seen primarily through the prism of their possible implications for the Iraqi question. With regard to the Saudi Initiative, Bush did not fully grasp its potential. He preferred implementation of the Tenet and Mitchell reports as they offered an immediate solution to the most urgent problems of violence, security, and lack of confidence. His national security adviser, Condoleezza Rice, thought that "it was a bold proposal and could have been an important point of departure for negotiations," but its timing "could not have been worse" (2011, 136). On February 21 the State Department defined the Saudi Initiative as a "significant and positive step." A few days later, Bush expressed publicly for the first time his support of the initiative, clarifying that only with the cessation of hostilities and terrorist attacks could it be implemented. On April 4 he made an important speech, which linked the summit's resolutions with the Israeli-Palestinian predicament:

> The recent Arab League support of Crown Prince 'Abdallah's initiative for peace is promising, is hopeful, because it acknowledges Israel's right to exist. And it raises the hope of sustained constructive Arab involvement in the

search for peace. This builds on a tradition of visionary leadership begun by President Sadat and King Hussein and carried forward by President Mubarak and King 'Abdallah. Now other Arab states must rise to this occasion and accept Israel as a nation and as a neighbor. Peace with Israel is the only avenue for prosperity and success for a new Palestinian state. The Palestinian people deserve peace and opportunity to better their lives. (Bush 2002)

At the end of his speech Bush announced his intention to send secretary of state Colin Powell to the Middle East to seek broad international support for his vision. Yet the tour was largely a blunder; it failed to stop the vicious circle of Palestinian suicide attacks and Israel's retaliation operations that undermined the chances of a dialogue. In the midst of the political impasse, Bush invited 'Abdallah to his ranch in Crawford, Texas—an honor reserved for special guests—on April 25. During this meeting the crown prince presented a modified peace plan. The new version was intended as a synthesis of the "vision" of the original Saudi Initiative and the necessity to deal with the "reality," as embodied in the Tenet and Mitchell reports. Significantly, it was more "friendly" to the United States and Israel: it did not mention the refugee problem and did not specify Israeli withdrawal to the 1967 borders. In presenting a plan that had not been approved by the Arab summit, 'Abdallah showed a measure of statesmanship. Though this behavior largely stemmed from the Saudi desire and need to improve its image in the US, it was an ingenious plan with potential to lead to the renewal of the peace process. Israel rejected the proposal, maintaining that there was "nothing new in the new initiative," and that it was basically devised to rescue 'Arafat and the Palestinian Authority.[4] Even Foreign Minister Peres was quoted to the effect that both Bush's and the Saudi visions are "like lights at the end of the tunnel—but with no tunnel" (Podeh 2014, 591; quoted in Friedman 2002a).

When Sharon visited the United States on May 5–8, he made every effort to delegitimize 'Arafat by exposing his responsibility for the Palestinian terrorist attacks. He also tried to malign Saudi Arabia while there. Based on documents seized during Defensive Shield, a special portfolio on alleged Saudi support for Hamas and the martyrs' families was delivered to officials and journalists. The Israeli campaign was timed to undermine Saudi credibility as a US ally and a possible peace partner. By the end of his visit, cut short by another terrorist attack, Sharon had achieved his aim: any serious negotiations were postponed to the distant future, while the immediate issue on the agenda was the question of reforms within the PA. A *New York Times* headline succinctly captured the situation: "Everyone Has a Peace Plan. And They Can All Wait" (Purdum 2002).

The fact that the Israeli decision makers attempted to besmirch the API can be explained by political considerations or unreceptiveness. Yet what was surprising was that even Military Intelligence (MI), which is not subordinate to political considerations, did not grasp its full meaning and potential. In a conference dealing with "the state of the nation," held in May 2002, the head of MI focused on the implications of Operation Defensive Shield and the looming threats from Iran, Syria, Hizballah, and Hamas. He noted the existence of moderate elements in the region such as Egypt, Saudi Arabia, and Jordan but completely ignored the API. In other words, even a short while after the proclamation of the API, MI did not attach due importance to the major change that had occurred in the Arab position since 1967 (Podeh 2014, 591; Ze'evi-Farkash 2002).

In May–June 2002, Egypt and Saudi Arabia, with the cooperation of both Jordan and the PLO, attempted to promote the API in Washington, but to no avail. On June 24, Bush delivered the Rose Garden speech that outlined the American view of a future Israeli-Palestinian settlement. The speech constituted a compromise between the positions of the State Department, the Pentagon, and the White House. "My vision," Bush declared, "is two states, living side by side in peace and security. There is simply no way to achieve that peace until all parties fight terror." But Bush's vision of a Palestinian state was with "a new and different Palestinian leadership." He talked about normalization of relations between Israel and the Arabs but ignored the Saudi Initiative. In many ways, this speech heralded the birth of a new American peace plan, the Road Map, which was formally launched in April 2003, in parallel to the occupation of Iraq (see chapter 22) (Meital 2006, 157; Golan 2007, 73–76; Podeh 2014, 592). In retrospect, Bush's speech did not trigger the anticipated reactions. The Arab states were particularly dismayed by the US position, which seemed, yet again, to dovetail with the Israeli posture. In many respects, the speech signaled the death knell for the Arab peace plan.

The Road Map referred only indirectly to the API. It was stated that the envisaged settlement would be based on the foundations of the Madrid Conference, the principle of land for peace, UN Resolutions 242, 338, and 1397, agreements previously reached by the parties, "and the initiative of Saudi Crown Prince Abdullah—endorsed by the Beirut Arab League Summit—calling for acceptance of Israel as a neighbor living in peace and security, in the context of a comprehensive settlement" (Golan 2007, 190; Elend-Rif 2009, 56–60). As expected, the parties to the conflict focused on advancing the Road Map, at the expense of the API. In Israel, the Sharon government continued to delegitimize the API. This was the situation until the outbreak of the Second Lebanon War in summer 2006. During this period important changes took place: 'Arafat had died in November 2004 and was replaced by Abu Mazen in January 2005, while Sharon completed his unilateral Disengagement Plan from Gaza in August 2005 before resigning from the Likud Party and founding a new party, Kadima, in November 2005. As a result, elections were brought forward to March 2006, but Sharon suffered a stroke and was replaced by his deputy, Ehud Olmert, who won an impressive victory in May and set up a new government with Tzipi Livni as foreign minister. At the same time, Hamas won the Palestinian elections to parliament and a government led by Ismaiʿl Haniyeh was formed (Podeh 2014, 592).

The US conquest of Iraq and Israel's Second Lebanon War brought about an implicit alliance between Israel, Egypt, Saudi Arabia, Jordan, and other moderate Arab countries. This was the result of Iran's growing influence in the Gulf and the Middle East, Iraq's coming under Shiʿite rule, the rising status of Hizballah following its perceived victory over the IDF, and the split in the Palestinian camp between Fatah and Hamas (Podeh 2014, 592; Bahgat 2007, 49–50). In light of these changes in the regional balance of power, coupled with the deadlock in the Palestinian track caused by the Fatah-Hamas rift, the API suddenly appeared as a possible instrument for igniting the peace process and building a new moderate coalition. In September 2006 there were rumors that Olmert had secretly met in Amman with Bandar bin-Sultan, the able Saudi ambassador to the US from 1983–2005 and now the chairman of the National Security Council, to discuss possible Saudi involvement in the peace process (Podeh 2014, 592–593; Bahgat 2007, 54). In the past, Bandar had played the role of a discreet messenger between Israelis and Arabs (see chapter 19). A few months later, on November 26, Olmert made a speech on the occasion of David Ben-Gurion's memorial at Sde Boker, in which he extended an invitation to Abu Mazen to hold "real, open, genuine and serious dialogue" following the cessation of violence. In this endeavor, Olmert promised to seek the assistance of Egypt, Jordan, Saudi Arabia, and the Gulf states. He further added that:

> The voices emanating from those states regarding the need for recognition and normalization of relations with the state of Israel—including, for example, some parts in the Saudi peace initiative—are positive, and I intend to invest efforts in order to advance the connection with those states and strengthen their support of direct bilateral negotiations between us and the Palestinians . . . The international circumstances which were created, specifically at this time, allow you and us to take a courageous step, which involves the need to make painful compromises and forgo those dreams which were part of our national ethos for so many years.[5] (quoted in Podeh 2014, 593)

The return of the Saudi Initiative, dressed as the API, was not coincidental; in March 2007, Riyadh was supposed to host the annual Arab summit. As the kingdom played a mediation role in the Iraqi and Palestinian scenes (in the latter it engineered the Mecca Agreement in February which led to the establishment of a Fatah-Hamas National Unity government), it was expected that it would play also a role in the Arab arena in promoting the API. Indeed, the pre-Riyadh summit saw hectic diplomatic activity by the United States, the European Union, and the United Nations aimed at persuading Saudi Arabia and the Arab League to adopt an "improved formula" of the API. Olmert reiterated his praise of the Saudi Initiative—making a distinction between it and the API—and ʿAbdallah's leadership qualities and personality (he was now king). In one interview he even bragged that "There is a real chance that in the next five years Israel will be able to reach a peace settlement with its enemies," adding that "things which have not happened before are taking place and ripening. We need to exploit this opportunity and to leverage it wisely and with responsibility" (quoted in Podeh 2014, 593). Olmert was not alone in his position; he was supported by leading members of the Labor and Kadima parties. Foreign Minister Livni expressed a more reserved position,[6] though the ministry's staff members were pushing for a more robust response. For the first time, the API received support from nonparliamentary elements in Israeli society. In contrast, the right-wing and religious parties repeated their opposition to any initiative—Saudi, Arab, or otherwise.

In tandem with the public diplomacy, there were some secret contacts between Israelis and Arabs regarding the possible promotion of the API. In the immediate aftermath of the Second Lebanon War, several Israeli civilian society members (including ex-minister Moshe Shachal; ex–chief of staff Amnon Lipkin-Shahak; Yuval Rabin, a businessman and son of the late prime minister Yitzhak Rabin; and businessmen Koby Huberman, Pini Meidan, Gil Berger, and others) established a group called "Circles of Peace," which attempted to exploit the opportunity created in the postwar period in order to promote a peaceful dialogue with the Arab world on the basis of the API. The group initially aimed at generating a more congenial atmosphere in Israeli society toward the Arab plan, which was hardly recognized.[7] The first opportunity it had to advance its ideas was when the Spanish Foreign Ministry organized an event marking the fifteenth anniversary of the Madrid Conference, on January 10–12, 2007, with the participation of leading Palestinian, Israeli, Jordanian, Syrian, and Lebanese diplomats who had been involved in the peace process since the Madrid Conference. The chairmen of the Arab League and the Gulf Cooperation Council (GCC) took part as well. In a speech delivered in Arabic, the Iraqi-born Shachal suggested that the Arab League invite Circles of Peace to offer its response to the API and investigate the possibility of furthering the peace process on its basis. Usama al-Baz, the close adviser of President Mubarak, enquired whether it would be possible to enlist the support of the

Olmert government to the API. During the personal meetings the possibility was raised for the first time that Olmert might be invited to a special session of the Arab League, at which he would express his willingness to negotiate with the Arab states on the basis of the API. Such a visit, it was thought, would have the same psychological effect on Israeli and Arab societies as had the Sadat visit in Jerusalem in November 1979 (Eldar 2012).[8]

Following the second Madrid Conference, Jibril Rajoub, the ex-Palestinian head of the security apparatus in the West Bank, flew to Cairo and received Mubarak's consent to the move. Upon his return, Rajoub met with Circles of Peace and notified them of the Egyptian nod. Later, it was further revealed that Mubarak elicited the consent of the Saudi, Jordanian, and Moroccan kings, as well as the Gulf sheikhdoms, to the idea. The consultations continued, and it was agreed that a preparatory meeting would take place in Cairo on April 15. Meanwhile, Circles of Peace met with Olmert on March 22 seeking his approval for the move. The Israeli prime minister thought that the idea was "worthwhile," but said that he did not enjoy enough political support for such a risky move; he suggested, therefore, that Shachal participate in the upcoming Cairo meeting "with the knowledge—though not the approval—of the prime minister." Shachal insisted that this approval was vital; Olmert said he would think it over (Eldar 2002). In the end, the Cairo meeting never took place and the idea soon evaporated. Just a week before an important Arab summit, a different response by Olmert might have made a difference.

Incidentally, the next day Thomas Friedman, who had played a role in introducing the 'Abdallah Initiative in February 2002, published an article in which he encouraged the king to fly from the Riyadh summit to Jerusalem and deliver the API personally to the Israeli people. Such a move, he opined, would resemble Sadat's historic visit and "could end this conflict once and for all" (Friedman 2007).

On March 29 the Arab summit convened in Riyadh. Its final communiqué reiterated the Arab commitment to the API, though the Arab leaders were unwilling to introduce changes in its text so long as Israel had not formally responded to it (Podeh 2014, 595; Elend-Rif 2009, 78–81). Yet the summit set up a follow-up committee (the Arab Quartet, composed of Egypt, Jordan, Saudi Arabia, and the Emirates) tasked to market the API in the US, the EU, and Israel. The Egyptian and Jordanian foreign ministers—representing the Arab League—arrived in Israel on July 25 for a short meeting with Olmert, Livni, and other officials. The visit took place a short while after the Hamas military takeover of Gaza, which led Abu Mazen to set up a rival Fatah government in the West Bank, thereby institutionalizing the separation between the two parts of the Palestinian homeland. This event largely overshadowed the Arab visit in Israel, leading many Israelis to doubt the API's chances of offering any

solution to the Israeli-Palestinian conflict in light of the institutional split between Fatah and Hamas (Podeh 2014, 595).

The renewed effort to launch the API did not receive any more of an enthusiastic response from the United States than had the original plan; in mid-
July, Bush called for the convening of an international meeting aimed at promoting the establishment of a Palestinian state. After prolonged consultations
regarding its agenda, the Annapolis Conference opened on November 27 with
an impressive participation of delegations from sixteen Arab countries, five
Islamic countries, as well as other states. At the end, the final communiqué
stated that the Israeli-Palestinian negotiations on the final status agreement
would commence in mid-December, with the aim of finalizing the discussions
at the end of 2008. The implementation of the agreement was conditioned
on the fulfillment of the obligations of the two parties within the Road Map
under American supervision. Though the final communiqué did not mention
the API, Olmert related to its importance in his speech at the conference. In
practical terms, the Annapolis Conference led to direct negotiations between
Olmert and Abu Mazen (see chapter 23), though the API again was thrown in
the dustbin (Podeh 2014, 595; Elend-Rif 2009, 86–88, 92–95).

On July 30, 2008, Olmert resigned as a result of charges of corruption
leveled against him. He remained as the head of a caretaker government until
the elections, scheduled for February 10, 2009. The impending elections in
both the US (November 2008) and Israel created an opportunity to advance
various political ideas that could serve as a possible basis for new policies in
their aftermath. Thus the candidate of the Democratic Party, Barack Obama,
was quoted to the effect that "The Israelis would be crazy not to accept this
initiative [the API]. It would give them peace with the Muslim world from
Indonesia to Morocco" (quoted in Elend-Rif 2009, 97). In Israel, President
Peres declared at the UN assembly in September that the Arab "three no's of
Khartoum" had been replaced by an Arab peace plan and called on the Saudi
king to promote his initiative, which might bring comprehensive peace. He
also invited Arab leaders to come to Jerusalem to initiate a dialogue. Visiting
Cairo a month later, Peres discussed with Mubarak possible ways of reviving
the API. The Saudi foreign minister, Saʿud al-Faysal, stated that Peres's support of the API was "better late than never" and expressed the hope that the
next Israeli prime minister would adopt the plan. When decorated with the
British knighthood in November, Peres stated that the initiative reflected a
"complete change" in the Arab position, and though it was not perfect, it
nevertheless allowed the signing of a peace agreement with the Arab states
for the price of an agreement with the Palestinians. Positive remarks were also
made by Minister of Defense Ehud Barak and Minister of the Interior Meir
Sheetrit. Foreign Minister Livni, however, vacillated: on the one hand, she

316 CHANCES FOR PEACE

described the API as "an historic opportunity that should not be missed"; on the other, she emphasized that it could not be accepted in its present form and text (Podeh 2014, 596–597; Elend-Rif 2009, 99–102).

In the period preceding the elections, there were attempts to boost Israeli society's awareness of the positive elements included in the API. To this end, the Geneva Initiative and the Council for Peace and Security published ads in the major newspapers, marketing the API as a revolution in Arab thinking and presenting a historical opportunity to Israel. Some ads were paid for by Daniel Abraham, a longtime proponent of peace and the API, in the *New York Times*. Surprisingly, at the same time the PA financed the advertisement of full-page ads in several Israeli newspapers, which presented a Hebrew version of the API, decorated with the flags of fifty-seven Islamic states; this was to symbolize that Israel's acceptance of the API would mean the recognition of not only twenty-two Arab states but also all Islamic countries, which endorsed the API on April 3, 2002. Likewise, Peace Now published an ad in the Palestinian *al-Quds* calling for acceptance of the API. It was not a surprise that this campaign aroused a lively dialogue in the Israeli media (Podeh 2014, 596; Elend-Rif 2009, 98–99, 103–106).

The results of the elections both in the United States and Israel brought disappointment to the pro-API camp: Obama's initial enthusiasm, as indicated above, seemed to evaporate and he did not embrace it as a possible vehicle for peace negotiations, while Netanyahu, now the prime minister for the second time, and his leading coalition parties—Avigdor Lieberman's Yisrael Beiteinu and Eli Yishai's Shas—were all against the API. Lieberman was even quoted to the effect that the API was "a recipe for the destruction of Israel."[9] With Olmert's disappearance from the political limelight, Peres remained the API's only active advocator. Participating in an interfaith conference in Kazakhstan in July 2009, he attempted to revive the initiative, calling upon ʿAbdallah "to meet in Jerusalem or in Riyadh or to travel to Kazakhstan, and together with other Arab leaders we will be able to realize your vision, our vision and the vision of all believers in our shared God of peace and justice."[10] Peres's call did not receive any official Saudi response. In fact, in the post-election political climate prevailing in Israel it became obvious that the API was doomed.

With the spate of spontaneous Arab revolutions (the so-called Arab Spring), which erupted in winter 2011, Israel became reentrenched in its position; the dominant position within the political and security establishment was that the time was not ripe to embark on new initiatives and that it was preferable to stick to the status quo. It was this lingering stalemate that prompted the previous Circles of Peace group (see above) to launch the Israeli Peace Initiative (IPI) in April 2011, which was meant as an Israeli counteroffer to the API, presented by nonpartisan, civil society elements.[11]

The new political climate in the Arab world allowed Israel to remain un-moved toward the API. Thus, the Arab states' reiteration of their commitment to the API at the Arab summit in Baghdad in March 2012 did not trigger any Israeli response. Moreover, at the end of a meeting between US secretary of state John Kerry and vice president Joe Biden with a delegation of the Arab League on April 29, 2013, the Qatari prime minister affirmed that peace be-tween the Palestinians and Israel is a strategic choice for the Arab states and that the agreement should be based on the two-state solution on the basis of the June 4, 1967, line, "with the possible comparable and mutual agreed minor swap of the land."[12] This concession indicated that the Israeli interpretation of the API as a take-it-or-leave-it plan was misguided. At a special session of the Knesset, called by the opposition members to discuss the API, on June 5, 2013, several members urged the government to see the API as an opportunity to advance a regional and multilateral peace process. Yet Netanyahu focused in his speech on the threats Iran, Islamic terror, and Syria pose to Israel. Thus the Netanyahu government, like previous Israeli governments, evaded the API.

ASSESSMENT

Observers of the Arab-Israeli conflict refer to the API as a plausible missed op-portunity. Marwan Muasher, the former Jordanian foreign minister involved in the drafting of the API in 2002, lamented on its tenth anniversary that it was indeed an Israeli missed opportunity.[13] In his book, he averred that "There was a time when Israel accused Arabs of not stepping forward and providing a partner for peace. The year 2002 showed that this was not true, with the core of the Arab world meeting the challenge and being fully engaged" (2006, 178). Nicola Nasser, a Palestinian journalist, concluded that "Israeli leaders used to mock Arab leaders as the masters of missing opportunities. This time, Israel is the party who seems determined to miss a real historic opportunity" (Nasser 2007).[14] Alon Ben-Meir, an academic and journalist, wrote that "The reintro-duction of the Saudi initiative . . . offers Israelis and Palestinians a momentous opportunity to end their century-old conflict. Israel and Palestinians will have only themselves to blame if they miss this historic opportunity" (Ben-Meir 2007). Finally, Gershon Baskin, a veteran peace activist, wrote that for the first time in the history of the Middle East "the possibility for genuine com-prehensive peace is much more real than fantasy. The opportunity is placed at our doorstep. If we miss it, we will have no one to blame for the next war than ourselves" (Baskin 2007).

To what extent has the API been a historical opportunity? By all accounts, the plan should have been considered as an attractive offer to Israel. A sober assessment of the Arab position toward Israel shows that the 2002 Beirut summit's resolutions, representing an Arab consensus, underwent a profound change. In comparison to the "three no's" of the summit in Khartoum in 1967, Beirut offered "three yes's": yes to peace with Israel, yes to recognizing Israel, and yes to negotiations with Israel. "For the first time since the beginning of the Arab-Israeli conflict," wrote Muasher, "the Arab states came up with a collective, proactive effort to solve the conflict by addressing not only their needs but also the needs of Israel" (2008, 132). The API, therefore, offered Israel a mega-incentive, as it promised full normal relations with Arab and Muslim countries, as well as integration in the region. The Israeli side, however, attempted to downplay its attractiveness, particularly by overemphasizing the demanded territorial concession and by exaggerating the meaning of the refugees clause.[15] The timing of the publication of the API unfortunately coincided with several suicide bombings in Israel, which did not allow the Israeli leadership to seriously consider it. Also, a short period after the failure of the Camp David summit, the Clinton Parameters, and the Taba Talks (see chapter 20), perhaps Israel was not yet ready for another peaceful ordeal. Yet with the completion of Operation Defensive Shield in the West Bank, and in light of the repeated reaffirmation of the API by Arab summits, Israel could have responded favorably on several occasions along the way. One such occasion was the revival of the Western-Arab-Israeli dialogue regarding the API in the aftermath of the Second Lebanon War in the summer of 2006, and in particular around the time of the convening of the Arab summit in Riyadh in March 2007. The war created a unique opportunity for tacit cooperation between Israel, Egypt, Saudi Arabia, Jordan, and other Arab-Sunni moderate countries against the rising Shi'i challenge of Iran, Iraq, and Hizballah. At that time, in the post-'Arafat and post-Intifada period, the chances that the PA would join the efforts to pursue peace talks were greater, since only a consensual Arab position could have overcome the divisions between Fatah and Hamas. The ingenious idea of Olmert appearing before a forum of the Arab League, introduced in March–April 2007, was another attractive opportunity that should have been embraced by Israeli leaders. Thus the historical processes and the attractiveness of the Arab initiative combined to offer a unique and rare opportunity to implement it.

To what extent was this opportunity missed? The first two variables in our definition relate to the level of the legitimacy of the leadership and their determination to take bold steps. On the Israeli side, during the period under review, there were governments headed by Sharon and Olmert. When the API was launched in March 2002, Sharon headed a National Unity government, with Likud, Labor (Peres replaced Barak as party leader, and was nominated both deputy prime minister and foreign minister), Shas, and many other small parties, accounting for more than eighty Knesset members. Though the government was a combination of disparate ideological parties, Sharon himself was elected to his post with a majority of 62 percent, according to the direct ballot system. Not only could Sharon be considered a leader enjoying wide legitimacy, but he also had a certain charisma that allowed him to sway large parts of the Israeli public, as was reflected in his ability to implement his unilateral Disengagement Plan from Gaza in February 2005 despite the opposition to this policy in his Likud Party and significant elements on the right. This means that Sharon had the ability and capability to deliver the API in Israeli society had he had the conviction and the desire to do so. Yet though he was able to take bold decisions (as seen in various decisions taken during his military and political careers), there is no indication that he was inclined to adopt the API as a viable diplomatic option for a settlement.[16] In contrast, Olmert seemed determined and bold enough to pursue the path of the API, yet he suffered from a shortage of legitimacy. Initially, he succeeded in presenting himself as the heir to Sharon's legacy. He also managed to lead Kadima to an impressive victory in the March 2006 elections, which led to a coalition of sixty-seven Knesset members. Yet the media reports of his alleged involvement in fraud and corruption eroded his legitimacy. In fact, for most of his premiership period Olmert operated under the gathering clouds of his impending impeachment. In such a political climate, it would have been more difficult to make a gigantic decision regarding the API. Yet it should be emphasized that several key Israeli politicians supported the API (Peres, Barak, Livni, Peretz, and Sheetrit, among others). The fact that Olmert and all these others were considered key politicians in both Kadima and Labor suggests that in spite of Olmert's own personal mishap, all these personalities could have created a critical mass able to shape public opinion in a meaningful way.

On the other side, the API was the product of a collective Arab decision. As such, its legitimacy derived from the fact that it carried the weight of an Arab consensus, unprecedented in the history of the conflict, including elements that had been part of the Arab radical camp opposing Israel (such as Syria, Libya, and Iraq). Though the Arab League had no mechanism to implement its decisions, it embodied a moral commitment of all Arab states to pursue a peaceful solution to the Arab-Israeli conflict. In addition, King ʿAbdallah, the initiator of the API, enjoyed the religious Islamic legitimacy as the custodian of the two holiest shrines in Mecca and Medina; it should not be forgotten that some two to three million Muslims make the pilgrimage to these places annually. Therefore, the fact that Saudi Arabia led the initiative—and not Egypt or Jordan, which had already signed peace agreements with Israel—boosted its legitimacy in the Arab and Islamic worlds. This fact should have prompted Israel to pursue this multilateral Arab track. At the same time it is worth noting that ʿAbdallah and Saudi Arabia did not display a determined effort to pursue the peace initiative. In many ways, they typically demonstrated what can be termed "reluctant leadership," which probably reflected the constraints of Saudi foreign policy.

The third variable relates to the history of past interactions that affects the level of trust between the parties. Israel had no previous contact with the Arab League. A reflection of the lowest common denominator in the Arab world, most of the Arab summits' decisions relating to the conflict were anti-Israeli. For the Israelis, the 1967 Khartoum resolutions were a constant reminder of the negative Arab position. Yet the API was not a complete innovation: the Fez summit in September 1982 had approved the first Arab peace plan (based on the Fahd Plan; see chapter 13). Therefore, the suspicion and skepticism with which the Israeli decision makers treated the API was only partially justified. Likewise, Israel had no previous contacts with Saudi Arabia. Politically and geographically remote from the center of the conflict, the hostility between the two was mainly expressed in negative rhetoric. In addition, anti-Semitic discourse often appeared in the Saudi media. The kingdom has never participated militarily in the Arab-Israeli wars, though it did use the oil weapon during the 1973 War. Saudi Arabia usually adopted moderate positions with regard to the Arab-Israeli conflict and since 1967 did not negate in principle the very existence of a Jewish state but rather insisted on full withdrawal from all the occupied territories in 1967, including Arab Jerusalem, and the establishment of a Palestinian state (Kostiner 2008, 15–27). Israelis, it seems, had a dual image of Saudi Arabia: on the one hand, they perceived it as a primitive, theocratic state governed by the Islamic shariaʿ, which sponsors Islamic terrorism. This image was strengthened after the discovery that fifteen Saudi citizens were involved in the 9/11 attacks and that Saudi money was transferred to ʿArafat during the Intifada and to families of martyrs killed in suicide bombings, as well as other Islamic projects (Gold 2004, 198–206, 256–262; Bergman 2002, 307–315). On the other hand, the image of King ʿAbdallah as reflected in the Israeli media was of a leader enjoying credibility and statesmanship; one that can be trusted to do business. The keen desire of Olmert, Peres, and others to meet a senior Saudi official attested that such a meeting—in their eyes—would be considered a positive step toward boosting their popularity and legitimacy. It should be emphasized that the API was not well enough recognized in Israeli politics and society and there was no serious attempt to acquaint the public with its essentials. The official text of the API was translated into Hebrew and distributed to a limited audience by the Jordanian embassy in Israel in 2005. Those familiar with the API willfully ignored it, employing a cognitive "iron wall" penetrated only by threatening and negative signals coming from the other side. Only in 2008, six years after its publication, was the API given appropriate coverage in the media. Had a more serious attempt been made to acquaint the public with the API then, the existing negative images of the Arab League and Saudi Arabia would have been mitigated.[17]

The fourth variable relates to the role of the mediator. The United States had never taken upon itself the role of mediator with respect to the API. The Bush administration welcomed the initiative and occasionally praised it, but the president had not considered the plan as a viable instrument for promoting dialogue or even an agreement. The autobiographies of both Bush and Rice indicate that they did not attach importance to the API as a manifestation of a significant change in the Arab position toward Israel.[18] This lukewarm attitude was probably connected with Sharon's refusal to deal with an initiative that subjected him to negotiations with the whole Arab world and which stood in sharp contrast to his worldview. The US joined Sharon in his quest for curbing the Palestinian Intifada and isolating ʿArafat. The most intense efforts were exerted in the Mitchell, Tenet, and Zinni missions, which focused on achieving an Israeli-Palestinian cease-fire. Yet the United States became convinced that only a detailed peace plan could achieve the desired end in the long run; therefore, in April 2003, when the US occupation and toppling of Saddam Hussein in Iraq had been completed, Bush launched the American peace plan called the Road Map (see chapter 22). Its publication was testimony that the US did not consider the API a viable diplomatic tool for igniting the peace process.[19] Even the revival of the API in 2007–2008, in the wake of the failure of the Road Map, did not convince the US to change its position. The Annapolis Conference, though held with the participation of Saudi Arabia in November 2007, did not reflect any change on the part of the United States regarding the API. Likewise, Obama did not embrace the API as a viable political tool in spite of his initial enthusiasm for the plan.[20]

Our analysis leads to the conclusion that the API episode constituted a historical opportunity mainly because, simply, it was a highly attractive offer, the likes of which had never before been offered to Israel. The original timing, however, was not propitious, as its publication coincided with bloody terrorist operations by Hamas at the height of Intifada, which led to the launching of Operation Defensive Shield by the IDF. In addition, Sharon, who enjoyed wide legitimacy, did not consider the API a viable diplomatic option. However, the plan's next round, after the Second Lebanon War, offered a new timing that could have been exploited. Indeed, Olmert grasped the magnitude of the change and went further than any other Israeli leader in promoting the API, yet he did not succeed either in transforming the public attitude or adopting a governmental decision. The number of variables supporting a missed opportunity in this case study are between two and three: Olmert's declining legitimacy and a certain lack of trust diminished its potentiality level from high to medium. It can be speculated that had Olmert accepted the idea of appearing before the Arab League, as suggested in March 2007, he might have dramatically affected Israeli perception toward the API and might have opened the road—as Sadat did in visiting Jerusalem—to an Israeli-Arab dialogue, possibly culminating in a peace treaty. The apathy, inaction, and indifference that characterized Israeli behavior during most of the time under review and the fact that the API had little effect on the Arab-Israeli peace process as a result of Israel's inaction strengthens our assessment that the level of the missed opportunity here should be high rather than medium.

NOTES

This chapter is based on "Israel and the Arab Peace Initiative, 2002–2014: A Plausible Missed Opportunity," *Middle East Journal* 68.4: 584–603.

1. Interestingly, a few days earlier, Friedman published an article that heralded the Saudi Initiative; it called on the Arab leaders in the Beirut Arab summit, to be held in late March, to adopt a resolution calling for full Israeli withdrawal to the 1967 borders—including Jerusalem and the Golan—in return for full Arab recognition of Israel, opening trade relations, and the signing of security guarantees. See "Dear Arab League," *New York Times*, February 6, 2002. See also Muasher 2008, 116.

2. Interview with Moshe Shachal, who served as minister in several Israeli governments, December 31, 2012.

3. Editorial, "From Khartoum to Beirut," *Haaretz*, March 27, 2002. The title referred to the long way the Arabs had gone from the Khartoum summit (familiar in Israel for its three "no's": no peace with Israel, no recognition, and no negotiations) to the current summit in terms of recognition of Israel.

4. The new Saudi proposal was presented to Sharon by US ambassador Dan Kurtzer on April 28; see *Yedioth Ahronoth*, May 3; *Haaretz*, April 29, 2002. Interestingly, though Bush writes of this meeting in his memoirs, he does not mention the new initiative. Bush 2011, 401–403; Rice 2011, 141.

5. http://www.mfa.gov.il/MFA/Government/Speeches+by+Israeli+leaders/2006/PM+Olmert.

6. Livni, however, published an article in the Saudi-owned *al-Sharq al-Awsat* (published in London), which attempted to offer an Israeli response to the API; see June 18, 2007 (Elend-Rif 2009, 89).

7. The main strategy of the group, devised by Huberman, was organized in circles—hence the name "Circles of Peace." The first circle devised peace among Israelis, mainly between the religious and secular sectors, and between Jews and Arabs in Israel. The second circle promoted peace with Israel's immediate neighbors, Palestine, Syria, and Lebanon. The third circle pitched a regional Middle Eastern Arab-Israeli alliance, with Egypt, Saudi Arabia, and other Arab countries; and the fourth circle included cooperation with the Islamic world. Interview with Koby Huberman, December 10, 2012, and original documents received from him; and interview with Moshe Shachal, December 31, 2012.

8. For reports on the Madrid Conference, see *Haaretz*, January 12, 14–15, 2007.

9. This quote is taken from *Ma'ariv*, April 22, 2009. Recently, however, Lieberman has proposed a regional approach to solving the conflict as an alternative to dealing with the PA or Hamas. See Barak Ravid, *Haaretz*, June 26, 2014.

10. http://www.mfa.gov.il/MFA/Government/Speeches+by+Israeli+leaders/2009/Ad dress_President_Peres_Interfaith_Conference_Kazakhstan_1-Jul-2009.htm.

11. For details on the group, see http://israelipeaceinitiative.com/.

12. http://www.cfr.org/peacekeeping/secretary-kerrys-qatari-prime-minister-hamads -remarks-april-2013/p30590.

13. Interviewed in Zvika Krieger, "Lost Moments: The Arab Peace Initiative, 10 Years Later," *Atlantic*, March 2012. A short while before, he published an article under the title "The Death of the Arab Peace Initiative?" in ibid., November 2011. The article was part of "Is Peace Possible?"—a special report on the Israeli-Palestinian conflict by the *Atlantic* and the S. Daniel Abraham Center for Middle East Peace.

14. The author was referring, of course, to Abba Eban's famous dictum mentioned in the Prologue.

15. A frequent Israeli allegation (repeated by Livni and other politicians) was that this clause was tantamount to calling for the implementation of the Right of Return, while the text, in fact, gave Israel a veto over the suggested solution to be agreed upon by both sides. See in this connection, Eyal Benvenisti, *Haaretz*, December 24, 2008; Steinberg 2008, 410–411.

16. An authoritative eight-hundred-page biography of Sharon does not mention the API even once. There is a long description of the reasons for Sharon's launching Operation Defensive Shield, but there is no mention of the API, which was adopted at the same time. See Hefez and Bloom 2005, 609–615.

17. According to the Peace Index Poll by the Tami Steinmetz Center for Peace Research, 62 percent of the Israeli public had heard of the API. Of those, 56 percent supported it, while 38 percent opposed it; 45 percent believed that it could serve as a basis for future peace talks, while 47 percent were of the opposite view. See Tamar Hermann, "The Iron Wall," *Bitterlemons* 12, vol. 2 (June 1, 2011). Another survey, in May 2013, indicated that 73.5 percent of Hebrew-speaking Israelis either had never heard of the API, or knew of its existence but were unfamiliar with it. See Akiva Eldar, *al-Monitor*, May 27, 2013 (Podeh 2014, 600).

18. Rice's 766-page autobiography does not mention the API except for a short reference to its reaffirmation in 2008; see Rice 2011, 575. As noted above, she did see the Saudi Initiative as "a bold proposal and could have been an important point of departure for negotiations." She thought that the timing of its publication "could not have been worse" (Rice 2011, 136). Bush (2011) did not mention the API at all in his autobiography.

19. The only mention of it in the plan was as a source of reference for the negotiations, such as UN Resolutions 242, 338, and 1397. See Meital 2006, 225–226.

20. In his Cairo speech on June 4, 2009, Obama noted the importance of the API, but later it did not play a role in his policy (Kurtzer et al. 2013, 250).

CHAPTER 22

THE US ROAD MAP

APRIL 2003

ON APRIL 30, 2003, a day before the US military operations in Iraq ended, President George W. Bush announced the Road Map, a new Israeli-Palestinian peace plan devised by the Quartet on the Middle East, that is, the United States, Russia, the European Union, and the United Nations. It was the first American peace initiative since the Reagan Plan of September 1982 (see chapter 13), though it did not carry the official endorsement of the president or the secretary of state so that it would not damage their prestige in case of failure. The Road Map was the consummation of a long process of negotiations and consultations between members of the Quartet and the relevant regional players that began right after Bush's Rose Garden speech on June 24, 2002, in which he outlined his vision of a two-state solution for Israel and Palestine. It was a performance-based and goal-driven plan, with clear phases, a timeline, target dates, and benchmarks aimed at offering substance to Bush's vision and bringing an end to al-Aqsa Intifada. Israel and the Palestinians accepted the plan with reservations. Though the Road Map was never formally abrogated or suspended, it was shelved for all practical purposes following Sharon's decision to pursue his Disengagement Plan from Gaza during the years 2003–2005. This chapter will analyze if and to what extent the Road Map marked a plausible missed opportunity.

THE EPISODE

Bush entered office in January 2001 with a mind-set already predisposed to disengaging the United States from the Arab-Israeli conflict. Condoleezza Rice, his national security adviser, admitted that "When we took office, our goal was simply to calm the region" (2011, 54). His predecessor's failures on the Israeli-Syrian and Israeli-Palestinian tracks, in addition to the outbreak of the Intifada, convinced Bush that the settlement of these conflicts should await better timing and opportunity. Thus the general tendency was to prefer conflict management over peacemaking (Kurtzer et al. 2013, 154–157; Abrams 2013, 6). In the post-9/11 period, the administration tended to see the Middle East problem as a clash of values rather than as a contest of interests. According to this line of thinking, peace was possible only with the end of terror and violence and the fall of terrorist regimes. The struggle, in essence, was between good and evil, democracy and authoritarianism, moderates and radicals, terrorists and anti-terrorists. In this struggle Israel was on the right side and Yasir ʿArafat on the wrong side (Miller 2008, 324–325, 336). The 9/11 syndrome and the raging terror of the Intifada put ʿArafat and Hamas, in the American mind, squarely in the terrorist camp. Bush entered office with a negative perception of ʿArafat, following Clinton's belief that he had turned down a generous offer by Barak at Camp David. What sealed ʿArafat's fate was the revelation that he was involved in the dispatch of a ship called *Karine A* to smuggle weapons from Iran to Gaza. In his memoirs, Bush was categorical: "Arafat had lied to me. I never trusted him again. In fact, I never spoke to him again" (2011, 400–401). Bush, therefore, concluded that peace would not be possible as long as ʿArafat was in power (Rice 2011, 54–55; Abrams 2013, 19–47; Kurtzer et al. 2013, 164–167).

The low priority given by the Bush administration to the Israeli-Palestinian conflict, needless to say, limited the US involvement in attempts to bring a cease-fire. In 2001–2002 there were three such attempts: by a US senator, George Mitchell; by the head of the CIA, George Tenet; and by a military general, Anthony Zinni. All these senior emissaries failed to achieve the declared target (Golan 2007, 63–68; Miller 2008, 331–332). Yet at the same time, the continuation of the Palestinian struggle for independence convinced Bush, like others, that only a two-state solution can offer a remedy to the conflict. Already in August 2001, in response to a harsh Saudi message rebuking the US hands-off approach, Bush committed himself to a "viable Palestinian state." It was the first time the United States formally supported the notion of a sovereign Palestinian state (Miller 2008, 333; Kurtzer et al. 2013, 163). In November, in his address to the United Nations, the president laid out a vision of two states, Israel and Palestine, living peacefully together. As the violence intensified in the occupied territories, the UN adopted Resolution 1397 on March 12, 2002, which demanded an immediate cessation of all acts of violence and the implementation of the Tenet Plan and Mitchell Report. In its preamble the resolution affirmed a "vision of a region where two states, Israel and Palestine, live side by side within secure and recognized boundaries."[1] At that point ʿArafat seemed to be contemplating, at least rhetorically, a Palestinian vision of peace (Arafat 2002).

Shortly after, the situation in the West Bank degenerated. In response to a series of terrorist attacks perpetrated by Hamas during the Jewish Passover holiday, the IDF—with US political support—launched Operation Defensive Shield in late March. The Israeli operation eclipsed the rather dramatic announcement in Beirut of the Arab summit's peace initiative; Israel largely ignored it, and the US response was lukewarm at best (see chapter 21). Meanwhile, pressure was exerted on the US by the Quartet and certain regional countries to do something to pacify the situation. In this regard, Egypt, Jordan, and Saudi Arabia played an important role; highly concerned about the possible regional ramifications of Israel's operation with its rising toll of civilian casualties and the continued Israeli blockade of 'Arafat in his presidential compound, they expected the United States to offer something tangible to arrest the deterioration (Miller 2008, 346). In his meetings with the Jordanian and Saudi kings, the Egyptian president, and the Israeli prime minister, Bush became acquainted with the positions of the different parties; and though 'Arafat was ostracized, Bush had also received a position paper from the Palestinians regarding final status talks (Muasher 2008, 140–151). All these meetings helped the administration to prepare the ground for a major speech delivered on June 24 at the White House Rose Garden. When the president makes a speech in the Rose Garden, wrote Rice, "it signals that the message is important" (2011, 144). Daniel C. Kurtzer and his coauthors assessed that it was "the most important statement on the Arab-Israeli conflict by Bush in his eight years as president" (2013, 172). To a large extent, the speech foreshadowed the publication of the Road Map.

The president's speech was preceded by a declaration by the European Union on June 22 calling for "an end to the occupation and the early establishment of a democratic, viable, peaceful and sovereign state of Palestine, on the basis of the 1967 borders, if necessary with minor adjustments agreed by the parties" (Muasher 2008, 152). Two days later, Bush outlined his vision for two states living side by side in peace and security. From the Palestinians he demanded the replacement of the current leadership with a new, elected leadership opposing terrorism. He also demanded the drafting of a constitution and the introduction of serious institutional reforms leading to democracy. "If Palestinians embrace democracy, confront corruption and firmly reject terror," Bush declared, "they can count on American support for the creation of a provisional state of Palestine." The final borders, the capital, and other aspects of the state's sovereignty were to be negotiated between the parties, with the help of the Arab states. This ambiguous phrasing was somewhat clarified by the statement that "The Israeli occupation that began in 1967 will be ended through a settlement negotiated between the parties, based on UN Resolutions 242 and 338, with Israeli withdrawal to secure and recognized boundaries." The agreement on final status issues was supposed to end within three years. Israel was asked to withdraw its military forces to the pre-Intifada

positions and to stop all settlement activity (Meital 2006, 158, 215–218; Muasher 2008, 152–154; Golan 2007, 73–76; Bush 2011, 404; Rice 2011, 142–145;
Christison 2004, 39; Abrams 2013, 41–42). Bush ended his speech with the
following passage:

> This moment is both an opportunity and a test for all parties in the Middle
> East: an opportunity to lay the foundations for future peace; a test to show
> who is serious about peace and who is not. The choice is here stark and
> simple. The Bible says, "I have set before you life and death; therefore, choose
> life." The time has arrived for everyone in the conflict to choose peace, and
> hope, and life. Thank you very much. (quoted in Meital 2006, 218)

Undoubtedly, it was not a balanced speech; it tilted toward the Israeli position. The Israelis, according to Miller, actually had significant input in shaping
the final version of the text, even providing some of the language (2008, 349–
350; Christison 2004, 39).[2] Indeed, the fact that Bush fully embraced Sharon's
position regarding the necessity to oust ʿArafat and the need for institutional
reforms was a victory for Israeli policy. In addition, the call for Israeli withdrawal to the 1967 line was in accordance with UN resolutions based on the accepted formula of recognized and secure boundaries (Hefez and Bloom 2005,
624). Even the notion of a Palestinian entity was not anathema to Sharon, as
already in September 2001 he delivered a speech in which he expressed for the
first time his readiness to accept an independent Palestinian state. Though
the Likud Party convention that year repudiated this idea, Sharon would not
budge (ibid., 614–615). So, the main Israeli criticism was of the clause regarding the settlements. The Palestinians, for their part, received with grati-
fication Bush's call for the establishment of a viable state, yet its provisional
borders raised fears regarding the end result of the negotiations. In addition,
the demand to replace the iconic ʿArafat was a condition bound to raise difficulties within Palestinian leadership and society. The speech, wrote Muasher,
"was far harsher on Arafat than we expected" (2008, 154). In the final analysis,
the speech stamped Bush as pro-Israeli, making it difficult for him to present
himself as an honest broker in the conflict.

No sooner had the president concluded his speech than the drumbeat
began about how this vision would be implemented. The pressure mainly
came from the European Union and the Arab states. Yet as the topic of
locating and eliminating weapons of mass destruction (WMD), expected to
be found in Iraq, was becoming the major focus of the administration, the
resolution of the Israeli-Palestinian conflict was not thought a pressing issue.
For some, wrote Miller, "the road to Jerusalem ran through Baghdad, so no
Arab-Israeli initiative made sense until the Iraq file could be closed" (2008,

350). It was precisely the combination of the Iraqi file and the ongoing Intifada that brought the Quartet and certain Arab leaders to press the United States to formulate a concrete plan. First came a declaration by the foreign ministers of the Quartet in mid-July; this was followed by a meeting of the foreign ministers of Jordan, Egypt, and Saudi Arabia with Bush, asking for the publication of a "road map" including benchmarks, timelines, obligations, and a monitoring group to supervise performance. The driving force behind this endeavor was Marwan Muasher, the Jordanian foreign minister (Miller 2008, 350–351; Rice 2011, 147; Muasher 2008, 157–159). When Jordan's king 'Abdallah II and Muasher met with Bush and Rice on August 1, they asked the president to translate his vision into steps; that meeting was important in persuading Bush to give a green light to furthering a concrete peace plan (Muasher 2008, 159–163).[3]

The first draft of the Road Map, devised at the State Department under the guidance of William Burns, the assistant secretary of state for Near Eastern affairs, was completed as early as October 2002. Then a process of consultations began with the Quartet, Israel, the moderate Arab countries, and the Palestinians. A final draft was completed on December 20, but only in late April 2003 was it formally presented to the parties. The long delay was a result of several factors. First was the need to consult and coordinate policies with the European Union and the moderate Arab leaders, including the Palestinians (preferably Abu Mazen, not 'Arafat). These consultations ended by December 2002 with agreement on most of the contested issues, and pressure was then applied to the US to make public its plan (Muasher 2008, 163–175). Second, the US needed to bring Israel on board, particularly with the looming war in Iraq, which necessitated its tacit cooperation. In other words, Bush wanted to ensure that an Iraqi missile attack against Israel would not be met by an Israeli counter-attack, as insinuated by Sharon (Hefez and Bloom 2005, 629)—a response that could badly affect American interests in the Arab world. The need to assuage Israel meant that the US sought a peace plan that would not antagonize the Sharon government. And since the next elections in Israel were due on February 28, 2003, Sharon asked Bush to postpone the publication of the plan until the composition of a new government, by which time the US preparations for the war were in high gear. In light of these considerations, the US approach was that serious work on the peace process could not start before military action on Iraq ended. The Arab view, in contrast, was that in light of the possible damage to the US position in the Arab world as a result of invading Iraq, "only a credible move to push the peace process forward might convince the Arab public that America meant what it said about democracy and freedom" (Muasher 2008, 166).

The Road Map was finally presented to the parties on April 30, 2003, a day before the United States announced the completion of its mission in Iraq. From an American perspective, the overthrow of Saddam Hussein marked an opportunity in the realm of democratic regime changes and the Arab-Israeli conflict similar to that created following the 1991 Gulf War, which led to the convening of the Madrid Conference and the resumption of several Israeli-Arab bilateral tracks (Rice 2011, 215–216; Rabinovich 2004, 207). With the nomination of Mahmoud ʿAbbas (Abu Mazen) by ʿArafat as prime minister in March 2003, it seemed that a new Palestinian leadership more suited to the American and Israeli demands was emerging.[4] These changes in the region, in addition to the election of a new Israeli government (albeit under the same prime minister), offered a historical opportunity that the Quartet attempted to seize.

Though the US played the primary role in the Road Map, it was presented as the Quartet's plan.[5] By the time it was published, the parties were already intimately acquainted with its details. In an attempt to satisfy everyone, it included all the necessary elements: sequence, mutual responsibility, and parallelism. In the preamble it was stated that the goal of the plan was a final and comprehensive settlement of the Israeli-Palestinian conflict by 2005. That, in turn, would result in the emergence of an independent, democratic, and viable Palestinian state living side by side in peace and security with Israel and its other neighbors. The settlement would resolve the conflict and end the occupation begun in 1967, on the basis of UN Resolutions 242, 338, and 1397 and the Arab Peace Initiative (API). The mention of the two latter resolutions was important, since they referred to the establishment of a Palestinian state, and the API also related to the Syrian and Lebanese tracks. The insertion of the API reference was due to the persistent efforts of Jordan and other moderate Arab leaders (Muasher 2008, 152–175). The plan set clear phases, timelines, target dates, and benchmarks aiming at progress through reciprocal steps by the two parties under the auspices of the Quartet. The first phase was to begin immediately and extend until May 2003. Within a month—hardly a realistic deadline—the parties were expected to implement the Tenet and Mitchell recommendations in the realm of security. Among these recommendations were the cessation of all forms of violence, the dismantling of terrorist infrastructure, and confiscation of all illegal weaponry. At the same time, a detailed program of institution building was to take place in the Palestinian Authority (PA), including the holding of free elections, the drafting of a constitution, and the appointment of Palestinian ministers (including a prime minister) capable of initiating institutional reforms. Israel was asked to withdraw progressively to the pre-Intifada lines (that is, the lines before September 28, 2000). In addition, it was asked to dismantle settlement outposts erected since March 2001 and freeze all other settlement activity. During this phase, the Quartet was to begin informal monitoring while consulting with the parties on the establishment of a formal monitoring mechanism. This instrument, which was missing from the Oslo Accords, was meant to supervise the actual implementation of the plan.

The second phase was a transition period theoretically slated for June to December, commencing as soon as the Quartet determined that both parties had fulfilled their obligations according to the plan. This stage would focus on the formation of an independent Palestinian state with provisional borders and attributes of sovereignty. The process would be launched by an international conference convened by the Quartet and aimed at comprehensive Middle East peace, including Syria and Lebanon. In addition, this phase would see the finalization of a constitution for a democratic Palestine; the restoration of pre-Intifada links among the Arab states; the creation of an empowered reform cabinet with the office of prime minister; the promotion of international recognition of the Palestinian state, including possible UN membership; and an enhanced international role in monitoring the transition phase.

The third phase was termed the "Permanent Status Agreement and End of the Israeli-Palestinian Conflict," scheduled to last for two years (2004–2005), commencing, as in phase II, after the Quartet determined that both parties had fulfilled their obligations. This stage too was to begin with the convening of an international conference, to endorse agreement reached on the provisional Palestinian state and to launch the process leading to a final and permanent agreement on Jerusalem, refugees and settlements, and continued negotiations on the Syrian and Lebanese tracks. As for the two contentious issues of refugees and Jerusalem, it offered "an agreed, just, fair, and realistic solution to the refugee issue, and a negotiated resolution on the status of Jerusalem that takes into account the political and religious concerns of both sides." Finally, the Arab states were asked to accept full normal relations with Israel, as prescribed by the API.

In principle, the Road Map had several drawbacks. First, like Oslo it was guided by the logic of graduality, yet unlike Oslo it provided mechanisms for testing and evaluating the performance of the obligations entailed in the Quartet's plan. It was unclear, however, how the monitors would interpret performance and with what authority. In addition, the existence of spoilers on both sides of the conflict indicated that they would attempt to obstruct the success of this process. Second, the promise of the establishment of a Palestinian state with provisional borders could be seen by the Palestinians as a device to limit the boundaries of the state to the existing areas A and B, which consisted of less than 50 percent of the envisaged Palestinian state in its 1967 borders. Should the negotiations collapse, it was noted, the Palestinians would find themselves controlling more or less the same amount of territory.

Third, the undisguised attempts at removing ʿArafat from power and the un-
democratic interference in Palestinian political life (setting dates for elections,
drafting a constitution, nominating a prime minister, etc.) were bound to
raise antagonism within the Palestinian leadership and society (Golan 2007,
85–89; Aruri 2003, 206–210).

In the period preceding the launch of the Road Map, the United States
clarified that it was open to "comments" from both sides that would not result in any changes to the text (Muasher 2008, 185; Ross 2005, 789). Thus on
May 25 the Israeli government officially accepted the document but attached
fourteen reservations (or comments). It was the first time that an Israeli government expressed its willingness to accept in principle the creation of a Palestinian state.[6] The comments included, inter alia, that the monitoring system
should be under American (not Quartet) management; full performance
would be a condition for progress between phases; there must be a Palestinian declaration of Israel's right to exist as a Jewish state and a waiver of any
right of return for Palestinian refugees to Israel; the end of the process would
lead to the end of all claims, not just the end of the conflict; there would be a
negation of reference to UN Resolution 1397 and the API; and no link would
be made between the Palestinian and Syrian and Lebanese tracks (Muasher
2008, 185–186; Golan 2007, 90–91; Meital 2006, 165). In Muasher's opinion,
Israel's reservations (he used the term "conditions") "amounted to rejecting
the plan" (2008, 185). The US, however, did not incorporate the Israeli reservations in the plan.

The "reservations" reflected the divergent views within the Israeli government. Sharon himself, as noted above, had already accepted the notion of
a Palestinian state in 2002. In his speech at the Herzliya Conference in late
December, he gave the nod to the essence of the Road Map, which had already
been presented to him in draft form (see above). He promised that "Israel is
prepared to make painful concessions for true peace" and accepted the establishment of a Palestinian state with borders yet to be finalized. Referring to
the Rose Garden speech, he said that Bush's vision "is a reasonable, pragmatic
and practicable one, which offers a real opportunity to achieve an agreement."
He also promised that "Israel will act to lift military pressure, create territorial
continuity between Palestinian population centers and ease daily life for the
Palestinians." In this plan, he declared, "there are risks involved but also opportunities." As for ʿArafat, he asserted that "This man is not—and never will
be—a partner for peace." Therefore, his role must be relegated to a symbolic
form (Meital 2006, 219–223). Following the stormy government session that
approved the Road Map, Sharon averred that "The idea that it is possible to
keep three and a half million Palestinians under occupation is wrong for Israel,
for the Palestinians and for the Israeli economy" (quoted in ibid., 167). The

fact that Sharon—perceived as the "father of the settlements"—termed Israeli control in the occupied territories as "occupation" was testimony to the ideological change he had undergone. Yet it seems that what he really sought was a long-term interim settlement that would guarantee the cessation of terror activity and the replacement of Palestinian leadership. This thinking led him to devise the Disengagement Plan from Gaza in December 2003. "Deep in his heart," wrote Sharon's biographers, he "did not give the Road Map a chance" (Hefez and Bloom 2005, 632).[7]

The PA officially accepted the Road Map with no reservations. This position reflected 'Arafat's predicament within the international community: ironically, he was compelled to accept a plan that called for stripping all his powers, if not for his abdication. But at the same time he was adamant to show that he still was master of his own domain, which meant that he would not cooperate with 'Abbas's attempts to reform the PA and disarm the military organizations. 'Arafat was also bothered by the conditionality of the plan, fearing that it might not get beyond the initial stage. The idea of a state with provisional borders looked much like the long-term interim agreement Sharon had in mind, which would be determined according to Israel's interests (Golan 2007, 91). Thus 'Arafat had his own reasons to procrastinate on implementing the plan.

The Road Map had an auspicious start, nevertheless; Sharon met with the new Palestinian prime minister 'Abbas twice in May. Sharon explained that the full acceptance of the Road Map would lead to the downfall of the Israeli government due to divisions regarding the establishment of an independent Palestinian state. He suggested that the two parties start implementing points of agreement and postpone the rest. He reiterated both his acceptance of Bush's Rose Garden speech and Israel's reservations regarding the Road Map. He was particularly concerned with the short time frame of three years. 'Abbas expressed his concern about the continuation of the settlement activity, the building of the separation wall, and the absence of a Palestinian state. The Palestinian side also presented a detailed security plan to cope with terror operations. The meeting demonstrated the limitations of both sides in implementing the Road Map (Muasher 2008, 187–188).

To give the Road Map a public push and to bolster 'Abbas's international standing, two international summits were organized within two days. On June 3, Egypt hosted a summit in Sharm al-Shaykh with the participation of Bush, 'Abbas, Jordanian king 'Abdallah II, Saudi crown prince 'Abdallah, the Bahraini emir Hamed, and, of course, Egypt's Husni Mubarak. The Moroccan king was expected as well, but as a result of a terror attack in Rabat he absented himself. The summit did not publish a joint communiqué as a result of disagreements between Bush and the Arab leaders regarding the inclusion of Syria and Lebanon in the Road Map and the introduction of confidence-building measures between Israel and the Arab states. In particular, the Saudi crown prince refused to move toward normalization until certain elements of the API were implemented (Muasher 2008, 190). Instead, Mubarak made a speech on behalf of the Arab leaders, expressing full support for the Road Map.[8] The next day another summit was held in ʿAqaba, with the participation of Bush, Sharon, ʿAbdallah II, and ʿAbbas. It was meant to be the official launch of the Road Map. There, ʿAbbas declared that

> This is an important moment. A new opportunity for peace exists, an opportunity based upon President Bush's vision and the Quartet's road map which we have accepted without any reservations. Our goal is two states, Israel and Palestine, living side by side in peace and security. The process is the one of direct negotiations to end the Israeli-Palestinian conflict and to resolve all the permanent status issues and end the occupation that began in 1967 under which Palestinians have suffered so much.

He promised that there was no military solution to the conflict and that the PA would do its utmost to fight against terrorism. Sharon, for his part, declared that Israel "welcomes the opportunity to renew direct negotiations according to the steps of the road map as adopted by the Israeli government to achieve this vision." He stressed that Israel's interest was not to govern the Palestinians, but for the Palestinians to govern themselves in their own state. "A democratic Palestinian state fully at peace with Israel," he said, "will promote the long-term security and well-being of Israel as a Jewish state." He emphasized, however, that there can be no peace without the abandonment and elimination of terrorism, violence, and incitement.[9]

The agreement in ʿAqaba, wrote Muasher, was clear: "The Palestinians will renounce violence and the Israelis will agree to the Road Map and to commence negotiations that will lead to the end of the occupation and the establishment of an independent Palestinian state" (2008, 191). At the end of the summit, Bush appointed a little-known career diplomat with no prior Middle East experience, John Wolf, to monitor the progress on the obligations the two sides had taken (Rice 2011, 219; Kurtzer et al. 2013, 178). In his memoirs, Bush summed up the events: "We had a long way to go, but it was a hopeful moment in the Middle East" (2011, 406). The Jordanian foreign minister concurred: "That day was a rare moment of hope" (Muasher 2008, 190). He added that the ʿAqaba summit "represented the pinnacle of peacemaking efforts in the region and the brightest point along that difficult, long and painful road" (ibid., 192). On the Israeli side, too, the feeling was that the Road Map indeed constituted a "political breakthrough" (Weissglas 2012, 198).

The positive atmosphere continued with the signing of the *Hudna* (cease-fire) agreement between the Palestinian factions—Fatah, Hamas, and Islamic Jihad—on June 29, 2003. Yet this agreement abruptly ended with the August 19 suicide bombing of a bus in Jerusalem in which twenty-three people were killed and over 130 wounded. Consequently, the Israeli cabinet decided on September 1 to wage an all-out war against Hamas and other terrorist elements and to freeze the diplomatic process with the PA. Shortly after, 'Abbas resigned as a result of his internal disputes. All the Jordanian attempts at reconciling the differences between 'Arafat and 'Abbas failed miserably (Muasher 2008, 194–195). 'Arafat quickly nominated Ahmad Qurei (Abu 'Ala)—'Abbas's longtime rival—as prime minister, attesting to his desire to exploit the bickering to his advantage.

Internationally, the Road Map, or the two-state solution, became the policy of the United Nations through UNSC Resolution 1515, adopted in November 2003 (Muasher 2008, 198; Rice 2011, 221). Yet on the ground, the Road Map encountered many problems. Wolf, the American diplomat tasked to monitor the plan's execution, had nothing to monitor, since neither side moved toward implementing it (Miller 2008, 353). Indeed, Rice gave a frank exposé of the situation:

> The efforts [to implement the plan] soon bogged down. I would learn valuable lessons about how frustrating it can be to get the Israelis to actually carry through on promises relating to the Palestinians. The illegal outposts were always going to be moved but were never quite moved. Gratuitous "security" roadblocks that kept the Palestinians from moving around in the West Bank were always going to be taken down but were never quite taken down. The Palestinians were frustrating too. Abbas meant well, but Yasser Arafat soon grew jealous of the prime minister's new international status. When the cautious Abbas tried to carry out reforms, he'd find resistance from Arafat's security chiefs and from the old guard of the ruling party, Fatah; he almost always backed off or simply postponed actions. (Rice 2011, 219)

The inability, or rather unwillingness, of both parties to implement the Road Map sealed its fate: though it was never formally aborted, the Palestinian domestic rivalries and Sharon's decision to gamble on the Gaza Disengagement Plan in December 2003 meant that, for all practical purposes, the Road Map was doomed. This was exacerbated by a wave of Palestinian terrorism and Israeli retaliatory targeted killings. It took the United States and the Quartet more than a year and a half to devise the plan, but it took the parties who were supposed to benefit from it only a few months to block it. The US, Israel, and the Palestinians kept affirming their commitment to the Road Map, most notably in Annapolis in November 2007. Its reiteration four and a half years later, wrote Kurtzer et al., "seemed an empty pledge at best, and at worst an incredulous statement that became fair game for critics" (2013, 224).

ASSESSMENT

"The Road Map had never a fighting chance," wrote Jordan's foreign minister Marwan Muasher, a close observer of the events (2008, 198). He blamed all the relevant parties for failing to live up to their commitments. The Palestinians were accused of not doing their share in the security field by closing arms factories, confiscating illegal weapons, freezing funds going to illegal organizations, and closing the cross-border tunnels used for smuggling. Israel, in contrast, was blamed for squandering a unique opportunity to help 'Abbas build his authority by allowing him to show that the Palestinians could benefit from his peace policy. Israel, Muasher concluded, "was never serious about accepting and implementing the Road Map as written. Instead, Israel created its own understanding of the Road Map whereby it would only accept a provisional Palestinian state comprising half of the occupied territories only and for an indefinite time" (2008, 197). Kathleen Christison, a former CIA analyst on the Palestinian issue, asserted that the history of the Road Map "is again the story of an opportunity bypassed" (2004, 39).[10] In contrast, Miller opined that "few people I know, and I'd put myself at the top of the list, really believed the road map had much of a chance to get the car out of the parking lot, let alone onto the highway" (2008, 351). So, to what extent was the Road Map an opportunity missed?

When the far-reaching plan was launched in late April 2003, it seems that there was a window of opportunity, caused by the coalescence of three developments in the region: the overwhelming US victory in Iraq, which led to the overthrow of the Saddam Hussein regime; the emergence of an alternative Palestinian leadership ('Abbas as prime minister), which allowed the US and Israel their preferred option of bypassing 'Arafat; and the reelection of Sharon as the Israeli prime minister with a coalition that allowed him more room to maneuver. The Road Map could have been considered as an attractive offer by both sides: for the Palestinians it offered a way out of the political deadlock caused by the Intifada, the establishment of a state in provisional borders in the short run, and a permanent state, with borders yet to be delineated, within no more than three years. Obviously, the plan was fraught with potential problems, but at least in theory it outlined a possible political horizon for the Palestinians. For the Israelis, it offered an immediate cessation of violence and terror, the acknowledgment of a provisional Palestinian state only on territories that had already been given to the Palestinians in the Oslo process, and a vague promise to deal with the permanent issues of refugees, Jerusalem, and borders within three years. In many ways, therefore, a historical opportunity existed.

And what was the potentiality level of the opportunity? The first variable relates to the legitimacy level of the leadership. On the Israeli side, Sharon enjoyed wide, arguably unprecedented, legitimacy as a result of what was perceived in Israeli society as his iron fist against the Intifada. In the January 2003 elections the Likud Party swept to a prominent position (soaring from nineteen to thirty-eight seats in the Knesset). The Labor Party and the left in general suffered a major defeat, which enabled Sharon to establish a sixty-six-strong coalition with two right-wing parties, as well as the surprising Shinui—a centrist, secularist, middle-class party (Rabinovich 2004, 212). Yet the changes in Sharon's position toward the notion of a Palestinian state aroused opposition within his party and among the other right-wing partners. With much difficulty he managed to get his government to approve the Road Map, though only by a small margin. His limited political room for maneuvering, however, could have been overcome by bringing Labor into the coalition—a move taken only in January 2005 when the Disengagement Plan from Gaza became relevant (it was approved by the Knesset in February and implemented in August). On the other side, 'Arafat was still recognized by the Palestinians as the elected leader and the symbol of their struggle for ending the occupation. Yet his leadership was now being questioned in his own society, particularly by those supporting the continuation of the military operations carried out by Hamas and Islamic Jihad. Hamas's popularity had particularly surged during the Intifada (Milton-Edwards and Crooke 2004, 39–52). Realizing the potential of armed struggle to increase his popularity, 'Arafat built and used the al-Aqsa Martyrs Brigade as a military arm of Fatah.[11] He was challenged by those who considered the suicide bombings as harmful to the Palestinian cause (like 'Abbas). Yet the fact that the United States and Israel, and to some extent the European Union, did not see 'Arafat as a possible partner for negotiations may have encouraged his tendency to sabotage the Road Map while stigmatizing his chosen heir ('Abbas) as a Western and Israeli stooge. By the time 'Arafat died, in November 2004, the Road Map was hardly valid.

The second variable relates to the level of determination of the leaders to take bold decisions. Neither Sharon nor 'Arafat—each for his own reasons—seemed determined or bold enough to pursue the Road Map. Though Sharon underwent a certain metamorphosis in his personal position toward the notion of a Palestinian state, he did not see the Road Map as the appropriate method for achieving this aim. The statement by his biographers Hefez and

Bloom that "deep in his heart Sharon did not give the Road Map a chance" is perhaps indicative of his way of thinking; he was more inclined to implement the first phase, which dealt with terrorism, and then adopt a long interim settlement that would build some trust between the parties, thereby postponing the establishment of a Palestinian state indefinitely (Weissglas 2012, 196). In other words, Sharon's demonstrated ability to harness reality to his worldview helped not in implementing the Road Map but rather in furthering the Disengagement Plan from Gaza. Likewise, ʿArafat, who had been declared irrelevant by the US and Israel, had no incentive to support the Road Map. Moreover, his newly appointed prime minister, ʿAbbas, who seemed determined to pursue this track, was blocked by ʿArafat's aides and was compelled to resign as a result of his inability to further his own policy. Ross concluded that "The roadmap reflected agreement with parties that had no responsibility for carrying out even one of the steps they were calling for" (2005, 788).

The third variable relates to the history of past interactions, which affects the level of trust existing between the parties. When the Road Map was launched, the Intifada had entered its third year. During the years of the uprising (2000–2004) more than one thousand Israelis and three thousand Palestinians were killed. The Palestinian suicide bombings, on the one hand, and the Israeli retaliatory policy of targeted assassinations and military operations, on the other, increased the mutual mistrust that had been building since the collapse of the Oslo Accords and the Camp David summit. Both leaders— Sharon and ʿArafat—epitomized the evil face of the other side. They had never met each other. Ironically, each carried with him the negative image of the other formed during the 1982 Lebanon War. Both had undergone a process of demonization in the other's society. This prevalent negativity made it more difficult to move forward. Moreover, the disbelief in the possibility of a peaceful solution was high; polls among Israeli society showed that while almost 60 percent supported the Road Map, only 34 percent believed that it could succeed in ending the Israeli-Palestinian conflict. At the same time, 51 percent believed that their chances of being hit in a terror attack were very high or relatively high (Golan 2007, 92).[12] In other words, suspicion, fear, and lack of trust in the other's intentions were evident on the Israeli side. Similar views, no doubt, could be found on the Palestinian side as well.

The fourth variable relates to the role of the mediating third party. In this case the United States, as part of the Quartet, initiated the peace plan and therefore was expected to fill the role of an involved mediator. Indeed, Bush initially promised he would steer the parties forward until they had reached agreements. Yet the US role proved to be problematic for two reasons. First, it was too closely identified with the Israeli position, and with Sharon's position in particular. This alienated the Palestinians to the point of jeopardizing the anticipated balanced US role in the negotiations. According to Christison, Bush "did virtually nothing to ensure Israel's compliance with the plan's demands" (2004, 39). From a Palestinian perspective, the American interference in choosing their own leadership was particularly annoying (Aruri 2003, 206–210). Second, in reality even Bush did not demonstrate a full commitment to implementing the Road Map. Mild disapproval was voiced by Muasher: "The United States also could have used its influence with the parties more effectively" (2008, 197). From Miller the criticism was more scathing; in his opinion, neither the Israelis nor the Palestinians were serious about implementing the plan. No less important, however, was that "No serious American diplomacy followed the president's speech on the Road Map for the remainder of the president's first term" (2008, 352). Bush's rather indifferent behavior probably stemmed from his preoccupation with the lingering Iraqi crisis, as well as his disappointment with the lack of cooperation from both the Israelis and the Palestinians in implementing the Road Map. Perhaps Clinton's legacy of "over-involvement" in the conflict led Bush to downplay the US role (Kurtzer et al. 2013, 188).

In the final analysis, the Road Map presented a historical opportunity, but the plausibility level of a missed opportunity was low. Only one variable, the lack of mediator involvement, was relevant; the other three variables — legitimacy deficiency on both sides, lack of determination to pursue the Road Map on both sides, and lack of trust — refute the notion that it was a missed opportunity. It is particularly important to emphasize that all the relevant parties here (the Quartet, including the United States, the Palestinians, and Israel) displayed apathy, inaction, and indifference with regard to the actual implementation of the Road Map. No party showed real enthusiasm for promoting it. Thus, in spite of the hard work invested in formulating this detailed peace plan, it is no wonder that it soon sank into oblivion.

NOTES

1. See the text in the *Guardian*, March 12, 2002.

2. Aruri even suggested that "Bush's repeated threats to the Palestinians would make anyone wonder whether his [Bush's] speech was written by Ariel Sharon" (2003, 206). The tilt toward Israel was confirmed by Abrams, who served as his deputy national adviser (2013, 2, 42).

3. Muasher's version was confirmed by Miller, who wrote of the meeting: "And with that the road map exercise was born. And it would remain just that — an exercise" (2008, 351).

4. 'Arafat had appointed 'Abbas on March 19 after considerable pressure by the US and EU. Yet the cabinet was approved only on April 23. The delay, according to Muasher, "revealed that Arafat's appointment of Abbas had not been done wholeheartedly. Nor, it seemed, was he enthusiastic about delegating his authority to the prime minister" (2008, 184).

5. For the text of the Road Map, see Meital 2006, 225–230. The analysis in this chapter is based on the following sources: Golan 2007, 77–92; Meital 2006, 163–165; Muasher 2008, 176–180; Bush 2011, 405; Rice 2011, 215–216; Rabinovich 2004, 212–219; Kurtzer et al. 2013, 174–178; Abrams 2013, 49–52.

6. The stormy government session took six hours. The final vote was a reflection of the divisions within the coalition: 12 voted in favor, 7 opposed, and 4 were absent; see Weissglas 2012, 188–189.

7. Weissglas, who served as Sharon's chief of staff, claimed that the prime minister was mainly interested in implementing the first phase of the Road Map, which dealt with the question of terror, but remained evasive regarding the last phase of establishing a Palestinian state, though he never protested against it (2012, 183–196).

8. *Haaretz*, June 4, 2003. Rice, who was responsible for drafting the text as Bush's national adviser, relates the whole story where the Saudi crown prince threatened to go home (2011, 217–218). See also Abrams 2013, 69–71.

9. For the texts of the speeches, see http://www.al-bab.com/arab/docs/pal/aqaba03 .htm; for the Hebrew version, see *Haaretz*, June 5, 2003.

10. For another assessment of the Road Map as an opportunity, see the article by influential *al-Ahram* editor Ibrahim Nafie', "No Evasions," *al-Ahram Weekly* 640 (May 29–June 4, 2003).

11. The reliability of polls on the Palestinian side is questionable. Still, a poll conducted by Bir Zeit University showed that 71 percent of respondents favored a halt in resistance operations in exchange for international guarantees for an equitable peace process. See Nafie', "No Evasions."

12. www.peaceindex.org, May 2003.

CHAPTER 23

THE ANNAPOLIS CONFERENCE AND ABU MAZEN–OLMERT TALKS

2007–2008

ENVOYS FROM FORTY-NINE countries and international organizations converged on Annapolis, Maryland, on November 27, 2007, in a major show of support for the relaunching of the Israeli-Palestinian peace negotiations on permanent status issues, with the two-state solution to the conflict as the desired outcome. The conference did indeed bring about the revival of the bilateral talks in December 2007; they lasted for a year, until the beginning of the Israeli military action in Gaza, Operation Cast Lead, against Hamas in December 2008 and the resignation of the Olmert government. These were the first official meetings between the Israelis and Palestinians since the collapse of the dialogue during the Clinton-Barak era. The protocols of the meetings between Foreign Minister Tzipi Livni, the head of the Israeli delegation, and Abu 'Ala, head of the Palestinian delegation, which were leaked to the media by al-Jazeera,[1] as well as the revelations of the Abu Mazen–Olmert Talks (Olmert 2011, Erekat 2009), show that the gaps between the parties on the key permanent issues were not substantial. The aim of this chapter is to assess if and to what extent an opportunity for peace was missed by the two parties.

THE EPISODE

The launching of the Road Map in April 2003 did not lead to a diplomatic breakthrough; the two parties did not fulfill the obligations specified in the first phase of the plan, which included a freeze on settlement activity on the Israeli side and the cessation of terror operations on the Palestinian side. As a result, they both remained bogged down in the vicious circle of Palestinian terror operations (mainly by the Hamas movement) and Israeli retaliatory attacks. The diplomatic deadlock led Sharon to declare on December 18, 2003, that in order to ensure "a Jewish and democratic Israel," he would unilaterally disengage from the Palestinians by redeploying Israeli forces and relocating settlements in the Gaza Strip elsewhere, while intensifying the construction of the security fence in the West Bank. The idea of a unilateral step came as a result of Sharon's realization that ʿArafat and the PA could not be counted on as a viable partner for peace. Sharon managed to overcome the fierce public debate regarding the wisdom of withdrawing from the Gaza Strip without an agreement with the PA; in June 2004 the government approved a plan to evacuate all twenty-one settlements in the Gaza Strip and four settlements in the northern West Bank. The disengagement was finally implemented in August 2005 amid heightened emotions among the settlers and indeed around Israel (Migdalovitz 2010, 12–14; Bar-Siman-Tov and Michael 2005, 346–374; Golan 2007, 119–130; Weissglas 2012, 208–217).

The United States fully supported Sharon's disengagement policy. In a letter sent on April 14, 2004, Bush reiterated the US commitment to the vision of a two-state solution as described in the Road Map. Offering Sharon a certain reward for the disengagement, the president noted that, with regard to the borders of the future Palestinian state, "It is unrealistic to expect that the outcome of the final status negotiations will be a full and complete return to the armistice lines of 1949," meaning that the 1967 borders would have to be modified to take account of Israeli settlement blocs. The letter also reiterated Clinton's position that the solution to the Palestinian refugee problem "will need to be found through the establishment of a Palestinian state, and the settling of Palestinian refugees there, rather than in Israel" (Golan 2007, 131–135, 217–220; Miller 2008, 355–356; Bush 2011, 406; Weissglas 2012, 231–243; Abrams 2013, 105–109).

Meanwhile, important changes were taking place among the Palestinians. ʿArafat had died in November 2004 and was replaced by Mahmoud ʿAbbas (Abu Mazen), who was elected president of the Palestinian Authority in January 2005. The challenge posed by Hamas to the PA materialized when the radical group won the parliamentary elections on January 25, 2006. As a result, ʿAbbas had no choice but to nominate Hamas leader Ismaʿil Haniyeh to form a government. The fact that Hamas did not recognize Israel, would not renounce terrorism, and vowed to liberate the whole of Palestine raised another major obstacle to a resumption of negotiations. The PA now had two heads, one advocating a peaceful solution and one bent on continuing the armed struggle for liberating Palestine. Israel began to treat the PA as a hostile entity, though it continued its contacts with the moderate Fatah faction. Meanwhile, terror operations inside Israel and shelling from the Gaza Strip continued on a sporadic basis throughout 2006 (Migdalovitz 2010, 15–17; Rabinovich 2011, 209–213; Kurtzer et al. 2013, 197–203).[2]

On the Israeli side, important changes took place as well. As a result of the fierce opposition to his disengagement policy within the Likud, Sharon decided to quit the party with which he had been strongly identified for over thirty years and found a new one called Kadima (meaning "forward" in Hebrew) in November 2005. Losing his majority in the Knesset as well, he opted for early elections, fixed for March 26, 2006. Kadima managed to attract many leading Likud members dissatisfied with the party's recent radical right-wing tendency who preferred instead to follow Sharon's charismatic personality. However, Sharon suffered an incapacitating stroke on January 4, 2006, and was replaced by his deputy, Ehud Olmert, another former Likud stalwart. Miller opined that Olmert was "smart, centrist, and pragmatic, but lacked the moral or historical legitimacy to sell big decisions" (2008, 356). However, Sharon's legacy was strong enough to push Kadima to victory in the elections, enabling Olmert to establish a coalition on May 4 that included between sixty-seven and seventy-eight members. The problem was that it was a heterogeneous government, composed of various—and even antagonistic— ideologies. Still, Olmert seemed determined to pursue a peaceful dialogue with the Palestinians (a key Kadima premise), with the aim of demarcating final borders for a state enjoying a Jewish majority (Rabinovich 2011, 208– 209). Olmert was elected on the basis of his "convergence" (or realignment) plan, which meant that in the absence of a Palestinian partner, Israel would unilaterally withdraw from most of the territories in the West Bank and retain the rest, thus incorporating the dense Jewish settlements into Israel. In many ways, this was an extension of Sharon's Gaza Disengagement Plan (ibid., 208; Weissglas 2012, 281–294; Abrams 2013, 170–174).

Yet the first problem that Olmert's government had to face was the growing challenge posed by the Hizballah organization along the Lebanese border, which included the occasional shelling of military and civil targets in northern Israel between May 2005 and June 2006. It culminated with an ambush by Hizballah on July 12 that resulted in the death of three Israeli soldiers and the kidnapping of another two (later it became known that they had been killed as well). This provocation brought the government to initiate a military operation (later known as the Second Lebanon War), which commenced on July 12 and ended on August 14, when the parties agreed to a cease-fire based on UN Security Council Resolution 1701. In the long run the war strengthened Israel's deterrence capability vis-à-vis Hizballah, though in the short run it was perceived as a setback for the IDF and a victory for Hizballah. In its wake, Chief of Staff Dan Halutz and other leading officers had to resign (January 2007). In April the interim report of the Winograd Commission, tasked to investigate the conduct of the decision makers and the army during the war, laid the responsibility for the mistakes made in the preparation, decision making, and conduct of the war squarely on the top political and defense echelons. Minister of Defense Amir Peretz resigned in June, though not as a result of the report but because Ehud Barak defeated him in the Labor Party primaries and consequently also replaced him in his post. Olmert managed to evade responsibility, but his legitimacy and credibility among the public were severely damaged (Harel and Issacharoff 2008, 451–456, 483–485; Shelah and Limor 2007, 406–416; Rabinovich 2011, 212–217; Kurtzer et al. 2013, 203–209).

The war affected the regional balance of power in a meaningful way. Iran's quest for a nuclear arsenal and its alliance with Hizballah and Syria brought Israel and the Sunni Arab moderate countries of Egypt, Jordan, and Saudi Arabia closer. In addition, the growing rift between Hamas and the Fatah (see below) led to the revival of the dialogue concerning the Arab Peace Initiative (API) as a possible avenue for solving the broader Arab-Israeli conflict (see chapter 21). At the same time, Olmert sought ways to reignite the diplomatic process with 'Abbas. A propitious moment presented itself when the two leaders agreed to a cease-fire in Gaza on November 25, 2006, which Hamas agreed also to honor (Migdalovitz 2010, 17). Two days later, Olmert used the occasion of the annual memorial ceremony for Israel's first prime minister, David Ben-Gurion, at his graveside in Sde Boker, to deliver a conciliatory speech, in which he quoted the founding father: "I would consider it a great sin, not only towards our generation but future generations as well, if we did not do everything in our power to reach a mutual understanding with our Arab neighbors, and if future generations had cause to blame the Government of Israel of missing an opportunity for peace." Olmert promised to invite Abu Mazen to meet with him "to conduct a real, open, genuine and serious dialogue," based on Bush's letter to Sharon of April 14, 2004.[3] This speech was important because it proved that Olmert now had a defined political agenda and that he was determined to pursue it. Indeed, the first meeting between the two leaders took place on December 23 at the prime minister's residence in Jerusalem. They then met no less than thirty-six times during the next eighteen months (Avishai 2011; Olmert 2011).

Yet the auspicious start was interrupted by important developments in the Palestinian political arena. In February 2007, Saudi Arabia managed to broker a deal—the Mecca Agreement—which led to the formation of a Palestinian unity government, headed by Haniyeh. The new government declared that it respects (rather than accepts) international resolutions and agreements signed by the PLO. Haniyeh was even quoted to the effect that he would work for the establishment of an independent Palestinian state, with Jerusalem as its capital, along the 1967 borders. This proved to be a temporary and misleading lull in the Hamas-Fatah dispute; in May, factional fighting in Gaza between the two organizations escalated, leading to the Hamas takeover of Gaza on June 14. Consequently, 'Abbas declared a state of emergency, dissolved the unity government, and named Salam Fayyad prime minister. On July 27,

Fayyad presented his new government, which vowed to establish a state on all lands occupied in 1967, with Jerusalem as its capital and a just and mutually agreed solution for the refugees (Migdalovitz 2010, 19–20; Miller 2008, 356–357; Kurtzer et al. 2013, 213–217; Abrams 2013, 217–232).

Aaron David Miller wrote that the June 2007 crisis did, as crises often do, "generate a good deal of peace-process motion" (2008, 358). Indeed, the institutionalization of the formal division of Gaza—under Hamas's control—and the West Bank—under the control of the PA, Fatah, and ʿAbbas—opened new opportunities in the realm of Israeli-Palestinian relations, which led to the adoption of a "West Bank-First" policy. Less than two weeks after the Hamas takeover of Gaza, Olmert, ʿAbbas, Egyptian president Mubarak, and Jordan's king ʿAbdallah II met in Sharm al-Shaykh with US encouragement. Olmert's speech at the summit reflected his determination:

> "I believe," he said, "that the conditions are ripe for this [resumption of negotiations]. I intend to exhaust every avenue, together with you [President ʿAbbas], so that we realize this hope, and transform it into reality. I am optimistic by nature, and it is precisely during these stormy days that I see a chance as well. An opportunity has been created to advance seriously the political process in the region and I do not intend to let this opportunity pass."

Olmert vowed to work with the PA to implement the Road Map. He promised to renew security and economic cooperation; to transfer tax monies; and to improve freedom of movement in the West Bank. He also acknowledged the suffering of the Palestinian people and promised to meet ʿAbbas regularly to advance mutual issues (Migdalovitz 2010, 19–20; Kurtzer et al. 2013, 218–220).[4]

Secretary of State Rice thought too that the developments in the Palestinian arena offered an opportunity: "ʿAbbas needed an agreement with Israel," she wrote, "and Olmert seemed ready to give him one" (2011, 600). She raised with Bush the idea of holding an international conference, which would "help sustain the good guys by giving international momentum to the process" (ibid., 601). The conference was meant to serve as a springboard for reviving bilateral negotiations between Israel and the Palestinians. Bush was initially skeptical: "The aftermath of a terrorist coup didn't seem the most opportune time for a peace summit. But I came to like the idea. If wavering Palestinians could see that a state was a realistic possibility, they would have an incentive to reject violence and support reform" (2011, 408).[5] On July 16, Bush called for an "international meeting this fall of representatives from nations that support a two-state solution, reject violence, recognize Israel's right to exist, and commit to all previous agreements between the parties" (Migdalovitz 2010, 20). It was to take place in Annapolis, Maryland, at the US Naval Academy.

Following this announcement, Rice attempted to form a broad coalition of moderate Arab and Muslim countries willing to abide by the conference's terms of reference: a two-state solution, rejection of violence, recognition of Israel's right to exist, and commitment to all previous agreements. Meanwhile, Israel and the PA, which expressed their willingness to take part, began a series of meetings to try to reach a declaration of principles before the conference. A negotiating team was formed, headed by Livni and Abu ʿAla. In addition, Olmert met periodically with Abu Mazen. However, the two sides could not bridge the gaps: Israel was unwilling to go beyond a general statement so as not to make major concessions before the formal start of the negotiations and prevent the crystallization of domestic opposition; the Palestinians, for their part, demanded a more detailed statement relating to the permanent status issues to show their public that negotiations could lead to tangible achievements (Migdalovitz 2010, 20; 2007, 2). Though little progress was achieved during these talks, it was apparent that the Israeli side was determined to move forward.[6] Eventually, in fact just one hour before the conference opened, Olmert and ʿAbbas succeeded in penning a "Joint Understanding," which amounted only to a document dealing with procedural matters (Kurtzer et al. 2013, 222; Rice 2011, 613–614; Bush 2011, 408–409).

In all, forty-nine countries and international organizations participated in the Annapolis Conference—the first-ever international parley held in the United States—on November 26–27, 2007. Most of the Arab countries took part, including Saudi Arabia and Syria. Saudi Arabia's participation was highly significant, as it had also played a role in promoting the API, which had most recently been reconfirmed as the Arab formula for a comprehensive Israeli-Arab peace at the Riyadh Arab summit in March that year (see chapter 21). Syria consented to attend only after it became clear that the issue of the Golan Heights would be on the agenda. It sent only the deputy foreign minister, while all the other delegations were led by their foreign ministers (except for the US, Israel, and the PA). The impressive Arab gathering can be attributed to their need for a strategic alliance with the US against Iran and may have indicated support for ʿAbbas over Hamas (Migdalovitz 2007, 2–3; Rice 2011, 617; Abdullah 2011, 278–279).

The public part of the conference included several speeches delivered on November 27. Bush began by reading the Joint Understanding reached between Olmert and ʿAbbas, which stipulated that they "shall make every effort to conclude an agreement before the end of 2008." For that purpose, a steering committee of both sides was to meet continuously, the first session to be held on December 12. Simultaneously, ʿAbbas and Olmert would meet on a biweekly basis to follow up on the negotiations. The parties also pledged to immediately implement their respective obligations under the Road Map. In addition, a tripartite committee, led by the United States, would monitor the implementation of the Road Map (Bush 2008). In his own speech, Bush noted the existence of a historical opportunity to promote peace, pledging to personally support the negotiations with the resources and resolve of the US.[7] ʿAbbas's speech emphasized the necessity of the talks to deal with all the permanent status issues, as well as the taking of tangible steps on the ground, which would serve as a proof to Palestinian society "of having embarked on an irreversible track toward a negotiated, comprehensive, and full peace." Such steps must involve freezing all settlement activities including natural growth, removing checkpoints, removing settlement outposts, releasing prisoners, and facilitating the mission of the PA in restoring law and order. ʿAbbas pledged to carry out the Palestinian responsibilities within the Road Map. He also acknowledged Olmert's determination for peace, as reflected in their bilateral talks. Olmert, for his part, emphasized Israel's sincere desire to achieve peace, vowing to address in the negotiations all and any issues that had been avoided thus far. Another statement was made by Saʿud al-Faysal, the Saudi foreign minister, who repeated ʿAbbas's demands for Israeli immediate steps on the ground while also declaring Saudi commitment to promoting peace in the Middle East. The formal public part concluded with Rice's speech. As the main architect of the conference, she ended with a personal touch, drawing some inspiration from the tough environment of her childhood in Birmingham, Alabama, to life for the Palestinians, which could be transformed as a result of peace (Rice 2011, 616). Considering that meaningful Israeli-Palestinian discussions or core issues had not been held for seven years, the conference could be seen as a success. The Palestinians were able to remove implementation of the Road Map as a precondition for final status negotiations, obtained a one-year target date, and brought in the United States as a judge to monitor the parties' fulfillment of their commitments. Israel, for its part, succeeded in making any peace treaty dependent upon the Road Map, particularly in the security field, and received some assurances from Bush regarding the Jewish character of the state (Rice 2011, 615; Bush 2011, 409; Kurtzer et al. 2013, 223–225; Abrams 2013, 253–256).

The Annapolis Conference allowed the parties to skip into phase III of the Road Map, discussing the final status issues. Both Israelis and Palestinians preferred to negotiate directly without US involvement. The formal talks began on December 12, 2007, though the opening was brief due to the Palestinian protest against a tender published by Israel for the construction of 307 new housing units in Har Homa (Jabal Abu Ghneim, in southeast Jerusalem)

(Migdalovitz 2010, 21–22). Serious talks between two parallel but often un-coordinated delegations (one led by Livni and Abu ʿAla and the other by Olmert and Abu-Mazen) took place in January–September 2008. In addition, twelve committees were set up to discuss the core issues of borders, water, settlements, refugees, Jerusalem, security, and other topics (including "culture of peace"). A major meeting between Olmert and Abu Mazen was held on September 16, the day before Livni was elected chair of the Kadima Party, following Olmert's decision not to run as a result of corruption charges he was facing. On September 21, Olmert submitted his resignation to the president.[8] On the basis of the available information (Swisher 2011; Olmert 2011; Erekat 2009; Kurtzer et al. 2013, 228–233; Abrams 2013, 274–275; Arieli 2013, 258–274, 337, 401, 462–464; Lehrs 2011, 52–63; Golan 2015, 179–182; Avishai 2011; Birnbaum 2013),[9] the main points that emerged in the talks were as follows:

Borders. Olmert suggested that Israel would annex 6.5 percent of the West Bank, including the four main settlement blocs of Gush Etzion, Maʿale Adumim, Givʿat Zeʾev, and Ariel, as well as the Jewish neighborhoods in East Jerusalem (including Har Homa), in exchange for the equivalent of 5.8 percent from Israeli territory. The rest (0.7 percent) would be given as a "safe passage" (territorial link) between Gaza and the West Bank (Olmert suggested a forty-kilometer tunnel) under Israeli sovereignty with Palestinian control. East Jerusalem would be divided along the lines of the Clinton Parameters, with the exception of the Holy Basin, the sovereignty of which would be finalized at a later stage (see below). During the talks Israel demanded a military presence in the Jordan Valley, while the Palestinians insisted on the deployment of international (that is, American) forces. In his final offer to ʿAbbas, Olmert demanded a military presence along the Jordanian-Palestinian border too, though he preferred not to specify the required security arrangement. It should be emphasized that Olmert was the first Israeli prime minister to agree that the 1967 boundaries would be the basis for negotiations over the meaning of "occupied territories." The Palestinians presented a consistent position with regard to the territory of the Palestinian state: all the land Israel occupied in 1967, whose total area is 6,238 square kilometers. That includes the no-man's-land near Latrun, East Jerusalem, and the Jordan Valley. Any amendments to these borders should keep Palestinian interests, geographical continuity, viability, and sovereignty within the context of a swap by the ratio of 1:1 with the same value and size, not exceeding 1.9 percent of the land. It was clarified that some settlements—such as Maʿale Adumim, Givʿat Zeʾev, Abu Ghneim, and Ariel—could not be included under any condition. This meant that the Palestinians accepted the Israeli demand for controlling all the Jewish neighborhoods in East Jerusalem except for Har Homa. In fact, the specific maps that the Palestinians submitted to the Israelis suggested that some 63–70 per-

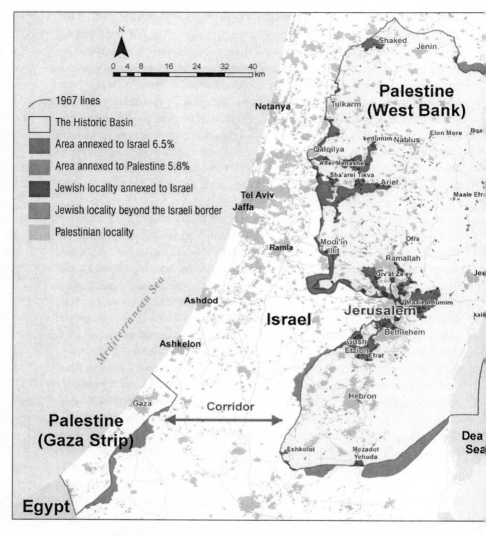

MAP 23.1. Post-Annapolis Talks, 2008: The Israeli Proposal. Courtesy of Shaul Arieli, 2013.

cent of the settlers would be included in the 1.9 percent annexed to Israel.[10] Thus, officially, the territorial gap between the parties was around 4 percent of the West Bank. No wonder that Livni, at the end of one of the sessions in April, concluded: "The gap is not big. It is about 350–450 square kilometers. Future generations will blame us and never forgive us if we lose this opportunity because of the gap" (Swisher 2011, 138).[11]

Security. Israel demanded that the future Palestinian state would be com-

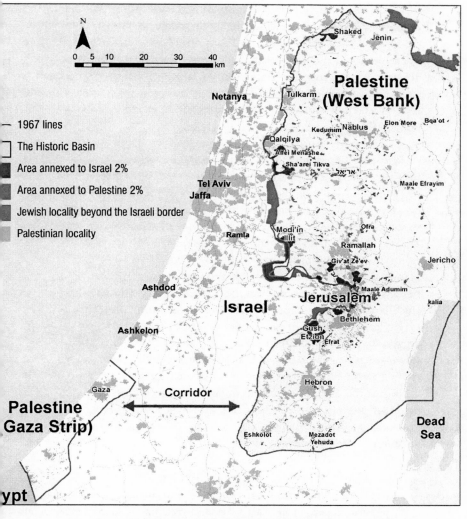

MAP 23.2. Post-Annapolis Talks, 2008: The Palestinian Proposal. Courtesy of Shaul
Arieli, 2013.

pletely demilitarized, while the Palestinians opted for a "limitedly militarized"
state. In any case, they agreed that they would have no army but rather an
army of a third party (preferably the United States) that would help build the
security capabilities and protect them from external threats. The logic of that
position was that a third-party force would never be seen as an occupier but
a helper. Israel demanded to control the Palestinian airspace; the Palestinians
rejected this demand, under the pretext that they could not accept "security

that breaches our right for sovereignty and the establishment of a truly Palestinian state." The same principle guided their objection to Israeli presence in the Jordan Valley and their demand to control border crossings.[12] The Palestinians accepted the Israeli demand for early warning stations connected to Tel Aviv, but not that they be manned by Israelis. Israel also asked for assurances that no foreign army would enter Palestine, while in case of invasion Israel would have the option of defending itself beyond the mutually agreed border. The negotiations in this field certainly left the impression that a deal was within reach (Kurtzer et al. 2013, 229; Arieli 2013, 337).

Jerusalem. Significantly, no separate committee was established to deal with the issue of Jerusalem, yet the subject was discussed by Olmert and ʿAbbas and by Livni and Abu ʿAla. The Israeli position was that all the Jewish neighborhoods in East Jerusalem would become Israeli, while the Arab neighborhoods would become Palestinian; in the Old City, the Jewish Quarter and Western Wall would remain under Israeli sovereignty, while neither party would exercise the sovereignty of the rest of the so-called "Holy Basin"—including al-Haram al-Sharif. The two sides would confer administrative powers to a third party, similar to the situation in the Vatican. The Palestinians agreed to include in the Israeli territory all the Jewish neighborhoods in East Jerusalem except for Jabal Abu Ghneim. In the words of Erekat, the Jews received "the biggest Yerushalayim in Jewish history" (Swisher 2010, 27). The Palestinian side insisted that the status of East Jerusalem should be identical to the rest of the Palestinian territory (that is, considered occupied territory) and that it become the capital of the Palestinian state. The discussion did not reveal the exact position of the Palestinians with regard to the Holy Basin. In his final offer to ʿAbbas, Olmert suggested the following, according to Rice's testimony:

> There will be two capitals, one for us in West Jerusalem and one for the Palestinians in East Jerusalem. The mayor of the joint city council will be selected by population percentage. That means an Israeli mayor, so the deputy should be a Palestinian. We will continue to provide security for the Holy sites because we can assure access to them . . . I've been thinking about how to administer the Old City. There should be a committee of people—not officials, but wise people—from Jordan, Saudi Arabia, the Palestinians, the United States and Israel. They will oversee the city but not in a political role. (Rice 2011, 651; Olmert 2011)

The parties narrowed their differences with regard to Israeli and Palestinian "borders" of Jerusalem, though the nature of the settlement in the Holy Basin was still to be negotiated.

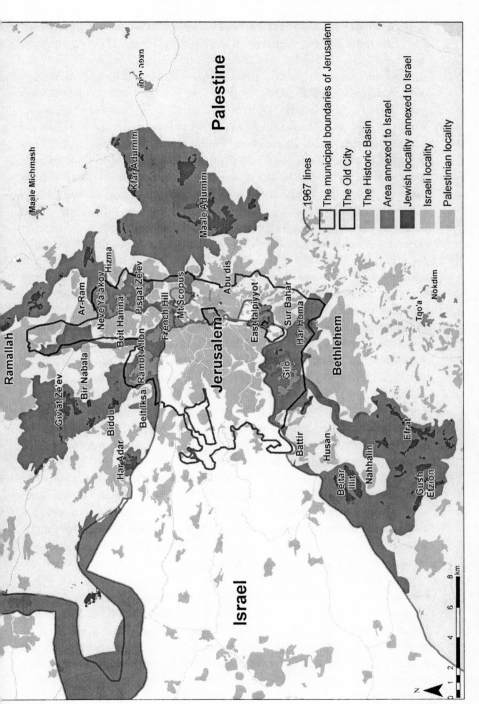

MAP 23.3. Jerusalem: The Israeli Proposal, 2008. Courtesy of Shaul Arieli, 2013.

The map shows:

Israel · **Palestine** · **Jerusalem** · **Ramallah** · **Bethlehem**

Localities labeled: Maale Michmash, Kfar Adumim, Maale Adumim, Ar-Ram, Hizma, Neve Ya'akov, Pisgat Ze'ev, Beit Hanina, Mt Scopus, French Hill, Abu dis, East talpiyyot, Sur Bahar, Har Homa, Gilo, Giv'at Ze'ev, Bir Nabala, Biddu, Beit Iksa, Ramot Allon, Har Adar, Battir, Husan, Nahhalin, Betar Illit, Gush Etzion, Efrat, Nokdim, Tqo'a

Legend:
- 1967 lines
- The municipal boundaries of Jerusalem
- The Old City
- The Historic Basin
- Area annexed to Israel
- Jewish locality annexed to Israel
- Israeli locality
- Palestinian locality

Scale: 0 1 2 4 6 8 km

Refugees. The talks on the refugee issue tended to be general and focused on the narrative and the modalities of solving the problem. Thus, for example, the Palestinians demanded that Israel acknowledge its "responsibility" for the problem, while the Israelis were willing to acknowledge the "suffering" of the refugees (Swisher 2010, 110, 172, 179, 206–210). It was Olmert who gave ʿAbbas a more detailed offer in their meeting on September 16: Israel would take in one thousand refugees per year for a period of five years on a "humanitarian" basis. In addition, "family reunification" programs would continue. Israel would act to establish an international fund that would offer "generous compensation" to the Palestinians, Jews, and Israelis suffering from the wars. Its budget would come from international donors willing to help end the conflict. In any case, compensation, not restitution or return, would be the only remedy for acceptable solution to the refugee problem (apart from the numbers cited above). In addition, as noted, Israel would acknowledge the suffering of—and not responsibility for—the Palestinian refugees. In parallel, mention must also be made of Israeli (or Jewish) suffering in the Arab countries. Olmert emphasized that this arrangement would be conditioned on a Palestinian written commitment that the agreement spelled the end of all claims and the end of the conflict. He further emphasized that it would be written that this part of the agreement was concluded in the spirit of the Arab Peace Initiative. The Palestinian response was that while it was willing to negotiate the number of returnees in consideration of Israel's capacity of absorption, the offer "is not serious and cannot be accepted" (Swisher 2010, 215). Erekat states that the Palestinian position was the return to Israel of fifteen thousand refugees per year for ten years, renewable thereafter at the agreement of both parties. The Israeli version was that this number was unofficially lowered to eighty thousand (Erekat 2009).[13]

The al-Jazeera protocols and Olmert's recollections give the essence of the talks between the Israeli and Palestinian parties. Conflicting narratives, however, emerged with regard to the end of these talks: Olmert said that ʿAbbas asked for some time to consult with his advisers but never came back (2011). This version is supported by Rice, who claims that in spite of the fact that both Olmert and Bush were considered "lame ducks," she was apprehensive lest the opportunity slip away. Therefore, Bush invited Olmert and ʿAbbas to Washington separately in November. "The President took Abbas into the Oval Office alone and appealed to him to reconsider," recalled Rice. "The Palestinians stood firm, and the idea died" (2011, 723–724). The Palestinian side, however, tells a different story; according to Erekat, Bush delivered to both parties a memo summing up the positions, along with maps, to be agreed upon and deposited with his administration to serve as a starting point for further negotiations. A meeting was scheduled for January 3, 2009, but when the

Olmert government launched Operation Cast Lead against Hamas in Gaza to end the years of rocket attacks on Israel, ʿAbbas canceled the meeting (Erekat 2009).

Bush, for his part, elaborated on the "deposit" issue:

We devised a process to turn the private offer [of Olmert to ʿAbbas] into a public agreement. Olmert would travel to Washington and deposit his proposal with me. Abbas would announce that the plan was in line with Palestinian interests. I would call the leaders together to finalize the deal.
The development represented a realistic hope for peace. But once again, an outside event intervened. Olmert had been under investigation . . . Abbas did not want to make an agreement with a prime minister on his way out of office. (Bush 2011, 409–410)[14]

Olmert attempted to strike a deal until his last day in office in the hope that a heroic achievement would turn into a referendum and save his premiership, or at least leave a legacy in the annals of the conflict. Aware of his tottering domestic legitimacy, Olmert's grand idea had an element of fantasy: to receive the unanimous support of the UN Security Council and General Assembly, the US Congress, and the European Parliament, to be followed by an official ceremony at the White House, ending with another ceremony at a certain point dividing East and West Jerusalem, where he and Abu Mazen would declare their commitment to support the agreement in all its aspects. Such ostentatious events, Olmert reasoned, would leave their marks on the Israeli public, leading to the approval of the agreement (Avishai 2011).

ʿAbbas's refusal or hesitancy to accept the deal stemmed from a combination of several factors: first, fear that the agreement would not be ratified by the Israeli government in its last days in office; second, signals received from Olmert's closest advisers and Livni's people not to sign but rather wait until she took over the country's top job (Abrams 2013, 285, 291; Rice 2011, 724); third, the domestic rivalries between Fatah and Hamas, which limited ʿAbbas's room to maneuver; and finally, ʿAbbas's hesitancy to take such a bold decision.

The elections in Israel, held on February 10, 2009, resulted in the formation of a new Netanyahu government on March 31. In their meetings with the US envoys following the Israeli and US elections, the Palestinians complained that they "are back to 1996–1999" (Swisher 2010, 249), referring to Netanyahu's first term as prime minister, when little progress was achieved in the diplomatic field. The new Israeli government's refusal to resume negotiations where they had left off sealed the fate of the Israeli-Palestinian negotiations.

ASSESSMENT

The Annapolis Conference and the ʿAbbas–Olmert Talks constituted a classic historical opportunity, as they combined a turning point in the conflict with the existence of an attractive offer. After the failure of the Camp David summit, the Clinton Parameters, and the Taba Talks, the parties were bogged down in the Intifada, which was followed by the Israeli Disengagement from Gaza (2005), the Hamas-Fatah rift, the Second Lebanon War (2006), and the Hamas takeover of Gaza (2007). The last two developments in particular created an opportune moment to form a moderate Arab and Islamic camp that would support the relaunching of the peace process and thus give legitimacy to the whole process. Olmert and Livni on the Israeli side and Abu Mazen, Abu ʿAla, and Fayyad on the Palestinian side were considered moderate leaders capable of delivering a negotiated settlement. The positions presented by the Palestinians and the Israelis during the post-Annapolis negotiations can be considered attractive enough, as they offered a new departure from previous offers.

What was the potentiality level of the opportunity? In terms of legitimacy, on the Israeli side there were serious problems; the Second Lebanon War caused Olmert's legitimacy to crumble in the public eye. The report of the Winograd Commission, which held the decision makers responsible for the failures of the IDF, only served to strengthen this trend. Olmert's coalition suffered from internal divisions as a result of political and ideological differences. In addition, the allegations against Olmert in various corruption cases further decreased his popularity and legitimacy in Israeli eyes. Bush and Rice were well aware that Olmert was a "lame duck" prime minister, yet they opted to bypass this problem. On the other side, ʿAbbas also suffered from a legitimacy deficiency as a result of the split, both physical and ideological, between Gaza, under Hamas's control, and the West Bank, under his/Fatah's control. Possibly demonstrating their thick politicians' skin, both leaders, however, believed that their legitimacy would be redeemed by the results of a referendum, which would overwhelmingly endorse a reasonable settlement. It is possible that Olmert thought—like Barak at Camp David—that a deal with the Palestinians ending all their claims might uplift his popularity. As late as November 2008, upon meeting Bush for the last time, Olmert was still optimistic about striking a deal despite his domestic problems (Abrams 2013, 287–288). For that purpose Olmert envisioned well-publicized media events that would help him to garner the necessary public support for his vision.

The second variable relates to the determination level of the leaders to make bold decisions. There are enough indications to attest that Olmert was highly determined to achieve a peaceful agreement. When Bush visited Israel in January 2008, Rice opined, "we'd both been impressed by Olmert's desire to get a deal" (2011, 650, 655). Later, when Rice met Olmert again, she reported to the president that "He wants a deal. And frankly, he might die trying to get one" (ibid., 652). Taking into account the volte-face that had occurred in Olmert's thinking with regard to the Palestinian issue since 2003 (see above), it is likely that he considered the Annapolis Conference and the subsequent negotiations as a historical opportunity to close a deal. The level of 'Abbas's determination to pursue the peace track was less clear-cut, though Rice was convinced that both parties "were trying very hard" (2011, 650). 'Abbas expressed his commitment to the talks, but he might have doubted Olmert's ability to deliver a deal. And in any case he did not consider Olmert's offer as a revolutionary Israeli position that necessitated an immediate response. Perhaps he was looking ahead, thinking that the United States under a new president, Barack Obama, and Israel under Livni as prime minister would display a more congenial attitude toward the Palestinians. The fact that 'Abbas did not embrace Bush's "deposit" idea was another indication of his hesitancy regarding the final deal.

The third variable relates to the level of trust existing between the parties. Israeli-Palestinian relations have gone through many ups and downs in the period since the Oslo Agreements. Yet the atmosphere in the post-Annapolis talks, as can be judged by the protocols of the negotiations, was cordial and respectful. 'Abbas sincerely related to Olmert as his "partner" (Swisher 2010, 214), and it appears that the feeling was mutual. Indeed, it can be safely assumed that in their thirty-six meetings, a certain trust was indeed developed between Olmert and Abu Mazen. Thus in contrast to the suspicion and deep mistrust that had developed between Israelis and Palestinians after the failure of the Camp David summit and the outbreak of al-Aqsa Intifada, Israeli and Palestinian leaders succeeded in developing a measure of trust.

The fourth variable relates to the role of the third party. The United States was involved in the organization of the Annapolis Conference, and yet Bush's involvement was limited; it was "Condi's issue," according to Miller. He emphasized that "This train [Annapolis] was driven by a secretary of state who saw an opportunity framed by the good (Olmert and Abbas), the bad (Hamas and Iran) and the ugly (a set of huge challenges that needed to be overcome if any Israeli-Palestinian agreement was to emerge)" (Miller 2008, 358). Indeed, Bush's own memoirs do not reveal a highly involved president à la Clinton. In 2008, he did visit Israel twice; however, he did not exploit those visits to initiate a major breakthrough. Bush was certainly updated about the negotiations, but he was less involved than his predecessor and definitely less committed. "When Bush did engage in peacemaking," wrote Kurtzer and his coauthors, "it was with little effect, halfhearted effort, and limited follow-through" (2013, 236). They termed the unique Bush-Rice style of involvement "facilitation from afar" (ibid., 220). It is possible that a more committed president, upon hearing of Olmert's surprising offer to ʿAbbas, would have invited the two leaders for a kind of Camp David summit. Kurtzer et al. believe that Bush missed a chance to develop this particular opportunity (2013, 275). In addition, most of the Israeli-Palestinian talks were held bilaterally without the participation of American officials (though they were kept abreast of developments). Thus the American role was helpful, but not decisive enough to make a change in the parties' behavior.

The preceding analysis suggests that the Israeli-Palestinian talks in the aftermath of the Annapolis Conference constituted a missed opportunity on a medium level. The variable that diminished the potentiality level of the opportunity from high to medium was Olmert's and perhaps ʿAbbas's lack of legitimacy. This was somewhat offset by a very high level of determination from Olmert to clinch an agreement. ʿAbbas's determination level was not as high as Olmert's; it did exist, though it perhaps diminished as a result of the circumstances. In contrast to other recent episodes, the two leaders enjoyed a measure of mutual trust. Finally, the mediator—the United States—did not invest sufficient efforts to bridge the gaps between the parties; this limited role enhanced the plausibility level of the missed opportunity.

The answer to the question of who missed the opportunity is complicated. The Israeli version throws the blame on ʿAbbas, who chose not to respond to the generous Israeli offer. Rabinovich claimed that ʿAbbas made "a serious mistake" by not giving formal expression to his understandings or agreements with Olmert (2011, 228). The Palestinian version claims that the war in Gaza and Olmert's nebulous political position prevented the consummation of this opportunity. ʿAbbas himself claimed on one occasion that the "gaps were [too] wide" (Diehl 2009), and on another that two additional months would have allowed the signing of an agreement (Ravid 2012). The American account supports the Israeli version. According to Rice, "had he [Abbas] expressed a willingness to accept the extraordinary terms he'd been offered, it might have been a turning point in the long history of the intractable conflict. It might be a long time before another Israeli prime minister offered anything as dramatic again" (2011, 724).

It is possible to "blame" the circumstances—the unfortunate timing of Cast Lead and Olmert's end of term, according to the Palestinian view. Yet the offer submitted by Olmert could have been reciprocated by the Palestinian side, either directly or through Bush's "deposit" idea, thereby, at the very least, setting in motion the first steps of the next Israeli and American administrations. By not formally securing the Israeli offer, ʿAbbas missed an opportunity to move forward in the peace negotiations.

NOTES

1. In January 2011, the al-Jazeera network released what it called the "Palestinian Papers," the largest disclosure of confidential negotiations documents—more than sixteen hundred files spanning the period 1999 to 2010, including minutes of high-level meetings between US, European, Israeli, and Palestinian officials. For the Internet site, see www.transparency .aljazeera.net. For a collection of important documents, see Swisher 2011.

2. These operations culminated in the Hamas kidnapping of an Israeli soldier, Gilad Shalit [and murder of two others], on June 25, 2006. He would remain a captive for five years. As a result, Israel arrested sixty-four Palestinian (Hamas) cabinet ministers, members of parliament, and other officials, while also destroying the offices of the Hamas prime minister, in addition to various other military operations in Gaza.

3. See the text of the speech: http://unispal.un.org/unispal.nsf/9a798adbf322aff3852561 7b006d88d7/boadf241625e4d3385257234006053cf?OpenDocument&Highlight=0,olmert,s de,boker,2006.

4. http://www.pm.gov.il/PMOEng/Archive/Speeches/2007/06/speechsharem250607 .htm.

5. Abrams wrote that he thought "the conference mania was a mistake. I was afraid that the negotiations would not succeed and leave us worse off" (2013, 251).

6. This is based on al-Jazeera's Palestine Papers, leaked in January 2011. For some of the protocols of the talks in the pre-Annapolis period, see Swisher 2010, 76–101.

7. For the text of the speeches, see Bush 2008, 77–91.

8. The president asked Livni to form a new government, but on October 26 she notified him that she was unable to do so. As a result, elections were called for February 10, 2009, and Olmert remained as head of a caretaker government until then.

9. Based also on an interview with Udi Dekel, the Israeli head of the negotiations team with the Palestinians during the Annapolis process, December 5, 2012.

10. The Palestinians presented detailed maps that were prepared by Dr. Samih al-Abed, a well-known geographer; see Swisher 2010, 143–148.

11. Unofficially, the Palestinians, according to Dekel, were willing to accept 4 percent annexation of the land.

12. The US thought to accommodate Israel by offering a regional solution; that is, Jordan would be persuaded to place its troops alongside others, even NATO forces, on that border (Rice 2011, 653).

13. See also Dekel's interview (footnote 9).

14. Abrams says that he and senior Israeli officials were unaware of the "deposit" idea (2013, 292); however, Dekel, in his interview, confirmed it.

The term "missed opportunity" is belabored by historians and laymen alike. The fact that it is impossible to verify whether an opportunity has been missed in a certain case study makes it easy to use the term uncritically. Opportunities of all kinds can be missed; this is a given. This book explores if and to what extent opportunities in the Arab-Israeli conflict that might have led to peace, or at least to progress in the diplomatic process, were lost in the course of this century-old tug-of-war. Furthermore, even when opportunities were not missed and ended instead in the signing of a peace treaty, the question arises as to whether the opportunity to reach a warmer peace has not eluded the parties who actually signed the treaty. This study does not delve into that question, though it arguably underscores the analysis of the two not-missed opportunities that culminated in Israel's peace treaties with Egypt and Jordan.[1]

The definition of what constitutes a missed opportunity, offered in the first chapter of the book, enables us to evaluate or measure more accurately the plausibility of the opportunity missed for peace. This definition is based on a three-tiered analysis: first, the existence of the necessary conditions for a historical opportunity are confirmed; second, if an opportunity is identified, the elements of plausibility are assessed; and finally, the long-term or legacy effect of the missed opportunity is evaluated. On the basis of this definition, twenty-eight historical case studies in the Arab-Israeli conflict were studied, beginning with the 1919 Faysal-Weizmann Agreement and ending with the 2008 Abu Mazen–Olmert Talks. Table 2 summarizes the main findings of our research.

On the basis of this table, it is possible to draw three important observations. One, the existence of a historical opportunity does not mean it is plausible or has high potential. In fact, most of the peace initiatives proposed during the period of study (twenty-five out of twenty-eight) presented an opportunity of some kind, but the circumstances and conditions were not necessarily conducive for a breakthrough in the negotiations. Of the twenty-eight analyzed case studies, the plausibility of the opportunity was low or non-existent in no less than eighteen episodes. Two, most of the peace initiatives were proposed by third parties, usually the United States; at least thirteen plans were devised by the superpowers and the United Nations. In addition, there were eight joint Israeli-Arab initiatives (the Oslo channel, for example, was a joint nonofficial Israeli-Palestinian endeavor). Israel proposed between four and five initiatives: the 1967 proposal, the Allon Plan, the 1983 Israeli-Lebanese Agreement, the 1989 Shamir Plan, and Barak's Camp David II. The

Table 2. Plausible Missed Opportunities

Episode	Historical Opportunity	Plausibility of Opportunity	Party/Parties Who Missed Opportunity
Faysal-Weizmann Agreement, 1919	Yes	Low	None
Peel Partition Plan, 1937	Yes	Low	None
UN Partition Plan, 1947	Yes	Medium-High	The Palestinians and Arabs
Israeli-Jordanian Negotiations, 1946–1951	Yes	Low	None
Israel and Syria: Husni Za'im Initiative, 1949	Yes	Low	None
Alpha Plan and Anderson Mission, 1955–1956	No		
Egyptian-Israeli Contacts, 1965–1966	Yes	Medium	Israel
Israeli Peace Plan, 1967	No		
Allon Plan, 1968	No		
Rogers Plan, 1969	Yes	Low	None
Jarring Mission and Sadat Initiative, 1971	Yes	High	Israel
Disengagement Agreements, 1974–1975	Yes	Low	None
Egyptian-Israeli Peace Treaty, 1979	Yes	High	An Opportunity Not Missed
Arab Peace Plan, 1982	Yes	Low	None
Reagan Plan, 1982	Yes	Low	None
Israeli-Lebanese Agreement, 1983	Yes	Nonexistent	None
London Agreement, 1987	Yes	Low	None
Shultz Initiative, 1988	Yes	Nonexistent	None
Shamir Plan, 1989	Yes	Nonexistent	None
Madrid Conference, 1991, and Oslo Agreements, 1993–2000	Yes	Medium-High until Rabin's Assassination	The Assassin
		Low after the Assassination	Both Parties
Israeli-Jordanian Peace Treaty, 1994	Yes	High	An Opportunity Not Missed

Table 2. Continued

Episode	Historical Opportunity	Plausibility of Opportunity	Party/Parties Who Missed Opportunity
Israeli-Syrian Negotiations, 1991–2000	Yes	High	1993–1995—Syria 1995–1996—Syria and Israel 1999–2000—Israel
Camp David Summit, July 2000	Yes	Low	The Palestinians
Clinton Parameters, December 2000	Yes	Medium	The Palestinians
Taba Talks, January 2001	Yes	Low	None
Arab Peace Initiative, March 2002	Yes	High	Israel
US Road Map, April 2003	Yes	Low	Both Parties
Annapolis Conference and Abu Mazen-Olmert Talks, 2007–2008	Yes	Medium	The Palestinians

Arabs were behind six initiatives—the Zaʿim Initiative, 1949; Egyptian-Israeli contacts, 1966; Sadat Initiatives, 1971 and 1977; Arab Peace Plan, 1982; and the Arab Peace Initiative, 2002.[2] Three, less than one-half (ten) of the identified opportunities had a moderate or high level of plausibility. Of these, two opportunities were seized (the Israeli-Egyptian and Israeli-Jordanian treaties), one was partially realized (Oslo), and seven were missed—three by Israel (contacts with Nasser in 1966, Sadat's 1971 initiative, and the API), three by the Palestinians (1947 Partition Plan, Clinton Parameters, and Abu Mazen-Olmert Talks), and one jointly missed (Israeli-Syrian negotiations in the 1990s). The opportunity that was partially seized (Oslo) was not realized due to Prime Minister Rabin's assassination. In the aftermath, both the Israelis and Palestinians were responsible for missing this opportunity, although by then its plausibility was low. The same applies to the Road Map: the Palestinians were also responsible for missing the opportunity at Camp David II, though its plausibility level was low.

These observations allow us to draw the following insights. One, in contrast to accepted Israeli mythology or the official position taken by Israeli decision makers, Israel has not been eager to extend its hand in peace, particularly since 1967. Its 1948 Declaration of Independence stated, "We extend the hand of peace and good neighborliness to all the neighboring States and their peoples and invite their cooperation and mutual assistance with the independent Jewish nation in its land."[3] Indeed, Israel's rhetoric in the post-1948 period included many statements by Ben-Gurion, Sharett, Eban, Eshkol, and Meir in favor of peace.[4] For example, in December 1952, Israel presented a draft of a "Blueprint for Peace" to the Ad Hoc Political Committee of the UN General Assembly.[5] Yet in reality, Israel offered four or five initiatives throughout the years of conflict: one was never passed on to its intended partners, Egypt and Syria (1967); one was unofficially delivered to Husayn; one was imposed unilaterally on the other party (Lebanon, 1983); and one was no more than a media spin (Shamir Plan, 1989). The only initiative that qualifies as a sincere Israeli peace overture is Barak's Camp David idea (2000). Yet even in this case, Barak came to the summit without a detailed peace initiative and instead improvised during the deliberations to an extent that surprised even himself, to say nothing of the political arena and the public. In other words, not only have Israel's actions been inconsistent with its rhetoric, but its initiatives have been neither generous nor sincere, representing only tactical maneuvers. Moreover, in some cases Israel blocked peaceful initiatives without good reason; thus, for example, when Nahum Goldmann, president of the World Jewish Congress, broached the idea of meeting with Egypt's president Nasser in response to the latter's suggestion, the Meir government torpedoed the initiative in April 1970.[6] This was reminiscent of the decision of the Eshkol government not to send the head of the Mossad, Meir Amit, to meet with Nasser in 1966—an opportunity missed by Israel, according to our analysis (see chapter 7).

Two, Israel missed at least three opportunities on a grand scale: Sadat's 1971 Initiative, the talks with Syria in Shepherdstown (1999), and the Arab Peace Initiative (2002); it also missed an opportunity with moderate plausibility (secret talks with Nasser). Another opportunity (Oslo), with moderate to high plausibility, was missed as a result of Rabin's assassination. Furthermore, Israel missed an opportunity to submit a peace proposal following the 1967 War, despite the fact that one had already been formulated (this event was not included in our list of missed opportunities because it had never actually been submitted to the other side). The findings of this study refute the thesis of several New Historians who argue that Israel missed several specific opportunities for peace following the 1948 War (particularly with Jordan's 'Abdallah and Syria's Za'im). Nor does this research support conventional wisdom that the Peres-Husayn London Agreement (1987) was a missed opportunity. Interestingly, Israel's missed opportunities always involved the Arab states but not the Palestinians.

Three, the Arab side proposed six independent initiatives of which at least three were significant and sincere: Sadat's two initiatives (1971, 1977) and the Arab Peace Initiative (2002). Though the Arab side also demonstrated intransigence, it made more peace overtures than did the Israeli side. Distinguishing between the Arab states and the Palestinians shows that the latter were part of two initiatives (Arab Peace Plan, 1982; Arab Peace Initiative, 2002) but offered none of their own, although one should bear in mind that in the post-1948 period the Palestinians (and the PLO from 1974) had no major cards in their possession to offer to Israel and the military and political asymmetry between the two sides weakened their bargaining position even further.

On the other hand, the Arab/Palestinian side missed five opportunities. The Arabs missed one highly plausible opportunity (Syrian talks with Asad). The rest were missed by the Palestinians: at Oslo, an opportunity of moderately high plausibility was missed (jointly with Israel), though the blame should primarily be attributed to Rabin's assassin. Three opportunities of moderate plausibility were also missed: the UN Partition Plan (jointly missed with the rest of the Arabs, 1947), the Clinton Parameters (2000), and the post-Annapolis talks (2008). In each of these case studies, circumstances reduced plausibility, yet these events still constitute significant missed opportunities in the Israeli-Palestinian conflict. Interestingly, in the four Israeli-Palestinian cases of medium-high plausibility, the Palestinians were responsible for missing the opportunity in three cases. The repetition of missed opportunities, particularly in the last decade, calls for a more critical view of the Palestinian decision-making process.

Four, not many historical opportunities existed prior to 1967. Among the six listed, only two cases contained a noticeable (moderate or high) measure of plausibility: one was missed by the Arabs (the UN Partition Plan) and one missed by Israel (the contacts with Nasser). In many ways, the historical conditions before 1967 were not ripe for a resolution of the conflict or even a serious peace proposal. Most of the historical opportunities occurred after 1967: two were realized, one was partially missed (Oslo), and a plethora of opportunities were completely missed. The reason for the relative proliferation of peace initiatives after the 1967 War is connected, of course, with the fact that Israel was now in possession of a crucial card (the occupied territories) that could have been played in the negotiation process. But Israel did not exploit its territorial assets to officially offer any meaningful peace initiatives. Interestingly, the two and a half opportunities that were seized in this period (Israel-Egypt, Israel-Jordan, and Oslo) were initiated largely by the parties to the conflict. The Israeli-Egyptian treaty was the culmination of a process triggered by Sadat's visit to Jerusalem in November 1977, which was unprecedented in its momentousness. Though the United States had played a significant role as mediator along the way, it was still the local parties that played the dominant roles. Similarly, the Israeli-Jordanian treaty was largely a product of the negotiations conducted between the parties themselves, specifically

Rabin and Husayn, while Oslo was the product of initial clandestine Israeli-Palestinian talks. The conclusion, therefore, is that peace plans offered by third parties have a smaller chance of success. Conversely, the study suggests that when the parties to the conflict themselves initiate a dialogue or peace plan, the chances that it will be successfully consummated are greater. This insight dovetails with Aaron David Miller's assertion that America cannot want peace more than the parties requiring it: "No matter how much will and skill US presidents possess, they cannot impose peace." What they can do is "sharpen choices, provide incentives, cajole with disincentives, and under certain circumstances even create new openings" (Miller 2012, 141).

The major exception to this generalization is the Arab Peace Initiative (2002), proposed by the Arab League, which received a cool Israeli response. Although this organization presumably represents all the Arab states and as such enjoys broad legitimacy, the fact that the plan was "faceless"—that is, no particular trustworthy Arab leader stood behind it—contributed to the suspicion and hesitancy on the Israeli side.

Nonetheless, opportunities do not usually appear suddenly and out of nowhere, but rather as a result of certain processes and circumstances. Indeed, wars, revolutions, regime changes—all these and more might create opportunities. This study confirms that most of the peace proposals were presented following major changes to the international and/or regional systems. In this context, therefore, Ilan Peleg and Paul Scham were correct to conclude that "A traumatic experience or a significant change might turn out to be a precondition for peacemaking in the Middle East in years to come" (2010, 220). Seldom do opportunities occur simply as a result of the existence of a sudden attractive offer presented by one of the parties to the conflict or by a third party (such as Sadat's gesture of visiting Jerusalem in 1977). The question of timing, then, is crucial; if the timing—or rather the moment—is not acknowledged and seized by the leaders, the opportunity will most probably disappear.[7] Such was the case with Za'im's offer to meet Ben-Gurion in 1949, the failure (1971) and success (1977) of Sadat's initiatives, Rabin's "deposit," the breakdown of the Shepherdstown Talks, the abortive Clinton Parameters, and the Abu Mazen–Olmert Talks. In contrast, the signing of the Oslo Agreements and the Israeli-Jordanian peace treaty were examples of the successful exploitation of a fortunate moment (ibid., 221). One of the lessons of Kurtzer and his coauthors is that "opportunities normally do not just happen, but need to be developed" (2013, 275). That may be so, but this book demonstrates that an ideal opportunity occurs when a major historical turning point meets an attractive offer.[8]

The two case studies in which it is clear that a plausible opportunity was seized—the Israeli-Egyptian and Israeli-Jordanian treaties—can be seen as ideal types. Their analysis proves that, in the context of the Arab-Israeli conflict at least, when the suggested four elements of plausibility—the legitimacy of the leadership, its determination to pursue peace, past relations and existing trust, and third-party involvement—are present and are sufficiently strong, there is a good chance that the opportunity will not be missed.

Still, it should be emphasized that the contributions of these four elements to an opportunity's plausibility are not always equal. In fact, it seems that their relative significance may vary from one opportunity to another. Thus, for example, the degree of a leader's legitimacy or determination occasionally played a more crucial role than did the role of trust or third-party involvement. In the final analysis, it is worth noting that domestic political constraints such as legitimacy may have acted as obstacles but never succeeded in preventing the formulation or implementation of peacemaking (Bar-Siman-Tov 1998, 27). This conclusion may indicate that though Barak (in Camp David, the Clinton Parameters, and the Taba Talks) and Olmert (in talks with 'Abbas) both suffered from serious legitimacy problems, this deficiency did not totally undermine the chances of the opportunity because a possible agreement could have turned the scheduled elections into a referendum. In other words, their determination to achieve a "mega-deal" could have swayed public opinion in an unexpected manner. It should be added that negotiations sometimes succeed in spite of the absence or paucity of a certain element: thus, for example, lack of trust and unfamiliarity with the Palestinian side did not hamper the signing of the Oslo Agreements. On the other hand, that deficiency thwarted the parties' efforts to walk that last mile.

In the Introduction to this volume, we asked whether there are moments that can be identified, in retrospect, as being more likely to develop into missed opportunities. Michael Greig's research on "moments of opportunity" offered examples of successful third-party mediations either early or late in negotiations (2001, 715–716). This study showed that late negotiations—that is, talks held close to the end of the ruler's term—are more likely to develop into missed opportunities. Such was the case with the Clinton Parameters, which were submitted at the end of President Clinton's term; the Syrian talks, held when Barak was losing his majority in the Knesset and Asad was nearing death; the revival of the API at the end of Olmert's and Bush's terms; and the Abu Mazen–Olmert Talks, which were held during the latter's last days in office. In contrast, Begin and Carter began the negotiations with Sadat early in their careers, and ended them within two years, while Rabin managed to sign the Oslo and Jordanian Agreements within less than two years in office. It may be concluded, then, that negotiations that begin at an early stage of a leader's term have a greater chance of success, as the perceived lack of time pressure allows greater flexibility and maneuverability. Conversely, the pressure that builds later in a leader's term in office does not facilitate favorable moments for leaders, who, experience shows, need more time to take bold decisions and to sway their peoples to do so.

In the absence of comparative studies of missed opportunities for peace in other conflicts around the globe, it is difficult to estimate whether the number of missed opportunities in the Arab-Israeli arena has been relatively high or low. The figures offered in table 2 suggest three conclusions. First, most of the historical opportunities did not embody a sufficient degree of plausibility for the conclusion of a peace agreement (eighteen out of twenty-eight). Second, the existence of a historical opportunity that has moderate or high plausibility is not a frequent phenomenon, though neither is it rare (ten out of twenty-eight, i.e., almost 35 percent). Finally, among the ten opportunities with a moderate or high level of plausibility, only two and a half opportunities (if we consider Oslo as an agreement partially succeeded) —i.e., merely 25 percent— were realized. The lessons of these numbers are twofold: first, that decision makers historically dismissed opportunities carrying the potential of leading to peace agreements or achieving some progress along the peaceful way; and second, that decision makers largely failed to transform these opportunities into successful agreements. The small proportion of realized opportunities should serve as a cautionary sign to both Israeli and Arab/Palestinian decision makers that more should be done to seize an opportunity once it appears.

Decision makers, consciously or not, engage in "what if?" kinds of questions. Some then dismiss the answers out of hand; others ponder—and even express regret and remorse—about possibilities missed. Israeli prime minister Barak belonged to the first category. In his own assessment of the opportunities presented during his term, he offered the following observation:

> Of all the trends in the public debate in Israel, my least favorite is that which I dub "sophists"—those who, no matter what happens, always say that if the opposite had been done, things would have been better. Life is nothing but a wide range of possibilities. In real life, each and every one of us, leaders included, are continually making choices, always leaving endless possibilities untried. This opens a wide scope for complaints: on the individual level, one can say: "If only I had been there, everything would have been different"; or on the collective level, "if only the government had done things differently, everything would have been better." These complaints are useless. (2005, 138)

Israeli prime minister Rabin belonged to the second category. In a speech to the Knesset delivered on October 3, 1994, in which he emphasized the need to exploit the opportunity for peace with Jordan, Syria, and the Palestinians, Rabin stated, "History does not recognize the concept of 'if.' But while we are still shackled by the bitter memory of that Yom Kippur [War], we cannot escape wondering what would have happened [had things gone differently]."⁹ These two schools of thought regarding "what if" presumably exist on both sides of the conflict; it is hoped, though, that decision makers will follow Rabin's approach, which will allow them not only to reflect on past events but also to be bold in their decision-making process. In a prophetic statement, Yigal Allon, Israel's deputy prime minister who initiated the Allon Plan in 1967, wrote, "Peace won't come on its own. But desperation will necessarily be followed by helplessness, which unfortunately will lead to avoidance and oversight in laying down the necessary conditions for peace, and to missed opportunities for peace that will appear in the future" (1968, 429). Unfortunately, however, the history of the Arab-Israeli conflict, as has been demonstrated in this book, is not only a story of wars, violence, and disasters, but also of opportunities that its leaders have failed to seize. In the above-mentioned speech in the Knesset, Prime Minister Rabin stated, "Our duty when facing the Israeli nation is to examine every option for peace." The conclusions of this study clearly show that successive Israeli governments failed to meet this obligation. Missed opportunities are "lost moments of history"; with every choice made, doors close and opportunities are lost, sometimes forever. Yet the final outcome is not the only possible result of an inevitable historical process, but rather the consequence of individual decisions that might have been averted, changed, or taken a different course. This is why the lessons of those missed opportunities should be explored and internalized. "The past is past," wrote Hugh Trevor-Roper. "It cannot be undone." But the past "is not dead but living; and unless we recognize that it is living, and live with it, and question it, and face the alternatives of the past as they were faced at the time, our history is dead too, and might as well be buried too" (Trevor-Roper 1988).

This book began with the story of Abba Eban's quip—that "The Arabs (or Palestinians) never miss an opportunity to miss an opportunity." At the end of this journey it is clear that this myth should be laid to rest: both sides— the Israelis, on the one hand, and the Arabs and Palestinians, on the other— have missed opportunities for peace during the many years of conflict. All leaders would be wise to take heed of André Brink's observation, quoted in the preface of this book, to be more attuned to the appearance of opportunities and then to invest all efforts into realizing them. Otherwise, our peoples are doomed to miss opportunities time and again.

NOTES

1. Thus, for example, Shimon Shamir, in a recent study (2012) of the Israeli-Jordanian peace treaty, explores the possibility that a real, warm peace was missed by the parties, particularly by Israel. In the Egyptian case, see Stein 1997; Podeh 2007b.

2. The reason for the gap between the number of analyzed case studies (twenty-eight) and initiatives (thirty-two) is because four case studies were divided into separate initiatives: the Jarring Mission, which was a UN initiative, and Sadat's Initiative were included in the same chapter (10); the Madrid Conference was initiated by the US and the Oslo Agreements were a joint Israeli-Arab initiative (chapter 17); the Camp David summit, which can be identified as both Israeli and US initiatives (chapter 20); the Annapolis Conference, a US initiative, led to the ʿAbbas-Olmert Talks, which are considered a joint Israeli-Arab initiative (chapter 23).

3. *Israel's Peace Offers to the Arab States 1948–1963* (Jerusalem: Ministry of Foreign Affairs, 1963), 19.

4. Ibid., 13–97.

5. Ibid., 33–37.

6. For a thorough analysis of the Goldmann episode, see Chazan 2009, 297–324. He concluded, "The idea of categorizing the initiative as one of the opportunities for peace that Israel let slip away is fundamentally flawed" (317).

7. Martin Indyk particularly emphasized this point, even mentioning in this regard a famous song by American actor and country singer Garrett Hedlund, "Timing Is Everything." Interview with Indyk, January 10, 2012.

8. I do not refute, however, the second part of their sentence, which says that "When such opportunities do open up, the US needs to be agile and determined to exploit whatever opening is provided" (Kurtzer et al., 2013).

9. *Divrei Haknesset*, Thirteenth Knesset, October 3, 1994, http://82.166.33.81/Tql//mark 01/h0021711.html#TQL.

After the failure of the Abu Mazen–Olmert Talks in late 2008, there were two attempts to reach an Israeli-Palestinian agreement. The first was the talks held between the Israeli president, Shimon Peres, and Abu Mazen; in this little-known episode the two leaders met secretly throughout 2011, with the knowledge of Prime Minister Netanyahu, with the aim of reaching a framework agreement. According to Peres's testimony, they reached some meaningful understandings that were rejected by Netanyahu.[1] A recent report revealed that an understanding was reached that the planned document would include a statement to the effect that a Palestinian state would be established based on the June 4, 1967, lines, with equal land swaps; the Palestinian state would be demilitarized, with a third party to be deployed at the borders and crossings; and that Jerusalem would be the capital of both states, remaining an open city, with the Jewish neighborhoods under Israeli sovereignty and the Arab neighborhoods under Palestinian sovereignty. The question of sovereignty over the Temple Mount remained disputed. As for the refugee problem, a vague formula was adopted, saying that the solution to the problem would be mutually agreed and just, similar to the formulation of the Arab Peace Initiative but with no mention of UN Resolution 194. The options for settling the refugee problem were based on the Clinton Parameters, with a Palestinian demand for Israel's absorption of some 10,000 refugees a year for fifteen years. However, when Peres was about to meet Abu Mazen in Amman, on July 28, 2011, to deliver a formal Israeli response, Netanyahu backed off.[2] If accurate, this episode recalls Netanyahu's use of the good offices of Ronald Lauder in his mediation attempt with Syrian president Asad in 1998, which was eventually repudiated by the Israeli prime minister (see chapter 19). Since Netanyahu's commitment to the Peres–Abu Mazen dialogue was doubtful from the very beginning, the impression is that a real opportunity to solve the Israeli-Palestinian conflict did not exist in this case and therefore it could not be missed.

The second episode was the nine-month Israeli-Palestinian negotiations, which commenced in July 2013 and were masterminded by US secretary of state John Kerry. Livni from the Israeli side, Erekat from the Palestinian, and Indyk from the American side were the chief negotiators. On the basis of the available information, we can offer a partial and tentative assessment of whether an opportunity to reach an agreement was missed.[3]

The Israeli-Palestinian talks occurred at a historic juncture that can be classified as an opportunity. Two developments converged at that point in time: Barack Obama's election to a second term, in November 2012, which relieved him from the pressure of domestic lobbies; and the formation of a more centrist coalition in Israel, headed by Benjamin Netanyahu, in March 2013. In addition, Obama's nomination of John Kerry as his secretary of state infused a sense of urgency, optimism, and energy into the process. Indeed, Kerry's avowed commitment and willingness to pursue the Israeli-Palestinian track convinced many that the parties are facing "an opportunity that should not be missed" (Birnbaum and Tibon 2014). The Israelis and Palestinians entered the talks with skepticism, which was temporarily overshadowed by Kerry's enthusiasm. "I was so impressed with the secretary's enthusiasm," Indyk said, "that I decided to suspend my disbelief" (ibid.).

The collapse of the talks in April 2014 did not come as a surprise to all involved. So, was an opportunity missed? On the Israeli side, Netanyahu possessed enough legitimacy at the time to pursue peace talks and perhaps even sign an agreement, yet the level of his commitment and willingness to pursue this track was questionable at best. In spite of Netanyahu's 2009 Bar-Ilan speech in favor of a two-state solution, it remained unclear whether his right-wing ideology had in fact undergone a major shift. Moreover, he was unwilling to take bold moves that put his coalition at risk, since a serious effort at peacemaking would have necessitated forming a more dovish coalition and confronting a vocal opposition from his own Likud Party and radical right-wing allies. On the other hand, Abu Mazen's legitimacy was in question in the West Bank and under challenge by Hamas in Gaza. In many ways, he was "a leader ahead of his public on the subject of peace with Israel" (ibid.). His determination to pursue peace was questionable not because he was not committed to this track, but because of his doubts regarding Netanyahu's sincerity. Indeed, the main obstacle for achieving a breakthrough was the deep mistrust between the two leaders in particular and the two peoples in general. In a recent interview, Indyk went as far as arguing that Netanyahu and Abu Mazen "loathed" each other (Friedman 2014). A repeated Palestinian comment throughout the talks was that "Netanyahu will take everyone for a ride" or that "Netanyahu is not a man of peace." On the Israeli side, right-wing politicians continued Netanyahu's "no partner" campaign, further discrediting the Palestinian leadership, while leading politicians in the coalition attempted to sabotage the negotiations in other ways (Birnbaum and Tibon 2014).

In this case, the US mediator was highly motivated and involved in the negotiations, time and again producing innovative ideas to overcome Israeli or Palestinian objections. In light of the mounting difficulties, in what became the final round of the talks, Kerry proposed to sign "a framework for negotiations"—a document spelling out parameters on all core issues that would enable the two sides to push for a new deadline for the talks. There were, at this point, signs of positive progress, particularly in the areas of security and borders, which led Kerry to believe that the gaps could be bridged with creativity and ambiguity. The Palestinians' sense of suspicion, however, increased as they felt that the United States—like in previous negotiation rounds—was not an honest broker, as if Kerry was privileging Israeli over Palestinian needs and that the US was coordinating its policy with Israel so as not to surprise it (Birnbaum and Tibon 2014; Drucker 2014). The result was that the proposal that had been submitted to Abu Mazen during his meeting with Obama in mid-March 2014 never received a response. The Palestinian leader, in Indyk's words, "had checked out of the negotiations" (Friedman 2014).

Shortly afterward, in response to Israel's delay in releasing the fourth tranche of prisoners promised at the beginning of the talks and the approval of the construction of new homes in the occupied territories, Abu Mazen renewed his bid to join the United Nations, signing fifteen international conventions. This was followed by reconciliation with Hamas, leading to the formation of a unity government. These steps sealed the fate of the talks. Their failure despite determined American mediation proved, once again, that the mediator cannot want peace more than the parties to the conflict. Thus insufficient legitimacy on the Palestinian side, lack of determination on the Israeli— and perhaps also on the Palestinian—side, the total mistrust existing on both sides, and the fact the mediator invested his best efforts to achieve a deal demonstrate that the chances for a successful consummation of the talks were not high and therefore an opportunity, in this case, was not missed.

On the basis of the many interviews they conducted, Birnbaum and Tibon concluded that few expect progress anytime soon: "With Netanyahu entrenched, Abbas on his way out, settlements and rocket ranges expanding, and the populations increasingly hardline, we seem to have reached the end of an era in the peace process" (2014). The results of the recent March 2015 elections, in which Netanyahu was reelected with a clear right-wing majority in the Knesset, confirm the assessment that the chances for a breakthrough in Israeli-Palestinian relations are remote. Yet, one should recall, and be encouraged by, Churchill's quotation cited at the beginning of this book: that optimists will find opportunities where others see problems.

NOTES

1. Peres's interview to Israeli TV, Channel 2, on the occasion of Independence Day, May 6, 2014.

2. Avi Issacharoff, "When Netanyahu Closed the Door on Peace Talks," *The Times of Israel*, February 13, 2015.

3. The most exhaustive source is Birnbaum and Tibon (2014). See also Indyk's interview in the *Atlantic*, July 3, 2014; Drucker 2014.

REFERENCES

Abbas, Mahmud (Abu Mazen). 1995. *Through Secret Channels*. Reading, UK: Garnet Publishing.
ʿAbd al-Hadi, Mahdi. 1975. *Al-Masʾala al-Filastiniyya wa-Mashariʿ al-Hulul al-Siyasiyya*. Beirut: Manshurat al-Maktaba al-ʿAsriya.
Abdullah II (King). 2011. *Our Last Best Chance: The Pursuit of Peace in a Time of Peril*. London: Viking.
Al-Abed, Samih. 2005. "The Israeli Proposals Were Not Serious." In *The Camp David Summit—What Went Wrong?* edited by Shimon Shamir and Bruce Maddy-Weitzman, 74–81. Brighton, UK: Sussex Academic Press.
Abraham, S. Daniel. 2006. *Peace Is Possible: Conversations with Arab and Israeli Leaders from 1988 to the Present*. New York: Newmarket.
Abrams, Elliott. 2013. *Tested by Zion: The Bush Administration and the Arab-Israeli Conflict*. Cambridge: Cambridge University Press.
Abu Amr, Ziad. 1992. "Palestinian-Israeli Negotiations: A Palestinian Perspective." In *The Arab-Israeli Search for Peace*, edited by Steven L. Spiegel, 27–36. Boulder, CO: Lynne Rienner Publishers.
Abu-Lughod, Ibrahim, ed. 1970. *The Arab-Israeli Confrontation of June 1967: An Arab Perspective*. Evanston, IL: Northwestern University Press.
Abu-Odeh, Adnan. 1999. *Jordanians, Palestinians and the Hashemite Kingdom in the Middle East Peace Process*. Washington, DC: US Institute of Peace Studies.
Aburish, Said K. 1998. *Arafat: From Defender to Dictator*. London: Bloomsbury.
Agha, Hussein, and Robert Malley. 2002. "The Last Negotiation: How to End the Middle East Peace Process." *Foreign Affairs* 81: 10–18.
———, Shai Feldman, Ahmad Khalidi, and Zeʾev Schiff. 2003. *Track-II Diplomacy: Lessons from the Middle East*. Cambridge, MA: MIT Press.
Ajami, Fouad. 1999. *The Dream Palace of the Arabs: A Generation's Odyssey*. New York: Vintage Books.
Albright, Madeleine. 2003. *Madam Secretary*. New York: Miramax Books.
ʿAli Kamal, Hasan. 1993. *Warriors and Peacemakers*. Translated from the Arabic by Abraham Robinson. Tel Aviv: Ministry of Defense. [Hebrew]
Allon, Yigal. 1968. *A Curtain of Sand*. Tel Aviv: Hakibbutz Hameuchad. [Hebrew]
———. 1989. *In Pursuit of Peace*. Tel Aviv: Hakibbutz Hameuchad. [Hebrew]
Amit, Meir. 1998. "Secret Contacts towards Peace: A Missed Opportunity." In *Intelligence for Peace*, edited by Hezi Carmel, 283–317. Tel Aviv: Yedioth Ahronoth. [Hebrew]
———. 1999. *Head On . . .* Tel Aviv: Hed Arzi. [Hebrew]
Antonius, George. 1965 [1938]. *The Arab Awakening*. New York: Capricorn Books.
Arafat, Yasir. 2002. "The Palestinian Vision of Peace." *New York Times*, February 3.
Arens, Moshe. 1995. *Broken Covenant: American Foreign Policy and the Crisis between the U.S. and Israel*. New York: Simon and Schuster.
Arian, Asher. 1995. *Security Threatened: Surveying Israeli Opinion on Peace and War*. Tel Aviv: Jaffe Center for Strategic Studies.
Arieli, Shaul. 2013. *A Border between Us and You*. Tel Aviv: Yedioth Ahronoth. [Hebrew]
Arnon-Ohanna, Yuval. 1984. "The Palestinian National Movement and the Partition Plan

of 1937." In *Studies in the Palestine Partition Plans*, edited by Meir Avizohar and Isaiah Friedman, 75–87. Sede Boqer: Ben-Gurion University of the Negev. [Hebrew]

Aronson, Shlomo. 1978. *Conflict and Bargaining in the Middle East: An Israeli Perspective*. Baltimore: Johns Hopkins University Press.

Arslan, Majid. 1983. *Mudhakirrat al-Amir 'Adil Arslan*, vol. 2, 1946–1950. Beirut: Dar al-Taqadum lil-Nashr.

Aruri, Naseer H. 1999. "The Wye Memorandum: Netanyahu's Oslo and Unreciprocal Reciprocity." *Journal of Palestine Studies* 28: 17–28.

———. 2003. *Dishonest Broker: The U.S. Role in Israel and Palestine*. Cambridge, MA: South End Press.

Ashrawi, Hanan. 1995. *This Side of Peace: A Personal Account*. New York: Simon and Schuster.

Ashton, Nigel. 2008. *King Hussein of Jordan: A Political Life*. New Haven, CT: Yale University Press.

Avishai, Bernard. 2011. "A Plan for Peace That Still Could Be." *New York Times*, February 7.

Avizohar, Meir, and Isaiah Friedman, eds. 1984. *Studies in the Palestine Partition Plans 1937–1947*. Sede Boqer: Ben-Gurion University of the Negev. [Hebrew]

Ayyad, Ahmad Y. 2012. "Uncovering Ideology in Translation: A Case Study of Arabic and Hebrew Translations of the 'Roadmap Plan.'" *Journal of Language and Politics* 11: 250–272.

Al-'Azm, Khalid. 1973. *Mudhakkirat Khalid al-'Azm*, vol. 1. Beirut: Dar al-Muttahida lil-Nashr.

Al-'Azm, Sadik J. 2000. "The View from Damascus." *New York Review of Books*, June 15.

Bahgat, Gawdat. 2007. "Saudi Arabia and the Arab-Israeli Peace Process." *Middle East Policy* 14.3: 49–59.

Baker, James A. 1995. With Thomas M. De Frank. *The Politics of Diplomacy: Revolution, War and Peace, 1989–1992*. New York: G. P. Putnam's Sons.

Ball, George W. 1976. *Diplomacy for a Crowded World: An American Foreign Policy*. Boston: Little, Brown.

Bar-Joseph, Uri. 1987. *The Best of Enemies: Israel and Transjordan in the War of 1948*. London: Frank Cass.

———. 2006. "Last Chance to Avoid War: Sadat's Peace Initiative of February 1973 and Its Failure." *Journal of Contemporary History* 41: 545–556.

Bar-On, Mordechai. 1994. *The Gates of Gaza: Israel's Road to Suez and Back, 1955–1957*. New York: St. Martin's.

Bar-Siman-Tov, Yaacov. 1980. *The Israeli-Egyptian War of Attrition, 1969–1970*. New York: Columbia University Press.

———. 1994. *Israel and the Peace Process 1977–1982: In Search of Legitimacy for Peace*. Albany: State University of New York.

———. 1997. "Peace-Making with the Palestinians: Change and Legitimacy." In *From Rabin to Netanyahu: Israel's Troubled Agenda*, edited by Efraim Karsh, 170–186. London: Frank Cass.

———. 1998. *Peace Policy as Domestic and as Foreign Policy: The Israeli Case*. Davis Occasional Papers. Jerusalem: Leonard Davis Institute.

———. 2005. "An Irresolvable Conflict or Lack of Ripeness?" In *The Camp David Summit— What Went Wrong?* edited by Shimon Shamir and Bruce Maddy-Weitzman, 189–199. Brighton, UK: Sussex Academic Press.

———. 2006. "Interlocking Conflicts in the Middle East: Structural Dimensions." In *Conflicts and Conflict Resolution in Middle Eastern Societies—Between Tradition and Modernity*, edited by Hans-Jorg Albrecht, Jan-Michael Simon, Hassan Rezaei, Holger-C. Rohne, and Ernesto Kiza. Berlin: Duncker and Humblot.

———. 2007. "The Arab League Initiative as a Historical Opportunity." In *The Arab Peace Initiative—A Historic Opportunity? Background, Meanings, and Possible Avenues of Exploration*, edited by Kobi Michael, 17–24. Jerusalem: Jerusalem Institute for Israel Studies. [Hebrew]

———, and Kobi Michael. 2005. "The Israeli Disengagement Plan as a Strategy for Conflict Management." In *The Israeli-Palestinian Conflict: From a Peace Process to a Violent Confrontation, 2000–2005*, edited by Yaacov Bar-Siman Tov, 346–374. Jerusalem: Jerusalem Institute for Israel Studies. [Hebrew]

Barak, Ehud. 2005. "The Myths Spread about Camp David Are Baseless." In *The Camp David Summit—What Went Wrong?* edited by Shimon Shamir and Bruce Maddy-Weitzman, 117–150. Brighton, UK: Sussex Academic Press.

Barak, Oren. 2005. "The Failure of the Israeli-Palestinian Peace Process, 1993–2000." *Journal of Peace Research* 42: 719–736.

Barari, Hassan A. 2004. *Israeli Politics and the Middle East Peace Process, 1988–2002*. London: Routledge.

Baskin, Gershon. 2007. "Accept the Saudi Initiative." *Jerusalem Post*, March 6.

Bavly, Dan. 2002. *Dreams and Missed Opportunities 1967–1973*. Jerusalem: Carmel. [Hebrew]

Beattie, Kirk J. 2000. *Egypt during the Sadat Years*. London: Palgrave.

Behrendt, Sven. 2007. *The Secret Israeli-Palestinian Negotiations in Oslo: Their Success and Why the Process Ultimately Failed*. London: Routledge.

Beilin, Yossi. 1994. "The Opportunity That Was Not Missed." In *From War to Peace: Arab-Israeli Relations 1973–1993*, edited by Barry Rubin, Joseph Ginat, and Moshe Ma'oz, 23–29. Brighton, UK: Sussex Academic Press.

———. 1997. *Touching Peace*. Tel Aviv: Yediot Ahronot. [Hebrew]

———. 2001. *Manual for a Wounded Dove*. Tel Aviv: Miskal–Yedioth Ahronoth. [Hebrew]

Ben-Aharon, Yossi. 2000. "Negotiating with Syria: A First-Hand Account." *Middle East Review of International Affairs* 4: 2.

Ben-Ami, Shlomo. 2004. *A Front without a Rearguard: A Voyage to the Boundaries of the Peace Process*. Tel Aviv: Miskal. [Hebrew]

———. 2005a. "So Close and Yet So Far." *Israel Studies* 10: 72–90.

———. 2005b. *Scars of War, Wounds of Peace: The Israeli-Arab Tragedy*. London: Weidenfeld and Nicolson.

Ben-Bassat, Yuval. 2009. "Proto-Zionist–Arab Encounters in Late Nineteenth-Century Palestine: Socio-Regional Dimensions." *Journal of Palestine Studies* 38: 42–63.

Ben-Elissar, Eliahu. 1995. *No More War*. Or Yehuda: Ma'ariv. [Hebrew]

Ben-Gurion, David. 1975. *Talks with Arab Leaders*. Tel Aviv: Am Oved. [Hebrew]

Ben-Meir, Alon. 2007. "Seizing on the Saudi Initiative." www.alonben-meir.com, March 20.

Ben-Zvi, Abraham. 1993. *The United States and Israel: The Limits of the Special Relationship*. New York: Columbia University Press.

Bentsur, Eytan. 2003. "A Prophet of Peace in the Absence of Peace." In *Abba Eban: A Statesman and a Diplomat: In Memory of the Former Prime Minister of Israel*, edited by Adam Ron, 161–166. Jerusalem: Ministry of Foreign Affairs. [Hebrew]

Benziman, Uzi. 1981. *Prime Minister under Siege*. Ramat-Gan: Dvir. [Hebrew]

Bergman, Ronen. 2002. *Authority Given*. Tel Aviv: Yedioth Ahronoth. [Hebrew]

Berlin, Isaiah. 1955. *Historical Inevitability*. London: Oxford University Press.

Binder, Leonard. 1982. "U.S. Policy in the Middle East: Toward a Pax Saudiana." *Current History* 81: 1–3.

Biran, Shraga. 2008. *The Praise of Opportunism: An Introduction to the Theory of Opportunities*. Tel Aviv: Yedioth Ahronoth. [Hebrew]

Birnbaum, Ben. 2013. "The End of the Two-State Solution." *New Republic*, March 11.

———, and Amir Tibon. 2014. "The Explosive, Inside Story of How John Kerry Built an Israel-Palestine Peace Plan—and Watched It Crumble." *New Republic*, July 20.

Blair, Tony. 2010. *A Journey: My Political Life*. London: Random House.

Bloch, Marc. 1984 [1954]. *The Historian's Craft*. Manchester: Manchester University Press.

Boutros-Ghali, Boutros. 1997. *Egypt's Road to Jerusalem: A Diplomat's Story of the Struggle for Peace in the Middle East*. New York: Random House.

Brecher, Michael. 1970. *The Foreign Policy System of Israel: Setting, Images, Process*. London: Oxford University Press.

Bregman, Ahron. 2005. *Elusive Peace: How the Holy Land Defeated America*. London: Penguin Books.

———. 2013. "The Deal That Never Was: Israel's Clandestine Negotiations with Syria, 1991–2000." In *Israel's Clandestine Diplomacies*, edited by Clive Jones and Tore T. Petersen, 225–240. London: Hurst & Company.

———. 2014. *Cursed Victory: A History of Israel and the Occupied Territories*. London: Allen Lane.

Brink, André. 1984. *The Wall of the Plague*. London: Faber and Faber.

Bunzl, Martin. 2004. "Counterfactual History: A User's Guide." *American Historical Review* 109: 845–858.

Bush, George W. 2002. *New York Times*, April 5.

———. 2008. "The Annapolis Conference." *Journal of Palestine Studies* 37: 76–77.

———. 2011. *Decision Points*. New York: Crown Publishers.

Caplan, Neil. 1983a. *Futile Diplomacy: Early Arab-Zionist Negotiations Attempts 1913–1931*. Vol. 1. London: Frank Cass.

———. 1983b. "Faisal Ibn Husain and the Zionists: A Reexamination with Documents." *International History Review* 5: 561–614.

———. 1986. *Futile Diplomacy: Arab-Zionist Negotiations and the End of the Mandate*. Vol. 2. London: Frank Cass.

———. 1993. *The Lausanne Conference, 1949: A Case Study in Middle East Peacemaking*. Tel Aviv: Moshe Dayan Center for Middle Eastern and African Studies.

———. 1997. *Futile Diplomacy: Operation Alpha and the Failure of Anglo-American Coercive Diplomacy in the Arab-Israeli Conflict, 1954–1956*. Vol. 4. London: Frank Cass.

———. 1999. *The Limitations of Third-Party Intervention in the Arab-Israeli Conflict: Lessons from Selected Episodes, 1949–1956*. Jerusalem: Leonard Davis Institute for International Relations.

Carmel, Hezi. 1998. "The First Attempt to Organize a Summit between Sharett and Nasser." In *Intelligence for Peace*, edited by Carmel Hezi, 69–80. Tel Aviv: Yedioth Ahronoth. [Hebrew]

Carr, Edward H. 1990. *What Is History?* London: Penguin Books.

Carter, Jimmy. 1982. *Keeping Faith: Memoirs of a President*. Toronto: Bantam Books.

Caspit, Ben. 1997. "This Is How We Missed Peace with Syria." *Ma'ariv*, December 12.

———. 2002. *Ma'ariv*, March 29.

Cattan, Henry. 1969. *Palestine, the Arabs and Israel: The Search for Justice*. London: Longman.

Chazan, Meir. 2009. "Goldmann's Initiative to Meet with Nasser in 1970." In *Nahum Gold-

mann: Statesman without a State, edited by Mark A. Raider, 297–324. Albany: State University of New York Press.

Christison, Kathleen. 2004. "'All Those Old Issues': George W. Bush and the Palestinian-Israeli Conflict." *Journal of Palestine Studies* 33: 36–50.

Christopher, Warren. 1998. *In the Stream of History: Shaping Foreign Policy for a New Era*. Stanford, CA: Stanford University Press.

———. 2001. *Chances of a Lifetime*. New York: Scribner.

Clark, Jonathan C. D. 2004. *Our Shadowed Present: Modernism, Postmodernism, and History*. Stanford, CA: Stanford University Press.

Clinton, Bill. 2004. *My Life*. New York: Alfred A. Knopf.

Cobban, Helena. 1991. *The Superpowers and the Syrian-Israeli Conflict: Beyond Crisis Management?* New York: Praeger.

———. 1999. *The Israeli-Syrian Peace Talks: 1991–96 and Beyond*. Washington, DC: US Institute of Peace Press.

Cohen, Aharon. 1970. *Israel and the Arab World*. Abridged ed. Boston: Beacon Press.

Cohen, Michael. 1978. *Palestine: Retreat from the Mandate — the Making of British Policy, 1936–1945*. London: Paul Elek.

———. 1982. *Palestine and the Great Powers 1945–1948*. Princeton, NJ: Princeton University Press.

———. 1987. *The Origins and Evolution of the Arab-Zionist Conflict*. Berkeley: University of California Press.

Cohen, Raymond. 1990. *Culture and Conflict in Egyptian-Israeli Relations: A Dialogue of the Deaf*. Bloomington: Indiana University Press.

Cohen, Yeroham. 1973. *The Allon Plan*. Tel Aviv: Hakibbutz Hameuchad. [Hebrew]

Collins, John, Ned Hall, and Laurie Ann Paul, eds. 2004. *Causation and Counterfactuals*. Cambridge, MA: MIT Press.

Copeland, Miles. 1969. *The Game of Nations: The Amorality of Power Politics*. New York: Simon and Schuster.

Cordesman, Anthony. 2007. *Lessons of the 2006 Israeli-Hizbollah War*. Washington, DC: CSIS Press.

Cowley, Robert, ed. 2006. *The Collected What If? Eminent Historians Imagine What Might Have Been*. New York: Putnam.

Daigle, Craig A. 2004. "The Russians Are Going: Sadat, Nixon and the Soviet Presence in Egypt, 1970–1971." *Middle East Review of International Affairs* 8: 1–15.

———. 2012. *The Limits of Détente: The United States, the Soviet Union and the Arab-Israeli Conflict, 1969–1973*. New Haven, CT: Yale University Press.

Dajani, Mohammed S. 2005. "The 'Blaming Game' Is Wrong." In *The Camp David Summit — What Went Wrong?* edited by Shimon Shamir and Bruce Maddy-Weitzman, 82–89. Brighton, UK: Sussex Academic Press.

Dajani, Munther S. 2005. "Wrong Assumptions." In *The Camp David Summit — What Went Wrong?* edited by Shimon Shamir and Bruce Maddy-Weitzman, 71–73. Brighton, UK: Sussex Academic Press.

———, and Mohammed S. Daoudi. 1986. "New Frontiers in the Search for Peace: The Saudi Initiative." *International Studies* 23: 63–74.

Dalal, Arie. 2012. *Yitzhak Rabin and the Arab-Israeli Conflict*. Azor: Reuveni Sifrei Tsameret. [Hebrew]

Daoudy, Marwa. 2008. "A Missed Chance for Peace: Israel and Syria's Negotiations over the Golan Heights." *Journal of International Affairs* 6: 215–234.

Darwaza, 'Izzat. 1993. *Mudhakkirat Muhammad 'Izzat Darwaza*. Vols. 1–6. Beirut: Dar al-Gharb al-Islami.

Dawisha, Adeed. 1983. "Saudi Arabia and the Arab-Israeli Conflict: The Ups and Downs of Pragmatic Moderation." *International Journal* 38: 674–689.

Dayan, Moshe. 1969. *New Map—Different Relations*. Tel Aviv: Ma'ariv. [Hebrew]

———. 1976. *Moshe Dayan: Story of My Life*. New York: William Morrow and Company.

———. 1981. *Breakthrough: A Personal Account of the Egypt-Israel Peace Negotiations*. London: Weidenfeld and Nicholson.

Dessouki, Ali E. Hillal. 1982. "The New Arab Political Order: Implications for the 1980s." In *Rich and Poor States in the Middle East: Egypt and the New Arab Order*, edited by Malcolm Kerr and El Sayed Yassin, 319–348. Boulder, CO: Westview Press.

Deutsch, Guy. 2010. "The Unripe Diplomacy: The Attempts to Sign an Interim Agreement between Israel and Egypt and Their Failure, 1971–1972." Master's thesis, Hebrew University of Jerusalem. [Hebrew]

Diehl, Jackson. 2009. Interview with 'Abbas. *Washington Post*, May 29.

Dowty, Alan. 2006. "Despair Is Not Enough: Violence, Attitudinal Change, and 'Ripeness' in Israeli-Palestinian Conflict." *Cooperation and Conflict* 41: 5–29.

Drucker, Raviv. 2002. *Harakiri—Ehud Barak: The Failure*. Tel Aviv: Yedioth Ahronoth. [Hebrew]

———. 2014. "How Abu Mazen Was Locked." *Haaretz*, July 6.

Drysdale, Alasdair, and Raymond Hinnebusch. 1991. *Syria and the Middle East Peace Process*. New York: Council on Foreign Relations Press.

Eban, Abba. 1969. "Die Sackgasse ist Arabisch," Spiegel-Gespräch mit Israels Außenminister Abba Eban. *Der Spiegel*, January 27.

———. 1973. Addresses at the Opening Meeting of the Geneva Peace Conference. VIII. The Yom Kippur War and Aftermath. http://www.mfa.gov.il/MFA/Foreign+Relations/Israels+Foreign+Relations+since+1947/1947–1974/21+Addresses+at+the+Opening+Meeting+of+the+Geneva.htm?DisplayMode=print, December 21.

———. 1977. *An Autobiography*. New York: Random House.

———. 1978. *An Autobiography*. Tel Aviv: Ma'ariv. [Hebrew]

———. 1983. *The New Diplomacy: International Affairs in the Modern Age*. London: Weidenfeld and Nicolson.

———. 1993. *Personal Witness: Israel through My Eyes*. London: Jonathan Cape.

———. 1998. *Diplomacy for the Next Century*. New Haven, CT: Yale University Press.

Eisenberg, Laura Zittrain. 1994. *My Enemy's Enemy: Lebanon in the Early Zionist Imagination 1900–1948*. Detroit: Wayne State University Press.

———, and Neil Caplan. 1998. *Negotiating Arab-Israeli Peace: Patterns, Problems, Possibilities*. Bloomington: Indiana University Press.

———. 2010a. *Negotiating Arab-Israeli Peace: Patterns, Problems, Possibilities*. 2nd ed. Bloomington: Indiana University Press.

———. 2010b. "History Revisited or Revamped? The Maronite Factor in Israel's 1982 Invasion of Lebanon." In *Conflict, Diplomacy and Society in Israeli-Lebanese Relations*, edited by Efraim Karsh, Rory Miller, and Michael Kerr, 54–78. London: Routledge.

Eldar, Akiva. 2012. Interview with Koby Huberman, December 10.

Elend-Rif, Ellen. 2009. "Israel's Reaction to the Arab Peace Initiative—A Missed Opportunity?" Master's thesis, Hebrew University of Jerusalem.

Elpeleg, Zvi. 1989. *Grand Mufti*. Tel Aviv: Ministry of Defense. [Hebrew]

————. 1995. *In the Eyes of the Mufti: The Essays of Haj Amin Translated and Annotated*. Tel Aviv: Kibbutz Meuchad Publishers. [Hebrew]

Enderlin, Charles. 2003. *Shattered Dreams: The Failure of the Peace Process in the Middle East, 1995–2002*. Translated by Susan Fairfield. New York: Other Press.

Erekat, Saeb. 2009. "The Political Situation in Light of Development with the US Administration and Israeli Government and Hamas' Continued Coup d'État: Recommendations and Options." Jerusalem: Center for Democracy and Community Development.

Eriksson, Jacob. 2013. "Israeli Track II Diplomacy: The Beilin–Abu Mazen Understandings." In *Israel's Clandestine Diplomacies*, edited by Clive Jones and Tore T. Petersen, 209–224. London: Hurst & Company.

Erlich, Reuven. 2000. *The Lebanon Tangle: The Policy of the Zionist Movement and the State of Israel towards Lebanon, 1918–1958*. Tel Aviv: Ministry of Defense. [Hebrew]

Evans, J. Richard. 1999. *In Defense of History*. New York: W. W. Norton.

Evron, Yair. 1987. *War and Intervention in Lebanon: The Israeli-Syrian Deterrence Dialogue*. Baltimore: John Hopkins University Press.

Fahmi, Ism'ail. 1983. *Negotiating for Peace in the Middle East*. Baltimore: John Hopkins University Press.

Al-Fara, Muhammad 'Ali. 2001. *Al-Salam al-Khadi': Min M'utamar Madrid ila Intifadat al-Aqsa*. Amman: Dar Majdalawi.

Ferguson, Niall, ed. 1997. *Virtual History: Alternatives and Counterfactuals*. New York: Picador.

Feste, Karen A. 1993. *Plans for Peace: Negotiations and the Arab-Israeli Conflict*. New York: Praeger.

Finklestone, Joseph. 1996. *Anwar Sadat: Visionary Who Dared*. London: Frank Cass.

Fishman, Henry, and Ephraim Lavie. 2010. *The Peace Process: Seventeen Plans in Ten Years*. Tel Aviv: Peres Center for Peace and the Palestine Center for Strategic Studies.

Flapan, Simha. 1979. *Zionism and the Palestinians*. London: Croom and Helm.

Friedman, Isaiah. 1992. *The Question of Palestine: British-Jewish-Arab Relations, 1914–1918*. 2nd expanded ed. New Brunswick, NJ: Transaction Publishers.

————. 2000. *Palestine: A Twice-Promised Land? The British, the Arabs and Zionism 1915–1920*. New Brunswick, NJ: Transaction Publishers.

————. 2010. *British Pan-Arab Policy 1915–1922: A Critical Appraisal*. New Brunswick, NJ: Transaction Publishers.

Friedman, Thomas. 2002a. "An Intriguing Signal from the Saudi Crown Prince." *New York Times*, February 17.

————. "Reeling, but Ready." 2002b. *New York Times*, April 28.

————. "Abdullah's Choice." 2007. *New York Times*, March 23.

Friedman, Uri. 2014. "Martin Indyk Explains the Collapse of the Middle East Peace Process." *Atlantic*, July 3.

Furlonge, Geoffrey. 1969. *Palestine Is My Country: The Story of Musa Alami*. London: John Murray.

Gabbay, Rony. 1959. *A Political Study of the Arab-Jewish Conflict: The Arab Refugee Problem*. Paris: Librairie Minard.

Gaddis, John L. 2002. *The Landscape of History: How Historians Map the Past*. Oxford: Oxford University Press.

Galnoor, Itzhak. 1995. *The Partition Plan of Palestine: Decision Crossroads in the Zionist Movement*. Albany: State University of New York.

El-Gamasy, Mohamed Abdel Ghani. 1993. *The October War: Memoirs of Field Marshal El-Gamasy of Egypt*. Translated by Gillian Potter, Nadra Morcos, and Rosette Frances. Cairo: American University in Cairo Press.

Garfinkle, Adam. 1992. *Israel and Jordan in the Shadow of War: Functional Ties and Futile Diplomacy in a Small Place*. New York: St. Martin's Press.

Gat, Moshe. 2012. *In Search of a Peace Settlement: Egypt and Israel between the Wars, 1967–1973*. Houndmills, Basingstoke, Hampshire: Palgrave/Macmillan.

Gause, F. Gregory III. 2002. "The Foreign Policy of Saudi Arabia." In *The Foreign Policies of Middle East States*, edited by Raymond Hinnebusch and Anoushiravan Ehteshami, 193–212. Boulder, CO: Lynne Rienner.

Gazit, Mordechai. *The Peace Process*. 1984. Tel Aviv: Hakibbutz Hameuchad. [Hebrew]

———. 1990. "The Middle East Peace Process." *Middle East Contemporary Survey* 12: 83–120. Boulder, CO: Westview Press.

———. 1991. "The Middle East Peace Process." *Middle East Contemporary Survey* 13: 65–97. Boulder, CO: Westview Press.

———. 1997. "Egypt and Israel—Was There a Peace Opportunity Missed in 1971?" *Journal of Contemporary History* 32: 97–115.

———. 1998. "The Israel-Jordan Peace Negotiations (1949–1951): King Abdallah's Lonely Effort." *Journal of Contemporary History* 23: 409–424.

Gelber, Yoav. 1997. *Jewish-Transjordanian Relations, 1921–48*. London: Frank Cass.

———. 2004. *Israeli-Jordanian Dialogue, 1948–1953: Cooperation, Conspiracy, or Collusion?* Brighton, UK: Sussex Academic Press.

Gemayel, Amine. 1992. *Rebuilding Lebanon*. Lanham, MD: University Press of America.

George, Alexander. 2006. "The Role of Counterfactuals in 'Missed Opportunities.'" In *On Foreign Policy: Unfinished Business*, 83–102. Boulder, CO: Paradigm Publishers.

———, and Jane E. Holl. 2000. "The Warning-Response Problem and Missed Opportunities in Preventive Diplomacy." In *Opportunities Missed Opportunities Seized: Preventive Diplomacy in the Post-Cold War World*, edited by Bruce W. Jentleson. London: Rowman and Littlefield Publishers.

Gershoni, Israel, and James P. Jankowski. 1995. *Redefining the Egyptian Nation, 1930–1945*. Cambridge: Cambridge University Press.

Giacaman, George, and Dag Jørund Lønning, eds. 1998. *After Oslo: New Realities, Old Problems*. London: Pluto Press.

Ginnosar, Yossi. 2005. "Factors That Impeded the Negotiations." In *The Camp David Summit—What Went Wrong?* edited by Shimon Shamir and Bruce Maddy-Weitzman, 51–59. Brighton, UK: Sussex Academic Press.

Golan, Galia. 2007. *Israel and Palestine: Peace Plans from Oslo to Disengagement*. Princeton, NJ: Markus Wiener Publishers.

———. 2015. *Israeli Peacemaking since 1967: Factors behind the Breakthroughs and Failures*. London: Routledge.

Golan, Matti. 1976. *The Secret Talks of Henry Kissinger*. Tel Aviv: Schocken. [Hebrew]

Gold, Dore. 2004. *Hatred's Kingdom: How Saudi Arabia Supports the New Global Terrorism*. Tel Aviv: Miskal. [Hebrew]

Goldmann, Nahum. 1969. *The Autobiography of Nahum Goldmann*. Translated by Helen Sebba. New York: Holt, Rinehart and Winston.

Goldstein, Dov. 1987. *Ma'ariv*, June 5.

Goldstein, Yossi. 2003. *Eshkol—Biography*. Tel Aviv: Keter. [Hebrew]

Goren, Nimrod. 2009. "The Role of External Incentives in Promoting Peace: The Cases of Israel and Turkey." PhD diss., Hebrew University of Jerusalem.

Greig, Michael. 2001. "Moments of Opportunity: Recognizing Conditions of Ripeness for International Mediation between Enduring Rivals." *Journal of Conflict Resolution* 45: 691–718.

Grinberg, Lev. 2007. *Imagined Peace, Discourse of War: The Failure of Leadership, Politics and Democracy in Israel, 1992–2006*. Tel Aviv: Rasling. [Hebrew]

Grosbard, Ofer. 2006. *Menachem Begin: A Portrait of a Leader—A Biography*. Tel Aviv: Rasling. [Hebrew]

Haass, Richard N. 2005. *The Opportunity: America's Moment to Alter History's Course*. New York: Public Affairs.

Habashana, Khalid ʿAbd al-Razzaq. 1999. *Al-ʿAlaqat al-Urduniyya al-Israʾiliyya fi Zill Muʿahadat al-Salam*. Beirut: Bisan lil-Nasr wa-al-Tawziʿ.

Hadari, Danny. 2011. *Israel Galili: A Biography*. Tel Aviv: Hakibbutz Hameuchad. [Hebrew]

Hadawi, Sami. 1991. *Bitter Harvest: A Modern History of Palestine*. 4th ed. New York: Olive Branch Press.

Hahn, Peter L. 1991. *The United States, Great Britain, and Egypt, 1945–1956: Strategy and Diplomacy in the Early Cold War*. Chapel Hill: University of North Carolina Press.

———. 2004. *Caught in the Middle East: U.S. Policy toward the Arab-Israeli Conflict, 1945–1961*. Chapel Hill: University of North Carolina Press.

Halevy, Efraim. 2006. *Man in the Shadow*. Tel Aviv: Matar. [Hebrew]

Hanieh, Akram. 2001. "The Camp David Papers." *Journal of Palestine Studies* 30: 75–97.

Harel, Amos, and Avi Issacharoff. 2008. *Spider Webs (34 Days)*. Tel Aviv: Yedioth Ahronoth. [Hebrew]

Harel, Isser. 1989. *Security and Democracy*. Tel Aviv: Yedioth Ahronoth. [Hebrew]

Harkabi, Yehoshafat. 1972. *Arab Attitudes to Israel*. Jerusalem: Keter Publishing House.

Hassan, bin Talal. 1984. *Search for Peace: The Politics of the Middle Ground in the Arab East*. New York: St. Martin's Press.

Hassassian, Manuel S. 1990. *Palestine: Factionalism in the National Movement (1919–1939)*. Jerusalem: PASSIA.

———. 2002. "Why Did Oslo Fail? Lessons for the Future." In *The Israeli-Palestinian Peace Process: Oslo and the Lessons of Failure*, edited by Robert L. Rothstein, Moshe Maʿoz, and Khalil Shikaki, 114–132. Brighton, UK: Sussex Academic Press.

Hawthorn, Geoffrey. 1991. *Plausible Worlds: Possibility and Understanding in History and Social Sciences*. Cambridge: Cambridge University Press.

Hefez, Nir, and Gadi Bloom. 2005. *The Shepherd: The Life Story of Ariel Sharon*. Tel Aviv: Yedioth Ahronoth. [Hebrew]

Heikal, Mohamed. 1972. *The Cairo Documents*. London: New English Library.

———. 1975. *The Road to Ramadan*. London: Collins.

———. 1978. *Sphinx and Commissar: The Rise and Fall of Soviet Influence in the Arab World*. London: Collins.

———. 1986. *Milaffat al-Suis*. Cairo: Markaz al-Ahram.

———. 1990. *1967: Al-Infijar*. Cairo: Markaz al-Ahram.

———. 1993. *Uktober 73: al-Silah wa-al-Siyasa*. Cairo: Markaz al-Ahram.

———. 1996a. *ʿAwatif al-Harb wa-ʿAwasif al-Salam: al-Mufawadat al-Sirriyya bayna al-ʿArab wa-Israʾil*. Vol. 2. Cairo: Dar al-Shuruk.

———. 1996b. *Secret Channels: The Inside Story of Arab-Israeli Peace Negotiations*. New York: HarperCollins.

Heller, Joseph. 1984. *The Struggle for the Jewish State, Zionist Politics 1936–1948*. Jerusalem: Zalman Shazar Center. [Hebrew]

Hermann, Tamar. 2011. "The Iron Wall." *Bitterlemons-api.org*, 12th ed., vol. 2, June 1.

Hinnebusch, Raymond. 1996. "Does Syria Want Peace? Syrian Policy in the Syrian-Israeli Peace Negotiations." *Journal of Palestine Studies* 26: 42–57.

Hirschfeld, Yair. 2000. *A Formula for Peace: From Negotiations to Implementation*. Tel Aviv: Am Oved. [Hebrew]

Hobsbawm, Eric. 1997. "What Can History Tell Us about Contemporary History?" In Hobsbawm, *On History*, 24–36. New York: New Press.

Hoffmann, Stanley. 1978. *Primacy or World Order: American Foreign Policy since the Cold War*. New York: McGraw-Hill Book Company.

Horowitz, David. 1953. *State in the Making*. Translated from the Hebrew by Julian Melzer. New York: Alfred A. Knopf.

Al-Hout, Nuwaihid Bayan. 1986. *Al-Qiyadat wa-al-Mu'asasat al-Siyasiyya fi Filastin 1917–1948*. Beirut: Dar al-Huda.

Hurewitz, J. C. 1976. *The Struggle for Palestine*. New York: Schocken Books.

Huwaidi, Amin. 1992. *Al-Furas al-Da'iah: al-Qararat al-Hasima fi Harbi al-Istinzaf wa-Uktober*. Beirut: Sharikat al-Matbu'at lil-Tawzi' wa-al-Nashr.

Inbar, Efraim. 1991. "Great Power Mediation: The USA and the May 1983 Israeli-Lebanese Agreement." *Journal of Peace Research* 28: 71–84.

———. 1999. *Rabin and Israel's National Security*. Washington, DC: Woodrow Wilson Center Press.

Indyk, Martin. 2009. *Innocent Abroad: An Intimate Account of American Peace Diplomacy in the Middle East*. New York: Simon and Schuster.

———. 2005a. "Camp David in the Context of US Mideast Peace Strategy." In *The Camp David Summit—What Went Wrong?* edited by Shimon Shamir and Bruce Maddy-Weitzman, 22–29. Brighton, UK: Sussex Academic Press.

———. 2005b. "Sins of Omission, Sins of Commission." In *The Camp David Summit—What Went Wrong?* edited by Shimon Shamir and Bruce Maddy-Weitzman, 100–107. Brighton, UK: Sussex Academic Press.

Israeli, Raphael. 1978. *The Public Diary of President Sadat*. Vols. 1–2. Leiden: E. J. Brill.

———. 1985. *Man of Defiance: A Political Biography of Anwar Sadat*. London: Weidenfeld and Nicolson.

———. 1998. *The Israel-Jordan Agreement—A Missed Opportunity*. Ariel: Ariel Center for Policy Research.

Joffe, Lawrence. 1996. *Keesing's Guide to the Mid-East Peace Process*. London: Cartermill Publishing.

John, Robert, and Sami Hadawi. 1970a. *The Palestine Diary, vol. 1, 1914–1945*. New York: New World Press.

———. 1970b. *The Palestine Diary*, vol. 2, *1945–1948*. New York: New World Press.

Kabha, Mustafa. 2004. *Journalism in the Eye of the Storm: The Palestine Press Shapes Public Opinion 1929–1939*. Jerusalem: Yad Ben-Zvi and Open University of Israel. [Hebrew]

Kacowicz, Marcelo Arie. 1994. *Peaceful Territorial Change*. Columbia: University of South Carolina Press.

———. 2005. "Rashomon in the Middle East: Clashing Narratives, Images and Frames in the Israeli-Palestinian Conflict." *Cooperation and Conflict* 40: 343–360.

Kadi, Leila S. 1966. *Arab Summit Conferences and the Palestine Problem (1936–1950), (1964–1966)*. Beirut: Research Center—Palestine Liberation Organization.

———. 1973. *The Arab-Israeli Conflict: The Peaceful Proposals, 1948–1972*. Beirut: Palestine Research Center.

Kamel, Mohamed Ibrahim. 1986. *The Camp David Accords: A Testimony*. London: KPI.

———. 2003. *Al-Salam al-Daiʿ*. Cairo: Markaz al-Ahram.

Kamil, Rashad. 2003. *ʿAbd al-Nasir wa-Isra'il: Sanawat al-Tafawudd al-Sirri*. Cairo: Dar al-Khial.

Karsh, Efraim. 1994. "Peace Not Love: Toward a Comprehensive Arab-Israeli Settlement." *Washington Quarterly* 17: 143–156.

———. 1999. "The Collusion That Never Was: King Abdallah, the Jewish Agency and the Partition of Palestine." *Journal of Contemporary History* 34: 569–585.

Katz, John. 2006. *The Dove That Failed: Israel between Mediation Initiatives of the US Government and the UN 1967–1973*. Tel Aviv: Yaron Golan. [Hebrew]

Katz, Yossi. 1998. *Partner to Partition: The Jewish Agency's Partition Plan in the Mandated Era*. London: Frank Cass. [Hebrew]

Kayyali, ʿAbd al-Wahhab. 1978. *Palestine: A Modern History*. London: Croom Helm.

———. 1990. *Ta'rikh Filastin al-Hadith*. 10th ed. Beirut: Al-Mu'asasa al-Arabiyya lil-Dirasat wa-al-Nashr.

Keith-Roach, Edward. 1994. *Pasha of Jerusalem: Memoirs of a District Commissioner under the British Mandate*. London: Radcliffe Press.

Kerr, Malcolm. 1982. "Introduction: Egypt in the Shadow of the Gulf." In *Rich and Poor States in the Middle East: Egypt and the New Arab Order*, edited by Kerr and El Sayed Yassin, 1–14. Boulder, CO: Westview Press.

Khalaf, Issa. 1991. *Politics in Palestine: Arab Factionalism and Social Disintegration 1939–1948*. Albany: State University of New York Press.

Khalidi, Rashid. 1997. *Palestinian Identity: The Construction of Modern National Consciousness*. New York: Columbia University Press.

———. 2006. *The Iron Cage: The Story of the Palestinian Struggle for Statehood*. Boston: Beacon Press.

Khalidi, Walid. 2007. "Revisiting the UNGA Partition Resolution." In *The Israel/Palestine Question: A Reader*. 2nd ed., edited by Ilan Pappe, 97–114. London: Routledge.

———. 2009. "The Hebrew *Reconquista* of Palestine: From the 1947 United Nations Partition Resolution to the First Zionist Congress of 1897." *Journal of Palestine Studies* 39: 24–42.

Khashan, Hilal. 2010. "The Evolution of Israeli-Lebanese Relations: From Implicit Peace to Explicit Conflict." In *Conflict, Diplomacy and Society in Israeli-Lebanese Relations*, edited by Efraim Karsh, Rory Miller, and Michael Kerr, 1–16. London: Routledge.

Khatib, Ghassan. 2010. *Palestinian Politics and the Middle East Peace Process*. London: Routledge.

Khouri, Fred. 1968. *The Arab-Israeli Dilemma*. Syracuse, NY: Syracuse University Press.

Khoury, Philip S. 1985. "Divided Loyalties? Syria and the Question of Palestine, 1919–39." *Middle Eastern Studies* 21: 324–348.

Kimche, David. 1991. *The Last Option: After Nasser, Arafat and Saddam Hussein, the Quest for Peace in the Middle East*. London: Weidenfeld and Nicolson.

Kimche, Jon. 1973a. *Palestine or Israel: The Untold Story of Why We Failed 1917–1923; 1967–1973*. London: Secker and Warburg.

———. 1973b. *There Could Have Been Peace*. New York: Dial Press.

Kimmerling, Baruch, and Joel S. Migdal. 2003. *The Palestinian People: A History*. Cambridge, MA: Harvard University Press.

Kipnis, Yigal. 2009. *The Mountain That Was as a Monster: The Golan between Syria and Israel.* Jerusalem: Magnes Press. [Hebrew]

———. 2012. *1973: The Way to the War.* Tel Aviv: Dvir. [Hebrew]

Kirkbride, Sir Alec. 1976. *From the Wings: Amman Memoirs 1947–1951.* London: Frank Cass.

Kissinger, Henry. 1979. *White House Years.* Boston: Little, Brown and Company.

———. 1999. "U.S. Mediation Essential." *Washington Post*, July 19.

Klieman, Aharon. 1980. "In the Public Domain: The Controversy over Partition for Palestine." *Jewish Social Studies* 42: 147–164.

———. 1983. *Divide or Rule: Britain, Partition and Palestine, 1936–1939.* Jerusalem: Yad Itzhak Ben-Zvi. [Hebrew]

———. 2000. *Compromising Palestine: A Guide to the Final Status Negotiations.* New York: Columbia University Press.

Klein, Menachem. 2001. *Shattering a Taboo: The Contacts toward a Permanent Status Agreement in Jerusalem 1994–2001.* Jerusalem: Jerusalem Institute for Israel Studies. [Hebrew]

———. 2003. *The Jerusalem Problem: The Struggle for Permanent Status.* Gainesville: University Press of Florida.

Kohn, Alexander. 1989. *Fortune or Failure: Missed Opportunities and Chance Discoveries.* Oxford: Basil Blackwell.

Korn, David. 1990. "US-Soviet Negotiations of 1969 and the Rogers Plan." *Middle East Journal* 44: 37–50.

———. 1992. *Stalemate: The War of Attrition and Great Power Diplomacy in the Middle East, 1967–1970.* Boulder, CO: Westview Press.

Kostiner, Joseph. 2005. "Coping with Regional Challenges: A Case Study of Crown Prince Abdullah's Peace Initiative." In *Saudi Arabia in the Balance: Political Economy, Society, Foreign Affairs*, edited by Paul Aarts and Gerd Nonneman, 352–371. New York: New York University Press.

———. 2008. *The Marginal Peace: The Attitudes of the Persian Arabian Gulf States towards Israel and the Peace Process.* Tel Aviv: Tami Steinmetz Center for Peace Research. [Hebrew]

———. 2009. "Saudi Arabia and the Arab-Israeli Peace Process: The Fluctuation of Regional Coordination." *British Journal of Middle Eastern Studies* 36: 417–429.

Kriesberg, Louis. 2001. "Mediation and the Transformation of the Israeli-Palestinian Conflict." *Journal of Peace Research* 38: 373–392.

Krispin-Peleg, Yael. 2010. "The Influence of the Level of Trust in the Rival on the Decision-Maker's Policy of Conflict Management or Resolution: Designing Israel's Policy towards the Palestinian Side and Jordan during Yitzhak Rabin's Premiership, 1992–1995." PhD diss., Hebrew University of Jerusalem. [Hebrew]

Kristianasen, Wendy. 1999. "Challenge and Counterchallenge: Hamas's Response to Oslo." *Journal of Palestine Studies* 28: 19–36.

Kurtzer, Daniel C., and Scott B. Lasensky. 2008. *Negotiating Arab-Israeli Peace: American Leadership in the Middle East.* Washington, DC: US Institute of Peace.

———, ed. 2012. *Pathways to Peace: America and the Arab-Israeli Conflict.* London: Palgrave/Macmillan.

———, Scott B. Lasensky, William B. Quandt, Steven L. Spiegel, and Shibley Z. Telhami. 2013. *The Peace Puzzle: America's Quest for Arab-Israeli Peace.* Ithaca, NY: Cornell University Press and US Institute of Peace.

Kyle, Keith. 1991. *Suez.* London: Weidenfeld and Nicholson.

Laham, Nicholas. 2004. *Crossing the Rubicon: Ronald Reagan and US Policy in the Middle East.* London: Ashgate.

Laqueur, Walter. 1972. *A History of Zionism*. New York: Holt, Rinehart and Winston.
———, and Barry Rubin, eds. 1984. *The Israel-Arab Reader: A Documentary History of the Middle East Conflict*. London: Penguin.
Larson, Deborah Welch. 1997. "Trust and Missed Opportunities in International Relations." *Political Psychology* 18: 701–734.
Lasensky, Scott. 2004. "Paying for Peace: The Oslo Process and the Limits of American Foreign Aid." *Middle East Journal* 58: 210–234.
Lebow, Richard Ned. 2000. "What's So Different about Counterfactual?" *World Politics* 52: 550–585.
———. 2010. *Forbidden Fruit: Counterfactuals and International Relations*. Princeton, NJ: Princeton University Press.
Lehrs, Lior. 2011. *Peace Talks over Jerusalem: A Review of Israeli-Palestinian Negotiations Concerning Jerusalem, 1993–2011*. Jerusalem: Jerusalem Institute for Israel Studies. [Hebrew]
Liddell-Hart, B. H. 1971. *Why Don't We Learn from History?* London: George Allen & Unwin.
Lipkin-Shahak, Amnon. 2005. "The Roles of Barak, Arafat and Clinton." In *The Camp David Summit—What Went Wrong?* edited by Shimon Shamir and Bruce Maddy-Weitzman, 42–50. Brighton, UK: Sussex Academic Press.
Little, Douglas. 1990. "Cold War and Covert Action: The United States and Syria, 1945–1958." *Middle East Journal* 44: 51–75.
Lukacs, Yehuda, ed. 1992. *The Israeli-Palestinian Conflict: A Documentary Record*. Cambridge: Cambridge University Press.
———. 1997. *Israel, Jordan, and the Peace Process*. Syracuse, NY: Syracuse University Press.
Maddy-Weitzman, Bruce. 1993. *The Crystallization of the Arab State System 1945–1954*. Syracuse, NY: Syracuse University Press.
Al-Madfai, Madiha Rashid. 1993. *Jordan, the United States, and the Middle East Peace Process, 1974–1991*. Cambridge: Cambridge University Press.
Mahler, S. Gregory, and Alden R. W. Mahler. 2010. *The Arab-Israeli Conflict: An Introduction and Documentary Reader*. London: Routledge.
Majali, Abdul Salam, Jawad A. Anani, and Munther J. Haddadin. 2006. *Peacemaking: The Inside Story of the 1994 Jordanian-Israeli Treaty*. Norman: University of Oklahoma Press.
Makovsky, David. 1996. *Making Peace with the PLO: The Rabin's Government Road to the Oslo Accord*. Boulder, CO: Westview Press.
Malley, Robert. 2005. "American Mistakes and Israeli Misconceptions." In *The Camp David Summit—What Went Wrong?* edited by Shimon Shamir and Bruce Maddy-Weitzman, 108–114. Brighton, UK: Sussex Academic Press.
———. 2002. "Camp David and After: An Exchange (2. A Reply to Ehud Barak)." *New York Review of Books*, June 13.
———, and Hussein Agha. 2001. "Camp David: The Tragedy of Errors." *New York Review of Books*, August 9.
Mandel, Neville J. 1976. *The Arabs and Zionism before World War I*. Berkeley: University of California Press.
Ma'oz, Moshe. 1995. *Syria and Israel: From War to Peace-Making*. Oxford: Clarendon Press.
———. 2002. "The Oslo Peace Process: From Breakthrough to Breakdown." In *The Israeli-Palestinian Peace Process: Oslo and the Lessons of Failure*, edited by Robert L. Rothstein, Moshe Ma'oz, and Khalil Shikaki, 133–148. Brighton, UK: Sussex Academic Press.
Maoz, Zeev. 2004. "Never Missing an Opportunity to Miss an Opportunity: The Israeli

Nonpolicy of Peace in the Middle East." In *Defending the Holy Land: A Critical Analysis of Israel's Security and Foreign Policy*. Ann Arbor: University of Michigan Press.

———. 2005. "The Strategy of Summit Diplomacy." In *The Camp David Summit—What Went Wrong?* edited by Shimon Shamir and Bruce Maddy-Weitzman, 203–209. Brighton, UK: Sussex Academic Press.

———, and Dan S. Felsenthal. 1987. "Self-Binding Commitments, the Inducement of Trust, Social Choice, and the Theory of International Cooperation." *International Studies Quarterly* 31: 177–200.

Marcus, Yoel. 1981. "To Learn to Respond." *Haaretz*, August 12.

Margalit, Dan. 1997. *I Have Seen Them All*. Tel Aviv: Zmora-Bitan. [Hebrew]

Mattar, Philip. 1988. *The Mufti of Jerusalem: Al-Hajj Amin al-Husayni and the Palestinian National Movement*. New York: Columbia University Press.

———. 1989. "The Critical Moment for Peace." *Foreign Policy* 76: 141–159.

Matz, David. 2003a. "Trying to Understand the Taba Talks (Part I)." *Palestine-Israel Journal of Politics, Economics and Culture* 10.3: 96–105.

———. 2003b. "Why Did Taba End?" *Palestine-Israel Journal of Politics, Economics and Culture* 10.4: 92–98.

———. 2006. "Reconstructing Camp David: Review Essay." *Negotiation Journal* 22.1: 89–103.

May, Ernest. 1973. *"Lessons" of the Past: The Use and Misuse of History in American Foreign Policy*. New York: Oxford University Press.

McGhee, George. 1983. *Envoy to the Middle East: Adventures in Diplomacy*. New York: Harper and Row.

McNamara, Robert S., James G. Blight, and Robert K. Brigham. 1999. *Argument without End: In Search of Answers to the Vietnam Tragedy*. New York: Public Affairs.

Medzini, Meron. 2008. *Golda: A Political Biography*. Tel Aviv: Yedioth Ahronoth. [Hebrew]

Meir, Golda. 1973. "Israel in Search of Lasting Peace." *Foreign Affairs* 51: 447–461.

———. 1976. *My Life: The Autobiography of Golda Meir*. London: Futura Publications.

Meital, Yoram. 1997. *Egypt's Struggle for Peace: Continuity and Change, 1967–1977*. Gainesville: University Press of Florida.

———. 2000. "The Khartoum Conference and Egyptian Policy after the 1967 War: A Reexamination." *Middle East Journal* 54: 64–82.

———. 2006. *Peace in Tatters: Israel, Palestine and the Middle East*. Boulder, CO: Lynne Rienner Publishers.

Melman, Yossi. 1987. *A Hostile Partnership: The Secret Relations between Israel and Jordan*. Tel Aviv: Yedioth Ahronoth. [Hebrew]

Mendes-Flohr, Paul R., ed. 1988. *A Land of Two Peoples: Martin Buber on Jews and Arabs*. Tel Aviv: Schocken. [Hebrew]

Merhav, Reuven. 2005. "Planning for Jerusalem." In *The Camp David Summit—What Went Wrong?* edited by Shimon Shamir and Bruce Maddy-Weitzman, 167–175. Brighton, UK: Sussex Academic Press.

Migdalovitz, Carol. 2007. *Israeli-Palestinian Peace Process: The Annapolis Conference*. Washington, DC: CRS Report for the Congress.

———. 2010. *Israeli-Arab Negotiations: Background, Conflicts, and U.S. Policy*. Washington, DC: CRS Report for the Congress.

Miller, Aaron David. 2005. "The Effects of 'Syria-First' Strategy." In *The Camp David Summit—What Went Wrong?* edited by Shimon Shamir and Bruce Maddy-Weitzman, 93–99. Brighton, UK: Sussex Academic Press.

——. 2008. *The Much Too Promised Land: America's Elusive Search for Arab-Israeli Peace*. New York: Bantam Books.

——. 2012. "Memorandum to the President: Thinking Through an Israeli-Palestinian Initiative." In *Pathways to Peace: America and the Arab-Israeli Conflict*, edited by Daniel C. Kurtzer, 135–156. London: Palgrave/Macmillan.

Milton-Edwards, Beverly, and Alastair Crooke. 2004. "Elusive Ingredient: Hamas and the Peace Process." *Journal of Palestine Studies* 33: 39–52.

Mitchell, Christopher. 2000. *Gestures of Conciliation: Factors Contributing to Successful Olive Branches*. London: Macmillan Press.

Mørk, Kjeang Hulda. 2007. "The Jarring Mission: A Study of the UN Peace Efforts in the Middle East, 1967–1971." Master's thesis, University of Oslo.

Morris, Benny. 1984. "Israel and the Lebanese Phalange: The Birth of a Relationship, 1948–1951." *Studies in Zionism* 5: 125–44.

——. 1993. *Israel's Border Wars: Arab Infiltration, Israeli Retaliation and the Countdown to Suez*. Oxford: Clarendon Press.

——. 1999. *Righteous Victims: A History of the Zionist-Arab Conflict, 1881–1999*. New York: Alfred A. Knopf.

——. 2001. *Righteous Victims: A History of the Zionist-Arab Conflict 1881–2001*. New York: Vintage Books.

——. 2002. "Camp David and After: An Exchange (1. An Interview with Ehud Barak)." *New York Review of Books*, June 13.

——. 2009. *One State, Two States: Resolving the Israel/Palestine Conflict*. New Haven, CT: Yale University Press.

Al-Moualem, Walid. 1997. "Fresh Light on the Syrian-Israeli Peace Negotiations: An Interview with Ambassador Walid al-Moualem." *Journal of Palestine Studies* 26: 81–94.

Muasher, Marwan. 2008. *The Arab Center: The Promise of Moderation*. New Haven, CT: Yale University Press.

Al-Mufawadat al-Suriayya al-Isra'iliyya: Ruwa Sahayuniyya wa-Gharbiyya. 2001. Beirut: Markaz al-Istisharat wa-al-Bukhuth.

Muslih, Muhammad. 1994. "Dateline Damascus: Asad Is Ready." *Foreign Policy* 96: 146–163.

Naor, Arye. 1993. *Begin in Power: A Personal Testimony*. Tel Aviv: Yedioth Ahronoth. [Hebrew]

Nashashibi, Nasser Eddin. 1990. *Jerusalem's Other Voice: Ragheb Nashashibi and Moderation in Palestinian Politics, 1920–1948*. Ithaca, NY: Ithaca Press.

Nasser, Nicola. 2007. "The Arab Peace Initiative: This Time, Israel Is Missing an Historic Opportunity." *Global Research*, http://nicolanasser.newsvine.com/, March 14.

Nevo, Joseph. 1984. "The Rejection of the White Paper of 1939 by the Palestinian Arab Leadership." In *Studies in the Palestine Partition Plans*, edited by Meir Avizohar and Isaiah Freidman, 128–142. Sede Boqer: Ben-Gurion University of the Negev. [Hebrew]

——. 1996. *King Abdallah and Palestine: A Territorial Ambition*. Oxford: Macmillan Press.

Nixon, Richard. 1978. *The Memoirs of Richard Nixon*. London: Sidgwick and Jackson.

Noor, Queen. 2003. *Leap of Faith: Memoirs of an Unexpected Life*. New York: Wheeler Publishing.

Nusseibeh, Sari. 2005. "There Could Have Been Another Way." In *The Camp David Summit—What Went Wrong?* edited by Shimon Shamir and Bruce Maddy-Weitzman, 18–21. Brighton, UK: Sussex Academic Press.

Oakeshott, Michael. 1933. *Experience and Its Modes*. Cambridge: Cambridge University Press.

O'Connell, Jack. 2011. *King's Counsel: A Memoir of War, Espionage, and Diplomacy in the Middle East*. New York: W. W. Norton.

Olmert, Ehud. 2011. "How I Almost Brought Peace." *Yedioth Ahronoth, 7 Days*, 24–40, January 28.

100 Years of Palestinian History: A 20th-Century Chronology. 2001. Jerusalem: PASSIA.

Al-O'ran, Mutayyam. 2009. *Jordanian-Israeli Relations: The Peacebuilding Experience*. London: Routledge.

Oren, Michael. 1990. "Secret Egypt-Israel Peace Initiatives Prior to the Suez Campaign." *Middle Eastern Studies* 26: 351–370.

——. 1992. *Origins of the Second Arab-Israel War: Egypt, Israel and the Great Powers*. London: Frank Cass.

——. 2007. *Power, Faith and Fantasy: America in the Middle East, 1776 to the Present*. New York: W. W. Norton.

Pappe, Ilan. 1994. *The Making of the Arab-Israeli Conflict 1947–1951*. London: I. B. Tauris.

——. 2006. "The Process That Never Was: Missed Opportunities in the Israeli-Palestinian Conflict, 1948–2000." In *Arab-Jewish Relations: From Conflict to Resolution? Essays in Honor of Prof. Moshe Ma'oz*, edited by Elie Podeh and Asher Kaufman. Brighton, UK: Sussex Academic Press.

Parker, B. Richard. 1993. *The Politics of Miscalculation in the Middle East*. Bloomington: Indiana University Press.

——, ed. 2001. *The October War: A Retrospective*. Gainesville: University Press of Florida.

Pedatzur, Reuven. 1996. *The Triumph of Embarrassment: Israel and the Territories after the Six-Day War*. Tel Aviv: Yad Tabenkin. [Hebrew]

Peleg, Ilan. 1987. *Begin's Foreign Policy, 1977–1983: Israel's Move to the Right*. New York: Greenwood Press.

——, and Paul Scham. 2010. "Historical Breakthroughs in Arab-Israeli Negotiations: Lessons for the Future." *Middle East Journal* 64: 215–233.

Peres, Shimon, with Arye Naor. 1993. *The New Middle East*. New York: Henry Holt and Company.

——. 1995. *Battling for Peace: Memoirs*. London: Weidenfeld and Nicolson.

Perlmann, M. 1944. "Chapters of Arab-Jewish Diplomacy." *Journal of Jewish Social Issues* 6: 123–154.

Podeh, Elie. 1995. *The Quest for Hegemony in the Arab World: The Struggle over the Baghdad Pact*. Leiden: E. J. Brill.

——. 1999. *The Decline of Arab Unity: The Rise and Fall of the United Arab Republic*. Brighton, UK: Sussex Academic Press.

——. 2000. *The Arab-Israeli Conflict in Israeli History Textbooks, 1948–2000*. Westport, CT: Bergin and Garvey.

——. 2003. *From Fahd to 'Abdallah: The Origins of the Saudi Peace Initiatives and Their Impact on the Arab System and Israel*. Jerusalem: Harry S. Truman Research Institute for the Advancement of Peace.

——. 2004. "Demonizing the Other: Israeli Perceptions of Nasser and Nasserism." In *Rethinking Nasserism: Revolution and Historical Memory in Modern Egypt*, edited by Elie Podeh and Onn Winckler, 72–99. Gainesville: University Press of Florida.

——. 2005. "Demonizing the Enemy: Nasser and Nasserism in the Eyes of the Israeli Decision Makers (1952–1970)." *Hamizrah Hehadash* 45: 151–208. [Hebrew]

——, and Asher Kaufman, eds. 2006. *Arab-Jewish Relations: From Conflict to Resolution? Essays in Honor of Prof. Moshe Ma'oz*. Brighton, UK: Sussex Academic Press.

———. 2007a. "The Arab Peace Initiative: A Missed Opportunity?" *Palestine-Israel Journal* 14.4: 5–11.

———. 2007b. "Normal Relations without Normalization: The Evolution of Egyptian-Israeli Relations, 1979–2006—the Politics of Cold Peace." In *The Search for Israeli-Arab Peace: Learning from the Past and Building Trust*, edited by Edwin G. Corr, Joseph Ginat and Shaul Gabbay, 107–129. Brighton, UK: Sussex Academic Press.

———. 2010. "Israel and the Arab Peace Plan—A Plausible Missed Opportunity?" In *Israel and the Arab Peace Initiative*, edited by Ephraim Lavie, 67–94. Tel Aviv: Tammy Steinmetz Center for Peace Research. [Hebrew]

———. 2011. *The Politics of National Celebrations in the Arab World*. Cambridge: Cambridge University Press.

———. 2014. "Israel and the Arab Peace Initiative, 2002–2014: A Plausible Missed Opportunity." *Middle East Journal* 68.4: 584–603.

Porath, Yehoshua. 1974. *The Emergence of the Palestinian-Arab National Movement 1918–1929*. London: Frank Cass.

———. 1977. *The Palestinian Arab National Movement: From Riots to Rebellion, vol. 2, 1929–1939*. London: Frank Cass.

Powell, Colin, with Joseph E. Persico. 1995. *My American Journey*. New York: Random House.

Pressman, Jeremy. 2003. "Visions in Collision: What Happened at Camp David." *International Security* 28: 4–43.

———. 2007. "Mediation, Domestic Politics, and the Israeli-Syrian Negotiations." *Security Studies* 16: 350–381.

Pundak, Ron. 2001. "From Oslo to Taba: What Went Wrong?" *Survival* 43: 31–45.

———. 2002. "From Oslo to Taba: What Went Wrong?" In *The Israeli-Palestinian Peace Process: Oslo and the Lessons of Failure*, edited by Robert L. Rothstein, Moshe Ma'oz, and Khalil Shikaki, 88–113. Brighton, UK: Sussex Academic Press.

———. 2013. *Secret Channel*. Tel Aviv: Yedioth Ahronoth. [Hebrew]

———, and Shaul Arieli. 2004. *The Territorial Aspect of the Israeli-Palestinian Final Status Negotiations*. Tel Aviv: Peres Center for Peace. [Hebrew]

Purdum, S. Todd. 2002. "Killing Time: Everyone Has a Peace Plan. And They Can All Wait." *New York Times*, May 12.

Quandt, William B. 1977. *Decade of Decisions: American Policy Toward the Arab-Israeli Conflict, 1967–1976*. Berkeley: University of California Press.

———. 1981. *Saudi Arabia in the 1980s: Foreign Policy, Security, and Oil*. Washington, DC: Brookings Institution.

———. 1986. *Camp David: Peacemaking and Politics*. Washington, DC: Brookings Institution.

———. 1988. "U.S. Policy toward the Arab-Israeli Conflict." In *The Middle East: Ten Years after Camp David*, edited by William B. Quandt, 357–386. Washington, DC: Brookings Institution.

———. 1993. *Peace Process: American Diplomacy and the Arab-Israeli Conflict since 1967*. Washington, DC: Brookings Institution.

———. 2005. *Peace Process: American Diplomacy and the Arab-Israeli Conflict since 1967*. 3rd ed. Washington, DC, and Berkeley: Brookings Institution Press and University of California Press.

Qurei, Ahmed (Abu 'Ala). 2006. *From Oslo to Jerusalem: The Palestinian Story of the Secret Negotiations*. London: I. B. Tauris.

————. 2008. *Beyond Oslo. The Struggle for Palestine: Inside the Middle East Peace Process from Rabin's Death to Camp David*. London: I. B. Tauris.

Rabbani, Mouin. 2001. "Rocks and Rockets: Oslo's Inevitable Conclusion." *Journal of Palestine Studies* 30: 68–81.

Rabil, Robert G. 2003. *Embattled Neighbors: Syria, Israel and Lebanon*. Boulder, CO: Lynne Rienner Publishers.

Rabin, Leah. 1997. *Rabin—Our Life, His Legacy*. Tel Aviv: Miskal—Yedioth Ahronoth. [Hebrew]

Rabin, Yitzhak. 1979. *Pinkas Sherut*. Vols. 1–2. Tel Aviv: Ma'ariv. [Hebrew]

Rabinovich, Itamar. 1991. *The Road Not Taken: Early Arab-Israeli Negotiations*. Oxford: Oxford University Press.

————. 1998. *The Brink of Peace: The Israeli-Syrian Negotiations*. Princeton, NJ: Princeton University Press.

————. 2004. *Waging Peace: Israel and the Arabs, 1948–2003*. Updated and revised. Princeton, NJ: Princeton University Press.

————. 2006. "From Deposit to Commitment: The Evolution of US-Israel-Syrian Peace Negotiations, 1993–2000." In *Arab-Jewish Relations: From Conflict to Resolution? Essays in Honor of Prof. Moshe Ma'oz*, edited by Elie Podeh and Asher Kaufman, 277–282. Brighton, UK: Sussex Academic Press.

————. 2011. *The Lingering Conflict: Israel, the Arabs, and the Middle East, 1948–2011*. Tel Aviv: Kinneret, Zmora-Bitan, Dvir. [Hebrew]

Rafael, Gideon. 1981. *Destination Peace: Three Decades of Israeli Foreign Policy—A Personal Memoir*. New York: Stein and Day Publishers.

Ran, Yaron. 1991. *The Roots of the Jordanian Option*. Tel Aviv: Zitrin. [Hebrew]

Rathmell, Andrew. 1995. *Secret War in the Middle East: The Covert Struggle for Syria, 1949–1961*. London: I. B. Tauris.

Ravid, Barak. 2012. *Haaretz*, October 15.

Raviv, Moshe. 2000. *Israel at Fifty*. Tel Aviv: Ministry of Defense. [Hebrew]

Raz, Avi. 2012. *The Bride and the Dowry: Israel, Jordan, and the Palestinians in the Aftermath of the June 1967 War*. New Haven, CT: Yale University Press.

————. 2013. "The Generous Peace Offer That Was Never Offered: The Israeli Cabinet Resolution of 19 June, 1967." *Diplomatic History* 37: 85–108.

Reagan, Ronald. 1990. *An American Life*. New York: Simon and Schuster.

Reich, Bernard. 1984. *The United States and Israel: Dynamics of Influence*. New York: Praeger.

————, and Rosemary Hollis. 1985. "Peacemaking in the Reagan Administration." In *Peace-Making in the Middle East: Problems and Prospects*, edited by Paul Marantz and Janice Gross Stein. London: Croom Helm.

Reinharz, Jehuda. 1993. *Chaim Weizmann: The Making of a Statesman*. Oxford: Oxford University Press.

Reiter, Yitzhak. 2008. *War, Peace and International Relations in Contemporary Islam: Muslim Scholars on Peace Treaty with Israel*. Jerusalem: Jerusalem Institute for Israel Studies. [Hebrew]

Rice, Condoleezza. 2011. *No Higher Honor: A Memoir of My Years in Washington*. New York: Simon and Schuster.

Riyad, Mahmoud. 1981. *The Struggle for Peace in the Middle East*. London: Quartet Books.

Roberts, Andrew, ed. 2004. *What Might Have Been? Leading Historians on Twelve "What Ifs" of History*. London: Phoenix.

Rosenfeld, Gavriel D. 2005. *The World Hitler Never Made: Alternate History and the Memory of Nazism*. Cambridge: Cambridge University Press.

Rosenthal, Yemima, ed. 2012. *Levi Eshkol—The Third Prime Minister: A Selection of Documents*. Jerusalem: Israeli State Archives. [Hebrew]

Ross, Dennis. 2005. *The Missing Peace: The Inside Story for the Fight for Middle East Peace*. New York: Farrar, Straus and Giroux.

———. 2007. *Statecraft and How to Restore America's Standing in the World*. New York: Farrar, Straus and Giroux.

Rothstein, Robert L. 2002. "A Fragile Peace: Are There Only Lessons of Failure?" In *The Israeli-Palestinian Peace Process: Oslo and the Lessons of Failure*, edited by Robert L. Rothstein, Moshe Ma'oz, and Khalil Shikaki, 161–169. Brighton, UK: Sussex Academic Press.

Rubin, Barry. 1994. *Revolution until Victory? The Politics and History of the PLO*. Cambridge, MA: Harvard University Press.

———, and Judith Colp Rubin. 2003. *Yasir Arafat: A Political Biography*. Oxford: Oxford University Press.

Rubinstein, Danny. 2001. *Arafat: A Portrait*. Ganei-Aviv: Zmora-Bitan. [Hebrew]

Rubinstein, Elyakim. 1992. *Paths of Peace*. Tel Aviv: Ministry of Defense. [Hebrew]

———. 2004. "Chapters in the Israeli-Jordanian Peace." In *Neighbors Caught in a Maze: Israel-Jordan Relations Before and After the Peace Treaty*, edited by Joseph Nevo, 135–169. Tel Aviv: Yitzhak Rabin Center for Israel Studies.

Rynhold, Jonathan. 2007. "Cultural Shift and Foreign Policy Change: Israel and the Making of the Oslo Accords." *Cooperation and Conflict* 42: 419–440.

———. 2008. *The Failure of the Oslo Process: Inherently Flawed or Flawed Implementation?* Ramat Gan: Begin-Sadat Center for Strategic Studies.

Saba, Alias. 2000. *Lubnan wa-al-Sira' al-'Arabi-al-Isra'ili*. Beirut: Dar al-Jadid.

El-Sadat, Anwar. 1972–1973. "Where Egypt Stands." *Foreign Affairs* 51: 114–123.

———. 1978. *In Search of Identity: An Autobiography*. New York: Harper and Row.

Safran, Nadav. 1988. *Saudi Arabia: The Ceaseless Quest for Security*. Ithaca, NY: Cornell University Press.

Sagie, Uri. 2011. *The Frozen Hand*. Tel Aviv: Yediot Ahronot. [Hebrew]

Sahliyeh, Emile. 1988. "Jordan and the Palestinians." In *The Middle East: Ten Years after Camp David*, edited by William B. Quandt, 279–318. Washington, DC: Brookings Institute.

Said, Edward. 1996. *Peace and Its Discontents: Essays on Palestine and the Middle East Peace Process*. New York: Vintage Books.

Salem, Walid. 2005. "Paradoxes of the U.N. 1947 Partition Plan." In *Shared Histories: A Palestinian-Israeli Dialogue*, edited by Paul Scham, Walid Salem, and Benjamin Pogrund, 182–187. Jerusalem: Harry S. Truman Research Institute for the Advancement of Peace.

Sanders, Ronald. 1983. *The High Walls of Jerusalem: A History of the Balfour Declaration and the Birth of the British Mandate for Palestine*. New York: Holt, Rinehart and Winston.

Sasson, Moshe. 2004. *Talking Peace*. Tel Aviv: Ma'ariv. [Hebrew]

Saunders, H. Harold. 1985. *The Other Walls: The Arab-Israeli Peace Process in a Global Perspective*. Princeton, NJ: Princeton University Press.

Savir, Uri. 1998. *The Process: 1,100 Days That Changed the Middle East*. New York: Random House.

Sayigh, Yezid. 1997. *Armed Struggle and the Search for State: The Palestinian National Movement, 1949–1993*. Oxford: Oxford University Press.

———. 2001. "Arafat and the Anatomy of Revolt." *Survival* 43.3: 47–60.

Schiff, Ze'ev. 1989. *Security for Peace: Israel's Minimal Security Requirements in Negotiations with the Palestinians*. Policy Papers, no. 15. Washington, DC: Washington Institute.

———, and Ehud Ya'ari. 1984. *A War of Deception*. Jerusalem: Schocken. [Hebrew]

Schoenbaum, David. 1993. *The United States and the State of Israel*. New York: Oxford University Press.

Schueftan, Dan. 1986. *A Jordanian Option: The Yishuv and the State of Israel vis-à-vis the Hashemite Regime and the Palestinian National Movement*. Tel Aviv: Yad Tabenkin. [Hebrew]

Schulze, Kirsten E. 1998. *Israel's Covert Diplomacy in Lebanon*. Oxford: Macmillan Press.

Seale, Patrick. 1987. *The Struggle for Syria: A Study of Post-War Arab Politics 1945–1958*. London: I. B. Tauris.

———. 1988. *Asad: The Struggle for the Middle East*. Berkeley: University of California Press.

———. 1996. "Asad's Regional Strategy and the Challenge from Netanyahu." *Journal of Palestine Studies* 26: 27–41.

———. 2000. "The Syria-Israel Negotiations: Who Is Telling the Truth?" *Journal of Palestine Studies* 29: 65–77.

Segev, Samuel. 2008. *The Moroccan Connection: The Secret Ties between Israel and Morocco*. Tel Aviv: Matar. [Hebrew]

Segev, Tom. 2000. *One Palestine, Complete: Jews and Arabs under the British Mandate*. Translated by Haim Watzman. New York: Metropolitan Books.

Sela, Avraham. 1972–1973. "Talks and Contacts between Zionist Leaders and Arab-Palestinian Leaders, 1933–1939." *Hamizrah Hehadash* 22: 401–423; 23: 1–21. [Hebrew]

———. 1985. *From Contacts to Negotiations: The Relations of the Jewish Agency and the State of Israel with King 'Abdallah, 1946–1950*. Tel Aviv: Moshe Dayan Center for Middle East and African Studies. [Hebrew]

———. 1998. *The Decline of the Arab-Israeli Conflict: Middle East Politics and the Quest for Regional Order*. Albany: State University of New York Press.

Seliktar, Ofira. 2009. *Doomed to Failure? The Politics and Intelligence of the Oslo Peace Process*. Santa Barbara, CA: ABC CLIO.

Serfaty, Simon. 1988. *After Reagan: False Starts, Missed Opportunities and New Beginnings*. Washington, DC: Johns Hopkins Foreign Policy Institute.

Shaaban, Bouthaina. 2013. *Damascus Diary: An Inside Account of Hafez al-Assad's Peace Diplomacy, 1990–2000*. Boulder, CO: Lynne Rienner Publishers.

Shafir, Gershon. 2006. "The Miscarriage of Peace: Israel, Egypt, and the United States and the 'Jarring Plan' in the Early 1970s." *Israel Studies Forum* 21: 3–26.

Shalev, Aryeh. 1989. *Cooperation under the Shadow of Conflict: The Israeli-Syrian Armistice Regime 1949–1955*. Tel Aviv: Ministry of Defense. [Hebrew]

Shalom, Zaki. 2001. "A Missed Opportunity? The Attempt to Form Direct Contacts between Israel and Egypt on the Eve of the Six-Day War." *Hatzionut* 22: 321–353. [Hebrew]

Shamir, Shimon. 1978. *Egypt under Sadat: The Search for a New Orientation*. Tel Aviv: Dvir. [Hebrew]

———. 1988. "Israeli Views of Egypt and the Peace Process: The Duality of Vision." In *The Middle East: Ten Years after Camp David*, edited by William B. Quandt, 187–216. Washington, DC: Brookings Institution.

———. 1989. "The Collapse of Project Alpha." In *Suez 1956: The Crisis and Its Consequences*, edited by Louis Roger and Roger Owen, 73–100. Oxford: Oxford University Press.

———. 1994. "The Yom Kippur War as a Factor in the Peace Process." In *From War to Peace:*

Arab-Israeli Relations 1973-1993, edited by Barry Rubin, Joseph Ginat, and Moshe Ma'oz, 33–40. Brighton, UK: Sussex Academic Press.

———. 2012. *The Rise and Decline of the Warm Peace with Jordan: Israeli Diplomacy in the Hussein Years*. Tel Aviv: Hakibbutz Hameuchad. [Hebrew]

———, and Bruce Maddy-Weitzman, eds. 2005. *The Camp David Summit—What Went Wrong?* Brighton, UK: Sussex Academic Press.

Shamir, Yitzhak. 1994. *Summing Up: An Autobiography*. Boston: Little, Brown and Company.

Al-Shara', Faruq. 2015. "Al-Risala al-Mafquda." *Al-'Arabi*, January 30–February 1.

Sharabi, Hisham. 1969. *Palestine and Israel: The Lethal Dilemma*. New York: Pegasus.

Al-Shazly, Saad. 1980. *The Crossing of the Suez*. San Francisco: American Mideast Research.

Sheehan, Edward R. F. 1976. *The Arabs, Israelis, and Kissinger: A Secret History of American Diplomacy in the Middle East*. New York: Reader's Digest Press.

Sheffer, Gabriel. 1974. "The Involvement of Arab States in the Palestine Conflict and British-Arab Relations before World War II." *Asian and African Studies* 10: 59–85.

———. 1996. *Moshe Sharett: Biography of a Political Moderate*. Oxford: Clarendon.

Shelah, Ofer, and Yoav Limor. 2007. *Captives of Lebanon*. Tel Aviv: Yedioth Ahronoth. [Hebrew]

Shemesh, Moshe. 2004. *From the Naqba to the Naksa: The Arab-Israeli Conflict and the Palestinian National Problem 1957-1967*. Sede Boqer: Ben-Gurion Research Institute. [Hebrew]

———. 2008. "The Origins of Sadat's Strategic *Volte-Face* (Marking 30 Years since Sadat's Historic Visit to Israel)." *Israel Studies* 13: 28–54.

Sher, Gilead. 2001. *Just Beyond Reach: The Israeli-Palestinian Peace Negotiations 1999-2001*. Tel Aviv: Yedioth Ahronot. [Hebrew]

———. 2005. "Lessons from the Camp David Experience." In *The Camp David Summit—What Went Wrong?* edited by Shimon Shamir and Bruce Maddy-Weitzman, 60–67. Brighton, UK: Sussex Academic Press.

———. 2006. *The Israeli-Palestinian Peace Negotiations, 1999-2001*. London. Routledge.

Shikaki, Khalil. 1998. "The Peace Process and Political Violence." *Middle East Review of International Affairs* 2: 8–11.

———. 2002. "Ending the Conflict: Can the Parties Afford It?" In *The Israeli-Palestinian Peace Process: Oslo and the Lessons of Failure*, edited by Robert L. Rothstein, Moshe Ma'oz, and Khalil Shikaki, 37–46. Brighton, UK: Sussex Academic Press.

Shilon, Avi. 2007. *Begin 1913-1992*. Tel Aviv: Am Oved. [Hebrew]

Shlaim, Avi. 1986. "Husni Za'im and the Plan to Resettle Palestinian Refugees in Syria." *Journal of Palestine Studies* 60: 68–80.

———. 1988. *Collusion across the Jordan: King Abdullah, the Zionist Movement and the Partition of Palestine*. New York: Columbia University Press.

———. 2000. *The Iron Wall: Israel and the Arab World since 1948*. New York: W. W. Norton.

———. 2003. "Interview with Abba Eban, 11 March 1976." *Israel Studies* 8: 153–178.

———. 2007. *Lion of Jordan: The Life of King Hussein in War and Peace*. London: Allen Lane.

Shultz, George P. 1993. *Turmoil and Triumph: My Years as Secretary of State*. New York: Charles Scribner's Sons.

Siegman, Henry. 2000. "Being Hafiz al-Assad: Syria's Chilly but Consistent Peace Strategy." *Foreign Affairs* 79: 2–9.

Simpson, William. 2006. *The Prince: The Secret Story of the World's Most Intriguing Royal Prince Bandar bin Sultan*. New York: Regan.

Sisco, Joseph J. 1982. "Middle East: Progress or Lost Opportunity?" *Foreign Affairs* 61.3: 611–640.

Slater, Jerome. 1990–1991. "The Superpowers and an Arab-Israeli Political Settlement: The Cold War Years." *Political Science Quarterly* 105: 557–77.

———. 2002. "Lost Opportunities for Peace in the Arab-Israeli Conflict." *International Security* 27: 79–106.

Smith, Charles D. 1996. *Palestine and the Arab-Israeli Conflict*. 3rd ed. New York: St. Martin's Press.

Sofer, Sasson. 1988. *Begin: An Anatomy of Leadership*. Oxford: Basil Blackwell.

Spiegel, L. Steven. 1985. *The Other Arab-Israeli Conflict: Making America's Middle East Policy from Truman to Reagan*. Chicago: University of Chicago Press.

———. 1990. "The United States and the Middle East in 1988." *Middle East Contemporary Survey* 12 (1988), 13–30. Boulder, CO: Westview Press.

———. 1992. *The Arab-Israeli Search for Peace*. Boulder, CO: Lynne Rienner Publishers.

———, and David J. Pervin. 1991. "The United States and the Middle East." *Middle East Contemporary Survey* 13 (1989), 13–30. Boulder, CO: Westview Press.

Squire, J. C. 1931. *If, or History Rewritten*. New York: Viking Press.

Stein, Kenneth. 1997. "Continuity and Change in Egyptian-Israeli Relations, 1973–97." In *From Rabin to Netanyahu: Israel's Troubled Agenda*, edited by Efraim Karsh, 296–320. London: Frank Cass.

———. 1999. *Heroic Diplomacy: Sadat, Kissinger, Carter, Begin and the Quest for Arab-Israeli Peace*. London: Routledge.

Steinberg, Matti. 2008. *Facing Their Fate: Palestinian National Consciousness 1967–2007*. Tel Aviv: Yedioth Ahronoth. [Hebrew]

Stewart, Dona. 2007. *Good Neighborly Relations: Jordan, Israel and the 1994–2004 Peace Process*. London: Tauris Academic Studies.

Swedenburg, Ted. 2003. *Memories of Revolt: The 1936–1939 Rebellion and the Palestinian National Past*. Fayetteville: University of Arkansas Press.

Swisher, Clayton E. 2004. *The Truth about Camp David: The Untold Story about the Collapse of the Middle East Peace Process*. New York: Nation Books.

———. 2011. *The Palestine Papers: The End of the Road?* London: Hesperus.

Sykes, Christopher. 1967. *Crossroads to Israel: Palestine from Balfour to Bevin*. London: New English Library.

Tal, David. 1998. *Israel's Day-to-Day Security Conception: Its Origins and Development 1949–1956*. Sede Boker: Ben-Gurion University of the Negev Press. [Hebrew]

Taleb, Nassim Nicholas. 2005. *Fooled by Randomness: The Hidden Role of Chance in Life and in the Markets*. New York: Random House.

Tamir, Avraham. 1988. *A Soldier in Search of Peace*. Tel Aviv: Idanim. [Hebrew]

Teitelbaum, Joshua. 2009. *The Arab Peace Initiative: A Primer and Future Prospects*. Jerusalem: Jerusalem Center for Public Affairs.

Telhami, Shibley. 1990. *Power and Leadership in International Bargaining: The Path to the Camp David Accords*. New York: Columbia University Press.

Tessler, Mark. 1994. *A History of the Israeli-Palestinian Conflict*. Bloomington: Indiana University Press.

———. 2009. *A History of the Israeli-Palestinian Conflict*. 2nd ed. Bloomington: Indiana University Press.

Tetlock, Philip E. 2005. *Expert Political Judgment: How Good Is It? How Can We Know?* Princeton, NJ: Princeton University Press.

———, and Aaron Belkin, eds. 1996. *Counterfactual Thought Experiments in World Politics:*

Logical, Methodological, and Psychological Perspectives. Princeton, NJ: Princeton University Press.

———, Richard Ned Lebow, and Geoffrey Parker, eds. 2009. *Unmaking the West: "What-If?" Scenarios That Rewrite World History*. Ann Arbor: University of Michigan Press.

———, and Geoffrey Parker. 2009. "Counterfactual Thought Experiments: Why We Can't Live without Them and How We Must Learn to Live with Them." In *Scenarios That Rewrite World History*, 14–44. Ann Arbor: University of Michigan Press.

Teveth, Shabtai. 1985. *Ben-Gurion and the Palestinian Arabs: From Peace to War*. Oxford: Oxford University Press.

Tibawi, A. L. 1978. *Anglo-Arab Relations and the Question of Palestine 1914–1921*. London: Luzac and Company.

Torrey, Gordon H. 1964. *Syrian Politics and the Military 1945–1958*. Athens: Ohio University Press.

Totten, Michael J. 2011. *The Road to Fatima Gate: The Beirut Spring, the Rise of Hezbollah, and the Iranian War against Israel*. New York: Encounter Books.

Touval, Saadia. 1982. *The Peace Brokers: Mediators in the Arab-Israeli Conflict, 1949–1979*. Princeton, NJ: Princeton University Press.

Trevor-Roper, Hugh. 1981. "History and Imagination." In *History and Imagination: Essays in Honor of H. R. Trevor-Roper*, edited by Hugh Lloyd-Jones, Valerie Pearl, and Blair Worden, 356–369. New York: Holmes and Meier.

———. 1988. "The Lost Moments of History." *New York Review of Books*, October 27.

Truman Institute Library. 1988. "Abba Eban on Peace and War." Eban's archives, serial no. 000008941. The article was originally published in *Jewish Frontier* 54.6 (1987): 11–14.

Tuchman, Barbara. 1984. *The March of Folly: From Troy to Vietnam*. London: Abacus.

Venetik, Boaz, and Zaki Shalom. 2012. *The Yom Kippur War: The War That Could Have Been Prevented*. Tel Aviv: Rasling. [Hebrew]

Waugh, Charles G., and Martin H. Greenberg, eds. 1986. *Alternative Histories: Eleven Stories of the World as It Might Have Been*. New York: Garland Publishing.

Wagge, Hilde Henriksen. 2004. *"Peacemaking Is a Risky Business": Norway's Role in the Peace Process in the Middle East 1993–1996*. Oslo: PRIO.

———. 2005. "Norway's Role in the Middle East Peace Talks: Between a Strong State and a Weak Belligerent." *Journal of Palestine Studies* 34: 6–24.

Walsh, Elsa. 2003. "The Prince." *New Yorker*, March 24.

Wasserstein, Bernard. 1991. *The British in Palestine: The Mandatory Government and the Arab-Jewish Conflict 1917–1929*. London: Basil Blackwell.

Weber, Max. 1949. "Objective Possibility and Adequate Causation in Historical Explanation." In *The Methodology of the Social Sciences*, 164–188. Glencoe, IL: Free Press.

Weinryb, Elazar. 2003. "What If?" In *History—Myth or Reality? Observations on the State of the Profession*, 375–414. Tel Aviv: Open University. [Hebrew]

———. 2011. "Divided Paths." *Zemanim* 115: 98–111. [Hebrew]

Weissglas, Dov. 2012. *Ariel Sharon—A Prime Minister*. Tel Aviv: Yedioth Ahronoth. [Hebrew]

Weizman, Ezer. 1982. *The Battle for Peace*. Tel Aviv: Idanim. [Hebrew]

Weizmann, Chaim. 1949. *Trial and Error: The Autobiography of Chaim Weizmann*. New York: Harper and Brothers.

Wittes, Tamara Cofman, ed. 2005. *How Israelis and Palestinians Negotiate: A Cross-Cultural Analysis of the Oslo Peace Process*. Washington: United States Institute of Peace Press.

Yaʿacobi, Gad. 1989. *On the Razor's Edge*. Tel Aviv: Yediot Ahronot. [Hebrew]

Yaari, Eliezer, Eitan Haber, and Zeʾev Schiff. 1980. *The Year of the Dove*. Tel Aviv: Zamora, Beitan, Modan. [Hebrew]

Yaari, Michal. 2012. "The Foreign Policy of Saudi Arabia—Between Power Politics, Culture and Regime Survival." PhD diss., Bar-Ilan University. [Hebrew]

Yakobson, Alexander, and Amnon Rubinstein. 2009. *Israel and the Family of Nations: The Jewish Nation-State and Human Rights*. London: Routledge.

Yaqub, Salim. 2007. "The Politics of Stalemate: The Nixon Administration and the Arab-Israeli Conflict, 1969–73." In *The Cold War in the Middle East: Regional Conflict and the Superpowers 1967–73*, edited by Nigel J. Ashton, 35–58. London: Routledge.

Yatom, Danny. 2005. "Background, Process and Failure." In *The Camp David Summit—What Went Wrong?* edited by Shimon Shamir and Bruce Maddy-Weitzman, 33–41. Brighton, UK: Sussex Academic Press.

———. 2009. *The Confidant: From Sayeret Matkal to the Mossad*. Tel Aviv: Yediot Ahronot. [Hebrew]

Zak, Moshe. 1996. *Husayn Makes Peace: Thirty Years and Another Year on the Road to Peace*. Ramat Gan: Bar-Ilan University Press. [Hebrew]

Zartman, I. William. 2000. "Ripeness: The Hurting Stalemate and Beyond." In *International Conflict Resolution after the Cold War*, edited by Paul C. Stern and Daniel Druckman, 225–250. Washington, DC: National Academies Press.

———. 2005. *Cowardly Lions: Missed Opportunities to Prevent Deadly Conflict and State Collapse*. Boulder, CO: Lynne Rienner Publishers.

———. 1997. "Explaining Oslo." *International Negotiations* 2: 195–215.

Zeʾevi-Farkash, Aharon. 2002. "Israel's Strategic Environment." *Strategic Assessment* 5.2: 32–36. [Hebrew]

Zisser, Eyal. 1996. "The Shattering of Illusions: The Maronite Community in Lebanon and Israel—First Initial Contacts." *Iyyunim Betkumat Israel* 6: 47–84. [Hebrew]

———. 2001. *Asad's Legacy: Syria in Transition*. London: Hurst and Company.

Zvielli, Alexander, and Calev Ben-David. 2002. "Abba Eban, the Father of Israeli Statesmanship, Dies at the Age of 87." *Jerusalem Post*, November 18.

CPSIA information can be obtained
at www.ICGtesting.com
Printed in the USA
FFOW03n1459160117
31366FF